PAPUA NEW GUINEA
4073
SOLOMON ISLANDS
Torres Strait
20:30
12:00
21:00
12:00
Iron Range
Cape York Peninsula
Great Barrier Reef
Cooktown
Coral Sea
Cairns
1611
Forsayth
Flinders
Townsville
Great Dividing Range
Mount Isa
Mackay
Diamantina
Queensland
Rockhampton
Pacific Ocean
Birdsville
Cooper Creek
Lake Eyre
Birdsville Track
Brisbane
Toowoomba
Gold Coast
Cunnamulla
Marree
New South Wales
Kempsey
Broken Hill
Darling
Port Augusta
Blue Mountains
Newcastle
Sydney
Rockdale
Wollongong
Mildura
Murrumbidgee
Murray
Adelaide
Canberra
Australian Capital Territory
Victoria
2230 Mount Kosciusko
Ballarat
Melbourne
Geelong
Tasmania
Hobart
North
East
South
northeast
southeast
0 100 200 300 400 500 km

NOTTING HILL GATE

5 Basic

Herausgegeben von
Prof. Dr. Torben Schmidt, Leuphana Universität Lüneburg, Mitglied THE ENGLISH ACADEMY

Erarbeitet von
Michael Biermann (Hamburg), Hannelore Debus (Mörfelden-Walldorf), Dr. David Gerlach (Marburg), Sascha Mohr (Wiesbaden), Susanne Quandt (Bremen), Dr. Ivo Steininger (Wetzlar)

sowie
Otfried Börner (Hamburg), Phil Mothershaw-Rogalla (Volkmarsen-Külte), Ingrid Preedy (Dortmund), Kathleen Unterspann (Halstenbek), Jürgen Wrobel (Oberursel)

Fachliche Beratung
Denise Arrandale (Neumünster), Rolf-Olaf Geisler (Oberhausen), Dr. Sandra Götz (Gießen), Semra Siyli (Hamburg), Kathleen Unterspann (Halstenbek)

Diesterweg
westermann

NOTTING HILL GATE
5 Basic

Für Klasse 9 an Gesamtschulen und anderen integrierenden Schulformen

Zusatzmaterialien zum vorliegenden Schülerbuch

Materialien für Schülerinnen und Schüler

- Workbook mit Audio-CD 978-3-425-14615-7
- Inklusions- und Fördermaterialien mit Audio-CD 978-3-425-14675-1
- Zoom-App www.zoom-app.de
- BiBox Schüler-Einzellizenz WEB-425-30008

Materialien für Lehrkräfte

- Lehrerfassung zum Schülerband 978-3-425-13998-2
- Teacher's Manual 978-3-425-14905-9
- Vorschläge für Lernerfolgskontrollen mit CD-ROM 978-3-425-14945-5
- Workbook mit Lösungen und Audio-CD 978-3-425-14915-8
- Audio-CD für Lehrkräfte 978-3-425-14935-6
- DVD für Lehrkräfte 978-3-425-14825-0
- BiBox – Digitale Unterrichtsmaterialien für Lehrkräfte 5
  Lehrer-Einzellizenz WEB-425-14995
  Lehrer-Einzellizenz auf DVD-ROM 978-3-425-14986
  Kollegiumslizenz WEB-425-14999

Fördert individuell – passt zum Schulbuch

Optimal für den Einsatz im Unterricht mit Notting Hill Gate! Stärken erkennen, Defizite beheben. Online-Lernstandsdiagnose und Auswertung auf Basis der aktuellen Bildungsstandards. Individuell zusammengestellte Fördermaterialien.

www.diesterweg.de/diagnose

Online-Diagnose

westermann GRUPPE

Druck P[1] / Jahr 2018

Redaktion: Doris Bos, Jutta Eckardt-Scheurig, Amy Frances Koerner, Dr. Katja Nandorf und Daniel Walker sowie Esther Morrison
Vokabelanhang: Doris Bos
Illustrationen: Ulf Marckwort, Kassel
Umschlaggestaltung: blum design und kommunikation GmbH, Hamburg
Umschlagfoto: Dirk Schmidt/dsphotos.de
Layoutkonzeption: tiff.any GmbH, Berlin
Druck und Bindung: westermann druck GmbH, Braunschweig

ISBN 978-3-425-**14605**-8

Being

In English-speaking countries people are usually very polite, so make sure you say 'excuse me', 'please', 'thank you' and 'sorry' a lot.

If you have a question, make sure you ask politely.

polite

When meeting an English-speaking friend, be polite and ask questions. When there is a problem, for example when your friend is late, be nice about it.

When you are invited to a party or at the dinner table, be polite and say thank you.

When someone apologizes, accept the apology politely.

Try and be enthusiastic when expressing feelings. 'OK', 'alright', 'nice' and 'interesting' are not very positive.

Inhalt

Inhalt

R = *revision*

Inhalt

Die Angebote in *Notting Hill Gate* sind nicht linear abzuarbeiten.
Die Auswahl richtet sich nach den Schwerpunkten des schulinternen Curriculums.

Inhalt

R = *revision*

Inhalt

In diesem Buch gibt es folgende Symbole:

A1 Diese Aufgabe gehört zum **Basisweg**.

A7 Diese Aufgabe gehört nicht zum Basisweg und ist **fakultativ**.

A8 Choose

Suche dir eine Aufgabe aus. Ihr könnt alleine arbeiten, zu zweit oder in einer Gruppe. Ihr könnt euch auch eine eigene Aufgabe ausdenken.

A9 Target task

Zielaufgabe der Sequenz

Diese Aufgabe eignet sich auch für Schülerinnen und Schüler mit **Förderbedarf**. Sie kann im Sinne eines inklusiven Unterrichts mit der ganzen Lerngruppe bearbeitet werden.

leichte Aufgabe

mittelschwere Aufgabe

schwierige Aufgabe

Diese Aufgabe eignet sich für die **kooperative Arbeit** in der Klasse mit allen Schülerinnen und Schülern.

Zu dieser Aufgabe gibt es einen Videoclip.

CD 1/1 — Der Hörtext ist auf der **Audio-CD** für Lehrkräfte (CD 1, Track 1).

CD 1 — Der Hörtext ist auf der **MP3-Audio-CD** für Schülerinnen und Schüler (Track 1).

DVD 1 — Der Videoclip ist auf der **DVD** für Lehrkräfte (Clip 1).

WB p. 5 A1, A2 — Hierzu gibt es im ***Workbook*** weitere Übungen.

p. 4 A1 — Hierzu gibt es Übungen in den **Inklusions- und Fördermaterialien**.

LiF p. 180 1 — Hierzu gibt es eine Erklärung im Grammatikteil ***Language in Focus***.

how to talk p. 147 — Hierzu gibt es eine Erklärung in den ***How to …***-Seiten.

wordbank jobs p. 169 — In den ***Wordbanks*** befinden sich die wichtigsten Wörter zu einem Thema.

model text — Ein ***model text*** ist eine Vorlage für deinen eigenen Text.

Webcode DSW-14605-xxx — Gehe zu www.diesterweg.de/webcodes und tippe den Webcode ein.

Tipp
Auf Seite 34 kannst du noch mehr über das Great Barrier Reef erfahren.

Hier bekommst du kleine **Tipps** und Hilfen.

Down under

1

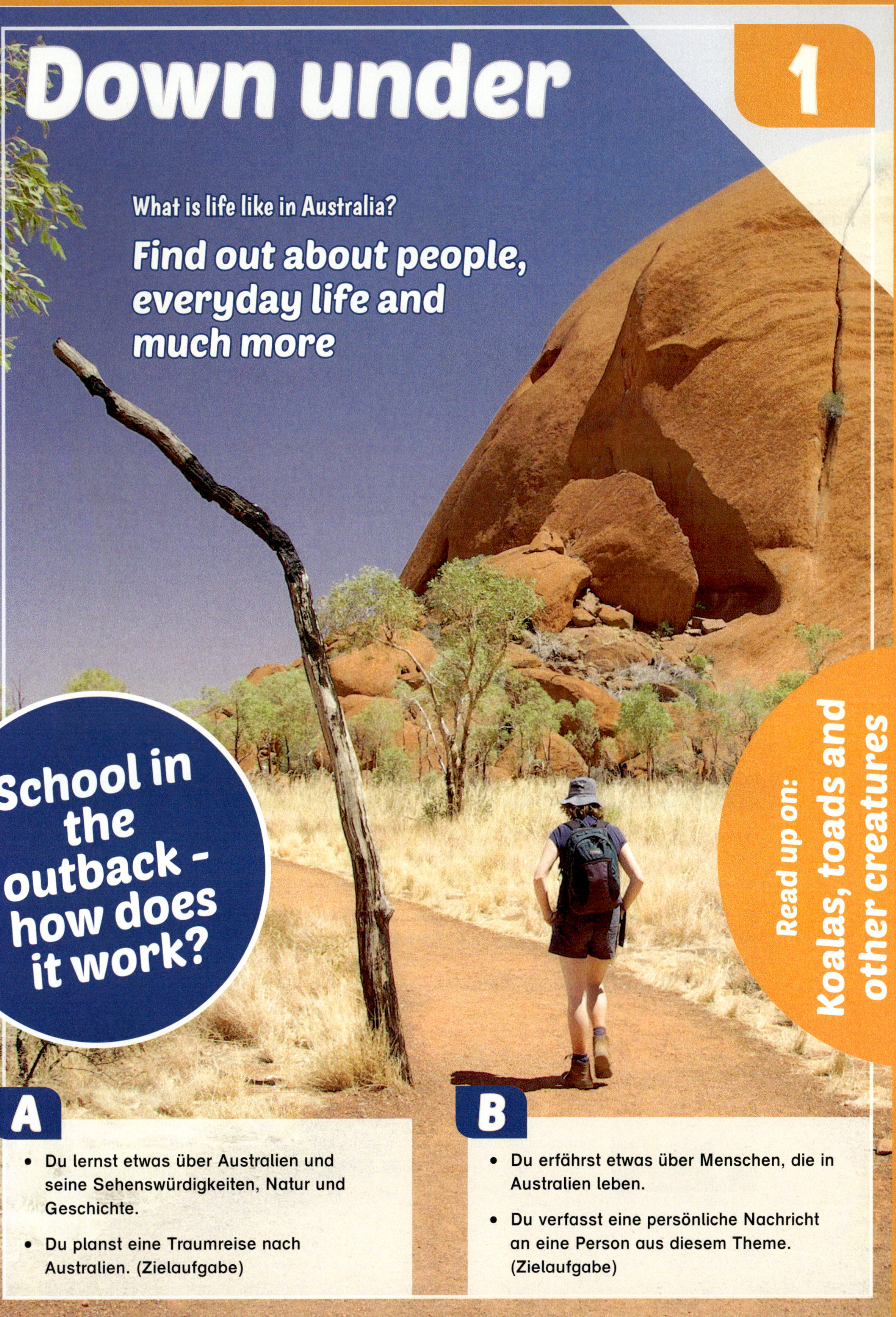

What is life like in Australia?

Find out about people, everyday life and much more

School in the outback – how does it work?

Read up on: **Koalas, toads and other creatures**

A

- Du lernst etwas über Australien und seine Sehenswürdigkeiten, Natur und Geschichte.
- Du planst eine Traumreise nach Australien. (Zielaufgabe)

B

- Du erfährst etwas über Menschen, die in Australien leben.
- Du verfasst eine persönliche Nachricht an eine Person aus diesem Theme. (Zielaufgabe)

A1 Australia – where in the world is that?

What comes to mind when you think of Australia?

a) Discover more about Australia on the inside covers of your book. Talk about it.

I think this is ...

I know that ...

I think ... is the capital of Australia.

Do you know ...?

...

WB p. XX
XX

b) What would you like to find out about Australia? Write down questions and share them in a group. Then put an "Our questions about Australia" poster on the wall. While working on the Theme, add your findings to the poster.

How many people live in Australia?
What is ...?
When was ...?
Where ...?
Why ...?
...

A2 Fascinating facts

Look at the article about Australia. Does it look interesting? Does it make you want to read it? Talk about it.

p. XX
XX

a) Read the article. Which of the facts did you already know?

Fascinating facts about Australia

Australia is more than kangaroos, koalas and crocodiles. Check out these fascinating facts about the only place in the world that is a continent, a country and an island at the same time.

■ **It takes** about 24 hours to fly to Australia from Europe. The first European settlers sailed there in eight months!

■ **Australia** is twenty times bigger than Germany.

■ **Australia** is the sixth biggest country in the world.

■ **The Australian flag** shows the British flag next to the Southern Cross, which is a formation of stars you can only see in the southern hemisphere.

■ **The capital city** is Canberra.

■ **Over 25%** of Australians were born in another country.

■ **The outback** covers one quarter of the country. Very few people live there.

■ **"The Royal** Flying Doctor Service of Australia" sends doctors by plane to patients in the outback.

■ **Over 200** different languages and dialects are spoken in Australia.

■ **Christmas** is celebrated in Australia in their summer time.

■ **There are** about 50 different species of kangaroo.

■ **There are** 1 million wild camels in the Australian deserts.

■ **The Great Barrier Reef** is the only living organism that can be seen from outer space.

b) Talk about the facts with a partner.

I knew that ...

I find it surprising that ... What about you?

I think it's interesting that ...

I had no idea that ...

...

wordbank Australia p. 164

c) What are the three most interesting facts for you? Share them with your partner or in a group.

My top three are ... Which are yours?

...

WB p. XX XX

A3 An Australian experience

Becky, a 15-year-old girl from Germany, has spent half a year in Newcastle 160 km from Sydney. Before she goes home, she talks about her experiences with a reporter of an Australian teenage radio programme.

a) Listen to the interview and find out why Becky speaks such good English.

CD X/XX

Reporter: G'day mates. This is Brian from Youthradio. Today I've got a special guest for you. It's Becky from Frankfurt in Germany. She came to Newcastle on a student exchange. Becky, you've been here for nearly half a year now and you're going back home next week. How do you feel?

Becky: I'm really sad. There are a lot of people and things I'm going to miss.

Reporter: Let's talk about it. ...

b) Listen again and take notes on what she liked about Australia. Compare your notes with a partner.

☼ **What does Becky say about different kinds of English? What countries does she mention? Look at the map of the English-speaking world at the back of your book and find out more. Report your findings to the class.**

A4 Sydney, wildlife and more

Look at the photos from Becky's trip to Sydney. What did she see and do there?

She saw ...

She went to ...

...

p. XX XX

how to read p. 146

a) Read Becky's blog entry. What do you find most interesting?

https://beckysdreamtime.com

Hi there!

Today I'm going to tell you about our trip to Sydney in my host family's camper trailer.

We had two days in Sydney. I think it's the most beautiful city in the world! We did the spectacular cliff walk to Bondi Beach for a swim in the ocean. No sharks to be seen! ☺ And if you think there's only a Hyde Park in London, you're quite wrong! There's also one in Sydney. I loved it there. We had a great picnic with some very spicy Asian takeaways. But the best thing was "Vivid Sydney", a great event of light and music and all for free! The Sydney Opera House looked amazing!

The next day we visited Taronga Zoo. From there you've got a fantastic view of the city. Of course you can find all these cuddly Australian marsupials there. The koala is still my favourite. It has to be protected though, which I find really sad.

At the zoo they also had an exhibition on invasive species – these are animals that are not originally from Australia. There was a picture of a cane toad. I took a photo of it. Have you ever seen anything like that? I think it's creepy! Cane toads are among the biggest toads in the world. The toads are dangerous for pets and other animals.

But back to Sydney. If you are interested in museums, visit their websites to find out more about their free entry days. On this trip there was no time left to go inside any museums - maybe next time ...

I really hope it's not going to be a once in a lifetime trip. I've already decided to do a one-year working holiday in Australia after school!!!! Then I'm definitely visiting Kakadu National Park. I heard so much about it. It must be an incredible place. The landscape is beautiful and you can learn a lot about the Aboriginal culture. Imagine, it's nearly half the size of Switzerland!

Next week my parents will come and see me and together we'll visit parts of the Great Barrier Reef.

b) ☆ **Complete the sentences.**

1. Becky thinks that Sydney is …
2. In Hyde Park Becky and her host family …
3. The takeaway was …
4. The thing Becky liked best was …
5. From Taronga Zoo you have …
6. Becky's favourite animal is …

☾ **Find the names of Australian sights and places in Becky's blog. What does she write about them? Take notes and compare with a partner.**

☼ **What does Becky write about sights, places and wildlife in Australia? Take notes and compare with a partner.**

WB p. XX XX

A5 Becky's blog

Unscramble the sentences and write them down.

1. visited – and her host family – Becky – Sydney.
2. too. – a Hyde Park – There is – in Sydney
3. in the world. – the most beautiful city – Sydney is – Becky thinks
4. is – of light and music. – a free event – Vivid Sydney
5. you can – in Sydney – find – In Taronga Zoo – all kinds of marsupials.
6. favourite animal – be protected. – Becky's – has to

LiF p. 178 1R

A6 Choose

1. **Make a quiz about Australia for a partner.**
2. **Find out more about Sydney or another Australian city.**
3. **Choose a typical Australian animal and present it in class. Find a way to make your presentation interesting.**
4. **Christmas on the beach: write a poem, a short story or a dialogue. Present it to the class.**

wordbank Australia p. 164

how to p. 150 present

A7 Great sights

Which of the places in the photos would you like to see in real life?

DVD X

how to p. 148 watch a video

p. XX XX

a) Watch the video clip and take notes on the places.

b) How do the impressions of Australia make you feel? Talk in class.

It makes me happy to see ...

I find it exciting to watch ...

When I see ... I would like to go there.

c) Read the texts and find out more about some of the sights. If you could visit two places, which would you choose and why? Talk in class.

Melbourne is the second largest city in Australia. It is a very multicultural city and famous for its trams. Melbourne also has many big parks and gardens.

Bondi Beach, only 15 minutes by car from the Sydney city centre, is one of the world's most famous beaches. Tourists and locals enjoy the ocean pool and the skate park. It's a great place for a seaside walk or a picnic.

Kakadu National Park is famous for its beautiful landscape and for what you can learn about Aboriginal culture. More than half the park is Aboriginal land. Kakadu is home to more than 10,000 crocodiles!

Tipp
Auf Seite 34 kannst du noch mehr über das Great Barrier Reef erfahren.

The Great Barrier Reef is a 2000 km long system of coral reefs. It consists of living rocks which are made up of billions of tiny creatures called polyps. About 1,500 kinds of fish live there.

Uluru, also called Ayers Rock, is a holy place for the Aboriginal people. It is in the middle of the Australian outback and was created over 600 million years ago. The Aboriginals don't climb Uluru and ask visitors to respect their culture by not climbing this holy place either.

WB p. XX XX

Find the places on the map. Suggest a route to see all the sights.

My route starts in ... The next stop would be ...

A8 A very short history of Australia

a) Read about the history of Australia. What do you find surprising?

More than 50,000 years ago the first people settled in Australia. They came from Asia and were later called Aborigines.
When the first European ships arrived, more than 300,000 Aborigines were living in Australia. Many were killed by the first European settlers. Many also died of diseases the settlers brought with them. **1**

In 1644 the Dutch explorer Abel Tasman found out that Australia is an island. Tasmania is named after the explorer. **2**

In 1770 the east coast of Australia was claimed as British territory by Captain James Cook. **3**

In January 1788 the first fleet with prisoners from Britain arrived at Port Jackson (now Sydney). At that time prisons in Britain were overcrowded. Today, the date of the prisoners' arrival is celebrated as Australia Day. **4**

After hearing reports about "the new continent" more people from Britain sailed to Australia. Many of them became sheep farmers. Wool was sent to British factories. **5**

In 1851 gold was discovered in New South Wales. More people came, hoping to become rich. **6**

Between 1869 and 1969 about 100,000 Aboriginal children were taken away from their families. The idea was to erase their Aboriginal cultural identity and replace it with the culture of white Australians. Today these children are called the "Stolen Generations." **7**

On 1st January 1901 the colonies of New South Wales, Victoria, Queensland, South Australia, Western Australia and Tasmania were formed to be the Commonwealth of Australia. Now Australia was independent. **8**

Only by 1965 Aborigines in all Australian states had been given the vote. They were now allowed to vote in their own country. **9**

On 13th February 2008 the Australian prime minister Kevin Rudd apologised to the Aborigines for the wrongs of the past in his famous "sorry speech". The National Sorry Day is celebrated every year on 26th May. **10**

b) Think of headlines for each box.

c) Make a timeline in class.

Make notes on what you learn about Aborigines or about European settlers.

wordbank Australia p. 164
WB p. XX XX

A9 What happened?

LiF p. 179 2R

Match the sentence halves.

Tipp
In Texten über historische Ereignisse wird oft das Passiv verwendet.

1. Many Aborigines
2. The Australian island state Tasmania
3. The Australian east coast
4. In 1788 prisoners from overcrowded prisons in Britain
5. The date of the prisoners' arrival
6. In New South Wales gold

a. was claimed by Cook as British territory.
b. was discovered in 1851.
c. were killed by white settlers.
d. is celebrated as Australia Day.
e. was named after the Dutch explorer Abel Tasman.
f. were sent to Australia.

LiF p. 179 2R

Write down the sentences with the correct passive forms from the box.

have been allowed were taken were told has been celebrated were sent were started

1. In 1788 the first British prisoners (send) to Australia.
2. They (take) to Australia because the British prisons were overcrowded.
3. Sheep farms (start) in the outback by many British settlers to make a living.
4. People (tell) that they could find gold in Australia and become rich.
5. Since 1965 the Aborigines (allow) to vote in elections.
6. The National Sorry Day (celebrate) every year on 26th May since 1998.

1. In 1788 the first British prisoners were sent to Australia.

LiF p. 179 2R

Change these sentences into passive sentences and write them down.

1. Diseases that the Europeans brought to Australia killed many Aborigines.
2. The British government sent prisoners to Australia.
3. Australians still celebrate the day of their first arrival in Australia.
4. The European settlers took animals unknown in Australia with them.
5. Some of these animals cause problems today.
6. In 1901 the six British colonies formed the Commonwealth of Australia.

1. Many Aborigines were killed by diseases that the Europeans brought to Australia.
2. Prisioners were ...
3. The day of ...

LAND & LEUTE 1

Der Commonwealth of Australia

Der Commonwealth of Australia besteht aus der australischen Hauptlandmasse, der Insel Tasmanien und mehreren kleineren Inseln.

Der Commonwealth of Australia wurde zu Beginn des 20. Jahrhunderts ein sich selbst regierendes Gebiet des britischen Königsreiches mit Canberra als Hauptstadt und der australischen Nationalflagge.

1986 wurde im Australia Act festgehalten, dass es keinerlei britischen Einfluss auf die australische Gesetzgebung mehr geben sollte. Das bedeutet, dass Australien seitdem völlig unabhängig von Großbritannien ist und seine eigenen Gesetze machen kann.

Dennoch ist der britische Monarch oder die britische Monarchin – wenn auch nur symbolisch – das Oberhaupt des Commonwealth of Australia.

Wegen der langen Geschichte der Besiedlung Australiens durch die Briten und den engen Verbindungen zu Großbritannien ist Englisch die Sprache, die von mehr als 70% der Einwohner gesprochen wird.

Finde heraus, wofür die einzelnen Teile des australischen Wappens stehen.

DVD XX

WB p. XX XX

A10 Target task: My dream trip to Australia

Plan your dream trip to Australia.

1. Decide if you would like to work in a group, with a partner or on your own.
2. Think about
   - where you would like to stay
   - what you would like to see and do
   - what you would like to know more about.
3. Collect information. You can use the information in this book and/or find out more in brochures, books or on the Internet.
4. Think about an interesting way to present your work. You could make a poster, a brochure or do a computer presentation.
5. Prepare your presentation.
6. Practise your presentation in your group or with a partner and give each other feedback.
7. Present your dream trip to the class.

Australia – my dream trip

- 3 weeks with my parents and my brother
- fly to Sydney
- 5 days in Sydney – visit Bondi Beach!
- 5 days in Melbourne
- fly to Brisbane – spend 4 days there
- visit Fraser Island – go whale watching!
- go to the Great Barrier Reef – scuba diving!
- fly back to Sydney
- then fly back to Germany
- rent an apartment and a car in each city

p. XX XX

WB p. XX XX

model text

how to p. 150 present, give feedback

P1 Explain

Explain what you have to do.

Ich soll ...

Wir sollen ...

...

1. Discover more about Australia on the inside covers of your book.
2. Unscramble the sentences and write them down.
3. Suggest a route to see all the sights.
4. Pay attention to the tenses.
5. Decide if you would like to work in a group, with a partner or on your own.

P2 What is it?

a) **Read the definitions and write down the words that are described. You can find the words in A2.**

1. the area in the centre of Australia where not many people live
2. a special group or type of people or animals living in an area
3. a town or city that is the centre of government of a country
4. animals that produce milk to feed their young
5. an Australian animal that jumps along on its strong hind legs
6. a person who is being punished by imprisonment

CD XX

b) **Listen to the CD and check your words.**

P3 Interesting facts

LiF p. 178 1R

a) **Unscramble the sentences.**

1. is about – Germany. – The Great Barrier Reef – the size of
2. in the Australian desert. – a lot of – You can see – wild camels
3. great picnics – You can have – in Hyde Park – in Sydney.
4. about eight months – the first European settlers – to sail – to Australia. – It took
5. was not born – a quarter of – the Australian population – in Australia. – More than
6. Cane toads are – to Australia – an invasive species – by farmers. – which was brought
7. amazing event – "Vivid Sydney" – of light and music – is an – for free. – which is
8. can kill – Cane toads are – that – they – cats and dogs. – so dangerous

CD XX

b) **Listen to the CD and check your sentences.**

c) **Write two more scrambled facts for a partner.**

Practice matters

P4 Important facts

a) What do you remember? Write down the facts.

LiF p. 179 2R

1. Over 25% of Australians 2. One quarter of the country 3. In Australia Christmas 4. Australian football 5. A lot of Australian camels 6. The first Australian police force	were is are can be was is	covered made up born played exported celebrated	in another country. by the outback. in bathing suits. with special Aussie rules. to Saudi Arabia. of convicts.

b) Listen to the CD and check your sentences.

CD XX

P5 Sound check: how to say the letter 'o'

a) Listen to the words and repeat them.

CD XX

b) Make three lists. Write the words in the correct list.

/ɒ/	/əʊ/	/ə/
population	snow	Aborigine

Aborigine • official • population • European • snow • opera • crocodile • rainforest • vote • continent • police • explore • blog • introduce • ocean

c) Listen to the CD and check your lists.

CD XX

d) Write six sentences using as many words of the lists as you can.

P6 Slip – slop – slap

how to p. 147 mediate

In the summer months Australia is closer to the sun than Europe during its summer. As too much sun can be really bad for your skin, Australia has one of the highest rates of skin cancer in the world.

Look at the poster. It tells Australians and tourists how to protect their skin from too much sun. Tell a classmate in German.

Es wird empfohlen ...

Man soll ...

...

SLIP on a shirt or other protective clothes.

SLOP on sunscreen. When you go swimming, use sunscreen that is water-resistant.

SLAP on a hat to protect your face, head, ears and neck.

SEEK some shade. It's one of the best ways to protect yourself from the sun.

SLIDE on some sunglasses to protect your eyes.

B1 A new life down under

People with many different cultural backgrounds and nationalities live in Australia.

Why do you think people leave their home countries to move to Australia?

p. XX XX

a) Look at the pictures and read the information. What else would you like to know about the people? Write down questions.

1

Lachlan (22) came to Sydney to study sport and stayed to teach surfing at Bondi Beach.

2

Jan is a journalist who came to Australia with his parents at the age of 18. He works for one of the many non-English newspapers published in Sydney.

3

Claire (16) was born in Germany and moved to Australia when she was five. She speaks two languages.

4

Hassan is the owner of the restaurant "Out of Africa" in Sydney. He left his friends and family in Casablanca, Morocco, to follow his dream.

5

Katie is 26. She came to Sydney three years ago to study. She is hoping to get a good job after she finishes. In the evenings she works as a waitress in a café.

CD X/XX
how to p. 145 listen

b) Listen to what the people say about life down under and take notes. Then talk about them with a partner. Were your questions from a) answered?

Lachlan	is	stay in Australia.
Jan	comes from	(always) welcome in Australia.
Claire	feels	German.
Hassan	wants to	from Scotland.
Katie	likes	Prague.
	…	…

wordbank jobs p. 167

c) Listen again. What else can you find out about the people? Take notes.

d) Write about one of the people. Use your notes and your imagination.

Lachlan is 22 years old. He came to …

WB p. XX XX

Write 40 words or more. **Write 60 words or more.** **Write 80 words or more.**

B2 All kinds of Australians

Look at the pie chart. Which of the countries are in Europe?

a) Read about immigration in Australia and look at the pie chart. What is the most important information for you? Copy it from the text and compare with a partner.

how to p. 156 work with statistics

- About 25 million people live in Australia.
- About 3% of the population are Aborigines. That's about 660,000 people.
- More than six million of the people who live in Australia were not born there. This diagram from 2015 shows where they mainly came from. In fact they are from around 200 different countries.

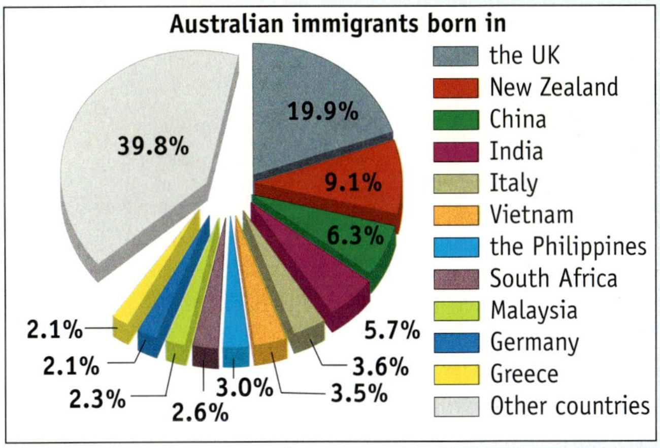

- Most of the immigrants come from other English-speaking countries, like the United Kingdom and New Zealand. But there are also many other people who have started a new life in Australia. They come, for example, from China, Indonesia, Japan, Thailand, Vietnam, Italy, France, Greece and many other parts of the world.

b) Listen to the CD and read along. Repeat the numbers and practise reading them with a partner.

CD X/XX XX

10% • 33.3% • 20% • 25% • 50%

... per cent

1/10 • 1/5 • 1/4 • 1/3 • 1/2

a tenth • a fifth • a quarter • a third • half

c) Look at the boxes in b) again. Which figures and words go together? Make a list.

figures	words
10%	ten per cent
33.3%	thirty-three point three per cent
...	...
1/10	...

d) Now talk about the statistics.

wordbank statistics p. 165

6.3% of Australian immigrants were born in China.

Almost 20% came from ...

...

WB p. XX XX

B3 My story

Look at the photo at the bottom of the page and talk about it. How does it make you feel?

Bindi is a 13-year-old Aboriginal girl. Here she talks about her life and culture.

CD X/XX XX

a) Listen to Bindi's story. How does she feel about being an Aborigine today?

p. XX XX

b) Now read the story. What do you learn about Aboriginal culture? Make a list.

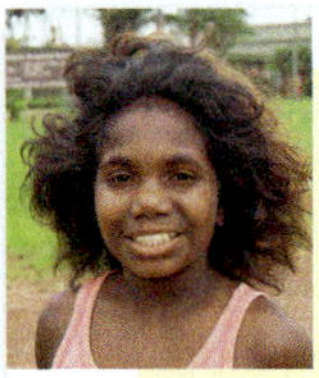

My story begins a long time ago, during what we Aborigines call "The Dreamtime".

I come from the oldest culture in the world – the Australian Aborigine culture, which my dad says goes back 100,000 years. It is really cool as we have such great stories, which we call "Dreaming stories". We also have great music and dance, which tell us about how our world started. How the Great Rainbow Serpent created the earth and all its plants and animals and how the mountains and the rivers were formed.

Tipp
Die Geschichte der Rainbow Serpent findest du im Book stop auf Seite 135.

My brother Jarly and I are in an Aboriginal dance group. I feel very lucky to be a part of this wonderful culture because I get to see many places when my family performs at cultural presentations. My dad plays the didgeridoo and tells Dreaming stories, and my brother and I dance. In February, I am going on my first international tour to Germany.

My dad told me that when he was a boy, being Aboriginal was not a good thing. Aboriginals did not have the same rights as white people and suffered from injustices. In February 2008, the Australian government said "sorry" to the Aboriginal people, which made my dad cry. Then I realised how lucky I am to be an Australian Aborigine today. It also made me sad because I began to understand that my culture was nearly destroyed.

Only last week I got my Australian passport in the mail. My dad was not a citizen of Australia until he was about 14 years old. Being a young Aboriginal girl today also gives me more educational and career opportunities. I have been able to develop my art – which I love doing – because I can share my culture with other people.

Being part of an Aboriginal family is great, as you have so many aunts and uncles and brothers and sisters. They are not my "real" aunts and uncles but in Aboriginal culture everyone is related to everyone else. When we all get together for events, we have a lot of fun. Then I really know that I am part of something great, and proud of it.

That is my story – what is yours?

WB p. XX XX

Explain why Bindi and Jarly are "lucky" to be Aboriginal today.

B4 The first people

a) Fill in the gaps with the simple past forms of the verbs in brackets.

LiF p. 180 3R

1. The first people who ??? in Australia are called Aborigines. (arrive)
2. They ??? from island to island in canoes or on rafts. (travel)
3. But at the end of the last ice age the sea level ???. (rise)
4. Australia ??? an isolated continent. (become)
5. The Aborigines lived off the land and ???, picked berries and fished. (hunt)
6. When the first settlers arrived the destruction of the culture ???. (begin)

b) Listen to the CD and check your sentences.

CD XX

B5 I am Australian

Listen to the song and read the lyrics. What kinds of people are mentioned?

CD X/XX XX

I came from the Dreamtime
From the dusty red soil plains
I am the ancient heart
The keeper of the flames
I stood upon the rocky shore
I watched the tall ships come
For forty thousand years I've been
the first Australian

I came upon the prison ships
Bound down by iron chains
I cured the land
Endured the lash
And waited for the rains
I'm a settler
I'm a farmer's wife
On a dry and barren run
A convict and a free man
I became Australian

I'm a daughter of a digger
Who sought the mother lode
The girl became a woman
On the long and dusty road
I'm a child of the depression
I saw the good time come
I'm a bushy I'm a battler
I am Australian

Chorus:
We are one
But we are many
And from all the lands on earth we come
We'll share a dream
And sing with one voice
I am, you are, we are Australian

I'm a teller of stories
I'm a singer of songs
I am Albert Namatjira
And I paint the ghostly gums
I'm Clancy on his horse
I'm Ned Kelly on the run
I'm the one who waltzed Matilda
I am Australian

I'm the hot wind from the desert
I'm the black soil of the plain
I'm the mountains and the valleys
I'm the drowned and flooding rains
I am the rock
I am the sky
The rivers when they run
The spirit of this great land
I am Australian

2x chorus

Lyrics: Bruce Woodley/Dobe Newton
Music: Bruce Woodley

What does "We are one but we are many" mean? Explain in your own words.

how to p. 161 talk about lyrics

B6 Rabbit-proof fence

Look at the title of the film in the film review. What do you think the film is about?

a) Read the film review. A friend who does not speak much English wants to watch the film. Tell him or her in German what the film is about and if the reviewer liked it.

WB p. XX XX

Rabbit-proof fence ★★★★☆

RELEASED: 2002
RUNNING TIME: 94 minutes
DIRECTOR: Phillip Noyce
CAST: Everlyn Sampi, Tianna Sansbury, Laura Monaghan, Kenneth Branagh
RATING: PG

Plot

There was a law in Australia in the 1930s that "mixed race" children must be separated from their Aboriginal families. But three young girls, the sisters Molly and Daisy and their cousin Gracie, escape from the detention centre 1,500 miles away from their home. They begin a long walk back across the country. Their guide is the rabbit-proof fence that crosses Western Australia.

Review

Film director Phillip Noyce illustrates the true story with beautiful locations. Kenneth Branagh plays the man from the Australian government who has to take the girls back to the detention centre. His performance is extremely sensitive. But in the end, the sad story really belongs to the girls. Everlyn Sampi, who plays Molly, is very convincing.

Verdict

Low on schmaltz with three great performances from the girls. A fascinating look at a piece of history that most Australians would prefer to forget.

INFO BUBBLE

The rabbit-proof fence was built between 1901 and 1907 to keep rabbits out of parts of Western Australia. There are three fences in Western Australia, together they are 3,256km long.

b) Would you like to watch the film? Why or why not?

c) Complete the word web.

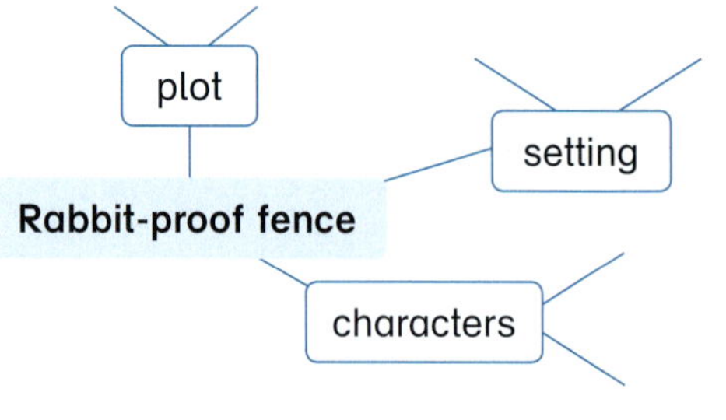

The girls have to walk for nine weeks. What difficulties could they face? Write down your ideas.

B7 A long way home

a) Watch the film "Rabbit-proof fence". What do you learn about life in the camp (0:13:40-0:28:08)? Why are some of the children sent to a 'proper' school?

b) On their long way home the girls face many dangers. What are they?

On their long way home the girls meet some strangers. Who are these people? How do they react when they see the girls?

What is special about Molly's family?

c) Do you think that the film has a happy ending? Can you think of a different title for the film? Discuss in small groups.

how to p. 160 talk about films

B8 Sorry

In February 2008 the Australian prime minister, Kevin Rudd, officially apologised for the wrongs that had been done to the Aborigines.

a) Watch the video clip and listen to the main part of his speech (until 0:03:30). How does it make you feel?

DVD XX

b) Read the following excerpt from Rudd's speech. Use a dictionary to look up words you cannot work out from the context.

how to p. 155 use a dictionary

p. XX XX

WB p. XX XX

"We apologise especially for the removal of Aboriginal and Torres Strait Islander children from their families, their communities and their country.

For the pain, suffering and hurt of these Stolen Generations, their descendants and for their families left behind, we say sorry.

To the mothers and the fathers, the brothers and the sisters, for the breaking up of families and communities, we say sorry.

And for the indignity and degradation thus inflicted on a proud people and a proud culture, we say sorry."

Tipp
Schau dir auch noch mal A8 zur Geschichte Australiens auf Seite 19 an.

c) Who does Kevin Rudd say sorry to? What is he apologising for? Why?

Find out how Aborigines reacted to Rudd's speech.

B9 Choose

DVD XX

1. **Watch the video clip "Uluru" on the DVD. Find out what Uluru (Ayers Rock) means to the Aborigines and present your findings.**
2. **Bindi mentions the story of the Rainbow Serpent. Read the story on page 135. Find your own way of presenting it to the class.**

wordbank Australia p. 164

3. **Aborigines have many interesting traditions. Find out more about one or more of the following topics: their music, art, symbols, ... Prepare a display or a short presentation.**

B10 Jack in the outback

Look at the photos. What do you think the children are doing?

Jack lives on a station in the outback. He is writing to David, a pupil from Germany, who needs information for a school project.

p. XX XX

a) **Read Jack's email and find out if you were right.**

Subject: Re: School of the Air

Hi David,

G'day mate. How're you going? It's really hot out here on our sheep station today. I had to help my dad earlier. We have some problems with dingoes at the moment. They killed some of our sheep and that means we lose quite a lot of money.

But you asked me about my school, the School of the Air. Sorry for answering late, I know you need the info for your project at school. I'm sending you a photo of my little brother "at school". Now you can see what it looks like, too. So, the SOA – the School of the Air – only exists in Australia! For people like me who live in the outback it's the only way to stay on the station and "go to school". In the past you had to leave your home and go to a boarding school for higher education. But that all changed with technology.

In 1951 the first SOA started at Alice Springs and made its first broadcast. Now there are more than sixteen schools of the air around Australia! And the SOA program now teaches all students and also adults so that all members of the family can finish school.

I found an old photo from the 1980s, it shows how pupils communicated back then. I'm so glad we don't have to use high frequency radio transceivers – a special kind of radio – anymore today!

Now we use more modern technology. There is a new interactive broadband satellite network that covers our area, too. I can even watch my teachers!

I use a web camera to watch and respond to lessons in real time! I can email teachers and the other students and I can interact with the whiteboard that they are using. We can also have group discussions! That's really great.

My teacher also visits me at home at least once a year! The best thing is the sports carnival we have every year. All the students and their families get together for a day and have so much fun!

So, that's it for now. I hope your presentation goes well.

Bye! Jack

b) **Read the email again.**

- **Explain what the School of the Air is. What is special about it?**
- **Why is Jack happy about the satellite network? How does it help him?**
- **Compare the SOA with a regular school. What is the same and what is different? Think of the students and the teachers.**

c) **Which school do you like better – your school or the School of the Air? Explain why.**

WB p. XX XX

B11 Target task: A personal message

In this Theme you read about many people and their lives in Australia. Imagine you could send a personal message to one of the people on pages 24 to 31, what would you say? React to something you found interesting in his or her life.

WB p. XX XX

1. Choose a person and first summarize what you have learnt about him or her.
2. Think about the contents of your message.
   - What would you like to say to that person?
   - What is your emotional reaction to what the person experienced, said or did?
3. Decide on the type of message (email, letter, audio recording, video message, ...).
4. Show your message to a partner. Give each other feedback on content and language.
5. Present your message to the class.

Dear Bindi,
I loved your report about your life as an Aboriginal. It sounds so interesting – especially the dance tour! Maybe I could come and see you when you visit Germany.
Your life sounds very exciting. I don't have many hobbies, but I like art, too.
It is cool that you have so many 'aunts' and 'uncles'. I have a very small family with just my mum, my dad and my little sister.
I can't imagine what it's like to have so many family members.
Do you ever get tired of having so many brothers and sisters?
Best wishes,
Louisa

model text

P7 Explain

Explain what you have to do.

Ich soll ...

Wir sollen ...

...

1. Use your notes and your imagination.
2. Repeat and practise reading the numbers with a partner.
3. Read the following excerpt from Rudd's speech.
4. Use a dictionary to look up words you cannot work out from the context.
5. Research how Aborigines live today and present your findings.

P8 A new life down under

LiF p. 180 3R

a) Complete the following sentences. Use the simple past.

1. Lachlan (live) in Glasgow until he (be) 20 years old.
2. He (study) sport and (fall) in love with life in Australia.
3. Jan (start) a new life in Australia because his parents (move) there.
4. He always (like) writing and (become) a journalist.
5. Claire (live) in Germany until she (be) five.
6. She (miss) her old friends but soon (make) new friends at her new school.
7. Hassan (leave) his home and (immigrate) to Australia when he (be) 21.
8. He (follow) his dream and (open) a restaurant in Sydney.
9. Katie (grow up) in Korea and (decide) to study in Sydney.
10. She (look) for a job and (find) one as a waitress in a restaurant.

1. Lachlan lived in Glasgow until he ...

CD XX

b) Listen to the CD and check your sentences.

P9 Numbers

a) With a partner, read the numbers and figures in the box. Take turns.

160 • 2018 • 1/4 • August 22 • 5 November 2012 • 1/3 • 5,999 • 8:45am • 3:30pm • 9.15% • 78.03% • 100% • 1/2 • 3/8 • 3/4 • 30p • £11 • £2.15 • €6 • €4.77 • $101.50

CD XX

b) Listen to the CD and check.

What do you think the numbers are used for? Think of some examples.

P10 Bindi's story

Look at Bindi's story on page 26 again and complete the following sentences.

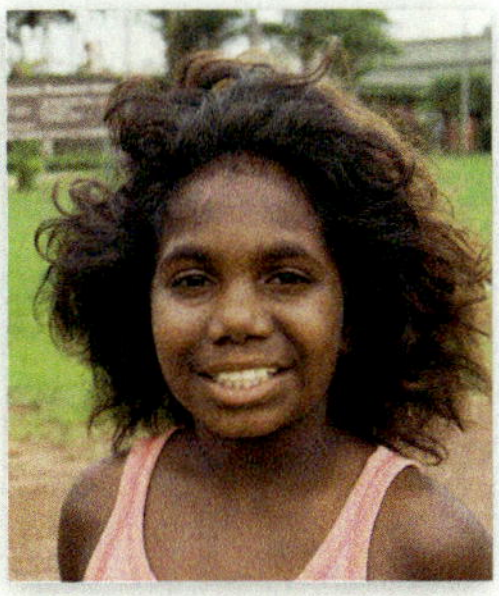

1. Bindi's story is about her …
2. Bindi is a descendant of the …
3. She loves her culture as it has such great … and …
4. "Dreaming stories" are always about …
5. As a member of a dance group she gets to …
6. When her dad was young …
7. Today it is different and Bindi has …
8. The great thing about being part of an Aboriginal family is …

P11 Questions for Jack

a) **Write questions for Jack about his life in the outback.**

1. ever – lonely? – feel – Do you
2. snow? – ever – Have you – seen
3. sheep – on the station? – do you have – How many
4. the station? – on – Can you – use a – mobile phone
5. go to – dad – a boarding school? – Did your
6. did you – get – When – new technology? – the
7. difficult to – get used – Was it – to the – new system?
8. your teacher – Has – already visited – this – year?
9. sports carnival? – was – How – the – last –
10. are – plans – for – the – What – future? – your –

1. Do you ever feel lonely?

b) **Read B10 on page 30 again. Write down what you think Jack would answer. Answer at least five of the questions.**

P12 Fun with words

Play a guessing game with a partner: Pick a word from the box and describe it. Your partner has to guess it as fast as possible.

newspaper • restaurant • surfing • waitress • immigrant • population • figure • didgeridoo • tradition • family • outback • fence • apology • station • dingo • boarding school • radio transceiver • web camera • whiteboard • sports carnival • teacher

Optional

O The Great Barrier Reef

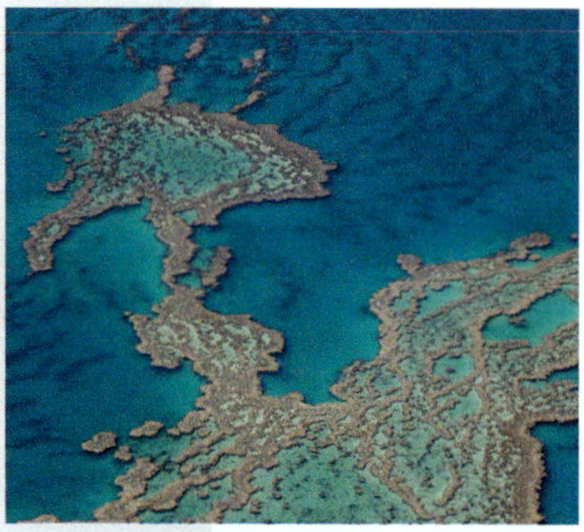

The Great Barrier Reef – A UNESCO World Heritage Site

- The Great Barrier Reef – more than 2000 km long – is situated off the north-east coast of Australia. It has got the world's largest collection of coral reefs.
- It is the only living organism that can be seen from outer space. Even the astronauts who walked on the moon could see it!
- 2 million tourists visit this famous World Heritage Site every year.
- It began to grow about 18 million years ago and consists of living rocks made up of colonies of billions of tiny creatures called polyps.
- There live around 1500 species of fish, over 400 species of coral, more than 4000 species of molluscs and over 1500 species of sponge.
- The Great Barrier Reef was named by Captain James Cook in 1770.
- The reef is a natural barrier against the strong tropical storms of the South Pacific.
- Environmentalists say that climate change is the main threat to the reef's future.

The Great Barrier Reef – a unique wonder of the natural world – is in danger!

Which of the facts do you find most interesting? Why?

Research what environmentalists such as "Friends of the Earth Far North Queensland" are doing to save the reef. Report to the class.

Extreme New Zealand

2

Maori culture - what do you know?

Find out about Maori war dances, tattoos and traditional meeting grounds on page 56.

Want to know how it feels to climb a glacier?

Check out page 40!

How dventurous are you?

Take the quiz on page 37 to find out!

Read about: the history of New Zealand

A

- Du sprichst über riskante Sportarten und findest heraus, welche Extremsportarten man in Neuseeland ausüben kann.
- Du präsentierst ein echtes oder ausgedachtes Abenteuer. (Zielaufgabe)

B

- Du lernst etwas über die Geschichte, Geografie und Kultur von Neeseeland.
- Du erstellst einen Radio-Dokumentarbericht über Neuseeland. (Zielaufgabe)

A1 Adventurous sports

Look at the pictures. Which of these sports do you think are cool? Can you say why?

Picture 1 is skateboarding. Skateboarding is ...

LiF p. 181 4R
p. XX XX

a) Look at the photos and name the different activities. Talk about them.

CD X/XX XX

street BMXing • paragliding • skateboarding • doing scooter stunts • snowboarding • skiing • surfing • indoor climbing • kayaking • kite surfing • ...

LiF p. 181 5R

b) Talk to a partner about the different sports. Which ones have you tried?

Have you ever tried ... ?

Yes, I have.

No, I haven't.

No, I've never ... but I have ...

What was it like?

It was ...

It was awesome! • It was hard – I was so proud of myself! • I was really scared. • It looks easy, but it's not! • I kept falling off/over. • I gave up after .... • You can do so many tricks! • ...

WB p. XX XX

c) Would you like to try out one of these sports or even do one on a regular basis?

I would like to ... because ... • I would love to ... • I wouldn't like to ... • My dream is to ... • ...

A2 How adventurous are you?

a) Do the quiz with a partner and write down your answers.

p. XX XX

How adventurous are you?

Are you open to new experiences? Are you a daredevil or a chicken? Do our quiz to find out!

1. Your school bus breaks down. It is raining. What do you do?
   A. You wait for the next bus.
   B. You text your mum to pick you up.
   C. You walk home through the fields.

2. You want to visit a friend who lives 80 km away, but you have no money. What do you do?
   A. You ask your father to drive you.
   B. You go on your bike!
   C. You tell your friend you can't come.

3. You go to an amusement park. What do you do?
   A. You ride all the roller coasters!
   B. You go on the less scary rides.
   C. You just watch but don't go on the rides.

4. You are planning your next class trip at school. What is your idea?
   A. A week of sailing in the Netherlands.
   B. A four star hotel at the beach.
   C. A camping trip with outdoor sports.

5. You and your family are on holiday. What do you want to do?
   A. Go paragliding over the mountains.
   B. Sunbathe by the pool.
   C. Go snorkelling and discover the sealife.

Work out your score on page 45!

b) Are you surprised at your result? Talk about it with a partner.

A3 Why we seek danger for fun

a) Why do people seek danger for fun? What do you think? Collect ideas.

I think it's because … | *I'm not sure, but maybe it's because …* | *…*

WB p. XX XX

b) Read the article. Compare your ideas with the ideas from the text.

Fight or flight – why we seek danger for fun

If you went to the top of a tall building and looked down, how would you feel? Would you be scared? Would you be excited? Many people might say that they feel unsafe – it's a long way down to the ground after all!

Why do people take risks?
It is normal for people to feel scared in dangerous situations. We know that we need to avoid risks, because they might end in disaster. As humans, we naturally want to survive. But there are people who love taking risks. Do you love roller coasters? Maybe you want to do a bungee jump? These are adventurous risks, but many people take them. Why is that? The answer is simple: adrenaline.

The "fight or flight" response
Adrenaline is released when our "fight or flight" response is triggered. Has this ever happened to you? You suddenly become more aware of your surroundings, your heart starts to beat a lot faster and you start breathing differently. That is when adrenaline kicks in.

What is adrenaline?
Adrenaline is a hormone. It is linked to the release of endorphins, like dopamine. Adrenaline helps you cope with pain. It also makes you want to come back for more!

Risk taking for fun
Although the sports and the situations seem dangerous, safety is always the first priority. Extreme risk-takers know how to cope with these situations and they know when to stop if a situation is too risky.

Risk taking is natural
Risk taking is not just for fun. Without risk-takers, the human race would not be able to survive. Humans and animals are naturally programmed to look for new things. For example, if an animal explored a new territory, which could be a huge risk, it might find food for its family, which would help its family survive.

So, actually, taking risks is maybe not as crazy as you think!

wordbank sports p. 166

WB p. XX XX

c) Look at the picture. Is the man a risk-taker? Use information from the article.

A4 New Zealand – the birthplace of extreme sports

Choose a picture and describe it. The others guess which one it is.

a) Match the sports with the descriptions and pictures.

p. XX
XX

New Zealand is the birthplace of extreme sports and adventure. Here are some of the exciting and crazy ways you can get your heart racing and blood pumping!

zorbing **bungy jumping** **ziplining** **jet boating**

A

B

1 This is a very popular tourist attraction in New Zealand. With a kind of elastic band tied around your ankles, you can jump from platforms and bridges all around New Zealand!

2 Roll down a hill in a big plastic ball. Inside the ball is a second, smaller ball – that's where you sit or stand. If you want to, you can even add in some water to the mix! Get ready to roll!

C

D

3 Start from 175 metres above a river canyon, then race down a one kilometre long zipline at up to 160 kilometres per hour. It literally takes your breath away!

4 On this exciting adventure you will speed down rivers and fly over the water. This is one activity that is sure to get the adrenaline flowing!

b) Which of these sports would you like to try? Which are too dangerous for you?

A5 My travel blog

Look at the pictures. Collect words and phrases that you expect in the text.

p. XX XX

a) Read the blog. Where did Emily go?

akiwiadventureforemily.blogs.co.uk

An icy adventure

Read the amazing story of my latest adventure!

I think all my friends and family would agree that it's not often I don't know what to say, but I have been trying since last week to find the right words to describe Fox Glacier on the South Island. It's amazing. Unforgettable.

Experienced mountaineers and ice-climbers have been exploring the glacier for years, but they're not the only ones – tourists can enjoy it too. You can go on guided hikes or take a helicopter up to the top! Wow! How cool is that!

I decided to do a heli-hike. I was so excited once it was booked! I couldn't wait to be on the ice.

I first saw the glacier from the window of the helicopter. It took my breath away, even then. Soon we landed and our adventure began!

There is something fascinating about glaciers. Something magical. Maybe it's because glaciers change, so you never know what you are going to find.

Walking on the ice, in glacier boots and using walking poles, was amazing. I think the highlight was when we found an ice cave. From inside the ice looks so blue, I couldn't believe it. I took so many photos!

We found some little streams of melted glacier water, too. The water is really clean, so I filled up my water bottle and tried it. It was really cold and so good! We spent a few hours exploring, and I loved every minute of it.

Before the heli-hike, I thought that being on a glacier would be a once-in-a-lifetime experience – but I loved it so much, I have already been thinking about when I can go back!

If you're ever in New Zealand, check it out!

WB p. XX XX

b) How does Emily express her enthusiasm and excitement? Collect words and phrases.

amazing, unforgettable, ...

c) Use the words and phrases.

- **Write a sentence about each photo.**
- **Write a blog comment.**
- **Write a postcard from Emily to one of her friends.**

A6 Choose

1. Choose one extreme sport from this Theme and collect all the information about it in a word web.
2. Make a list of extreme sports. Sort them from least risky to most risky. Compare your list with a partner.
3. Present an extreme sport of your choice. You could give a computer presentation.
4. Make your own quiz about extreme sports for the class.

how to p. 150 present

A7 Sports and the environment

Doing sports is a great way to keep fit and make new friends – but have you ever thought about how sports affect the environment? Some are environmentally friendly, others are not.

a) Which sports do you think are environmetally friendly? Which are not?

b) Work with a partner. Listen to two people discussing a sport. Which environmental impacts do they talk about? Take notes.

CD X/XX
WB p. XX XX

c) Look at the sports in A1, A4 and A5 again. Choose one and talk to a partner about the impact of this sport on the environment. How environmentally friendly is it?

I think ... is bad for the environment because ...

... is environmentally friendly if you ...

...

It is obvious that ... • It is not a good idea to ... • ... is not ... • Is it really necessary to ... ? • ...

harmless • harmful • need a lot of equipment • need little equipment • fly long distances • enjoy sport locally • change the countryside • destroy areas of wildlife • ...

how to p. 152 write your opinion

Write your opinion about the environmental impact of a sport of your choice. You can use the model text and a dictionary for help.

Hiking is quite a green sport. You don't need much special equipment, just a good pair of shoes and a backpack. If hikers follow the rules and don't walk in protected areas then they should not harm any plants or wildlife. Hiking is even greener if people take trains or buses to where they want to hike.

model text

WB p. XX XX

A8 Safe and sound

a) Read the brochure and find out about the Outdoor Safety Code.

Have a great time on a Great Walk

New Zealand is a great place to go walking, and many people go there especially to enjoy the great outdoors. Some of the most popular walks are the nine Great Walks. These hikes take three or four days and lead you through national parks and forests, into valleys, up mountains and much more.

You can stay in huts or tents along the way.

Put safety first when you hike a Great Walk. It is important to plan and prepare your trip well and be well-equipped. So before you go, know the Outdoor Safety Code.

The Outdoor Safety Code – 5 simple rules to help you stay safe when hiking

1. Plan your trip.
2. Tell someone.
3. Be aware of the weather.
4. Know your limits.
5. Take sufficient supplies.

LiF p. 182 7R

b) What do the rules mean? Match the speech bubbles and talk to a partner.

'Plan your trip' means you have to …

You should tell someone …

You shouldn't go hiking if …

You must always check …

…

'Take sufficient supplies' means you need to …

… the weather forecast before you go.

… where you will be walking.

… take enough food and drink for the hike.

… you are not fit enough.

… look at a map and work out all the details.

…

wordbank sports p. 166

c) Write five safety rules for a sport of your choice. Think of rules to follow before doing the sport, whilst doing it and after doing it.

check • use • wear • learn • tell • practise • take care not to • …

never • always • …

For hockey: 1. You must check your equipment.
2. …

d) Now talk to a partner and explain your safety rules.

You must remember to …

Never play football without …

You shouldn't …

…

WB p. XX XX

A9 Rescue on Routeburn

a) Look at the photo. What sort of landscape do you see? What problems could there be if you walk in that landscape?

b) Listen to the report about a couple who went walking on the Routeburn Track, one of New Zealand's Great Walks. Take notes on the weather conditions, the couple's behaviour and how the woman was saved. You can find help in your workbook.

CD X/XX XX
how to p. 145 listen

c) What happened? Compare your notes in a group.

WB p. XX XX

Look at the Outdoor Safety Code in A8. Then listen to the report again and check whether the couple followed all the rules.

A10 Target task: An adventurous experience

You are going to give an oral presentation about a real or imaginary adventurous experience.

p. XX XX
WB p. XX XX

1. Think about what experience you want to present.
2. Write a text or a dialogue about it. This will form the basis for your presentation. Use words and phrases from A5.
3. Ask a partner to edit your text or dialogue.
4. Practise reading out your text or talking about your experience.
5. Present your experience. You could make a recording. Ask for feedback.

CD X/XX XX
model text

Bungee at the harbour
I got a bungee jump for my birthday! It was on my wishlist but when I got the present, at first it felt weird. Now I really had to go and do it!
When I arrived at the port crane, I was enthusiastic about the location. But most importantly: from below, the crane did not look that high. I watched some jumps, which made me want to try!
But as soon as I started to climb the crane, I was really scared. When I finally got to the top ...

An awesome skydive
Me: Hi, Mum, it's me.
Mum: Hello! How are you?
Me: I'm so excited, Mum! Today I did the most awesome thing. I went skydiving!
Mum: You ... you what?
Me: I went skydiving – with Dad! And it was amazing, the coolest thing I have ever done! Before we went up in the plane I was so scared, but my instructor was really nice. ...

P1 Explain

Explain what you have to do.

Ich soll ...

Wir sollen ...

...

1. Match the sports with the descriptions and pictures.
2. Collect words and phrases that you expect in the text.
3. Write a comment about the environmental impact of a sport of your choice.
4. Retell the story.
5. Ask someone to edit your text or dialogue.

P2 Extreme questions

LiF p. 181 5R

Interview a partner.

Have you ever	tried been to heard of eaten ...	kangaroo? bungy jumping? Australia? zorbing? New Zealand? ...

Yes, I have.

No, I haven't.

No, never.

P3 Being adventurous means ...

LiF p. 181 4R

a) **What does 'being adventurous' mean to you? Write 5 to 7 sentences. You can use A2 for help.**

Being adventurous means riding the biggest, scariest roller coaster.
Being adventurous means going ...
...

b) **Share your sentences with a partner. Do you have similar ideas?**

P4 The right preposition

a) **Copy the phrases into your exercise book and add the correct preposition from the box.**

of • with • in • for • to • to

1. be full ??? fear
2. be attracted ??? extreme sports
3. cope ??? pain
4. look crazy ??? an outsider
5. be highly valuable ??? society
6. a recipe ??? survival

be full of fear, ...

CD XX

b) **Listen to the CD and check your phrases.**

P5 Active people

a) Use the sentence parts to write sentences with for and since.

LiF p. 182 6

1. Diego / doing parkour / last year
2. Robin and Janis / surfing / two hours
3. Anthony / mountain biking / last summer
4. Carla / skateboarding / half an hour
5. Frank / surfing / lunchtime
6. Layla / skiing / she was four
7. Jo / bouldering / two weeks
8. Adam / street BMXing / 1.30 pm

Diego has been doing parkour since last year.

b) Listen to the CD and check your sentences.

CD XX

P6 So many questions

Work with a partner. One of you is Liz. Ask questions about her adventure on the glacier and give short answers.

Was it easy to walk on the glacier?
No, it wasn't.
Would you like to go back to the glacier again?
Yes, I would.
Does the ice really look blue in caves?
Yes, ...
... ?
...

P7 Especially sporty

a) Complete the sentences with the modal verbs in the box. Look at A4 for help.

shouldn't • shouldn't • must • can • need • shouldn't • can't

LiF p. 182 7R

1. If you want to go bungee jumping, you ??? be scared of heights.
2. You ??? to listen carefully to the safety instructions when you go bungee jumping.
3. If you don't like water, you ??? go jet boating.
4. There are different kinds of zorbing that you ??? do.
5. Before you go bungee jumping, you ??? check the equipment.
6. If you ??? swim, maybe you ??? go jet boating.

b) Listen to the CD and check your sentences.

CD XX

Quiz results for A2

1. a) 2 pts, b) 1 pt, c) 3 pts
2. a) 2 pts, b) 3 pts, c) 1 pt
3. a) 3 pts, b) 2 pts, c) 1 pt
4. a) 2 pts, b) 1 pt, c) 3 pts
5. a) 3 pts, b) 1 pt, c) 2 pts

5–9
You could be a bit more confident. Do not always stay away from things you find scary. Try taking a risk now and again. It can be fun!

6–12
You are not a daredevil at heart, but you like taking a few risks. You seek challenges, but you like to think first. Things are looking good for you.

13–15
You like taking risks. You are brave and bold – a real daredevil! But have you thought about the dangers involved?

B1 Impressions of New Zealand

What do you know about New Zealand? Collect information.

p. XX
XX

a) Look at the pictures and the three topics. Which ones go together?

History and culture | Nature and geography | Maori traditions and legends

Auckland

A kiwi

Maori Haka dance

Maori waka (canoe)

A geyser in Rotorua

The All Blacks playing rugby

Mount Cook National Park

Maori legends

b) What would you be interested in finding out more about? Talk to a partner.

I'd be interested in finding out more about ...

...

I'd be interested in learning about ...

Auckland and other cities • the animals • Maori culture • the landscape • the All Blacks • ...

WB p. XX
XX

B2 Where New Zealand began

The first people to come to New Zealand were the Maori. It is thought that they came from other islands in Polynesia around 1,000 years ago. It is believed that they reached New Zealand in large canoes – the so-called *waka* – and navigated using the stars and the ocean currents.

a) Look at the map. Talk about where the Maori came from.

b) What skills do you need to survive such a dangerous journey?

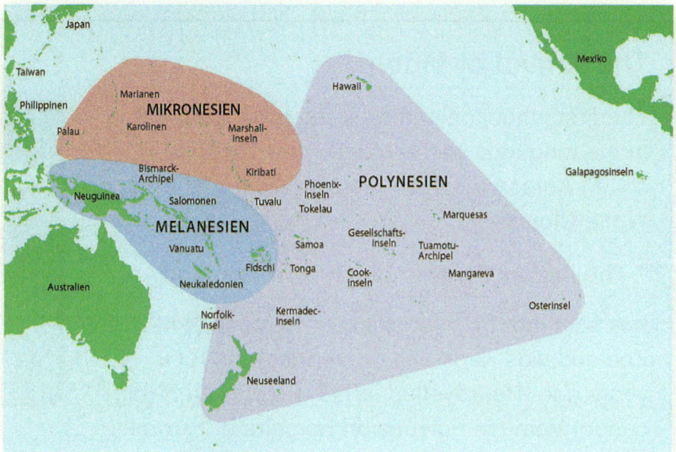

You need to be good at navigating.

You should be capable of working ...

You must know a lot about building waka.

...

prepare • navigate • repair • catch fish • row a boat • build • ...

LiF p. XX 4R

WB p. XX XX

DVD XX

LAND & LEUTE 2

Neuseeland

Neuseeland liegt im südwestlichen Pazifik. Es besteht aus zwei größeren Hauptinseln und zahlreichen kleineren Inseln. Neuseeland liegt etwa 1.500 km östlich von Australien. Heute leben ca. 4,4 Millionen Menschen auf den Inseln. Die Hauptstadt ist Wellington und die größte Stadt heißt Auckland. Beide Städte liegen auf der Nordinsel. Neuseeländer werden häufig als ‚Kiwis' bezeichnet. ‚Kiwi' ist auch der Name eines einheimischen Vogels, der zudem eines der nationalen Symbole Neuseelands ist.
Als Amtssprachen gelten in Neuseeland Englisch, die Sprache der Maori und die neuseeländische Zeichensprache. Die Währung ist der New Zealand Dollar.

Heutzutage ist Neuseeland offiziell ein zweisprachiges Land. Die Gesellschaft besteht nicht nur aus der Maori- und der europäischstämmigen Kultur, sie ist multikulturell, da in den letzten Jahren viele Menschen von den Pazifischen Inseln und aus Asien zugewandert sind. Insbesondere Auckland ist eine multikulturelle Stadt. Neuseelands außergewöhnliche und abwechslungsreiche Landschaft zieht viele Touristen an. Das macht Neuseeland auch als Kulisse für die Filmindustrie attraktiv. Viele Filmemacher haben Neuseeland als Drehort für ihre Filme gewählt. Der vielleicht berühmteste ist Peter Jackson, der die Trilogie Der Herr der Ringe in Neuseeland gedreht hat.

Finde mehr über die Geschichte der Fahne von Neuseeland heraus und berichte der Klasse.

p. XX XX

WB p. XX XX

B3 History of New Zealand

a) **Skim the two texts. Which topic do you find more interesting? Why?**

how to read p. 146

b) **Read one of the texts. Take notes in two colours: green for what you find important or interesting, and red for things you don't understand or have questions about.**

The Arrival of Māori

The first inhabitants in New Zealand were Māori. In the language of the Māori, New Zealand is called Aotearoa, which means 'Land of the Long White Cloud'.

The first explorer to reach New Zealand

It is said that the first explorer to reach New Zealand was Kupe. He arrived around 1000 years ago. He travelled in his *waka hourua* (big canoe) from his Polynesian homeland, Hawaiki.

What did Māori eat?

Māori were good hunters and fishermen. They made fishing nets and they used bone and stone to make fish hooks. They also hunted birds and they grew vegetables from Polynesia, including the *kumara* (sweet potato), but they also ate native food, such as berries. They made baskets to carry food. They created little storehouses, called *pataka*, as you can see in the picture, so they could protect their food from water.

Māori and the British Empire

In 1840, Māori and British representatives signed the Treaty of Waitangi. With this treaty, the Māori accepted British government and were given the same rights as British people. One year later, in 1841, New Zealand became a British colony. More and more settlers came to New Zealand and received land. This led to conflicts between Māori and the Europeans. By 1872, wars over land ended.

Maori culture in New Zealand

Until the end of the Second World War in 1945, most Māori lived in rural communities. Then there was a trend of Māori-migration to the cities. Māori claimed more representation and raised awareness for their difficult economic situation. Then, from the 1970s onwards, the Māori language became more important in urban New Zealand. The first bilingual school (Māori and English) opened in 1978. The Māori language and culture began to play a bigger role in everyday life.

WB p. XX XX

The Arrival of Europeans

A Dutch visitor

Abel Tasman, a Dutch explorer, was the first European to discover New Zealand. He was on an expedition looking for minerals. He first sighted parts of the South Island in 1642.

The first contact Tasman had with Māori was at the top of the South Island. He was spotted by groups of Māori men who were in two canoes. Tasman sent out some of his men in small boats, but four of them were killed by the Māori men due to misunderstandings.

Tasman never set foot on New Zealand. Due to the attack, he and his men sailed further north. Tasman's employers, the Dutch East India Company, declared his expedition unsuccessful, as he didn't find any minerals.

A British Captain

British Captain James Cook was another European who went on an expedition in the Pacific, a little later than Tasman. Whilst on this expedition, Cook's cabin boy saw part of the North Island near Gisborne in 1769. After that, Cook travelled around the island and mapped the country.

European settlers

It was mostly sealers, whalers and missionaries who went to New Zealand before 1840. They had lots of contact with Māori, especially near the coast and traded items with them. Some of the items that they traded were guns which the Māori used to fight against other tribes. The use of guns led to the deaths of several thousands of Māori. Diseases brought by the Europeans also led to many deaths of Māori.

c) Work with classmates who read the same text. Compare your notes and help each other with anything you don't understand.

WB p. XX XX

d) Work with a partner who read the other text. Present your findings to one another.

e) ☆ Work with a partner. Make a timeline of the history of New Zealand.

☾ Work with a partner who read the same text as you. Make a quiz about New Zealand. Swap with another pair.

☼ Use your notes and write a short text about the text you read.

B4 New Zealand geography

Look at the photos. What landscapes do you see? *A lake, ...*

p. XX
XX
CD X/XX
how to p. 145
listen

a) Listen to the tour guides. Match the photos to the names in the box.

Southern Alps • Lake Taupo • Pancake Rocks • Champagne Pool • Fiordland • Wharariki Beach

b) Listen again. Match the sentence halves.

1. The North Island is warmer
2. Lake Taupo is the biggest
3. The water in the Champagne Pool
4. Wharariki Beach is known for
5. The Southern Alps cross almost
6. Some Mountains in the Southern Alps are

a. lake in New Zealand.
b. is around 75 degrees celsius.
c. than the South Island.
d. over 3,000 metres high.
e. its sand dunes and beautiful scenery.
f. the complete length of the South Island.

c) Which of the places would you like to see? Why?

I would like to see ... because ...

I find ... very interesting because ...

...

B5 Kiwi culture

a) Get into groups of three. Each group member reads a text. Find out more about it by listening to the CD. For one text there is a video clip, too. Take notes about:

p. XX XX

Amiria: Where does she live? What does she say about her family? What does she say about her life? What do you learn about Maori culture?

Food: What is it called? When was first produced? What is special about it? Why is it typical for New Zealand?

Haka: What is special about the dance? What do you find out about the history of it? Why do players perform it before rugby matches?

CD X/XX XX

My name is Amiria and I am part Maori and part Pakeha – that means European New Zealander. My grandparents on my mum's side are Maori, my dad's side are Pakeha. I'm proud of my heritage, and can speak both English and the Maori language – although my English is better. In school we learn Te reo Maori – the Maori language. I find this important. There are a lot of kids like me, living between two cultures. And learning the language not only at home, but in school, is very important for understanding our heritage.

CD X/XX XX

When people think about traditional Kiwi food, they might think of roast lamb, fish and chips or seafood like green lipped muscles. But have you heard of L & P or Anzac biscuits?

L & P (full name: Lemon and Paeroa) is a soft drink made in New Zealand. It was created in 1907 in the town of Paeroa. It was made by combining lemon juice with fizzy water from the town.

Anzac biscuits are sweet biscuits popular in New Zealand and Australia. They are associated with the Australian and New Zealand Army Corps (ANZAC) that was established in World War 1.

CD X/XX XX
DVD XX

The haka is a traditional Maori dance. There are many different types of haka. The most famous one is called Ka Mate, which is the haka that the New Zealand Rugby Team performs before their matches.

b) Compare and complete your notes.

c) What have you found out about Kiwi culture? Inform the others in your group.

WB p. XX XX

B6 Choose

1. Make a word web about one of the topics on New Zealand, such as food, geography, history, culture, ...
2. The film industry not only uses New Zealand as a film set, the country also produces many films. Go online, choose a film and tell the class about characters, setting and plot.
3. Rugby is a very popular sport in New Zealand. Find out the rules and tell the class.
4. Act out a scene from the history of New Zealand.

B7 Sensitive nature

how to p. 147 mediate

You have just arrived in New Zealand and are travelling with someone who doesn't speak very much English. He wants to check whether he needs to declare any goods but he doesn't understand the poster. Explain to him in German what it says.

PLEASE READ THIS GUIDE CAREFULLY

When you fly to New Zealand from overseas, it's important to follow New Zealand law. That means you must declare or dispose of risk goods at our international borders. You might have goods with you that could be carrying pests and diseases. These pests and diseases could cause millions of dollars in damage to our country's environment and economy.

RISK GOODS YOU MUST DECLARE INCLUDE

All of these goods are a risk for New Zealand and must be declared. (If you are not sure, ask an Inspector).

DECLARE

Ingredients used in cooking, all dairy products, honey, honeycombs and other bee products.

DECLARE

Any plants, plant cuttings, bulbs, corms and seeds.

DECLARE

Traditional or herbal medicines or remedies, health supplements and homeopathic remedies that include animal or plant products.

DECLARE

All outdoor, camping, sports equipment, hiking boots and other sporting footwear that could be contaminated with soil, seeds or water.

DECLARE

All wooden items, drums, carvings, spears and masks, items stuffed with seeds or straw, made of bamboo, cane, coconut or straw, or hair, fur, unprocessed wool, skin, feathers and bone.

DECLARE

Fruit and vegetables, fresh or dried.

DECLARE

Any meat, fish or poultry.

Note: For a full list of risk goods that must be declared see your Passenger Arrival Card or visit www. biosecurity.govt.nz.

Talk in class about why 'biosecurity' is so important in New Zealand.

New Zealand ..., which means that ...

It is important that New Zealand ...

...

B8 Kiwi lingo

The English spoken in New Zealand is very similar to the English spoken in Australia. However, there are words, phrases and expressions that are typical Kiwi lingo or slang.

a) **Look at the Kiwi words and phrases in the blue box. What could they mean?**

flip flops – an open, flat shoe | 'no problem' or 'OK' | Maori word for food

jandals • bro • togs • hot chips • kai • sweet as

friend or brother | French fries | swimsuit or swimming trunks

b) **Listen to the CD and check the meanings. Were you right? Take notes.**

CD XX

c) **Check your notes with a partner.**

Are there any expressions in the language you use that are slang or typical youth lingo? Collect words and phrases and write English explanations.

B9 Target task: A radio feature on New Zealand

In a group, you are going to create a radio feature on New Zealand. It should be a recording that lasts several minutes and you should present different aspects about New Zealand. You could record it. But first, find out what a radio feature is!

p. XX XX
WB p. XX XX

1. As a group, think about what you want to present. Think about:
   - which facts are especially interesting about New Zealand? What did you find out in this Theme?
   - your opinion! Don't just include facts. Talk about what you found interesting. Talk about your view on ideas, values, beliefs and the way people interact.

how to work on a target task p. 149

2. Each member of your group decides on at least one topic. Make notes on your topic.
3. Find other people in class who are working on the same topic as you. Share your ideas and findings with them. You are now the experts on that topic (expert groups).
4. Go back to your home group.
5. Script the radio feature.
6. Rehearse it with your group.
7. Record your radio feature.
8. Share your radio features in class.

New Zealand geography
- lots of different kinds of landscape, such as beaches, fiords, mountains, lakes
- suprising that there are so many different landscapes – the country is quite small
- nature and countryside is important for tourism
- ...

CD X/XX XX

P8 Explain

Explain what you have to do.

Ich soll …

Wir sollen …

…

1. Skim the two texts.
2. Make a timeline of the history of New Zealand.
3. Swap with a pair who worked on the other text.
4. Inform each other about what you have found out about Kiwi culture.
5. Read the quotes about what biosecurity means in everyday life.

P9 Interest in New Zealand

LiF p. 181
4R

a) **You have learnt a lot about New Zealand. If you could go there, what would you be interested in seeing and doing? Write sentences.**

I would be interested in seeing the Pohutu Geyser.
I would be keen on visiting …
…

b) **Share your sentences with a partner. Are you interested in the same things?**

P10 Moving to New Zealand

LiF p. 181
4R

Imagine you and your family were moving to New Zealand. What would you look forward to, dream of, be happy about, … ? Write about it.

I would	dream of look forward to be interested in …	going heli-hiking on Fox Glacier. exploring our new home. getting to know some Kiwis. making new friends. discovering the Maori culture. being in a new place. going bungee jumping. …

P11 The history of New Zealand

a) **Unscramble the sentences about the history of New Zealand.**

1. to reach New Zealand – the first explorer – was Kupe. – According to Maori legend,
2. were – The first Maori explorers – expert hunters – and fishermen.
3. to sight New Zealand – was Dutch explorer – Abel Tasman. – The first European
4. James Cook – The British captain – in 1779. – around – travelled – the island
5. European whalers – Before 1840, – mostly – came – and missionaries – to New Zealand.
6. government. – British – the Maori – accepted – In 1840

b) **Compare your sentences with a partner.**

Practice matters

P12 Working with words

a) Read the sentences and decide on the best word to fill the gaps. Write down the sentences.

1. New Zealand is a ??? society. People from different countries come to live here. *(multicultural, agricultural, bicultural)*
2. ??? is part of a law that all foreign visitors have to follow. It is there to protect New Zealand's natural environment. *(data security, biosecurity, biology)*
3. New Zealand's ??? is largely based on agriculture and tourism. Money is made by selling goods like butter, wool and meat and by providing services. *(diversity, economy, government)*
4. The ??? of New Zealand is diverse and unique. The beautiful landscape makes New Zealand famous around the world. *(geography, industry, produce)*

b) Listen to the CD and check your sentences.

CD XX

P13 New Zealand word webs

a) Copy the following word webs into your exercise book. Complete them with information about New Zealand.

b) Make it into a game: read words from one of your word webs to a partner. How quickly can he or she work out which word web it is?

P14 Sound check

a) How many syllables do the following words have? Copy the table and complete it.

1. culture
2. adventurous
3. journey
4. expedition
5. languages
6. multicultural
7. landscape
8. tradition

two	three	four	five
culture ...	...	...	...

b) Listen to the CD and check your lists.

CD XX

Optional

O Maori culture

Hangi – the traditional way to cook

Maori hangi is cooked in the ground. Meat and vegetables were traditionally wrapped in leaves but today, aluminium foil and wire baskets are often used instead. The wrapped food is placed on hot stones and covered with a wet cloth and earth. The food takes about three to four hours to cook, and tastes smokey and earthy.

Ta Moko – Maori tattoos

Ta Moko are tattoos that reflect a person's personal history. It was also a symbol of social rank, skill, knowledge and marriage. Men had *moko* on their faces, buttocks and thighs, whereas women had them on their lips and chins. Today, *moko* is becoming popular again in traditional and modern forms.

Marae – Maori meeting grounds

A *marae* is a collection of buildings and grounds that is owned by a tribe or family. These meeting grounds are seen as a place to stand and belong. They are used for celebrations, funerals and other tribal events. In order to become one with the people of the marae, a visitor has to take part in a formal welcoming ceremony called a *powhiri*.

Go online and find out more on one of the three topics. Prepare a presentation for your classmates.

Off to work

3

A career expert talks about hard and soft skills on p. 62

Happy with your job?

People explain what they like about their job

Find out what a vlogger says about his job on p. 70

Read about: **How to apply for a job**

A

- Du unterhältst dich über deine Erfahrungen im Berufspraktikum und übst, wie man eine Bewerbung schreibt.
- Du erstellst deine eigene Bewerbungsmappe. (Zielaufgabe)

B

- Du sprichst über die Bedeutung von Geld und darüber, was im Berufsleben wichtig ist.
- Du diskutierst über Kriterien für ein zufriedenes Berufsleben. (Zielaufgabe)

A1 Jobs and work experience

p. XX
XX

Play a guessing game. Think about your work experience. Describe or mime what you did.

wordbank
jobs p. 167

a) Talk to a partner about a work experience you did.

- Where did you do it?
- What did you do?
- What was good?
- What was not so good?
- …

I did my work experience at …

I really liked my colleagues.

At first it was … but then …

…

LiF p. 184
8R

WB p. XX
XX

b) Could you imagine doing the same job in the future? What are your plans after leaving school?

I'm going to start …

I am definitely not going to …

I will probably …

Maybe I'll …

…

A2 Adverts for summer jobs abroad

how to p. 146
read

p. XX
XX

a) Skim the job adverts. Which of these jobs sound interesting or unusual to you? Say why.

CHILDCARE IN IRELAND

The Childcare Experience in Ireland is looking for young people who love children and want to gain experience working in childcare. You will stay with host families and help children at day care centres or in private homes. You will play educational games with the children, help to run the soup kitchen or prepare meals in private households, and clean. Every other weekend you will have a day off. If you are between 16 and 19 years old, have patience, can work in a team, have good communication skills and are reliable, you can have the time of your life in Ireland. Pay: Homestay + 100€ a week.

Find out more and apply at www.childcare-experience.co.ireland

FARMHANDS NEEDED IN GODARVILLE, BELGIUM

We are looking for farm workers to pick fruit (strawberries, cherries) and check it for quality. The more you pick, the more you earn! You will have to work six days a week, so you must be able to work hard and enjoy a challenge. Some knowledge of English and French would be useful as you will live and work with our team of young people from many countries. We provide mobile homes for our workers (shared bathroom and kitchen) on the farm, which is in a beautiful area of Belgium.

Info and application forms at www.farmhand_godarville.co.belg/summer.htm

WORKING WITH ANIMALS IN AN ANIMAL SHELTER IN THE CZECH REPUBLIC

Many animals are homeless. We at Breclav Animal Shelter look after them – and you can help us. You will feed animals and take dogs for walks. You will also help our team with other tasks in the office. If you are reliable, organised and have the ability to work hard, this is the ideal summer job for you. Office skills are not essential but some computer knowledge would be useful. A working knowledge of English is required. This is a voluntary position (free room and board, but no pay) and a great opportunity for students who want to work with animals.

Apply at www.animalshelter.org.czech

b) How are these German phrases expressed in the adverts? Work with a partner and make a list.

1. Erfahrungen sammeln
2. ein Tag frei
3. Bewirb dich bei …
4. hart arbeiten können
5. eine unbezahlte Stelle
6. freie Unterkunft und Verpflegung

WB p. XX XX

c) Read at least two of the adverts again and take notes in a grid.

job offered	location	wages	accommodation	tasks	skills needed	my opinion

d) Mill around and use your grid to talk to your classmates about the jobs.

I think the job in … sounds fun.

I think the job in … is a … job.

I wouldn't like to do that job because …

…

Collect arguments for or against doing a summer job abroad.

An argument for a summer job abroad is …

An argument against a summer job abroad is …

A3 Good advice on hard and soft skills

What are you good at? Collect ideas.

CD X/XX
how to p. 145 listen

a) Listen to Mr Baker, a career expert, talking to pupils about hard and soft skills. Copy the table and take notes.

hard skills	soft skills
foreign languages	being punctual
…	…

b) Compare your table with a partner and add more examples.

WB p. XX XX

Identify the hard and soft skills needed for the jobs in A2. Mark them in your table.

A4 Writing a CV

model text
p. XX XX

a) Look at this CV. What does it tell you about the person? Which job in A2 do you think he is applying for? Write it down.

wordbank jobs p. 167

b) Complete the sentences.

The person's name is …
He lives in …
He was born in …
He goes to …
He is good at …
He speaks …
…

CURRICULUM VITAE

Personal information

Name	Oliver Schmidt
Address	Steinweg 18, 28717 Bremen, Germany
Telephone	+49-178-29
Email	oliver.schmidt@
Nationality	German
Date of birth	14 July 2005
Place of birth	Bremen

Work experience

since 2018	Babysitting on a regular basis for a neighbour's children (aged 4 and 6)
October 2018	Two-week work experience in the AWO-Kindergarten in Bremen

Education

2015 – now	Gesamtschule an der Lesum (Secondary Comprehensive School), Bremen
2011 – 2015	Grundschule Heisterbusch (Primary School), Bremen

Skills

Languages	German (mother tongue) and English (B1)
Computer	Competent in word processing and presentation software
Other skills	Very reliable, great teamworking skills, creative

Interests

Music	Playing the guitar, member of the school band
Sport	Team sports (basketball, hockey), since 2019 assistant coach with the under 7 basketball team

References available on request

WB p. XX XX

A5 Your CV

Write your own CV. Don't forget to include examples of your soft skills. Then swap your CV with a partner and give each other feedback on information, spelling and layout.

how to p. 158 write a CV
WB p. X XX
p. XX XX

A6 Oliver's cover letter

a) Oliver wrote this cover letter. Read it and find out why he wants to work in childcare.

model text

Oliver Schmidt
Steinweg 18
28717 Bremen
Germany

Childcare Experience
110 Duff Street
Dublin D08 C8CN
Ireland

27 March 2019

Dear Sir or Madam,

p. XX XX
WB p. X XX

I learnt from Mrs Wiese, the careers officer at my school, Gesamtschule an der Lesum, that you offer students the chance to do work experience in Ireland this summer. I am very interested in doing childcare either at a day care centre or in a private home and would like to apply for a placement from July to mid-August.

My work experience in the Kindergarten and my experience as a babysitter have taught me to be a good listener. In the Kindergarten I was able to accompany musical games on the guitar and I enjoyed helping out at mealtimes. As a basketball coach I have to motivate young children. Since I am considering a career in elementary education, I would be grateful for the opportunity of working with your company in Ireland.

I enclose my CV and the address of Mr and Mrs Grabow, who are my neighbours and the family where I babysit at least once a week. They will be pleased to send you a reference.

I am available for an online video interview at any time. Thank you for considering my application.

I look forward to hearing from you soon.

Yours faithfully,

Oliver Schmidt

Enclosed: CV, address of referee

b) Do you think this is a good cover letter? Look at layout, language and content.

how to p. 159 write a cover letter

A7 Cover letter phrases

a) **Read Oliver's cover letter in A6 again.**

p. XX XX

b) ☆ **Match the sentence halves.**

1. I enclose my CV
2. They will be pleased to
3. I would like to
4. I am available for an online

a. apply for a placement in July.
b. video interview at any time.
c. send you a reference.
d. and the address of Mr and Mrs Grabow.

☾ **Unscramble the sentences.**

1. doing – very – I am – interested – in – childcare – .
2. my – I – CV – enclose – .
3. the guitar – I was – on – accompany – able to – musical games – .
4. for – my – considering – application – Thank you – .
5. look forward – from you – soon – I – hearing – to – .

WB p. XX XX

☼ **Find the phrases for the beginning and the end of a cover letter.**

A8 Some advice from a career expert

Oliver is going to have an interview. So he looks on the Internet to find some advice and finds this video clip.

DVD XX

a) **Watch the video clip of Cara Hall, a career expert, giving advice to young people. Write down three tips she gives.**

wordbank jobs p. 167

b) **Compare your tips with a partner and add some more.**

☼ **Which of the tips do you find most useful? Say why.**

A9 Choose

1. **Write a job advert for an unusual job, for example an ice cream tester or working for "Rent-a-friend". You can also look at the text "The best job in the world" on page 74.**

model text

2. **Look at the adverts in A2 again. Choose one and think of at least three questions you would ask the employer.**
3. **What should you do to prepare for a job interview? Write a to-do list.**

Job interview to-do list

- read the company's website
- practise ...
- ...

A10 What went wrong?

a) Look at the cartoon. What do you think about it?

b) How do you think the woman will respond? Collect ideas.

"Yes, I think I have good people skills. What kind of idiot question is that?"

WB p. XX XX

A11 Target task: My application folder

You are going to collect all your papers for a job application and present them in an application folder.

1. Look for a summer job advert you find interesting. You can look online or in the book. You could even use your or one of your classmates' adverts from A9.
2. Use or adapt your CV from A5.
3. Write a cover letter. Remember to include the relevant information for the job you have chosen. You can find help in your workbook.
4. Swap your texts with a partner and give each other feedback.
5. Edit your texts.
6. Put everything together in an attractive folder. If you like you can put it on display in your classroom.
7. Keep your application folder for future use.

Dear Sir or Madam,

I read on your website that you offer students the chance to do work experience at your company.
I am very interested in ... and would like to apply for a placement in ...

I enjoy working in a team and ...
So, I think I would be an ideal candidate.
I would be grateful for the opportunity to do my work experience with you.

I enclose my CV and ...
I am available for an interview at any time. Thank you for considering my application.

I look forward to hearing from you soon.

Yours faithfully,

p. XX XX

WB p. XX XX

how to p. 158 write a CV, write a cover letter

model text

wordbank jobs p. 167

P1 Explain

Explain what you have to do.

1. Mill around and use your grid to talk to your classmates about the jobs.
2. Identify the hard and soft skills needed for the jobs.
3. Use or adapt your CV.
4. Swap your texts with a partner and give each other feedback.
5. Edit your texts.

Ich soll ...

Wir sollen ...

...

P2 What are their plans?

LiF p. 184 8R

a) Write sentences about what you think is going to happen.

I My friend ... My friend ... and I My classmates ...	am going to is going to are going to	get a summer job. find a nice work placement. travel after finishing school. start a job training. do a lot of sports to keep fit. work on getting better at school. work on communication skills. take driving lessons. ...

b) Write about your plans in more detail.

P3 A dream summer job

LiF p. 184 8R

a) Copy the text and fill in will or won't.

I am dreaming of a summer job abroad next year. I ??? be in a country with extremely good weather, perhaps France or Italy. I ??? sleep long and have breakfast and then I ??? only work for an hour or two a day, the rest of the day I ??? work but I ??? go to the beach or a swimming pool. I ??? have parties every night and ??? be able to talk to the other people from all over Europe who spend their time there. We ??? have a very good time together and ??? be tired or stressed from work.

It is such a shame that this ??? happen like that and ??? stay a dream!

CD XX

b) Listen to the CD and check your sentences.

P4 A summer job in a German vineyard

Your friend from England would like to get a summer job in Germany. You have found this job advert and want to let him know what it is about and how to apply. Write an email.

how to mediate p. 147

Sommerjob in einem deutschen Weingut

Weingut sucht einen Jugendlichen, der sich nicht vor harter Arbeit scheut. Dein Job beinhaltet, unser Haus sauber zu machen, ein bisschen zu kochen, im Garten zu arbeiten und dabei zu helfen, die Trauben zu ernten. Teenager jeglichen Alters sind willkommen.

- Teilzeit
- flexible Dauer (Minimum vier Wochen)
- freie Unterkunft und Verpflegung
- Reisekosten werden bezahlt
- 25€ pro Tag
- Bewirb dich per E-Mail bei: job@moselweingut.de

P5 Hard and soft skills

Make two lists, one for hard skills and one for soft skills. Write the words in the correct list.

being on time • having good maths marks • having a driving licence • being reliable • being creative • having good school marks • playing an instrument • having computer skills • speaking English well • being a good teamworker • being polite • being respectful

P6 Word pairs

a) **Match the word pairs.**

job • work • telephone • first • primary • date • foreign • computer • cover • basketball

coach • advert • number • of birth • language • school • letter • name • experience • skills

b) **Listen to the CD and check your word pairs.**

CD XX

P7 In the right order

a) **The green parts of the sentences are in the wrong places. Put them in the correct places and rewrite this letter of application.**

b) **Listen to the CD and check your letter.**

CD XX

Dear Sir working in a team,

I learned very well with others that you are looking for a cook. I am my CV. I would like to hearing from you soon. I enjoy apply for the job. I can communicate for an interview at any time. I would be grateful from my neighbour. I am available Becca Finn. I enclose an experienced cook. I look forward to for the opportunity to work with you.

Yours faithfully, or Madam

B1 What do you spend your money on?

What do you spend your money on? Talk about it.

p. XX
XX

a) Read the article. What is it about? Think of a title.

Tipp
Englisch:
1 billion =
Deutsch:
1 Milliarde

Children and teenagers today have a lot of money to spend. That makes them important for big companies who want to sell them all kinds of products.

Australian kids for example get 14 Australian dollars pocket money a week on average. German kids receive around 29 Euros per month. It's a fact that boys get more pocket money than girls. In both countries they have to help out at home, for example they take the rubbish out or tidy up.

Most kids in Germany save up some pocket money to buy more expensive things like sneakers and computer games. The rest they spend on sweets, cookies and chewing gum (66%), followed by magazines, comics and mangas (49%) and ice-cream (39%). To earn some extra money they can do things like babysitting, taking care of animals, or gardening.

how to p. 145
talk

b) Talk to a partner. What do you find interesting or surprising?

I find surprising that ...

I had no idea that ...

c) Read the article again. What is similar to your situation? What is different?

I also ...

I never have to ...

At home we ...

d) Where does your money come from?

I get pocket money every ...

To earn some extra money I ...

I don't get any pocket money, but I ...

...

walk the dog
babysit
do paper rounds
sell old toys
repair bikes
help in the garden
make ...
...

WB p. XX
XX

B2 How important is money to you?

How important is money to you on a scale from 1 to 5?
(1 = not important, 5 = very important)

I would say three. What about you?

…

a) Explain why money is important or not important to you.

I think money is very important because …

Money is not important to me because …

…

b) Listen to the Teentalk interview with teenagers talking about money. Match the names and the photos.

CD X/XX

Grace · Chloe · Ben · Jake

c) Copy the table. Then listen again and take notes. Where do the teenagers get their money from? What do they do with it? Compare your notes with a partner.

WB p. XX XX

name	where he/she gets his/her money from	what he/she does with it

d) ☆ Match the sentence parts.

1. Jake feels lucky because
2. Jake argues with his parents because
3. Chloe wants to save money because
4. Chloe likes having her own business because this helps her
5. Ben doesn't save any money because
6. Grace stopped working because

a. to learn about managing her money.
b. he wants to have fun now.
c. they feel treated like a money machine.
d. she needed time for school and her friends.
e. she wants to go to college.
f. his parents pay for his phone bill.

☾ **Imagine Teentalk asked you about money. What would you say? Make some notes and prepare a short presentation.**

☼ **Jake would like to earn some extra money but his parents want him to focus on school instead. Write a dialogue between Jake and his parents.**

B3 Happy with your job?

What do you think: what makes people happy with their jobs?

p. XX
XX

a) A magazine asked different people about their work life. Read what they said. Are they happy with their jobs or not?

Pari (24)

Being a nurse is one of the most rewarding but also stressful jobs in the world. I was trained in India. I came to Australia because there aren't enough qualified nurses here. So I got the chance to start a new life down under. It was hard to leave my friends and family and I missed them terribly at first. On my first day at the hospital I was very nervous but everyone made me feel welcome.
Nursing is hard work. It means a lot of physical activity like lifting patients. You also have to get used to night shifts and long working hours. The pay is not great but it's enough to live on and more than I would earn back home.
However, I am not in this profession for the money but because I like helping people. Seeing patients get better and be able to go home makes me feel happy and satisfied.

Mason (22)

I really hate my job as a shop assistant. Working at the cash register and filling shelves is so frustrating and boring. I never liked school and when I finished highschool I just wanted to earn my own money. I didn't want a career and started working in a department store.
I have to work long hours and still don't earn a lot of money. Sometimes the customers are so rude, but I still have to be friendly. The worst part is that I have to work on weekends and holidays when all my friends are off!
To find a better job I could go to a vocational school and learn a trade. My parents always told me that they would help me if I decided to go back to school. Maybe I should think about that to make a better future for myself.

Thomas (25)

I've worked as an underground diamond driller for five years now and I love it. After school I didn't know what to do so I searched the Internet for unusual jobs in Australia and found this job.
Everyone starts as a helper and it takes years to become a driller. As a diamond driller you have to be strong and fit. You also have to get used to working underground and in a dangerous environment. It also means that you have to live away from your family for longer periods of time. Sometimes I miss my wife and my daughter, but we stay in touch via video phone calls.
But the pay is good and drillers can find jobs all over the world. I like the company that I work for now, but who knows what will happen in the future.

b) **Read the texts again. Make a list of reasons why people like or dislike their jobs. Think of more reasons and add them to your list.**

reasons why people like their job	reasons why people dislike their job
the job is rewarding ...	the job is stressful ...

wordbank jobs p. 167

c) **What do you think? What is important for you in a job? Think of**
- **working hours**
- **pay**
- **location**
- **...**

Make notes and talk to a partner.

I want a job that ...

For me the most important thing about a job is ...

...

WB p. XX XX

B4 Who said it?

Read the texts in B3 again and report who said what. Write it down.

LiF p. 185 9R

1. Sometimes I miss my wife and my daughter.
2. The pay is good.
3. Nursing is hard work.
4. I have to work long hours and still don't earn a lot of money.
5. I like helping people.

1. Thomas said that sometimes he missed his wife and his daughter.

Pari

Mason

Thomas

6. I was trained in India.
7. I searched the Internet for unusual jobs in Australia.
8. It was hard to leave my friends and family.
9. I just wanted to earn my own money.

6. Pari said that she had been trained in India.

B5 Choose

1. **Interview people about their work life and present your findings.**
2. **Do a class survey about what your classmates spend their money on. Present your findings.**
3. **Find out more about one of the jobs mentioned in B3 and report to the class.**
4. **Find and present a song about jobs. What is said about the job in the song?**

Interview questions:
- What do you like about your job?
- What don't you like?
- What can you say about ...?
- When did you ...?
- How ...?
- ...

how to p. 161 talk about song lyrics

B6 Vlogger – a dream job?

p. XX
XX

a) A teen magazine did an interview with John Valencia, a 20-year-old vlogger. Read it and find out what he says about vlogging.

REPORTER: We all know about the vlogging giants. But what about all of the smaller vloggers? After all they represent the majority of people posting video blogs on social networks. Most of them can only dream of earning enough money to live on it. So why do they constantly produce videos for little or no pay? We talked to John Valencia, who vlogs about topics like teenage problems or coming out as gay or lesbian. Hi, John.

JOHN: Hi there!

REPORTER: Why do you make video blogs? Is it the dream of getting that viral hit that brings in millions of views?

JOHN: I don't make videos to become famous or to earn money. I do it to entertain. I love to make people happy. If I can do that, I'm happy, too.

REPORTER: How do your viewers react to your videos?

JOHN: I love communicating with my viewers. People have sent me pictures of drawings they've done for me. I get fanmail all the time from all over the world. People have told me that my videos have helped many young people come out and accept who they are. When I hear stories like that I feel motivated.

REPORTER: How much work is it to make the videos?

JOHN: It's a lot of work really! Creating my videos takes hours. When you watch a 3-4 minute video it doesn't take long. But to create it takes some time. From thinking of ideas, to filming, to editing, to uploading it can take up to four hours or more.

REPORTER: What equipment do you use?

JOHN: I want to produce high quality content, so I need good cameras. I also need lighting equipment, tripods, and microphones.

REPORTER: How do you measure success?

JOHN: One of my videos had over 40,000 views! That's one way of measuring success. But a supportive and encouraging community is most important for me.

REPORTER: How long do you think you are going to be a vlogger?

JOHN: I've been vlogging for three years now. I will keep doing it as long as it's fun and I feel inspired. For me it is more than just a vlog. It's a chance to express myself. I can't think of a better way to do that!

REPORTER: What advice can you give to anyone who wants to start vlogging?

JOHN: First of all, always make content that you would want to watch. Be yourself and don't give up. Upload videos regularly to get more followers. Don't do it for fame, attention, or money because you will be disappointed very quickly. Do it because you have a message and you love it.

REPORTER: Is there a dark side to being a vlogger that our readers should know about?

JOHN: Yes, unfortunately there is! The Internet is full of hate and negative posts. Be aware that some people will write horrible things and try to hurt you, too. You have to learn to accept yourself as you are before asking others to do the same.

REPORTER: So keep that in mind, folks. John, thank you very much for your time.

JOHN: Cheers. No worries.

b) What does John mean when he says "I never make videos for the fame or the money"?

c) ☆ Why does John like what he does? Collect reasons and write them down.

☾ What are John's skills? What is he good at? What other jobs do you think he could do?

☼ Write down what it takes to be a good vlogger. Use John's statements and tips.

WB p. XX XX

B7 Language detective

a) John Valencia told a friend about the interview and the reporter's questions. Read what the reporter asked and what John told his friend. What do you notice?

LiF p. 187 11

What the reporter asked:	What John told his friend:
"Why do you make video blogs?"	First she asked me why I made video blogs.
"Is it the dream of getting that viral hit ...?"	She wanted to know if it was the dream of getting that viral hit.
"How do your viewers react to your videos?"	She asked me how my viewers reacted to my videos.

b) Write down more questions that the reporter asked. Continue John's account of the questions he was asked.

What equipment do you use? – She asked me what equipment I used. After that ...

B8 Target task: A happy work life

In a group you are going to take part in a 'tweet' discussion about criteria for a happy work life.

p. XX XX
WB p. XX XX

1. Get together in small groups.
   As a group decide on a statement that you want to discuss. You can use one of the statements in B3 and B6 or make up your own.
2. Write the statement at the top of a poster.
3. Now take turns to write 'tweets' in which you express your opinion. Your list of reasons from B3b) may be helpful. Keep your tweets short and precise.
4. Put up the posters in the classroom. Read them and choose the discussion you like best. Give reasons.

I love to make people happy and if I can do that, I'm happy, too.

I am not in this profession for the money but because I like helping people.

P8 Explain

Explain what you have to do.

1. Read the statements.
2. Use your notes and your own ideas.
3. Make a list of reasons why people like or dislike their jobs.
4. Present your findings.
5. Continue John's account of the questions he was asked.

P9 Words

a) Match the words with the explanations.

1.	pocket money	a.	Nice extras that your company offers to you.
2.	chores at home	b.	Working hours when other people sleep.
3.	night shift	c.	Often teenagers do them for money they get from their parents.
4.	benefits	d.	Many people keep their money in it.
5.	wallet	e.	Many teenagers think they don't get enough of it.

CD XX **b) Listen to the CD and check your matches.**

P10 Nouns and adjectives

a) Look at the nouns in the box and find the adjectives that go with them. Write them down in pairs. If you need help, check with your word list or with a dictionary.

possibility • ability • responsibility • nationality • personality • similarity • difficulty • activity

CD XX **b) Listen to the CD and check your pairs.**

P11 Say it in German

A friend needs help to understand the statements about jobs in B3 on page 68. Answer his or her questions in German.

1. Wie war es denn für Pari, ihre Heimat zu verlassen?
2. Und was sagt sie über ihre Arbeitszeiten und ihre Bezahlung?
3. Oh, ist sie denn glücklich in ihrem Beruf?
4. Ich verstehe, dass Mason seine Arbeit nicht mag. Warum eigentlich?
5. Warum sucht er sich dann keine andere Arbeit?
6. Thomas hat ja einen sehr ungewöhnlichen Beruf! Wie kam er denn auf die Idee?
7. Er ist ja oft nicht bei seiner Familie. Wie geht er damit um?

Practice matters

P12 Meet the vloggers

Six vloggers talked to an online magazine about their "job". Report what they said. Use reported speech. Remember the time shift.

LiF p. 185 9R

1. Alana: "I just love being a vlogger. I love filming, I love editing, I love seeing the people's reactions to my content."
2. Helen: "If I can make one person happy, I've done my job."
3. Nigel: "I never make videos for the fame or the money. I don't have millions of subscribers, and to me that's OK."
4. Damon: "People have sent me photos of drawings they've made for me. Some have sent me emails. I make sure I answer all of them."
5. Becky: "I can see myself vlogging as long as the Internet is around! This is the first time in history that anyone can put themselves out there to the world.
6. Anita: "Unfortunately it is true that women receive more insulting comments than men. You have to be ready for that!"

1. Alana said that she just loved being a vlogger. She added that she loved filming and editing. She also said that she loved seeing the people's ...

P13 What viewers said

A journalist interviewed two young people who subscribe to vlogs on the Internet. Put the questions and the answers in reported speech.

LiF p. 185 9R, 11

1. Reporter: What are your favourite vlogs?
2. Harry: I only follow vlogs about online games and skateboarding.
3. Scarlett: I don't like online games at all. I'm mainly interested in life hacks.
4. Reporter: What are your favourite life hacks?
5. Scarlett: I used teabags to treat my sunburn last summer and it worked perfectly.
6. Harry: I don't believe in life hacks. I tried to use toothpaste on mosquito bites and it didn't work at all.
7. Reporter: How many hours do you usually spend online?
8. Scarlett: I usually watch video blogs in the afternoon after I have finished my chores at home.
9. Reporter: Have you ever communicated with a vlogger?
10. Harry: I've sent fanmail to Andy Schrock, a famous skateboarder.

1. The reporter asked what their favourite vlogs were.
2. Harry told the reporter that he ...

Optional

O The best job in the world

In January 2009 the Queensland Tourism Board started a competition for a job they described as "the best job in the world". Instead of a traditional newspaper job advert, the tourism board used their website and social networking sites to tell people about it.

A tourism official said: "It doesn't sound too bad, does it? We are looking for someone to tell the stories of the Great Barrier Reef and we have created what we think is a dream job."

They advertised a six-month job for an "island caretaker" on Hamilton Island in Australia's Whitsunday Islands, off the Queensland coast. No formal qualifications were needed but candidates had to be physically fit, able to swim, snorkel, dive and sail. The winner would get 150,000 Australian dollars for the six months and free accommodation in a three-bedroom villa. He or she would have to work for just twelve hours a month. The job would include feeding some of the hundreds of species of fish and collecting the island's mail. He or she would also have to prepare a blog, a photo diary and video updates to make the area even more popular with tourists.

Interested candidates had to send a sixty-second video application explaining why they were the ideal person for the job. Although Queensland Tourism Board had expected a lot of interest, they were surprised at the enormous number of applicants. In one week's time, there were over 34,000 applicants from 200 countries.

Queensland Tourism Board chose sixteen finalists who were then flown to Hamilton Island for their final "job interview". They had to take on lots of different tasks like swimming and snorkelling and had formal job interviews and tests. The applicants also had to show their personalities and skills in front of cameras from all over the world.

In the end it was 34-year-old Ben Southall from Britain who got the job. In his application video Mr Southall was not only shown riding on an ostrich, he also described himself as "the adventurous, crazy, energetic type" and "practically a fish". He convinced the jury with a combination of his outdoor abilities and his excellent media skills.

What do you think about "the best job in the world"? Would you like to have a job like this?

Webcode DSW-14605-xxx

Go online and look for Ben Southall's application video. Watch it. What do you think about it?

Technology and the future

Is there anything the Internet can't do?

Find out about the exciting genre of

SCIENCE FICTION

and read a short story and a mini-saga!

Got an idea for an app?

Design it using our guide on page 81!

Read about: **Staying safe online**

A

- Du beschäftigst dich mit Internetanwendungen und Internetsicherheit.
- Du entwirfst deine eigene App. (Zielaufgabe)

B

- Du liest und analysierst eine Science-Fiction-Kurzgeschichte und Mini-saga.
- Du schreibst deine eigene Science-Fiction-Geschichte oder schreibst eine Geschichte um. (Zielaufgabe)

A1 Internet use

What do you do online?

LiF p. 188 12R

a) **How often do you do each online activity?**

I often share pictures with my friends.

I usually ...

I sometimes chat ...

always • regularly • normally • never • ...

how to p. 156 work with statistics

wordbank statistics p. 165

b) **Look at the bar chart below. What do you find out about the Internet use of young people?**

31% of girls use the Internet for entertainment.

Reasons for Internet use in Germany (2016)

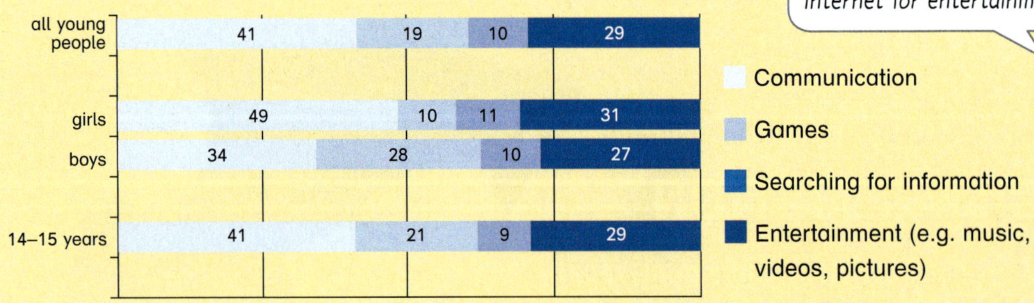

Source: JIM 2016, figures in per cent, Base: 1188 young people (aged 12-19 years old)

WB p. XX XX

c) **Compare your own Internet use with the bar chart.**

I am a girl and I use the Internet for games, but only 10% of girls use the Internet for games. I often use the Internet for communication and 41% of all young people also ...

A2 Being online

p. XX XX

a) **Look at the photos. What do you think the people use the Internet for?**

1 Maria, 15, pupil

2 Sultan, 27, software developer

3 John, 23, trainee

how to p. 145 listen

CD X/XX

b) **Listen to the three people. What role does the Internet play for each of them? Choose the right phrases from the box and write them down.**

use it to check things • chat with people • it's my job • couldn't do without it • improve my English • ...

Listen again and add more things that the people say to your notes.

A3 What's in an app?

Which social network apps do you use?

a) Listen to Sam and her mum. What are they talking about?

CD X/XX XX
p. XX XX

Mum: Hey Sam, what are you up to?
Sam: Hey, Mum. I'm just trying out this new app I found. It's called FriendsShare.
Mum: Don't you already have lots of other social network apps? Why do you need another one?
Sam: Well, this one is different. You just use your login details from one of the other apps and then it imports all your pictures, videos, friends lists and other things from everywhere! It's really simple, and it looks really cool, too.
Mum: Hmm... OK...
Sam: It makes keeping in touch with everybody much easier. Look. Here are all the pictures that I've shared in my photo community, here I can see all the messages that I've sent to my classmates, ... oh, and here are my high scores against my friends who are in my gaming community. You just need this one app for everything. And I only need one password.
Mum: But then everybody can see all of your information! And how does the app get all the information and the permission to use your data?
Sam: Um ... Well, I think they work together with other companies ...
Mum: Hmm ... Didn't you have to click on a button to accept their privacy policy?
Sam: Oh, come on, Mum. Nobody reads those huge legal documents. Everyone just clicks on 'Agree' and carries on with signing up. These privacy policies are always the same.
Mum: Sam, if you aren't careful, anybody will be able to see your location when you use the app. So if we go on holiday and you post photos on the app, everyone will see that we're away. That is the perfect opportunity for burglars to break into our house!
Sam: Oh ... well, maybe you're right ...
Mum: And haven't you heard about criminals who steal people's identities? They could pretend to be you and send insulting messages to your friends. Just one error on one of the app's servers could allow criminals to see all of your information!
Sam: You're being dramatic, Mum.
Mum: I just worry about these things sometimes. Please just be careful, OK?
Sam: Yes, Mum ...

b) Listen again and read along.

Collect arguments from the text for and against the new app and write them down.

how to p. 152 write your opinion

Collect arguments from the text for and against the new app. Choose Sam or her mum and write down what the person thinks about the app.

Collect arguments from the text for and against the new app. Write down your own opinion and give reasons.

c) Talk about the app in small groups.

WB p. XX XX

A4 Favourite apps

What is your favourite app? Why?

LiF p.189 13R

Write about apps you like. You can work with a partner.

... is an app that plays music.
... is an app which takes photos.
... is an app I use to chat with my friends.
...

A5 Digital awareness

Have you heard of any dangers on the Internet? Which ones?

p. XX XX

a) Write a list of statements about how to stay safe online. Compare your list with a partner. Agree on the most important statements.

wordbank Internet p.169

You have to use strong passwords.
Do not share personal information.
...

- use strong passwords
- share personal information
- read privacy policies
- check security settings
- accept friend requests
- use social media sites
- meet online friends
- report upsetting material
- ...

how to p.147 mediate

b) Imagine you want to tell your younger brother or sister the main things you can do to protect yourself while surfing the Internet. Talk to him or her in German.

LiF p.190 14R

c) Read about the following situations. What could go wrong? What would you do? Write about at least two of them.

- If an online friend asked me for my address, I would ...
- If I received insulting messages, I would ...
- If I found upsetting material or pictures online, I would ...
- If I wanted to order something online, ...
- If I wanted to meet an online friend in real life, ...
- If I knew someone who did illegal things on the Internet, ...

If an online friend asked me for my address, I would make sure that I know the person in real life. If I didn't know the person, I wouldn't give him or her my address. ...

WB p. XX XX

A6 Choose

1. Work with a partner. Tell him or her about your favourite app, but don't mention its name. Let your partner guess which app it is. If he or she doesn't know it, say why you think it is good. Take turns.
2. Make a poster for your classroom on how to be safe online.
3. Many people will always first look on Wikipedia to get information. Give a summary on what Wikipedia is and find out how it tries to ensure the quality of its entries. Then collect reasons why you might need more good sources than just Wikipedia for presentations and homework.

model text

how to p. 149 research online

A7 Gamification and the future of technology

Webcode DSW-14605-xxx

a) Have you heard of gamification? What do you think it might be?

It is probably …

It could also be …

b) Watch the video clip. As a class, try to summarise in German what happens.

c) Collect examples of gamification from the video.

d) Sort the examples of gamification into two lists: positive and negative.

positive	negative
fun exercise games	…
…	

INFO BUBBLE

Gamification means that real-life situations are mixed with game-like elements. Examples include rewards, such as earning points or unlocking a new level, or taking part in competitions against your friends or your own personal records.

Can you think of (good) examples of gamification in your everyday life? Report to the class.

I've heard of an app that rewards you when …

I know of …

WB p. XX XX

A8 The Internet of things

p. XX
XX

wordbank
Internet
p. 169

a) **Look at the photos of the devices. They all connect to the Internet. How do you think they use the Internet?**

I think the fridge can ...

car

TV

fridge

security camera

fitness tracker

game console

b) **Read the sales pitch for a new everyday product with Internet access. What problem does it solve?**

Remember the last time you went to the supermarket? You thought you had everything that you needed? But once you got home you realised: "Whoops! I forgot the milk!"

Well, look no further! With our new CoolX3000 you will never have to worry about anything in your fridge ever again! The CoolX3000 will notice every product that you have in your fridge.

It will recognise when you're nearly out of something and automatically order it on the Internet. Your new fridge will even warn you when your food is about to go out of date! It's the perfect solution to your problem.

Make your life easier – with CoolX3000.

WB p. XX
XX

c) **What words and phrases does the sales representative use to sell her product? Take notes.**

CD
X/XX

d) **Now listen to the sales pitch. Does the product sound good? What do you think of it?**

A9 Target task: Designing an app

Apps play an important role in our everyday lives. We use them to get information, chat and play with friends, and we can even use them to connect other technical devices to the Internet to make them 'smarter'. You are going to design your own app.

p. XX XX

1. Work together in small groups and think about a problem that you would like to solve.

DVD XX

2. Think about these questions:
   - What problem does it solve? How?
   - When and how do you use it?
   - What does it need (a camera, ...)?
   - Can you include gamification elements?

wordbank Internet p. 169

3. Think about issues such as data and privacy protection. Could there be any problems or difficulties?
4. Draw a picture of your app with buttons, the menu and a logo. How can you use the English language in your app?
5. Present your app concept to the class and listen to the other groups' concepts. Ask the other groups questions about their concepts.
6. Give the other groups feedback. What did they do well? What could they do better next time?

WB p. XX XX

Which apps do you think would be useful?

how to give feedback p. 151

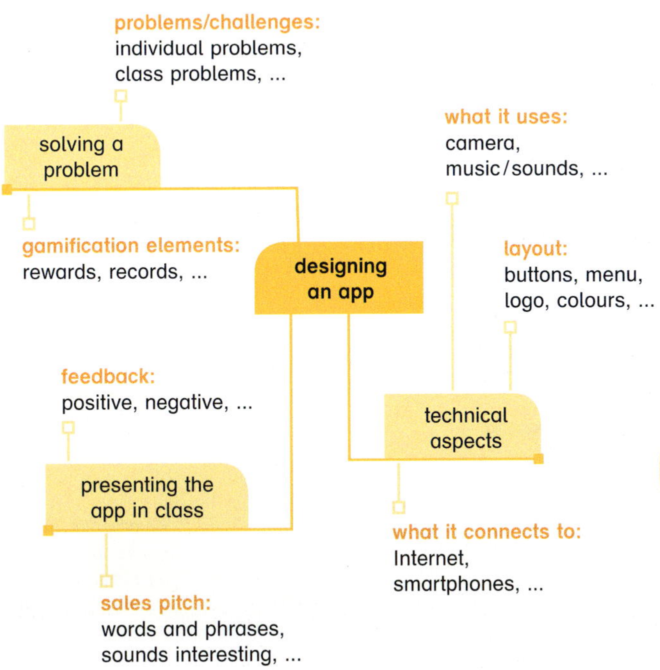

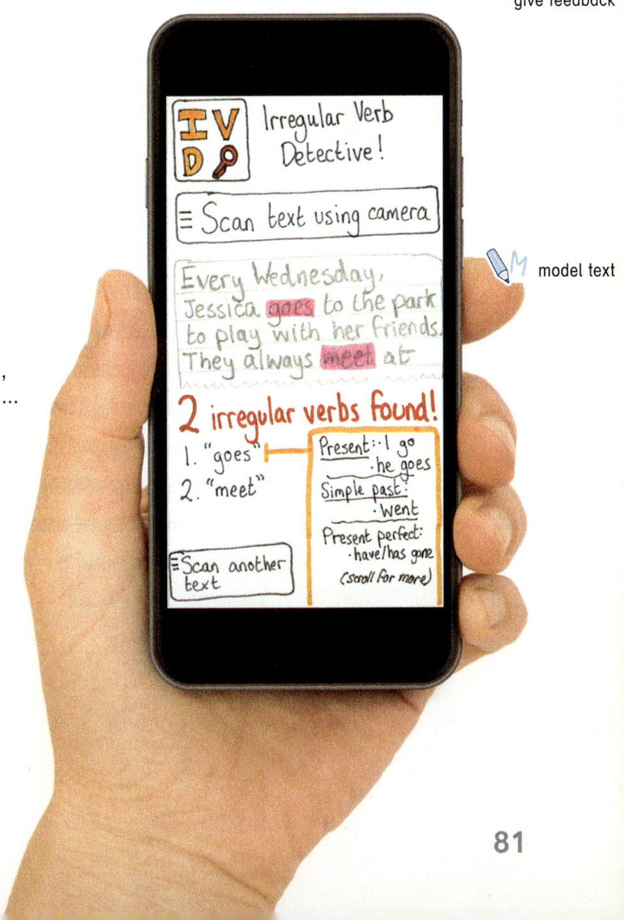

model text

Practice matters

P1 Explain

Explain what you have to do.

1. Compare your own Internet use with the bar chart.
2. Collect arguments from the text for and against the new app.
3. Write about apps you like.
4. Write a list of statements about how to stay safe online.
5. Think about a problem you would like to solve.

Ich soll ...

Wir sollen ...

...

P2 Using apps

LiF p. 188 12R

a) **Write down five sentences in which you explain which apps you use for what purpose and how often.**

always • often • regularly • normally • usually • sometimes • never • ...

I sometimes use my gaming app to play online games.

b) **Think of another person and rewrite your sentences. How often do you think he or she uses the apps that you use?**

I think Sara often uses the gaming app.

P3 Talking about statistics

wordbank statistics p. 165

how to p. 156 work with statistics

Look at the bar chart and explain it in English. Work with a partner and take turns. You can use the wordbank for help.

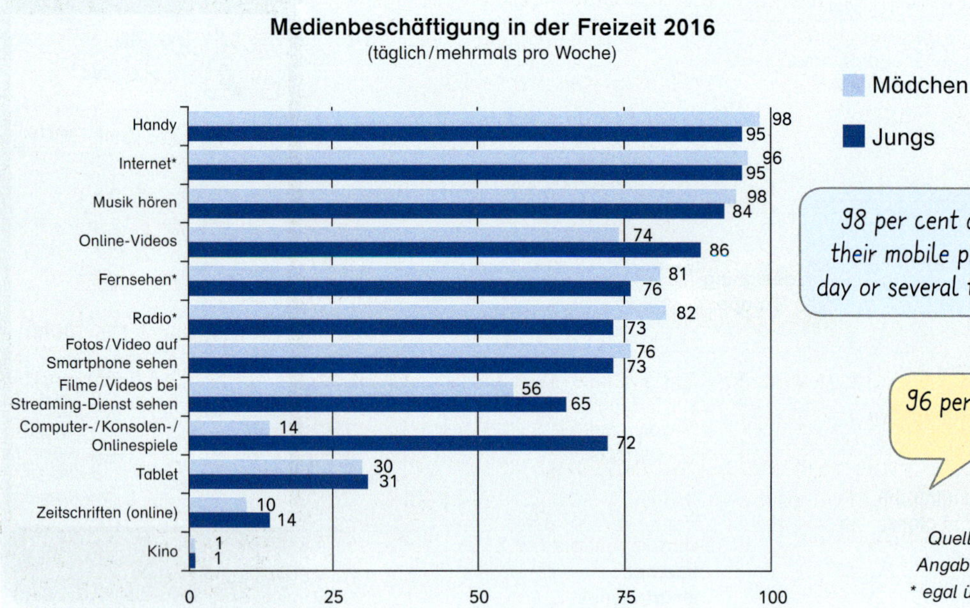

98 per cent of girls use their mobile phones every day or several times a week.

96 per cent of boys also ...

*Quelle: JIM 2016, Angabe in Prozent, * egal über welchen Verbreitungsweg Basis: alle Befragten n=1.200*

P4 FriendsShare

Read the dialogue in A3 again and write sentences about the story.

LiF p. 181 13R

Sam is the girl FriendsShare is the new app Sam can see all the messages The privacy policy is the part Sam's mum is worried about criminals ...	who which that	that she has sent to her classmates. has found a new app. is really simple. steal peoples' identities. tells you how the app uses your data. ...

Sam is the girl who has found a new app.

P5 Technology vocabulary

Think of and write down definitions for the terms in the box.

social media sites • username • password • privacy policy • security settings • login details • gaming community

On social media sites you can connect with friends and share pictures with them.

P6 What would you do?

Work with a partner. Ask each other what you would do in certain situations when being online. You could use the situations in A5 or think of your own.

LiF p. 190 14R

What would you do if you forgot your password?

If I forgot my password, I would contact the website. What would you do if you wanted to order something online?

I would ... And what would you do if ...?

P7 Your dream app

What would your dream app be like? Write about it. Use the following sentences for ideas on what to write.

LiF p. 190 14R

- If I could design my own dream app, I would ...
- If I had enough time, I could ...
- If I needed help, ...
- It would need to use the camera if ...
- Pupils could use it at school if ...
- The app might be able to ... if ...

If I could design my own dream app, I would design a fashion app. It would need to use the camera if people wanted to take photos of their clothes. If I needed help, I would ask ...

B1 School of the future

Imagine what school will be like in 50 years. Collect ideas.

p. XX
XX

a) Look at the photos. Which technology is used in your school? What could change in the school of the future?

wordbank
Internet
p. 169

In class we use …

We often use …

In the school of the future, maybe they will have …

b) Think about the school of the future. What would be better? What would be worse?

Maybe the books could be different. They could be …

I think … would be better.

… would be worse.

B2 Reading a short story

how to read p. 146

a) Look at the title of the story on the next page. What do you think is fun about school? Talk to a partner.

WB p. XX
XX

b) Copy the cluster or use the one in your workbook. Fill in as much information as you can while you read: characters (who), plot (what, how and why), setting (where and when).

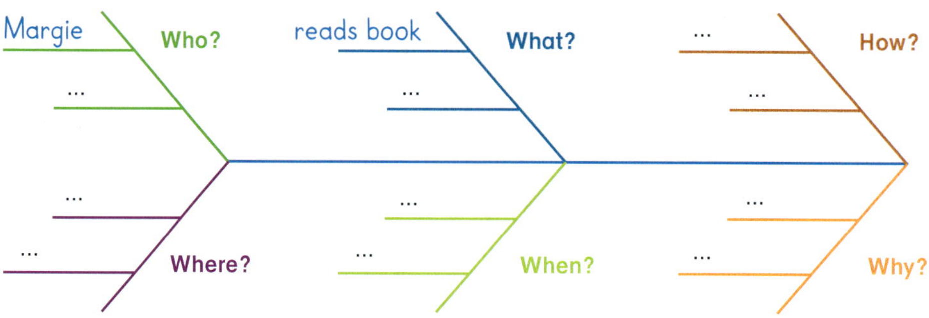

The Fun They Had

Margie even wrote about it that night in her diary. On the page headed May 17, 2157, she wrote, "Today Tommy found a real book!"

It was a very old book. Margie's grandfather once said that when he was a little boy his grandfather told him that there was a time when all stories were printed on paper.

They turned the pages, which were yellow and crinkly, and it was awfully funny to read words that stood still instead of moving the way they were supposed to – on a screen, you know. And then, when they turned back to the page before, it had the same words on it that it had had when they read it the first time.

"Gee," said Tommy, "what a waste. When you're through with the book, you just throw it away, I guess. Our television screen must have had a million books on it and it's good for plenty more. I wouldn't throw it away."

"Same with mine," said Margie. She was eleven and hadn't seen as many textbooks as Tommy had. He was thirteen. She said, "Where did you find it?"

"In my house." He pointed without looking, because he was busy reading. "In the attic."

"What's it about?"

"School."

Margie was scornful. "School? What's there to write about school? I hate school." Margie always hated school, but now she hated it more than ever. The mechanical teacher had given her test after test in geography and she had been doing worse and worse until her mother had shaken her head sorrowfully and sent for the County Inspector.

He was a round little man with a red face and a whole box of tools with dials and wires. He smiled at Margie and gave her an apple, then took the teacher apart. Margie had hoped he wouldn't know how to put it together again, but he knew how all right, and, after an hour or so, there it was again, large and black and ugly, with a big screen on which all lessons were shown and the questions were asked. That wasn't so bad. The part Margie hated most was the slot were she had to put homework and test papers. She always had to write them out in a punch code they made her learn when she was six years old, and the mechanical teacher calculated the mark in no time.

The Inspector had smiled after he was finished and patted Margie's head. He said to her mother, "It's not the little girl's fault, Mrs. Jones. I think the geography sector was geared a little too quick. Those things happen sometimes. I've slowed it up to an average ten-year level. Actually, the overall pattern of her progress is quite satisfactory." And he patted Margie's head again.

Margie was disappointed. She had been hoping they would take her teacher away altogether. They had once taken Tommy's teacher away for nearly a month because the history sector had blanked out completely. So she said to Tommy, "Why would anyone write about school?"

c) Talk about what you have filled into your cluster. Why do *you* think anyone would want to write about school?

d) Add information to your cluster while you read the second part of the story.

Tommy looked at her with very superior eyes. “Because it’s not our kind of school, stupid. This is the old kind of school they had hundreds and hundreds of years ago.” He added loftily, pronouncing the word carefully, “Centuries ago.”

Margie was hurt. “Well, I don’t know what kind of school they had all that time ago.” She read the book over his shoulder for a while, then said, “Anyway, they had a teacher.”

“Sure they had a teacher, but it wasn’t a regular teacher. It was a man.”

“A man? How could a man be a teacher?”

“Well, he just told the boys and girls things and gave them homework and asked them questions.”

“A man isn’t smart enough.”

“Sure he is. My father knows as much as my teacher.”

“He can’t. A man can’t know as much as a teacher.”

“He knows almost as much, I betcha.”

Margie wasn’t prepared to dispute that. She said, “I wouldn’t want a strange man in my house to teach me.”

Tommy screamed with laughter.

“You don’t know much, Margie. The teachers didn’t live in the house. They had a special building and all the kids went there.”

“All the kids learned the same thing?”

“Sure, if they were the same age.”

“But my mother says a teacher has to be adjusted to fit the mind of each boy and girl it teaches and that each child has to be taught differently.”

“Just the same they didn’t do it that way then. If you don’t like it, you don’t have to read the book.”

“I didn’t say I didn’t like it,” Margie said quickly. She wanted to read about those funny schools.

They weren’t even half finished when Margie’s mother called,

“Margie! School!”

Margie looked up. “Not yet, Mamma.”

“Now!” said Mrs. Jones. “And it’s probably time for Tommy, too.”

Margie said to Tommy, “Can I read the book some more with you after school?”

“Maybe,” he said nonchalantly. He walked away whistling, the dusty old book tucked beneath his arm.

Margie went into the schoolroom. It was right next to her bedroom, and the mechanical teacher was on and waiting for her.

It was always on at the same time except Saturday and Sunday, because her mother said little girls learned better if they learned at regular hours.

The screen was lit up, and it said: “Today’s arithmetic lesson is on the addition of proper fractions. Please insert yesterday’s homework in the proper slot.”

Margie did so with a sigh. She was thinking about the old schools they had when her grandfather’s grandfather was a little boy. All the kids from the whole neighbourhood came, laughing and shouting at the schoolyard, sitting together in the schoolroom, going home together at the end of the day. They learned the same things, so they could help one another on the homework and talk about it.

And the teachers were people …

The mechanical teacher was flashing on the screen: “When we add the fractions 12 and 14 …”.

Margie was thinking about how the kids must have loved it in the old days. She was thinking about the fun they had.

e) Compare your clusters in class and edit them.

f) Were your speculations from a) correct?

For 'who' I have written Margie, ...

... is different from what I thought.

... is similar to our ideas.

It is in lines ... to ... that ...

In line ... we see ...

What do you think about the story? Write a short text (50-80 words). Think about:

- what you like
- what you find interesting
- what you find surprising
- what you don't like
- what you find boring
- what you don't understand

WB p. XX XX

B3 The central conflict

In the last two lines of the story, we learn that Margie is thinking about "the fun they had". How does Margie feel in her 'school'? What does she miss? Collect ideas.

Think about the story and answer at least two of these questions:

- Can a teacher know as much as a machine/robot/computer?
- Can we learn more from a machine/robot/computer than we can from people?
- What can we learn from people that we cannot learn from machines/robots/computers?

What do you think the message of the story is? Think about Margie's thoughts on her 'school' and the school of the past, as well as the title of the short story. Give reasons.

I think the message of the story is ...

B4 Summarising a story

a) Complete the sentences about 'The Fun They Had' using the words in the box.

where • first • then • because • in order to • when • even though

LiF p. 191 15

how to p. 153 write a summary

1. ??? have the mechanical teacher examined, Margie's mother sends for the inspector.
2. Margie's mother thinks that the mechanical teacher is broken, ??? Margie has bad results in geography all the time.
3. ??? Margie reads the book, ??? she talks to Tommy about it.
4. ??? Margie is sceptical first, she wonders about the fun the children had at school.
5. Tommy has been in the attic, ??? he finds an old book.
6. ??? Tommy tells her the book is about school, Margie thinks about how she hates school and her mechanical teacher.

b) Write down the sentences in the correct order to get a very short summary of the story.

Tipp
Wenn man über eine Geschichte spricht oder schreibt, verwendet man die einfache Gegenwart oder die Zeitform, die in der Geschichte verwendet wird.

LAND & LEUTE 3

DVD XX

Science fiction als Genre

Science Fiction, oder sci-fi, wird von einer Vielzahl von Autoren überall auf der Welt geschrieben. Die Science-Fiction-Geschichte „The Fun They Had" wurde 1951 von dem russischstämmigen US-Amerikaner Isaac Asimov geschrieben. Als weitere sehr erfolgreiche US-amerikanische Beispiele sind die „Star Wars"-Reihe und die Serie „Star Trek" zu zählen. Star Trek wurde das erste Mal 1966 ausgestrahlt und Star Wars im Jahr 1977. Beide erlangten sehr schnell Bekanntheit in den USA und sind heute noch weltweit sehr erfolgreich.

Aus Großbritannien stammt eine Reihe sehr populärer Science-Fiction-Geschichten, z. B. „The Hitchhiker's Guide to the Galaxy" (Per Anhalter durch die Galaxis), das ursprünglich als Radiohörspiel im Jahr 1978 produziert wurde. „Doctor Who" ist eine britische Science-Fiction-TV-Serie, die erstmals 1963 im Fernsehen ausgestrahlt wurde. Die Serie, die sich um Zeitreisen dreht, ist weltweit sehr erfolgreich und wird auch heute noch gedreht.

Science-Fiction-Geschichten spielen häufig in der Zukunft, und Technologie nimmt eine wichtige Rolle ein, z. B. Roboter, Raumschiffe und Zeitreisen. Manchmal werden Probleme thematisiert, die es auch in der realen Welt gibt – z. B. was in der Zukunft geschehen könnte, wenn wir nicht auf unseren Planeten achten.

Welche Probleme der realen Welt thematisiert Asimov in „The Fun They Had"? Welche anderen Science-Fiction-Geschichten kennst du noch?

B5 A science fiction mini-saga

Will humans someday live in space? What do you think?

how to read p. 146
p. XX XX

a) **Read the mini-saga and find out what colony 4 is. Talk about it in small groups.**

Colony 4

As the star ship hit warp speed Jake studied the in-flight brochure. He didn't want to move home, away from everything he'd ever known – live on Colony 4 – some reclaimed[1] rock.

"It'll be OK," Mum reassured[2] him.

"Yeah," he said despondently[3] as they docked on planet Earth.

[1] to get back something that was lost or taken away
[2] to make someone feel less afraid, unhappy or hopeless
[3] unhappy and with no hope

b) Imagine what Jake's old life was like. Write down your ideas.

Think about the setting of the mini-saga. If you had to turn it into a film, what would the setting be like? What props and objects would you need? Write down your ideas.

What has happened to planet Earth in the mini-saga? Why do you think people have had to leave it? Write down your ideas.

INFO BUBBLE

Mini-sagas are a relatively new genre. Invented by Brian Aldiss – a British science fiction writer – in 1982, mini-sagas are extremely short stories with a beginning, a middle and an ending. They have to have exactly 50 words and a title that is no longer than 15 words. Mini-sagas are quite popular for writing contests.

B6 Working with the mini-saga

Write down information about the mini-saga on characters (who), the setting (where) and the plot (what).

Make a cluster like in B2 for the mini-saga.

Which problems of the real world does the mini-saga address? Collect ideas with a partner.

p. XX XX

B7 Target task: Science fiction writing

Short stories and mini-sagas concentrate on one single situation because they are so short. In order to understand them, the reader has to think about:

p. XX XX

WB p. XX XX

- why the characters are in the situation
- what is special about the situation
- what the characters think, feel, believe, hope for, wish for
- why they act the way they do
- what consequences their actions have.

You are going to write your own piece of science fiction or transform 'The Fun They Had' or 'Colony 4'. Choose one of the tasks in one of the two boxes. Keep the above information in mind while you plan and write.

how to write a story p. 157

Writing a piece of science fiction:

- Write a mini-saga that is set before the situation in 'The Fun They Had' or 'Colony 4'.
- Write a mini-saga that is set after the situation in 'The Fun They Had' or 'Colony 4'.
- Write your own science fiction short story or mini-saga.

1

Transform the stories:

- Turn the stories into a play or a short film.
- Change the characters, the setting and the plot of the stories and rewrite them.
- Turn 'The Fun They Had' into a mini-saga.
- Turn 'Colony 4' into a short story.

2

Tipp
Eine Geschichte wird normalerweise in der einfachen Vergangenheit geschrieben.

LiF p. 180 3R

If you like, you can share your story with a partner or in class.

P8 Explain

Explain what you have to do.

1. Imagine what school will be like in 50 years.
2. Fill in as much information as you can.
3. Write down the sentences in the correct order to get a very short summary of the story.
4. Read the mini-saga and talk about it in small groups.
5. Keep the above information in mind while you plan and write.

P9 What might they say?

LiF p. 180 3R

a) In 50 years, what might people find strange about our schools today? What might they say? Fill in the gaps using the simple past forms of the verbs in the box.

do • be • take • go • spend • wear • have • use

1. 50 years ago, pupils ??? to a place called 'school'.
2. They all ??? school uniforms.
3. The pupils ??? time together during breaks.
4. They ??? a teacher who ??? a real person.
5. When they ??? their homework, they ??? a pen and paper.
6. Some pupils ??? the bus to school.

CD XX

b) Listen to the CD and check your sentences.

What else might the people say? Write down more sentences with a partner.

P10 Elements of a story

how to p. 162 work with words

Match the words in the box with the definitions.

setting • middle • ending • beginning • motives

1. The place, the scene, the time and the objects described in a story are all part of this.
2. This is the part of the story in which the reader is introduced to the characters and the setting.
3. This part of the story is where the action starts. It tells the most exciting part of the story.
4. This part of the story can be very open, or it explains the situation.
5. This is the reason why a character acts a certain way.

P11 What is a mini-saga?

how to p. 147 mediate

a) Read the info bubble on page 89 again. In German, write down a short summary of what a mini-saga is.

b) Compare your summary with a partner. Have you both included all the important pieces of information?

P12 The author of 'The Fun They Had'

a) **Use the words in the box to complete the sentences about Isaac Asimov, the author of 'The Fun They Had'.**

where • since • then • when • while • first • even though • in order to

LiF p. 191 15

1. Russia is ??? Isaac Asimov was born.
2. The family moved to the USA ??? Isaac was three years old.
3. ??? help his parents in the shop, Isaac spent a lot of time there.
4. ??? he was going to school and university, he started writing science fiction stories.
5. ??? he wrote short stories for magazines, ??? he began publishing books.
6. ??? he wrote 'The Fun They Had' as a favour for a friend, it became one of his best-known stories.

b) **Listen to the CD and check your sentences.**

CD XX

P13 Writing about a story

a) **Read this part of the short story 'The Fun They Had' again. Rewrite it as a summary of what happens using the simple present.**

how to write a summary p. 153

They turned the pages, which were yellow and crinkly, and it was awfully funny to read words that stood still instead of moving the way they were supposed to – on a screen, you know. And then, when they turned back to the page before, it had the same words on it that it had had when they read it the first time.

LiF p. 188 12R

Margie and Tommy turn the pages, which are yellow ...

b) **Swap with a partner and edit his or her summary.**

P14 Working with words

a) **Look at the words in the box. Sort them into two lists: positive and negative feelings.**

happy • sad • glad • optimistic • despondent • sorry • hopeful • pessimistic • cheerful • excited • pleased

positive	negative
happy	sad
...	...

b) **Work with a partner. Sort your words in order from negative to positive. Can you agree on one order?**

Optional

O The history of communication

Papyrus was first used around 3000 BC. It is made from thinly-cut strips of the stalks of the dried papyrus reed. For the first time stories could be written down, carried around and exchanged. When paper was invented in China in 105 AD, papyrus production came to a stop.

Johannes Gutenberg created the printing press in the 15th century. The printing press enabled people to communicate and read about other countries and events that changed people's lives. Less than 200 years later, the first newspaper in Germany, the Avisa, was published in 1609 in Wolfenbüttel.

People have always been sending messages and documents to each other. Messengers brought news to others. In Britain the post began in the 17th century, but only rich people could afford it. It was not until the 19th century that a cheap and efficient postal system was available to everybody.

In 1844, Samuel Morse sent the first telegraph message from Washington to Baltimore. A little more than 30 years later, in 1876, Alexander Graham Bell invented the telephone. People could talk to one another over long distances. In 1901 Guglielmo Marconi sent radio signals across the Atlantic Ocean and in 1925 John Logie Baird sent the first experimental TV signal.

Between 1930 and 1940 scientists were working on a revolutionary invention: the computer. The first computers were so large they took up whole rooms. They were mainly used to store information. In the 1950s the first computers were sold commercially, however they were still large and very expensive.

The first e-mail was sent in 1965 by Ray Tomlinson. He also decided to use the @-sign for e-mail addresses.

The first mobile phone call was made from the streets of New York in 1973. Martin Cooper, back then a manager at Motorola, called one of the company's biggest rivals to demonstrate the new freedom of communication.

In 1991 the World Wide Web (www) was born when Tim Berners-Lee developed Hyper Text Markup Language. HTML allowed the Internet to expand into the World Wide Web.

The first smartphone was sold around the globe in 2007. A touch screen enables the user to input information through a virtual keyboard and function buttons.

Which inventions do you think were the most important? Find out more about them.

War and peace

5

Famous people's thoughts on war and peace

Discover some war pictures and discuss
the importance of war photographers

Working for peace

Find out how organisations are working for peace on pages 104-107

Read about:
War memories from World War II

A

- Du liest und lernst etwas über die Realität und die Auswirkungen von Krieg.
- Als Klasse gestaltet ihr einen *gallery walk*, um eure Gedanken zum Thema Krieg zu präsentieren. (Zielaufgabe)

B

- Du findest heraus, wie Menschen weltweit für den Frieden arbeiten.
- Du erarbeitest ein Produkt, das anderen erklärt, wie man sich für Frieden engagieren kann. (Zielaufgabe)

A1 Thoughts on war

What comes to mind when you think about war?

p. XX
XX

a) Read the quotes and talk about them. With which do you agree or disagree?

We make war that we may live in peace.

Aristotle

Establishing lasting peace is the work of education; all politics can do is keep us out of war.

Maria Montessori

Older men declare war. But it's the youth who must fight and die!

Herbert Hoover

Mankind must put an end to war before war puts an end to mankind.

John F. Kennedy

You can no more win a war than you can win an earthquake.

Jeanette Rankin

b) Choose one of the quotes. What can you find out about the person who said it?

WB p. XX
XX

c) Have you heard any quotes about war in German or another language you speak? Explain what they mean.

how to p. 152
write your opinion

Write down your opinion on one of the quotes.

A2 War memories

What do you think war memories are?

INFO BUBBLE
Oral history collects personal memories and commentaries of historical importance by interviewing people. The interview is recorded, transcribed, summarised and put into libraries and archives. Then the interview can be used for things such as research or for museum exhibitions. Witnesses of historic events are keen on letting future generations know what happened to them.

Several years ago some English pupils did an oral history project. They interviewed people who had experienced World War II in Britain. They wanted to learn more about war memories. This is what the older people told the pupils.

a) Read at least one of the texts. What do you find out about the people and the situations?

"I stayed in Bow* and was working in the hospital all through the Blitz until 1945, even though I married in 1943. At the time my room overlooked Bromley-by-Bow station and I remember watching the children of the local schools setting out from the station with their teachers, suitcases, bags and a label attached to their lapels. There was a great sad silence after they left."
(M. Fugill)

Bow – *a part of London*

"I was just nine years old when war was declared. [...] I was taken into the drawing room to hear Mr Chamberlain speak on the wireless. I can still recall his tired, dispirited voice. Air raid sirens were tested soon afterwards. There was a sense of anti-climax. My brother and I went out to play in the garden not quite understanding what had happened, but knowing that it would affect our lives."
(Sir Crispin Tickell)

"I was on holiday in the Wirral* with my family on the day the war broke out, staying at our grandparents' house. I was sixteen and still at school. My younger brother and I were by the sea and heard people talking. We were at war! We rushed back to tell our father. He didn't believe us until he heard it soon after on the radio. Mother and I rushed to the nearest haberdasher's to buy blackout material – someone had had great forethought and there was a good supply in the shop. We quickly covered our grandparents' windows and still had enough to do our own at home!" *(Nancy Smith)*

the Wirral – *a place close to Liverpool*

WB p. XX
XX

b) Read the texts again and take notes on how the people were affected by the war.

c) Work with a partner and compare your notes. Add more information to your notes if necessary.

Why do you think people can't forget a war? Write your opinion.

wordbank war and peace p. 17
how to p. 15 write your opinion

LAND & LEUTE 4

Kriegserinnerungen in Großbritannien

Für viele Briten bleibt der erste Weltkrieg „The Great War“, vor allem, weil sie als Nation größere Verluste hinzunehmen hatten als in jedem anderen Krieg zuvor oder danach. Auch der zweite Weltkrieg bleibt immer noch in Erinnerung, denn die Vielzahl deutscher Luftangriffe haben nachhaltig Spuren hinterlassen.

DVD XX

Die Erinnerung an beide Kriege wird in Großbritannien beispielsweise durch den jährlich am 11. November stattfindenden *Remembrance Day* wachgehalten. An diesem Tag wird an die in den Schlachten gefallenen Soldaten gedacht. Es finden viele Veranstaltungen statt, und jedes Jahr wird überall in den Städten Geld für *The Royal British Legion* gesammelt. Jeder, der spendet, bekommt eine

Anstecknadel in Form einer Mohnblume (*poppy*). Die Mohnblume ist ein Symbol für die gefallenen Soldaten und ein Zeichen für neues Leben. Auf den Schlachtfeldern des Ersten Weltkriegs blühten nach Beendigung der Kämpfe Tausende von Mohnblumen.

Finde mehr über Veranstaltungen heraus, die in Großbritannien und anderen Ländern im Zusammenhang mit dem Remembrance Day stattfinden.

A3 Children and landmines

What can you see in the picture? How do you feel about it?

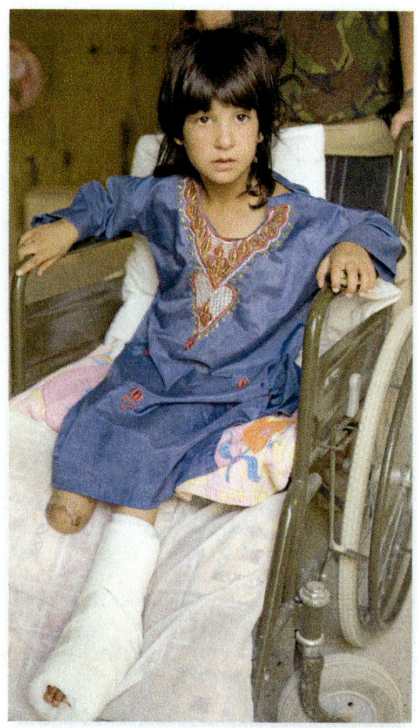

p. XX XX

a) Read about Amalia. What happened to her?

Amalia is from Afghanistan and she was a victim to a landmine. She lost her right leg when she was only seven years old.

“My mother had always warned me about the mines. When I played just outside of our house, she was quite calm. But if we went out of the village, there was the risk of stepping on a mine hidden in the ground. Most of the landmines are leftovers from past wars. They are very dangerous, because you cannot see them very well. They are designed to injure and hurt, but they do not kill.

The sad thing about my story is that I took a risk when I shouldn't have. My mother was suffering from a fever, so I went to collect wood because I wanted to prepare a soup for her. I thought that soup would make her better. When I left home, she was not feeling very well at all. I didn't want to leave her alone for a long time, so I went to the closest field next to our house. All the signs said, "Danger Mines". But I had seen other children play there before, so I thought it was safe. I had almost collected enough wood when suddenly, just as I was pulling the last piece of wood out of a larger pile, the landmine exploded."

b) **How do you think Amalia was feeling when she woke up at the hospital?**

was trying to • was wondering if • was hoping that • was crying about • was losing hope because

I think Amalia was feeling ...
She ...
...

LiF p. 192 16R

c) **Listen to the interview with landmine expert Christian Sanders. He works for the United Nations. What do you learn about landmines?**

CD X/XX

d) **Listen again and take notes.**

e) **Make a fact file on landmines.**

Make a fact file on landmines. Swap with a partner. Suggest things that your partner can add to his or her fact file.

Make a fact file on landmines. Research how landmines are cleared and add this information to your fact file.

Fact file on landmines
- can be hidden in ground for years
- planted as ...
- produced ...
- ...

wordbank war and peace p. 171

how to p. 149 research online

WB p. XX XX

A4 Choose

1. **Choose one of the pictures of children in war zones. Write about the picture. You could write his or her story.**

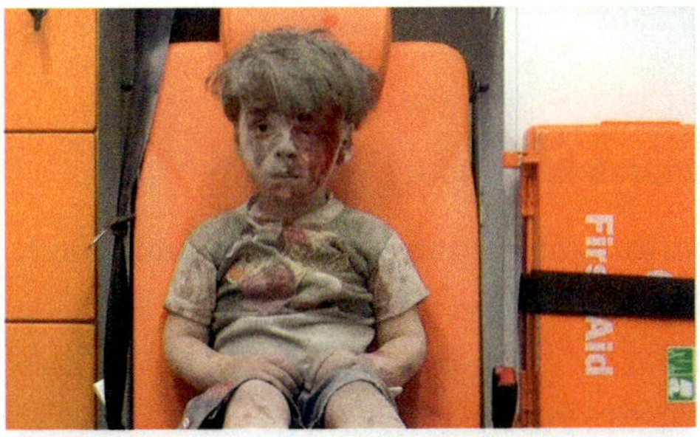

2. **Do you know someone who has a war memory that he or she might be willing to share? Prepare interview questions and interview him or her. Record the interview or make notes. Bring your recording or notes to school to share with the class.**

how to p. 147 mediate

3. **"Playing war games on game consoles or computers makes the gamer violent." Do you agree or disagree with this statement? Work in small groups and collect arguments. Discuss or write your opinion.**

how to p. 152 write your opinion, discuss

A5 War pictures

Look at the pictures and talk about them. How do they make you feel?

p. XX XX

a) Work with a partner and choose one of the pictures. Share your ideas about the picture in a silent discussion in written form. One of you starts with the first sentence, the other reads it and responds or adds a new aspect.

Adam Ferguson, Afghanistan, 2009
"As a photographer, you feel helpless. Around you are medics, security personnel, people doing good work. It can be agonisingly painful to think that all you're doing is taking pictures."

Dar Yasin, India, 2017
"Here (in Kashmir) we are not telling one story. We are telling our story through pictures, the whole story, not one part of the story."

Unknown photographer, Iraq, 2009

CD X/XX

b) Listen to the news report. Which of the three pictures is it about?

c) Listen again. What strikes you as the most important information about the situation? Write down key words.

d) Read the photographers' quotes.

Look at the third picture. Write a statement from the point of view of the photographer.

Work with a partner. Make a list of the differences between the news report and the photographer's statement. Present them to the class.

Work in a group. Think about how the newspaper reports and the photographers' statements differ. What are the good and the bad effects of photographers working in war situations? Present your results to the class.

WB p. XX XX

A6 War in the media

a) Read the article about the 2003 invasion of Iraq. What does it tell you about modern wars?

The 2003 invasion of Iraq is known as one of the first wars which was covered by the media. TV stations showed live streams of attacks on the city of Baghdad. Reporters travelled with soldiers as they made their way through Iraq to defeat Saddam Hussein.

The reporters were criticised because of biased reports on the war. People accused some US news outlets of a pro-war and sensationalist reporting. They said that some of the reporting was very patriotic and emphasised the soldiers' risking their lives.

This criticism was possibly a result of the journalists being 'embedded' in the army and reporting from the front lines of the conflict. In earlier decades, journalists were much more independent. They visited war zones on their own and not with the army. However, this lead to more critical reporting about the war events. 'Embedded journalism' seems to influence the way events are shown in the media.

b) Read the text again. What is the difference between 'embedded journalism' and journalists who are independent?

WB p. XX XX

Where do you hear or read news? Do you believe everything you see or hear? How can you be sure that the information you see or hear is true? Discuss in class.

A7 Target task: A statement against war

As a class, you are going to present your statements against war in a gallery walk.

p. XX XX

WB p. XX XX

1. Think about your own opinion and take notes.
2. Share your thoughts with others and decide whether you want to work alone, with a partner or in a small group of 3-4 people.
3. Think about ways of making your statement. Your statement could take the form of:
   - pictures
   - words or quotations collected on a poster
   - a series of questions with or without answers
   - a collection of authentic material
   - an exhibition of objects
   - a video clip
   - ...
4. Prepare your statement. Make cue cards to help you explain your statement.
5. Display your statements and do the gallery walk. You might also want to invite other classes to visit your gallery.
6. Invite your visitors to react to your statement and share their comments and opinions.

Let's not make war!
Let's talk about our problems and bring peace to the world!

model text

Practice matters

P1 Explain

Explain what you have to do.

Ich soll …

Wir sollen …

…

1. Read the quotes and talk about them.
2. Take notes on the texts you read.
3. Make a fact file on landmines.
4. Share your ideas about the picture in a silent discussion in written form.
5. Think about your own opinion and take notes.

P2 Talking about war memories

a) **Work with a partner. Choose one of the texts you read in A2 and read it again. Rewrite it as an interview with an interviewer.**

Interviewer: How old were you when war was declared?
Sir Crispin Tickell: I was just nine years old.
Interviewer: Can you explain what happened?
Sir Crispin Tickell: I was taken into the drawing-room.
Interviewer: And what happened then?
Sir Crispin Tickell: Well, I heard …

b) **Swap your interview with another pair. Have they got any questions that you don't have? Write them down. You can use these questions and your own questions to ask people about their war memories.**

P3 Amalia's story

LiF p. 192
16R

a) **Complete the sentences using the words in the box.**

was playing • was walking • was pulling • was feeling • was looking

1. When Amalia ??? just outside of the house, her mother knew she was safe.
2. Amalia's mother ??? ill, so Amalia wanted to make her some soup.
3. When she ??? for wood, she decided to go to the closest field.
4. As she ??? towards the field, she saw signs saying, "Danger Mines".
5. As she ??? the last piece of wood out of a big pile, a landmine exploded.

1. When Amalia was playing just outside of the house, her mother knew she was safe.

b) **Swap with a partner and check his or her sentences.**

Practice matters

P4 Facts about landmines

Listen to the interview with the landmine expert again. Are these facts about landmines right or wrong?

CD XX

1. Every year, thousands of people are affected by landmines.
2. Most of the landmines that explode today haven't been in the ground for many years.
3. Since 1975 there have been more than one million victims worldwide.
4. Landmines are designed to kill people.
5. Landmines can only be found in large cities.
6. The process of clearing areas of landmines is cheap and easy.

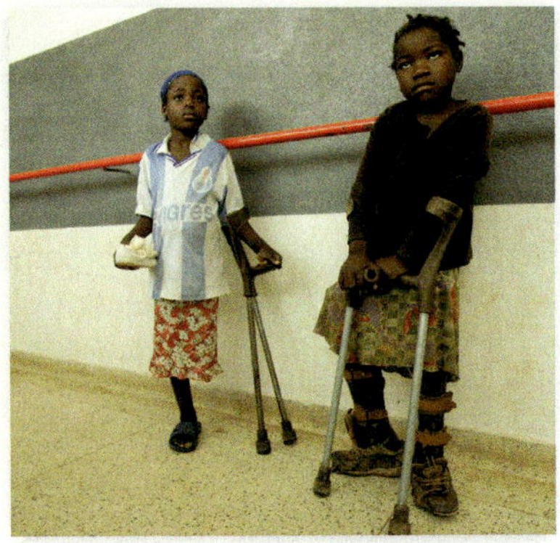

Correct the wrong sentences.

P5 Sound check

CD XX

a) **Listen to the words and repeat them.**

b) **Use a dictionary to check the meaning of the words you don't know.**

invasion • defeat • criticise • biased • accuse • patriotic • emphasise • criticism

c) **Which words are difficult? Practise saying them with a partner.**

P6 War vocabulary

Make a word web of words and phrases from this Theme. You can use it to help you with your statement against war.

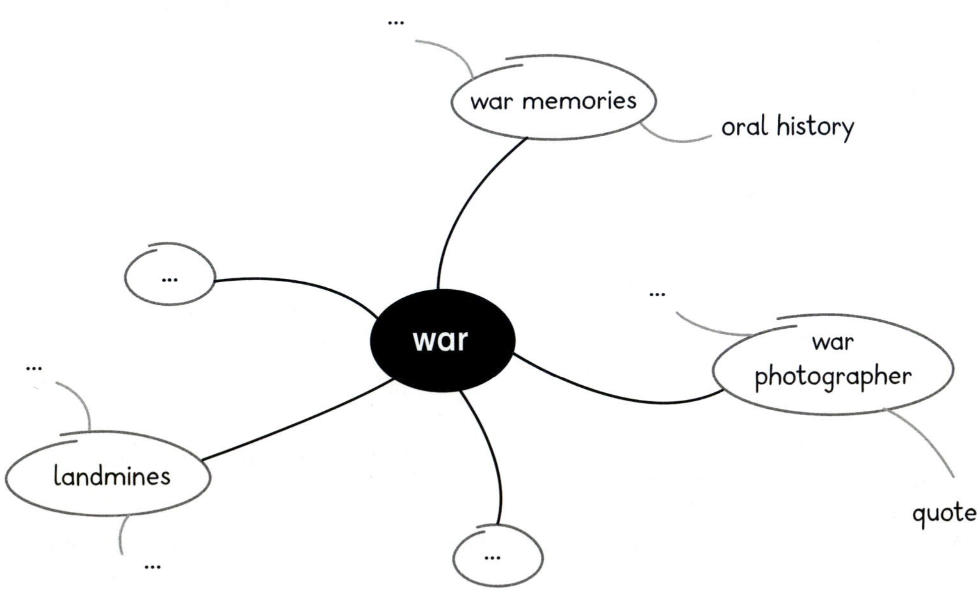

B1 Thoughts on peace

Draw something that symbolises peace to you and talk about your drawing.

p. XX
XX

a) Read these quotes about peace. Choose the one you like best. Read it to a partner.

When the power of love overcomes the love of power the world will know peace.

Jimi Hendrix (1942–1970)

If we are to teach real peace in this world, and if we are to carry on a real war against war, we shall have to begin with the children.

Mahatma Gandhi (1869–1944)

You cannot shake hands with a clenched fist.

Indira Gandhi (1917–1984)

We have learned to fly the air like birds and swim the sea like fish, but we have not learned the simple art of living together as brothers.

Martin Luther King, Jr. (1929–1968)

It isn't enough to talk about peace. One must believe in it. And it isn't enough to believe in it. One must work on it.

Eleanor Roosevelt (1884–1962)

b) Have you heard any peace quotes in German or another language you speak? Explain what they are about.

WB p. XX
XX

c) Make a list of keywords to do with peace. Add words to your list that describe what peace means to you. Work in groups.

B2 Imagine

Listen to the song. What do you think of the melody, the instruments and the tone of the song?

CD X/XX

Imagine there's no heaven
It's easy if you try
No hell below us
Above us only sky
Imagine all the people
Living for today

Imagine there's no countries
It isn't hard to do
Nothing to kill or die for
And no religion too
Imagine all the people
Living life in peace

You may say I'm a dreamer
But I'm not the only one
I hope someday you'll join us
And the world will be as one

Imagine no possessions
I wonder if you can
No need for greed or hunger
A brotherhood of man
Imagine all the people
Sharing all the world

You may say I'm a dreamer
But I'm not the only one
I hope someday you'll join us
And the world will live as one

Music and lyrics: John Lennon

how to p. 161 talk about song lyrics

a) Work with a partner and answer the questions.

1. What does the singer imagine? Name three things.
2. Do you like the song? Say why or why not.

1. What do you think the singer wants to say?
2. Do you agree with the message of the song?

1. What do you think the world would be like if it didn't have different countries?
2. In your opinion: is the singer a dreamer? Why do you think so?

b) What is your vision of a peaceful word? Think, pair, share.

WB p. XX XX

B3 Working for peace

Get together in small groups (home groups). Everyone skims the four texts on the next four pages, chooses one of them and reads it in detail. Then get together in an expert group with classmates who have read the same text. After that inform your home group what your text is about. Give the main ideas by thinking of who, what, when, where, how and why.

p. XX
XX

The Maidstone Mediation Scheme: Peer Mediation in English schools

Peer mediators are young people trained to help others sort out student disputes.

We train a selected group of Year 9 students (about 10 or 12) to become peer mediators so that they can offer the service to younger students.

The process of mediation is simple and anyone can follow it to help others to reach an agreement.

Why develop peer mediation in schools?

- It teaches life skills to all students.
- It promotes an ethos of problem solving and cooperation.
- It raises self-esteem and self-confidence.
- It develops empathy and valuing others.
- It gives opportunities to young people to take responsibility.
- It opens discussions on bullying and how it can be dealt with.
- It promotes equal opportunities because everyone is respected.
- It allows young people to resolve conflicts for themselves without involving adults.

Client comments ...

"It was brilliant!"

"School attendance greatly improved as a result of mediation."

"This is probably the happiest I have seen these pupils together."

teaching mindfulness

There are many 'mindfulness programmes' in the USA, and one particular one, the Holistic Life Foundation, is based in Baltimore, Maryland. It was co-founded by Ali Smith, Atman Smith and Andres Gonzalez in 2001.

Their non-profit organization aims to help people, both young and old, develop **compassion** and **empathy** in everyday situations. They want to look after the wellness of children and adults in low-income communities through **yoga** and **mindfulness**.

The Holistic Life Foundation are working at Patterson High School in Baltimore. They were quite shocked about the following statistics about the school:
- end-of-year suspension rates up to 16% of students
- a 4-year graduation rate of only 86% of students
- more than 60% of students are absent more than 20 days each year

Their aim is to take their yoga and mindfulness curriculum into Patterson High School in order to **improve participation** in class, **students' grades**, and **graduation rates**. They also want the students to find some inner **peace** of their own.

Patterson High students come from families that don't earn a lot of money. This kind of program will change their lives (and there are over 1,000 of them!).

The organization's first afterschool program of 20 children was very successful. After 2 months, the students who usually get detentions all the time were showing up to their classes and they were passing all of their classes.

Since then, the organization has been teaching all over the place - from children at kindergardens to senior citizens. This kind of work with inner-city youth makes a huge impact, not just now while they're in school, but in the future in their community.

Webcode
DSW-14605-xxx

The German War Graves Commission

Beyond all borders!

You would like to
- live as part of an international group for a while?
- get to know Germany?
- explore historical and political topics?
- enjoy and arrange leisure activities?
- work voluntarily for two to three weeks to maintain war graves or memorials to preserve them as a peace memorial?

You are the right person for us! The German War Graves Commission (Volksbund Deutsche Kriegsgräberfürsorge e.V.) organises many work camps across Germany each summer. Young people between the ages of 16 and 25 years from all over Europe can take part.

I had a really amazing time at the work camp in Magdeburg. Before I went, I thought it might be weird hanging around war graves, but it was a great experience. It was so moving and shocking to see all those graves of soldiers who died in the wars. Reading the headstones, I realised that many of the soldiers were hardly older than me. It got me wondering how I'd feel if I had to fight and risk getting killed.

And of course, we Brits were working alongside German kids, having campfire evenings, discos and playing football. Anyone who fought in the Second World War – like my grandad, for example – could never have imagined it! And I still find it unbelievable that Brits and Germans were at war with each other not so long ago. We're close neighbours, just across that bit of water. We go to the Black Forest or the Rhine for our holidays, and back then we were killing each other.

But I also enjoyed the work. It was good fun and I made lots of new friends from all over Europe. Some of us still text each other. And it was good to have the feeling that we'd done something practical and useful, and to work for peace …

Mike Charles, Canterbury, UK

WB p. XX
XX

United Nations Children's Fund (UNICEF)

unicef

for every child

The United Nations Children's Fund or UNICEF is an international organization.

The United Nations established UNICEF on 11 December 1946.

UNICEF has its headquarters in New York, USA. It provides many types of assistance and help to children and mothers. It receives money from different governments and private persons.

Purpose

UNICEF has decided the following 5 areas as priority or main areas:

- Young child survival and development
- Primary education and gender equality
- Child protection
- HIV/AIDS
- Early childhood

Some other priority areas are the child in the family, and sports for development.

UNICEF has been working for over 60 years in different countries all over the world.

In 1965, this organization received the Nobel Peace Prize for its work. It is the world's leading organization for the development of children. It operates in 190 countries around the world.

WB p. XX
XX

B4 A glimpse of peace: The Christmas truce

a) Read the text and find out what the Christmas truce was.

World War I took place between 1914 and 1918. It caused pain to millions of people. Many people from different nations in Europe lost their lives. On and around Christmas Day in 1914, there were reported incidents showing glimpses of hope, humanity and peace. These incidents are referred to as the Christmas truce. It showed how important it is for people to be brave; people who will step out and shake hands, although there are restrictions and hate around them.

According to accounts from both sides, soldiers from the German and British armies along the Western Front left their trenches and went into no-man's-land. They wished each other a Merry Christmas, gave each other food and souvenirs and sang Christmas songs together. There were even reports of soldiers playing a game of football together. Some soldiers used the time to retrieve bodies of soldiers who had fallen in no-man's-land.

The incidents of the Christmas truce were described in letters and diaries of soldiers, so the truce was very well-documented. It is widely used to portray a glimpse of peace in one of the most brutal wars in history.

b) Read the text again.

- ☆ **What did the German and British soldiers do together? Name at least three things.**
- ☾ **What did the German and British soldiers do during the Christmas truce?**
- ☼ **Why do you think the soldiers did what they did? Was it a brave thing to do?**

B5 A Christmas truce advert

In 2014, the Christmas truce was used in an advert.

Webcode DSW-14605-xxx

a) What do you think the advert might be about? Collect ideas in class.

b) Watch the advert. Whilst you watch it, pay attention to how it makes you feel.

c) What do you think of the advert? How did it make you feel? Talk to a partner.

d) Read the two comments about the advert.

■ What a wonderful idea! Sainsbury's, one of Britain's largest supermarket chains, has shown the true meaning of Christmas in this advert. Christmas is about spending time with others and spreading peace and love around the world. Sainsbury's sold the chocolate bars for £1 each, and all the money was donated to The Royal British Legion. Fantastic! Well done, Sainsbury's! ■

[...] a short three minute clip does rather gloss over the actual horrors of the trenches. This is war for the Instagram generation. Two incredibly attractive, chiselled young men, without a spot of mud or a smear of blood in sight, merrily frolic together in the sunshine, before swapping Sainsbury's own brand chocolates (yours for just one pound; in stores now).

e) What do *you* think? Is it OK to use war as a topic to advertise chocolate?

B5 Choose

1. Design your own piece of anti-war graffiti.
2. Find more anti-war songs or poems and present them in class. You can also write your own song or poem.
3. Look at B1 again. Find out about the peaceful resistance that either Mahatma Gandhi or Martin Luther King Jr. practised. Present your findings to the class.

B6 A survey about peace

a) Watch the video clip. What questions are asked in the survey?

b) Write down words that show what peace means to the people being interviewed.

Choose at least two of the people in the video and write down what peace means to them. Do you agree with them?

Write down what peace means to each of the people who are interviewed in the video. Which person do you agree with?

c) What does peace mean to you? Have a discussion in class.

DVD XX
p. XX XX
wordbank war and peace p. 171
how to discuss p. 154

B7 Target task: Working for peace

What can you personally do to work for peace? You should think about what you can change in your everyday life to make life more peaceful for everyone. Here are some suggestions:

- Carry out a survey in your school or town on the subject of war and peace. Decide on 10 questions.
- Find out what is going on in your area. Are there any campaigns that promote peace?
- Find out more about mindfulness programmes in the USA. Make some recommendations for your own school.
- Use your results from B4 and present some examples of peaceful resistance.
- Describe the activities for solving conflicts in your school for English readers (e.g. *Klassenrat*, ...)

Get into groups and decide how you want to present what you have done. You could:

- add a new page to your school's website about your programme for peace in English and in German.
- produce a podcast.
- make a class presentation for parents' evening.

p. XX XX
WB p. XX XX
Webcode DSW-14605-xxx

Tipp
Sieh dir für ein gutes Beispiel einer Präsentation den Ted-Talk an. Nutze den Webcode.

Practice matters

P7 Explain

Ich soll ...

Wir sollen ...

...

Explain what you have to do.

1. Draw something that symbolises peace to you.
2. Skim the four texts on the next four pages.
3. Give the main ideas by thinking of who did what, when, where, how and why.
4. Read the text and find out what the Christmas truce was.
5. Get into groups and decide which activity you want to work on.

P8 Working for peace

a) Complete the sentences using the words in the box.

Europe • peace • wellness • children • truce • countries

1. There are many organisations that work for ???.
2. The Maidstone Mediation Scheme is used to help ??? in schools.
3. The Holistic Life Foundation want to look after the ??? of children and adults.
4. Young people from all over ??? can take part in the German War Graves Commission.
5. UNICEF operates in over 190 ??? around the world.
6. The Christmas ??? took place in 1914.

There are many organisations that work for peace.

CD XX

b) Listen to the CD and check your sentences.

P9 The German War Graves Commission

how to mediate p. 147

Look at the brochure for the German War Graves Commission on page 106. Your German friend is interested in the summer camp, but he has some questions. Answer her questions in German.

LiF p. 188
12R

P10 The Christmas truce

a) Read the text in B4 again. Then answer the questions.

1. When does the story take place?
2. Where does the story take place?
3. Which sport do the soldiers play for a while?
4. What do the soldiers give each other?
5. Why do the soldiers leave their trenches?
6. What makes the soldiers go back to their trenches?

b) Compare your answers with a partner.

Write down at least two more questions about the Christmas truce. Swap with a partner and write down the answers to his or her questions as fast as you can.

P11 Sound check

a) Listen to the CD and repeat the words.

CD XX

**b) Copy the lists and fill in the words.
Is the stress on the first or the second syllable?
Which word isn't stressed like the others?**

c) Listen to the CD and check your lists.

CD XX

dreamer • achieve • believe • imagine • peaceful • mediation • attitude • empathy • commission • memorial • Europe • humanity

first syllable	second syllable
dreamer	achieve
...	...

P12 Peace vocabulary

Make a word web of words and phrases about peace. Share your ideas with a partner.

wordbank war and peace p. 171

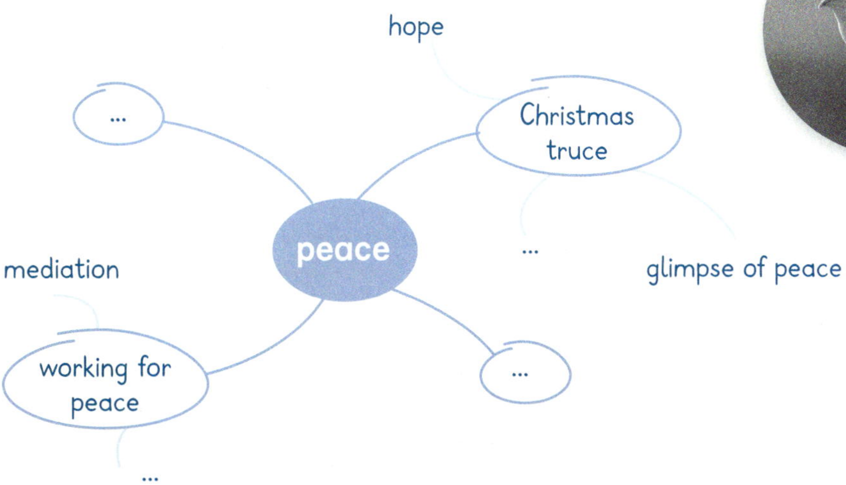

Optional

O A tale of two brothers

When they were childen, Luis Samacumbi and his brother Amaral were kidnapped and forced to fight. They almost killed each other. Luckily they both survived.

This is what happened.

In 1987, 14-year-old Luis Samacumbi was kidnapped on his way to school and forced to serve in an army fighting a civil war in Angola. He was trained to hate but he felt he had no choice. Luis survived. He did not know at the time that his older brother, who had also been kidnapped, had been forced to fight for the other side.

In 1992 when the first peace treaty was signed, Luis left the army. "It was hard. I had no skills, but I attended nursing school, started working with young people and founded a youth movement for peace." He later earned a degree in peace studies and conflict resolution in South Africa. He said he drew his strength to start a new life from a traditional healing process, undertaken in his village in 1995.

In 2004, Luis heard from his brother Amaral, who was in a Zambian refugee camp, and the victim of a landmine. "When I went home to meet him, he hugged me and started crying. 'I'm back,' he said, 'but I am useless now because I have only one leg. From now on, you will have to be my big brother.'"

Now they fight for peace together. Luis worries that the gap between rich and poor could cause further conflict. "Violence will always generate violence," he warns. "No one knows that better than a man who fought his own brother."

INFO BUBBLE

Child soldiers

There are hundreds of thousands of children who fight and die in conflicts around the world. In Africa in particular there is a tradition of using children in wars and armed conflicts. As there are so many children who live very poor lives, it is easy for army chiefs to find new recruits. With the offer of food, a gun and a uniform and after a few weeks of brainwashing, many children are happy to join the army.

Why are child soldiers used in wars? Where does this happen today? What are the lives of child soldiers like? Research online and present some facts or stories.

Projects: Be yourself

What does it mean to be yourself? Share your ideas on page 114.

Topic A
Music and dance

Topic B
Fashion and style

Topic C
Attitudes and values

With a handy navigation bar!

Music and fashion are important for many teens. Why? Find out on pages 119 and 123!

Choose a topic and do your own project. Find tips on pages 130 and 131!

Before you get into the project, take some time to find out what it's all about. The following pages will give you an idea.

Be yourself

p. XX
XX

WB p. XX
XX

Look at the photos. What do they tell you about the teenagers? What does it mean to be yourself?

What is important in your life?

listening to music | following an idol | being vegetarian | doing things with friends or family | taking part in political activities | having my own style | having tattoos or piercings | keeping fit | looking good | living with traditions | having a job | ...

wordbank
be yourself
p. 172

... is really important to me. •
... plays a big role in my life. •
... is not important to me. •
I can't imagine my life without ... • ...

For me, listening to music is really important. Listening to ... makes me feel ...

What is important to me? Sometimes I don't really know.

...

Read this post by a youth magazine blogger. Collect keywords and statements. Talk about them with a partner or in a group.

www.teenmag/blog

Posted by Martin, Wednesday, June 20

Teenagers can sometimes feel like aliens from another planet. They don't know who they are. They don't know what they want. They feel like nobody understands them. But why is this? I wanted to find out more, so I talked to youth psychologist Dr. M. Rosen.

M: Dr. Rosen, why is being a teenager sometimes so hard?

Dr.R.: Well, Martin, your teenage years, we also say puberty, are a time of change. For many teens it is a time when they feel uncertain. They are no longer children but also not yet adults. Teenagers want to find out who they are. They try to form their identity – and that's not easy.

M.: What does 'identity' actually mean?

Dr.R.: Qualities that make you who you are, that make you different from other people, that's your identity. There are many different elements to your identity, such as your social identity, national identity, ethnic identity, gender identity and, for your generation, your online identity.

M: OK ... but we work on our identities during our whole lives, don't we? Not just as teens?

Dr.R.: Yes, we do, but during your teenage years this process is the most dynamic. Think of being a teenager as a trial and error period. You can try things out and explore who you want to be.

M: So teens can choose their own identity?

Dr.R.: Yes and no. Yes because teens are free to make their own decisions. No because society, or traditions, also influence a teen's identity and they are out of their control.

M.: Out of control – that sounds a bit scary.

Dr.R.: Well, yes, it is an exciting time. Teenagers often rebel against rules or get into conflicts with parents and teachers. The way a teenager sees himself or herself changes as they are influenced by the people around them.

M.: Is that why friends are so important to many teens?

Dr.R.: Yes, friends and peer group play a very important role in the development of a teenager's identity. Many teens loosen their relationship with their parents and get much closer with friends.

M.: One last question, Dr Rosen. What advice would you give a teenager reading this?

Dr. R.: Follow your dreams, and be tolerant of others. Everyone is on a journey to finding out who they are.

M.: Thanks a lot for the interview, Dr. Rosen. It's been really interesting.

Project steps

1 Choose a topic

Look through the three topics in this Theme:

Topic A Music and dance p. 118–121
Topic B Fashion and style p. 122–125
Topic C Attitudes and values p. 126–129

DVD XX-XX

Watch the video clips for each topic. Then decide which topic you want to find out more about. Get into a group with classmates who want to work on the same topic as you.

2 Get into your topic

Look at the first page of your topic. Do the activities together to get a first impression of what the topic is all about.

3 Explore your topic

On the second and third pages of each topic there are pictures, facts and figures, newspaper articles, podcasts, and much more, for example:

EPISODE 1:
Ballet for boys

Is ballet just for girls and boxing just for boys? What do you think? This week we will look at the story of a young boy - Billy Elliot - who loves to dance.

0:00:00

How to be cruelty-free

1. Reduce your waste, especially your food waste.
2. Recycle products because nothing really just 'goes away'.

Putting myself first

My name is Sam and I'm 16 years old. I know it sounds selfish, but for me it's important to put myself first.

You don't all have to read every text! Split up your group so that different people explore different texts.

Webcode DSW-14605-XXX

If you want to find out even more, go to www.diesterweg.de/webcodes and type in the webcode of your topic. You will find a list of links to useful websites. You can also search for other useful websites yourself.

As a group, start a wordbank for your topic. Add to it during the project.

Inform other group members about what you found out.

4 Spotlight on ...

On the fourth page you will find a text called 'Spotlight on ...'. This is a detailed report about a young person in the field of music, fashion or environmental activism. Read the text as a group, take notes and talk about it. There are also links to websites to find out more information.

5 Get ready to share

You and your group now know quite a lot about your topic. It is time to share your knowledge with your class.

Prepare a presentation. You could make a poster, a computer presentation, a fact file, ... Decide on the aspects you want to focus on. Be prepared for questions and feedback from the other groups.

If as a class you want to go further and carry out your own projects, do step 6.
If not, go straight to step 7.

Steps

6 Over to you!

Each group now has to plan their own project based on their topic. If you prefer one of the other topics, you can change groups at this point.

Each group will need to:

- identify a problem
- research it
- think of a solution
- put their plan into action
- present their project to the class.

how to p. 149 work on a project

All the details for this part of the project are on pages 130 and 131.

7 Reflection

After the project is over, you have a chance to think about how it went and reflect on the work you have done.

You can find a questionnaire to help you with this in your workbook.

WB p. XX XX

On pages 132-134 you will find useful words and phrases for each topic. These pages can be helpful to you during or after your project.

Topic A Music and dance

wordbank music and dance p.172

p. XX XX

DVD XX-XX

CD X/XX XX

What can music and dance mean to teenagers? Why are they so important? Look at the photos and read the statements. Talk about them with a partner.

Dancing can be a way of ...

Teenagers listen to music when ...

For teenagers, music can mean ...

...

I'm a ballet dancer, so I like to listen to classical music a lot.

I like bands that have emotion in their lyrics. It takes your mind off problems.

I like music with good lyrics – lyrics that I could think about or that I can talk to people about.

Hip hop and rap is my favourite kind of music.

music

rap • hip hop • folk • pop • metal • jazz • techno • soul • dance • classical • blues • alternative • disco • rock 'n' roll • country • R&B • reggae • latin • punk • ...

dance

ballet • salsa • tango • waltz • B-boying/-girling • folk dance • street dance • zumba • tap dance • ...

Share your ideas in your group. Agree on three reasons why music or dance can play such a big role in a teenager's life.

Why teens need music

During the teen years, teenagers are on their way to becoming independent individuals. They question values and rules set by adults. Youth cultures help them to express their personal feelings and lifestyle.

Clothes are obviously important, as are sports, behaviour and a specific vocabulary. Their attitudes, values and beliefs are different from those of other age groups.

But above all music seems to be a common need during the teenage years. How come? Why do teens need their music? There are many reasons ...

Did you know ...?

p. XX
XX

Many teens use music as an **escape**. Music helps them express **feelings** and **emotions** like anger and rage, but also love, longing and loneliness.

For teens, finding others who like the same band gives them a sense of **belonging**, of no longer being "alone". Music lets them experience **close friendship**.

Generation after generation of music – especially rock music – has revolutionized youth culture. It's all about **rebellion.**

There are so many different teenage music scenes. A shared love of music gives teenagers a basis for **friendship**.

EPISODE 1:
Ballet for boys

Is ballet just for girls and boxing just for boys? What do you think? This week we will look at the story of a young boy – Billy Elliot – who loves to dance.

0:00:00

Music – my first love

Music will always be my first love. Being part of an orchestra has changed my life. You make music together. It's a group effort – we have to listen to each other to play together. Orchestra has taught me how to be patient with others. I learnt to cooperate. And it has shown me the beauty of classical music.

CD
X/XX XX

Real, personal and honest: hip hop is right here, right now.

Hip hop has become a lifestyle, culture and form of expression for thousands of young people all around the world. You can find hip hop culture in fashion, design, movies and many other aspects of modern life.

'Real, personal and honest: hip hop is right here, right now.' What does this mean? Well, hip hop culture rebels against elements of modern society and adult culture. It is aggressive and often rude. But it is real.

Hip hop is also creative – an aspect of the culture that is sometimes forgotten. It offers young people a chance to show their talents at competitions such as the World Hip Hop Dance Championship.

Every year, thousands of the world's best dancers come together to celebrate the hip hop culture. Dancers compete for the world title. Famous hip hop artists and celebrities also perform. It's a great opportunity for hip hop dancers to meet people with the same interests and ideas from around the world.

www.allthingsclassical.com/forum

Posted by Joe, Wednesday, May 21, Bristol

Hey everyone. I was driving home with my fifteen-year-old son tonight, and I put on some classical music. My son immediately turned it off and said it was boring. He would rather listen to no music than classical music. Why do teenagers hate classical music so much?

Comment posted by Karla: The pace and rhythm of classical music is not what most teens go for. Teens talk, play and think fast, so it's no wonder that they want their music fast, too.

Comment posted by Jake: That's not totally true. I'm sixteen and I love playing classical music in our school orchestra – I just don't really like to listen to it in my free time. I usually listen to rap and hip hop, music with electrical instruments and a good beat.

Comment posted by Scott: Classical music makes you want to sit next to a nice fire and, like a good book, simply enjoy. What teen wants to sit still for a whole hour?!

Comment posted by Miriam: I bet most teens can't even name a single classical composer!

Comment posted by Zani: I'm a music teacher. In my experience, there are teens who like classical music, but they just don't want to admit it to their peers.

Webcode DSW-14605-XXX

Want to find out more? Use the webcode or do your own research online. Here are some ideas for search terms.

- hip hop
- x-factor UK (guitar audition)
- Tina S plays Vivaldi
- hip hop dance moves
- Irish folk dance
- ballet dancing

sPOTlight on ...

Lizzie Sider – a singer, songwriter and anti-bullying activist

p. XX
XX

Lizzie Sider is a 19-year-old singer/songwriter, actress, dancer and anti-bullying activist. She uses her music to share her anti-bullying message.

Music and acting have been important to Lizzie since she saw her first musical when she was five. She started playing the piano when she was six and the guitar a few years later.

But not everything was perfect for Lizzie when she was younger. In elementary school, Lizzie was bullied. She was in tears every day. One day, her dad said to her, 'No one has the power to ruin your day'. This a phrase that she didn't forget.

When she was 13, Lizzie recorded her first single, 'Butterfly'. The song is about the bullying she experienced when she was younger and how she overcame it. It was a huge success.

A few years later, Lizzie decided to try and stop other kids from being bullied like she was. She organized her National Bully Prevention School Tour, which she called 'Nobody has the power to ruin your day'. As part of the tour, Lizzie has so far performed at over 400 schools all around the USA.

When she goes into a school, she performs her own Bully Prevention Assembly. In these positive assemblies, Lizzie talks to students about bullying, tells them her own story and, of course, sings and performs her songs. She also gives students bracelets that say, 'Nobody has the power to ruin your day'.

Lizzie has already met and worked with over 150,000 students, but she isn't stopping there! She has made a DVD version of her anti-bullying assembly and she's offering it to every school across the USA for free, so that her message can reach even more students at even more schools.

At just 19 years old, this special teen is spreading her message and making a difference student by student, school by school.

Topic
A
B
C

Webcode
DSW-14605-XXX

Topic B Fashion and style

p. XX
XX

wordbank
fashion and
style p. 173

Look at the photos and read the statements. Talk about them with a partner. Which of these styles do you like?
Why are fashion and style important to many teenagers? Make notes. Think about different attitudes towards fashion and style.

trendy • casual • ethnic • punk • gothic • emo • sporty • skater • …

CD
X/XX XX

My friends and I often wear similar clothes. I don't need to look different from anyone else.

I love fashionable clothes. A stylish outfit is a big part of my lifestyle.

I don't really care about fashion.

I think it is a good idea to buy eco-fashion.

Don't judge me by what I wear. I just want to be myself.

A special look makes me who I am.

Share your ideas in your group. Agree on five ideas about what fashion and style can mean to young people.

p. XX
XX

Why fashion matters

Your mum doesn't understand why you need a new pair of jeans. Your dad finds it hard to believe that you needed an hour to pick an outfit and get ready to meet your friends. But fashion and style really are important during your teenage years.

Read on to find out why – then tell your parents!

What is 'fashion'?

'Fashion' means a style of clothing, footwear or hairstyle that is 'in' at a given time. Not all teens care about fashionable clothes – but their style can still be important to them.

What your style says about you

Some teens want to look different from others. Their style underlines their individuality. Other teens use their clothing to fit in with their peer group. They want to show that they belong to a special group. What about you? Do you want to look different, or blend in with a group? No matter what – it's YOUR style, there's no right or wrong!

Why do teenagers care so much?

As a teenager, you explore your identity, your independence and your image. Fashion is one of the ways that you can express yourself and show the world who you are. What to wear is one of the things that most of you can control, which is why it feels so important. Your clothing shows the world your developing identity.

Is it OK to experiment with it?

It is not only OK to experiment with your style as a teenager, it is normal! Try out different looks and styles and develop your own sense of identity. Have fun!

Topic
B

EPISODE 2:
I do it my way

This week, lifestyle and fashion presenter Tina Marks is talking with five young people about their lifestyles. They also talk about their problems when other people judge them.

0:00:00

CD
X/XX XX

FASHIONISTA HAUL GIRLS

Some teens love **shopping** and the **latest fashions**. Others are more into **ethical fashion** and are **critical of consumerism**. Here's a topic that is sure to create a strong reaction in either group: **haul girls**.

What's a haul girl?
A haul girl goes shopping for clothes, shoes or beauty products. Then she makes a haul video and uploads it online.

What's in a haul video?
Haul girls show their viewers what they have bought – in detail. They tell them where they bought the item, and what they like about it. By doing so they show viewers what their style is and what's important to them.

How do you make a haul video?
There's a lot to think about, such as background music, sound, different camera shots and a lot more. It can be a really creative process.

Why make haul videos?
Haul girls enjoy communicating with people who feel and think the same way they do.

What do critics say?
Haul girls think it's a lot of fun to make and present these videos. Others don't agree. They view haul girls critically. They don't think it's OK to make viewers think that this kind of consumerism is normal.

how to p. 156 work with statistics

American teenager spending 2014

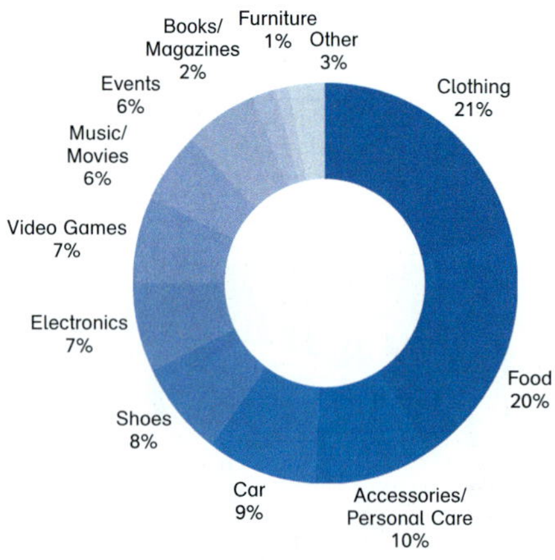

- Average teen spending (per person) on clothing and fashion: $1,069
- Average number of shopping trips per year: 28.7
- Average parent contribution to teen spending in average income families: 66 per cent
- Top clothing brands include: Nike, American Eagle, Forever 21, Ralph Lauren.

Webcode DSW-14605-XXX

Want to find out more? Use the webcode or do your own research online. Here are some ideas for search terms.

- teenage lifestyles
- hipsters
- teenage fashion
- 'Fashion' by Lady Gaga
- popular clothing brands
- fashion hacks

sPOTlight on ...

p. XX
XX

Madeline Stuart

Madeline Stuart is a 20-year-old model from Brisbane, Australia, but she's no ordinary model. She has been called 'the world's most famous model with Down syndrome'. This talented young woman is very successful and even has her own fashion label.

In 2015 Madeline started doing a lot of sport and dance to lose weight. Later that year, she went to a Fashion Parade with her mum. This inspired her to become a model herself.

The rest, as they say, is history. Madeline has modelled all around the world, from the USA to China, Dubai to the UK. Madeline was named Model of the Year 2016 by World Fashion Media. She launched her fashion label, '21 Reasons Why by Madeline Stuart', in February 2017.

Madeline is also the ambassador of a dance school called 'Inside, Outside Dance Ensemble'. This dance school gives young people with disabilities the chance to learn different kinds of dance styles and be involved in perfomances and shows.

Madeline is changing how society views people with disabilities and challenging the stereotypes that surround beauty and modelling. This determined young woman is not only a model, but also a role model for people of all ages, all around the world.

Topic
B

Webcode
DSW-14605-XXX

Topic C Attitudes and values

p. XX
XX

wordbank attitudes and values p. 173

DVD XX-XX

CD X/XX XX

Look at the photos and read the statements. Talk about them with a partner. What are these young people doing? Which of these attitudes and values do you share?

demonstrate • campaign • fight for animal rights • volunteer • help • ...

I'm vegan. I don't want dead animals on my plate. I try to live cruelty-free.

I volunteer at a primary school once a week.

Last summer I volunteered to plant trees with an environmental organisation. This is my way of connecting with people.

I think it's important to support the LGBTQ community even though I'm not gay. Equal rights for everybody!

Let's take action for our world and fight for our environment!

I help some old people in our neighbourhood with their shopping. I want to be an active part of our community.

Share your ideas in a small group. Come up with five ideas about what can make life meaningful for young people on which all your group members agree.

Attitudes and values – what are they and why are they important?

When we talk to someone, we hear what they say and see how they act. But **why** do they say certain things, or act in a certain way?

Think of a person as being like an iceberg. Above the water are the things you can see or hear: words, body language and actions.

Below the water are their attitudes, beliefs and values. Attitudes, beliefs and values influence how people act and what they say.

We learn a lot of our attitudes and values from our family, our friends, our culture, and so on. They influence how we see ourselves and develop our identity during our lives.

Iceberg model of culture

Our values are the things that we think are right or wrong or the things we believe in. Things like honesty and respect are values that many people share, although sometimes in different ways.

An attitude is the way you express your values and beliefs. Maybe it's very important to you to respect animal rights. So if you see a man kicking his dog, you might shout at him to stop. He hears your words and sees your anger, but he doesn't see the attitudes and values that are behind it.

It's worth thinking about your values and attitudes – they are shaping your identity!

EPISODE 3:
Why I'm vegan

Every Monday, Trevor Wright, a well-known environmental activist, talks to young people who have made a difference by changing their lives or communities. Today he talks with Jamila, a 15-year-old girl who is a vegan.

0:00:00

"SO, BJORN, I HEAR YOU'VE GONE VEGAN!"

CartoonStock.com

CD X/XX XX

Topic A B C

p. XX XX

Putting myself first

My name is Sam and I'm 16. I know it sounds selfish, but for me it's important to put myself first. If you don't look after yourself, no one else will. That's also what my Dad says and I think he's right.

It's not that I don't care about other people – I do. I have lots of friends and family that I care about a lot. But I try to do things that are right for me. I don't worry too much about others.

Training youngsters

My name is Phil, I'm 15 and my hobby is basketball. One day my trainer asked me to train a group of youngsters in our club.

At first I was a bit unsure. But then I just tried and I found out that I'm good at training others. I've learned so much! Now I'm more self-confident than before.

This way I can also give something back to my club. That is also important to me.

Helping out at a local animal shelter

My name is Sandy and I love animals. Since my 9th birthday I've wanted to become a vet. So I took the chance when some people from the local animal shelter came to our school because they really needed help.

For more than a year now I've been walking dogs, cleaning cages and a lot more. I love it and at the same time I can develop skills I'll need as a vet. I also meet people with the same attitudes and values. Last month my colleagues from the animal shelter and I went on a march for animal rights.

How to be cruelty-free

Top 6 easy ideas to live a cruelty-free lifestyle

1. Reduce your waste, especially your food waste.
2. Recycle products because nothing really just 'goes away'.
3. Stop buying plastic water bottles, use water from the tap instead.
4. Find cosmetics not tested on animals.
5. Try to understand other people's feelings and experiences. Show empathy!
6. Buy and eat locally and seasonally.

Webcode DSW-14605-XXX

Want to find out more? Use the webcode or do your own research online. Here are some ideas for search terms.

- volunteering
- cruelty-free lifestyle
- attitudes and values
- community activities for teens
- environmental groups for teenagers
- iceberg model of culture

sPOTlight on ...

p. XX
XX

Tipp
Man spricht Xiuhtezcatl /ˈʃuːtezkæt/ aus.

Xiuhtezcatl Martinez

Xiuhtezcatl Martinez is seventeen years old and a climate activist, a hip hop artist, and the Youth Director of Earth Guardians, an environmental movement led by young people.

Since he was a child, Xiuhtezcatl has felt a close connection with nature. He has been involved in climate activism since he was six, when he started speaking at events all around the world.

Xiuhtezcatl has worked to fight the use of pesticides in parks and has been fighting against fracking in his state since he was eleven. He has even written, and now performs, an anti-fracking rap.

Xiuhtezcatl wants to educate people, particularly young people, about the state of the planet. He wants young people to take action to protect the Earth. One way that he does this is by writing and performing rap music that reflects his message. His work has taken him all across the USA and to many different countries. He also works to grow the Earth Guardian network. There are now groups in more than 30 countries.

His work has been featured on many television programs and in magazines and newspapers. He has also won awards and prizes, such as the 2015 Peace First Prize and the 2016 Children's Climate Prize from Sweden. In 2013 he was asked to serve on President Obama's youth council.

Xiuhtezcatl is an important spokesman for ideas the whole world needs to hear. This teenager and his fantastic movement show what can happen once young people get involved.

Webcode DSW-14605-XXX

Over to you – Your project

1. In class, talk about your reactions to the three topics. What did you find interesting or surprising? What was new for you? How do you feel about what you found out?

WB p. XX XX

wordbank be yourself p. 172

Our school dance club is mostly full of girls. Almost no boys go. That seems a shame.

I'd never really thought about why fashion was so important for me – I found that really interesting.

I was not surprised that many teenagers spend their money on clothes.

I think our school could be more involved in the community.

Topic C made me feel like I can actually do something important and help to change things I believe in.

My topic made me think about how many different kinds of people, and teenagers, there are!

2. Agree on one aspect that you want to work on as a project. You can stay in your topic groups or work as a class. What form could your project take?

A B C For me, the most important thing that we just talked about is how different we all are. We should celebrate that. Maybe we could organise a school 'identity day' to show we are proud of all the different kinds of pupils at our school.

A B C We've learnt a lot about why things like fashion and music are important to young people. Maybe we could put together a presentation or book for other pupils at the school to share what we've learnt?

A I want to start a campaign to get more boys to join the school dance club.

B Let's organise an inclusive school fashion show, where we celebrate all kinds of fashion – goth, sporty, trendy, ethnic, everything!

C There are a lot of older people in our community. We have a fantastic choir and orchestra. Maybe we could ask to put on regular concerts for them, like at Christmas?

3. Talk about your project in more detail. Discuss and decide:

- Who do you need to talk to?
- What do you need to find out?
- What do you need to do?
- How much would it cost?
- How will you inform people?
- …

4. Create an action plan for your project like this:

Aspect we want to focus on:
How different we all are, with our own tastes in music and fashion, and different values.

What we want to do:
Have a big party celebrating our similarities and differences. We can present our school with its different and unique students to our community.

Why we want to do this:
We want to be part of a sharing community, to be proud of our school because it respects all students no matter what they look like, where they come from and what their likes and dislikes are. We want to build up trust and respect by getting to know each other better, by communicating what and who we are.

Project details:
- What we will need to do: talk to all kinds of students from different groups; do interviews with many different pupils; take photos to make displays; talk to teachers about how to organise the party; make posters
- How long the project will take: we hope to have the party in 3 months' time
- How much it will cost: posters: 20 €; photos: 10 €; food and drink for party: contributions
- Who will be involved: pupils, at least one teacher, secretary, local newspaper reporter?

5. Now put your plan into action.
Use English where you can!

TAKE ACTION!

To carry out your action plan in your school, home or community, you could:

- Advertise what you are doing (posters, leaflets, school website, local newspaper, ...).
- Present the action plan to a wider audience, such as parents, other classes or the local community.
- Organise some fundraising activities to raise the money you need.
- Find more people who want to help.
- Make an action plan diary and take photos of your progress.

6. Once you have put your plan into action, maybe you would like to share what you have done. If you stayed in your three topic groups, you could tell the other two groups about your project. If you worked as a class, you could tell other classes or the rest of the school about what you have done.

how to p. 149 present

A1 Emotions

a) **Match the words and phrases in the box with the definitions below.**

emotion • B-boying • lyrics • X-factor • salsa •

breakdancing, an athletic style of street dancing

the words of a song

Latin American music and dance

feelings like sadness, happiness, anger or fear

a talent show in the UK

b) **Compare your answers in your group.**

A2 Prepositions

a) **Choose the correct preposition from the box for each phrase.**

of • for • of • of • in • about • to • in • for •

a shared love ??? music
a basis ??? friendship
a wide range ??? emotions
the beauty ??? classical music
emotion ??? their lyrics
talk ??? lyrics
listen ??? rap and hip hop
go ??? ??? music

b) **Write sentences about music using the phrases.**

My best friend and I have a shared love of rap music.

A3 Discussion

how to p. 154 discuss

Talk about your music taste and what music means to you.

I like bands/songs that ...

I grew up with ...

Music gives me ...

I am a huge ... fan because ...

Music means ...

Music lets me experience ...

Without music I would ...

I think my music taste is ...

Music is ... for me.

A4 Share

Share the words and expressions that you as a group find most important with your class. Think of an interesting way of presenting them.

Practice matters

B1 New words

a) **Match the words and phrases in the box to the definitions below.**

stylish outfit • label a person • shape one's identity • blend in • empower people

- describe and classify someone
- a set of clothes worn together in a popular way
- form who you are
- fit in
- give people the opportunity to do something

b) **Compare your answers in your group.**

B2 Adjectives and nouns

a) **Match the parts of the following phrases. There is more than one solution.**

b) **Write sentences using the phrases. Compare with a partner.**

Some people are very critical of consumerism.

be critical of	different styles and looks
belong to	independence
explore your	a special group
try out	consumerism

Help

B3 Discussion

Talk about fashion, lifestyle and consumerism with a partner or in a small group.

I think that ... as a way of building self-confidence is ...

I believe that ...

Could you explain that a bit more?

I think it's important that everyone ...

I agree with you. I don't think that ...

Fashion is something many teens ... but ...

I'm not really sure whether ...

how to discuss p. 154

B4 Share

Share the words and expressions that you as a group find most important with your class. Think of an interesting way of presenting them.

C1 New words

a) **Match the words and phrases in the box to the definitions below.**

empathy • attitude • beliefs • values • like-minded people • campaign

moral principles

a way of thinking

planned activities with a special aim

people who think and feel the same

things accepted as true or real

ability to imagine or share another person's feelings and experiences

b) **Check your answers in your group.**

C2 Words and nouns

a) **Match the words to make phrases that have something to do with expressing your values and attitudes. There is more than one solution.**

b) **Write sentences about values and attitudes using these phrases. You can also use the ing-form of the verbs:**

volunteer to fight for support get take	animal rights responsibility an environmental group help out in your community active

Fighting for animal rights is something I feel strongly about.

C3 Discussion

how to p. 154 discuss

Talk about the role that attitudes and values play for your identity or the identity of teenagers. Talk with a partner or in a small group.

I believe that your attitudes and values …

I think … is so important for many teens because …

Do you really think that … ?

I'm not really sure if …

I think it is important that …

Could you explain what you mean a bit more, please?

…

C4 Share

Share the words and expressions that you as a group find most important with your class. Think of an interesting way of presenting them.

BS1 The Rainbow Serpent

Long ago in the Dreamtime when the earth lay sleeping and nothing moved or grew, lived the Rainbow Serpent. Then one day the Rainbow Serpent woke up and came out from beneath the earth. Refreshed from her long sleep she travelled far and wide leaving winding tracks from her huge body and then returned to the place she had first appeared.

When she returned she called to the frogs, "Come out!" The frogs came out slowly as they were full of water which they had stored during their long sleep. The Rainbow Serpent tickled their stomachs and when the frogs laughed, the water spilled out all over the earth to fill the tracks of the Rainbow Serpent. This is how the lakes and the rivers were first formed.

With water, grass and trees began to grow, waking all the animals. They followed the Rainbow Serpent across the land and were happy on earth. Each animal lived and gathered food with its own tribe. Some animals lived in rocks, some on the huge plains, and others in trees and in the sky.

The Rainbow Serpent made laws but some animals began to make trouble and argue. The Rainbow Serpent said,
"Those who keep my laws will be rewarded; I will give them human form. Those who break my laws will be punished. They will be turned to stone and will never walk the earth again."

Those who broke the law were turned to stone and mountains and hills. Those who followed the laws were turned into human form and were each given their own totem of the animal, bird or reptile from when they began. The tribes knew themselves by their totems - kangaroo, emu, carpet snake, and many, many more. So that no one would be hungry, the Rainbow Serpent ruled that no man should eat of his totem, but only of other totems. This way there was food for everyone.

The tribes lived together on the land given to them by the Rainbow Serpent or Mother of Life and knew the land would always be theirs, and no one should ever take it from them.

BS2 The dingo

His gun at his side, Nick Walker moved carefully through the country.

It was a good place for hunting, but his father had often told him not to go there.

Suddenly he noticed something orange-coloured moving among the trees. Too big for a fox. Could it be a dingo?

A moment later he saw the flash of orange again. This time he was quite sure: a big dingo came out of the high grass. It was carrying the fat, grey body of a rabbit in its mouth. This must be a mother dingo carrying food to her little ones.

Nick had always wanted to shoot a dingo, but his father had forbidden him to do so. But the Government paid twenty shillings for a dead dingo and if he could find the nest he would perhaps get five dollars. He'd give them to his father and say: "This can help with the new machines, Dad." So his father surely would not punish him.

Nick knew what to do. He had to find the nest. A dingo can kill thirty sheep in a night. In a few weeks there would be five or six dingoes running free to destroy his father's flocks.

Nick went to the place where the dog had come out of the grass and followed its footprints in the sand. He walked on and on and suddenly felt lonely in the bush. He hadn't left a message to tell his father where he had gone. If anything happened to him, nobody would find him. No, nothing would happen. He was twelve years old and he was a good bushman.

Suddenly, from behind a fallen tree, the mother dingo appeared. She jumped on the tree and sat down. From behind the tree the boy heard the sounds of the little dingoes.

Nick took his gun and shot. The dingo fell from the tree trunk and lay still. The boy ran to the trunk and looked over. He saw three of the little dingoes at the edge of the grass and shot them one by one.

Night was coming and he had to hurry to find his way home. In the morning he'd ride there with his father and show him the nest.

Suddenly he heard a small sound in the grass. He looked down and saw a little dingo running towards him. Before he had taken his gun from his shoulder the little dingo pressed itself against his legs. Suddenly he had pity on the little animal and couldn't kill it. He picked it up and the dingo licked his face. He carried the dingo home. On the way home the little dog slept inside his shirt. It was warm and soft. Once it sneezed.

At home the boy said to his father: "I was going to shoot him, but he ran right up to me. He's so small, Dad. He can't be killed. I'll look after his food myself. He won't do anything wrong, Dad, I promise. Feel his nose, he's so soft and he can even sneeze ..."

"He's a nice little fellow," his father said, "but he's a wild animal and not a dog. You can't trust him. If you want a little dog, I'll buy you one."

But finally Mr Walker allowed Nick to keep the dingo. "But remember this," he said, "don't let him run free. If you take him out, put him on a lead."

The boy was very happy with the dingo and trained him. The little dingo grew older and became a beautiful animal which obeyed the boy better than a normal dog. But Nick didn't obey his father. He had found an interesting game: he hunted rabbits with the dingo.

One afternoon Nick was out with the dingo, which was on the lead as usual. Suddenly the animal stood still and listened, and the boy heard the sound of sheep from behind the hill. The dingo ran away so fast that the boy could not hold him. Nick shouted, "Come back! Here! Here!" but the dingo did not obey.

Nick ran after the animal, but when he reached the sheep behind the hill, five of them were already dead, and the dingo came proudly back to him.

At that moment Mr Walker rode up. "That's enough," he said.

"Don't shoot him," said the boy, "it was my fault. I taught him the game with the rabbits."

But Mr Walker took his gun. Before he had aimed, Nick took off the lead and shouted "Run away, quickly!"

The man fired over the boy's head, but the dingo felt the danger and ran away as fast as he could.

"You've done a bad thing, son," said his father. "Now he knows."

In the next few days the men looked for the dingo, but they did not find him. A fortnight later Mr Walker came home and said: "This time I've hit him. I'm not sure I killed him, but I hope so."

Next winter dingoes broke into their neighbour's farm and killed lots of sheep. Everybody helped the sheep-farmer. Men with guns were posted over a wide area, waiting to see if the dingoes would come again. Nick – with his gun and an old revolver – was among them. He sat in the high grass and waited. After a long time the moon came up behind the trees.

The boy began to make sounds like a dingo. Suddenly a dingo answered. He answered the dingo, but this time there was no answer. Suddenly Nick felt a big head under his arm and a big warm body at his side. It was his dingo. In the moonlight he could see that his fur had been torn by a hunter. The dingo had heard Nick's voice and had come back to his friend.

But while one of the boy's hands was stroking him as softly as in former times, the other hand took the old revolver out of his pocket and pressed it behind the dingo's ear.

That was the coldest night which the boy had ever spent.

BS3 Only in New Zealand

New Zealand is a great place for people who like nature. There are many plants and animals that are only found in New Zealand and nowhere else in the world! Because New Zealand has been isolated for so long, its plants and animals have developed in isolation for millions of years. Check out these five species only found in New Zealand!

KEA

The kea is a parrot that lives in the mountains of the South Island. Keas are the only mountain parrots in the world. They are very intelligent but also very cheeky. They are not always that popular with New Zealanders because they sometimes attack cars to steal windscreen wipers or steal food.

TUATARA

Tuatara are reptiles that look a lot like lizards. However, tuatara are much more unique than that. They are the only reptiles that still exist from the dinosaur era, and they look pretty much the same as they did over 220 million years ago!

They are only found on some of the islands around New Zealand. From head to tail, they can be as long as 80 cm and can weigh up to 1.3 kilograms.

KIWI

The kiwi is the oldest of all New Zealand birds. It evolved over 70 millions years ago. Kiwis sleep during the day and are awake at night, so not many people actually get to see this little bird that gave the New Zealanders their nickname.

Kiwis have no tail and cannot fly. They use their beaks to smell and catch food, such as insects and spiders. They can be found in diffferent environments, such as in forests, on farmland and near rivers.

BS4 Monkey business

One day an out of work actor was visiting the zoo, where he attempted to earn some money as a street performer. Unfortunately as soon as people started to watch him, a zoo-keeper grabbed him and took him to his office.

The zoo-keeper explained to the actor that the zoo's most popular animal, a gorilla named Sparky, had died suddenly and the keeper was worried that without him the zoo wouldn't get so many visitors. The zoo-keeper offered the actor a job – to dress up as Sparky until they could get a new gorilla. The actor accepted.

The next morning, the actor put on a gorilla suit and entered the cage before the people arrived. He discovered that it was a great job! He could sleep all he wanted, could play and make fun of people.

However, eventually the people got tired of him, and he was getting bored just swinging on tyres. He began to notice that the people were paying more attention to the lion in the cage next to his. Not wanting to lose the attention of his audience, he climbed to the top of his cage, crawled across the wall between them and hung from the top over the lion's cage. Of course, this made the lion furious, but the people loved it. At the end of the day the zoo-keeper was very pleased, and even gave the actor more money for being such a good attraction.

This went on for some time, the actor kept making fun of the lion, the crowds grew larger, and his salary kept going up. Then one terrible day when he was hanging over the furious lion, he lost his balance and fell. The actor was terrified. Watching him, the lion got ready to jump. The actor was so scared that he began to run round and round the cage with the lion close behind. When no help came, and the crowd looked on in shock, the actor started screaming and yelling.

"Help, help me!" he screamed, but the lion was too quick and jumped. The actor found himself flat on his back looking up at the angry lion, who was just inches away from his face when the lion whispered, "Shut up, you idiot! Do you want to get us both fired?"

BS5 Carrie's War

This is an excerpt from Nina Bawden's novel *Carrie's War* (1973).

Carrie (...) stared crossly out of the carriage window at the big mountain on the far side of the valley. It was brown and purple on the top and green lower down; streaked with silver trickles of water and dotted with sheep.

Sheep and mountains. 'Oh, it'll be such fun,' their mother had said when she kissed them goodbye at the station. 'Living in the country instead of the stuffy old city. You'll love it, you see if you don't!' As if Hitler had arranged this old war for their benefit, just so that Carrie and Nick could be sent away in a train with gas masks slung over their shoulders and their names on cards round their necks. Labelled like parcels – Caroline Wendy Willow and Nicholas Peter Willow – only with no address to be sent to. None of them, not even the teachers, knew where they were going. 'That's part of the adventure,' Carrie's mother had said, and not just to cheer them up: it was her nature to look on the bright side. If she found herself in Hell, Carrie thought now, she'd just say, 'Well, at least we'll be *warm*.'

Thinking of her mother, always making the best of things (or pretending to: when the train began to move she had stopped smiling) Carrie nearly did cry. There was a lump like a pill stuck in her throat. She swallowed hard and pulled faces.

The train was slowing. 'Here we are,' Miss Fazackerly said. 'Collect your things, don't leave anything. Take care of Nick, Carrie.'

Carrie scowled. She loved Nick, loved him so much sometimes that it gave her a pain, but she hated to be told to do something she was going to do anyway. (...)

They all seemed to have more luggage than when they had started. Suitcases that had once been quite light now felt as if they were weighed down with stones. And got heavier as they left the small station and straggled down a steep, cinder path. Carrie had Nick's case as well as her own and a carrier bag with a broken string handle. She tucked it under one arm, but it kept slipping backwards and her gas mask banged her knee as she walked.

'Someone help Caroline, please,' Miss Fazackerly cried, rushing up and down the line of children like a sheep dog. Someone did – Carrie felt the carrier bag go from under her arm, then one suitcase.

It was a bigger boy. Carrie blushed, but he wasn't a Senior: he wore a cap like all boys under sixteen, and although he was tall, he didn't look very much older than she was. She glanced sideways and said, 'Thank you *so* much,' in a grown-up voice like her mother's.

He grinned shyly back. He had steel-rimmed spectacles, a few spots on his chin. He said, 'Well, I suppose this is what they call our ultimate destination. Not much of a place, is it?'

They were off the cinder track now, walking down a hilly street where small, dark houses opened straight on to the pavement. There was sun on the mountain above them, but the town was in shadow; the air struck chill on their cheeks and smelled dusty.

'Bound to be dirty,' said Carrie. 'A coal-mining town.'

'I didn't mean dirt. Just that it's not big enough to have a good public library.'

It seemed a funny thing to bother about at the moment. Carrie said, 'The first place was bigger. Where we stopped at the junction.' She peered at his label and read his name. Albert Sandwich. She said, 'If you came earlier on in the

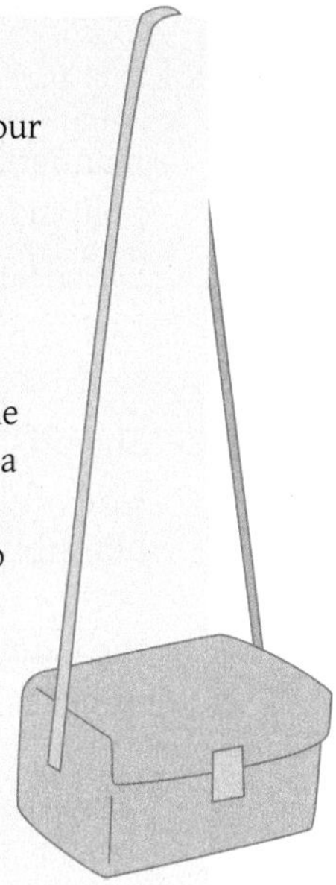

alphabet you could have stayed there. You only just missed it, they divided us after the Rs. Do your friends call you Ally, or Bert?'

'I don't care for my name to be abbreviated,' he said. 'Nor do I like being called Jam, or Jelly, or even Peanut Butter.'

He spoke firmly but Carrie thought he looked anxious.

'I hadn't thought of sandwiches,' she said. 'Only of the town Sandwich in Kent, because my granny lives there. Though my dad says she'll have to move now in case the Germans land on the coast.' She thought of Germans landing and her grandmother running away with her things on a cart like a refugee in a newspaper picture. She gave a loud, silly laugh and said, 'If they did, my gran 'ud give them What For. She's not frightened of anyone, I bet she could even stop Hitler. Go up on her roof and pour boiling oil down!'

Albert looked at her, frowning. 'I doubt if that would be very helpful. Old people aren't much use in a war. Like kids – best out of the way.'

His grave tone made Carrie feel foolish. She wanted to say it was only a joke, about boiling oil, but they had arrived at a building with several steps leading up and told to get into single file so that their names could be checked at the door. Nick was waiting there, holding Miss Fazackerly's hand. She said, 'There you are, darling. There she is, didn't I tell you?' And to Carrie, 'Don't lose him again!'

She ticked them off on her list, saying aloud, 'Two Willows, One Sandwich.'

Nick clung to Carrie's sleeve as they went through the door into a long, dark room with pointed windows. It was crowded and noisy. Someone said to Carrie, 'Would you like a cup of tea, bach? And a bit of cake, now?' She was a cheerful, plump woman with a sing-song Welsh voice. Carrie shook her head; she felt cake would choke her. 'Stand by there, then,' the woman said. 'There by the wall with the others, and someone will choose you.'

Carrie looked round, bewildered, and saw Albert Sandwich. She whispered, 'What's happening?' and he said, 'A kind of cattle auction, it seems.'

He sounded calmly disgusted. He gave Carrie her suitcase, then marched to the end of the hall, sat down on his own, and took a book out of his pocket.

Carrie wished she could do that. Sit down and read as if nothing else mattered. But she had already begun to feel ill with shame at the fear that no one would choose her, the way she always felt when they picked teams at school. Suppose she was left to the last! She dragged Nick into the line of waiting children and stood, eyes on the ground, hardly daring to breathe. When someone called out, 'A nice little girl for Mrs Davies, now,' she felt she would suffocate. She looked up but unfocused her eyes so that passing faces blurred and swam in front of her.

Nick's hand tightened in hers. She looked at his white face and the traces of sick round his mouth and wanted to shake him. No one would take home a boy who looked like that, so pale and delicate. (...)

Minutes passed, feeling like hours. Children left the line and were taken away. Only unwanted ones left, Carrie thought. She and Nick, and a few tough-looking boys, and an ugly girl with a squint who had two little sisters. And Albert Sandwich who was still sitting quietly on his suitcase, reading his book and taking no notice. He didn't care! Carrie tossed her head and hummed under her breath to show she didn't either.

Someone had stopped in front of her. Someone said, 'Surely you can take two, Miss Evans?' (...)

BS6 Jeannette Rankin

JEANNETTE RANKIN

Jeannette Rankin was an American politician and the first female member of Congress in the USA.

Early life

She was born on June 11, 1880 in Montana, USA. As a teenager she helped look after her siblings and also helped around the family ranch. Rankin studied biology at the University of Montana and graduated in 1902.

First involvement in women's rights movement

Whilst working in Spokane, Washington, Rankin became involved in the women's rights movement. She started to speak out about her beliefs that women should have the right to vote.

First female member of Congress

In 1916 Rankin became the first female member of Congress. Not long after that, President Woodrow Wilson asked Congress to vote on declaring war on Germany. Out of the 50 people who voted, Rankin was the only one who voted against starting a war.

An anti-war attitude

In the following years, she was asked to vote on declaring war two more times. Once she voted against it and once she refused to vote. This basically ended her political career. When, years later, she was asked if she regretted the decision, she said, "Never. If you're against war, you're against war regardless of what happens. It's a wrong method of trying to settle a dispute."

Her pacifist work

Rankin continued her pacifist work, though. She frequently travelled to India to learn about the teachings of Mahatma Gandhi. In 1968, she led five thousand women on an anti-war march in Washington.

The legacy of Jeannette Rankin

Rankin died on May 18, 1973. She died at the age of 92. She never married and had no children. She left her money and house to help "mature, unemployed women workers". Today, the Jeannette Rankin Women's Scholarship Fund still gives educational scholarships to low-income women aged 35 and older. Rankin continues to be remembered for her fight for pacifism.

BS7 Martin Luther King Jr.

Martin Luther King Jr. was an American civil rights activist. He was born on January 15, 1929 and was shot and killed on April 4, 1968.

WHAT HE FOUGHT FOR
Martin Luther King's dream was to live in a society in which all people are equal. He fought for African Americans to have the same rights as white Americans.

RISE TO FAME
King played a large role in the Montgomery bus boycott. This was a peaceful protest that took place in 1955. At that time, African Americans had to ride at the back of buses in Montgomery, Alabama, whilst the white passengers sat at the front. King led a campaign to change these rules.

After protesting for thirteen months, the boycott was successful: a new law was passed and bus companies had to change their rules. King became well-known as an important figure of the American civil rights movement.

'I HAVE A DREAM' SPEECH
On August 28, 1963, King took part in a huge civil rights march in Washington, D.C. The speech he gave, known as his 'I have a dream' speech, is one of the most famous speeches in US history. King spoke of his dream for the future of the country.

One of the most famous lines is: 'I have a dream that my four little children will one day live in a nation where they will not be judged by the color of their skin, but by the content of their character'.

NON-VIOLENT PROTESTS
In all of Martin Luther King's campaigns and protests, he practiced the idea of non-violence. This means that he never used violence or violent actions. This non-violent approach was based on the teachings of Mahatma Ghandi.

THE LEGACY OF KING
Today there are hundreds of streets and roads around the world named after Martin Luther King. On the third Monday in January, around the date of King's birthday, Americans celebrate Martin Luther King Day. Because it was important to King to help people in need, many people spend the day volunteering in the community and giving something back to society.

BS8 A Poem For Being Yourself

I see far too many people walking through life with their heads down,
time passing by, not noticing their fellow man's smile or frown.
What a world it would be,
if people were just free.
Free to be themselves, without worrying about others around,
not caring if they fail or just fall down.
Society, why are we so afraid?
To stand up for what we believe in each and every day?
I want to make this change, so the world can be free,
and when we walk down the streets, each other's souls are what we see.
Stop hiding behind the eyes of a fearful soul,
or hiding your face because you have a beautiful mole.
Your differences are good, they make you stand out.
Please don't try to fit in, that's not what this life is about.
You are you, and we love you for that,
and for all the haters out there, pick up the bat.
Take your swing, because I am strong.
I know who I am and I will sing my song.
If you don't like the tune you don't have to listen,
but please be kind because I want my soul to glisten.
This life is ours for the taking.
What fun is it if I'm hiding and not waking?
This is my time, to live my life and I will not stand down.
Everyone hear me, be yourself and you will wear the crown.
We can all be successful and we all have something to give.
Show your authenticity, stay focused on your vision, and just live.
Breathe in the fresh air and be confident in who you are,
you are beautiful and a unique shining star.
If you believe in this message then begin today,
to be yourself and give your gifts away.
Spread this message of positivity,
so more people can choose to be *free*.

Alexa Carlin

Do you remember?

Zu vielen Themen wie etwa zu *How to talk* oder *How to listen* hast du in Klasse 5 bis 8 schon einiges erfahren. Auf den folgenden Seiten findest du Zusammenfassungen wichtiger Punkte:

Remember? – How to talk

- Trau dich zu sprechen und hab keine Angst vor Fehlern!
- Die *classroom phrases* auf Seite 174 und auf dem Einleger können dir bei der Partner- und Gruppenarbeit und beim Klassengespräch helfen.
- Nutze jede Gelegenheit, Englisch zu sprechen. Hör dir zum Beispiel die CD an und lies Texte laut mit.
- Wenn du einen Vortrag, ein Interview oder ein Gespräch vorbereiten willst, mache dir dazu vorher auf Kärtchen Notizen.
- Versuche aber immer, frei zu sprechen. Lies nicht einfach deine Notizen ab.
- Achte auch auf deine Aussprache, Betonung und die Satzmelodie, damit das, was du sagst, lebendig klingt.
- Das Sprechen wird dir leichter fallen, wenn du ein Gespräch oder einen Vortrag vorher gut vorbereitest und übst.
- Achte beim Sprechen auch auf deine Körpersprache, deinen Gesichtsausdruck und deine Gesten.
- Schau deine Zuhörerinnen und Zuhörer beim Sprechen an.

Remember? – How to listen

- Wenn du einem Gesprächspartner zuhörst, schau ihn dabei an.
- Achte im Gespräch auf Körpersprache, Gesichtsausdruck und Gesten.
- Wenn es eine Aufgabe zu einem Hörtext gibt, dann lies dir die Aufgabe vorher genau durch. Überlege, was du zu dem Thema schon weißt.
- Sieh dir Überschrift und Bilder an: Was verraten sie über das Thema?
- Denk beim Hören daran, dass du nicht jedes einzelne Wort verstehen musst.
- Versuche, beim ersten Hören herauszufinden, worum es geht.
- Achte auch auf Geräusche und darauf, wie die Personen sprechen.
- Folgende Fragewörter können dir helfen, das Wichtigste zu verstehen: *Who? What? Where? When? Why?* Du kannst dir hierzu zum Beispiel Notizen in einer Tabelle oder in einem *word web* machen.
- Konzentriere dich beim Notizenmachen auf die wichtigsten Informationen.
- Schreibe Schlüsselwörter *(keywords)* auf und nicht ganze Sätze.

Who?	What?	Where?	When?	Why?
Becky	talks about her year abroad	in Australia	...	...

- Beim zweiten Hören kannst du dann weitere Informationen ergänzen.

Remember? – How to read

Bevor du liest

- Schau dir Überschriften und Bilder zum Text an, sie verraten oft etwas über den Inhalt.
- Die Art der Gestaltung verrät etwas über die Textsorte: Handelt es sich z. B. um einen Zeitungsartikel, eine Werbeanzeige, eine E-Mail oder einen Blogeintrag?

Während des Lesens

- Überfliege dann zunächst den Text *(skimming)*. Du musst dabei nicht jedes Wort verstehen. Achte auf die Wörter, die du schon kennst. Beim *skimming* kommt es darauf an, sich schnell einen ersten Eindruck zu verschaffen, worum es geht.
- Beim *scanning* suchst du in einem Text gezielt nach bestimmten Informationen, zum Beispiel nach dem Alter von Personen oder den Daten von Ereignissen. Dabei helfen dir Schlüsselwörter *(keywords)*, die zu deinem Suchauftrag passen, also zum Beispiel *age* oder *old*, wenn es um das Alter von Personen geht.
- Achte auch beim detaillierten Lesen auf Schlüsselwörter *(keywords)*.
- Bei einem Text im Workbook oder auf einem Arbeitsblatt kannst du wichtige Wörter und Passagen auch farbig markieren oder unterstreichen. Du kannst auch grün markieren, was du verstanden hast, und rot, was nicht.
- Es kann auch hilfreich sein, wenn du dir Zwischenüberschriften für einzelne Abschnitte des Textes überlegst.

Wörter erschließen

- Versuche, beim Lesen unbekannte Wörter aus dem Zusammenhang zu erschließen. Auch Bilder und Illustrationen können eventuell helfen, die Bedeutung unbekannter Wörter zu erraten.
- Manchmal kannst du die Bedeutung von Wörtern auch erschließen, weil sie so ähnlich geschrieben werden wie im Deutschen oder in einer anderen Sprache, die du kennst.
- Auch Vor- oder Nachsilben von Wörtern können Hinweise auf die Bedeutung von Wörtern geben, wie zum Beispiel die Vorsilben *un-* oder *im-*, die das Gegenteil bedeuten, wie in *happy – unhappy*, *possible – impossible* (siehe auch *How to work with words* auf Seite 162).

Notizen machen

- Die Fragewörter *who*, *what*, *where*, *when* und *why* helfen auch beim Lesen von Texten.
- Du kannst dir hierzu zum Beispiel Notizen in einer Tabelle oder in einem *word web* machen.
- Konzentriere dich beim Notizenmachen auf die wichtigsten Informationen.
- Schreibe Schlüsselwörter *(keywords)* auf und nicht ganze Sätze.

Who?	What?	Where?	When?	Why?
Becky	sights and activities	in Sydney	...	...

- Lies den Text nicht nur einmal. Beim nochmaligen Lesen wirst du sicher noch mehr Details verstehen und kannst so deine Notizen ergänzen.

Remember? – How to write

- Wenn du einen Text (zum Beispiel eine Geschichte oder einen Zeitungsartikel) schreiben willst, kannst du mit Hilfe von *who, what, where, when* (und eventuell auch *why*) Ideen sammeln und deinen Text planen.
- Überlege dir vorher, wie du deinen Text gliedern möchtest und sammle wichtige Wörter, zum Beispiel in einem *word web*.
- Du kannst auch in den *wordbanks* im Buch oder in einem Wörterbuch nach passenden Wörtern suchen.
- Bei jeder Art von Texten gilt, dass du zunächst einen Entwurf schreiben solltest *(draft)* – entweder handschriftlich oder am Computer.
- Überarbeite und verbessere dann deinen Text *(edit)*. Du kannst auch andere nach ihrer Meinung zu deinem Text und nach Verbesserungsvorschlägen fragen.
- Wenn du deinen Text fertig hast, schreibe ihn ins Reine. Das kannst du handschriftlich oder mithilfe eines Textverarbeitungsprogramms am Computer machen.
- Dein fertiger Text sollte „veröffentlicht" werden *(publish)*. Zeige ihn einem Partner, einer Partnerin oder der Klasse.
- Gelungene Texte kannst du in deinem Portfolio aufbewahren.
- Tipps zum Schreiben findest du auch auf den Seiten *How to write a CV* (Seite 158), *How to write a cover letter* (Seite 159), *How to write your opinion* (Seite 152), *How to write a summary* (Seite 153) und *How to write a story* (Seite 157).

Remember? – How to mediate

- Bei der Sprachmittlung kommt es darauf an, die wichtigsten Informationen von einer Sprache in eine andere zu übertragen.
- Es kommt dabei nicht darauf an, alles wortgetreu zu übersetzen. Wichtig ist, dass du das Wesentliche auf Deutsch wiedergibst.
- Bilde einfache, kurze Sätze, wenn du den Sinn wiedergibst.
- Schwieriger ist die Sprachmittlung vom Deutschen ins Englische, also wenn du etwas auf Englisch wiedergeben musst.
- Es kann zum Beispiel vorkommen, dass du in deiner Stadt einen englischsprachigen Reisenden triffst, der deine Hilfe beim Lesen eines Fahrplans braucht. Ihm kannst du auf Englisch erklären, wie er zu seinem Ziel kommt.
- Hab keine Angst vor Fehlern. Es kommt darauf an, verstanden zu werden, der andere freut sich auf jeden Fall über deine Hilfe.
- Wenn dir Wörter fehlen, kannst du versuchen, diese zu umschreiben, und Gesten benutzen.

Remember? – How to watch a video clip

Vor dem Sehen

- Gibt es Bilder zu dem Videoclip in deinem Buch oder Workbook? Was ist zu sehen?
- Lies den Titel des Videoclips. Welche Hinweise gibt er auf den Inhalt?
- Worum könnte es in dem Videoclip gehen? Stelle Vermutungen an.

Währenddessen

- Schau dir den Videoclip in Ruhe an. Dabei ist es nicht schlimm, wenn du nicht alles verstehst.
- Konzentriere dich zunächst vor allem auf das, was du siehst:

Who?	Wer ist zu sehen? Um wen geht es?
Where?	Wo findet das Geschehen statt?
When?	Wann findet das Geschehen statt?
What?	Um was geht es? Was passiert?

- Was ist dein erster Eindruck? Mache dir Notizen.
- Konzentriere dich beim zweiten Anschauen stärker auf das, was du hörst. Gibt es Wörter, die immer wieder vorkommen? Notiere sie dir.
- Gibt es eine Aufgabe zu dem Videoclip in deinem Buch oder dem Workbook? Behalte die Frage im Kopf, während du zuschaust. Versuche, gleich danach die Frage zu beantworten.
- Wenn nötig, schau dir dann den Clip ein weiteres Mal an. Überprüfe dabei deine Antworten.

Nach dem Sehen

- Tausche dich mit deinen Klassenkameradinnen und -kameraden aus. Was habt ihr herausgefunden?

Außerdem

- Schau dir an, wie die Personen aussehen und wie sie sich verhalten.
- Achte auf den Gesichtsausdruck und die Gesten der Personen. Ändert sich der Gesichtsausdruck? Wie fühlen sie sich? Wie ist das Verhältnis der Personen zueinander?
- Auch die Musik in einem Videoclip oder Film drückt Stimmungen aus. Ist die Musik lustig oder spannend? Wie fühlst du dich aufgrund der Musik?
- Man kann sich viele Videoclips auch mit Untertiteln ansehen. Es gibt sie auf Englisch und auf Deutsch. Das kann eine große Hilfe sein, denn nach und nach lernt man so besser zu verstehen, was auf Englisch gesagt wird.
- Schau dir doch auch Filme oder Videoclips aus dem Internet auf Englisch an.

Remember? – How to work on a project or target task

Plan it

- Wenn du mit anderen zusammenarbeiten möchtest, dann überlegt gemeinsam, wie euer Endprodukt bzw. eure Präsentation aussehen soll: Poster, Tonaufnahme, Videoaufnahme, Computerpräsentation, ...?
- Überlegt in der Gruppe, welche Informationen, Materialien und Geräte ihr braucht.
- Teilt die Arbeit sinnvoll und gerecht auf.
- Erstellt gemeinsam einen Zeitplan.

Do it

- Recherchiere Informationen und sammle Material.
- Werte dein gesammeltes Material aus. Entscheide, welche Materialien wichtig sind und welche Ergebnisse du vorstellen möchtest.
- Überlege dir, wie du deine Informationen anschaulich präsentieren kannst und erstelle dann dein Produkt oder deine Präsentation.

Check it

- Sind alle wichtigen Informationen enthalten? Sind die Texte verständlich? Sind die Bilder groß genug? Gibt es Fehler? Lest eure Texte gegenseitig durch und besprecht sie.
- Überarbeite und verbessere dann nochmal deine Präsentation, wenn nötig.

Present it

- Planst du eine mündliche Präsentation, dann übe vorher mit einem Stichwortzettel (siehe auch *How to present* auf Seite 150).

Remember? – How to research online

- Benutze eine Suchmaschine. Versuche, möglichst genau zu formulieren, wonach du suchst, und zwar auf Englisch.
- Suche auf englischsprachigen Seiten, damit dir der nötige Wortschatz gleich zur Verfügung steht. Bei den Einstellungen der meisten Suchmaschinen kannst du Englisch als Sprache wählen.
- Halte nützliche Informationen fest. Überfliege dafür zunächst einmal die Seiten, die dir interessant erscheinen.
- Wenn du interessante Webseiten gefunden hast, kannst du die Informationen in einem Dokument speichern. Denk daran, auch die Internetadresse festzuhalten, damit du später noch weißt, wo du die Informationen gefunden hast.
- Wenn du Textausschnitte unverändert übernimmst, musst du sie als Zitat kenntlich machen und die Quelle (die Internetadresse) angeben.
- Sei kritisch: Weder inhaltlich noch sprachlich ist alles richtig, was im Internet steht. Überprüfe angegebene Fakten in einer anderen Quelle.
- Einfache und kurze Texte auf Englisch gibt es bei simple.wikipedia.org.

Remember? – How to present

Die Präsentation vorbereiten

- Überlege: Was ist dein Thema? Wie viel Zeit hast du für deinen Vortrag?
- Überlege auch, was deine Zuhörer schon wissen und berücksichtige dies in deiner Präsentation.
- Sammle deine Gedanken und schreibe sie in Stichpunkten auf, zum Beispiel in einem *word web* oder auf Karteikarten.
- Entscheide, in welcher Reihenfolge du die Dinge sagen und wie du anfangen möchtest.
- Fertige zum Beispiel ein Poster an, um deinen Vortrag anschaulich zu machen.
- Übe deinen Vortrag mehrmals, bevor du ihn hältst.

Bei der Präsentation

- Sprich langsam und deutlich.
- Sieh deine Zuhörer an, wenn du sprichst.
- Versuche, frei zu sprechen. Du kannst die wichtigsten Punkte aber von deinen Notizen ablesen.
- Zeige deinen Zuhörern auf deinem Poster, worüber du gerade sprichst.
- Fasse zum Schluss die wichtigsten Punkte noch einmal zusammen.

Nützliche Redewendungen

Für die Einleitung:

- *Hello, everybody. My talk is about …*
- *First of all, I'm going to …*
- *Then I'll talk about …*
- *Finally I'll …*

Etwas Neues einleiten:

- *So let's start with …*
- *OK, my first/next/last point is …*

Auf Hilfsmittel hinweisen:

- *On my poster you can see …*
- *Look at this picture. It shows …*

Wenn du mal den Faden verlierst:

- *Just a moment, please.*
- *Wait a second, please.*

Etwas anders ausdrücken:

- *In other words, …*
- *What I'm saying is …*

Aufmerksamkeit aufrechterhalten:

- *You see?*
- *Do you see what I mean?*
- *Don't you agree?*
- *What do you think?*

Zum Schluss kommen:

- *So, to summarise …*
- *So my main points are …*
- *Thank you for listening.*
- *Have you got any questions?*

Remember? – How to give feedback

- Versuche immer, zuerst etwas Positives zu sagen.
- Formuliere Kritik und Verbesserungsvorschläge vorsichtig, höflich und sachlich.
- Bei Präsentationen kannst du zu verschiedenen Kategorien Feedback geben:

Körpersprache und Augenkontakt

Der/die Präsentierende

- lächelt das Publikum freundlich an
- hält Augenkontakt
- dreht dem Publikum nicht zu lange den Rücken zu

You looked at the audience most of the time.

You turned your back to the audience too much.

Sprache

Der/die Präsentierende

- spricht laut und deutlich
- verwendet kurze, gut verständliche Sätze
- spricht eher frei, liest nicht ab

You spoke loudly and clearly.

You read a lot word-by-word. Maybe you could try to speak more freely next time.

Struktur und Inhalt des Vortrags

Der/die Präsentierende

- führt gut in das Thema ein
- bezieht das Publikum mit ein
- fasst am Schluss noch einmal das Wichtigste zusammen

You introduced your topic very well.

The questions you asked us were very interesting.

You didn't summarise your main points. Maybe you could do that next time.

Die Gestaltung des Materials

Der/die Präsentierende

- hat das Poster/die Seiten/das Handout übersichtlich angelegt
- die Schrift ist gut zu lesen
- hat passende Bilder verwendet

Your poster was easy to read.

I think you packed a little bit too much information on your poster.

How to write your opinion

In einer Meinungsäußerung nimmst du Stellung zu einem bestimmten Thema oder einem Problem. Dabei kannst du auch Argumente sowie Vor- und Nachteile vergleichen, um deine Meinung zu begründen.

1. Bevor du anfängst zu schreiben

- Notiere dir Ideen, sammle Informationen und bilde dir deine eigene Meinung.
- Eine Liste mit *pros and cons,* Beispielen und Argumenten kann dir dabei helfen.

2. Beim Schreiben

- Beginne mit einer kurzen Einleitung, die das Thema vorstellt und Interesse weckt.
- Bringe die Argumente in eine sinnvolle Reihenfolge. Finde Beispiele oder Belege.
- Begründe deine Meinung und drücke diese klar aus.

Formuliere am Anfang einen Satz, der Interesse weckt und das Thema einleitet.

Ordne deine Ideen:
Firstly, …
Secondly, …
Finally, …

Today lots of people want to leave the city and move to a village in the countryside.
The question is: Is village life good or bad?
If you ask me, there are a lot of good and bad things about village life. Let's start with the good things: Firstly, I think it is good for people with children. It's a fact that there are fewer cars and the air is much cleaner.
In my opinion, the countryside looks nicer – there are more trees and fields and normally there is less rubbish. Some people say that cities are better though – there are more shops and the public transport is better. Cities also have a better choice of schools and libraries. All in all, I would say village life is the right thing for me – it's nice to have some peace and quiet!

Drücke deine Meinung klar aus:
I think …
In my opinion, …
I'm sure …

Begründe deine Meinung:
I think so because …
The reason is …
It's a fact that …
Let me give an example: …

Wäge deine Argumente gegeneinander ab:
Some people say …, but I think …
On the one hand …, but on the other hand …

So kannst du enden:
That's why I think …
All in all, I would say …

3. Überarbeite deinen Text

- Überprüfe, ob du alles beachtet hast, und verbessere sprachliche Fehler.

Remember? – How to write a summary

In einer Zusammenfassung eines Textes, Buches oder Videoclips gibst du kurz den Inhalt wieder, es geht dabei nicht um Details oder eigene Interpretationen.

1. Bevor du die Zusammenfassung schreibst

- Finde die wichtigsten Aussagen und Inhalte des Buches, Textes oder Videoclips heraus.
- In deinem Workbook oder auf einer Kopie kannst du wichtige Stellen in einem Text farbig markieren oder unterstreichen, ansonsten solltest du dir stichwortartig Notizen machen.
- Um den Aufbau eines Buches oder Textes zu erkennen, ist es hilfreich, Stichworte oder Überschriften für die einzelnen Absätze oder Kapitel zu formulieren.
- Außerdem kannst du dir zum Beispiel bei einer Geschichte oder einem Film gezielt Notizen zu den folgenden Aspekten machen:
  - *setting*
  - *characters*
  - *time*
  - *action*.

2. Schreibe deinen Text

- Beginne deine Zusammenfassung mit einem Einleitungssatz, in dem du kurz beschreibst, wovon der Text oder Videoclip handelt.

  The book '...' by ... is about ...
  The poem '...' deals with ...
  In the article '...' the author writes about ...
  The video clip shows ...

- Gib nur die wesentlichen Informationen an, lasse alle Beispiele, detaillierten Beschreibungen, direkte Rede oder deine eigene Meinung weg.
- Zitiere nicht aus dem Text oder Videoclip, sondern benutze eigene Formulierungen.
- Benutze *time words* wie *first, then, afterwards, while, …*
- Achte auf die Zeitform: Die Zusammenfassung steht in der Regel in der einfachen Gegenwart *(simple present)*.

3. Überarbeite deinen Text

- Hast du alle wesentlichen Informationen wiedergegeben?
- Sind sie in der richtigen Reihenfolge angeordnet?
- Stimmen Satzbau, Grammatik und Rechtschreibung?
- Du kannst auch eine Mitschülerin oder einen Mitschüler um Feedback zu deiner Zusammenfassung bitten.

Remember? – How to discuss

In einer Diskussion tauscht man Meinungen zu einem Thema aus. Oft geht es auch darum, den oder die anderen von der eigenen Ansicht zu überzeugen.

1. Bevor du diskutierst

- Wie stehst du zu dem Thema der Diskussion? Mache dir Gedanken über mögliche Argumente.
- Notiere Stichpunkte oder erstelle ein *word web*.
- Denke auch an Argumente, die gegen deine Meinung sprechen.
- Überlege dir Antworten auf diese Argumente.

2. Während der Diskussion

- Schau die Person an, die gerade spricht.
- Höre den anderen genau zu.
- Falle niemandem ins Wort.
- Frage höflich nach, wenn du etwas nicht verstanden hast.
- Äußere deine Meinung. Bleibe dabei immer höflich und freundlich.

TIPP

- Bestimmt einen Diskussionsleiter. Er/Sie sollte darauf achten, dass alle Gesprächsteilnehmer zu Wort kommen können, beim Thema bleiben und die vereinbarte Redezeit einhalten.
- Bildet eine neutrale Gruppe, die während der Diskussion Notizen macht und nachher Feedback gibt.

3. Nützliche Redewendungen

Eine Meinung äußern:

- *I think …*
- *I believe …*
- *In my opinion, …*
- *I'm sure …*

Eine Meinung begründen:

- *I think so because …*
- *The reason is …*
- *Well, it's a fact that …*

Jemandem zustimmen:

- *Yes, that's true.*
- *I think you're right.*
- *I agree (with you).*
- *I think so, too.*
- *That's a good point.*

Jemandem widersprechen:

- *I know, but …*
- *Sorry, I don't agree with you.*
- *I disagree.*
- *I don't think so.*

Nachfragen:

- *Could you say that again, please?*
- *Could you repeat that, please?*
- *Do you mean that …?*
- *Can you please explain what you mean?*

Einen abschließenden Satz einleiten:

- *In general, …*
- *All in all, …*

Remember? – How to use a dictionary

Englisch-deutsche Wörterbücher

- Wörterbücher haben oben auf jeder Seite Leitwörter, die angeben, welches der erste und der letzte Eintrag auf der jeweiligen Seite ist.
- Nach dem fett gedruckten Wort gibt es Erklärungen und Übersetzungen.
- Die Lautschrift verrät dir, wie ein Wort ausgesprochen wird. Sie steht direkt hinter dem englischen Wort.
- Die Abkürzungen geben dir unter anderem Auskunft über die Wortarten.
- Schau dir immer alle Einträge an und entscheide dann, welche Übersetzung in dem Zusammenhang am besten passt.

Lautschrift

Verb

Substantiv / Nomen

sea•son ['si:zn] I *s.* **1.** (Jahres) Zeit *f.*; **2.** (Reife- *etc.*)Zeit *f.*, rechte Zeit *(für et.)*; **3.** Saison *f.*; II *v/t* **4.** *Speisen* würzen; III *v/i* **5.** reifen; **6.** ablagern

Deutsch-englische Wörterbücher

- Auch hier gilt: Nimm nicht gleich die erste Übersetzung. Für viele deutsche Wörter gibt es mehrere Übersetzungen.
- Die Abkürzungen und Ergänzungen geben weitere Informationen zu dem Eintrag.
- Wenn du ein bestimmtes Verb suchst, musst du zunächst die Grundform bilden, da nur dieses im Wörterbuch verzeichnet ist.
- Wenn du nicht sicher bist, ob das englische Wort wirklich passt, mache die Gegenprobe und überprüfe es in einem englisch-deutschen Wörterbuch. Dort findest du auch die Lautschrift, wenn du Hilfe bei der Aussprache brauchst.

m gibt an, dass das Wort maskulin (männlich) ist.

Zusätze in Klammern verraten, in welchem Zusammenhang ein Wort gebraucht wird.

Boden *m* **1.** *(Erdoberfläche)* ground; *(Erdreich, lockerer ~)* soil, *(Fuß~)* floor *(Grundbesitz)* land; **2.** *(Dach~)* attic, loft

Online-Wörterbücher

- Der Vorteil von elektronischen Wörterbüchern ist unter anderem, dass du dir die Aussprache von Wörtern anhören kannst. Meist musst du dafür auf ein Lautsprechersymbol klicken.
- Im Internet gibt es verschiedene Online-Wörterbücher, bei denen du schnell eine Übersetzung finden kannst.
- Oft findest du dort auch weiterführende Informationen und Diskussionforen, in denen die Verwendung und Übersetzung der Wörter von verschiedenen Nutzern diskutiert werden.

Remember? – How to work with statistics

Es gibt verschiedene Möglichkeiten, statistische Daten in Diagrammen darzustellen.

1. Säulen- oder Balkendiagramm *(bar chart)*:

- Mit Säulen- oder Balkendiagrammen lassen sich übersichtlich Zahlen darstellen, vergleichen und Veränderungen darstellen.

Tipp
Bei Säulendiagrammen sind die Balken vertikal angeordnet, bei Balkendiagrammen horizontal.

In 1850, the majority of immigrants were born in ..., but in 2000 ...

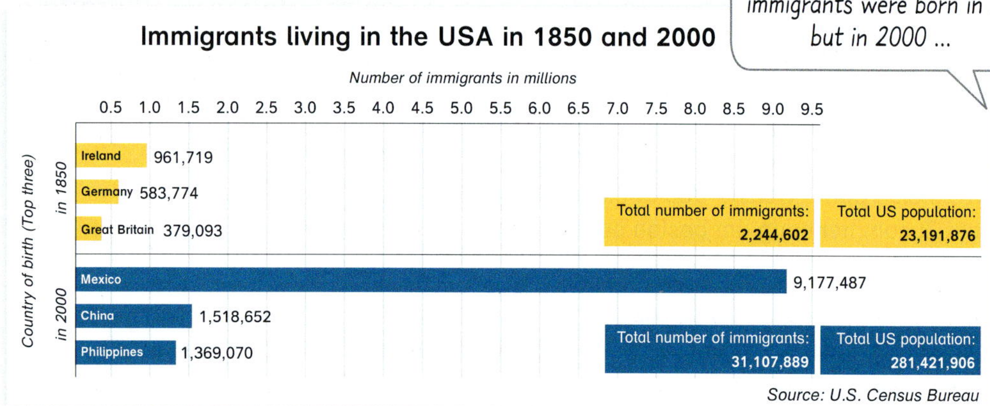

2. Tortendiagramm *(pie chart)*:

- Mit einem Tortendiagramm kann man gut Prozentanteile veranschaulichen.

6.3% of Australian immigrants were born in China.

Almost a fifth of the immigrants came from ...

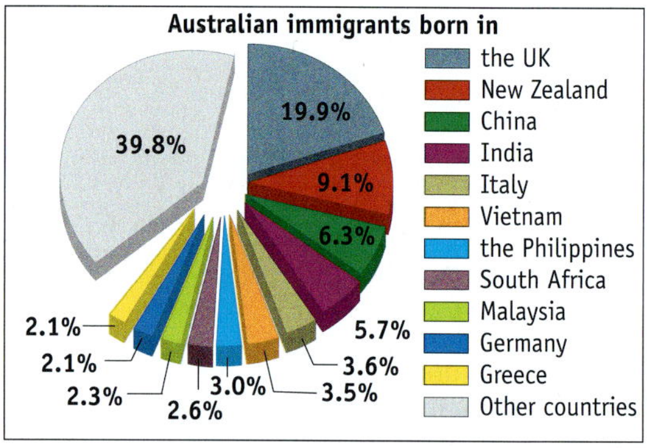

Nützliche Redewendungen:

So kannst du über ein Diagramm sprechen oder schreiben:

- *The ... chart shows ...*
- *In the ... chart you can see ...*
- *When you compare ... and ..., you can see ...*
- *The total number of ... is ...*
- *The total amount ...*
- *The majority of ...*
- *The biggest/smallest group ...*
- *Most of the ...*
- *About half/one third/two thirds/ a quarter/three quarters of ...*
- *There has been a huge increase in the number of ...*
- *Fewer than ...*

Remember? – How to write a story

Plane zunächst deine Geschichte. Du kannst dich an den Fragewörtern *who, what, where, when* und *why* orientieren und Ideen sammeln.
Denke dabei besonders an folgende Dinge:

Die Figuren

- Beginne mit der Hauptfigur oder den Hauptfiguren. Überlege dir Name, Alter, Aussehen, Interessen, Freunde, ...
- Überlege dir, wer die Nebenfiguren sein könnten. Wie ist ihre Beziehung zu den Hauptfiguren?

Der Ort

- Überlege dir, wo deine Geschichte spielen soll: In einer Stadt oder in einem Dorf? In einem anderen Land? Auf einem anderen Planeten? Die Geschichte kann natürlich auch an mehreren Orten spielen.
- Vielleicht spielt deine Geschichte sogar hauptsächlich in einem Gebäude oder bei einer Science-fiction-Geschichte in einem Raumschiff. Beschreibe den Ort, damit die Leserinnen und Leser ihn sich gut vorstellen können. Überlege etwa, was man dort sehen, hören, fühlen oder riechen kann.

Die Handlung

- Denke dir eine Handlung *(plot)* aus. Beachte dabei die folgenden fünf Teile einer Geschichte:
- *Exposition* – Überlege dir den Anfang deiner Geschichte. Wie weckst du Interesse? Fällt dir ein spannender erster Satz ein?
- *Rising action* – Hier beginnt die eigentliche Handlung. Denke dir zum Beispiel etwas Spannendes oder Lustiges aus, das passieren könnte.
- *Climax* – Dies ist der spannendste Teil deiner Geschichte. Hier könnte etwas Dramatisches passieren.
- *Falling action* – Nach dem *climax* der Geschichte kannst du zum Beispiel erzählen, wie es zu dem Ereignis kommen konnte oder was danach passiert ist.
- *Resolution* – Wie soll deine Geschichte enden? Entscheidest du dich für ein offenes Ende oder ein *happy ending*? Überlege, was am Ende mit den Figuren in deiner Geschichte passiert.

Der Schreibprozess: *draft – edit – publish*

- Schreibe zunächst einen Entwurf.
- Gib deinen Entwurf jemandem zu lesen und lass dir Feedback geben.
- Überarbeite dann deinen Entwurf.
- Wenn deine Geschichte fertig ist, dann „veröffentliche“ sie – hänge sie zum Beispiel in deiner Klasse aus oder gestalte ein Heft.
- Du kannst deine Geschichte auch in deinem Portfolio aufbewahren.

How to write a CV

Ein Lebenslauf *(CV = curriculum vitae)* stellt knapp und übersichtlich dar, welche Ausbildung, Arbeitserfahrungen und Kenntnisse ein Bewerber oder eine Bewerberin hat.

CURRICULUM VITAE

In vielen englischsprachigen Ländern ist es unüblich, ein Foto beizulegen.

Informationen zur Person

PERSONAL INFORMATION

Name	Oliver Schmidt
Address	Steinweg 18, 28717 Bremen, Germany
Telephone	+49-178-29
Email	oliver.schmidt@
Nationality	German
Date of birth	14 July 2005
Place of birth	Bremen

Arbeitserfahrungen / Praktika, die neuesten zuerst

WORK EXPERIENCE

since 2018	Babysitting on a regular basis for a neighbour's children (aged 4 and 6)
October 2014	Two-week work experience in the AWO-Kindergarten in Bremen

Schul- / Ausbildung

EDUCATION

2015 – now	Gesamtschule an der Lesum (Secondary Comprehensive School), Bremen
2011 – 2015	Grundschule Heisterbusch (Primary School), Bremen

Sprachen sowie andere Kenntnisse und Fähigkeiten

SKILLS

Languages	German (mother tongue) and English (B1)
Computer	Competent in word processing and presentation software
Other skills	Very reliable, great teamworking skills, stamina, creative

Interessen, vor allem die, die für die Bewerbung relevant sind

INTERESTS

Music	Playing the guitar, member of the school band
Sport	Team sports (basketball, hockey), since 2019 assistant coach with the under 7 basketball team

References available on request

Ein bis zwei Personen sollten für eine Referenz zur Verfügung stehen.

Tipps:

- Erstelle eine Vorlage für deinen Lebenslauf und halte sie immer auf dem neuesten Stand in Bezug auf neue Kenntnisse, besuchte Kurse usw.
- Wenn du dich bewirbst, informiere dich genau über die Firma und die Stellenanforderungen.
- Schreibe für jede Bewerbung auf der Basis deiner Vorlage einen neuen Lebenslauf, den du genau auf die Firma und die Stellenanforderungen abstimmst:
  - Welche deiner Fähigkeiten und Kenntnisse sind für diese Stelle besonders wichtig?
  - Wieso bist du genau der richtige Kandidat oder die richtige Kandidatin für diese Stelle?
- Ein Lebenslauf sollte nicht länger als eine oder zwei Seiten sein.
- Lass deinen Lebenslauf immer von jemandem Korrektur lesen, damit sich keine Rechtschreib- oder Sprachfehler einschleichen.

How to write a cover letter

Für eine Bewerbung brauchst du einen Bewerbungsbrief, den du zusammen mit deinem Lebenslauf abschickst. Der Bewerbungsbrief ist ein formelles Anschreiben.

Name und Anschrift der Firma stehen oben links

Wenn du den Namen des Empfängers nicht kennst, dann schreibe *Dear Sir or Madam*. Kennst du den Namen, dann schreibe *Dear Mr/Ms/Mrs ...*

Oliver Schmidt
Steinweg 18
28717 Bremen
Germany

Childcare Experience
110 Duff Street
Dublin D08 C8CN
Ireland

Die erste Zeile beginnt immer mit einem Großbuchstaben.

27 March 2019

Dear Sir or Madam,

Erkläre zu Beginn, warum du den Brief schreibst. Fasse dich dabei kurz.

I learnt from Mrs Wiese, the careers officer at my school, Gesamtschule an der Lesum, that you offer students the chance to do work experience in Ireland this summer. I am very interested in doing childcare either at a day care centre or in a private home and would like to apply for a placement from July to mid-August.

My work experience in the Kindergarten and my experience as a baby-sitter have taught me to be a good listener. In the Kindergarten I was able to accompany musical games on the guitar and I enjoyed helping out at mealtimes. As a basketball coach I have to motivate young children. Since I am considering a career in elementary education, I would be grateful for the opportunity of working with your company in Ireland.

Denke daran, auch deine *soft skills* darzustellen.

I enclose my CV and the address of Mr and Mrs Grabow, who are my neighbours and the family where I babysit at least once a week. They will be pleased to send you a reference.

Sei immer höflich.

I am available for an online video interview at any time. Thank you for considering my application.

I look forward to hearing from you soon.

Schreibe, dass du dich über eine Antwort freuen würdest.

Yours faithfully,

Oliver Schmidt

Enclosed: CV, addresses of referees

Beende den Brief mit *Yours faithfully,* wenn du die Person nicht kennst, und mit *Yours sincerely*, wenn du sie kennst.

Nenne am Ende die beigefügten Anlagen

Unterschreibe den Brief.

How to talk about films

Mit Filmkritiken hast du dich schon beschäftigt und vielleicht hast du auch schon selbst eine geschrieben. Dabei geht es neben den Fakten zu dem Film, wie etwa Titel, Thema und Inhalt, auch um deine Meinung und Empfehlung.

Wenn du einen Film genauer beschreiben, analysieren oder bewerten möchtest, ist es wichtig, die richtigen Begriffe zu kennen.

Hier findest du einige Beispiele.

Einleitung *(introduction)*:
- *The film ... was made in ... by director ...*

Genre *(genre)*:
- *The film is a (historical) drama/an action film/a thriller/a love story/ a comedy/ a science fiction film ...*
- *The film is a typical ...*

Thema *(topic)*:
- *The film ... is about ...*
- *The film tells the story of ...*
- *It describes the life of ...*

Besetzung *(cast)*:
- *The film was directed by ...*
- *The main characters of the film are ...*
- *The part of ... is played by ...*

Schauplatz *(setting)*:
- *The story is set in a house/a city/ the USA/the 20th century ...*
- *The story takes place in ...*

Szenen/Atmosphäre *(scenes/atmosphere)*:
- *The scene where ..., is very funny/exciting/sad ...*
- *There are amazing special effects ...*
- *The film's mood is sad/cheerful/... because ...*
- *... creates a sad/scary/... atmosphere.*

Ton *(soundtrack)*:
- *The (background) music matches ...*
- *The music supports/disturbs ...*
- *Some sound effects ...*

Persönliche Meinung *(personal opinion)*:
- *This film made me laugh/sad/happy/...*
- *I enjoyed watching ...*
- *... was/wasn't what I expected.*
- *I really liked ... but I didn't like ... because ...*
- *The actor/actress ... did a great job/was very good playing the role of ...*
- *The film was exciting because there were a lot of special effects ...*
- *All in all I think the film is really funny/scary/boring/exciting ...*
- *The film is worth watching.*
- *I recommend this film for people who like ...*

How to talk about song lyrics

In Liedern – wie auch in Gedichten – werden Inhalte oft anders ausgedrückt als zum Beispiel in einem Sachtext oder einer Geschichte. Die Sprache wird anders – auch freier – eingesetzt, um Stimmungen, Gefühle und Inhalte zu vermitteln. Folgende Fragen können dir helfen, einen Liedtext besser zu verstehen:

- **Thema**: Was ist das Thema des Liedes? Wird es im Titel genannt?

  The topic of the song is ...

- **Inhalt:** Erzählt der Liedtext eine Geschichte *(story)*? Oder wird eine bestimmte Erfahrung *(experience)* geschildert? Fasse den Inhalt in wenigen Worten zusammen.

  The song ... is about ...
  The song lyrics give a description of ...

- **Gefühle**: Welche Gefühle *(feelings)* drückt der Liedtext aus? Mit welchen Ausdrücken werden die Gefühle dargestellt? Werden konkrete Bilder *(images)* benutzt, um die Gefühle auszudrücken?

  The song writer uses the image of ... to express ...

- **Erzähler**: Gibt es in dem Liedtext direkte oder indirekte Hinweise auf den Erzähler *(narrator, speaker)*?

  The speaker seems to be ...
  The speaker talks to ...

- **Klang**: Lies den Liedtext laut oder höre dir das Lied an. Konzentriere dich dabei auf die Klänge. Markiere die betonten Silben und schreibe die Wörter auf, die sich reimen. Gibt es Alliterationen (d. h. Wörter, die mit dem gleichen Laut beginnen)?

  There are many rhyming words in the lyrics, for example ...

- **Ungewöhnlicher Sprachgebrauch** *(unusual language)*: Kommen ungewöhnliche Wortkombinationen vor? Oder eine ungewöhnliche Wortstellung? Oder grammatikalische Konstruktionen, die wiederholt werden *(repetition)*? Werden Symbole (*symbols*) verwendet (wie Taube für Frieden oder Herz für Liebe)?

  In the song ... the dove is used as a symbol of peace.
  Repetition is used to ...
  ... is used in an unusual way.

- **Wirkung**: Wie fühlst du dich, wenn du den Liedtext liest bzw. das Lied anhörst? Was drückt es für dich aus? Welche Wörter drücken für dich das meiste aus?

  The image of ... reminds me of ...
  When I read the lyrics ... I feel ...

How to work with words

Um die Bedeutung von Wörtern abzuleiten (oder auch Wörter selbst zu bilden) ist es hilfreich zu wissen, wie Wörter zusammengesetzt sind.

- So lassen sich zum Beispiel Gegenteile bilden, indem eine Vorsilbe *(prefix)* wie *un-*, *im-* oder *dis-* hinzugefügt wird.
- Nomen können gebildet werden, indem an ein Verb eine Nachsilbe *(suffix)* wie *-ion*, *-tion* oder *-er* gehängt wird.
- Hier findest du eine Übersicht über häufige Vor- und Nachsilben:

happy → unhappy
polite → impolite
agree → disagree

invent → invention
produce → production
play → player

suffixes					
adjectives			nouns		
-ful/-less	-al	-y	-tion	-er	-ing
careful/-less	personal	lucky	information	firefighter	feeling
useful/-less	normal	noisy	celebration	teacher	cycling
helpful/-less	traditional	foggy	reservation	farmer	painting
...	...	...	...	...	...

prefixes		
dis-	im-/in-	un-
disabled	impolite	unfriendly
disagree	imperfect	unhappy
disadvantage	incredible	unhealthy
...	...	...

- Einige Wörter haben dieselbe Form, auch wenn die Wortart unterschiedlich ist:

<u>noun – verb</u>
answer – answer
change – change
damage – damage
hate – hate

<u>verb – adjective</u>
clean – clean
correct – correct
empty – empty
open – open

<u>noun – adjective</u>
cold – cold
fun – fun
right – right
secret – secret

How to describe pictures

Um ein Bild zu beschreiben, gehst du am besten so vor:

1. Fange allgemein an

- Sage erst einmal, was du auf dem Bild oder Foto allgemein siehst:

  The picture shows a street scene.

2. Beschreibe, was sich wo befindet

- Sage nun, wen oder was du siehst und wo sich Personen, Tiere, Gegenstände usw. befinden. Benutze zum Beispiel Präpositionen wie *in, inside, on, in front of, behind, next to, between, over* oder *under*:

  There is a man with a blue shirt in front of a shop. There is another man inside the shop. …

3. Beschreibe, was passiert, und gehe mehr ins Detail

- Beschreibe, was die abgebildeten Personen tun. Benutze dazu das *present progressive*:

  A man is walking down the street.

- Beschreibe auch die Haltung, Körpersprache und Gesichtsausdrücke der Personen.

  The man in the blue shirt is leaning against the wall.

- Überlege, wo sich die Szene befinden könnte:

  Perhaps the photo shows a street scene in a small town in Africa.

- Beschreibe auch die Atmosphäre, die das Bild transportiert.

  The atmosphere seems a bit depressing to me because …

Australia

Australian and British English

Australian English	British English
Aussie	person from Australia/Australian
barbie	barbecue
bonza	great
station	big farm
Oz	Australia
G'day	hello
G'day mate!	Hello!
How are you going?	How are you?

animals in Australia

kangaroo • koala • dingo • cane toad • crocodile

places in Australia

Great Barrier Reed • Canberra • Melbourne • Sydney • Bondi Beach • Sydney Opera House • Taronga Zoo • Uluru (Ayers Rock) • Kakadu National Park

talking about Aboriginal culture

didgeridoo
in the outback
Aboriginal
Aborigine
The Dreamtime
Dreaming stories
Rainbow Serpent
National Sorry Day
Stolen Generations

Statistics

reading statistics

What per cent of Australian immigrants come from the UK?

Around 23 per cent come from the UK.

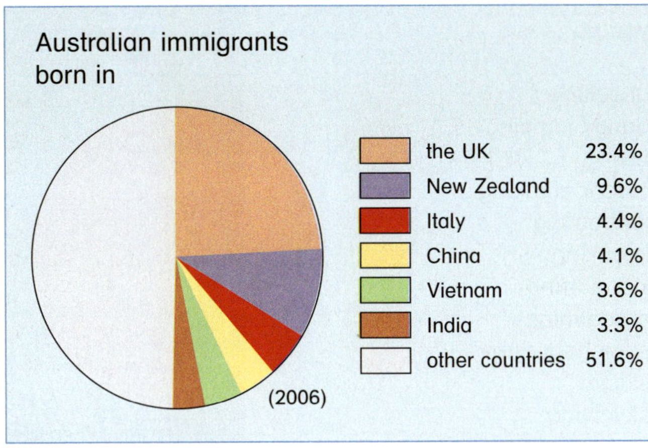

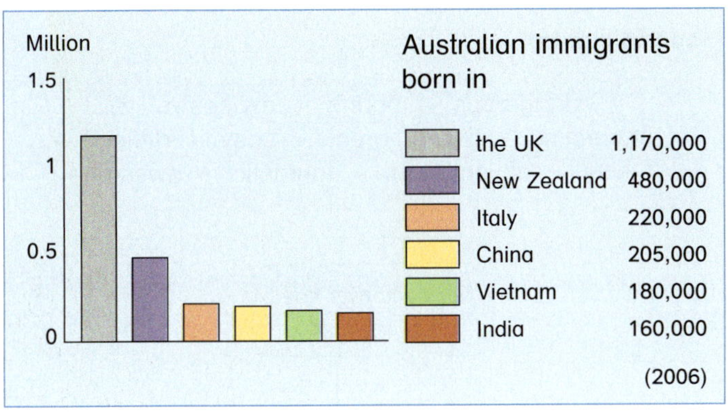

How many people moved from Italy to Australia?

About 220,000 people.

talking about statistics

- Almost a quarter of the Australian population come from ...
- 480,000 Australians are ...
- More than 2.5% of Australian immigrants are ...
- This diagram shows that ...
- In the pie chart, less than half of ...
- More than 40% ...
- 180,000 Australian immigrants come from ...
- Most people in the class ...
- 40% of the girls in my class ...

numbers

One quarter is the same as 25%.

3.3 means "three point three".

75% is three quarters.

one and a half

One fifth is the same as 20%

One third is the same as 33.3%.

Sports

you go ...

abseiling
bungy jumping
hiking
indoor climbing
jet boating
kayaking
kite surfing
paragliding
skateboarding
skiing
skydiving
snowboarding
street BMXing
surfing
zip-lining
zorbing

you do ...

scooter stunts

sports can be ...

dangerous • boring • expensive • interesting • fun • great • easy • difficult • silly • adventurous • fantastic • awesome

Have you ever tried kite surfing?

No, I haven't. It looks too dangerous.

Yes, I have. It's hard – I was so proud of myself!

Yes, I have. It was awesome!

sports and the environment

sports can ...

- be good or bad for the environment
- be environmentally friendly
- need a lot of equipment
- need no equipment
- change the countryside
- destroy areas of wildlife

Jobs

job/work placement adverts

- We are looking for ...
- gain experience ...
- You will help ...
- You will have to work six days a week.
- A working knowledge of English is required.
- You can help us.
- Office skills are not essential.
- Some computer knowledge would be useful.
- This is a voluntary position.
- We provide ...
- Find out more and apply at ...
- You can have the time of your life ...
- a great opportunity
- a day off
- homestay
- free room and board

writing a curriculum vitae (CV)

personal details:
- name
- address
- telephone number
- email address
- nationality
- date of birth
- place of birth

personal profile:
- work experience
- education
- qualifications
- skills
- interests
- references

letter of application

- read an advert
- apply for a job
- apply for a work experience placement
- be available for an interview
- consider a career in ...
- enclose a CV
- send a reference
- be grateful for an opportunity

Wordbank

examples of hard skills

computer programming • cooking • school qualifications • repairing cars • speaking a foreign language

examples of soft skills

be reliable • be creative • organisational skills • listening skills • ability to work alone/in a team • being on time • office skills

formal language

- Dear Sir or Madam, ...
- I am very interested in a work placement at your company.
- I would like to apply for a work placement.
- I enclose my CV and ...
- Since I am considering a career in ...
- I would be grateful for the opportunity of working with your company.
- I am available for an (online video) interview at any time.
- I look forward to hearing from you soon.
- Yours faithfully, ...
- References are available on request.

Where does your money come from?

I get extra money for cleaning the dishes.

I get pocket money every month.

To earn extra money I help my neighbour with her grocery shopping.

Wordbank

Internet

staying safe online

- Use strong passwords.
- Do not share personal information.
- Read privacy policies.
- Check security settings.
- Do not accept friend requests from people you don't know.
- Report upsetting material.

social network • social media site • login details

an app can ...

- play music
- share pictures
- send messages
- solve a problem
- play videos
- send pictures and videos
- connect to a smart gadget
- order something
- use a mobile phone's camera
- import pictures and videos
- edit pictures and videos
- need a password
- have friends lists

FriendsShare is an app which allows you to share pictures.

My favourite app plays music.

I use an app to chat with my friends.

devices that can connect to the Internet

smartphone/mobile phone • tablet • computer • laptop • car • TV • security camera • fridge • fitness tracker • game console • whiteboard

Science fiction

Science fiction stories ...

- are often set in the future
- include advanced technology
- can be very different from the real world
- include things that could be possible
- sometimes address problems of the real world

technology • machine • robot • computer • mechanical teacher • space • planet Earth • star ship

Writing texts

sentence • phrase • noun • verb • adjective • direct speech • title • illustrations • heading • paragraph • character • point of view

write • plan • edit • publish • read • give feedback • connect • rewrite • present • discuss • summarise

A long time ago ... • One day ... • First ...

One year later ... • Next ... • The next day ... • That night ... • Then ... • After some time ... • After that ... • Afterwards ...

Before that ... • Suddenly ...

Finally ...

and • or • but • however • instead • although • when • first ... then ... • while • in order to • where • whereas • even though • because

characters • plot • setting • situation • summary • central conflict • message of the story • short story • mini-saga

who • where • what • when • how • why

First Margie reads the book, then she talks to Tommy about it.
The attic is where Tommy found the book.

War and peace

- World War I (The Great War)
- World War II
- the Blitz
- declare war
- start a war
- be at war with ...
- air raids
- the fighting ended
- war is over

risk one's life • risk getting killed •
lose one's life • get killed •
death • loss of life •

conflict • landmines • mines •
lose one's leg • leftovers from past wars •
designed to injure, not kill •
the landmine exploded • "Danger Mines"

medics • security personnel • soldiers •
military forces • war photographers •
reporters • propaganda

air raid sirens • blackout material •
(civilian) gas masks • fill sandbags

Remembrance Day •
11 November •
The Royal British Legion

oral history •
war memories •
personal memories

working for peace • peace memorial •
a glimpse of peace • hope • empathy •
humanity • compassion •
resolve conflicts •
ceasefire • the Christmas truce •
spread peace and love around the world

yoga • mindfulness program • mediation •
The German War Graves Commission •
Youth Peace Ambassadors •
peace-building activities • human rights

Be yourself

being yourself • having tattoos or piercings • having my own style • looking good • following an idol • doing things with friends and family • living with traditions • taking part in political activities • listening to music • having a job

- ... plays a big role in my life.
- ... is really important to me.
- ... isn't that important to me.
- I can't imagine my life without ...

Music and dance

- I like music with good lyrics.
- I like to listen to classical music a lot.
- A shared love of music gives those in the group a basis for friendship.
- Music will always be my first love.
- Rap is pretty much all I listen to.
- I love playing classical music.
- You can find hip hop culture in fashion, design, movies and many other aspects of modern life.

lyrics • emotion • sense of belonging • rebellion • common interest • appreciation • stereotypes • creative • like-minded

Wordbank

Fashion and style

- My friends and I often wear similar clothes.
- I love fashionable clothes.
- I don't really care about fashion.
- A special look makes me who I am.
- Fashion is one of the ways you can express yourself and show the world who you are.
- Your clothing shows the world your developing identity.
- I just want to be myself.

clothing • footwear • hairstyle • individuality • image • explore who you want to be • try out different looks and styles • latest fashions • ethical fashion

Attitudes and values

- I'm vegan.
- It's important to support the LGBT community.
- I want to be an active part of our community.
- For me it's important to put myself first.
- Try to understand other people's feelings and experiences.
- Let's take action for our world and fight for our environment!

demonstrate • campaign • fight for animal rights • volunteer • equal rights • beliefs • values • honesty • respect • way of connecting with people • shape your identity • like-minded people

Working together

Which topic have you chosen?	Welches Thema hast du dir ausgesucht?
Which topic are you going to work on?	An welchem Thema hast du vor zu arbeiten?
Who is going to work on topic A/B/...?	Wer hat vor, an Thema A/B/... zu arbeiten?
I haven't decided yet.	Ich habe mich noch nicht entschieden.
I can't make up my mind.	Ich kann mich nicht entscheiden.
Do you want to work with me?	Willst du mit mir zusammenarbeiten?
Sorry, I haven't got ... with me.	Tut mir leid, ich habe ... nicht dabei.
Sorry, I forgot to bring ...	Tut mir leid, ich habe vergessen ... mitzubringen.
I've got a question.	Ich habe eine Frage.
Can you help me, please?	Können Sie/Kannst du mir bitte helfen?
I don't understand this.	Ich verstehe das hier nicht.
What's ... in English/German?	Was heißt ... auf Englisch/Deutsch?
What does ... mean?	Was bedeutet ...?
Can you spell that, please?	Kannst du das bitte buchstabieren?
Can you say that again, please?	Kannst du das bitte noch einmal sagen?
Sorry, I don't know.	Tut mir leid, das weiß ich nicht.
What page is it on?	Auf welcher Seite ist das?
Let's do the activities together.	Lass uns die Aktivitäten zusammen machen.
Let's compare ...	Lass uns ... vergleichen.
What do you think?	Was meinst du?
Whose turn is it?	Wer ist dran?
Are we allowed to use a dictionary?	Dürfen wir ein Wörterbuch benutzen?
Let's look it up in the dictionary.	Lass uns im Wörterbuch nachschlagen.
What else do we need?	Was brauchen wir noch?

First we have to read up on/investigate the idea about/...	Als Erstes müssen wir uns über ... informieren/die Idee über ... untersuchen/...
I think we should first watch/read/explore/...	Ich meine, wir sollten zuerst ... anschauen/lesen/untersuchen/...
Do you know how to use the webcode?	Weißt du, wie man den Webcode benutzt?
Why don't we have a look at the website/on the Internet/...?	Warum schauen wir nicht auf der Website/im Internet/...?

Classroom phrases

Who wants to keep the word list/take notes/prepare the fact file/…?	Wer will die Wortliste führen/Notizen machen/den Steckbrief vorbereiten/…?
Who is doing the presentation?	Wer übernimmt die Präsentation?
Who is writing down the results?	Wer notiert die Ergebnisse?
What do you think is the biggest problem/the most important fact/…?	Was hältst du für das größte Problem/die wichtigste Tatsache/…?
I think it would be a good idea to …	Ich finde, es wäre eine gute Idee, wenn wir …
Can I be the one to call/do the interview with/talk to/…?	Kann ich … anrufen/das Interview mit … führen/mit … sprechen/…?
You're good at … Why don't you …?	Du kannst gut … Warum machst du nicht …?

Let me give you an example.	Lass mich dir ein Beispiel geben.
Well, it's a fact that …	Es ist nun mal eine Tatsache, dass …
I think that's a good point.	Ich denke, das ist ein guter Hinweis.
I wouldn't say so.	Das würde ich nicht sagen.
I see what you mean, but …	Ich verstehe, was du meinst, aber …
Sorry, I don't agree with you.	Tut mir leid, aber ich stimme dir nicht zu.
I'd rather focus on …	Ich würde mich lieber auf … konzentrieren.
We should do some more research on …	Wir sollten … besser untersuchen.
I'm sure there's more to it.	Ich glaube, da steckt mehr dahinter.
Only two of us seem to think that it's best to …	Nur zwei von uns scheinen der Ansicht zu sein, dass es am besten ist, wenn wir …
I agree with your idea/suggestion/…	Ich stimme deiner Idee/deinem Vorschlag/… zu.
You could make your text more interesting if you …	Du könntest deinen Text interessanter machen, wenn du …
I would use a different word here.	Ich würde hier ein anderes Wort verwenden.
We are running out of time.	Uns läuft die Zeit davon.
Well done!	Gut gemacht!

Deutscher Begriff	Englischer Begriff mit Aussprache	Beispiele	LiF
Adjektiv (Eigenschaftswort)	adjective /ˈædʒɪktɪv/	green, expensive, boring	
Adverb	adverb /ˈædvɜːb/	quickly, fast, well, often, sometimes, here	1R, 5R, 9R
Bedingungssatz	conditional clause /kənˈdɪʃənl klɔːz/	If you miss the bus, you will be late.	14R
direkte Rede	direct speech /dɪˌrekt ˈspiːtʃ/	"Close the door, please!"	9R
einfache Gegenwart (Präsens)	simple present /ˌsɪmpl ˈpreznt/	Becky lives in Germany.	7R, 9R, 12R
einfache Vergangenheit (Präteritum)	simple past /ˌsɪmpl ˈpɑːst/	It was warm and sunny.	2R, 3R, 7R, 9R
Entscheidungsfrage (Ja/Nein-Frage)	yes/no-question /jesˈnəʊˌkwestʃn/	Are you from Australia?	3R, 5R, 6, 8R
Frage mit Fragewort	wh-question /ˌdʌbljuː ˈeɪtʃ ˌkwestʃn/	What's your name?	3R, 5R, 6, 8R
Futur mit *will*	will-future /ˈwɪl ˌfjuːtʃə/	I'll find a good job.	8R
Gerundium	gerund /ˈdʒerənd/	Dancing can be fun.	4R
Grundform des Verbs (Infinitiv)	infinitive /ɪnˈfɪnətɪv/	be, go, like	3R, 5R, 8R, 14R
Hauptsatz	main clause /ˈmeɪn klɔːz/	If you miss the bus, you will be late.	14R
Imperativ (Befehlsform)	imperative /ɪmˈperətɪv/	Close the door, please!	
Indirekter Befehlssatz	reported command /rɪˌpɔːtɪd kəˈmɑːnd/	Mr Cameron told Nick to be on time.	
Indirekte Rede	reported speech /rɪˌpɔːtɪd ˈspiːtʃ/	John told the reporter that he liked his job.	9R, 16
Indirekter Fragesatz	reported question /rɪˌpɔːtɪd ˈkwestʃn/	The reporter asked if he liked his job.	11
Komparativ (1. Vergleichsform)	comparative /kəmˈpærətɪv/	faster, better, more beautiful, more loudly	
Modalverb	modal verb /ˈməʊdl vɜːb/	can, must	6
Nomen (Substantiv, Hauptwort)	noun /naʊn/	apple, friend, milk, water	4R

Glossary

Deutscher Begriff	Englischer Begriff mit Aussprache	Beispiele	LiF
Objekt	object /ˈɒbdʒɪkt/	Becky is writing an email.	1R, 2R, 13R
direktes Objekt	direct object /dɪˌrekt‿ˈɒbdʒɪkt/	He gave her a book.	
indirektes Objekt	indirect object /ɪndɪˌrekt‿ˈɒbdʒɪkt/	He gave her a book.	
Partizip Perfekt	past participle /ˌpɑːst ˈpɑːtɪsɪpl/	played, been, taken	2R, 5R, 10R
Passiv	passive /ˈpæsɪv/	A tower is built.	2R
Perfekt	present perfect /ˌpreznt ˈpɜːfɪkt/	have gone, has been, has visited	5R
Personalpronomen	personal pronoun /ˌpɜːsnl ˈprəʊnaʊn/	I, you, we, they	9R
Plural (Mehrzahl)	plural /ˈplʊərəl/	apples	
Reflexivpronomen	reflexive pronoun /rɪˌfleksɪv ˈprəʊnaʊn/	myself, yourself, ourselves	
Singular (Einzahl)	singular /ˈsɪŋgjʊlə/	apple	12R
Steigerung (Vergleichsformen) von Adverbien	comparison of adverbs /kɒmˌpærɪsn‿əv‿ˈædvɜːbz/	more quickly than …, as beautifully as …, the most quickly	
Stützwort	prop word /ˈprɒp wɜːd/	the blue one, the red ones	
Subjekt (Satzgegenstand)	subject /ˈsʌbdʒekt/	Becky is writing an email.	1R, 2R, 13R
Superlativ (2. Vergleichsform)	superlative /suːˈpɜːlətɪv/	biggest, nicest, most interesting, best	
Verb (Tätigkeitswort)	verb /vɜːb/		1R, 2R
regelmäßig	regular /ˈregjʊlə/	play, like, watch, walk	5R, 3R
unregelmäßig	irregular /ɪˈregjʊlə/	go, do, have	5R, 3R
Vergangenheitsform	past form /ˈpɑːst fɔːm/	played, liked, went, did	7R
Verlaufsform der Gegenwart	present progressive /ˌpreznt prəʊˈgresɪv/	We are having a party.	9R, 16R
Verlaufsform der Vergangenheit	past progressive /ˌpɑːst prəʊˈgresɪv/	was reading, were running	16R
Verlaufsform des Perfekt	present perfect progressive /ˌpreznt ˌpɜːfɪkt prəʊˈgresɪv/	She has been running for half an hour.	6
Vorvergangenheit (Plusquamperfekt)	past perfect /ˌpɑːst ˈpɜːfɪkt/	had left, had gone, had been	9R, 10R

Theme 1

LiF1R Die Stellung der Satzglieder – *word order (revision)*

a Satzstellung Subjekt – Verb – Objekt

Im englischen Aussagesatz ist die Satzstellung meist:

Subjekt (*subject*) S	Verb (*verb*) V	Objekt (*object*) O
Becky	likes	koalas.
We	are planning	a trip to Australia.

b Verben mit zwei Objekten

Manche Verben können zwei Objekte haben, z. B. *give, offer, show, ask, send*. Das indirekte Objekt steht entweder vor dem direkten Objekt oder unmittelbar danach. Wenn es nachgestellt wird, muss das indirekte Objekt durch *to* oder *for* eingeleitet werden.

Subjekt	Verb	indirektes Objekt	direktes Objekt
Becky	sent	her parents	an email.
She	bought	her friend	a souvenir.

Subjekt	Verb	direktes Objekt	indirektes Objekt
Becky	sent	an email	to her parents.
She	bought	a souvenir	for her friend.

c Aussagesätze mit Häufigkeitsadverbien

Im Englischen stehen Häufigkeitsadverbien meist zwischen Subjekt und Verb:

Subjekt	Häufigkeitsadverb	Verb	
Becky	often	talks	to her parents.
She	never	felt	lonely.

In Sätzen mit einer Form von *be* (*is, was* etc.) steht das Adverb jedoch hinter der Form von *be*:
It is always quite hot in the north of Australia.

In Sätzen mit *can* steht das Häufigkeitsadverb hinter *can*:
You can often see kangaroos in the outback.

Einige Häufigkeitsadverbien, wie z. B. *sometimes*, können vorangestellt werden, um sie zu betonen:
Sometimes Becky missed her family in Germany.

d Ortsangaben und Zeitangaben

Orts- und Zeitangaben stehen in der Regel am Ende eines Satzes. Wenn sie zusammen in einem Satz vorkommen, steht die Ortsangabe vor der Zeitangabe („Ort“ vor „Zeit“).

	Ortsangabe	Zeitangabe
I was born	in Sydney	in 2004.
My parents came	to Australia	twenty years ago.

Um eine Zeitangabe stärker zu betonen, kannst du sie auch an den Satzanfang stellen.

Zeitangabe		Ortsangabe
In 2010	we moved	to Newcastle.
Last year	my grandparents went	to Sydney.

LiF2R Das Passiv – *the passive (revision)*

Mit dem Passiv drückst du aus, dass etwas mit einer Person, einer Sache oder einem Tier getan wird. Man benutzt es vor allem dann, wenn es nicht wichtig oder wenn es unklar ist, wer handelt.

Aktiv	Passiv
They discovered **gold**.	**Gold** was discovered.

Passivsätze werden so gebildet: Form von *be* + **Partizip Perfekt *(past participle)***

*Doctors are **flown** to the outback.*
*Many Australians were **born** in other countries.*
*Australia Day has been **celebrated** for many years.*

Mit *by* („von“, „durch“) kannst du in einem Passivsatz die handelnde Person oder die Ursache hinzufügen.

*Diseases had been **introduced** by the settlers.*

Du kannst einen Aktivsatz in einen Passivsatz umformen und umgekehrt. Das Objekt des Aktivsatzes ist das Subjekt des Passivsatzes. Außerdem musst du im Passivsatz die richtige Form von *be* und das Partizip Perfekt des Verbes verwenden.

Subjekt	Verb	Objekt
The settlers	*discovered*	*gold.*

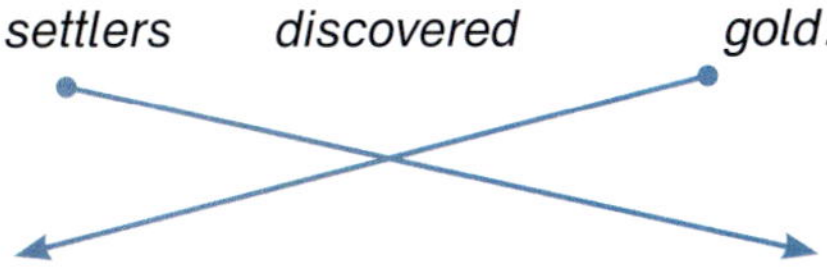

Gold	*was **discovered***	*by the settlers.*

Der Satz steht hier im *simple past*, daher verwendet man *was* (*simple past* von *be*) und das Partizip Perfekt des Verbs *discover*, also *discovered*.

LiF3R Die einfache Vergangenheit – *simple past (revision)*

Das *simple past* verwendest du, wenn du über etwas sprechen willst, das in der Vergangenheit liegt und abgeschlossen ist.

a Regelmäßige Formen

Das *simple past* der regelmäßigen Verben bildest du, indem du die Endung *-ed* an den Infinitiv anhängst:

talk + ed → talked *Becky talked about her trip to Sydney.*

b Unregelmäßige Formen

Die unregelmäßigen Verben haben im *simple past* eine eigene Form, die du lernen musst, zum Beispiel:

Infinitiv	*simple past*	
leave	left	Becky left Germany in August.
go	went	She went to Australia.
be	was/were	Becky was in Sydney for a few days.

Eine Liste mit unregelmäßigen Verben findest du auf den Seiten 340 bis 342.

c Verneinung

Vollverben verneinst du im *simple past* mit *didn't (did not)*. *Didn't* ist die Vergangenheitsform von *don't* und *doesn't* und ist in allen Personen gleich. Das Verb selbst bleibt im Infinitiv. Bei *was/were* hängst du *not* bzw. die Kurzform *n't* an.

simple past: bejahter Satz	*simple past:* verneinter Satz
Becky talked to her parents on Saturday.	Becky didn't talk to her parents on Sunday.
I went to Sydney.	I didn't go to Melbourne.
We were happy.	We weren't sad.
He was in Melbourne.	He wasn't in Sydney.

d Fragen

Entscheidungsfragen im *simple past* stellst du im Allgemeinen mit *did*.
Bei *was* oder *were* brauchst du jedoch kein *did*, wenn du eine Frage bildest.

Did you go to Australia?	Yes, I did.	No, I didn't.
Was the weather good?	Yes, it was.	No, it wasn't.

Bei Fragen mit Fragewort steht das Fragewort am Satzanfang:

How did Becky travel to Sydney?
What did she do there?
Why was Becky sad?

Theme 2

LiF 4R Das Gerundium – *the gerund (revision)*

Wird ein Verb durch Anhängen von *-ing* zu einem Nomen, nennt man es Gerundium *(gerund)*:
Running keeps you fit.

Das Gerundium folgt oft nach bestimmten Verben wie *like, love, start*:
She loves hiking.

Du benutzt es auch nach bestimmten Ausdrücken wie zum Beispiel *proud of* und *good at*:
He is good at skiing.

LiF 5R Das Perfekt – *present perfect (revision)*

Das *present perfect* verwendest du, wenn etwas bis zum jetzigen Zeitpunkt irgendwann, noch nie oder noch nicht geschehen ist, oder wenn ein Vorgang in der Vergangenheit noch Auswirkungen auf die Gegenwart hat.

Das *present perfect* bildest du mit *have/has* + **Partizip Perfekt *(past participle)***.
Die Verneinung bildest du mit *haven't/hasn't* + **Partizip Perfekt *(past participle)***.

*I have **been** to Australia before, but I have never **been** to New Zealand.*
*I've already **cooked** dinner, you don't have to do it!*

Das *present perfect* kannst du mit Adverbien der unbestimmten Zeit verwenden, z. B. mit *already, just, ever, never, yet, not yet*. Es ist in solchen Sätzen nicht wichtig, wann genau etwas geschehen ist. Die Adverbien stehen dann direkt vor dem Partizip Perfekt, nur *yet* steht am Satzende.

I have already tried skydiving.
I haven't been to New Zealand yet.

Entscheidungsfragen im *present perfect* bildest du, indem du *have* oder *has* an den Satzanfang stellst.

present perfect: Entscheidungsfragen und Kurzantworten	+	–
Have you finished your homework? Has Becky been to Hong Kong?	Yes, I have. Yes, she has.	No, I haven't. No, she hasn't.

Bei Fragen mit Fragewörtern steht das Fragewort am Satzanfang:

Where have you travelled so far?

Bei regelmäßigen Verben bildest du das Partizip Perfekt *(past participle)* mit dem Infinitiv + *-ed*.
Unregelmäßige Verben haben unregelmäßige Formen. Lerne sie wie Vokabeln.
Auf den Seiten 340 bis 342 findest du eine Liste mit unregelmäßigen Verben.

LiF 6 Die Verlaufsform des Perfekts – *present perfect progressive*

Das *present perfect progressive* verwendest du, wenn du über etwas sprechen möchtest, das in der Vergangenheit begonnen hat und immer noch andauert.

Tim has been running for thirty minutes (and he is still running).

a Aussagesätze im *present perfect progressive*

So bildest du das *present perfect progressive*:

have/has + *been* + *-ing*-Form:

I have been doing parkour since I was twelve.
Jacob has been surfing for an hour.

She has been doing her homework for two hours.

Bei Verneinungen fügst du *not* hinter *have* oder *has* ein:

have/has + *not* + *been* + *-ing*-Form:

I haven't been mountain biking for long.
He hasn't been skating for a long time.

b Fragen und Kurzantworten im *present perfect progressive*

Entscheidungsfragen im *present perfect progressive* bildest du, indem du *have* oder *has* an den Satzanfang stellst. *Have* bzw. *has* wird in den Kurzantworten aufgegriffen.

Have you been working for long? – *Yes, I have./No, I haven't.*
Has he been going to school for six years? – *Yes, he has./No, he hasn't.*

Bei Fragen mit Fragewörtern steht das Fragewort vor *have* oder *has*.

What have you been doing all day?

LiF 7R Modalverben – *modal verbs (revision)*

Mithilfe von Modalverben kannst du z. B. ausdrücken, was jemand tun kann, darf, muss oder sollte. Die meisten Modalverben haben nur Formen für das *simple present*. In den anderen Zeitformen verwendest du deshalb die Ersatzformen.

a Fähigkeit: *can/can't/be able to*

Mit *can* kannst du sagen, was jemand tun kann. Die Ersatzform von *can* ist *be able to*. Im *simple past* kannst du auch *could* benutzen.

Kiwis can't fly.
He wasn't able to go to New Zealand because he didn't have enough money.
He couldn't afford it.

b Erlaubnis: *can/can't – be allowed to/not be allowed to – may/may not – must not*

Mit *can/can't, (not) be allowed to, may/may not* und *must not* kannst du sagen, was jemand tun bzw. nicht tun darf.

*You **can** swim in this lake, it is not forbidden.*
*He **wasn't allowed to** use a mobile phone on the plane.*
*You **mustn't** climb this mountain, it is too dangerous.*

! ***Must not*** oder die Kurzform ***mustn't*** klingt wie im Deutschen „muss nicht", heißt aber „nicht dürfen".

Ihr dürft jetzt nicht sprechen.

c Notwendigkeit: *must/have to – don't have to/needn't*

Must bedeutet „müssen". In der Regel kannst du ***must*** auch durch ***have to/has to*** ersetzen. Da ***must*** keine eigene Vergangenheitsform hat, wird die *simple past*-Form von ***have to*** benutzt.

*In New Zealand you **must** drive on the left.*
*In New Zealand you **have to** drive on the left.*
*In New Zealand we **had to** drive on the left.*

Wenn du sagen willst, was jemand *nicht* tun muss oder musste, benutzt du ***don't/doesn't have to*** bzw. ***didn't have to***. Auch mit ***needn't*** (Kurzform von ***need not***) kannst du ausdrücken, dass jemand etwas nicht tun muss.

*We **didn't have to** pay a lot for our hotel in New Zealand.*
*You **needn't** stay there long if you don't want to.*

d Empfehlung: *should/shouldn't*

Mit *should/shouldn't* drückst du aus, dass etwas deiner Ansicht nach passieren oder nicht passieren sollte. Mit *should* kannst du auch die Meinung einer anderen Person erfragen.

*You **should** go to New Zealand one day, it's a really beautiful country.*
*Where do you think I **should** go first?*

e Übersicht über die Ersatzformen der Modalverben

simple present	substitute	simple past	present perfect	future
can	be able to	was able to; could	have been able to	will be able to
can't	not be able to	was not able to; couldn't	haven't been able to	won't be able to
must	have to	had to	have had to	will have to
mustn't	not be allowed to	wasn't allowed to	haven't been allowed to	won't be allowed to
needn't	don't have to	didn't have to	haven't had to	won't have to

Theme 3

LiF8R Formen des Futurs – *forms of the future (revision)*

Im Englischen gibt es mehrere Möglichkeiten, Zukünftiges auszudrücken.

a Futur mit *going to*

Wenn du sagen willst, was jemand für die Zukunft plant oder beabsichtigt, benutzt du das Futur mit *going to*: *We are going to have a party this weekend*.

Auch bei Ereignissen, die wahrscheinlich eintreten werden, verwendet man das *going to-future*. Im Deutschen gibt es keine Zeitform, die dem *going to-future* entspricht.

Du bildest es mit einer Form von **be** + **going to** + Infinitiv:

I ***am going to*** *study.*

Für die Verneinung stellst du *not* hinter die Form von *be*. Oft benutzt man Kurzformen.

I'm ***not*** *going to study.*

Bei Entscheidungsfragen rückt die Form von *be (am, is, are)* an den Satzanfang. In der Kurzantwort steht dann die entsprechende Form.

Are *you going to study?* ***Yes, I am./No, I'm not.***

Bei Fragen mit Fragewort steht das Fragewort an erster Stelle:

What *are you going to do?*

b Futur mit *will*

Wenn du über die Zukunft sprechen möchtest, kannst du auch das *will-future* verwenden. Damit kannst du Vermutungen ausdrücken, Vorhersagen machen und Versprechen äußern. Das *will-future* bildest du mit *will* und dem Infinitiv des Verbs. *Will* hat die Kurzform *'ll*. Die Form *will* ist in allen Personen gleich.

I hope the weather ***will be*** *nice tomorrow.*

Für die Verneinung fügst du einfach ein ***not*** hinter *will* ein. Die Kurzform von ***will not*** ist ***won't***. *Won't* ist für alle Personen gleich.

The weather forecast says it ***won't*** *rain tomorrow.*

Tomorrow it ***will*** *be sunny. It* ***won't*** *rain.*

In Entscheidungsfragen stellst du *will* an den Satzanfang. Du verwendest *will* und *won't* auch in den Kurzantworten.

Will *it rain tomorrow?* ***Yes, it will./No, it won't.***

Bei Fragen mit Fragewörtern stellst du auch beim *will-future* das Fragewort an den Satzanfang.

What *will the weather be like tomorrow?*

LiF9R Zeitverschiebung in indirekter *Rede – tense shift in reported speech (revision)*

Wenn du berichten willst, was jemand sagt oder gesagt hat, verwendest du die indirekte Rede *(reported speech)*.

Wenn das Verb im Begleitsatz in der Vergangenheit steht, dann musst du die Zeitform in der indirekten Rede anpassen. Sie rückt dann sozusagen eine Stufe weiter in die Vergangenheit (Zeitverschiebung = *backshift of tenses*).

Mr Cameron: You have to be on time.

→ *Mr Cameron told Nick that he had to be on time.*

Mr Cameron: You will have to work later this evening.

→ *Mr Cameron told Nick that he would have to work later that evening.*

Nick: I'm cleaning the floor.

→ *Nick said that he was cleaning the floor.*

Nick: I will be on time tomorrow.

→ *Nick said that he would be on time the next day.*

Denke daran, Bezugswörter, die nur aus dem Zusammenhang richtig zu verstehen sind, in der wiedergegebenen Aussage anzupassen. Dies sind zum Beispiel Personalpronomen und Adverbien wie *tomorrow* und *here*.

Mr Cameron: "I'm not happy." → *Mr Cameron said that he wasn't happy.*
Nick: "I'll work harder tomorrow." → *Nick said that he would work harder the next day.*
Caroline: "I like working here." → *Caroline said that she liked working there.*

Aus dieser Tabelle kannst du ablesen, wie sich die Zeiten verändern.

Direkte Rede		Indirekte Rede
simple present	→	*simple past*
present progressive	→	*past progressive*
will	→	*would*
can	→	*could*
should	→	*should*
simple past	→	*past perfect*
present perfect	→	*past perfect*

LiF10R Die Vorvergangenheit – *past perfect (revision)*

Das *past perfect* verwendest du, wenn du über eine Handlung sprechen möchtest, die vor einer anderen Handlung in der Vergangenheit stattgefunden hat.
Die zweite Handlung steht im *simple past*. Beide Handlungen sind abgeschlossen.

*After Anna's parents **had gone** to Australia, they found jobs in Sydney.*
Nachdem Annas Eltern nach Australien gegangen waren, fanden sie Arbeit in Sydney.

Anna's parents had gone to Australia.	*They found jobs in Sydney.*
↓	↓
1. Handlung: *past perfect*	2. Handlung: *simple past*

Das *past perfect* bildest du so: ***had*** + **Partizip Perfekt *(past participle)***.

1. Handlung ***past perfect***	**2. Handlung** ***simple past***
After Anna **had boarded** the plane, *Nachdem Annie an Bord gegangen war,*	her journey began. *begann ihre Reise.*
Anna's family **had lived** in England *Annas Familie hatte in England gelebt,*	before they came to Australia. *bevor sie nach Australien kam.*

Die Verneinung bildest du mit ***hadn't*** + **Partizip Perfekt *(past participle)***.

1. Handlung ***past perfect***	**2. Handlung** ***simple past***
Anna's parents **hadn't had** any money *Annas Eltern hatten kein Geld gehabt,*	before they moved to Sydney. *bevor sie nach Sydney zogen.*

Wenn du das *past perfect* bildest, musst du auf das Partizip Perfekt achten.
Bei regelmäßigen Verben endet es auf *-ed*.
Bei unregelmäßigen Verben musst du die Formen wie neue Vokabeln lernen.

Auf den Seiten 340 bis 342 findest du eine Liste mit unregelmäßigen Verben.

LiF11 Indirekte Fragesätze 2 – *reported questions 2*

Wenn du eine Frage wiedergeben willst, die jemand anderes gestellt hat, benutzt du *if* oder *whether*. Wenn der Einleitungssatz in der Vergangenheit steht, dann musst du auch hier die Zeiten verändern (*tense shift*, siehe auch LiF9R).

Do you like your job? — *The reporter wanted to know **whether** he liked his job.*

Do you make a lot of money? — *The reporter asked **if** he made a lot of money.*

Wenn die Frage mit einem Fragewort eingeleitet wird, übernimmst du das Fragewort:

When did you start your job? — *The reporter asked **when** he had started his job.*

What will you do next? — *The reporter asked **what** he would do next.*

Wie bei der indirekten Rede müssen die Bezugswörter angepasst werden:

*"Are **you** happy with **your** job?"*	→	*The reporter asked the woman if **she** was happy with **her** job.*
*"Will **you** give a presentation **tomorrow**?"*	→	*He wanted to know whether **she** would give a presentation **the next day**.*
*"Do **you** like working **here**?"*	→	*He asked if **he** liked working **there**.*

Theme 4

LiF12R Die einfache Gegenwart – *simple present (revision)*

Das *simple present* verwendest du unter anderem, wenn du über Gewohnheiten oder regelmäßige Handlungen sprichst. Bei *I, you, we* und *they* hat das *simple present* dieselbe Form wie die Grundform des Verbs (Infinitiv).

*I often **share** pictures with my friends.*

In der 3. Person Singular hängst du ein ***-s*** an.
*My sister sometimes share**s** pictures with her friends.*

Sätze im *simple present* verneinst du, indem du *don't* (= *do not*) vor das Verb stellst. Bei der 3. Person Singular verwendest du *doesn't* (= *does not*). Dabei verliert das Verb das *-s* am Ende.

*I **don't** use my tablet very often.*

! Bei der Verneinung von Sätzen mit *be*, *have got,* und Modalverben wie *can* etc. brauchst du *don't* oder *doesn't* nicht:

*My brother **isn't** online very often.*

Fragen werden so gebildet:

***Do** you use your smartphone for searching the Internet?*
***How** often **do** you check your emails?*

Wie bei der Verneinung brauchst du kein *do* oder *don't* bei Sätzen mit *be*:

***Are** you online every day?*
***How** often **are** you online?*

Achte auf die Satzstellung: Häufigkeitsadverbien stehen im Aussagesatz meist vor dem Verb (siehe auch LiF1R):

*I **sometimes** share pictures with my friends.*

My sister often uses her tablet for researching information.

LiF13R Relativsätze – *relative clauses (revision)*

Relativsätze sind Nebensätze, die Personen oder Dinge näher beschreiben.
Ein Relativsatz beginnt meist mit einem Relativpronomen: ***who***, ***which*** oder ***that***.

Dabei verwendest du ***who*** für Personen und ***which*** für Dinge.

Relativsatz

This is the man **who** developped the app.	*Das ist der Mann, der die App entwickelt hat.*
This is the app **which** I like best.	*Das ist die App, die ich am liebsten mag.*

Das Relativpronomen ***that*** kannst du sowohl für Dinge als auch für Personen benutzen.

Relativsatz

There are many people **that** use this app.	*Es gibt viele Leute, die diese App benutzen.*
The app only uses data **that** you are willing to share.	*Die App verwendet nur Daten, die man bereit ist zu teilen.*

Relativsätze können auch in der Mitte eines Satzes stehen:

*The app **that I like best** has many interesting features.*

Wann kann man das Relativpronomen weglassen?

Wenn ein Relativpronomen (*who*, *which* oder *that*) das Objekt eines Relativsatzes ist, kann man es weglassen:

*These are the apps **that** my classmates use the most.*
oder:
These are the apps my classmates use the most.

that bezieht sich hier auf *the apps* (= Objekt).
Hier kannst du es gut sehen:

Subjekt Objekt

My classmates *use* ***the apps***.

Relativsätze ohne Relativpronomen heißen *contact clauses*.

Wenn das Relativpronomen das Subjekt eines Relativsatzes ist, kann man es nicht weglassen: *I downloaded an app that was free of charge.*

LiF14R Bedingungssätze 2 – *conditional 2 (revision)*

Bedingungssätze können realistische oder unrealistische Bedingungen nennen. Ist eine Bedingung erfüllbar, verwendet man den Bedingungssatz 1:

If you study hard, you will get a good mark.

Ist eine Bedingung jedoch unwahrscheinlich oder unmöglich, verwendet man den Bedingungssatz 2.

If my mom had the money, she would send me to art school.

Da die Mutter das Geld im Moment nicht hat, ist die Bedingung nicht erfüllbar.

Bei dieser zweiten Art von Bedingungssätzen steht der *if*-Satz im *simple past*. Im Hauptsatz steht *would* (oder auch *could*) mit einem Hauptverb im Infinitiv.

if-Satz (*simple past*)	Hauptsatz (*would/could* + Infinitiv)
If Emma's brother didn't help her,	Emma would fail completely in math.
If she was fitter,	she would choose basketball.
If Emma chose graphic design,	she would be happier.
If Emma's mother had more money,	Emma could go to art school.

Mr Batson would be very happy if he found a new job.

If I were …

Bei *if*-Sätzen heißt es manchmal *If I were …*, aber du kannst auch *If I was …* sagen. Beide Formen sind hier möglich.

If I were Emma, I would choose graphic design.
oder:
If I was Emma, I would choose graphic design.

LiF 15 Adverbialsätze – *adverbial clauses*

Adverbialsätze sind Nebensätze, die mit Konjunktionen (z. B. *because, while, before*) beginnen und durch diese eine bestimmte Bedeutung erhalten. Es gibt verschiedene Arten von Adverbialsätzen. Für jede Art sind bestimmte Konjunktionen typisch.

Adverbialsatz der Zeit *(time)*

after • as soon as • before • since • till • until • when • whenever • while

After she had finished her first book she started her second one.

Nachdem sie ihr erstes Buch beendet hatte, begann sie mit ihrem zweiten.

Adverbialsatz des Grundes *(reason)*

because • as

He became a writer because he loved inventing stories.

Er wurde Schriftsteller, weil er gerne Geschichten erfand.

Adverbialsatz der Folge *(result)*

so that • so ... that • such ... that

The book was so exciting that I couldn't stop reading.

Das Buch war so spannend, dass ich nicht aufhören konnte zu lesen.

Adverbialsatz des Zwecks *(purpose)*

so that • in order to

Tom worked really hard in order to get a good mark.

Tom arbeitete sehr hart, um eine gute Note zu bekommen.

Adverbialsatz des Gegensatzes *(contrast/concession)*

although • even if • though • whereas

He became a writer although his parents didn't want him to.

Er wurde Schriftsteller, obwohl seine Eltern das nicht wollten.

Adverbialsatz des Ortes *(place)*

where • wherever

He always lived in the city where he was born.

Er lebte immer in der Stadt, in der er geboren worden war.

Theme 5

LiF16R Die Verlaufsform der Vergangenheit – *past progressive (revision)*

Mit dem *past progressive* kannst du ausdrücken, was zu einem bestimmten Zeitpunkt in der Vergangenheit gerade passierte oder was gerade vor sich ging, als etwas anderes geschah.

We were staying at our grandparents' house when the war broke out.

Das *past progressive* wird ganz ähnlich gebildet wie das *present progressive*, nur dass die Form von *be* im *simple past* steht (*was* bzw. *were*):

***Simple past*-Form von *be* (*was/were*)** + ***ing*-Form**:

*The children **were playing** in the garden.* – Die Kinder spielten (gerade) im Garten.

So kannst du beschreiben, was gerade vor sich ging, als etwas anderes geschah:

past progressive	*simple past*
The pupils **were running** around *Die Schüler rannten herum,*	when the teacher came. *als der Lehrer kam.*
was gerade passierte: *past progressive*	**neues Ereignis:** ***simple past***

Für die Verneinung fügst du einfach ***not*** hinter die Form von *be* (*was* bzw. *were*) ein:

*The children were**n't** playing in the garden.*

Bei Fragen rückt *was/were* nach vorne:

***Were** the children playing in the garden?*

Fragewörter stehen am Satzanfang:

***What** were the children doing?*

Words

Erläuterung der Wortlisten

Alphabetische Wortlisten *(Dictionary)*

Du kannst in der alphabetischen Liste *(Dictionary English-German)* ab Seite 273 die Bedeutung von Wörtern, die im Buch vorgekommen sind, oder von Lernwörtern aus Band I, II, III oder IV (5., 6., 7. oder 8. Klasse) nachschlagen. Unbekanntes Vokabular aus den Arbeitsanweisungen findest du ebenfalls dort. Die wichtigsten Arbeitsanweisungen findest du in der Liste auf den Seiten 196-199 und in Kästen innerhalb der Wortlisten nach Kapiteln. Einige Wörter, die im Englischen wie im Deutschen gleich sind, findest du mit ihrer Lautschrift auf Seite 195. Im *Dictionary German-English* ab Seite 319 kannst du nachschlagen, wenn dir eins der englischen Lernwörter nicht einfällt.

Wortlisten nach Kapiteln *(Words)*

Hier werden die neuen Vokabeln an der Stelle aufgelistet, an der sie zum ersten Mal vorkommen oder zum Lernwort werden. Die Lernwörter sind fett gedruckt. Du solltest sie dir auf jeden Fall merken. Hier siehst du, wie du die Wortlisten nach Kapiteln (ab Seite 201) benutzen kannst:

Links stehen die englischen Wörter mit ihrer Lautschrift.

Die Lautschrift zeigt an, wie man ein Wort ausspricht.

Hier findest du die Übersetzungen.

Fett gedruckte Wörter solltest du dir merken.

Zu dieser Aufgabe gehören die folgenden Wörter.

(pl) weist auf eine unregelmäßige Mehrzahlform hin oder darauf, dass ein Wort in seiner Mehrzahlform vorkommt.

(no pl) bedeutet: Dieses Wort hat keine Mehrzahl.

(AusE) bedeutet: Dies ist ein Wort aus dem australischen Englisch.

(informal) bedeutet: Dieses Wort ist umgangssprachlich.

Kleine Bilder und Beispielsätze helfen dabei, dir Wörter besser einzuprägen.

Hier findest du wichtige Vokabel-Lerntipps.

(irr) bedeutet: Dieses Verb hat unregelmäßige Formen. Du findest sie in der Liste ab S. 340.

W

Words

photographer /fəˈtɒɡrəfə/	Fotograf/in	
silence /ˈsaɪləns/	Stille, Ruhe	She asked for *silence*. 
drawing room /ˈdrɔːɪŋ ruːm/	Empfangszimmer, Salon, Gesellschaftszimmer	
wireless /ˈwaɪələs/	Radio, (Rund)funk	
recall /rɪˈkɔːl/	sich erinnern an	
dispirited /dɪˈspɪrɪtɪd/	niedergeschlagen, entmutigt	
A1 air raid /ˈeə reɪd/	Luftangriff	*siren*
siren /ˈsaɪrən/	Sirene	
anticlimax, anti-climax /ˌæntiˈklaɪmæks/	Antiklimax, Enttäuschung	
memory /ˈmemri/	Erinnerung, Gedächtnis	
the rains *(pl)* /ðə ˈreɪnz/	Regenzeit	
forethought /ˈfɔːˌθɔːt/	Weitblick	
vacation /vəˈkeɪʃn/	Ferien, Urlaub	
central /ˈsentrəl/	zentral, wesentlich, Zentral-	
announcement /əˈnaʊnsmənt/	Bekanntmachung, Mitteilung, Durchsage	The teacher made an important *announcement*.
civilian /səˈvɪliən/	Zivil-; *hier:* für Zivilisten	
gas mask /ˈɡæs mɑːsk/	Gasmaske	
chorus (*pl* choruses) /ˈkɔːrəs, ˈkɔːrəsɪz/	Refrain	
biosecurity *(no pl)* /ˈbaɪəʊsɪˌkjʊərəti/	*Sicherheitsvorkehrungen gegen biogene Probleme*	
set to work /ˌset‿tʊ ˈwɜːk/	sich an die Arbeit machen	
spade /speɪd/	Spaten	
dusk /dʌsk/	(Abend)dämmerung	
stiff /stɪf/	steif	
stand up /ˌstænd‿ˈʌp/	aufstehen; *hier:* gerade stehen	
blister /ˈblɪstə/	Blase	
wallow /ˈwɒləʊ/	ausgiebig baden	
bath /bɑːθ/	Bad	
bomb /bɒm/	Bombe	
weary /ˈwɪəri/	müde, erschöpft	*weary* = very tired
blackout /ˈblækaʊt/	Verdunkelung	
seek *(irr)* /siːk/	suchen, streben nach	
rush /rʌʃ/	eilen	to *rush* = to hurry
haberdasher /ˈhæbəˌdæʃə/	Kurzwarenhändler/in	
sandbag /ˈsænˌbæɡ/	Sandsack	
station *(AusE)* /ˈsteɪʃn/	große Farm	
down under *(informal)* /ˌdaʊn‿ˈʌndə/	Australien, Neuseeland	

Bilde das Gegenteil!
Man kann aus vielen Wörtern neue bilden, indem man eine Vorsilbe setzt, die die Bedeutung des Wortes ins Gegenteil verändert. Diese Vorsilben können sein: **„un-"**, **„im-"**, **„in-"** oder **„ir-"** z. B.

usual ≠ *unusual*
possible ≠ *impossible*
direct ≠ *indirect*
regular ≠ *irregular*

The English alphabet

/eɪ/ a	/biː/ b	/siː/ c	/diː/ d	/iː/ e	/ef/ f	/dʒiː/ g	/eɪtʃ/ h	/aɪ/ i
/dʒeɪ/ j	/keɪ/ k	/el/ l	/em/ m	/en/ n	/əʊ/ o	/piː/ p	/kjuː/ q	/ɑː/ r
/es/ s	/tiː/ t	/juː/ u	/viː/ v	/ˈdʌbljuː/ w	/eks/ x	/waɪ/ y	/zed/ z	

English sounds

Im Englischen spricht man Wörter oft anders aus, als man sie schreibt. Die Aussprache der Wörter wird mit Hilfe der Lautschrift in jedem Wörterbuch angegeben. Man kann so auch neue Wörter richtig aussprechen, ohne sie vorher gehört zu haben.
Die Lautschrift ist eine Schrift, deren Symbole jeden Laut genau bezeichnen.
Hier ist eine Liste mit den Symbolen dieser Lautschrift zusammen mit Beispielwörtern, in denen der entsprechende Laut vorkommt.

Vokale

/ɑː/ **ar**m
/ʌ/ b**u**t
/e/ d**e**sk
/ə/ **a**, **a**n
/ɜː/ g**ir**l, b**ir**d
/æ/ **a**pple
/ɪ/ **i**n, **i**t
/i/ happ**y**
/iː/ **ea**sy, **ea**t
/ɒ/ **o**range, s**o**rry
/ɔː/ **a**ll, c**a**ll
/ʊ/ l**oo**k
/u/ Jan**u**ary
/uː/ b**oo**t

Doppellaute

/aɪ/ **eye**, b**y**, b**uy**
/aʊ/ **our**
/eə/ **air**, th**ere**
/eɪ/ t**a**ke, th**ey**
/ɪə/ h**ere**
/ɔɪ/ b**oy**
/əʊ/ g**o**, **o**ld
/ʊə/ t**ou**rist

Konsonanten

/b/ **b**ag, clu**b**
/d/ **d**uck, car**d**
/f/ **f**ish, lau**gh**
/g/ **g**et, do**g**
/h/ **h**ot
/j/ **y**ou
/k/ **c**an, du**ck**
/l/ **l**ot, sma**ll**
/m/ **m**ore, mu**m**
/n/ **n**ow, su**n**
/ŋ/ so**ng**, lo**ng**
/p/ **p**resent, to**p**
/r/ **r**ed, a**r**ound
/s/ **s**ister, cla**ss** (stimmlos)
/z/ no**s**e, dog**s** (stimmhaft)
/t/ **t**ime, ca**t**
/ʒ/ televi**s**ion
/dʒ/ sausa**ge**
/ʃ/ fre**sh**
/tʃ/ **ch**ild, **ch**eese
/ð/ **th**ese, mo**th**er (stimmhaft)
/θ/ ba**th**room, **th**ink (stimmlos)
/v/ **v**ery, ha**v**e
/w/ **wh**at, **w**ord

/ˈ/ Betonungszeichen für die folgende Silbe (Hauptbetonung)
/ˌ/ Betonungszeichen für die folgende Silbe (Nebenbetonung)

Words

Viele Wörter, die im Englischen wie im Deutschen so gut wie gleich sind und in deinem Buch vorkommen, findest du hier. Sie sind nicht in den Wortlisten der einzelnen Kapitel, weil sie dir ja nicht neu sind. Bei denen, die anders ausgesprochen werden als im Deutschen, haben wir die Lautschrift farbig hervorgehoben.

addition /əˈdɪʃn/
alternative /ɔːlˈtɜːnətɪv/
anti- /ˈænti/
app /æp/
argument /ˈɑːgjʊmənt/
arm /ɑːm/
astronaut /ˈæstrəˌnɔːt/
ball /bɔːl/
band /bænd/
bank /bæŋk/
bio /baɪəʊ/
blog, blogger /blɒg, ˈblɒgə/
blues /bluːz/
bravo /ˌbrɑːˈvəʊ/
brutal /ˈbruːtl/
bungee /ˈbʌndʒiː/
bungee jump /ˈbʌndʒiː ˌdʒʌmp/
bungee/bungy jumping /ˈbʌndʒiː ˌdʒʌmpɪŋ/
bus /bʌs/
café /ˈkæfeɪ/
camping /ˈkæmpɪŋ/
cartoon /kɑːˈtuːn/
CD, DVD /ˌsiːˈdiː, ˌdiːviːˈdiː/
clip /klɪp/
clique /kliːk/
cluster /ˈklʌstə/
coach /kəʊtʃ/
code /kəʊd/
comic /ˈkɒmɪk/
community /kəˈmjuːnəti/
computer /kəmˈpjuːtə/
cool /kuːl/
country /ˈkʌntri/
definition /ˌdefəˈnɪʃn/
designer /dɪˈzaɪnə/
detail /ˈdiːteɪl/
digital /ˈdɪdʒɪtl/
dollar /ˈdɒlə/
element /ˈelɪmənt/
email /ˈiːmeɪl/
emo /ˈiːməʊ/
emotional /ɪˈməʊʃnəl/
emu /ˈiːmjuː/
endorphin /enˈdɔːfɪn/
ensemble /ɒnˈsɒmbl/
episode /ˈepɪsəʊd/
euro /ˈjʊərəʊ/
expedition /ˌekspəˈdɪʃn/
explosion /ɪkˈspləʊʒn/
extra /ˈekstrə/
fan /fæn/
fashionista /ˌfæʃəˈniːstə/
film /fɪlm/
finalist /ˈfaɪnlɪst/
fitness tracker /ˈfɪtnəs ˌtrækə/
folk /fəʊk/
follower /ˈfɒləʊə/
form /fɔːm/
formation /fɔːˈmeɪʃn/
forum /ˈfɔːrəm/
franchise /ˈfræntʃaɪz/
front /frʌnt/
funk /fʌŋk/
gamification /ˌgeɪmɪfɪˈkeɪʃn/
gaming /ˈgeɪmɪŋ/
gap year /ˈgæp jɪə/
generation /ˌdʒenəˈreɪʃn/
global /ˈgləʊbl/
gold /gəʊld/
gorilla /gəˈrɪlə/
gothic /ˈgɒθɪk/
graffiti /grəˈfiːti/
hand /hænd/
haul video /ˈhɔːl ˌvɪdiəʊ/
hipster /ˈhɪpstə/
hit /hɪt/
hobby /hɒbi/
horror /ˈhɒrə/
hotel /həʊˈtel/
hotspot /ˈhɒtˌspɒt/
hunger /ˈhʌŋgə/
ideal /aɪˈdɪəl/
idiot /ˈɪdiət/
idol /ˈaɪdl/
illegal /ɪˈliːgl/
image /ˈɪmɪdʒ/
in-app /ˈɪnˌæp/
info /ˈɪnfəʊ/
initiative /ɪˈnɪʃətɪv/
instrument /ˈɪnstrʊmənt/
integration /ˌɪntɪˈgreɪʃn/
intelligent /ɪnˈtelɪdʒnt/
international /ˌɪntəˈnæʃnəl/
Internet /ˈɪntəˌnet/
interview /ˈɪntəˌvjuː/
interviewer /ˈɪntəˌvjuːə/
intolerant /ɪnˈtɒlərənt/
intro /ˈɪntrəʊ/
isolation /ˌaɪsəˈleɪʃn/
jeans /dʒiːnz/
journalist /ˈdʒɜːnəlɪst/
jr. = junior /ˈdʒuːniə/
kindergarten /ˈkɪndəˌgɑːtn/
koala /kəʊˈɑːlə/
land /lænd/
landmine /ˈlænˌmaɪn/
legion /ˈliːdʒn/
link /lɪŋk/
live /laɪv/
live stream /ˌlaɪv ˈstriːm/
login /ˈlɒgɪn/
logo /ˈləʊgəʊ/
manga /ˈmæŋgə/
material /məˈtɪəriəl/
metal /ˈmetl/
migration /maɪˈgreɪʃn/
million /ˈmɪljən/
mine /maɪn/
mineral /ˈmɪnrəl/
mini /ˈmɪni/
minute /ˈmɪnɪt/
mission /ˈmɪʃn/
model /ˈmɒdl/
modern /ˈmɒdən/
monarch /ˈmɒnək/
move /muːv/
museum /mjuːˈziːəm/
musical /ˈmjuːzɪkl/
name /neɪm/
national /ˈnæʃnəl/
navigation /ˌnævɪˈgeɪʃn/
norm /nɔːm/
normal /ˈnɔːml/
online /ˈɒnlaɪn/
organisation /ˌɔːgənaɪˈzeɪʃn/
outfit /ˈaʊtfɪt/
parade /pəˈreɪd/
park /pɑːk/
parkour /pɑːˈkʊə/
partner /ˈpɑːtnə/
party /ˈpɑːti/
patient /ˈpeɪʃnt/
peer group /ˈpɪə gruːp/
penny /ˈpeni/
person /ˈpɜːsn/
phase /feɪz/
piercing /ˈpɪərsɪŋ/
plan /plæn/
planet /ˈplænɪt/
podcast /ˈpɒdˌkɑːst/
polyp /ˈpɒlɪp/
pool /puːl/
pop /pɒp/
position /pəˈzɪʃn/
poster /ˈpəʊstə/
pro- /prəʊ/
problem /ˈprɒbləm/
propaganda /ˌprɒpəˈgændə/
protagonist /prəʊˈtægənɪst/
protest /ˈprəʊtest/
pudding /ˈpʊdɪŋ/
quiz /kwɪz/
radio /ˈreɪdiəʊ/
rate /reɪt/
rebellion /rɪˈbeljən/
region /ˈriːdʒn/
religion /rɪˈlɪdʒn/
reporter /rɪˈpɔːtə/
rest /rest/
restaurant /ˈrestrɒnt/
ring /rɪŋ/
routine /ruːˈtiːn/
sand /sænd/
satire /ˈsætaɪə/
server /ˈsɜːvə/
show /ʃəʊ/
sightseeing /ˈsaɪtˌsiːɪŋ/
situation /ˌsɪtʃuˈeɪʃn/
skate park /ˈskeɪt pɑːk/
skater /ˈskeɪtə/
slang /slæŋ/
smartboard /ˈsmɑːt bɔːd/
smartphone /ˈsmɑːtˌfəʊn/
so /səʊ/
social networking /ˌsəʊʃl ˈnetwɜːkɪŋ/
software /ˈsɒfˌweə/
soul /səʊl/
sound /saʊnd/
sound check /ˈsaʊnd‿tʃek/
souvenir /ˌsuːvəˈnɪə/
star /stɑː/
stress /stres/
stunt /stʌnt/
super /ˈsuːpə/
symbol /ˈsɪmbl/
system /ˈsɪstəm/
talent /ˈtælənt/
tattoo /tæˈtuː/
teamworking /ˈtiːmˌwɜːkɪŋ/
techno /ˈteknəʊ/
teenager /ˈtiːnˌeɪdʒə/
test /test/
text /tekst/
thermometer /θəˈmɒmɪtə/
thermostat /ˈθɜːməʊstæt/
tolerant /ˈtɒlərənt/
totem /ˈtəʊtəm/
tour, tourist /tʊə, ˈtʊərɪst/
tradition /trəˈdɪʃn/
training /ˈtreɪnɪŋ/
trance /trɑːns/
trendy /ˈtrendi/
trip /trɪp/
uniform /ˈjuːnɪfɔːm/
update /ˈʌpdeɪt/
verb /vɜːb/
video clip /ˈvɪdiəʊ klɪp/
villa /ˈvɪlə/
viral /ˈvaɪrəl/
vlog, vlogger /vlɒg, ˈvlɒgə/
vlogging /ˈvlɒgɪŋ/
voucher /ˈvaʊtʃə/
webcode /ˈwebˌkəʊd/
website /ˈwebˌsaɪt/
whiteboard /ˈwaɪtˌbɔːd/
wild /waɪld/
windsurfing /ˈwɪnˌsɜːfɪŋ/
workshop /ˈwɜːkˌʃɒp/

Übersicht über in diesem Buch verwendete Arbeitsanweisungen

Adapt your CV.	Passe deinen Lebenslauf an.
Add further information/more examples/statements to your checklist/your opinion.	Füg weitere Informationen/Beispiele/Aussagen zu deiner Checkliste/deine Meinung hinzu.
Add the correct preposition/missing figures.	Füg die richtige Präposition/fehlenden Zahlen hinzu.
Add to it during the project.	Ergänzt es während des Projekts.
Agree on five ideas/one aspect/three reasons why ...	Einigt euch auf fünf Ideen/einen Aspekt/drei Gründe, warum ...
Answer his or her questions in German.	Beantworte seine oder ihre Fragen auf Deutsch.
Ask each other what you would do in certain situations.	Fragt euch gegenseitig, was ihr in bestimmten Situationen tun würdet.
Ask for feedback.	Bitte um Rückmeldung.
Ask questions about ...	Stellt Fragen über ...
Ask someone to edit your text or dialogue.	Bitte jemanden, deinen Text oder Dialog zu bearbeiten.
Be prepared for questions and feedback.	Seid auf Fragen und Feedback vorbereitet.
Bring it to school.	Bring es mit zur Schule.
Change these sentences into passive sentences.	Verändere diese Sätze zu Passivsätzen.
Check whether ...	Überprüft, ob ...
Check your definitions/explanations/letter/lists/notes/phrases.	Überprüf deine Definitionen/Erklärungen/deinen Brief/deine Listen/Notizen/Ausdrücke.
Choose a picture/word from the box/another text/one aspect.	Wähl ein Bild/ein Wort aus dem Kasten/einen anderen Text/einen Aspekt aus.
Choose one of the tasks/the one you like best/your favourite authors.	Sucht euch eine der Aufgaben aus/das aus, das euch am besten gefällt/einen eurer Lieblingsautoren aus.
Choose the correct preposition from the box for each phrase.	Wähl die richtige Präposition aus dem Kasten für jeden Ausdruck.
Collect arguments for or against .../examples.	Sammle Argumente für oder gegen .../Beispiele.
Collect ideas and arguments/information/keywords and statements/reasons.	Sammle Ideen und Argumente/Informationen/Schlüsselwörter und Äußerungen/Gründe.
Collect reasons why ...	Sammle Gründe, warum ...
Come up with five ideas.	Denkt euch fünf Ideen aus.
Comment on them.	Kommentiere sie.
Compare the bar chart/your answers/ideas/list/notes/summary/table/your clusters in class.	Vergleicht das Balkendiagramm/eure Antworten/Ideen/Liste/Notizen/Zusammenfassung/Tabelle/eure Cluster in der Klasse.
Complete the following sentences/your notes.	Vervollständige die folgenden Sätze/eure Notizen.
Consider issues such as data and privacy protection.	Denkt über Themen wie Datenschutz und Privatsphäreschutz nach.
Consider the past and the present.	Denk an die Vergangenheit und die Gegenwart.
Continue ...	Führe ... fort.
Copy the cluster/lists/table.	Schreib das Cluster/die Listen/Tabelle ab.
Correct the wrong sentences.	Verbessere die falschen Sätze.
Create a crossword puzzle.	Mach ein Kreuzworträtsel.
Create a dialogue.	Denk dir einen Dialog aus.
Create an action plan.	Erstellt einen Aktionsplan.
Decide if ...	Entscheidet euch, ob ...
Decide on a statement that you want to discuss.	Entscheidet euch für eine Aussage, über die ihr diskutieren wollt.
Decide on the aspects you want to focus on/the best words to fill the gaps.	Entscheidet euch, auf welche Aspekte ihr euch konzentrieren wollt/für die besten Wörter, um die Lücken zu füllen.
Describe ...	Beschreib ...
Design your own piece of anti-war graffiti.	Entwirf dein eigenes Anti-Kriegs-Graffiti.
Discover more on the inside covers of your book.	Entdecke mehr auf den Einbandinnenseiten eures Buchs.
Discuss in small groups/your findings.	Diskutiert in Kleingruppen/eure Ergebnisse.
Display your statements.	**Hängt eure Aussagen aus.**
Do a class survey/computer presentation/role play.	Mach eine Umfrage/Computerpräsentation/ein Rollenspiel.

Words

Do the activities together/the gallery walk/quiz.	Macht die Aktivitäten zusammen/den Galeriegang/das Quiz.
Don't mention its name.	Erwähne seinenNamen nicht.
Draw a picture.	Zeichnet ein Bild.
Draw something that symbolises …	Zeichne etwas, das … symbolisiert.
Edit his or her summary/your texts.	Bearbeite seine oder ihre Zusammenfassung/deine Texte.
Explain it in English/the term in German.	Erklär es auf Englisch/den Begriff auf Deutsch.
Explain what …/why …	Erklär, was …/warum …
Fill in …	Trag … ein.
Fill in the gaps.	Füll die Lücken aus.
Fill in the information while you read.	Trag die Informationen ein, während du liest.
Find all the phrases you could use for a cover letter.	Finde alle Ausdrücke, die du für ein Anschreiben benutzen könntest.
Find help in your workbook.	Finde in deinem Arbeitsheft Hilfe.
Find other people in class who are working on the same topic as you.	Finde andere Leute in der Klasse, die am gleichen Thema wie du arbeiten.
Find out about …	Finde etwas über … heraus.
Find out how …/if you were right.	Finde heraus, wie …/ob du Recht hattest.
Find out in what historical context the quote was made.	Finde heraus, in welchem historischen Kontext das Zitat gemacht wurde.
Find out more about …	Finde mehr über … heraus.
Find the odd one out in each group.	Finde in jeder Gruppe das Wort, das nicht zu den anderen passt.
Find the places on the map.	Finde die Orte auf der Karte.
Find your own way of presenting it to the class.	Finde deine eigene Art, wie du es der Klasse präsentieren kannst.
Get into a group with classmates who want to work on the same topic as you.	Kommt in einer Gruppe mit Klassenkameraden/Klassenkameradinnen zusammen, die dasselbe Thema bearbeiten wollen wie du.
Get together in small groups.	Kommt in Kleingruppen zusammen.
Give a presentation to the class.	Halte der Klasse eine Präsentation.
Give a summary on …	Mach eine Zusammenfassung von …
Give each other feedback on content and language.	Gebt einander Rückmeldung zu Inhalt und Sprache.
Give reasons.	Gib Gründe an.
Give shorts answers.	Gebt kurze Antworten.
Give the main ideas.	Gib die Hauptideen wieder.
Give the other groups feedback.	Gebt den anderen Gruppen Feedback.
Go back to …/online.	Geh zurück zu …/online.
Guess which one it is.	Ratet, welches es ist.
Have a discussion in class.	Diskutiert in der Klasse.
Help each other with anything you don't understand.	Helft einander mit allem, was ihr nicht versteht.
Identify …	Identifiziere …
Imagine …	Stell dir vor, …
Inform each other about …	Informiert einander über …
Interview …	Befrage …
Invite your visitors to react to your statement.	Ladet eure Besucher/Besucherinnen ein, auf eure Aussagen zu reagieren.
Keep the above information in mind while you plan and write.	**Behalte die oben gegebenen Informationen im Gedächtnis, während du planst und schreibst.**
Keep your application folder for future use.	Behalte deine Bewerbungsmappe für zukünftigen Gebrauch.
Let your partner gues which app it is.	Lass deinen Partner/deine Partnerin raten, welche App es ist.
Listen to the five people/tour guides.	Hör den fünf Leuten/Reiseleitern/Reiseleiterinnen zu.
Listen to the interview/news report/song.	Hör dir das Interview/die Nachrichtenmeldung/das Lied an.
Listen to the sales pitch.	Hört euch das Verkaufsgespräch an.
Look at … for help.	Sieh dir … zur Hilfe an.
Look at layout, language and content.	Sieh dir Aufbau, Sprache und Inhalt an.

Look for …	Such nach …
Look through the three topics in this Theme.	Sieh durch die drei Themen in diesem Kapitel.
Make a fact file / list of keywords / list of reasons.	Fertige einen Steckbrief / eine Liste mit Schlüsselwörtern / eine Liste mit Gründen an.
Make a word web / cue cards.	Erstell ein Wortnetz / Stichwortkarten.
Make notes.	Mach dir Notizen.
Make up your own statement.	Denk dir deine eigene Aussage aus.
Match … with / to …	Ordne … … zu.
Mill around.	Lauft umher.
Mime what you did.	Stell pantomimisch dar, was du gemacht hast.
Name at least three things / the activities.	Benenne mindestens drei Dinge / die Aktivitäten.
Pay attention to the tenses / verbs.	Achte auf die Zeiten / Verben.
Plan your dream trip to Australia.	Plant eure Traumreise nach Australien.
Play a guessing game.	Spielt ein Ratespiel.
Practise it with a partner.	Übt es mit einem Partner / einer Partnerin.
Practise reading out your text.	Üb, deinen Text laut vorzulesen.
Prepare a display / presentation / an interview.	Bereitet eine Ausstellung / Präsentation / ein Interview vor.
Present your dream trip / experience / findings / message.	Stellt eure Traumreise / Erfahrung / Ergebnisse / Botschaft vor.
Put a poster on the wall.	Hängt ein Poster an die Wand.
Put everything together in an attractive folder.	Leg alles in einer ansprechenden Mappe zusammen.
Put it on display in your classroom.	Stell es in deinem Klassenzimmer aus.
Put the parts in the correct places.	Setz die Teile an die richtigen Stellen.
Put the questions and the answers in reported speech.	Setz die Fragen und die Antworten in die indirekte Rede.
Put up the posters in the classroom.	Hängt die Poster im Klassenzimmer auf.
Put your plan into action.	Setzt euren Plan in die Tat um.
React to something you found interesting about him or her.	Reagier auf etwas, das du interessant an ihm oder ihr fandest.
Read … on page … again.	Lies … auf Seite … noch einmal.
Read about …	Lies über …
Read along.	Lies mit.
Read it in detail in your home group.	Lies ihn im Detail in deiner Ursprungsgruppe.
Read the article / blog / dialogue / following excerpt / lyrics / text.	Lies den Artikel / Blog / Dialog / folgenden Auszug / Liedtext / Text.
Read the brochure / definitions / email / film review / mini-saga / numbers and figures / quotes / sentences / statements / story.	Lies die Broschüre / Definitionen / Email / Filmkritik / Minisaga / Zahlen und Werte / Zitate / Sätze / Aussagen / Geschichte.
Read the sales pitch for a new everyday product with Internet access.	Lies das Verkaufsgespräch für ein neues Alltagsprodukt mit Internetzugang.
Record it.	Nehmt es auf.
Rehearse it.	Probt es.
Remember the time shift.	Denk an die Zeitverschiebung.
Remember to include the relevant information for the job you have chosen.	Denk daran, die wichtigen Informationen für den von dir gewählten Job einzubeziehen.
Repeat the numbers / words.	Wiederhole die Zahlen / Wörter.
Report them.	Gib sie wieder.
Report to the class.	Berichte der Klasse davon.
Research …	Recherchiere …
Retell the story.	Erzähl die Geschichte nach.
Rewrite it as an interview.	Schreib es als Interview um.
Rewrite lines … as a summary of what happens using the simple present.	Schreib die Zeilen … zu einer Zusammenfassung darüber um, was passiert, indem du die einfache Gegenwart benutzt.
Say why or why not.	Sag, warum oder warum nicht.
Script the audio feature.	Schreibt das Drehbuch zum Hörbeitrag.
Share the words and expressions that you as a group find most important with your class.	Teilt die Wörter und Ausdrücke mit eurer Klasse, die ihr als Gruppe am wichtigsten findet.

Words

Share your audio features/findings in a group.	Teilt eure Hörbeiträge/Ergebnisse in einer Gruppe.
Share your ideas about the picture in a silent discussion in written form.	Teilt eure Ideen über das Bild in einer stillen Diskussion in schriftlicher Form.
Show your message to …	Zeig … deine Nachricht.
Skim the five texts/job adverts.	Überfliege die fünf Texte/Stellenanzeigen.
Sort them from least risky to most risky.	Sortiere sie von am wenigsten riskant zu am riskantesten.
Sort them into two lists.	Sortiere sie in zwei Listen ein.
Start a wordbank for your topic.	Beginnt ein Wortfeld für euer Thema.
Stay in your topic groups or work as a class.	Bleibt in euren Themengruppen oder arbeitet als Klasse.
Suggest a route to see all the sights.	Schlag eine Route vor, um alle Sehenswürdigkeiten zu sehen.
Summarise the views.	Fasse die Ansichten zusammen.
Swap with a pair who worked on the other text.	Tauscht mit einem Paar, das an dem anderen Text gearbeitet hat.
Take notes about …	Macht euch Notizen über …
Take notes in a grid.	Mach dir in einem Raster Notizen.
Take time to get familiar with the topic.	Nimm dir Zeit, dich mit dem Thema vertraut zu machen.
Take turns.	Wechselt euch ab.
Talk about the statistics/your reactions.	Sprecht über die Statistik/eure Reaktionen.
Talk in class.	Redet in der Klasse darüber.
Tell him or her about it in German.	Erzähl ihm oder ihr auf Deutsch darüber.
Tell the class about the characters, setting, and plot.	Erzähl der Klasse von den Figuren, dem Schauplatz und der Handlung.
Think about …	Denkt über … nach.
Think of …	Denk an …
Think of a title.	Denk dir eine Überschrift aus.
Transcribe it.	Transkribiere es.
Try to summarise what happens.	Versucht zusammenzufassen, was passiert.
Turn to page …	Blätter um zu Seite …
Type in the webcode of your topic.	Tippt den Webcode eures Themas ein.
Unscramble the sentences.	Ordne die Sätze.
Use a dictionary to check the meaning of any of the words you don't know.	Benutz ein Wörterbuch, um die Bedeutung aller Wörter zu überprüfen, die du nicht kennst.
Use a dictionary to find out the meaning of words in the text that you find good to know.	Benutz ein Wörterbuch, um die Bedeutung von den Wörtern im Text herauszufinden, die deiner Meinung nach gut zu wissen sind.
Use a dictionary to look up words you cannot work out from the context.	Benutz ein Wörterbuch, um Wörter nachzuschlagen, die du dir nicht aus dem Kontext erschließen kannst.
Use reported speech/the given information/your CV.	Benutze die indirekte Rede/die gegebenen Informationen/deinen Lebenslauf.
Use your list of reasons from … to justify your opinion.	Benutz deine Liste mit Gründen aus …, um deine Meinung zu rechtfertigen.
Watch a film/the advert/the video clip.	Sieh dir einen Film/die Werbung/den Videoclip an.
Work on a concept for your app.	Arbeitet an einem Konzept für eure App.
Write a comment/dialogue/report.	Schreib einen Kommentar/Dialog/Bericht.
Write a cover letter/poem.	Schreib ein Anschreiben/Gedicht.
Write a definition for them in your own words in English/an explanation/a job advert/list of statements/postcard/short story/summary/to-do-list.	Schreib eine Definition für sie in deinen eigenen Worten auf Englisch/Erklärung/Stellenanzeige/Liste mit Aussagen/Postkarte/Kurzgeschichte/ Zusammenfassung/To-do-Liste.
Write a short text advertising …	Schreib einen kurzen Text, der Werbung für … macht.
Write about …	Schreib über …
Write as the person/your own CV.	Schreib als die Person/deinen eigenen Lebenslauf.
Write captions for the photos.	Schreib Bildunterschriften für die Fotos.
Write down …	Schreib… auf.
Write two more scrambled facts.	Schreib zwei weitere durcheinander gebrachte Sätze.
Write your own true or false sentences.	Schreib deine eigenen wahren oder falschen Sätze.

Numbers

0 oh, zero, nil /əʊ, 'zɪərəʊ, nɪl/
1 one /wʌn/
2 two /tuː/
3 three /θriː/
4 four /fɔː/
5 five /faɪv/
6 six /sɪks/
7 seven /sevn/
8 eight /eɪt/
9 nine /naɪn/
10 ten /ten/
11 eleven /ɪ'levn/
12 twelve /twelv/
13 thirteen /ˌθɜː'tiːn/
14 fourteen /ˌfɔː'tiːn/
15 fifteen /ˌfɪf'tiːn/
16 sixteen /ˌsɪks'tiːn/
17 seventeen /ˌsevn'tiːn/
18 eighteen /ˌeɪ'tiːn/
19 nineteen /ˌnaɪn'tiːn/
20 twenty /'twenti/
21 twenty-one /ˌtwenti'wʌn/
22 twenty-two /ˌtwenti'tuː/
30 thirty /'θɜːti/
33 thirty-three /ˌθɜːti'θriː/
34 thirty-four /ˌθɜːti'fɔː/
40 forty /'fɔːti/
45 forty-five /ˌfɔːti'faɪv/
50 fifty /'fɪfti/
56 fifty-six /ˌfɪfti'sɪks/
60 sixty /'sɪksti/
67 sixty-seven /ˌsɪksti'sevn/
70 seventy /'sevnti/
78 seventy-eight /ˌsevnti'eɪt/
80 eighty /'eɪti/
89 eighty-nine /ˌeɪti'naɪn/
90 ninety /'naɪnti/
100 a/one hundred /ə/wʌn 'hʌndrəd/
101 one hundred and one /wʌn ˌhʌndrəd‿ən 'wʌn/
102 one hundred and two /wʌn ˌhʌndrəd‿ən 'tuː/
110 one hundred and ten /wʌn ˌhʌndrəd‿ən 'ten/
200 two hundred /tuː 'hʌndrəd/

1,000 a/one thousand /ə/wʌn 'θauznd/
1,001 one thousand and one /wʌn ˌθauznd‿ən 'wʌn/
1,111 one thousand one hundred and eleven /wʌn ˌθauznd wʌn ˌhʌndrəd‿ən‿ɪ'levn/
2,000 two thousand /tuː 'θauznd/
10,000 ten thousand /ten 'θauznd/
100,000 a/one hundred thousand /ə/wʌn ˌhʌndrəd 'θauznd/
1,000,000 a/one million /ə/wʌn 'miljən/
1,000,000,000 a/one billion /ə/wʌn 'biljən/

1st first /fɜːst/
2nd second /'sekənd/
3rd third /θɜːd/
4th fourth /fɔːθ/
5th fifth /fɪfθ/
6th sixth /sɪksθ/
7th seventh /'sevnθ/
8th eighth /eɪtθ/
9th ninth /naɪnθ/
10th tenth /tenθ/
11th eleventh /ɪ'levnθ/
12th twelfth /twelfθ/
13th thirteenth /ˌθɜː'tiːnθ/
14th fourteenth /ˌfɔː'tiːnθ/
15th fifteenth /ˌfɪf'tiːnθ/
16th sixteenth /ˌsɪks'tiːnθ/
17th seventeenth /ˌsevn'tiːnθ/
18th eighteenth /ˌeɪ'tiːnθ/
19th nineteenth /ˌnaɪn'tiːnθ/
20th twentieth /'twentiəθ/
21st twenty-first /ˌtwenti'fɜːst/
22nd twenty-second /ˌtwenti'sekənd/
23rd twenty-third /ˌtwenti'θɜːd/

30th thirtieth /'θɜːtiəθ/
40th fortieth /'fɔːtiəθ/
50th fiftieth /'fɪftiəθ/
60th sixtieth /'sɪkstiəθ/
70th seventieth /'sevntiəθ/
80th eightieth /'eɪtiəθ/
90th ninetieth /'naɪntiəθ/
100th hundredth /'hʌndrədθ/

$\frac{1}{2}$ a/one half /ə/wʌn 'hɑːf/
$\frac{1}{3}$ a/one third /ə/wʌn 'θɜːd/
$\frac{1}{4}$ a/one quarter /ə/wʌn 'kwɔːtə/
$\frac{1}{8}$ a/one eighth /ə/wʌn‿'eɪtθ/
$\frac{3}{4}$ three quarters /θriː 'kwɔːtəz/

Months

January /'dʒænjuəri/	Januar	July /dʒʊ'laɪ/	Juli
February /'februəri/	Februar	August /'ɔːgəst/	August
March /mɑːtʃ/	März	September /sep'tembə/	September
April /'eɪprəl/	April	October /ɒk'təʊbə/	Oktober
May /meɪ/	Mai	November /nəʊ'vembə/	November
June /dʒuːn/	Juni	December /dɪ'sembə/	Dezember

Theme 1

I	down under *(informal)* /ˌdaʊn‿ˈʌndə/	Australien, Neuseeland	
	Australia /ɒˈstreɪliə/	Australien	*Australia* is a beautiful country.
	everyday /ˈevriˌdeɪ/	alltäglich, Alltags-	*everyday* = common or normal
	outback /ˈaʊtˌbæk/	Hinterland (Australiens)	
	read up on /ˌriːd‿ˈʌp‿ɒn/	sich informieren über	Dingos are very interesting *creatures*.
	toad /təʊd/	Kröte	
	creature /ˈkriːtʃə/	Kreatur, Lebewesen	

A1	What comes to mind when you think of Australia?	Was fällt dir ein, wenn du an Australien denkst?
	Discover more about Australia on the inside covers of your book.	Entdecke mehr über Australien auf den Einbandinnenseiten deines Buchs.
	Write down what you would like to find out about Australia.	Schreibt auf, was ihr gerne über Australien herausfinden würdet.
	Then put an 'Our questions about Australia' poster on the wall.	Hängt dann ein ‚Unsere Fragen über Australien'-Poster an die Wand.
	While working on the Theme, add your findings to the poster.	Während ihr das Kapitel bearbeitet, ergänzt eure Ergebnisse auf dem Poster.

A2	fascinating /ˈfæsɪneɪtɪŋ/	faszinierend	There are lots of *kangaroos* in Australia.
	kangaroo /ˌkæŋɡəˈruː/	Känguru	
	check out *(informal)* /ˌtʃek‿ˈaʊt/	sich etwas ansehen	
	be considered /ˌbiː kənˈsɪdəd/	gelten als	
	continent /ˈkɒntɪnənt/	Kontinent	
	at the same time /æt‿ðə ˌseɪm ˈtaɪm/	gleichzeitig	
	sail /seɪl/	segeln	
	mainland /ˈmeɪnˌlænd/	Festland	
	Australian /ɒˈstreɪliən/	Australier/in; australisch	This is the *Australian* flag.
	star /stɑː/	Stern	
	southern /ˈsʌðən/	südliche(r, s)	
	hemisphere /ˈhemɪˌsfɪə/	Halbkugel	
	compromise /ˈkɒmprəmaɪz/	Kompromiss	
	km (= kilometre) /ˈkɪləˌmiːtə/	Kilometer	
	royal /ˈrɔɪəl/	königlich	
	dialect /ˈdaɪəlekt/	Dialekt	
	indigenous /ɪnˈdɪdʒənəs/	einheimisch	*Christmas* is my favourite holiday.
	Christmas /ˈkrɪsməs/	Weihnachten	
	flowering plant /ˌflaʊərɪŋ ˈplɑːnt/	Blütenpflanze, Zierpflanze	A *mammal* is an animal that is not born from an egg, but from its mother's body.
	mammal /ˈmæml/	Säugetier	

species *(pl)* /ˈspiːʃiːz/	Art, Spezies	
camel /ˈkæml/	Kamel	
roam /rəʊm/	umherstreifen, umherziehen	
desert /ˈdezət/	Wüste	It is very hot in the *desert*.
Saudi Arabia /ˌsaʊdi‿əˈreɪbiə/	Saudi-Arabien	
living /ˈlɪvɪŋ/	lebend	
organism /ˈɔːgəˌnɪzm/	Organismus	
outer space /ˌaʊtə ˈspeɪs/	Weltraum, Weltall	The film had a very *surprising* ending.
surprising /səˈpraɪzɪŋ/	überraschend	
idea /aɪˈdɪə/	*hier:* Ahnung	
A3 teenage /ˈtiːnˌeɪdʒ/	jugendlich, Teenager-	

Listen to the interview and find out why Becky speaks such good English.	Hör dir das Interview an und finde heraus, warum Becky so gut Englisch spricht.

G'day *(informal)* /gəˈdeɪ/	Tag, Hi	
mate /meɪt/	Freund/in; Kumpel	An *exchange student* goes to school in another country for some time.
Youthradio /ˈjuːθ ˌreɪdiəʊ/	Jugendradio	
exchange /ɪksˈtʃeɪndʒ/	Austausch-	

Listen again and take notes on what she liked about Australia and what she found most interesting.	Hör noch mal zu und mach dir Notizen darüber, was ihr an Australien gefallen hat und was sie am interessantesten fand.
Collect them in pairs and write them down.	Sammelt sie paarweise und schreibt sie auf.
What countries does she mention?	Welche Länder erwähnt sie?
Report to the class.	Berichte der Klasse davon.

A4 wildlife /ˈwaɪldˌlaɪf/	Tier- und Pflanzenwelt, Flora und Fauna	*wildlife* = animals and plants

Look at the photos from Becky's trip to Sydney.	Sieh dir die Fotos von Beckys Ausflug nach Sydney an.
Read Becky's blog entry.	Lies Beckys Blogeintrag.

trip /trɪp/	*hier:* Ausflug	
host family /ˈhəʊst ˌfæmli/	Gastfamilie	
camper trailer /ˈkæmpə ˌtreɪlə/	Wohnwagenabstellplatz	
spectacular /spekˈtækjʊlə/	atemberaubend, spektakulär	The view of the mountains was *spectacular*.
walk /wɔːk/	*hier:* Wanderung, Wanderweg	A *walk* is a short journey that you make on foot.
cliff /klɪf/	Klippe, Kliff	

swim *(no pl)* /swɪm/	Schwimmen	
ocean /ˈəʊʃn/	Ozean, Meer	The second biggest *ocean* is the Atlantic.
shark /ʃɑːk/	Hai	
be wrong /ˌbiː ˈrɒŋ/	sich irren	
picnic /ˈpɪknɪk/	Picknick	
spicy /ˈspaɪsi/	würzig, scharf	
Asian /ˈeɪʒn/	Asiat/in; asiatisch	
takeaway /ˈteɪkəˌweɪ/	Essen zum Mitnehmen	
though *(nachgestellt)* /ðəʊ/	jedoch	
vivid /ˈvɪvɪd/	anschaulich; leuchtend	
unique /juːˈniːk/	einzigartig	
opera /ˈɒprə/	Oper	
stunning /ˈstʌnɪŋ/	toll, fantastisch	
view /vjuː/	Ansicht, Meinung; Aussicht	I like your *view* of things. = I like your opinion. You have a fantastic *view* from the top of a mountain!
cuddly /ˌkʌdli/	knuddelig	
marsupial /mɑːˈsuːpiəl/	Beuteltier	
threatened /ˈθretnd/	bedroht	Wild tigers are *threatened* with extinction. 
invasive /ɪnˈveɪsɪv/	invasiv	
cane toad /ˈkeɪn təʊd/	Agakröte	
creepy /ˈkriːpi/	gruselig	
impact /ˈɪmpækt/	Auswirkung	Farming has a big *impact* on the environment.
biodiversity /ˌbaɪəʊdaɪˈvɜːsəti/	Artenvielfalt	
cane /keɪn/	Zuckerrohr	
grower /ˈgrəʊə/	Pflanzer/in	
South America /ˌsaʊθ‿əˈmerɪkə/	Südamerika	
beetle /ˈbiːtl/	Käfer	
crop /krɒp/	Ernte	
in case /ˌɪn ˈkeɪs/	für den Fall, dass	
entry /ˈentri/	Eintritt	 The museum has free *entry* on Wednesdays.
art gallery /ˈɑːt ˌgæləri/	Kunstgalerie	
New South Wales /ˌnjuː saʊθ ˈweɪlz/	Neusüdwales	
once in a lifetime /ˌwʌns‿ɪn‿ə ˈlaɪfˌtaɪm/	einmalig	
definitely /ˈdefnətli/	eindeutig, definitiv	
national park /ˌnæʃnl ˈpɑːk/	Nationalpark	
landscape /ˈlænˌskeɪp/	Landschaft	
Aboriginal /ˌæbəˈrɪdʒənəl/	austral. Ureinwohner/in; der Aboriginals	The didgeridoo is an *Aboriginal* instrument.
Switzerland /ˈswɪtsələnd/	Schweiz	
Great Barrier Reef /ˌgreɪt ˈbæriə riːf/	Großes Barriereriff	

	Take notes and compare with a partner.	Mach dir Notizen und vergleich mit einem Partner/einer Partnerin.
	What does Becky write about sights, places and wildlife in Australia?	Was schreibt Becky über Sehenswürdigkeiten, Orte und die Tier- und Pflanzenwelt in Australien?
	Choose one aspect and write a comment.	Wähl einen Aspekt aus und schreib einen Kommentar.
A5	Unscramble the sentences and write them down.	Ordne die Sätze und schreib sie auf.
A6	Find out more about an Australian city or animal and report to the class.	Finde mehr über eine australische Stadt oder ein australisches Tier heraus und berichte der Klasse davon.
	Find out more about one of the animals that threaten biodiversity in Australia.	Finde mehr über eines der Tiere heraus, die die Artenvielfalt in Australien bedrohen.
	Christmas on the beach: write a poem, a short story or a dialogue.	Weihnachten am Strand: Schreib ein Gedicht, eine Kurzgeschichte oder einen Dialog.

A7	tram /træm/	Straßenbahn, Tram	
	multicultural /ˌmʌltiˈkʌltʃərəl/	multikulturell	Manchester is a very *multicultural* city.
	run *(irr)* /rʌn/	*hier:* fließen	There is too much traffic in the *city centre*.
	city centre /ˌsɪti ˈsentə/	Innenstadt	
	local /ˈləʊkl/	Ortsansässige/r, Heimische/r	
	seaside /ˈsiːˌsaɪd/	(Meeres)küste, Meer	 A banana is a *type* of fruit.
	type /taɪp/	Art	
	guided /ˈɡaɪdɪd/	geführt	
	talk /tɔːk/	Gespräch; Vortrag	
	coral reef /ˌkɒrəl ˈriːf/	Korallenriff	
	extend /ɪkˈstend/	sich erstrecken	
	be made up of /biː ˌmeɪd‿ˈʌp‿əv/	zusammengesetzt sein aus	The Union Jack flag is *made up of* three colours.
	colony /ˈkɒləni/	Kolonie	
	billion /ˈbɪljən/	Milliarde	
	holy /ˈhəʊli/	heilig	
	tribe /traɪb/	Stamm	
	sandstone /ˈsænˌstəʊn/	Sandstein	
	visitor /ˈvɪzɪtə/	Besucher/in	
	respect /rɪˈspekt/	respektieren	
	rainforest /ˈreɪnˌfɒrɪst/	Regenwald	
	wave (at/to sb) /weɪv/	jdm zuwinken	
	sanddune /ˈsænddjuːn/	Sanddüne	She found the *perfect* gift for her mum.
	perfect /ˈpɜːfɪkt/	perfekt	
	wild /waɪld/	Wildnis	
	whale /weɪl/	Wal	

Words

cruise /kruːz/	Kreuzfahrt	
rainwater /ˈreɪnˌwɔːtə/	Regenwasser	

Suggest a route to see all the sights.	Schlag eine Route vor, um alle Sehenswürdigkeiten zu sehen.

route /ruːt/	Strecke, Route	
A8 **settle** /ˈsetl/	sich niederlassen; sich einigen	After moving from country to country, his family finally *settled* in France.
Asia /ˈeɪʒə/	Asien	
Aborigine /ˌæbəˈrɪdʒəni/	(austral.) Ureinwohner/in	
drive *(irr)* /draɪv/	treiben, vertreiben	
introduce /ˌɪntrəˈdjuːs/	*hier:* einschleppen	
Dutch /dʌtʃ/	holländisch, niederländisch	
explorer /ɪkˈsplɔːrə/	Forscher/in	
Tasmania /tæzˈmeɪniə/	Tasmanien	
name /neɪm/	(be)nennen	to *name* = to give a name to
claim /kleɪm/	Anspruch erheben auf	The settlers *claimed* the land as British *territory*.
territory /ˈterətri/	Gebiet, Territorium	
captain /ˈkæptɪn/	Kapitän/in; Mannschaftsführer/in	
fleet /fliːt/	Flotte	
overcrowded /ˌəʊvəˈkraʊdɪd/	überfüllt	
report /rɪˈpɔːt/	Bericht	A *sheep farmer* works with sheep. 
sheep farmer /ˈʃiːp ˌfɑːmə/	Schafzüchter/in	
wool /wʊl/	Wolle	
turn into /ˌtɜːn‿ˈɪntʊ/	umwandeln in	
educate /ˈedjʊkeɪt/	ausbilden, unterrichten	
erase /ɪˈreɪz/	auslöschen	I'm going to *replace* the old poster in my room with a new one.
identity /aɪˈdentɪti/	Identität	
replace /rɪˈpleɪs/	ersetzen	
South Australia /ˌsaʊθ‿ɒˈstreɪliə/	Südaustralien	
Western Australia /ˌwestən‿ɒˈstreɪliə/	Westaustralien	
form /fɔːm/	bilden	
commonwealth /ˈkɒmənwelθ/	Staat, Republik	52 countries *form* the *commonwealth*.
independent /ˌɪndɪˈpendənt/	unabhängig	*independent* = ruled by its own government rather than by another country
only /ˈəʊnli/	erst	
vote /vəʊt/	*hier:* Wahlrecht; wählen, abstimmen	
election /ɪˈlekʃn/	Wahl	People *vote* in an *election* for a government to represent them. 
prime minister /ˌpraɪm‿ˈmɪnɪstə/	Premierminister	
wrong /rɒŋ/	Unrecht	

past /pɑːst/	Vergangenheit	
speech /spiːtʃ/	Rede	

A9
Make notes on what you learn about … — Mach dir Notizen darüber, was du über … erfahren hast.
Texts about historical facts often make use of the passive. — Texte über historische Fakten benutzen oft das Passiv.

prison /ˈprɪzn/	Gefängnis	

Write down the sentences with the passive forms. — Schreib die Sätze mit den Passivformen auf.
Pay attention to the tenses. — Achte auf die Zeiten.

make a living /ˌmeɪk‿ə ˈlɪvɪŋ/	seinen Lebensunterhalt verdienen	He *makes a living* selling fruit.
refugee /ˌrefjʊˈdʒiː/	Flüchtling	
unknown /ʌnˈnəʊn/	unbekannt	
so far /ˈsəʊ fɑː/	bisher	
policy /ˈpɒləsi/	Programm; Politik	
discrimination /dɪˌskrɪmɪˈneɪʃn/	Diskriminierung, Benachteiligung	
P1 Practice matters. /ˌpræktɪs ˈmætəz/	*etwa:* Übung macht den Meister.	
P2 young /jʌŋ/	Junge	
along /əˈlɒŋ/	vorwärts	
hind /haɪnd/	Hinter-	
punish /ˈpʌnɪʃ/	bestrafen	If you do something against the law, you *will be punished*, sometimes with *imprisonment*.
imprisonment /ɪmˈprɪznmənt/	Gefängnisstrafe	

P3
Unscramble the sentences. — Ordne die Sätze.

population /ˌpɒpjʊˈleɪʃn/	Bevölkerung	

Write two more scrambled facts for your partner. — Schreib zwei weitere durcheinander gebrachte Sätze für deinen Partner/deine Partnerin.

P4 police force /pəˈliːs fɔːs/	Polizei	
export /ˈekspɔːt/	exportieren	*export* ≠ import
bathing suit /ˈbeɪðɪŋ suːt/	Badeanzug	
Aussie *(informal)* /ˈɒzi/	Australier/in; australisch	A *convict* can't walk around freely.
convict /ˈkɒnvɪkt/	Sträfling	

P5
Listen to the words and repeat them. — Hör dir die Wörter an und wiederhol sie.

introduce /ˌɪntrəˈdjuːs/	einführen	

P6

slip – slop – slap /ˌslɪp slɒp ˈslæp/	*Name einer austral. Gesundheitskampagne*	
cancer /ˈkænsə/	Krebs	*'Cancer'* is the word for a serious illness.

It tells Australians and tourists how to protect their skin from too much sun.	Es zeigt Australiern/Australierinnen und Touristen/Touristinnen, wie man die Haut vor zu viel Sonne schützen kann.

slip on /ˌslɪp‿ˈɒn/	anziehen	When you ride a motorbike, you should wear *protective clothing*.
protective clothing /prəˌtektɪv ˈkləʊðɪŋ/	Schutzkleidung	
slop on *(informal)* /ˈslɒp‿ɒn/	schütten; *hier:* großzügig auftragen	
sunscreen /ˈsʌnˌskriːn/	Sonnenschutzmittel	
water-resistant /ˌwɔːtərɪˈzɪstənt/	wasserbeständig	
slap on *(informal)* /ˈslæp‿ɒn/	draufklatschen	
protect /prəˈtekt/	schützen	
seek *(irr)* /siːk/	suchen	
shade /ʃeɪd/	Schatten	
slide on *(informal)* /ˈslaɪd‿ɒn/	*hier:* aufsetzen	
B1 background /ˈbækˌgraʊnd/	Hintergrund	
nationality /ˌnæʃəˈnæləti/	Nationalität	

Zwei in einem Wort
Manchmal wirst du auf Wörter stoßen, deren einzelne Bestandteile dir bereits bekannt sind. Dann kannst du die Bedeutung längerer Wörter mühelos erraten, z. B.:
wheelchair = wheel + chair
spaceship = space + ship
housework = house + work

Why do you think people leave their home countries to move to Australia? Take notes and talk to a partner.	Warum, denkst du, verlassen Menschen ihre Heimatländer, um nach Australien umzuziehen? Mach dir Notizen und sprich mit einem Partner/einer Partnerin.

non- /nɒn/	nicht	When you buy something, you *own* it.
own /əʊn/	besitzen	
surfing /ˈsɜːfɪŋ/	Surfen	Refugees have to *leave* their homes *behind*.
leave behind /ˌliːv bɪˈhaɪnd/	zurücklassen	
torn /tɔːn/	hin- und hergerissen	
advantage /ədˈvɑːntɪdʒ/	Vorteil	
accent /ˈæksnt/	Akzent	

Use the given information and your imagination.	Benutz die gegebenen Informationen und deine Fantasie.
B2 Look at the pie chart.	Sieh dir das Kreisdiagramm an.

pie chart /ˈpaɪ tʃɑːt/	Kreisdiagramm	
diagram /ˈdaɪəgræm/	Diagramm	People *mainly* speak English in an *English-speaking* country.
mainly /ˈmeɪnli/	hauptsächlich	

in fact /ɪn ˈfækt/	tatsächlich, in Wirklichkeit	
English-speaking /ˈɪŋɡlɪʃ‿ˌspiːkɪŋ/	englischsprachig	*New Zealand* is an *English-speaking* country.
New Zealand /nju ˈziːlənd/	Neuseeland	
Indonesia /ˌɪndəʊˈniːʒə/	Indonesien	
Italy /ˈɪtəli/	Italien	*Italy* is a European country.
France /frɑːns/	Frankreich	
Greece /ɡriːs/	Griechenland	

Repeat the numbers and practise reading them with a partner.	Wiederhol die Zahlen und üb mit einem Partner/einer Partnerin, sie zu lesen.

third /θɜːd/	Drittel
fifth /fɪfθ/	Fünftel
tenth /tenθ/	Zehntel

Which figures and words go together?	Welche Zahlen und Wörter passen zusammen?
Now talk about the statistics.	Sprecht nun über die Statistik.

statistics *(pl)* /stəˈtɪstɪks/	Statistik

B3

Think of language, culture, immigration policy, ...	Denk an Sprache, Kultur, Einwanderungspolitik, ...
How does she feel about being an Aborigine today?	Wie findet sie es, in der heutigen Zeit ein Aborigine zu sein?
Make notes of what you learn about Aboriginal culture.	Mach dir Notizen darüber, was du über die Kultur der Aborigines erfährst.

Dreamtime /ˈdriːmˌtaɪm/	*zentraler Begriff der Aborigine-Mythologie, etwa: Traumzeit*
descendant /dɪˈsendənt/	Nachkomme
BC (= before Christ) /ˌbiː ˈsiː, bɪˌfɔː ˈkraɪst/	v. Chr. (= vor Christus); *hier: Wortspiel mit Bezug auf die Ankunft Cooks in Australien*
pop *(informal)* /pɒp/	Paps, Papa
nana *(informal)* /ˈnænə/	Oma
blackfella *(informal)* /ˈblækˌfelə/	*austral. Ureinwohner/in*
dreaming story /ˈdriːmɪŋ ˌstɔːri/	*Traumzeitgeschichte*
rainbow /ˈreɪnbəʊ/	Regenbogen
serpent /ˈsɜːpənt/	Schlange
wipe out /ˌwaɪp‿ˈaʊt/	auslöschen
all but /ˈɔːl bʌt/	*hier:* fast komplett

Achtung! Der Begriff *‚blackfella'* gilt als abwertend oder sogar beleidigend, wenn er von Nicht-Aborigines verwendet wird. Nur die Aborigines selber verwenden ihn untereinander, ohne ihn als beleidigend anzusehen.

rainbow

citizen /ˈsɪtɪzn/	Bürger/in	
recently /ˈriːsntli/	vor Kurzem, neulich	
passport /ˈpɑːspɔːt/	(Reise)pass	My *passport* is still valid.
mail /meɪl/	Post	
plenty of /ˈplenti‿əv/	reichlich, genug	
educational /ˌedjʊˈkeɪʃnəl/	Bildungs-, pädagodisch	
opportunity /ˌɒpəˈtjuːnəti/	Gelegenheit; Chance, Möglichkeit	*opportunity* = chance
as /əz/	weil, da	
related /rɪˈleɪtɪd/	verbunden; verwandt	

B4

Fill in the gaps with the simple past forms of the correct verbs.	Füll die Lücken mit den Vergangenheitsformen der richtigen Verben aus.

canoe /kəˈnuː/	Kanu	
raft /rɑːft/	Floß	
ice age /ˈaɪs‿eɪdʒ/	Eiszeit	
sea level /ˈsiː ˌlevl/	Meeresspiegel	
sink *(irr)* /sɪŋk/	sinken	
isolated /ˈaɪsəˌleɪtɪd/	isoliert, einsam; abgelegen	
hunt /hʌnt/	jagen	A lion has to *hunt* to get food.
berry /ˈberi/	Beere	
fish /fɪʃ/	fischen, angeln	The bears *have been fishing*.
pick /pɪk/	aussuchen; pflücken, sammeln	
bury /ˈberi/	begraben; vergraben	
destruction /dɪˈstrʌkʃn/	Zerstörung	
official, officially /əˈfɪʃl, əˈfɪʃli/	offiziell	

B5

Listen to the CD and check your sentences.	Hör dir die CD an und überprüf deine Sätze.
Read the lyrics.	Lies den Liedtext.

dusty /ˈdʌsti/	staubig	
the plains *(pl)* /ðə ˈpleɪnz/	Flachland	
ancient /ˈeɪnʃnt/	alt, antik	
keeper /ˈkiːpə/	Inhaber/in, Wärter/in	
flame /fleɪm/	Flamme	*Flames* are very hot.
upon /əˈpɒn/	auf, an	
rocky /ˈrɒki/	felsig	
shore /ʃɔː/	Küste, Ufer	
bind *(irr)* /baɪnd/	binden, fesseln	
iron /ˈaɪən/	Eisen	
chain /tʃeɪn/	Kette	
cure /kjʊə/	heilen	People go to hospitals to have their illnesses *cured*.
endure /ɪnˈdjʊə/	ertragen	

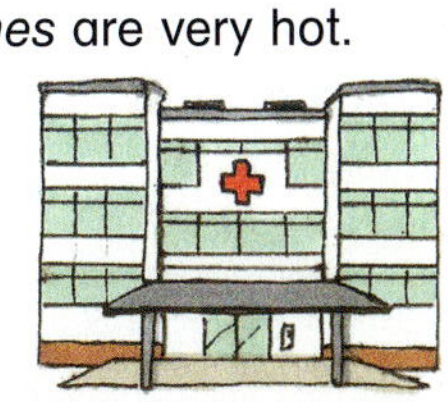

lash /læʃ/	Peitsche	
the rains *(pl)* /ðə ˈreɪnz/	Regenzeit	
dry /draɪ/	trocken	*dry* ≠ wet
barren /ˈbærən/	unfruchtbar	
run /rʌn/	*hier:* Land	
digger /ˈdɪgə/	(Gold)gräber/in	
seek *(irr)* /siːk/	suchen, streben nach	
mother lode /ˈmʌðə ləʊd/	*hier:* Goldader	
depression /dɪˈpreʃn/	Wirtschaftskrise	
bushy /ˈbʊʃi/	Hinterwäldler/in	
battler /ˈbætlə/	Kämpfer/in	
chorus (*pl* choruses) /ˈkɔːrəs, ˈkɔːrəsɪz/	Refrain	He has a nice *voice* when he sings.
voice /vɔɪs/	Stimme	
teller /ˈtelə/	Erzähler/in	
ghostly /ˈgəʊsli/	geisterhaft, gespenstisch	
gum /gʌm/	Gummibaum	‚Waltzing Matilda' ist wohl das bekannteste Volkslied Australiens, das die Geschichte eines Wanderarbeiters erzählt.
on the run /ˌɒn ðə ˈrʌn/	auf der Flucht	
waltz Matilda /ˌwɔːls məˈtɪldə/	*umherreisen auf der Suche nach Arbeit*	
plain /pleɪn/	Ebene	
valley /ˈvæli/	Tal	
drown /draʊn/	ertränken, überfluten	
flood /flʌd/	überschwemmen	*Valleys* are at risk of *flooding*.
spirit /ˈspɪrɪt/	Geist; Stimmung	
B6 rabbit-proof fence /ˌræbɪt ˌpruːf ˈfens/	*Schutzzaun in Westaustralien, der gezogen wurde, um die Ausbreitung von Kaninchen auf Ackerland zu vermeiden*	The *running time* of a film is the amount of time that it takes to watch the film.
running time /ˈrʌnɪŋ taɪm/	Laufzeit	
cast /kɑːst/	Besetzung	
rating /ˈreɪtɪŋ/	Bewertung	
PG (= parental guidance) /ˌpiː ˈdʒiː, pəˌrentl ˈgaɪdəns/	nicht jugendfrei	It is against the *law* to sell alcohol to under 18s.
law /lɔː/	Gesetz, Recht	
state /steɪt/	*hier:* festlegen	
mixed /mɪkst/	gemischt	
snatch /snætʃ/	schnappen	
native /ˈneɪtɪv/	beheimatet; einheimisch	
settlement /ˈsetlmənt/	Siedlung	
internment camp /ɪnˈtɜːnmənt kæmp/	Internierungslager	
mile /maɪl/	Meile	A marathon is 26.2 *miles*.
make one's way /ˌmeɪk wʌnz ˈweɪ/	sich seinen/ihren Weg bahnen	

hostile /ˈhɒstaɪl/	feindselig, *hier:* gefährlich
wire /ˈwaɪə/	Draht
fence /fens/	Zaun
cross /krɒs/	*hier:* durchqueren
illustrate /ˈɪləstreɪt/	illustrieren
location /ləʊˈkeɪʃn/	Lage; Standort
official /əˈfɪʃl/	Amtsperson; Beamte/Beamtin
whose /huːz/	dessen
camp /kæmp/	*hier:* Lager
surprisingly /səˈpraɪzɪŋli/	überraschenderweise
sensitive /ˈsensətɪv/	verständnisvoll
evil /ˈiːvl/	böse
misguided /mɪsˈgaɪdɪd/	fehlgeleitet
determined /dɪˈtɜːmɪnd/	entschlossen
verdict /ˈvɜːdɪkt/	Urteil
schmaltz *(informal)* /ʃmɔːlts/	Schmalz
terrific /təˈrɪfɪk/	großartig, fantastisch
moving /ˈmuːvɪŋ/	bewegend
recent /ˈriːsnt/	jüngste(r, s), letzte(r, s)

Their holiday home is in the perfect *location*.

evil = morally wrong or bad, wicked

He is *determined* to learn Spanish.

terrific = great, amazing, super

recent = not long ago

What difficulties could they encounter?	Welchen Schwierigkeiten könnten sie begegnen?
Why does the reviewer say that most Australians would probably prefer to forget this part of their history?	Warum sagt der Kritiker/die Kritikerin, dass es die meisten Australier/Australierinnen wahrscheinlich bevorzugen würden, diesen Teil ihrer Geschichte zu vergessen?
B7 Why are some of the children sent to a 'proper' school?	Warum werden manche der Kinder auf eine ‚richtige' Schule geschickt?
On their long way home the girls meet some strangers.	Auf ihrem langen Weg nach Hause treffen die Mädchen einige Fremde.
How do they react?	Wie reagieren sie?
Molly, her mother, her grandmother, Daisy and Gracie have a special relationship.	Molly, ihre Mutter, ihre Großmutter, Daisy und Gracie haben eine besondere Beziehung.
Do you think that the ending is happy or not?	Glaubst du, dass das Ende glücklich ist oder nicht?
B8 Watch the video clip and listen to the main part of his speech.	Sieh dir den Videoclip an und hör dir den Hauptteil seiner Rede an.
Read the following excerpt from Rudd's speech.	Lies den folgenden Auszug aus Rudds Rede.
Use a dictionary to look up words you cannot work out from the context.	Benutz ein Wörterbuch, um Wörter nachzuschlagen, die du dir nicht aus dem Kontext erschließen kannst.

turn a page /ˌtɜːn‿ə ˈpeɪdʒ/	*hier:* ein neues Kapitel aufschlagen

right /raɪt/ — *hier:* wiedergutmachen
move forward /ˌmuːv‿ˈfɔːwəd/ — vorrücken
confidence /ˈkɒnfɪdns/ — Vertrauen, Zuversicht — *confidence* = belief that you are able to do things well
successive /səkˈsesɪv/ — aufeinanderfolgend
parliament /ˈpɑːləmənt/ — Parlament
inflict /ɪnˈflɪkt/ — zufügen
profound /prəˈfaʊnd/ — tief
grief /griːf/ — Trauer
suffering /ˈsʌfərɪŋ/ — Leiden
fellow /ˈfeləʊ/ — Mitbürger/in
removal /rɪˈmuːvl/ — Umzug; Beseitigung
Torres Strait Islander /ˌtɒrɪs‿ˌstreɪt‿ˈaɪləndə/ — der Torres Strait Insulaner

Since the death of her rabbit she has been struggling with *profound grief*.

hurt /hɜːt/ — Schmerz
break up /ˌbreɪk‿ˈʌp/ — zerstören
indignity /ɪnˈdɪgnəti/ — Demütigung
degradation /ˌdegrəˈdeɪʃn/ — Erniedrigung
thus /ðʌs/ — so, diese Weise
people *(pl)* /ˈpiːpl/ — Volk
respectful /rɪˈspektfl/ — respektvoll
request /rɪˈkwest/ — um etwas bitten
apology /əˈpɒlədʒi/ — Entschuldigung
receive /rɪˈsiːv/ — *hier:* entgegennehmen
healing /ˈhiːlɪŋ/ — Heilung

B9

Find out what Uluru (Ayers Rock) means to the Aborigines and present your findings.	Finde heraus, was Uluru (Ayers Rock) für die Aborigines bedeutet und präsentiere deine Ergebnisse.
Bindi mentions the story of the Rainbow serpent.	Bindi erwähnt die Geschichte von der Regenbogenschlange.
Aborigines have many interesting traditions.	Aborigines haben viele interessante Traditionen.
Find out more about one or more of the following topics: their music, art, symbols, 'songlines'.	Finde mehr über eins oder mehrere der folgenden Themen heraus: ihre Musik, Kunst, Symbole, ‚Liedzeilen'.

songline /ˈsɒŋlaɪn/ — *Begriff aus der Aborigine-Kultur*

Prepare a display or a short presentation.	Bereite eine Ausstellung oder eine kurze Präsentation vor.

display /dɪˈspleɪ/ — *hier:* Ausstellung
B10 station *(AusE)* /ˈsteɪʃn/ — große Farm
subject /ˈsʌbdʒɪkt/ — Thema
re /riː/ — betrifft, Betreff

The bakery has a delicious *display* of cakes.

Words

G'day *(AusE, informal)* /gəˈdeɪ/	Tag, hi	
mate *(informal)* /meɪt/	Kumpel, Freund/in	*mate* = friend
How're you going? *(AusE, informal)* /ˌhaʊəjə ˈgəʊɪŋ/	Wie geht es dir?	
earlier /ˈɜːliə/	vorhin	
attach /əˈtætʃ/	befestigen, verbinden, *hier:* anfügen	
in the back of beyond /ˌɪn ðə ˌbæk‿əv bɪˈjɒnd/	am Ende der Welt	
boarding school /ˈbɔːdɪŋ skuːl/	Internat	
complete /kəmˈpliːt/	*hier:* absolvieren	
by /baɪ/	*hier:* per	
separate /ˈsepəreɪt/	trennen	
interaction /ˌɪntərˈækʃn/	Interaktion	
broadcast /ˈbrɔːdˌkɑːst/	Übertragung, Sendung	*broadcast*
program *(AusE)* /ˈprəʊgræm/	Programm	
secondary student /ˈsekəndri ˌstjuːdnt/	*Schüler/in einer weiterführenden Schule*	Mobile phones allow us to keep in touch, *no matter where* you are in the world.
no matter where /nəʊ ˌmætə ˈweə/	wo auch (immer)	
studies *(pl)* /ˈstʌdis/	Studium	
back then /ˌbæk ˈðen/	damals	*back then* = at that time
high frequency /haɪ ˈfriːkwənsi/	Hochfrequenz-	
transceiver /trænˈsiːvə/	Sende- und Empfangsgerät	to *enable* = to give someone the ability or opportunity to do something
enable /ɪnˈeɪbl/	ermöglichen	
class /klɑːs/	hier: (Unterrichts)stunde	
interactive /ˌɪntərˈæktɪv/	interaktiv	
broadband /ˈbrɔːdˌbænd/	Breitband	
satellite /ˈsætəlaɪt/	Satellit	
network /ˈnetˌwɜːk/	Netzwerk	
cover /ˈkʌvə/	*hier:* abdecken	
web /web/	Netz	He usually *responds* to his emails within a day.
respond /rɪˈspɒnd/	antworten; reagieren	
real time /ˌrɪəl ˈtaɪm/	Echtzeit	
email /ˈiːmeɪl/	mailen	
interact /ˌɪntərˈækt/	interagieren, kommunizieren	
discussion /dɪˈskʌʃn/	Diskussion	They are having a *discussion* about their homework.
annual /ˈænjuəl/	jährlich, Jahres-	
sports carnival *(AusE)* /ˈspɔːts ˌkɑːnɪvl/	*Sportfest*	

for now /fə ˈnaʊ/ — für den Augenblick

What are the advantages of the new broadband satellite network?	Was sind die Vorteile des neuen Breitband-Satelliten-Netzwerks?
What are the similarities and differences for the students and for the teachers?	Was sind die Gemeinsamkeiten und Unterschiede für die Schüler/Schülerinnen und Lehrkräfte?
B11 If you could send a personal message to one of the people on pages 24 to 31, what would you say?	Wenn du eine persönliche Nachricht an einen der Menschen auf den Seiten 24 bis 31 schicken könntest, was würdest du sagen?
React to something you found interesting about him or her.	Reagier auf etwas, das du interessant an ihm oder ihr fandest.
Think about the contents of your message.	Denk über die Inhalte deiner Nachricht nach.
What is your emotional reaction to what the person experienced, said or did?	Was ist deine emotionale Reaktion auf das, was die Person erlebt, gesagt oder gemacht hat?
Decide on the type of message (email, letter, audio recording, video message, ...).	Entscheide dich für eine Art der Nachricht (Email, Brief, Audioaufnahme, Videonachricht, ...).
Show your message to a partner.	Zeig deine Nachricht einem Partner/einer Partnerin.
Give each other feedback on content and language.	Gebt einander Rückmeldung zu Inhalt und Sprache.
P8 Use the simple past.	Verwende die einfache Vergangenheit.

taste /teɪst/ — Geschmack

P9 With a partner, read the numbers and figures in the box.	Lies mit einem Partner/einer Partnerin die Zahlen und Werte im Kasten.
Take turns.	Wechselt euch ab.
P12 Play a guessing game with a partner.	Spielt ein Ratespiel mit einem Partner/einer Partnerin.
Your partner has to guess it as fast as possible.	Dein Partner/Deine Partnerin muss es so schnell wie möglich raten.

figure /ˈfɪgə/ — Zahl, Wert

Use words from the box and create a crossword puzzle.	Verwende Wörter aus dem Kasten und mach ein Kreuzworträtsel.

A2 Theme 2

I meeting ground /ˈmiːtɪŋ graʊnd/	Begegnungsort	The skatepark is our *meeting ground*.
glacier /ˈglæsiə/	Gletscher	
adventurous /ədˈventʃrəs/	abenteuerlich; risikofreudig	
take a quiz /ˌteɪk‿ə ˈkwɪz/	ein Quiz machen	
A1 **extreme sport** /ɪkˈstriːm spɔːt/	Extremsportart	*Extreme sports* can be very dangerous.
skateboarding /ˈskeɪtbɔːdɪŋ/	Skateboardfahren	

> Look at the photos and name the different activities. — Sieh dir die Fotos an und benenne die verschiedenen Aktivitäten.

mountain biking /ˈmaʊntɪn ˌbaɪkɪŋ/	Mountainbike fahren	
BMXing /ˌbiː‿em‿ˈeksɪŋ/	BMX-Rad fahren	
paragliding /ˈpærəˌglaɪdɪŋ/	Gleitschirmfliegen	
scooter /ˈskuːtə/	Roller	
snowboarding /ˈsnəʊˌbɔːdɪŋ/	Snowboardfahren	
skydiving /ˈskaɪˌdaɪvɪŋ/	Fallschirmspringen	
skiing /ˈskiːɪŋ/	Skifahren	He loves *skiing*.
bouldering /ˈbəʊldərɪŋ/	Bouldern	
white-water rafting /ˌwaɪtwɔːtə ˈrɑːftɪŋ/	Wildwasserrafting	
indoor climbing /ˌɪndɔː ˈklaɪmɪŋ/	Hallenklettern	
kayaking /ˈkaɪækɪŋ/	Kajakfahren	
kite surfing /ˈkaɪt ˌsɜːfɪŋ/	Lenkdrachensegeln	
fairly /ˈfeəli/	ziemlich, recht	
hard /hɑːd/	schwierig	The pupils found the test *fairly hard*.
fall over /ˌfɔːl‿ˈəʊvə/	(um)fallen; *hier:* hinfallen	
be on a high *(informal)* /ˌbiː‿ɒn‿ə ˈhaɪ/	*hier:* einen Adrenalinstoß haben	
trick /trɪk/	Trick, Kunststück	

> Would you like to try out one of these sports or even do one on a regular basis? — Würdest du gerne eine dieser Sportarten ausprobieren oder sogar eine regelmäßig ausüben?

that's why /ˈðæts ˌwaɪ/ — deshalb

> A2 Do the quiz with a partner and write down your answers. — Mach das Quiz mit einem Partner/einer Partnerin und schreib deine Antworten auf.

daredevil /ˈdeəˌdevl/	Draufgänger/in	
chicken /ˈtʃɪkɪn/	*hier:* Angsthase	
daring /ˈdeərɪŋ/	kühn, wagemutig	He *texts* his girlfriend every day. 
break down /ˌbreɪk ˈdaʊn/	liegen bleiben	
text /tekst/	eine SMS schreiben	
give a lift /ˌɡɪv‿ə ˈlɪft/	mitnehmen	
grab /ɡræb/	sich schnappen	
take a rain check *(informal)* /ˌteɪk‿ə ˈreɪn tʃek/	verschieben	
amusement park /əˈmjuːzmənt pɑːk/	Freizeitpark	
scary /ˈskeəri/	Furcht erregend, unheimlich	
roller coaster /ˈrəʊlə ˌkəʊstə/	Achterbahn	We went on the *scariest ride* in the park.
ride /raɪd/	Fahrt	
sailing /ˈseɪlɪŋ/	Segeln	
the Netherlands /ðə ˈneðələndz/	die Niederlande	If you like being *outdoors*, then camping is ideal.
outdoor /ˌaʊtˈdɔː/	draußen, im Freien	
paraglide /ˈpærəˌɡlaɪd/	Paragliding machen	
sunbathe /ˈsʌnˌbeɪð/	sonnenbaden	
get a tan /ˌɡet‿ə ˈtæn/	braun werden	
snorkelling /ˈsnɔːklɪŋ/	Schnorcheln	
sealife /ˈsiːlaɪf/	*hier:* Unterwasserwelt	
high rope course /ˈhaɪ rəʊp ˌkɔːs/	Hochseilgarten	
choice /tʃɔɪs/	Auswahl	*choice* = selection
survival /səˈvaɪvl/	Überleben	
work out /ˌwɜːk‿ˈaʊt/	errechnen, ausarbeiten	
score /skɔː/	Punktestand	
A3 danger /ˈdeɪndʒə/	Gefahr	A red flag signals *danger*.

Why do people seek danger for fun?	Warum suchen Leute zum Spaß Gefahr?

for sure *(informal)* /fə ˈʃɔː/	ganz sicher, bestimmt

Read the article.	Lest den Artikel.
Compare your ideas with the ideas from the text.	Vergleicht eure Ideen mit den Ideen aus dem Text.

since /sɪns/	da, weil	
human /ˈhjuːmən/	Mensch	*human* = person
naturally /ˈnætʃrəli/	natürlich	
programme /ˈprəʊɡræm/	programmieren	
major /ˈmeɪdʒə/	*hier:* groß	*major* = important or great
risk /rɪsk/	Risiko, Gefahr	

understandable /ˌʌndəˈstændəbl/	verständlich	*understandable* = easy to understand
unnatural /ʌnˈnætʃrəl/	unnatürlich	
take a risk /ˌteɪk‿ə ˈrɪsk/	ein Risiko eingehen	
sane /seɪn/	geistig gesund, normal	*sane* ≠ crazy 
nurture /ˈnɜːtʃə/	Erziehung	
trigger /ˈtrɪɡə/	auslösen	
physiological /ˌfɪziəˈlɒdʒɪkl/	physiologisch	
reaction /riˈækʃn/	Reaktion	What she said made no *sense* to him.
sense /sens/	Sinn; Gefühl	
heighten /ˈhaɪtn/	steigern, erhöhen, verstärken	
pupil /ˈpjuːpl/	Pupille	The *pupil* is a part of your eye.
dilate /daɪˈleɪt/	sich weiten	
heart rate /ˈhɑːt reɪt/	Pulsfrequenz	Your *heart rate increases* when you are excited.
increase /ɪnˈkriːs/	(an)steigen, zunehmen	
adrenaline /əˈdrenəlɪn/	Adrenalin	
hormone /ˈhɔːməʊn/	Hormon	*Adrenaline* is a *hormone*.
closely /ˈkləʊsli/	eng	
linked /lɪŋkt/	gekoppelt, verbunden	*linked* = related
release /rɪˈliːs/	Entlassung, Freigabe, *hier:* Entweichen	
dopamine /ˈdəʊpəmiːn/	Dopamin	
chemical /ˈkemɪkl/	Chemikalie	
euphoric /juːˈfɒrɪk/	euphorisch	
cope	zurechtkommen	
brain /breɪn/	Gehirn	
handle /ˈhændl/	bewältigen, regeln, behandeln	
relaxed /rɪˈlækst/	entspannt	
focused, focussed /ˈfəʊkəst/	fokussiert	
risk-taker /ˈrɪsk ˌteɪkə/	*risikofreudiger Mensch*	She is very *skilled* at her job. = She is very good at her job.
skilled /skɪld/	ausgebildet, geschickt	
assess /əˈses/	einschätzen	
capable /ˈkeɪpəbl/	fähig	
ongoing /ˈɒnˌɡəʊɪŋ/	laufende(r, s)	
intense /ɪnˈtens/	intensiv	*intense* = very great or extreme
preparation /ˌprepəˈreɪʃn/	Vorbereitung	
expert /ˈekspɜːt/	Experte/Expertin	
as well as /əz ˈwel‿əz/	ebenso wie	
influence /ˈɪnfluəns/	Einfluss	
cautious /ˈkɔːʃəs/	vorsichtig, achtsam	*cautious* = careful
sudden /ˈsʌdn/	plötzlich	
environmental /ɪnˌvaɪrənˈmentl/	Umwelt-	Pollution can cause *environmental change*.
change /tʃeɪndʒ/	Veränderung	

ease /iːz/	Leichtigkeit, Mühelosigkeit	
valuable /ˈvæljʊbl/	wertvoll	
society /səˈsaɪəti/	Gesellschaft	
human /ˈhjuːmən/	menschlich	
prosper /ˈprɒspə/	gedeihen	
novelty /ˈnɒvlti/	Neuheit, Neuartigkeit	
seeking /siːkɪŋ/	Suchen	
behaviour /bɪˈheɪvjə/	Benehmen, Verhalten	
advantageous /ˌædvənˈteɪdʒəs/	günstig, vorteilhaft	
explore /ɪkˈsplɔː/	erforschen, untersuchen	Which book did you use as your *source* of information?
source /sɔːs/	Quelle	
biological /ˌbaɪəˈlɒdʒɪkl/	biologisch	
craving /ˈkreɪvɪŋ/	heftiges Verlangen	
essential /ɪˈsenʃl/	unbedingt erforderlich, unverzichtbar	*essential* = completely necessary

What do you learn about risk-takers?	Was erfährst du über riskiofreudige Menschen?
Make notes.	Mach dir Notizen.

A4 **birthplace** /ˈbɜːθˌpleɪs/ — Geburtsort

The others guess which one it is.	Die anderen raten, welches es ist.
Match the sports with the descriptions and pictures.	Ordne die Sportarten den Beschreibungen und Bildern zu.

race /reɪs/	*hier:* heftig schlagen, rasen	
blood /blʌd/	Blut	
pump /pʌmp/	pumpen	
jet boating /ˈdʒet ˌbəʊtɪŋ/	Jetbootfahren	
caving /ˈkeɪvɪŋ/	Höhlenexpedition; *hier:* Höhlenerforschen	
above /əˈbʌv/	über	We are holidaying in the *countryside*.
countryside /ˈkʌntriˌsaɪd/	Landschaft	
drift /drɪft/	treiben, schweben	
parachute /ˈpærəˌʃuːt/	Fallschirm	
attraction /əˈtrækʃn/	Attraktion	
elastic /ɪˈlæstɪk/	elastisch, flexibel	
ankle /ˈæŋkl/	(Fuß)knöchel	
all around /ˌɔːl‿əˈraʊnd/	überall	
roll down /ˌrəʊl ˈdaʊn/	hinunterrollen, herunterrollen	
hill /hɪl/	Hügel	She is taking a photo of the *hills*.
water baby /ˈwɔːtə ˌbeɪbi/	*hier:* Wasserratte	
add in /ˌæd‿ˈɪn/	hinzufügen	

inner /ˈɪnə/	innere(r, s)	
caver /ˈkeɪvə/	Höhlensportler/in	
spelunker /spɪˈlʌŋkə/	Hobbyhöhlenforscher/in	
cave /keɪv/	Höhle	
float /fləʊt/	schwimmen, sich treiben lassen	
require /rɪˈkwaɪə/	brauchen; verlangen, erfordern	
abseiling /ˈæbseɪlɪŋ/	Abseilen	
keep one's eyes peeled for /ˌkiːp wʌnz‿ˌaɪz ˈpiːld fə/	Ausschau halten nach	
glow-worm /ˈgləʊ wɜːm/	Glühwürmchen	
flying fox /ˌflaɪɪŋ ˈfɒks/	*eine der schnellsten Stahlseilrutschen der Welt*	
experience /ɪkˈspɪəriəns/	erleben, kennenlernen	to *experience* = to live through something
canyon /ˈkænjən/	Schlucht	
zip-line /ˈzɪplaɪn/	Seilrutsche	
literally /ˈlɪtrəli/	(wort)wörtlich	
take one's breath away /ˌteɪk wʌnz ˈbreθ‿əˌweɪ/	jemandem den Atem rauben	
speed *(irr)* /spiːd/	sausen, flitzen	
be prepared /ˌbiː prɪˈpeəd/	vorbereitet sein auf	The pupils *were* not *prepared* for the surprise test.

Bilde das Gegenteil!
Man kann aus vielen Wörtern neue bilden, indem man eine Vorsilbe setzt, die die Bedeutung des Wortes ins Gegenteil verändert. Diese Vorsilben können sein: ‚un-', ‚im-', ‚in-' oder ‚ir-' z. B.

usual ≠ ***unusual***
possible ≠ ***impossible***
direct ≠ ***indirect***
regular ≠ ***irregular***

Which are too daring or dangerous for you? — Welche sind zu wagemutig oder gefährlich für dich?

A5 travel blog /ˈtrævl blɒg/ — Reiseblog

Collect words and phrases that you expect in the text. — Sammle Wörter und Ausdrücke, die du im Text erwartest.

kiwi, Kiwi /ˈkiːwiː/	*Vogel, Frucht und Spitzname für* Neuseeländer/in	*kiwi* = bird or fruit *Kiwi* or *kiwi* = person from New Zealand
icy /ˈaɪsi/	eisig (kalt)	
struggle /ˈstrʌgl/	sich abmühen, sich quälen	
speechless /ˈspiːtʃləs/	sprachlos	
west coast /ˌwest ˈkəʊst/	Westküste	
unforgettable /ˌʌnfəˈgetəbl/	unvergesslich	It was an *unforgettable* summer of fun for him.
life-changing /ˈlaɪf ˌtʃeɪndʒɪŋ/	lebensverändernd	
experienced /ɪkˈspɪəriənst/	erfahren	A *mountaineer* climbs high mountains.
mountaineer /ˌmaʊntɪˈnɪə/	Bergsteiger/in	
ice-climber /ˈaɪs ˌklaɪmə/	Eiskletterer/in	

hike /haɪk/	Wanderung	
helicopter /ˈhelɪˌkɒptə/	Hubschrauber, Helikopter	
heli-hike /ˈheli haɪk/	Heli-Wanderung	
book /bʊk/	buchen, reservieren	
ice axe /ˈaɪs‿æks/	Eispickel	
climbing /ˈklaɪmɪŋ/	Kletter-	
bottom /ˈbɒtəm/	Boden, Grund	
land /lænd/	landen	
set off /ˌset‿ˈɒf/	aufbrechen, auf den Weg machen	They *set off* on their adventure.
magical /ˈmædʒɪkl/	magisch	
ice /aɪs/	Eis	
stream /striːm/	(Berg)bach, Flüsschen	
truly /ˈtruːli/	wirklich, wahrhaftig	
surreal /səˈrɪəl/	surreal, (traumhaft-) unwirklich	
get lucky /ˌget ˈlʌki/	Glück haben	
glow /gləʊ/	leuchten, glühen	The eyes *glowed* in the dark.
pure /pjʊə/	rein, klar	
trickle /ˈtrɪkl/	sickern, tröpfeln	
clumsy /ˈklʌmzi/	ungeschickt, unbeholfen	
fail *(informal)* /feɪl/	*etwa:* Dumm gelaufen!	
freezing /ˈfriːzɪŋ/	frostig, eiskalt	
fill /fɪl/	füllen	Their basket *is filled* with food.
ice cube /ˈaɪs kjuːb/	Eiswürfel	
demanding /dɪˈmɑːndɪŋ/	anstrengend	
traverse /trəˈvɜːs/	*hier:* queren	to *traverse* = to cross
have the bug *(informal)* /ˌhæv ðə ˈbʌg/	jemanden hat es gepackt	

How does Liz express her enthusiasm and excitement about her adventure on the ice? Copy the table.	Wie drückt Liz ihren Enthusiasmus und ihre Aufregung über ihr Abenteuer auf dem Eis aus? Schreib die Tabelle ab.

adjective /ˈædʒɪktɪv/	Adjektiv	*Adjectives* describe nouns in a sentence.
exclamatory remark /ˌeksˌklæmətəri rɪˈmɑːk/	Ausruf	

Write a short text advertising heli-hiking.	Schreib einen kurzen Text, der Werbung für Heli-Hiking macht.
A6 Make a list of extreme sports. Sort them from least risky to most risky.	Erstell eine Liste von Extremsportarten. Sortiere sie von am wenigsten riskant zu am riskantesten.
What extreme sports can you do in your area? Give a presentation to the class.	Welche Extremsportarten kannst du in deiner Region machen? Halte der Klasse eine Präsentation.

Words

You could give a computer presentation.	Du könntest eine Computer-Präsentation halten.
Make your own quiz about extreme sports for the class.	Mach dein eigenes Quiz über Extremsportarten für die Klasse.

A7

whilst /waɪlst/	während	*whilst* = while
catastrophe /kəˈtæstrəfi/	Katastrophe	

Which environmental impacts do they talk about?	Über welche Auswirkungen auf die Umwelt reden sie?
How environmentally friendly are they?	Wie umweltfreundlich sind sie?

obvious, obviously /ˈɒbviəs, ˈɒbviəsli/	offensichtlich	
involve /ɪnˈvɒlv/	beinhalten, umfassen	Smoking is *harmful* to your health.
doubt /daʊt/	(be)zweifeln	
harmful /ˈhɑːmfl/	schädlich	
harmless /ˈhɑːmləs/	harmlos	
consume /kənˈsjuːm/	konsumieren; verbrauchen	
resource /rɪˈzɔːs/	Quelle, Ressource	The *distance* is the amount of space between things or people.
distance /ˈdɪstəns/	Distanz, Entfernung	
locally /ˈləʊkli/	am Ort, vor Ort	
habitat /ˈhæbɪtæt/	Lebensraum	

You can use the model texts and a dictionary for help.	Du kannst die Modelltexte und ein Wörterbuch zur Hilfe nehmen.

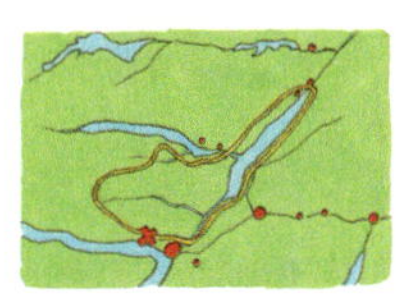

The X marks our *destination*.

She *made an effort* with her costume for the party.

go hiking /ˌgəʊ ˈhaɪkɪŋ/	wandern gehen
remote /rɪˈməʊt/	fern, abgelegen
protected /prəˈtektɪd/	geschützt
hiker /ˈhaɪkə/	Wanderer/Wanderin
destination /ˌdestɪˈneɪʃn/	Ziel
hiking /ˈhaɪkɪŋ/	Wandern
harm /hɑːm/	Schaden zufügen, schaden
downhill /ˈdaʊnhɪl/	Abfahrt
variation /ˌveərɪˈeɪʃn/	*hier:* Variante
resort /rɪˈzɔːt/	Urlaubsort
-consuming /kənˈsjuːmɪŋ/	verzehrend
giant /ˈdʒaɪənt/	Riese
manufacture /ˌmænjʊˈfæktʃə/	herstellen
make an effort /ˌmeɪk‿ən‿ˈefət/	sich bemühen
renewable /rɪˈnjuːəbl/	erneuerbar
carpooling /ˈkɑːpuːlɪŋ/	*Bildung einer Fahrgemeinschaft*
implement /ˈɪmplɪˌment/	einführen, umsetzen

	skier /ˈskiːə/	Skifahrer/in
	take to /ˈteɪk tʊ/	Gefallen finden an
	sustainable /səˈsteɪnəbl/	nachhaltig
	back country skiing /ˈbæk‿kʌntri ˌskiːɪŋ/	Skilanglauf
A8	sound /saʊnd/	gesund; vernünftig

They arrived home safe and *sound*.

Read the brochure and find out about the Outdoor Safety Code. — Lies die Broschüre und finde etwas über den Outdoor-Sicherheitscode heraus.

the great outdoors *(only pl)* /ðə ˌgreɪt‿aʊtˈdɔːz/	die freie Natur
multi- /mʌlti/	multi-, viel-
hut /hʌt/	Hütte
tent /tent/	Zelt
New Zealander /nju ˈziːləndə/	Neuseeländer/in
walker /ˈwɔːkə/	*hier:* Wanderer
paradise /ˈpærədaɪs/	Paradies
trail /treɪl/	Weg, Pfad
the outdoors *(only pl)* /ði‿ˌaʊtˈdɔːz/	Natur
coastal /ˈkəʊstl/	Küsten-
overnight stay /ˌəʊvəˈnaɪt steɪ/	Übernachtung
tramping /ˈtræmpɪŋ/	*neuseeländisch für Wandern*
well-equipped /ˌwel‿ɪˈkwɪpt/	gut vorbereitet
simple /ˈsɪmpl/	einfach, simpel
limit /ˈlɪmɪt/	(Höchst)grenze, Limit
sufficient /səˈfɪʃnt/	genug, ausreichend, genügend
supply /səˈplaɪ/	Vorrat

The island was *paradise* on earth.

The *speed limit* is 70 on this road.
sufficient = enough

Write five safety rules for a sport of your choice.
Think of rules to follow before doing the sport, whilst doing it and after doing it.
Explain your safety rules.

Schreib fünf Sicherheitsregeln für eine Sportart deiner Wahl.
Denk dir Regeln aus, die es vor, während und nach dem Ausüben des Sports zu befolgen gilt.
Erklär deine Sicherheitsregeln.

A9	rescue /ˈreskjuː/	Rettung

Listen to the report about a couple who went walking on the Routeburn Track, one of New Zealand's Great Walks. — Hört euch den Bericht über ein Paar an, das auf dem *Routeburn Track*, einer von Neuseelands größten Wanderwegen, gewandert ist.

Look at the Outdoor Safety Code in …	Seht euch den Outdoor-Sicherheitscode in … an.
Check whether the couple followed all the rules.	Überprüft, ob das Paar alle Regeln befolgt hat.
A10 You are going to give an oral presentation about a real or imaginary adventurous experience.	Ihr werdet eine mündliche Präsentation über eine tatsächliche oder eingebildete abenteuerliche Erfahrung halten.
This will form the basis of your presentation.	Dies wird die Grundlage eurer Präsentation bilden.
Practise reading out your text or talking about your experience.	Übt, euren Text zu präsentieren oder über eure Erfahrung zu sprechen.
Your voice and intonation should show your feelings, excitement, enthusiasm, and maybe relief or pride in the end.	Eure Stimme und Intonation sollten eure Gefühle, Aufregung, euren Enthusiasmus und vielleicht Erleichterung oder Stolz am Ende zeigen.
You could make a recording.	Ihr könntet eine Aufnahme machen.

harbour /ˈhɑːbə/	Hafen	
at first /ət ˈfɜːst/	zuerst	
punishment /ˈpʌnɪʃmənt/	Bestrafung, Strafe	
port /pɔːt/	Hafen	
crane /kreɪn/	Kran	
enthusiastic /ɪnˌθjuːziˈæstɪk/	enthusiastisch, begeistert	 The crowd was very *enthusiastic*.
that /ðæt/	so	
jump /dʒʌmp/	Sprung	
sway /sweɪ/	schwanken, sich wiegen	
tremble /ˈtrembl/	zittern, beben	
skydive /ˈskaɪˌdaɪv/	Fallschirmsprung	
go kayaking /ˌɡəʊ ˈkaɪækɪŋ/	Kajak fahren	 He *goes kayaking* every weekend.
go skydiving /ˌɡəʊ ˈskaɪˌdaɪvɪŋ/	Fallschirmspringen gehen	

P3

What does 'being adventurous' mean to you?	Was bedeutet es für dich, ‚risikofreudig' zu sein?
Share your sentences with a partner.	Teil deine Sätze mit einem Partner/einer Partnerin.

P4 preposition /ˌprepəˈzɪʃn/ — Präposition

Copy the phrases into your exercise book and add the correct preposition from the box.	Schreib die Ausdrücke in dein Heft ab und füg die richtige Präposition aus dem Kasten hinzu.

P5 active /ˈæktɪv/ — aktiv

P6

Ask questions about her adventure on the glacier and give short answers. — Stellt Fragen über ihr Abenteuer auf dem Gletscher und gebt kurze Antworten.

P7

sporty /ˈspɔːti/	sportlich	

Complete the sentences with the modal verbs in the box. — Vervollständige die Sätze mit den Modalverben im Kasten.

confident /ˈkɒnfɪdnt/	selbstsicher, selbstbewusst	
shy away /ʃaɪ‿əˈweɪ/	zurückschrecken vor, scheuen	She doesn't *shy away* from attention – she doesn't seem to feel uncomfortable.
scary /ˈskeəri/	unheimlich	
brave /breɪv/	mutig	
now and again /ˌnaʊ‿ən‿əˈgen/	ab und zu	
at heart /ˌæt ˈhɑːt/	im Grunde seines/ihres Herzens	
live on the edge /ˌlɪv‿ɒn ði‿ˈedʒ/	ein extremes Leben führen	A stuntman *is living on the edge*.

B1

What do you know about New Zealand? Which ones go together? — Was wisst ihr über Neuseeland? Welche passen zusammen?

legend /ˈledʒnd/	Legende	A *legend* is an old story.
geyser /ˈgiːzə/	Geysir	

B2

Polynesian /ˌpɒlɪˈniːziən/	polynesisch	

What skills do you need to survive a journey like this? — Welche Fähigkeiten braucht man, um so eine Reise zu überleben?

navigate /ˈnævɪgeɪt/	navigieren	
row /rəʊ/	rudern	

B3

Skim the two texts. Take notes in two colours: green for what you find important or interesting, and red for things you don't understand or have questions about. — Überflieg die zwei Texte. Mach dir Notizen in zwei Farben: grün für das, was du wichtig oder interessant findest, und rot für Dinge, die du nicht verstehst oder zu denen du Fragen hast.

current /ˈkʌrənt/	Strömung	A *current* is a strong movement of water.
homeland /ˈhəʊmˌlænd/	Heimat(land)	
Polynesia /ˌpɒlɪˈniːziə/	Polynesien	
South Pacific Ocean /ˌsaʊθ pəˌsɪfɪk‿ˈəʊʃn/	südpazifischer Ozean, Südpazifik	
similarity /ˌsɪməˈlærəti/	Ähnlichkeit, Parallele	There are a lot of *similarities* between Germany and the UK.

hunter /ˈhʌntə/	Jäger/in	
gatherer /ˈgæθərə/	Sammler/in	
grower /ˈgrəʊə/	Züchter/in	
expert /ˈekspɜːt/	erfahren, ausgezeichnet	
fisherman (*pl* fishermen) /ˈfɪʃəmən/	Fischer, Angler	
weave *(irr)* /wiːv/	weben, flechten	
fishing net /ˈfɪʃɪŋ net/	Fisch(er)netz	
carve /kaːv/	schnitzen, meißeln	
fish hook /ˈfɪʃ hʊk/	Angelhaken	
extinct /ɪkˈstɪŋkt/	ausgestorben	Dinosaurs are *extinct*.
cultivate /ˈkʌltɪveɪt/	anbauen	
sweet potato /ˌswiːt pəˈteɪtəʊ/	Süßkartoffel	
root /ruːt/	Wurzel	There were only vegetables in her shopping *basket*.
basket /ˈbaːskɪt/	Korb	
store /stɔː/	lagern	
storehouse /ˈstɔːˌhaʊs/	Warenhaus, Schatzkammer	
stilt /stɪlt/	Pfahl	They *signed* the Maastricht *treaty* in 1992.
treaty /ˈtriːti/	Vertrag, Abkommen	
sign /saɪn/	unterschreiben, unterzeichnen	
representative /ˌreprɪˈzentətɪv/	(Stell)vertreter/in	
secure /sɪˈkjʊə/	(ab)sichern	
subject /ˈsʌbdʒɪkt/	*hier:* Staatsbürger/in	
conflict /ˈkɒnflɪkt/	Konflikt	
the Second World War /ðə ˌsekənd ˌwɜːld ˈwɔː/	Zweiter Weltkrieg	
rural /ˈrʊərəl/	ländlich	
trend /trend/	Trend, Tendenz	
representation /ˌreprɪzenˈteɪʃn/	Vertretung; Darstellung	There is a protest to *raise awareness* about animal cruelty.
raise awareness /ˌreɪz‿əˈweənəz/	Bewusstsein schärfen	
problematic /ˌprɒbləˈmætɪk/	problematisch	
economic /ˌiːkəˈnɒmɪk/	wirtschaftlich	
prominent /ˈprɒmɪnənt/	deutlich sichtbar	
everyday life /ˌevrideɪ ˈlaɪf/	Alltag	
sight /saɪt/	sichten	
Southern /ˈsʌðən/	südliche(r, s)	
search for /ˈsɜːtʃ fɔː/	suchen nach	
annex /əˈneks/	annektieren, einverleiben	
mapmaker /ˈmæpˌmeɪkə/	Kartograph/in, Kartenhersteller/in	She is struggling with bags *full of* shopping.
full of /ˈfʊl‿əv/	voller	

Dinosaurs are *extinct*.

There were only vegetables in her shopping *basket*.

There is a protest to *raise awareness* about animal cruelty.

She is struggling with bags *full of* shopping.

misunderstanding /ˌmɪsʌndəˈstændɪŋ/	Missverständnis	
set foot on /ˌset ˈfʊt‿ɒn/	betreten	
unsuccessful /ˌʌnsəkˈsesfl/	erfolglos	
East India /ˌiːst‿ˈɪndiə/	ostindisch	
treasure /ˈtreʒə/	Schatz	*treasure* 
matter /ˈmætə/	Materie, Stoff	
cabin boy /ˈkæbɪn bɔɪ/	Schiffsjunge	
map /mæp/	kartografieren, eine Karte machen von	
whaler /ˈweɪlə/	Walfänger/in	A *whaler*'s job is to hunt whales.
sealer /ˈsiːlə/	Robbenfänger/in	
missionary /ˈmɪʃnri/	Missionar/in	
considerable /kənˈsɪdrəbl/	erheblich, beträchtlich	They ate a *considerable* amount of pizza. = They ate a lot of pizza.
trade /treɪd/	Geschäft machen, handeln	
gun /gʌn/	Waffe	
amongst /əˈmʌŋst/	unter, zwischen	
along with /əˈlɒŋ wɪð/	zusammen mit	*along with* = together with

Work with a partner who read the other text.	Arbeitet mit einem Partner/einer Partnerin, der/die den anderen Text gelesen hat.
Present your findings to one another.	Präsentiert einander eure Ergebnisse.
Swap with a pair who worked on the other text.	Tauscht mit einem Paar, das an dem anderen Text gearbeitet hat.

B4

Alps /ælps/	Alpen

Listen to the tour guides.	Hör den Reiseführern/Reiseführerinnen zu.

appealing /əˈpiːlɪŋ/	attraktiv, verlockend	
rolling /ˈrəʊlɪŋ/	sanft ansteigend	You call an area of land filled with trees *'woodland'*.
woodland /ˈwʊdlənd/	Waldgebiet	
agricultural /ˌægrɪˈkʌltʃrəl/	landwirtschaftlich	*produce* = fruit, vegetables and other things that farmers grow
produce *(pl)* /ˈprɒdjuːs/	Erzeugnisse, Produkte	
model /ˈmɒdl/	Modell	
diameter /daɪˈæmɪtə/	Durchmesser	
fiord /ˈfiːɔːd/	Fjord	
cover /ˈkʌvə/	*hier:* Dickicht, Unterholz	

B5

Correct the wrong sentences.	Verbessere die falschen Sätze.
Each group member chooses two texts.	Jedes Gruppenmitglied wählt zwei Texte.
Take notes about …	Macht euch Notizen über …

heritage /ˈherɪtɪdʒ/	Erbe	
roast lamb /ˌrəʊst ˈlæm/	Lammbraten	We eat *roast lamb* on Sundays.
seafood /ˈsiːˌfuːd/	Meeresfrüchte	
lolly /ˈlɒli/	Lolli, Lutscher	

bed and breakfast /ˌbed‿ən ˈbrekfəst/	Frühstückspension	Many people worship their *God* in a church. The national *anthem* of Great Britain is '*God* save the Queen'.
God (= god) /gɒd/	Gott	
defend /dɪˈfend/	verteidigen	
anthem /ˈænθəm/	Hymne	
common /ˈkɒmən/	üblich	
nowadays /ˈnaʊəˌdeɪz/	heutzutage	
relatively /ˈrelətɪvli/	relativ	

Inform each other about what you have found out about Kiwi culture.	Informiert einander darüber, was ihr über die neuseeländische Kultur herausgefunden habt.
New Zealand is not only often used as a film set, the country also produces many films.	Neuseeland wird nicht nur oft als Filmkulisse verwendet, das Land produziert auch viele Filme.

B6

set /set/	Drehort

Imagine you were an exchange student living with a Maori family.	Stell dir vor, du wärst ein Austauschschüler/eine Austauschschülerin, der/die bei einer Maori-Familie lebt.

exchange student /ɪksˈtʃeɪndʒ ˌstjuːdnt/	Austauschschüler/in

In their/your everyday life, what do you think would be influenced by Maori culture, what by Western culture?	Was, denkst du, wäre in ihrem/deinem Alltag von der Maori-Kultur beeinflusst, was von der westlichen Kultur?
What similarities and differences can you find between the Aborigines and the Maori?	Welche Ähnlichkeiten und Unterschiede kannst du zwischen den Aborigines und den Maori finden?
Consider the past and the present.	Denk an die Vergangenheit und die Gegenwart.

B7

sensitive /ˈsensətɪv/	empfindlich

You have just arrived in New Zealand and are travelling with someone who doesn't speak very much English.	Du bist gerade in Neuseeland angekommen und reist mit jemandem, der nicht viel Englisch spricht.
He wants to check whether he needs to declare any goods but he doesn't understand the poster.	Er möchte prüfen, ob er irgendwelche Waren verzollen muss, aber er versteht das Poster nicht.

declare /dɪˈkleə/	deklarieren, verzollen	*Goods* are things that are produced for sale.
goods *(pl)* /gʊds/	Waren	
guide /gaɪd/	Reiseführer	
overseas /ˈəʊvəsiːz/	Übersee-, aus Übersee	

dispose of /dɪˈspəʊz‿əv/	entsorgen	
border /ˈbɔːdə/	Grenze	The hurricane caused
pest /pest/	Schädling	considerable *damage* to the
damage /ˈdæmɪdʒ/	Schaden	town.

> Explain the term 'biosecurity'.
> Tip: Work with both parts of the word – 'bio' and 'security'.
>
> Erklär den Begriff ‚biosecurity'.
> Tipp: Arbeite mit beiden Teilen des Wortes – ‚bio' und ‚security'.

move /muːv/	umziehen	
moving company /ˈmuːvɪŋ ˌkʌmpni/	Umzugsfirma	
get in somebody /ˌget‿ˈɪn ˌsʌmbədi/	jemanden kommen lassen	
pack up /ˌpæk‿ˈʌp/	zusammenpacken	
bug /bʌg/	Wanze, Ungeziefer	Do you mind if I open the window?
mind /maɪnd/	etwas dagegen haben	
pack /pæk/	packen	
customs officer /ˈkʌstəmz‿ˌɒfɪsə/	Zollbeamter/in	
biosecurity (*no pl*) /ˈbaɪəʊsɪˌkjʊərəti/	*Sicherheitsvorkehrungen gegen biogene Probleme*	
rely on /rɪˈlaɪ‿ɒn/	*hier:* abhängen von	
natural /ˈnætʃrəl/	natürlich	*natural* = not produced by people
crop /krɒp/	*hier:* Feldfrucht	
B8 lingo *(informal)* /ˈlɪŋgəʊ/	Sprache, Jargon	
jandal /ˈdʒændl/	*neuseel. für Flip-Flop*	Another informal word for *'bro'* is 'mate'.
bro *(informal)* /brəʊ/	Bruder, Kumpel	
togs *(pl)* /tɒgz/	*austral./neuseel. für Schwimmsachen*	
kai *(informal)* /kaɪ/	*austral./neuseel. für Essen, Futter*	
sweet as *(informal)* /ˈswiːt‿əz/	super, klasse	
to the days *(informal)* /ˌtʊ ðə ˈdeɪz/	*nachgestellt:* sehr	
B9 audio feature /ˈɔːdiəʊ ˌfiːtʃə/	Hörbeitrag	

> In a group, you are going to create an audio feature on New Zealand.
> It should be a recording that lasts several minutes, in which you present different aspects about New Zealand.
>
> In einer Gruppe werdet ihr einen Hörbeitrag über Neuseeland erstellen.
> Es sollte eine Aufnahme sein, die einige Minuten lang dauert, in welcher du verschiedene Aspekte über Neuseeland vorstellst.

introduce /ˌɪntrəˈdjuːs/	einführen	
value /ˈvæljuː/	Wert	A *belief* is a strong feeling that
belief /bɪˈliːf/	Glaube	something is true.

Words

	consider /kən'sɪdə/	denken an, in Betracht ziehen	to *consider* = to think about

Share your ideas and findings (expert groups).	Teilt eure Ideen und Ergebnisse (Expertengruppen).
Script the audio feature.	Schreibt das Drehbuch zum Hörbeitrag.
Then rehearse it and finally record it.	Probt es dann und nehmt es schließlich auf.

P9	be keen on doing something /ˌbiː ˌkiːn‿ɒn 'duːɪŋ ˌsʌmθɪŋ/	etwas mit Begeisterung tun	
P10	heli-hiking /'heli ˌhaɪkɪŋ/	Heli-Wandern	

P11	Unscramble the sentences about the history of New Zealand.	Ordne die Sätze über die Geschichte Neuseelands.

	travel /'trævl/	*hier:* bereisen	

P12	Read the sentences and decide on the best word to fill the gaps.	Lies die Sätze und entscheide dich für das beste Wort, um die Lücken zu füllen.

	data security (*no pl*) /'deɪtə sɪˌkjʊərəti/	Datensicherheit, Datenschutz	
	biology /baɪ'ɒlədʒi/	Biologie	The study of *biology* is the study of living things.
	be based on /biː 'beɪst‿ɒn/	basieren auf	

Make your own sentences with gaps.	Bilde deine eigenen Sätze mit Lücken .

P13	word web /'wɜːd web/	Wortnetz	

	Copy the following word webs into your exercise book and complete them with information about New Zealand.	Schreib die folgenden Wortnetze in dein Heft ab und vervollständige sie mit Informationen über Neuseeland.
	Make it into a game: read words from one of your word webs to a partner.	Mach es zu einem Spiel: lies einem Partner/einer Partnerin Wörter aus einem deiner Wortnetze vor.
	How quickly can he or she work out which word web it is?	Wie schnell kann er oder sie sich erschließen, welches Wortnetz es ist?
P14	How many syllables do the following words have?	Wie viele Silben haben die folgenden Wörter?
	Copy and complete the table.	Schreib die Tabelle ab und vervollständige sie.
	In English the stress is always on one syllable.	Im Englischen ist die Betonung immer auf einer Silbe.
	Find the odd one out in each group (where the stress is on a different syllable).	Finde in jeder Gruppe das Wort, das nicht zu den anderen passt (bei dem die Betonung auf einer anderen Silbe liegt).

Theme 3

I off to work /ˌɒf tʊ ˈwɜːk/ — *hier:* auf zur Arbeit

A1 Play a guessing game. Describe or mime what you did. — Spielt ein Ratespiel. Beschreib oder stell pantomimisch dar, was du gemacht hast.

placement /ˈpleɪsmənt/	Stelle; *hier:* Praktikumsstelle	A *colleague* is someone you work with.
colleague /ˈkɒliːg/	Kollege/Kollegin	

A2 Skim the job adverts. — Überfliege die Stellenanzeigen.

childcare /ˈtʃaɪldˌkeə/	Kinderbetreuung	
opening /ˈəʊpnɪŋ/	*hier:* Möglichkeit	
anyone /ˈeniˌwʌn/	jede(r, s), (irgend)jemand	
gain experience /ˌgeɪn‿ɪkˈspɪəriəns/	Erfahrungen sammeln	to *gain experience* = to get experience
day care centre /ˈdeɪ keə ˌsentə/	*hier:* Kindertagesstätte	
private /ˈpraɪvət/	privat	A *diary* is very private.
household /ˈhaʊsˌhəʊld/	Haushalt	*Patience* is the ability to accept situations that you do not like without getting angry.
off /ɒf/	*hier:* frei	
patience /ˈpeɪʃns/	Geduld	
homestay /ˈhəʊmˌsteɪ/	*Aufenthalt in einer Gastfamilie*	
farmhand /ˈfɑːmˌhænd/	Landarbeiter/in	
Belgium /ˈbeldʒəm/	Belgien	*Belgium* is a European country.
worker /ˈwɜːkə/	Arbeiter/in	
strawberry /ˈstrɔːbri/	Erdbeere	The *quality* of something is how good or bad it is.
quality /ˈkwɒləti/	Qualität	
payment /ˈpeɪmənt/	Bezahlung, Vergütung	
piecework /ˈpiːsˌwɜːk/	Akkordarbeit	
basis /ˈbeɪsɪs/	Grundlage, Basis	
require somebody to do something /rɪˌkwaɪə ˌsʌmbədi tə ˈduː ˌsʌmθɪŋ/	von jemandem verlangen, etwas zu tun	
stamina /ˈstæmɪnə/	Durchhaltevermögen, Ausdauer	
working knowledge /ˌwɜːkɪŋ ˈnɒlɪdʒ/	Grundkenntnisse	
French /frentʃ/	Franzose/Französin; französisch	
provide /prəˈvaɪd/	zur Verfügung stellen	She *is providing* drink at the party.
mobile home /ˌməʊbaɪl ˈhəʊm/	Wohnwagen	

Words

form /fɔːm/ — Formular
animal shelter /ˈænɪml ˌʃeltə/ — Tierheim
Czech Republic /ˌtʃek riˈpʌblɪk/ — Tschechische Republik
homeless /ˈhəʊmləs/ — heimatlos, obdachlos
conscientious /ˌkɒnʃiˈenʃəs/ — gewissenhaft, pflichtbewusst — If you are *conscientious*, you work carefully and hard.
essential /ɪˈsenʃl/ — unbedingt erforderlich
required /riˈkwaɪəd/ — erforderlich
voluntary /ˈvɒləntri/ — freiwillig
board /bɔːd/ — *hier:* Verpflegung

How are these German phrases expressed in the adverts?	Wie werden diese deutschen Ausdrücke in den Anzeigen ausgedrückt?
Read the adverts again, take notes in a grid and add your opinion.	Lies die Anzeigen nochmal, mach dir in einem Raster Notizen und füg deine Meinung hinzu.

wage /ˈweɪdʒ/ — Lohn — The *wage* is an amount of money that you earn for working.
accommodation /əˌkɒməˈdeɪʃn/ — Unterkunft

Mill around and use your grid to talk to your classmates about the jobs.	Lauft umher und benutzt euer Raster, um mit euren Klassenkameraden/Klassenkameradinnen über die Jobs zu sprechen.

A3 career expert /kəˈrɪər‿ˌekspɜːt/ — Berufsberater/in
foreign /ˈfɒrɪn/ — ausländisch, fremd — *foreign* = from another country
A4 **CV (= curriculum vitae)** /ˌsiː ˈviː/ — Lebenslauf
surname /ˈsɜːˌneɪm/ — Nachname
address /əˈdres/ — Adresse
telephone /ˈtelɪˌfəʊn/ — Telefon
place of birth /ˌpleɪs‿əv ˈbɜːθ/ — Geburtsort
babysit /ˈbeɪbiˌsɪt/ — babysitten
on a regular basis /ˌɒn‿ə ˈregjʊlə ˌbeɪsɪs/ — regelmäßig
aged /eɪdʒd/ — alt
comprehensive school /kɒmprɪˈhensɪv skuːl/ — Gesamtschule
secondary school /ˈsekəndri skuːl/ — weiterführende Schule
primary school /ˈpraɪməri skuːl/ — Grundschule

Den richtigen Ton treffen
Im gesprochenen Englisch gibt es viele umgangssprachliche Wörter und Ausdrücke. Ihre Verwendung hängt sehr von der Situation und der Herkunft des Sprechers ab. Wenn du nicht weißt, ob ein Wort oder Ausdruck angemessen ist, benutze ihn lieber nicht. Verwende stattdessen ein Wort oder einen Ausdruck, der dir vertraut ist.

mother tongue /ˌmʌðə ˈtʌŋ/	Muttersprache	
competent /ˈkɒmpɪtənt/	fähig, kompetent	
word processing /ˈwɜːd ˌprəʊsesɪŋ/	Textverarbeitung	
creative /kriˈeɪtɪv/	kreativ	He is very *creative*.
assistant coach /əˌsɪstnt ˈkəʊtʃ/	Kotrainer/in	
reference /ˈrefrəns/	Referenz, Zeugnis	
on request /ˌɒn rɪˈkwest/	auf Anfrage	

A5

Then swap your CV with a partner and give each other feedback on information, spelling and layout.	Tausche dann deinen Lebenslauf mit einem Partner/einer Partnerin und gebt einander Feedback zu den Informationen, der Rechtschreibung und dem Layout.

A6

cover letter /ˈkʌvə ˌletə/	Anschreiben	You should send a *cover letter* with your *CV* when applying for jobs.
Dear Sir or Madam, ... /ˌdɪə ˌsɜːr‿ɔː ˈmædəm/	Sehr geehrte Damen und Herren, ... *(als Anrede in Briefen, wenn der Empfänger namentlich nicht bekannt ist)*	You start a formal letter with *'Dear Sir or Madam, ...'*.
mid-August /ˌmɪd‿ˈɔːgəst/	Mitte August	
babysitter /ˈbeɪbiˌsɪtə/	Babysitter/in	
listener /ˈlɪsnə/	Zuhörer/in	to *accompany* = to go with someone to a place or event
accompany /əˈkʌmpni/	begleiten	
musical /ˈmjuːzɪkl/	musikalisch, Musik-	
help out /ˌhelp‿ˈaʊt/	aushelfen	
mealtime /ˈmiːlˌtaɪm/	Essenszeit	The trainer always *motivates* them.
motivate /ˈməʊtɪveɪt/	motivieren	
set a positive example /ˌset‿ə ˌpɒzətɪv‿ɪgˈzɑːmpl/	mit gutem Beispiel vorangehen	
elementary education /elɪˌmentri‿edjʊˈkeɪʃn/	Elementarbildung, Grundschulausbildung	
enclose /ɪnˈkləʊz/	*hier:* beilegen, beifügen	
pleased /pliːzd/	erfreut, zufrieden	
mentor /ˈmentɔː/	Mentor/in	
referee /ˌrefəˈriː/	Referenz	
at any time /ət‿ˈeni taɪm/	jederzeit	At the end of a formal letter, write *'Yours faithfully'*.
yours faithfully /ˌjɔːz ˈfeɪθfli/	mit freundlichen Grüßen	

Look at layout, language and content.	Sieh dir Aufbau, Sprache und Inhalt an.

A8	conduct /kənˈdʌkt/	(durch)führen	

	Watch the video clip of Cara Hall, a career expert, giving advice to young people.	Sieh dir den Videoclip von Cara Hall, einer Berufsberaterin, an, in dem sie jungen Leuten Ratschläge gibt.
	Compare your notes with a partner and write down Cara Hall's tips.	Vergleich deine Notizen mit einem Partner/einer Partnerin und schreib dir Cara Halls Tipps auf.
A9	Write a job advert for an unusual job, for example an ice cream tester or working for 'Rent-a-friend'.	Schreibe eine Stellenanzeige für einen ungewöhnlichen Job, zum Beispiel als Eiscreme-Tester oder für ‚Miete dir einen Freund/eine Freundin'.
	Write a to-do list.	Schreib eine To-do-Liste.

	to-do list /tə ˈduː ˌlɪst/	To-do-Liste	
A10	go wrong /ˌɡəʊ ˈrɒŋ/	schiefgehen	

How do you think the woman will respond?	Wie wird die Frau deiner Meinung nach reagieren?
Present it to the class.	Stelle ihn der Klasse vor.

A11	**folder** /ˈfəʊldə/	Mappe, Schnellhefter, Ordner	Put the word web in your *folder*!

	You can look online, look in the book or you could even write your dream summer job advert yourself.	Du kannst online oder im Buch nachschauen, oder du könntest sogar eine Anzeige für deinen Traum-Sommerjob selbst schreiben.
	Use or adapt your CV from A5.	Benutze oder passe deinen Lebenslauf von A5 an.
	Write a cover letter.	Schreib ein Anschreiben.
	Swap your texts with a partner and give each other feedback.	Tausche deine Texte mit einem Partner/einer Partnerin und gebt einander Feedback.
	Put everything together in a nice looking folder and put it on display in your classroom.	Leg alles in einer ansprechenden Mappe zusammen und stell sie in deinem Klassenzimmer aus.
P1	Explain what you have to do.	Erklär, was du tun sollst.

P2	driving lesson /ˈdraɪvɪŋ ˌlesn/	Fahrstunde	

P3	Fill in 'will' or 'won't'.	Trag *‚will'* oder *‚won't'* ein.
P4	Your friend from England would like to get a summer job in Germany.	Dein Freund aus England hätte gern einen Sommerjob in Deutschland.
	You have found this job advert and want to let him know what it is about and how to apply.	Du hast diese Anzeige gefunden und möchtest ihn wissen lassen, worum es geht und wie er sich bewerben soll.

P5	driving license /ˈdraɪvɪŋ ˌlaɪsns/	Führerschein	
	emotion /ɪˈməʊʃn/	Emotion, Gefühl	*emotion* = feeling
P7	order /ˈɔːdə/	Reihenfolge	

The green parts of the sentences are in the wrong places.	Die grünen Teile der Sätze sind an den falschen Stellen.
Put the parts in the correct places and rewrite this letter of application.	Setz die Teile an die richtigen Stellen und schreib das Anschreiben neu.
B1 What do you spend your money on?	Wofür gibst du dein Geld aus?

spending power /ˈspendɪŋ ˌpaʊə/	Kaufkraft	
around /əˈraʊnd/	ungefähr	
chore /tʃɔː/	lästige Aufgabe, Hausarbeit	Taking the bins out is his least favourite *chore*.
save up /ˌseɪv‿ˈʌp/	sparen	
purchase /ˈpɜːtʃəs/	Kauf, Einkauf	
sneaker *(AE)* /ˈsniːkə/	Turnschuh	
sweet /swiːt/	Süßigkeit	
cookie /ˈkʊki/	Keks, Plätzchen	
chewing gum /ˈtʃuːɪŋ ˌgʌm/	Kaugummi	
extra /ˈekstrə/	zusätzlich	
possibility /ˌpɒsəˈbɪləti/	Möglichkeit	
gardening /ˈgɑːdnɪŋ/	Gartenarbeit, Gärtnern	
toy /tɔɪ/	Spielzeug	He *saved up* to buy a new *toy*.
jewellery *(no pl)* /ˈdʒuːəlri/	Schmuck	

Talk to a partner about what you find interesting or surprising.	Sprich mit einem Partner/einer Partnerin darüber, was du interessant oder überraschend findest.
Read the article again and compare the information with your situation.	Lies den Artikel nochmal und vergleich die Informationen mit deiner Situation.

mow /məʊ/	mähen	to *mow* the *lawn* = to cut grass with a machine
lawn /lɔːn/	Rasen	
do a paper round /ˌduː‿ə ˈpeɪpə ˌraʊnd/	Zeitungen austragen	

Talk to a partner and make notes.	Sprich mit einem Partner/einer Partnerin und mach dir Notizen.
B2 Read the statements.	Lies die Aussagen.

go round /ˌgəʊ ˈraʊnd/	*hier:* sich drehen	Family and friends are the *key* to *happiness*.
key /kiː/	Schlüssel	
happiness /ˈhæpinəs/	Glück; Zufriedenheit	

Words

Listen again and take notes. What are their views about money? Compare your notes with a partner.	Hör noch einmal zu und mach dir Notizen. Was sind ihre Ansichten über Geld? Vergleiche deine Notizen mit einem Partner/einer Partnerin.

save /seɪv/	sparen; aufheben	To *save* money, spend less!
treat /triːt/	behandeln	
money machine /ˈmʌni məˌʃiːn/	Bankautomat	
college /ˈkɒlɪdʒ/	Universität, College	
manage /ˈmænɪdʒ/	verwalten, organisieren	to *manage* = to organise

Jake would like to earn some extra money but his parents want him to focus on school instead.	Jake würde gern etwas zusätzliches Geld verdienen, aber seine Eltern wollen, dass er sich stattdessen auf die Schule konzentriert.
B3 A magazine asked different people about their working life satisfaction.	Eine Zeitschrift fragte verschiedene Leute nach ihrer Zufriedenheit mit ihrem Berufsleben.

rewarding /rɪˈwɔːdɪŋ/	befriedigend, dankbar	
stressful /ˈstresfl/	stressig, anstrengend	
India /ˈɪndiə/	Indien	
qualified /ˈkwɒlɪfaɪd/	qualifiziert, ausgebildet	*Nursing* can be a very *stressful* job.
nursing /ˈnɜːsɪŋ/	Krankenpflege, Pflege	
pay /peɪ/	Lohn	He loves his *profession* as a dentist.
live on /ˌlɪv‿ˈɒn/	leben von	
profession /prəˈfeʃn/	Beruf	
satisfied /ˈsætɪsfaɪd/	zufrieden	
shop assistant /ˈʃɒp‿əˌsɪstnt/	Verkäufer/in	
cash register /ˈkæʃ ˌredʒɪstə/	Registrierkasse	
stock /stɒk/	füllen, bestücken	
frustrating /ˈfrʌˌstreɪtɪŋ/	frustrierend	
high school *(AE)* /ˈhaɪ skuːl/	Highschool, weiterführende Schule	
retail /ˈriːteɪl/	Einzelhandel, Kleinhandel	
rude /ruːd/	unhöflich; primitiv	Using bad words is very *rude*.
holiday /ˈhɒlɪdeɪ/	*hier:* Feiertag	
be off /ˌbi‿ˈɒf/	*hier:* frei haben	
unfortunately /ʌnˈfɔːtʃnətli/	unglücklicherweise	
college education /ˈkɒlɪdʒ‿edjʊˌkeɪʃn/	Hochschulbildung, Hochschulstudium	
be stuck /ˌbiː ˈstʌk/	*hier:* feststecken, festhängen	
vocational school /vəʊˈkeɪʃnəl skuːl/	Berufsschule	She always wanted to be a doctor, *even though* she hates the sight of blood.
trade /treɪd/	Handwerk	
even though /ˌiːvn ˈðəʊ/	obwohl	

reconsider /ˌriːkən'sɪdə/	überdenken, neu erwägen	
underground /'ʌndəˌgraʊnd/	*hier:* unter der Erde	
diamond /'daɪəmənd/	Diamant	
driller /'drɪlə/	Bohrarbeiter/in	
search /sɜːtʃ/	suchen	
come up /'kʌm‿ʌp/	aufkommen	
helper /'helpə/	Helfer/in	
strength /streŋθ/	Kraft, Stärke	
period /'pɪəriəd/	Zeitspanne, Zeitraum	
stay in touch /ˌsteɪ‿ɪn 'tʌtʃ/	in Verbindung/Kontakt bleiben	*Cellphones* help us *stay in touch* with our friends.
via /'vaɪə/	über	
be in high demand /ˌbi‿ɪn ˌhaɪ dɪ'mɑːnd/	sehr gefragt sein	
all over the world /ˌɔːl‿ˌəʊvə ðə 'wɜːld/	auf der ganzen Welt	English is spoken *all over the world*.
end up *(informal)* /ˌend‿'ʌp/	schließlich landen	
sales rep *(informal)* /'seɪlz rep/	Vertreter/in	
straight /streɪt/	gerade(aus); direkt	
insurance /ɪn'ʃʊərəns/	Versicherung	
cellphone *(AE)* /'sel fəʊn/	Handy	
at the time /ˌæt‿ðə 'taɪm/	damals, zu dem Zeitpunkt	
benefit /'benɪfɪt/	Vorteil; *hier:* Sozialleistung	
security /sɪ'kjʊərəti/	Sicherheit	
challenging /'tʃælɪndʒɪŋ/	(heraus)fordernd	Teaching is a *challenging* job.
intelligence /ɪn'telɪdʒns/	Intelligenz	
potential /pə'tenʃl/	Potenzial	
advisor /əd'vaɪzə/	Berater/in, Ratgeber/in	
therefore /'ðeəfɔː/	deshalb, deswegen, daher	*therefore* = that's why
advertising /'ædvəˌtaɪzɪŋ/	Werbung, Werbebranche	

	Think of more reasons and add them to your list.	Denk dir weitere Gründe aus und füg sie deiner Liste hinzu.
	Think of working hours, pay and benefits, location, stress levels, …	Denk an Arbeitszeiten, Lohn und Sozialleistungen, Standort, Stress, …
	Make notes and talk to a partner.	Mach dir Notizen und sprich mit einem Partner/einer Partnerin.
B4	Read the texts in B3 again and report who said what.	Lies die Texte in … nochmal und berichte, wer was gesagt hat.
	Write it down.	Schreib es auf.
B5	Present your findings.	Stell deine Ergebnisse vor.
	Find out more about one of the jobs mentioned in … and report to the class.	Finde über einen der in … erwähnten Jobs mehr heraus und berichte der Klasse davon.
	Interview people about their worklife and present your findings.	Befrage Leute über ihr Berufsleben und präsentiere deine Ergebnisse.

Words

part-time /ˌpɑːt‿ˈtaɪm/ Teilzeit-

B6

Do you agree or disagree?	Stimmst du zu oder nicht?
Read it and find out what he says about vlogging.	Lies es und finde heraus, was er über *vlogging* sagt.

make one's living /ˌmeɪk wʌnz ˈlɪvɪŋ/	leben können von	
content /ˈkɒntent/	Inhalt, *hier:* Content	
constantly /ˈkɒnstəntli/	ständig, dauernd	*constantly* = all the time
little /ˈlɪtl/	*hier:* wenig	Die Begriffe ‚vlog' bzw. ‚vlogger' sind Kunstwörter aus ‚video' und ‚blog'.
vlog /vlɒg/	vloggen	
come out /ˈkʌm‿aʊt/	herauskommen; *hier:* sich outen	
gay /geɪ/	homosexuell	
lesbian /ˈlezbiən/	lesbisch	
bring in /brɪŋ/	*hier:* einbringen	
view /vjuː/	*hier:* Betrachtung, Klick	
fame /feɪm/	Ruhm	
subscriber /səbˈskraɪbə/	Abonnent/in	
entertain /ˌentəˈteɪn/	unterhalten	
achieve /əˈtʃiːv/	erreichen	TV should *entertain* the *viewers*.
viewer /ˈvjuːə/	Zuschauer/in	
react /riˈækt/	reagieren	
fanmail /ˈfænmeɪl/	Fanpost	
take up time /ˌteɪk‿ʌp ˈtaɪm/	Zeit beanspruchen	
process /ˈprəʊses/	Prozess, Verlauf	Be careful when you *upload* pictures to the Internet!
upload /ˈʌpˌləʊd/	laden, hochladen	
lens /lenz/	Objektiv, Linse	
lighting /ˈlaɪtɪŋ/	Beleuchtung	
tripod /ˈtraɪpɒd/	Stativ	
microphone /ˈmaɪkrəˌfəʊn/	Mikrofon	
needless to say /ˌniːdləs tə ˈseɪ/	selbstverständlich	
measure /ˈmeʒə/	messen	
supportive /səˈpɔːtɪv/	unterstützend	
encouraging /ɪnˈkʌrɪdʒɪŋ/	ermutigend	She is *passionate* about baking.
passionate /ˈpæʃnət/	leidenschaftlich	
continue /kənˈtɪnjuː/	fortführen, weitermachen	
inspired /ɪnˈspaɪəd/	inspiriert	
inspire /ɪnˈspaɪə/	inspirieren	
tool /tuːl/	Mittel, Instrument	
aspiring /əˈspaɪərɪŋ/	aufstrebend, ambitioniert	
first of all /ˌfɜːst‿əv‿ˈɔːl/	zuallererst	
consistent /kənˈsɪstənt/	beständig, gleich bleibend	
attention /əˈtenʃn/	Aufmerksamkeit	They were *disappointed* that they couldn't go to the beach.
disappointed /ˌdɪsəˈpɔɪntɪd/	enttäuscht	

case /keɪs/	Fall
hate /heɪt/	Hass
harassment /ˈhærəsmənt/	Belästigung, Schikane
take a toll on /ˌteɪk‿ə ˈtəʊl‿ɒn/	seinen/ihren Tribut fordern von
self-esteem /ˌself‿ɪˈstiːm/	Selbstwertgefühl
keep something in mind /ˌkiːp ˌsʌmθɪŋ‿ɪn ˈmaɪnd/	etwas im Gedächtnis behalten
folks *(informal)* /fəʊks/	Leute
cheers *(informal)* /tʃɪəz/	danke; tschüss
No worries. *(informal)* /ˈnəʊ ˌwʌriz/	Gern geschehen., Kein Problem.

Collect reasons and write them down.	Sammle Gründe und schreib sie auf.
Money vs. job satisfaction – summarise John's views and comment on them.	Geld gegen Zufriedenheit im Beruf – fasse Johns Ansichten zusammen und kommentiere sie.
B7 Continue John's account of the questions he was asked.	Führe Johns Bericht über die Fragen, die ihm gestellt wurden, fort.

B8

working life /ˈwɜːkɪŋ laɪf/	Berufsleben
tweet /twiːt/	*eine über Twitter verbreitete Kurznachricht*
criterion (*pl* criteria) /kraɪˈtɪəriən/	Kriterium

Working life was more stressful than John had expected.

As a group decide on a statement that you want to discuss.	Entscheidet euch als Gruppe für eine Aussage, über die ihr diskutieren wollt.

be around *(informal)* /ˌbi‿əˈraʊnd/	da sein

Write the statement at the top of a poster.	Schreibt die Aussage oben auf ein Poster.
Now take turns to write 'tweets' in which you express your opinion.	Wechselt euch nun damit ab, *‚tweets'* zu schreiben, in denen ihr eure Meinung ausdrückt.
Use your list of reasons to justify your opinion.	Benutz deine Liste mit Gründen, um deine Meinung zu rechtfertigen.
'Tweets' may not be longer than 280 characters so keep them short and precise.	*‚Tweets'* dürfen nicht länger als 280 Zeichen sein, also halte sie kurz und präzise.
Read them and choose the discussion you like best.	Lest sie und wählt die Diskussion aus, die euch am besten gefällt.

P9

night shift /ˈnaɪt ʃɪft/	Nachtschicht
wallet /ˈwɒlɪt/	Brieftasche

P10	A friend needs help to understand the statements.	Ein Freund/Eine Freundin braucht Hilfe, um die Aussagen zu verstehen.
P11	Six vloggers talked to an online magazine about their 'job'.	Sechs Vlogger haben mit einer Online-Zeitschrift über ihren ‚Job' gesprochen.
	Report what they said.	Gib wieder, was sie gesagt haben.
	Use reported speech.	Benutze die indirekte Rede.
	Remember the time shift.	Denk an die Zeitverschiebung.

tool /tu:l/	Werkzeug
insulting /ɪn'sʌltɪŋ/	beleidigend

P12	A journalist interviewed two young people who subscribe to vlogs on the Internet.	Ein Journalist/Eine Journalistin hat zwei junge Menschen befragt, die Vlogs im Internet abonniert haben.
	Put the questions and the answers in reported speech.	Setz die Fragen und die Antworten in die indirekte Rede.

Theme 4

I	**use** /ju:s/	Verwendung; Einsatz; Nutzung	A smartphone has many *uses*, like listening to music or taking photos.
	The Internet of things /ði‿ˌɪntənet‿əv 'θɪŋz/	*Vision einer durch Technologie vernetzten Infrastruktur von Alltagsgegenständen*	
	genre /'ʒɒnrə/	Genre, Gattung	
	saga /'sa:gə/	Saga, Geschichte	
	analyse /'ænəlaɪz/	analysieren, untersuchen	
	transform /træns'fɔ:m/	verwandeln; umwandeln	
A1	chat /tʃæt/	chatten	She *seldom* eats sweets. = She rarely eats sweets.
	seldom /'seldəm/	selten, fast nie	
	occasionally /ə'keɪʒnəli/	gelegentlich, hin und wieder	

Look at the bar chart below.	Sieh dir unten das Balkendiagramm an.

entertainment /ˌentə'teɪnmənt/	Unterhaltung	
source /sɔ:s/	Quelle	
figure /'fɪgə/	Zahl, Wert	*figure* = number, amount
base /beɪs/	Grundlage, Basis	

	Is anything similar?	Ist etwas ähnlich?
	What is different?	Was ist unterschiedlich?
A2	Look at the photos.	Sieh dir die Fotos an.

software developer /ˈsɒfˌweə dɪˌveləpə/	Softwareentwickler/in	
trainee /treɪˌniː/	Auszubildende/r	
A3 be up to something /ˌbi‿ˈʌp tə ˌsʌmθɪŋ/	etwas vorhaben	
social network /ˌsəʊʃl ˈnetwɜːk/	soziales Netzwerk	Many young people use *social network* sites.
details *(pl)* /ˈdiːteɪls/	Personalien, persönliche Daten	
everywhere /ˈevriweə/	überall	Her things are *everywhere*. 
high score /ˈhaɪ skɔː/	Highscore *(erreichter Punktestand bei der Wertung von Computer-spielen)*	
plus /plʌs/	plus, zuzüglich	
password /ˈpɑːsˌwɜːd/	Passwort	When you forget your *password*, you can't log on to your computer.
permission /pəˈmɪʃn/	Erlaubnis, Genehmigung, Berechtigung	
data *(pl)* /ˈdeɪtə/	Daten	
click /klɪk/	klicken	
button /ˈbʌtən/	Knopf	
privacy policy /ˈprɪvəsi ˌpɒləsi/	Datenschutzbestimmungen, Datenschutzrichtlinie	
come on /ˌkʌm‿ˈɒn/	*hier etwa:* Jetzt hör(t) aber auf!, Komm(t) schon	
legal /ˈliːgl/	rechtlich, gesetzlich	
document /ˈdɒkjʊmənt/	Dokument	
yeah /jeə/	ja	My brother helped me *sign up* to the site.
sign up /ˌsaɪn‿ˈʌp/	*hier:* sich anmelden	
no one /ˈnəʊ wʌn/	keiner	*No one* was in the room.
stick to /ˈstɪk tʊ/	an etwas (fest)halten	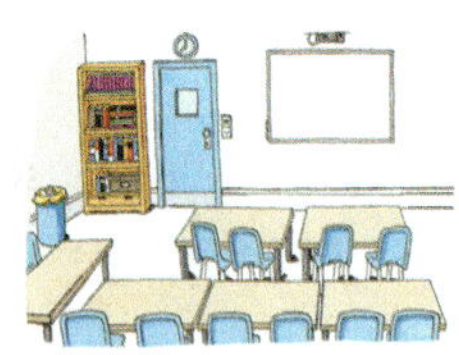
post /pəʊst/	posten, bekannt geben	
break into /ˌbreɪk‿ˈɪntuː/	einbrechen	
put *(irr)* /pʊt/	*hier:* ausdrücken	
criminal /ˈkrɪmɪnl/	Verbrecher/in	
network /ˈnetˌwɜːk/	Netzwerk	
site /saɪt/	*hier:* Seite	I made an *error*. = I made a mistake.
error /ˈerə/	Fehler	
dramatic /drəˈmætɪk/	dramatisch	
go for /ˈgəʊ fɔː/	gelten für	

Listen again and read along.	Hör noch einmal zu und lies mit.
Collect arguments from the text for and against the new app.	Sammle Argumente aus dem Text für und gegen die neue App.
Write a summary of what Sam and her mum think.	Schreib eine Zusammenfassung davon, was Sam und ihre Mutter denken.
With whom do you agree? Explain why.	Wem stimmst du zu? Erklär, warum.

Words

A5 awareness /ə'weənəs/ Bewusstsein

Write a list of statements about how to stay safe online.	Schreibt eine Liste mit Aussagen darüber, wie man online sicher bleibt.
Agree on the most important statements.	Einigt euch auf die wichtigsten Aussagen.

setting /'setɪŋ/	Einstellung	If you are *anonymous*, no one knows your name.
anonymous /ə'nɒnɪməs/	anonym	
request /rɪ'kwest/	Wunsch, Anfrage	
social media /ˌsəʊʃl 'miːdiə/	soziale Medien	
username /'juːzəˌneɪm/	Benutzername	
provider /prə'vaɪdə/	Anbieter/in	
upsetting /ʌp'setɪŋ/	schlimm, erschütternd	

Imagine you want to tell your younger brother or sister the main things you can do to protect yourself while surfing the Internet.	Stell dir vor, du wolltest deinem jüngeren Bruder oder deiner jüngeren Schwester die Hauptdinge erzählen, die man machen kann, um sich zu schützen, während man im Internet surft.
When preparing your checklists in a), did you think about all the situations in c)?	Hast du, als du deine Checkliste bei a) vorbereitet hast, an alle Situationen bei c) gedacht?
Add more statements to your checklist.	Füge weitere Aussagen zu deiner Checkliste hinzu.
A6 Tell him or her about your favourite app, but don't mention its name.	Erzähl ihm oder ihr von deiner Lieblings-app, aber erwähne den Namen nicht.
Give a summary on what Wikipedia is and find out how it tries to ensure the quality of its entries.	Mach eine Zusammenfassung darüber, was Wikipedia ist, und finde heraus, wie es versucht, die Qualität der Einträge sicherzustellen.
Then collect reasons why you might need more good sources than just Wikipedia for presentations and homework.	Sammle dann Gründe, warum du weitere gute Quellen als nur Wikipedia für Präsentationen und Hausaufgaben brauchen könntest.
Research online what is meant by 'privacy policies' and find examples of privacy policies of apps or other online services.	Recherchiere online, was mit ‚Datenschutzbestimmungen' gemeint ist und finde Beispiele für Datenschutzbestimmungen von Apps oder anderen Online-Diensten.
Do any of the privacy policies have anything in common?	Haben irgendwelche der Datenschutzbestimmungen etwas miteinander gemeinsam?
Discuss your findings in class.	Diskutiert eure Ergebnisse in der Klasse.
Watch the video clip.	Sieh dir den Videoclip an.

A7

As a class, try to summarise what happens.	Versucht als Klasse zusammenzufassen, was passiert.
Based on what you could see in the video, what are the possible dangers of the future of technology?	Was sind, basierend auf dem, was ihr im Video gesehen habt, mögliche Gefahren der Zukunft der Technologie?

reward /rɪ'wɔ:d/	belohnen	
info bubble /'ɪnfəʊ ˌbʌbl/	Info-Blase	
real-life /ˌrɪəl‿'laɪf/	real	
like /laɪk/	ähnlich	*like* = similar
reward /rɪ'wɔ:d/	Belohnung	
level /'levl/	Stufe, Level	
unlock /ʌn'lɒk/	aufschließen; *hier:* freisetzen	

A8

Look at the photos of the devices.	Sieh dir die Fotos der Geräte an.
They all connect to the Internet.	Sie verbinden sich alle mit dem Internet.

security camera /sɪ'kjʊərəti ˌkæmrə/	Überwachungskamera
console /kən'səʊl/	Konsole

Read the sales pitch for a new everyday product with Internet access.	Lies das Verkaufsgespräch für ein neues Alltagsprodukt mit Internetzugang.

grocery /'grəʊsəri/	Lebensmittel-
damn *(informal)* /dæm/	verdammt, verflucht
be out of something /ˌbi‿ˌaʊt‿əv 'sʌmθɪŋ/	etwas nicht mehr haben
automatically /ˌɔ:tə'mætɪkli/	automatisch
go out of date /ˌgəʊ‿ˌaʊt‿əv 'deɪt/	*hier:* ablaufen
set up /ˌset‿'ʌp/	einrichten

My brother *has set up* a blog.

What words and phrases does the sales representative use to sell her product?	Welche Wörter und Ausdrücke benutzt die Vertreterin, um das Produkt zu verkaufen?

sales representative /'seɪlz reprɪˌzentətɪv/	Vertreter/in

Does the sales representative sound convincing?	Hört sich die Vertreterin überzeugend an?
A9 Apps play an important role in our everyday lives.	Apps spielen in unserem Alltagsleben eine wichtige Rolle.

We use them to get information, chat and play with friends, and we can even use them to connect other technical devices to the Internet to make them 'smarter'.	Wir nutzen sie, um Informationen zu bekommen, zu chatten und mit Freunden zu spielen, und wir können sie sogar nutzen, um andere technische Geräte mit dem Internet zu verbinden, um diese ‚schlauer' zu machen.
You are going to take on the role of app designers and design your own app.	Ihr werdet die Rolle von App-Designern übernehmen und eure eigene App entwerfen.
Work on a concept for your app.	Arbeitet an einem Konzept für eure App.
Consider issues such as data and privacy protection.	Denkt über Themen wie Datenschutz und Privatsphäreschutz nach.
Could there be any problems or difficulties?	Könnte es irgendwelche Probleme oder Schwierigkeiten geben?
Draw a picture of your app with buttons, the menu and a logo.	Zeichnet ein Bild von eurer App mit Knöpfen, dem Menü und einem Logo.
How is the English language used in your app?	Wie wird die englische Sprache in eurer App benutzt?

aspect /ˈæspekt/	Aspekt, Gesichtspunkt
layout /ˈleɪaʊt/	Layout, Aufbau
positive /ˈpɒzətɪv/	positiv
negative /ˈnegətɪv/	negativ

Access to information is a very *positive aspect* of the Internet.

P2

Write down five sentences in which you explain which apps you use for what purpose and how often.	Schreib fünf Sätze auf, in denen du erklärst, welche Apps du zu welchem Zweck nutzt und wie oft.
Think of another person and rewrite your sentences.	Denk an eine andere Person und schreib deine Sätze um.

P3

Look at the bar chart and explain it in English.	Sieh dir das Balkendiagramm an und erklär es auf Englisch.
Work with a partner and take turns.	Arbeitet mit einem Partner/einer Partnerin und wechselt euch ab.

P5

vocabulary /vəʊˈkæbjʊləri/	Vokabular, Wortschatz
connect /kəˈnekt/	verbinden

P6

Ask each other what you would do in certain situations when online.	Fragt euch gegenseitig, was ihr in bestimmten Situationen tun würdet, wenn ihr online seid.

B2

short story /ˌʃɔːt ˈstɔːri/	Kurzgeschichte

Copy the cluster or use the one in your workbook.	Schreib das Cluster ab oder benutze das in deinem Arbeitsheft.
Fill in the information while you read: characters (who), plot (what, how and why), setting (where and when).	Trag die Informationen ein, während du liest: Charaktere (wer), Handlung (was, wie und warum), Schauplatz (wo und wann).

headed /ˈhedɪd/	mit der Überschrift
print /prɪnt/	drucken
turn /tɜːn/	*hier:* umblättern
crinkly /ˈkrɪŋkli/	zerknittert
still /stɪl/	reglos, bewegungslos
screen /skriːn/	Bildschirm
turn back /ˌtɜːn ˈbæk/	zurückblättern
gee *(AE, informal)* /dʒiː/	Wahnsinn, Mannomann
What a …! /ˈwɒt‿ə/	Was für ein/eine …!
waste /weɪst/	Verschwendung, Vergeudung; Abfall
television /ˈtelɪˌvɪʒn/	Fernseher, Fernsehen
plenty *(informal)* /ˈplenti/	viel
textbook /tekst bʊk/	Lehrbuch, Schulbuch
attic /ˈætɪk/	Dachboden
scornful /ˈskɔːnfl/	verächtlich
mechanical /mɪˈkænɪkl/	mechanisch
shake one's head /ˌʃeɪk wʌnz ˈhed/	den Kopf schütteln
sorrowfully /ˈsɒrəʊfli/	traurig, betrübt
send for /ˈsend fɔː/	rufen
county /ˈkaʊnti/	(Verwaltungs)bezirk, (Stadt)bezirk
inspector /ɪnˈspektə/	Inspektor/in
round /raʊnd/	rund
dial /ˈdaɪəl/	Skala
take apart /ˌteɪk‿əˈpɑːt/	auseinandernehmen
slot /slɒt/	Schlitz
write out /ˌraɪt‿ˈaʊt/	aufschreiben, ausschreiben
punch code /ˈpʌntʃ kəʊd/	Stanzcode, Lochcode
calculate /ˈkælkjʊleɪt/	berechnen
pat /pæt/	tätscheln, einen Klaps geben
sector /ˈsektə/	Bereich, Sektor
gear /gɪə/	*hier:* einstellen, schalten
slow up /ˌsləʊ‿ˈʌp/	verlangsamen
overall /ˌəʊvərˈɔːl/	allgemein, Gesamt-
satisfactory /ˌsætɪsˈfæktri/	zufriedenstellend
blank out /ˌblæŋk‿ˈaʊt/	verdrängen, ausstreichen
superior /sʊˈpɪəriə/	überlegen, überheblich
stupid *(informal)* /ˈstjuːpɪd/	Blödmann, Dummkopf
loftily /ˈlɒftili/	hochmütig, stolz
pronounce /prəˈnaʊns/	aussprechen
hurt /hɜːt/	gekränkt, verletzt
for a while /fər‿ə ˈwaɪl/	eine Weile

Turn to page 4.

Looking at a *screen* can be bad for your eyes.

What a waste to throw away food!

Bilde Hauptwörter!
Durch Hinzufügen der Silbe ‚-er' ans Wortende kannst du mit einigen Wörtern neue Hauptwörter bilden.
Du kennst schon *‚dance'* (‚tanzen' bzw. ‚der Tanz'); *‚dancer'* bedeutet ‚Tänzer/Tänzerin'.
Sieh dir die folgenden Wörter an und probiere es dann selbst einmal. Du kannst im Lexikon nachgucken, ob es bei deinen Beispielen funktioniert.

dream — *dreamer*
sleep — *sleeper*
read — *reader*

Bei einigern Wörtern gibt es Besonderheiten bei der Schreibweise:

swim — *swimmer*
travel — *traveller*

Umgekehrt funktioniert es natürlich auch! Du kennst schon ‚settler' (‚Siedler/in'). Lässt du die Silbe ‚-er' weg und fügst das stumme *‚e'* hinzu, bekommst du *‚settle'* (‚siedeln, besiedeln').

prisoner — *prison*
farmer — *farm*

sure /ʃɔː/	*hier:* natürlich, na klar	
man (*pl* **men**) /mæn, men/	Mensch	
smart /smɑːt/	schlau	*smart* = intelligent
I betcha *(informal)* /aɪ ˈbetʃə/	ich wette darauf	
prepared /prɪˈpeəd/	vorbereitet	
dispute /dɪˈspjuːt/	bestreiten, über etwas streiten	
strange /streɪndʒ/	fremd, unbekannt	*strange* = unusual
scream with laughter /ˌskriːm wɪð ˈlɑːftə/	vor Lachen brüllen	
special /ˈspeʃl/	*hier:* besonders, speziell	
adjust to /əˈdʒʌst‿tʊ/	anpassen an	
fit /fɪt/	entsprechen	
mind /maɪnd/	Geist, Verstand	Keep your mind active!
differently /ˈdɪfrəntli/	verschieden, unterschiedlich	
then /ðen/	damals	
look up /ˌlʊk‿ˈʌp/	nach oben sehen	
nonchalantly /ˈnɒnʃləntli/	gleichgültig	
whistle /ˈwɪsl/	pfeifen	
tuck /tʌk/	stecken, klemmen	
schoolroom /ˈskuːlruːm/	Klassenzimmer	
bedroom /ˈbedruːm/	Schlafzimmer	
hour /ˈaʊə/	Zeit	
lit up /ˌlɪt‿ˈʌp/	beleuchtet	
arithmetic /əˈrɪθmətɪk/	Rechen-	
proper fraction /ˌprɒpə ˈfrækʃn/	echter Bruch *(mathematisch)*	
fraction /ˈfrækʃn/	Bruch *(mathematisch)*	
insert /ɪnˈsɜːt/	einwerfen, (hinein)stecken, einfügen	
proper /ˈprɒpə/	richtig	
sigh /saɪ/	Seufzer	
schoolyard /ˈskuːlˌjɑːd/	Schulhof	
one another /ˌwʌn‿əˈnʌðə/	einander	
flash /flæʃ/	*hier:* anzeigen	
add /æd/	addieren	

She isn't wearing *proper* uniform.

B3

Were your speculations on the title correct?	Waren eure Vermutungen zum Titel richtig?
What is similar and what is different to what you expected?	Was ist ähnlich und was ist unterschiedlich zu dem, was ihr erwartet habt?
In the last two lines of the story, we learn that Margie is thinking about 'The fun they had'.	Auf den letzten zwei Zeilen der Geschichte erfahren wir, dass Margie über ‚The fun they had' nachdenkt.

robot /ˈrəʊbɒt/	Roboter

What do you think the central conflict of the story is?	Was ist deiner Meinung nach der zentrale Konflikt der Geschichte?
Think about school, the way people learn, the way people interact and the way people use technology.	Denk an Schule, die Art, wie Leute lernen, interagieren und Technologie benutzen.
Give reasons.	Gib Gründe an.

point of view /ˌpɔɪnt‿əv‿ˈvjuː/	Ansicht, Perspektive	*point of view* = opinion
B4 summarise /ˈsʌməraɪz/	zusammenfassen	

Write a summary of the story with the help of your cluster.	Schreib mit Hilfe deines Cluster eine Zusammenfassung der Geschichte.
B5 Will humans someday live in space?	Werden Menschen irgendwann im Weltall leben?

starship (= star ship) /ˈstɑːˌʃɪp/	Raumschiff	*starship* 
warp speed /ˈwɔːp spiːd/	*Geschwindigkeit, die schneller als Lichtgeschwindigkeit ist*	
in-flight /ˌɪnˈflaɪt/	Bord-	
brochure /ˈbrəʊʃə/	Broschüre	*brochure* = flyer
reclaim /rɪˈkleɪm/	*hier:* zurückholen, zurückfordern	
reassure /ˌriːəˈʃʊə/	beruhigen	
despondently /dɪˈspɒndəntli/	niedergeschlagen	
dock /dɒk/	anlegen	

Consider …	Zieh … in Betracht.
Take on her perspective and write about it.	Nimm ihren Blickwinkel ein und schreib darüber.

bubble /ˈbʌbl/	Blase	
beginning /bɪˈɡɪnɪŋ/	Anfang	
ending /ˈendɪŋ/	Ende, Schluss	*beginning ≠ ending*
contest /ˈkɒntest/	Wettbewerb	
submit /səbˈmɪt/	einreichen	

B6 Write down information about the mini-saga on characters (who), the setting (where) and the plot (what).	Schreib Informationen über die Mini-Saga zu Figuren (wer), dem Schauplatz (wo) und der Handlung (was) auf.
At the end of the mini-saga, we learn that they dock onto planet Earth.	Am Ende der Mini-Saga erfahren wir, dass sie auf dem Planeten Erde andocken.
Which problems of the real world does the mini-saga address?	Welche Probleme der realen Welt spricht die Mini-Saga an?

Words

	twist /twɪst/	*hier:* Wendung	Juliet is my favourite *character* in the play. 
B7	**single** /ˈsɪŋgl/	einzige(r, s)	
	reader /ˈriːdə/	Leser/in	
	character /ˈkærəktə/	Charakter, Wesen, Figur	
	wish for /ˈwɪʃ fɔː/	sich wünschen	
	consequence /ˈkɒnsɪkwəns/	Konsequenz, Folge	Every action has a *consequence*.

Keep the above information in mind while you plan and write.	Behalte die oben gegebenen Informationen im Gedächtnis, während du planst und schreibst.

rewrite *(irr)* /ˌriːˈraɪt/ — überarbeiten, umschreiben

P9

Fill in the gaps using the simple past forms of the verbs in the box.	Füll die Lücken aus, indem du die Formen der einfachen Vergangenheit der Verben im Kasten benutzt.

ink /ɪŋk/ — Tinte

Write down more sentences with a partner.	Schreib weitere Sätze mit einem Partner auf.

P10	motive /ˈməʊtɪv/	Motiv	
	narrator /nəˈreɪtə/	Erzähler/in	*Narrators* tell a story.
	introduce /ˌɪntrəˈdjuːs/	vorstellen	
	lead *(irr)* /liːd/	führen	to *lead* = to show someone the way
	certain /ˈsɜːtn/	bestimmt, gewiss	

P11

Write down a summary of what science fiction is in German.	Schreib auf Deutsch eine Zusammenfassung darüber, was Science Fiction ist.

P12 Russia /ˈrʌʃə/ — Russland

P13

Turn to page 85 and read lines 10–17 again.	Blätter um zu Seite 85 und lies die Zeilen 10–17 nochmal.
Rewrite lines 10–17 as a summary of what happens using the simple present.	Schreib die Zeilen 10–17 zu einer Zusammenfassung darüber um, was passiert, indem du die einfache Gegenwart benutzt.
Pay attention to the verbs.	Achte auf die Verben.
Swap with a partner and edit his or her summary.	Tausche mit einem Partner/einer Partnerin und bearbeite seine oder ihre Zusammenfassung.

P14

Sort them into two lists: positive and negative feelings.	Sortiere sie in zwei Listen ein: positive und negative Gefühle.

depressed /dɪ'prest/	deprimiert	The break-up left her feeling *heartbroken*.
heartbroken /'hɑ:tˌbrəʊkən/	todunglücklich, untröstlich	
optimistic /ˌɒptɪ'mɪstɪk/	optimistisch	
despondent /dɪ'spɒndənt/	niedergeschlagen	
sorry /'sɒri/	traurig	She was *sorry* she had to go.
hopeful /'həʊpfl/	zuversichtlich	
pessimistic /ˌpesə'mɪstɪk/	pessimistisch	
cheerful /'tʃɪəfl/	fröhlich, vergnügt, heiter	

Theme 5

I	photographer /fə'tɒgrəfə/	Fotograf/in	A *photographer*'s job is to take photos.
	World War II /ˌwɜ:ld ˌwɔ: 'tu:/	der Zweite Weltkrieg	
	reality /ri'æləti/	Realität, Wirklichkeit	in *reality* = in real life
	effect /ɪ'fekt/	Effekt, Wirkung	
	gallery walk /'gæləri wɔ:k/	*Gruppendiskussion in Stationsarbeit*	

A1 Read the quotes and talk about them. With which do you agree or disagree? — Lest die Zitate und sprecht über sie. Welchen stimmt ihr zu und welchen stimmt ihr nicht zu?

glazed /gleɪzd/	glasig	
soldier /'səʊldʒə/	Soldat/in	
battlefield /'bætlˌfi:ld/	Schlachtfeld	
think hard /ˌθɪŋk 'hɑ:d/	scharf nachdenken	
establish /ɪ'stæblɪʃ/	schaffen, einführen, durchsetzen	
lasting /'lɑ:stɪŋ/	dauerhaft, andauernd	New school rules *had been established* and *were declared* on a piece of paper.
politics *(pl)* /'pɒlətɪks/	Politik	
declare /dɪ'kleə/	verkünden, erklären	
mankind /mæn'kaɪnd/	Menschheit	
put an end to /ˌpʊt‿ən‿'end‿tʊ/	ein Ende setzen	
earthquake /'ɜ:θˌkweɪk/	Erdbeben	

Find out in what historical context the quote was made. Write a statement on one of the quotes. — Finde heraus, in welchem historischen Kontext das Zitat gemacht wurde. Schreib eine Stellungnahme zu einem der Zitate.

A2	**memory** /'memri/	Erinnerung, Gedächtnis	My *memory* is so bad I can't remember what I ate for lunch.

Words

What do you find out about the people and the situations? | Was findest du über die Leute und die Situationen heraus?

the Blitz /ðə ˈblɪts/	*deutsche Luftangriffe auf britische Städte im Zweiten Weltkrieg*	
overlook /ˌəʊvəˈlʊk/	überblicken	
set out /ˌset‿ˈaʊt/	aufbrechen, sich auf den Weg machen	
suitcase /ˈsuːtˌkeɪs/	Koffer	The *suitcase* is empty.
label /ˈleɪbl/	Etikett, Schildchen	
lapel /ləˈpel/	Kragen(aufschlag), Revers	
silence /ˈsaɪləns/	Stille, Ruhe	She asked for *silence*. 
drawing room /ˈdrɔːɪŋ ruːm/	Empfangszimmer, Salon, Gesellschaftszimmer	
wireless /ˈwaɪələs/	Radio, (Rund)funk	
recall /rɪˈkɔːl/	sich erinnern an	
dispirited /dɪˈspɪrɪtɪd/	niedergeschlagen, entmutigt	
air raid /ˈeə reɪd/	Luftangriff	
siren /ˈsaɪrən/	Sirene	This is a *siren*.
anticlimax, anti-climax /ˌæntiˈklaɪmæks/	Antiklimax, Enttäuschung	After all the excitement, the film was an *anticlimax*.
not quite /nɒt ˈkwaɪt/	nicht ganz	
affect /əˈfekt/	betreffen, beeinflussen	to *affect* = to have an effect on
sir, Sir /sɜː/	Sir; Herr *(Anrede vor Vornamen)*	
break out /ˌbreɪk‿ˈaʊt/	ausbrechen	
by /baɪ/	*hier:* an	
rush /rʌʃ/	eilen	to *rush* = to hurry
haberdasher /ˈhæbəˌdæʃə/	Kurzwarenhändler/in	
blackout /ˈblækaʊt/	Verdunkelung	
forethought /ˈfɔːˌθɔːt/	Weitblick	
vacation /vəˈkeɪʃn/	Ferien, Urlaub	
central /ˈsentrəl/	zentral, wesentlich, Zentral-	
announcement /əˈnaʊnsmənt/	Bekanntmachung, Mitteilung, Durchsage	The teacher made an important *announcement*.
civilian /səˈvɪliən/	Zivil-; *hier:* für Zivilisten	
gas mask /ˈɡæs mɑːsk/	Gasmaske	
sandbag /ˈsænˌbæɡ/	Sandsack	She logged onto her computer and *set to work*.
set to work /ˌset‿tʊ ˈwɜːk/	sich an die Arbeit machen	
spade /speɪd/	Spaten	
dusk /dʌsk/	(Abend)dämmerung	
stiff /stɪf/	steif	
stand up /ˌstænd‿ˈʌp/	aufstehen; *hier:* gerade stehen	

blister /ˈblɪstə/	Blase	
wallow /ˈwɒləʊ/	ausgiebig baden	
bath /bɑːθ/	Bad	
bomb /bɒm/	Bombe	
weary /ˈwɪəri/	müde, erschöpft	*weary* = very tired

Take notes on the texts you read.	Mach dir Notizen zu den Texten, die du gelesen hast.
How were the people affected by the war?	Wie waren die Menschen vom Krieg betroffen?
Work with a partner and compare your notes.	Arbeitet mit einem Partner/einer Partnerin und vergleicht eure Notizen.

oral /ˈɔːrəl/	mündlich	
commentary /ˈkɒməntri/	Kommentar, Stellungnahme	
historical /hɪˈstɒrɪkl/	historisch	
transcribe /trænˈskraɪb/	umschreiben, transkribieren	
archive /ˈɑːkaɪv/	Archiv	The government spends millions on *research*.
research /rɪˈsɜːtʃ/	Forschung	
public /ˈpʌblɪk/	öffentlich	
witness /ˈwɪtnəs/	Zeuge/Zeugin	
A3 take a step /ˌteɪk‿ə ˈstep/	einen Schritt machen	
blow off /ˌbləʊ‿ˈɒf/	wegreißen, abreißen	
horrifying /ˈhɒrɪˌfaɪɪŋ/	schrecklich, grauenhaft	
threat /θret/	Bedrohung, Gefahr	The boy on the right is a *victim* of bullying.
victim /ˈvɪktɪm/	Opfer	
cabin /ˈkæbɪn/	Hütte	
calm /ˌkɑːm/	ruhig, gelassen	
leftovers *(pl)* /ˈleftˌəʊvəz/	(Über)reste, Überbleibsel	I've been really busy these *past* few weeks.
past /pɑːst/	vergangen, letzte	
injure /ˈɪndʒə/	verletzen	
suffer from /ˈsʌfə frəm/	leiden an, erleiden	
fever /ˈfiːvə/	Fieber	They sat by the *fireplace* to keep warm.
infection /ɪnˈfekʃn/	Infektion	
fireplace /ˈfaɪəˌpleɪs/	Kamin	
pile /paɪl/	Stapel, Haufen	
explode /ɪkˈspləʊd/	explodieren	

What do you think her mother's reaction was?	Was denkst du, was die Reaktion ihrer Mutter war?
Listen to the interview with a landmine expert who works for the United Nations.	Hör dir das Interview mit einem Experten für Landminen an, der für die Vereinten Nationen arbeitet.

the United Nations /ðə juːˌnaɪtɪd ˈneɪʃnz/	die Vereinten Nationen

	What do you learn about landmines in addition to Amalia's story?	Was erfährst du zusätzlich zu Amalias Geschichte über Landminen?
	Make a fact file on landmines and explain why children can be easily harmed by them.	Fertige einen Steckbrief über Landminen an und erklär, warum Kindern leicht durch sie Schaden zugefügt werden kann.
	Research how landmines are cleared and add this information to your fact file.	Recherchiere, wie Landminen beseitigt werden und füge diese Information deinem Steckbrief hinzu.
	Share with the class what you find out about the procedure of clearing landmines.	Teil mit der Klasse, was du über den Vorgang des Beseitigens von Landminen herausfindest.
A4	Choose one of the pictures of children in war zones.	Wähl eines der Bilder von Kindern in Kriegsgebieten.
	Do you know someone who has a war memory that he or she might be willing to share?	Kennst du jemanden, der eine Kriegserinnerung hat, welche er oder sie bereit sein könnte zu teilen?
	You could transcribe it or record it.	Du könntest es transkribieren oder aufnehmen.
	"Playing war games on game consoles or computers makes the gamers violent."	„Das Spielen von Kriegsspielen auf Spielkonsolen oder Computern macht die Spieler/Spielerinnen gewalttätig."
	Do you agree or disagree with this statement?	Stimmst du dieser Äußerung zu oder nicht?
	Find out more about organisations that try to clear regions of landmines.	Finde mehr über Organisationen heraus, die versuchen, Gebiete von Landminen zu reinigen.
A5	Share your ideas about the picture in a silent discussion in written form.	Teilt eure Ideen über das Bild in einer stillen Diskussion in schriftlicher Form.
	One of you starts with the first sentence, the other reads it and responds or adds a new aspect.	Eine/r von euch beginnt mit dem ersten Satz, der/die andere liest ihn und reagiert oder fügt einen neuen Aspekt hinzu.

helpless /ˈhelpləs/	hilflos	
medic /ˈmedɪk/	Mediziner/in	A doctor is a *medic*.
personnel /ˌpɜːsəˈnel/	Personal	
agonising /ˈæɡənaɪzɪŋ/	qualvoll	She is in *agonising* pain.
painful /ˈpeɪnfl/	schmerzhaft	
take pictures /ˌteɪk ˈpɪktʃəs/	Bilder machen, fotografieren	
estimate /ˈestɪmeɪt/	schätzen, einschätzen	We can only *estimate* because we do not know.
glimpse /ɡlɪmps/	flüchtiger Blick	
normality /nɔːˈmæləti/	Normalität	
ruin /ˈruːɪn/	Ruine	This castle is a *ruin*.
dangerously /ˈdeɪndʒərəsli/	gefährlich	
fragile /ˈfrædʒaɪl/	brüchig, unsicher, zerbrechlich	

long-term /ˌlɒŋ ˈtɜːm/	langfristig	
occupant /ˈɒkjʊpənt/	Bewohner/in	
Iraq /ɪˈrɑːk/	Irak	

Listen to the news report.	Hört euch die Nachrichtenmeldung an.
Which of the above situations is it about?	Über welche der obigen Situationen ist sie?
What details do you learn about the situation in the picture?	Welche Einzelheiten erfahrt ihr über die Situation auf dem Bild?
Read the photographers' quotes underneath the pictures.	Lies die Zitate der Fotografen unter den Bildern.
Work with a partner.	Arbeitet mit einem Partner/einer Partnerin zusammen.
Write a statement from the point of view of the photographer.	Schreib eine Aussage aus der Sicht des Fotografen/der Fotografin.
Write about why society needs war reporters and photographers.	Schreib darüber, warum die Gesellschaft Kriegsreporter/Kriegsreporterinnen und Fotografen/Fotografinnen braucht.

A6	the media /ðə ˈmiːdiə/	die Medien

Read the text about the 2003 invasion of Iraq.	Lies den Text über die Invasion in den Irak 2003.

invasion /ɪnˈveɪʒn/	Invasion, Eindringen	to *cover* = to give a report on TV or radio
cover /ˈkʌvə/	sich befassen mit, behandeln	
TV station /ˌtiːˈviː ˌsteɪʃn/	Fernsehsender	
attack /əˈtæk/	Angriff	
the armed forces *(pl)* /ˌɑːmd ˈfɔːsɪz/	Streitkräfte	
disempower /ˌdɪsɪmˈpaʊə/	entmachten	
criticise /ˈkrɪtɪsaɪz/	kritisieren	If you are *biased* then you show unfair support for something.
biased /ˈbaɪəst/	voreingenommen	
coverage /ˈkʌvrɪdʒ/	Berichterstattung	*coverage* = reporting by the media
outlet /ˈaʊtˌlet/	Medien, Verlag, Fernsehsender	to *accuse* = to say that someone has done something wrong
accuse /əˈkjuːz/	anklagen, beschuldigen	
sensationalist /senˈseɪʃnəˌlɪst/	Sensations-	
reporting /rɪˈpɔːtɪŋ/	Berichterstattung	
broadcasting /ˈbrɔːdˌkɑːstɪŋ/	Rundfunk, Fernsehen	
patriotic /ˌpætriˈɒtɪk/	patriotisch	
emphasise /ˈemfəsaɪz/	betonen, hervorheben	
risk /rɪsk/	riskieren	

Words

criticism /ˈkrɪtɪˌsɪzm/	Kritik	
embedded /ɪmˈbedɪd/	eingebettet	
army /ˈɑːmi/	Armee	
front line /ˌfrʌnt ˈlaɪn/	Frontlinie, vorderste Front	Soldiers on the *front line risk* death every day.
war zone /ˈwɔː zəʊn/	Kriegsgebiet	
military forces *(pl)* /ˌmɪlɪtri ˈfɔːsɪz/	Streitkräfte	
critical /ˈkrɪtɪkl/	kritisch	
actual /ˈæktʃuəl/	eigentlich, tatsächlich; echt	
influence /ˈɪnfluəns/	beeinflussen	to *influence* someone = to affect the way that someone thinks or behaves

Explain what is meant by 'embedded journalism'.	Erklär, was mit *‚embedded journalism'* gemeint ist.
What is problematic about it?	Was ist daran problematisch?

A7	**statement** /ˈsteɪtmənt/	Äußerung, Stellungnahme; Aussage	The man refused to give a *statement* to the police.

As a class, you are going to present your statements against war in a gallery walk.	Ihr werdet als Klasse eure Aussagen gegen den Krieg in Stationsarbeit präsentieren.
You must be prepared to answer questions about your statement.	Ihr müsst darauf vorbereitet sein, Fragen zu eurer Aussage zu beantworten.
Think about your own opinion and take some notes.	Denk über deine eigene Meinung nach und mach dir ein paar Notizen.

authentic /ɔːˈθentɪk/	authentisch	*authentic* = real

	Make cue cards to help you explain your statement.	Erstell Stichwortkarten, die dir dabei helfen, deine Aussage zu erklären.
	Display your statements and do the gallery walk.	Hängt eure Aussagen aus und macht einen Galeriegang.
	You might also want to invite other classes to visit your gallery.	Ihr könntet auch andere Klassen dazu einladen wollen, eure Galerie zu besuchen.
	Invite your visitors to react to your statement and share their comments and opinions.	Ladet eure Besucher/Besucherinnen ein, auf eure Aussagen zu reagieren und ihre Kommentare und Meinungen zu teilen.
P2	Rewrite it as an interview with an interviewer.	Schreib es als Interview mit einem Interviewer um.
	Swap your interviews with a partner and write down any questions that you don't have.	Tausch deine Interviews mit einem Partner/einer Partnerin und schreib alle Fragen auf, die du nicht hast.
P3	Complete the sentences using the past progressive forms of the verbs in the box.	Vervollständige die Sätze, indem du die Verlaufsform der Vergangenheit der Verben aus dem Kasten benutzt.

mine /maɪn/	Mine, Bergwerk, Fundgrube	

Swap with a partner and check his or her sentences.	Tausche mit einem Partner/einer Partnerin und kontrolliere seine oder ihre Sätze.
P4 Listen to the interview with the landmine expert again.	Hör dir das Interview mit dem Landminen-Experten noch einmal an.
Are these facts about landmines true or false?	Sind diese Fakten über Landminen wahr oder falsch?
Correct the false ones.	Verbessere die falschen.

today /tə'deɪ/	heutzutage	
number /'nʌmbə/	Anzahl	

Write your own true or false sentences for a partner.	Schreib deine eigenen wahren oder falschen Sätze für einen Partner/eine Partnerin.
They can be about the interview or about another text from this Theme.	Sie können über das Interview oder über einen anderen Text aus diesem Kapitel sein.
P5 Use a dictionary to check the meaning of any of the words you don't know.	Benutz ein Wörterbuch, um die Bedeutung aller Wörter zu überprüfen, die du nicht kennst.
Which words are difficult?	Welche Wörter sind schwierig?
P6 Make a word web of words and phrases about war.	Mach ein Wortnetz aus Wörtern und Ausdrücken über den Krieg.
You can use it to help you with your statement against war.	Du kannst es benutzen um dir bei deiner Stellungnahme gegen den Krieg zu helfen.

B1 peace /piːs/	Frieden	

Draw something that symbolises peace to you and talk about your drawing.	Zeichne etwas, das für dich Frieden symbolisiert, und sprich über deine Zeichnung.

overcome *(irr)* /ˌəʊvə'kʌm/	bewältigen, überwinden	
force /fɔːs/	Gewalt	*force* = violence
understanding /ˌʌndə'stændɪŋ/	Verständnis, Übereinkunft	
shake *(irr)* /ʃeɪk/	schütteln	
clenched fist /ˌklentʃt 'fɪst/	geballte Faust	
absence /'æbsns/	Abwesenheit, Fehlen	*absence* = a period of time when someone is not there when they should be
peaceful, peacefully /'piːsfl, 'piːsfli/	friedlich, friedfertig, ruhig	
mean /miːn/	Mittel	

Words

B2	Make a list of keywords concerning peace.	Erstell eine Liste mit Schlüsselwörtern bezüglich Frieden.
	What do you think of the melody, the instruments and the voice of the singer?	Was hältst du von der Melodie, den Instrumenten und der Stimme des Sängers?

heaven /ˈhevn/	Himmel	
hell /hel/	Hölle	
dreamer /ˈdriːmə/	Träumer/in	
someday /ˌsʌm ˈdeɪ/	irgendwann (einmal)	
possession /pəˈzeʃn/	Besitz	
need /niːd/	Notwendigkeit, Bedürfnis	Food and water are daily *needs*.
greed /ˈɡriːd/	Gier	
brotherhood /ˈbrʌðəˌhʊd/	Brüderlichkeit	
lyrics *(pl)* /ˈlɪrɪks/	Liedtext	
unrealistic /ˌʌnrɪəˈlɪstɪk/	unrealistisch	
go together /ˌɡəʊ təˈɡeðə/	zusammenpassen	to *go together* = to match

B3	What is your vision of an ideal peaceful world?	Was ist deine Vorstellung von einer idealen friedlichen Welt?
	Skim the five texts on the next four pages.	Überfliege die fünf Texte auf den nächsten vier Seiten.
	Choose one of them and read it in detail in your home group.	Entscheide dich für einen von ihnen und lies ihn im Detail in deiner Ursprungsgruppe.

home group /ˈhəʊm ɡruːp/	*Ursprungsgruppe*

Inform your home group what the text is about.	Informiere deine Ursprungsgruppe, worüber der Text ist.
Give the main ideas by thinking of who did what, when, where, how and why.	Gib die Hauptideen wieder, indem du daran denkst, wer was wann, wo, wie und warum gemacht hat.

mediation /ˌmiːdiˈeɪʃn/	Vermittlung, Mediation	
scheme /skiːm/	Projekt, Programm, Plan	*scheme* = plan
peer /ˈpɪə/	Kollege/Kollegin, Mitschüler/in	
mediator /ˈmiːdieɪtə/	Vermittler/in, Schlichter/in	
scripted /ˈskrɪptɪd/	vorbereitet	
sort out /ˌsɔːt‿ˈaʊt/	klären	
dispute /dɪˈspjuːt/	Streit	*dispute* = fight
selected /sɪˈlektɪd/	ausgewählt	
lower school /ˌləʊə ˈskuːl/	*hier:* Unterstufe	
reach an agreement /ˌriːtʃ‿ən‿əˈɡriːmənt/	sich einigen, zu einer Einigung kommen	
vital /ˈvaɪtl/	essenziell, entscheidend	*vital* = very important

promote /prəˈməʊt/	fördern, werben für; befördern	Junk food does not *promote* a healthy lifestyle.
ethos /ˈiːθɒs/	Gesinnung, Ethos	
cooperation /kəʊˌɒpəˈreɪʃn/	Kooperation, Zusammenarbeit	
raise /reɪz/	heben, erhöhen	
self-confidence /ˌselfˈkɒnfɪdəns/	Selbstvertrauen, Selbstbewusstsein	She has a lot of of *self-confidence*.
empathy /ˈempəθi/	Einfühlungsvermögen, Empathie	
value /ˈvæljuː/	schätzen, wertschätzen	
take *(irr)* /teɪk/	hier: übernehmen	
increase /ɪnˈkriːs/	erhöhen, verstärken	
equal /ˈiːkwəl/	gleich	
resolve /rɪˈzɒlv/	lösen	
involve somebody in something /ɪnˈvɒlv ˌsʌmbədi‿ɪn ˌsʌmθɪŋ/	jemanden an etwas beteiligen	
client /ˈklaɪənt/	Kunde/Kundin	She is a regular *client*.
attendance /əˈtendəns/	Anwesenheit	
greatly /ˈgreɪtli/	sehr	
result /rɪˈzʌlt/	Folge, Resultat	
mindfulness /ˈmaɪnfəlnəs/	Achtsamkeit	
holistic /həʊˈlɪstɪk/	ganzheitlich	A *foundation* is an organisation
foundation /faʊnˈdeɪʃn/	Stiftung	that provides money for charity.
be based /biː ˈbeɪst/	seinen Sitz haben	to *found* = to start an
found /faʊnd/	gründen	organisation, company etc.
non-profit /ˌnɒn ˈprɒfɪt/	gemeinnützig, nicht gewinnorientiert	
aim /eɪm/	zielen auf	
compassion /kəmˈpæʃn/	Mitgefühl, Mitleid	
be committed /ˌbiː kəˈmɪtɪd/	sich widmen	
nurture /ˈnɜːtʃə/	fördern	
wellness /ˈwelnəs/	Wohlbefinden	
low-income /ˌləʊ ˈɪnkʌm/	einkommensschwach	He was *shocked* at how late it
shocked /ˈʃɒkt/	schockiert, entsetzt	was.
suspension /səˈspenʃn/	Suspendierung	
graduation /ˌgrædʒuˈeɪʃn/	(Studien)abschluss	
absent /ˈæbsnt/	abwesend	
testing /ˈtestɪŋ/	Testen, Prüfen	
average /ˈævərɪdʒ/	Durchschnitt	
aim /eɪm/	Ziel	*aim* = purpose
proven /ˈpruːvn/	nachgewiesen, bewährt	
curriculum /kəˈrɪkjʊləm/	Lehrplan	
participation /pɑːˌtɪsɪˈpeɪʃn/	Teilnahme, Beteiligung	

Words

academic /ˌækəˈdemɪk/	akademisch, *hier:* schulisch	
scoring /ˈskɔːrɪŋ/	Abschneiden	*deal* = an agreement to do business
deal /diːl/	Geschäft	
unemployment /ˌʌnɪmˈplɔɪmənt/	Arbeitslosigkeit	*Unemployment* is the state of not having a job.
program *(AE)* /ˈprəʊgræm/	Programm	
phenomenally /fəˈnɒmɪnli/	phänomenal	
get detention /ˌget ˈdɪˈtenʃn/	nachsitzen müssen	
show up /ʃəʊ ʌp/	erscheinen	If you *pass* a test, you are successful in a test.
pass /pɑːs/	bestehen	
senior /siːniə/	Oberstufenschüler/in, Senior/in	
center *(AE)* /ˈsentə/	Zentrum	
since then /sɪns ˈðen/	seitdem, seither	
all over the place /ˌɔːl‿ˌəʊvə ðə ˈpleɪs/	überall	
range from … to … /ˈreɪndʒ frəm … tʊ …/	eine Bandbreite von … bis … haben	
kindergartener /ˈkɪndəˌgɑːtnə/	Kindergartenkind	
senior citizens *(pl)* /ˌsiːniə ˈsɪtɪznz/	ältere Menschen	
inner-city /ˌɪnə ˈsɪti/	Innenstadt-, innerstädtisch	
tremendous /trəˈmendəs/	enorm, riesig	
grave /greɪv/	Grab	
commission /kəˈmɪʃn/	Kommission, Ausschuss	There are hills *beyond* those trees.
beyond /bɪˈjɒnd/	jenseits	
border /ˈbɔːdə/	Grenze	
actively /ˈæktɪvli/	aktiv	
while /waɪl/	Weile	
arrange /əˈreɪndʒ/	arrangieren, organisieren	
leisure /ˈleʒə/	Freizeit, Freizeit-	
voluntarily /ˌvɒlənˈteərɪli/	freiwillig	
maintain /meɪnˈteɪn/	erhalten, pflegen	
memorial /məˈmɔːriəl/	Denkmal, Ehrenmal	He brings sandwiches to work every day *so as to* save money.
so as to /ˈsəʊ‿əz tʊ/	dass, damit; um	
preserve /prɪˈzɜːv/	erhalten	
numerous /ˈnjuːmərəs/	zahlreich	
work camp /ˈwɜːk‿kæmp/	*Lager, in dem Freiwillige gemeinnützige Arbeiten verrichten*	People celebrate Chinese New Year *all over* the world. 
across /əˈkrɒs/	quer durch	
all over /ˌɔːl‿ˈəʊvə/	überall	
kind of *(informal)* /ˈkaɪnd‿əv/	irgendwie, ziemlich	
weird /wɪəd/	merkwürdig, seltsam	

hang around *(informal)* /ˌhæŋ‿əˈraʊnd/	rumhängen
for a start /fər‿ə ˈstɑːt/	zunächst (einmal)
moving /ˈmuːvɪŋ/	bewegend, ergreifend
shocking /ˈʃɒkɪŋ/	schockierend
headstone /ˈhedˌstəʊn/	Grabstein
of course /əv ˈkɔːs/	natürlich
Brit *(informal)* /brɪt/	Brite/Britin
alongside /əˈlɒŋˌsaɪd/	neben, Seite an Seite
campfire /ˈkæmpˌfaɪə/	Lagerfeuer
disco /ˈdɪskəʊ/	Disko
unbelievable /ˌʌnbɪˈliːvəbl/	unglaublich
Black Forest /ˌblæk ˈfɒrɪst/	Schwarzwald
Rhine /raɪn/	Rhein
by the thousand /ˌbaɪ ðə ˈθaʊznd/	zu Tausenden
United Nations Children's Fund (UNICEF) /juːˌnaɪtɪd ˌneɪʃnz ˈtʃɪldrəns fʌnd (ˈjuːnɪsef)/	Kinderhilfswerk der Vereinten Nationen
fund /fʌnd/	Fonds, finanzielle Mittel
at that time /æt ˈðæt‿taɪm/	zu jener Zeit
thus /ðʌs/	folglich, so, diese Weise
in short /ɪn ˈʃɔːt/	in der Kurzform
drop /drɒp/	weglassen
headquarters *(pl)* /hedˈkwɔːtəz/	Hauptquartier, Zentrale
assistance /əˈsɪstns/	Hilfe
area /ˈeəriə/	Bereich
priority /praɪˈɒrəti/	Priorität
primary education /ˌpraɪməri ˈedjʊˈkeɪʃn/	Grundschul(aus)bildung
gender /ˈdʒendə/	Geschlecht, Geschlechter-
equality /ɪˈkwɒləti/	Gleichberechtigung, Gleichheit
protection /prəˈtekʃn/	Schutz
childhood /ˈtʃaɪldˌhʊd/	Kindheit
the Nobel Peace Prize /ðə nəʊˌbel ˈpiːs praɪz/	Friedensnobelpreis
leading /ˈliːdɪŋ/	führend
operate /ˈɒpəreɪt/	tätig sein
ambassador /æmˈbæsədə/	Botschafter/in
council /ˈkaʊnsl/	Rat
carry out /ˌkæri‿ˈaʊt/	durchführen, betreiben
build *(irr)* /bɪld/	*hier:* schaffen, aufbauen
contribute /kənˈtrɪbjuːt/	beitragen
dignity /ˈdɪgnəti/	Würde, Achtung

Gleich ist nicht immer gleich

Manche englischen Wörter sind in ihrer äußeren Form gleich, können aber sowohl Verb als auch Hauptwort sein, z. B.

change
offer
cost
shop

Bei einigen von ihnen musst du allerdings aufpassen, weil die Aussprache unterschiedlich ist:

record	rɪˈkɔːd	aufzeichnen
record	ˈrekɔːd	Rekord
use	juːz	benutzen
use	juːs	Verwendung, Gebrauch

A *priority* is something important that has to be done before something else.

The whole class must *contribute* to the project.

human rights *(pl)* /ˌhjuːmən ˈraɪts/	Menschenrechte	
intercultural /ˌɪntəˈkʌltʃrəl/	interkulturell	
democratic /ˌdeməˈkrætɪk/	demokratisch	
citizenship /ˈsɪtɪznʃɪp/	Staatsbürgerschaft	
affected /əˈfektɪd/	betroffen	
civil society /ˌsɪvl səˈsaɪəti/	Zivilgesellschaft	
advocate /ˈædvəkeɪt/	sich einsetzen, unterstützen	They are *participants* in a demonstration for animal rights.
participant /pɑːˈtɪsɪpənt/	Teilnehmer/in	
committed /kəˈmɪtɪd/	engagiert	
multiplier /ˈmʌltɪplaɪə/	Multiplikator/in	An *institution* is a large organisation.
institution /ˌɪnstɪˈtjuːʃn/	Einrichtung, Institution	
informal /ɪnˈfɔːml/	informell	
last but not least /ˌlɑːst bət nɒt ˈliːst/	nicht zuletzt, nicht zu vergessen	
armed /ɑːmd/	bewaffnet	*armed* = carrying a gun
racism /ˈreɪˌsɪzm/	Rassismus	
aggressive /əˈgresɪv/	aggressiv, angriffslustig	
nationalism /ˈnæʃnəˌlɪzm/	Nationalismus	
hate speech /ˈheɪt spiːtʃ/	Hassrede, Hetzrede	A *migrant* is someone who travels to another place in order to find work.
violation /ˌvaɪəˈleɪʃn/	Verletzung, Verstoß	
migrant /ˈmaɪgrənt/	Zuwanderer/in	
B4 truce /truːs/	Waffenstillstand	
hardship /ˈhɑːdʃɪp/	Not, Elend	
death toll /ˈdeθ təʊl/	Zahl der Todesopfer	
report /rɪˈpɔːt/	berichten	
humanity /hjuːˈmænəti/	Menschlichkeit, Menschheit	
refer to /rɪˈfɜː tu/	*hier:* bezeichnen als	
record /riˈkɔːd/	aufzeichnen, festhalten	
courageous /kəˈreɪdʒəs/	mutig	
step out /ˌstep‿ˈaʊt/	*hier:* heraustreten, sich hervortun	
in spite of /ɪn ˈspaɪt‿əv/	trotz	
restriction /rɪˈstrɪkʃn/	Begrenzung, Einschränkung	She wrote her *account* of the event.
account /əˈkaʊnt/	Bericht	
Western /ˈwestən/	West-, westlich	
trench /trentʃ/	Schützengraben	
venture /ˈventʃə/	sich vorwagen	
No Man's Land /ˈnəʊ mænz lænd/	Niemandsland	
wish /wɪʃ/	wünschen	to *wish* = to want or hope something to happen
merry /ˈmeri/	fröhlich	
exchange /ɪksˈtʃeɪndʒ/	austauschen	

	Christmas carol /ˌkrɪsməs ˈkærəl/	Weihnachtslied	
	opposing /əˈpəʊzɪŋ/	entgegengesetzt, gegnerisch	
	gesture /ˈdʒestʃə/	Geste	
	goodwill /ɡʊdˈwɪl/	guter Wille	
	ceasefire /ˈsiːsˌfaɪə/	Waffenruhe	To *retrieve* something is to get it back or rescue it.
	retrieve /rɪˈtriːv/	bergen	
	body /ˈbɒdi/	*hier:* Leiche	
	fellow /ˈfeləʊ/	Mit-	to *document* = to record something in written form
	document /ˈdɒkjʊmənt/	dokumentieren, belegen	
	widely /ˈwaɪdli/	weit verbreitet	
	portray /pɔːˈtreɪ/	porträtieren, darstellen	
	a touch of /ə ˈtʌtʃ‿əv/	ein bisschen	

Name at least three things.	Benenne mindestens drei Dinge.

B5	spread *(irr)* /spred/	verbreiten	If you *spread* news, you tell many people.
	bar /bɑː/	Riegel	
	cause /kɔːz/	Grund, Ursache; *hier:* Sache	
	gloss over /ˌɡlɒs‿ˈəʊvə/	flüchtig abhandeln	
	chiselled /ˈtʃɪzld/	scharf geschnitten	
	mud /mʌd/	Schlamm	*Mud* is very soft wet earth.
	smear /smɪə/	Fleck	
	in sight /ɪn ˈsaɪt/	in Sicht	
	merrily /ˈmerəli/	vergnügt	
	frolic /ˈfrɒlɪk/	herumtollen	
	swap /swɒp/	tauschen	to *swap* = to exchange
	brand /brænd/	Marke	

	Is it morally sound to use war as a topic to advertise chocolate?	Ist es moralisch vertretbar, Krieg als Thema zu benutzen, um Schokolade zu bewerben?
B6	You can also write your own song or poem.	Du kannst auch dein eigenes Lied oder Gedicht schreiben.
	Find out about the concept of peaceful resistance that Mahatma Gandhi and Martin Luther King Jr. practised.	Finde etwas über das Konzept friedlichen Widerstands heraus, welches Mahatma Gandhi und Martin Luther King Jr. praktizierten.
	Write a report and present it in class.	Schreib einen Bericht und präsentiere ihn in der Klasse.
	Watch a film on promoting peace (for example ‘Gandhi’) and write a film review.	Sieh dir einen Film an, der für Frieden wirbt, (zum Beispiel ‚Gandhi‘), und schreib eine Filmkritik.

B7	**survey** /ˈsɜːveɪ/	Umfrage	They did a class *survey*.

Words

Write down words that show what peace means to the people being interviewed.	Schreib Wörter auf, die zeigen, was Frieden für die Leute, die interviewt werden, bedeutet.
What do you think of their answers?	Was hältst du von ihren Antworten?
Which person do you agree with most?	Welcher Person stimmst du am meisten zu?
Have a discussion in class.	Diskutiert in der Klasse.
B8 What can you personally do to work for peace?	Was kannst du persönlich tun, um für Frieden zu arbeiten?
You should think about what you can change in your everyday life to make life more peaceful for everyone.	Du solltest darüber nachdenken, was du in deinem Alltag verändern kannst, um das Leben für jeden friedlicher zu machen.

produce /prəˈdjuːs/	*hier:* produzieren
campaign /kæmˈpeɪn/	Kampagne
recommendation /ˌrekəmenˈdeɪʃn/	Empfehlung
resistance /rɪˈzɪst(ə)ns/	Widerstand
award /əˈwɔːd/	Preis, Auszeichnung

She won an *award* for her performance.

P8 Complete the sentences about the founders of the Holistic Life Foundation using the correct form of the verbs in the box.	Vervollständige die Sätze über die Gründer/Gründerinnen der *Holistic Life Foundation*, indem du die korrekte Form der Verben aus dem Kasten benutzt.

detention /dɪˈtenʃn/	Nachsitzen
pass /pɑːs/	*hier:* erfolgreich absolvieren
P9 the German Graves Commission /ðə ˌdʒɜːmən ˈgreɪvz kəˌmɪʃn/	Volksbund Deutsche Kriegsgräberfürsorge

Look at the brochure for the German Graves Commission on page 106.	Sieh dir die Broschüre für den Volksbund Deutscher Kriegsgräberfürsorge auf Seite 106 an.
P10 Then write down the answers to as many questions as you can within 10 minutes.	Schreib dann die Antworten auf so viele Fragen wie du kannst innerhalb von 10 Minuten auf.

indirect /ˌɪndəˈrekt/	indirekt

Swap with a partner and write down the answers to his or her questions as fast as you can.	Tausche mit einem Partner/einer Partnerin und schreib die Antworten auf seine oder ihre Fragen so schnell wie du kannst auf.
P11 Listen to the CD and repeat the words.	Hör dir die CD an und wiederhol die Wörter.

Copy the lists and fill in the words. | Schreib die Listen ab und trag die Wörter ein.

Is the stress on the first or the second syllable? | Ist die Betonung auf der ersten oder der zweiten Silbe?

Which two words are not stressed like the others? | Welche zwei Wörter werden nicht wie die anderen betont?

P12 Make a word web of words and phrases about peace. | Erstell ein Wortnetz mit Wörtern und Ausdrücken über Frieden.

Share your ideas with a partner. | Teilt eure Ideen mit einem Partner/einer Partnerin.

Theme 6

I	navigation bar /ˌnævɪˈgeɪʃn bɑː/	Navigationsleiste	
	teen /tiːn/	Teenager	*teen* = teenager
	tip /tɪp/	Tipp	

P p. 114

Before you get into the project, take time to get familiar with the topic. | Bevor du dich näher mit dem Projekt auseinandersetzt, nimm dir Zeit, dich mit dem Thema vertraut zu machen.

get into /ˌget‿ˈɪntʊ/	*hier:* sich auseinandersetzen mit	
take time /ˌteɪk ˈtaɪm/	Zeit lassen/beanspruchen; dauern	
get familiar with /ˌget fəˈmɪliə wɪð/	vertraut werden mit	
certain /ˈsɜːtn/	bestimmt, gewiss	I am *certain* of it. = I know for sure.
role model /ˈrəʊl ˌmɒdl/	Vorbild	
vegan /ˈviːgən/	Veganer/in; vegan	
reject /rɪˈdʒekt/	ablehnen	to *reject* ≠ to accept

P p. 115

Read this post by a youth magazine blogger. | Lies diesen Post von einem Blogger für ein Jugendmagazin.

What can you relate to? | Womit kannst du dich identifizieren?

relate to /rɪˈleɪt‿tʊ/	*hier:* sich identifizieren mit	

Collect keywords and statements and talk about them with a partner or in a group. | Sammle Schlüsselwörter und Äußerungen und sprich mit einem Partner/einer Partnerin oder in einer Gruppe darüber.

teen mag *(informal)* /ˈtiːn mæg/	Jugendzeitschrift	She seems to like *teen mags*.
alien /ˈeɪliən/	Außerirdische/r	

Words

psychologist /saɪˈkɒlədʒɪst/	Psychologe/Psychologin	
Dr (= Doctor) /ˈdɒktə/	Dr. (= Doktor)	
puberty /ˈpju:bəti/	Pubertät	
adolescence /ˌædəˈlesns/	Adoleszenz, Jugend(zeit)	There has been a *change* of plan, we are now leaving at 2pm, not at 3pm.
change /tʃeɪndʒ/	Veränderung	
uncertainty /ʌnˈsɜ:tnti/	Ungewissheit, Zweifel	
sense /sens/	Sinn; Gefühl	
adulthood /ˈædʌltˌhʊd/	Erwachsensein, Erwachsenenalter, Volljährigkeit	The term 'refugee' *refers to* people who are running away from danger in their own country.
refer to /rɪˈfɜ: tu/	betreffen, sich beziehen auf	
ethnic /ˈeθnɪk/	ethnisch, Volks-	
gender /ˈdʒendə/	Geschlechter-	
dynamic /daɪˈnæmɪk/	dynamisch	
trial and error /ˌtraɪəl‿ən‿ˈerə/	Ausprobieren	
influence /ˈɪnfluəns/	beeinflussen	
out of control /ˌaʊt‿əv kənˈtrəʊl/	außer Kontrolle	The party got *out of control*.
potentially /pəˈtenʃəli/	potenziell	
authority /ɔ:ˈθɒrəti/	Autorität	
loosen /ˈlu:sn/	lockern	
final /ˈfaɪnl/	letzte(r, s), endgültig	*final* = last

P
p. 116

Get into a group with classmates who want to work on the same topic as you.	Kommt in einer Gruppe mit Klassenkameraden/Klassenkameradinnen zusammen, die dasselbe Thema bearbeiten wollen wie du.
On the second and third pages there are pictures, facts and figures, newspaper articles, podcasts, and much more, for example …	Auf der jeweils zweiten und dritten Seite gibt es Bilder, Fakten und Zahlen, Zeitungsartikel, Podcasts und viel mehr, zum Beispiel …

ballet /ˈbæleɪ/	Ballett	She *is surrounded* by her friends.
stereotype /ˈsteriəˌtaɪp/	Stereotyp, Klischee	
surround /səˈraʊnd/	umgeben	
cruelty-free /ˌkru:əlti ˈfri:/	*nicht an Tieren getestet*	You should *reduce* the amount of plastic that you use.
reduce /rɪˈdju:s/	reduzieren	
selfish /ˈselfɪʃ/	selbstsüchtig	

If you want to find out even more, go to www.diesterweg.de/webcodes and type in the webcode of your topic.	Wenn ihr sogar noch mehr herausfinden wollt, geht auf www.diesterweg.de/webcodes und tippt den Webcode eures Themas ein.
You can also search for other useful websites yourself.	Du kannst auch selbst nach weiteren nützlichen Websites suchen.

Add to it during the project.	Ergänzt es während des Projekts.

P p. 117

spotlight /ˈspɒtˌlaɪt/	Scheinwerfer, Aufmerksamkeit	

On the fourth page you will find a text called 'Spotlight on …'.	Auf der vierten Seite findest du einen Text, der ‚Spotlight on …' heißt.
This is a detailed report about a young person in the field of music, fashion or environmental activism.	Dies ist ein detaillierter Bericht über einen jungen Menschen aus dem Bereich Musik, Mode oder Umweltaktivismus.
Read the text as a group, take notes and talk about it.	Lest als Gruppe den Text, macht euch Notizen und sprecht darüber.
It is time to share your knowledge with your class.	Es ist Zeit, dass ihr euer Wissen mit eurer Klasse teilt.
Decide on the aspects you want to focus on.	Entscheidet euch, auf welche Aspekte ihr euch konzentrieren wollt.
If as a class you want to go further and carry out your own projects, do step 6.	Wenn ihr als Klasse weitermachen und eure eigenen Projekte durchführen wollt, macht Schritt 6.
If not, go straight to step 7.	Falls nicht, geht direkt zu Schritt 7.

put into action /ˌpʊt‿ɪntʊ ˈækʃn/	in die Tat umsetzen	
reflection /rɪˈflekʃn/	Reflexion	A *reflection* is what you see when you look into a mirror.

You can find a questionnaire to help you with this in your workbook.	Ihr könnt in eurem Arbeitsheft einen Fragebogen finden, der euch dabei helfen kann.

PA p. 118

Look at the photos and read the statements.	Sieh dir die Fotos an und lies die Äußerungen.

dancer /ˈdɑːnsə/	Tänzer/in	
classical /ˈklæsɪkl/	klassisch	
take somebody's mind off something /ˌteɪk ˌsʌmbədiz ˈmaɪnd‿ɒf ˌsʌmθɪŋ/	jemanden auf andere Gedanken bringen, jemanden ablenken	Shopping *takes her mind off* her problems.
empowerment /ɪmˈpaʊəmənt/	Stärkung, Unterstützung	
no matter what /nəʊ ˌmætə ˈwɒt/	was auch (immer) passiert	
pretty much *(informal)* /ˌprɪti ˈmʌtʃ/	ziemlich	The project is *pretty much* finished. = The project is very nearly finished.
disco /ˈdɪskəʊ/	Diskomusik	
vocal /ˈvəʊkl/	Vokalmusik	
waltz /wɔːls/	Walzer	A *waltz* is a dance.
tap dance /ˈtæp ˌdɑːns/	Stepptanz	

Words

Agree on three reasons why music or dance can play such a big role in a teenager's life.	Einigt euch auf drei Gründe, warum Musik oder Tanz so eine große Rolle in dem Leben eines Teenagers spielen kann.

PA p. 119	teen /ti:n/	jugendlich, Teenager-	
	in search of /ɪn ˈsɜ:tʃ‿əv/	auf der Suche nach	
	individual /ˌɪndɪˈvɪdʒuəl/	Einzelperson, Einzelne/r	
	medium /ˈmi:diəm/	Medium, Mittel	
	question /ˈkwestʃn/	*hier:* hinterfragen	to *question* = to doubt
	lifestyle /ˈlaɪfˌstaɪl/	Lebensstil	
	set apart /ˌset‿əˈpɑ:t/	abheben von	
	above all /əˌbʌv‿ˈɔ:l/	vor allem	
	How come? *(informal)* /ˌhaʊ ˈkʌm/	Wieso?	*How come?* = Why?
	for /fɔ:/	*hier:* aus	
	various /ˈveəriəs/	verschieden	
	turn out /ˌtɜ:n‿ˈaʊt/	*hier:* heraustellen	
	escape /ɪˈskeɪp/	Flucht, Entkommen	
	channel /ˈtʃænl/	Kanal	
	range /reɪndʒ/	*hier:* Bandbreite	
	anger /ˈæŋgə/	Ärger, Wut	She slammed the door in a fit of *rage*.
	rage /reɪdʒ/	Wut, Zorn	
	longing /ˈlɒŋɪŋ/	Sehnsucht, Verlangen	
	affinity /əˈfɪnəti/	Verbundenheit, Affinität	
	sense of belonging /ˌsens‿əv bɪˈlɒŋɪŋ/	Zusammengehörigkeitsgefühl	
	closeness /ˈkləʊsnəs/	Nähe	
	revolutionize /ˌrevəˈlu:ʃəˌnaɪz/	revolutionieren	
	break *(irr)* /breɪk/	hier: überschreiten	
	boundary /ˈbaʊndri/	Grenze	
	head /hed/	*hier:* Hörer/in	
	common /ˈkɒmən/	*hier:* gemeinsam	The girl on the right plays the violin in the school *orchestra*.
	orchestra /ˈɔ:kɪstrə/	Orchester	
	profound /prəˈfaʊnd/	tief, tiefgehend, heftig	
	effort /ˈefət/	Mühe, Anstrengung	
	cue /ˈkju:/	Stichwort; *hier:* Zeichen	
	note /nəʊt/	Note, Ton	
	section /ˈsekʃn/	*hier:* Gruppe	
	entire /ɪnˈtaɪə/	ganz, gesamt	*entire* = whole
	appreciation /əˌpri:ʃiˈeɪʃn/	Anerkennung, Verständnis	
	beauty /ˈbju:ti/	Schönheit	An *honest* person does not tell lies.
PA	honest /ˈɒnɪst/	ehrlich	
p. 120	originate /əˈrɪdʒəneɪt/	entstehen, seinen Anfang nehmen	
	rebel /ˈrebl/	rebellieren	
	controversial /ˌkɒntrəˈvɜ:ʃl/	umstritten, kontrovers	

rebellious /rɪˈbeljəs/	aufsässig, widerspenstig	
championship /ˈtʃæmpiənʃɪp/	Meisterschaft	
come together /ˌkʌm təˈgeðə/	zusammenkommen	
compete /kəmˈpiːt/	wetteifern, kämpfen	This is a magazine about *celebrities*.
celebrity /səˈlebrəti/	Berühmtheit, Star	
like-minded /ˌlaɪk ˈmaɪndɪd/	gleich gesinnt	
pace /peɪs/	Tempo	
rhythm /ˈrɪðəm/	Rhythmus	
teen /tiːn/		
go in for *(informal)* /ˌgəʊ‿ˈɪn fə/	abfahren auf, mögen	
totally /ˈtəʊtli/	völlig, total	
electrical /ɪˈlektrɪkl/	elektrisch	
beat /biːt/	Takt	The cat was *curled up* asleep whilst he cleaned.
curl up /ˌkɜːl‿ˈʌp/	sich einrollen	
sit still /ˌsɪt ˈstɪl/	stillsitzen	
bet *(irr)* /bet/	wetten	A *composer* is someone who writes music.
composer /kəmˈpəʊzə/	Komponist/in	

Use the webcode or do your own research online.	Benutz den Webcode oder recherchier selbst online.
Here are some ideas for search terms.	Hier sind ein paar Ideen für Suchbegriffe.

audition /ɔːˈdɪʃn/	Vorsprechen, Vorsingen, Vortanzen	
Irish /ˈaɪrɪʃ/	irisch	
PA songwriter /ˈsɒŋˌraɪtə/	Texter/in; Songwriter	
p. 121 activist /ˈæktɪvɪst/	Aktivist/in	
theme song /ˈθiːm sɒŋ/	Titelmelodie	
teasing /ˌtiːzɪŋ/	Hänseln, Ärgern	
elementary school /elɪˈmentri skuːl/	Grundschule	
tease /tiːz/	hänseln, ärgern	
ridicule /ˈrɪdɪˌkjuːl/	verspotten	The girl on the left *was excluded* from the group.
exclude /ɪkˈskluːd/	ausschließen	
recess /rɪˈses/	(Schul)pause	
frequently /ˈfriːkwəntli/	häufig	
habitually /həˈbɪtʃuəli/	ständig	
make fun of /ˌmeɪk ˈfʌn‿əv/	sich lustig machen über	
ruin /ˈruːɪn/	zerstören, verderben	
go through /ˌgəʊ ˈθruː/	durchmachen	
specialize in /ˈspeʃəlaɪz‿ɪn/	sich spezialisieren auf	
contemporary /kənˈtempri/	zeitgenössisch	
perform /pəˈfɔːm/	*hier:* auftreten	The band *is performing*.
prevention /prɪˈvenʃn/	Verhinderung, Vorbeugung	

issue /ˈɪʃuː/	Frage, Thema, Problem
distribute /dɪˈstrɪbjuːt/	verteilen
bracelet /ˈbreɪslət/	Armband
contain /kənˈteɪn/	enthalten
gonna (= going to) *(informal)* /ˈɡʌnə, ˈɡəʊɪŋ tʊ/	werden
spread *(irr)* /spred/	ausbreiten
'em = them *(informal)* /em/	sie, ihnen
take up /ˌteɪk‿ˈʌp/	*hier:* hinaufbringen; aufheben
plain /pleɪn/	einfach
all along /ˌɔːl‿əˈlɒŋ/	die ganze Zeit, von Anfang an
PB p. 122 casual /ˈkæʒuəl/	lässig
stand out /ˌstænd‿ˈaʊt/	herausstechen aus
look /lʊk/	Aussehen, Look
fashionable /ˈfæʃnəbl/	modisch; extravagant
stylish /ˈstaɪlɪʃ/	modisch
fit /fɪt/	passen, anpassen
judge /dʒʌdʒ/	(be)urteilen, (ein)schätzen

Konditionstraining
Schreibe einen kleinen Text mit den Wörtern, die du lernen willst. Die Liste hängst du in deinem Zimmer auf – möglichst weit weg von deinem Schreibtisch. Gehe zu dem Blatt und merke dir einen Teil des Textes. Setze dich wieder an deinen Schreibtisch und notiere, was du behalten hast.
Das wiederholst du, bis du den gesamten Text geschrieben hast. Um zu sehen, ob du alles richtig geschrieben hast, gehst du wieder los und vergleichst den Text nach und nach.

Agree on five ideas about what fashion and style can mean to young people.	Einigt euch auf fünf Ideen darüber, was Fashion und Stil für junge Leute bedeuten kann.

PB p. 123 footwear /ˈfʊtˌweə/	Schuhe, Schuhwerk	Designer *footwear* is expensive.
hairstyle /ˈheəˌstaɪl/	Frisur	
accessory /əkˈsesəri/	Accessoire	
necessarily /ˈnesəsərəli/	notwendigerweise, unbedingt	
individuality /ˌɪndɪˌvɪdʒuˈæləti/	Individualität	She expresses her *individuality* with her hair.
self (*pl* selves) /ˈself, selvz/	Selbst, Ich	
fit in /ˌfɪt‿ˈɪn/	*hier:* dazugehören	
blend in /ˌblend‿ˈɪn/	sich vermischen, passen zu	
imitate /ˈɪmɪteɪt/	imitieren, kopieren	
independence /ˌɪndɪˈpendəns/	Unabhängigkeit	
developing /dɪˈveləpɪŋ/	sich entwickelnd, heranreifend	
experiment /ɪkˈsperɪˌment/	experimentieren	
completely /kəmˈpliːtli/	völlig, absolut	The *presenter* is dressed very smartly.
presenter /prɪˈzentə/	*hier:* Moderator/in	
label /ˈleɪbl/	*hier:* abstempeln	

PB p. 124	ethical /ˈeθɪkl/	ethisch	
	consumerism /kənˈsjuːməˌrɪzm/	Konsum, Konsumdenken	
	either /ˈaɪðə/	*hier:* jede/r	
	in detail /ɪn ˈdiːteɪl/	ausführlich	*in detail* = including many facts
	item /ˈaɪtəm/	Artikel	
	camera shot /ˈkæmrə ʃɒt/	Aufnahme, (Film)sequenz	
	shape /ʃeɪp/	(aus)formen, prägen	
	convinced /kənˈvɪnst/	überzeugt	
	view /vjuː/	betrachten	
	parent contribution /ˈpeərənt kɒntrɪˌbjuːʃn/	Elternbeitrag	
	income /ˈɪnkʌm/	Einkommen	
	furniture /ˈfɜːnɪtʃə/		
	personal care /ˌpɜːsnəl ˈkeə/	Körperpflege	 *Personal care* is very important.
	electronics *(pl)* /ˌelekˈtrɒnɪks/	Elektronik	
	video game /ˈvɪdiəʊ geɪm/	Videospiel	
	fashion hack /ˈfæʃn hæk/	*Modetrick*	
PB p. 125	ordinary /ˈɔːdnri/	gewöhnlich, normal	*ordinary* = normal
	Down's syndrome /ˈdaʊnz‿ˌsɪndrəʊm/	Down-Syndrom, Trisomie 21	
	model /ˈmɒdl/	modeln	
	talented /ˈtæləntɪd/	talentiert	
	launch /lɔːntʃ/	*hier:* starten, einführen	Many stars *launch* their own fashion *label*.
	label /ˈleɪbl/	*hier:* Label, Marke	
	Fashion Parade /ˈfæʃn pəˌreɪd/	Modenschau	
	dedication /ˌdedɪˈkeɪʃn/	Engagement	
	feature /ˈfiːtʃə/	zeigen, erscheinen	
	aside from /əˈsaɪd frəm/	abgesehen von	*aside from* = apart from
	modelling /ˈmɒdlɪŋ/	Modeln	
	empower /ɪmˈpaʊə/	stärken, befähigen	
	disability /ˌdɪsəˈbɪləti/	Behinderung, Einschränkung	
	shoot /ʃuːt/	Aufnahme	
	perception /pəˈsepʃn/	Wahrnehmung, Auffassung	
	walk of life /ˌwɔːk‿əv ˈlaɪf/	Gesellschaftsschicht, soziale Schicht	from *all walks of life* = from all different social backgrounds, rich or poor
PC p. 126	Which of these attitudes and values do you share?	Welche dieser Einstellungen und Werte teilt ihr?	
	demonstrate /ˈdemənˌstreɪt/	*hier:* demonstrieren	
	campaign /kæmˈpeɪn/	kämpfen, sich engagieren	

volunteer /ˌvɒlənˈtɪə/	sich freiwillig melden; ehrenamtlich arbeiten	to *volunteer* = to work without getting paid
plant /plɑːnt/	pflanzen	
environmental organisation /ɪnvaɪrənˌmentl‿ɔːɡənaɪˈzeɪʃn/	Umweltschutzorganisation	*Environmental organisations* try to raise awareness about climate change.
nutrition /njuːˈtrɪʃn/	Ernährung	Your *diet* is the food that you usually eat.
diet /ˈdaɪət/	Ernährung, Diät	
turn /tɜːn/	werden	
join in /ˌdʒɔɪn‿ˈɪn/	sich beteiligen an, mitmachen bei	
eco- /ˈiːkəʊ/	Öko-	
take action /ˌteɪk‿ˈækʃn/	handeln	to *take action* = to act

Come up with five ideas about what can make life meaningful for young people on which all your group members agree.	Denkt euch fünf Ideen aus, was das Leben für junge Leute bedeutsam machen kann, mit denen alle eure Gruppenmitglieder übereinstimmen.

PC	iceberg /ˈaɪsˌbɜːɡ/	Eisberg	
p. 127	body language /ˈbɒdi ˌlæŋɡwɪdʒ/	Körpersprache	
	behave /bɪˈheɪv/	sich verhalten, sich benehmen	
	and so on /ænd ˈsəʊ‿ɒn/	und so weiter	
	guide /ɡaɪd/	führen, leiten	
	honesty /ˈɒnɪsti/	Ehrlichkeit	
	shout at somebody /ˈʃaʊt‿ət ˌsʌmbədi/	jemanden anschreien	Her mum always *shouts at* her if her music is too loud.
	make a difference /ˌmeɪk‿ə ˈdɪfrəns/	einen Unterschied machen, verändern	
	soy /sɔɪ/	Soja	A selfless person is someone who always *puts* other people *first*.
	pose /pəʊz/	posieren	
PC	put first /ˌpʊt ˈfɜːst/	an die erste Stelle setzen	
p. 128	make a decision /ˌmeɪk‿ə dɪˈsɪʒn/	eine Entscheidung treffen	
	first /fɜːst/	zuerst	
	youngster /ˈjʌŋstə/	Jugendliche/r	
	trainer /ˈtreɪnə/	Trainer/in	
	be willing to /ˌbiː ˈwɪlɪŋ tʊ/	bereit sein	
	unsure /ʌnˈʃʊə/	unsicher	
	self-confident /ˌselfˈkɒnfɪdnt/	selbstsicher, selbstbewusst	
	take a chance /ˌteɪk‿ə ˈtʃɑːns/	die Gelegenheit nutzen	
	march /mɑːtʃ/	Demonstration	
	go away /ˌɡəʊ‿əˈweɪ/	weggehen, verschwinden	

There is an animal rights *march* on Sunday.

tap /tæp/	Wasserhahn	
cosmetics *(pl)* /kɒzˈmetɪks/	Kosmetika, Kosmetikartikel	
seasonally /ˈsiːznəli/	saisonbedingt, saisonal	*seasonally* = not throughout the whole year
PC p. 129 build up /ˌbɪld‿ˈʌp/	aufbauen	
movement /ˈmuːvmənt/	Bewegung	
take responsibility /ˌteɪk rɪˌspɒnsəˈbɪləti/	Verantwortung übernehmen	
climate /ˈklaɪmət/	Klima	
speak out /ˌspiːk‿ˈaʊt/	seine Meinung deutlich vertreten	
General Assembly /ˌdʒenrəl‿əˈsembli/	(UNO-)Vollversammlung	
pesticide /ˈpestɪsaɪd/	Pestizid, Schädlingsbekämpfungsmittel	A *pesticide* is toxic.
youth-led /ˈjuːθ led/	*von der Jugend durchgeführt*	
lawsuit /ˈlɔːˌsuːt/	Klage, Gerichtsverfahren, Prozess	
federal government /ˌfedrəl ˈɡʌvənmənt/	Bundesregierung	
failure /ˈfeɪljə/	Scheitern	
atmosphere /ˈætməsˌfɪə/	Atmosphäre	
change-maker /ˈtʃeɪndʒ ˌmeɪkə/	*jemand, der eine Veränderung in die Wege leitet*	
serve on /ˈsɜːv‿ɒn/	angehören	
youth council /ˈjuːθ ˌkaʊnsl/	Jugendrat	
halo /ˈheɪləʊ/	Heiligenschein	
Sweden /ˈswiːdn/	Schweden	
spokesman /ˈspəʊksmən/	Sprecher	
get involved /ˌɡet‿ɪnˈvɒlvd/	sich engagieren	There are lots of school clubs you can *get involved* in.

P p. 130

In class, talk about your reactions to the three topics.	Sprecht in der Klasse über eure Reaktionen auf die drei Themen.
What did you find interesting or surprising?	Was fandet ihr interessant oder überraschend?
How do you feel about what you found out?	Was haltet ihr von dem, was ihr herausgefunden habt?

shame /ʃeɪm/	Schande

Agree on one aspect that you want to work on as a project.	Einigt euch auf einen Aspekt, an dem ihr als Projekt arbeiten wollt.
What form could your project take?	Welche Gestalt könnte euer Projekt annehmen?

put together /ˌpʊt‿təˈɡeðə/	zusammenstellen, zusammensetzen, zusammenbauen	
inclusive /ɪnˈkluːsɪv/	allumfassend	
fashion show /ˈfæʃn ʃəʊ/	Modenschau	
goth /ɡɒθ/	Gothic	
choir /ˈkwaɪə/	Chor	They are singing in a *choir*.
put on /ˌpʊt‿ˈɒn/	*hier:* veranstalten	

P p. 131

Talk about your project in more detail.	Sprecht ausführlicher über euer Projekt.
Create an action plan for your project like this.	Erstellt einen solchen Aktionsplan für euer Projekt.

focus on /ˈfəʊkəs‿ɒn/	sich konzentrieren auf	Their *tastes* in music are very similar – they both like pop music.
taste /teɪst/	Geschmack	
like /laɪk/	Vorliebe	
dislike /dɪsˈlaɪk/	Abneigung	
trust /trʌst/	Vertrauen	
contribution /ˌkɒntrɪˈbjuːʃn/	Beitrag, Spende	
secretary /ˈsekrətri/	Sekretär/in	

Now put your plan into action.	Setzt nun euren Plan in die Tat um.

take action /ˌteɪk‿ˈækʃn/	handeln	We must *take action* to stop pollution! 
action plan /ˈækʃn plæn/	Handlungsplan, Maßnahmenplan	
advertise /ˈædvətaɪz/	für etwas Werbung machen	
fundraising *(no pl)* /ˈfʌndreɪzɪŋ/	*Geldbeschaffung zu Wohltätigkeitszwecken*	
breakdancing /ˈbreɪkˌdɑːnsɪŋ/	Breakdance	
athletic /æθˈletɪk/	athletisch, sportlich	
Latin American /ˌlætɪn‿əˈmerɪkən/	Lateinamerikaner/in, lateinamerikanisch	The *way of living* in the future will be very different.
way of living /ˌweɪ‿əv ˈlɪvɪŋ/	Lebensweise	
sadness /ˈsædnəs/	Traurigkeit	
characteristic /ˌkærɪktəˈrɪstɪk/	charakteristisch	*characteristic* = typical

PA p. 132

Choose the correct preposition from the box for each phrase.	Wähl die richtige Präposition aus dem Kasten für jeden Ausdruck.

belonging /bɪˈlɒŋɪŋ/	Zugehörigkeit

Talk about your music taste and what music means to you.	Sprich über deinen Musikgeschmack und was dir Musik bedeutet.

PB p. 133	label /ˈleɪbl/	*hier:* kategorisieren	
	set /set/	Set, Garnitur	
	classify /ˈklæsɪfaɪ/	klassifizieren	
	noun /naʊn/	Hauptwort, Substantiv, Nomen	
	challenge /ˈtʃælɪndʒ/	*hier:* infrage stellen	The word *'challenge'* can both be a *noun* and a verb.

Talk about fashion, lifestyle and consumerism with a partner or in a small group.	Sprich mit einem Partner/einer Partnerin oder in einer Gruppe über Mode, Lebensstil und Konsumdenken.

PC p. 134	moral /ˈmɒrəl/	moralisch, ethisch	
	principle /ˈprɪnsəpl/	Prinzip	
	way of thinking /ˌweɪ‿əv ˈθɪŋkɪŋ/	Denkweise	They have different *ways of thinking* but still agree.
	share /ʃeə/	(An)teil	
	get involved in /ˌget‿ɪnˈvɒlvd‿ɪn/	sich engagieren	

Talk about the role that attitudes and values play for your identity or the identity of teenagers.	Sprich über die Rolle, die Einstellungen und Werte für deine Identität oder die Identität von Teenagern spielen.

Dictionary

Hier findest du alphabetisch sortiert alle Wörter aus dem vorliegenden Buch sowie die Lernwörter aus den vorigen Bänden.
I bedeutet: Dieses Wort kommt in Band I (5. Klasse) vor, entsprechend steht II für Band 2, III für Band 3, IV für Band 4 und V für Band 5.
V:5/A3 bedeutet: Dieses Wort kommt in Band V, *Theme* 5, Aufgabe A3 das erste Mal vor oder wird erst an dieser Stelle zum Lernwort gemacht. Die **fett gedruckten** Lernwörter solltest du dir merken.
BS markiert ein Wort aus einem *Book stop*-Text. O markiert ein Wort aus einem *Optional*.
Diese Wörter sind zusätzlich mit einem ° versehen.
Folgende Abkürzungen werden verwendet:
sth = something, sb = somebody, etw = etwas, jd = jemand, jdm = jemandem, jdn = jemanden

A

a/an /ə, eɪ/ən/ ein(e) I
a /ə/ pro III
°a lot /ə 'lɒt/ viel, sehr V:3/O
ability /ə'bɪləti/ Fähigkeit IV
be able to do sth /ˌbi‿ˌeɪbl tə 'du: ˌsʌmθɪŋ/ etw tun können II
Aboriginal /ˌæbə'rɪdʒɪnəl/ austral. Ureinwohner/in; der Aboriginals V:1/A4
Aborigine /ˌæbə'rɪdʒəni/ austral. Ureinwohner/in V:1/A8
about /ə'baʊt/ über; an; ungefähr I
above /ə'bʌv/ über V:2/A4
above /ə'bʌv/ obige(r, s); oben genannte(n) V:4/B7
above all /əˌbʌv‿'ɔ:l/ vor allem V:6/Project A p. 119
abroad /ə'brɔ:d/ im Ausland, ins Ausland II
abseiling /'æbseɪlɪŋ/ Abseilen V:2/A4
absence /'æbsns/ Abwesenheit; Fehlen V:5/B1
absent /'æbsnt/ abwesend V:5/B3
academic /ˌækə'demɪk/ akademisch; *hier:* schulisch V:5/B3
accent /'æksnt/ Akzent V:1/B1
accept /ək'sept/ anerkennen; akzeptieren IV
°accept /ək'sept/ annehmen V:BS/4
accessory /ək'sesəri/ Accessoire V:6/Project B p. 123
accident /'æksɪdnt/ Unfall III
accommodation /əˌkɒmə'deɪʃn/ Unterkunft V:3/A2
accompany /ə'kʌmpni/ begleiten V:3/A6
according to /ə'kɔ:dɪŋ ˌtu:/ nach; gemäß II
account /ə'kaʊnt/ Bericht V:5/B4
accuse /ə'kju:z/ anklagen; beschuldigen V:5/A6
achieve /ə'tʃi:v/ erreichen V:3/B6
across /ə'krɒs/ über II; quer durch V:5/B3
act /ækt/ handeln; spielen II
act /ækt/ *hier:* dienen V:1/O
act out /ˌækt‿'aʊt/ nachspielen; vorspielen II
action /'ækʃn/ Handlung I
action plan /'ækʃn plæn/ Handlungsplan, Maßnahmenplan V:6/Project p. 131
active /'æktɪv/ aktiv V:2/P5
actively /'æktɪvli/ aktiv V:5/B3
activism /'æktɪvɪzm/ Aktivismus V:6/Project p. 117
activist /'æktɪvɪst/ Aktivist/in V:6/Project A p. 121
activity /æk'tɪvəti/ Aktivität II
actor/actress /'æktə, 'æktrəs/ Schauspieler/in II
actual /'æktʃuəl/ eigentlich; tatsächlich; echt V:5/A6
actually /'æktʃuəli/ eigentlich; übrigens II
°actually /'æktʃuəli/ tatsächlich V:BS/3
adapt /ə'dæpt/ anpassen V:3/A11
add /æd/ hinzufügen III
add /æd/ *hier:* ergänzen V:1/A1; addieren V:4/B2
add in /ˌæd‿'ɪn/ hinzufügen V:2/A4
address /ə'dres/ Adresse V:3/A4
adjective /'ædʒɪktɪv/ Adjektiv V:2/A5
adjust to /ə'dʒʌst‿tʊ/ anpassen an V:4/B2
admit /əd'mɪt/ zugeben IV
adolescence /ˌædə'lesns/ Adoleszenz; Jugend(zeit) V:6/Project p. 115
adrenaline /ə'drenəlɪn/ Adrenalin V:2/A3
adult /'ædʌlt/ Erwachsene/r II
adulthood /'ædʌltˌhʊd/ Erwachsensein; Erwachsenenalter; Volljährigkeit V:6/Project p. 115
advantage /əd'vɑ:ntɪdʒ/ Vorteil V:1/B1
advantageous /ˌædvən'teɪdʒəs/ günstig; vorteilhaft V:2/A3
adventure /əd'ventʃə/ Abenteuer III
adventurous /əd'ventʃrəs/ abenteuerlich; risikofreudig V:2/I
advertise /'ædvətaɪz/ für etw Werbung machen V:5/B5
advertisement (= advert) /əd'vɜ:tɪsmənt, 'ædvɜ:t/ Werbung; Anzeige III
advertising /'ædvəˌtaɪzɪŋ/ Werbung; Werbebranche V:3/B3
advice *(no pl)* /əd'vaɪs/ Rat(schlag) III
advise /əd'vaɪz/ raten, beraten; informieren IV

advisor /əd'vaɪzə/ Berater/in; Ratgeber/in V:3/B3
advocate /'ædvəkeɪt/ sich einsetzen; unterstützen V:5/B3
affect /ə'fekt/ betreffen; beeinflussen V:5/A2
affinity /ə'fɪnəti/ Verbundenheit; Affinität V:6/Project A p.119
afford /ə'fɔ:d/ sich leisten III
°afraid /ə'freɪd/ verängstigt V:BS/8
°Africa /'æfrɪkə/ Afrika V:5/O
African American /ˌæfrɪkən‿ə'merɪkən/ Afroamerikaner/in; afroamerikanisch IV
after /'ɑ:ftə/ nachdem IV; nach I
after all /ˌɑ:ftər‿'ɔ:l/ immerhin; schließlich III
after that /ˌɑ:ftə 'ðæt/ danach II
afternoon /ˌɑ:ftə'nu:n/ Nachmittag I
afterwards /'ɑ:ftəwədz/ anschließend; später III
again /ə'gen/ wieder; noch einmal I
against /ə'genst/ gegen II:5/A8
age /eɪdʒ/ Alter I
aged /eɪdʒd/ alt V:3/A4
aggressive /ə'gresɪv/ aggressiv, angriffslustig V:5/B3
ago /ə'gəʊ/ vor III
agonising /'ægənaɪzɪŋ/ qualvoll V:5/A5
agree /ə'gri:/ zustimmen II
agree on /ə'gri:‿ɒn/ sich einigen auf V:4/A5
agricultural /ˌægrɪ'kʌltʃrəl/ landwirtschaftlich V:2/B4
ahead /ə'hed/ voraus IV
aim /eɪm/ Ziel V:5/B3
aim /eɪm/ zielen auf V:5/B3
air /eə/ Luft III
air raid /'eə reɪd/ Luftangriff V:5/A2
airport /'eəpɔ:t/ Flughafen II
alarm clock /ə'lɑ:m klɒk/ Wecker II
alien /'eɪliən/ Außerirdische/r V:6/Project p.115
all /ɔ:l/ alle; alles I; ganz; völlig III
most of all /'məʊst‿əv‿ˌɔ:l/ am allermeisten III
all afternoon /ˌɔ:l‿ˌɑ:ftə'nu:n/ den ganzen Nachmittag lang II
all along /ˌɔ:l‿ə'lɒŋ/ die ganze Zeit; von Anfang an V:6/Project A p.121
all around /ˌɔ:l‿ə'raʊnd/ überall V:2/A4
all but /'ɔ:l bʌt/ *hier:* fast komplett V:1/B3
all kinds of /ˌɔ:l 'kaɪndz‿əv/ alle möglichen II
all over /ˌɔ:l‿'əʊvə/ überall V:5/B3
all over the place /ˌɔ:l‿ˌəʊvə ðə 'pleɪs/ überall V:5/B3
all over the world /ˌɔ:l‿ˌəʊvə ðə 'wɜ:ld/ auf der ganzen Welt V:3/B3
all right /ˌɔ:l 'raɪt/ in Ordnung III
all the time /ˌɔ:l ðə 'taɪm/ die ganze Zeit II
all week /ˌɔ:l 'wi:k/ die ganze Woche lang II
allow /ə'laʊ/ erlauben II:5/A8
almost /'ɔ:lməʊst/ fast; beinahe III
alone /ə'ləʊn/ allein III
along /ə'lɒŋ/ vorwärts V:1/P2
along with /ə'lɒŋ wɪð/ zusammen mit V:2/B3
alongside /ə'lɒŋˌsaɪd/ neben; Seite an Seite V:5/B3
Alps /ælps/ Alpen V:2/B4
already /ɔ:l'redi/ schon II
also /'ɔ:lsəʊ/ auch I
although /ɔ:l'ðəʊ/ obwohl IV
altogether /ˌɔ:ltə'geðə/ insgesamt I
°aluminium foil /ˌælə'mɪniəm fɔɪl/ Alufolie V:2/O
always /'ɔ:lweɪz/ immer I
am (= ante meridiem) /ˌeɪ'em, ˌænti mə'rɪdiəm/ morgens, vormittags *(nur hinter Uhrzeit zwischen Mitternacht und 12 Uhr mittags)* I
amazing *(informal)* /ə'meɪzɪŋ/ toll III
ambassador /æm'bæsədə/ Botschafter/in V:5/B3
America /ə'merɪkə/ Amerika II
American /ə'merɪkən/ Amerikaner/in; amerikanisch IV
among /ə'mʌŋ/ unter; zwischen II
amongst /ə'mʌŋst/ unter; zwischen V:2/B3
amount /ə'maʊnt/ Menge; Betrag II
amusement park /ə'mju:zmənt pɑ:k/ Freizeitpark V:2/A2
analyse /'ænəlaɪz/ analysieren; untersuchen V:4/I
°ancestry /'ænsestri/ Abstammung V:2/O
ancient /'eɪnʃnt/ alt; antik V:1/B5
and /ænd/ und I
and so on /ænd 'səʊ‿ɒn/ und so weiter V:6/Project C p.127
anger /'æŋgə/ Ärger; Wut V:6/Project A p.119
angry /'æŋgri/ verärgert II
animal /'ænɪml/ Tier I
animal shelter /'ænɪml ˌʃeltə/ Tierheim V:3/A2
ankle /'æŋkl/ (Fuß)knöchel V:2/A4
annex /ə'neks/ annektieren; einverleiben V:2/B3
announce /ə'naʊns/ bekannt geben IV
announcement /ə'naʊnsmənt/ Bekanntmachung; Mitteilung; Durchsage V:5/A2
annoyed /ə'nɔɪd/ verärgert II
annual /'ænjuəl/ jährlich V:1/B10
anonymous /ə'nɒnɪməs/ anonym V:4/A5
another /ə'nʌðə/ noch ein/e I; ein/e andere(r,s) II
answer /'ɑ:nsə/ (be)antworten I; Antwort I
answer the phone /ˌɑ:nsə ðə 'fəʊn/ ans Telefon gehen I
anthem /'ænθəm/ Hymne V:2/B5
anticlimax, anti-climax /ˌænti'klaɪmæks/ Antiklimax; Enttäuschung V:5/A2
any /'eni/ (irgend)ein(e) I
any /'eni/ *hier:* jede(r,s); alle V:5/P2

anybody /ˈenibɒdi/ irgendjemand; jede(r, s) I
anyone /ˈeniˌwʌn/ jede(r, s); (irgend)jemand V:3/A2
anything /ˈeniˌθɪŋ/ irgendetwas III
anything else /eniˌθɪŋ‿ˈels/ noch etwas I
anyway /ˈeniweɪ/ jedenfalls I; sowieso; überhaupt II
anywhere /ˈeniˌweə/ irgendwo II
apologise /əˈpɒlədʒaɪz/ sich entschuldigen IV
apology /əˈpɒlədʒi/ Entschuldigung V:1/B8
appealing /əˈpi:lɪŋ/ attraktiv; verlockend V:2/B4
appear /əˈpɪə/ erscheinen, auftauchen IV
appearance /əˈpɪərəns/ Erscheinen, Aussehen IV
apple /ˈæpl/ Apfel I
°applicant /ˈæplɪkənt/ Bewerber/in V:3/O
application /ˌæplɪˈkeɪʃn/ Bewerbung IV
apply for /əˈplaɪ fɔ:/ sich bewerben um IV
appreciation /əˌpri:ʃiˈeɪʃn/ Anerkennung; Verständnis V:6/Project A p. 119
°approach /əˈprəʊtʃ/ Zugang V:BS/7
April /ˈeɪprəl/ April I
archive /ˈɑ:kaɪv/ Archiv V:5/A2
area /ˈeəriə/ Gebiet, Region III; Bereich V:5/B3
argue /ˈɑ:gju/ sich streiten III
argument /ˈɑ:gjʊmənt/ Streit IV
arithmetic /əˈrɪθmətɪk/ Rechen- V:4/B2
armed /ɑ:md/ bewaffnet V:5/B3
the armed forces *(pl)* /ˌɑ:md ˈfɔ:sɪz/ Streitkräfte V:5/A6
army /ˈɑ:mi/ Armee V:5/A6
around /əˈraʊnd/ um; herum, umher II; ungefähr V:3/B1
arrange /əˈreɪndʒ/ arrangieren; organisieren V:5/B3
arrival /əˈraɪvl/ Ankunft IV
arrive /əˈraɪv/ ankommen II
art /ɑ:t/ Kunst I

art gallery /ˈɑ:t ˌgæləri/ Kunstgalerie V:1/A4
article /ˈɑ:tɪkl/ Artikel I
artist /ˈɑ:tɪst/ Künstler/in III
as /əz/ als; wie; während II; weil; da V:1/B3
as ... as /æz æz/ so ... wie II
as a result /əz‿ə rɪˈzʌlt/ als Folge IV
as well /ˌəz‿ˈwel/ auch II
as well as /əz ˈwel‿əz/ ebenso wie V:2/A3
Asia /ˈeɪʒə/ Asien V:1/A8
Asian /ˈeɪʒn/ Asiat/in; asiatisch V:1/A4
aside from /əˈsaɪd frəm/ abgesehen von V:6/Project B p. 125
ask /ɑ:sk/ fragen; bitten I
ask questions /ˌɑ:sk ˈkwestʃnz/ Fragen stellen III
aspect /ˈæspekt/ Aspekt; Gesichtspunkt V:4/A9
aspiring /əˈspaɪərɪŋ/ aufstrebend; ambitioniert V:3/B6
assembly /əˈsembli/ (Schüler) versammlung I
assess /əˈses/ einschätzen V:2/A3
assistance /əˈsɪstns/ Hilfe V:5/B3
assistant coach /əˌsɪstnt ˈkəʊtʃ/ Kotrainer/in V:3/A4
at /æt/ an; in; bei; um I
at all /ət‿ˈɔ:l/ überhaupt II
at any time /ət‿ˈeni taɪm/ jederzeit V:3/A6
at first /ət ˈfɜ:st/ zuerst V:2/A10
at heart /ˌæt ˈhɑ:t/ im Grunde seines/ihres Herzens V:2/P7
at home /ˌæt ˈhəʊm/ zu Hause I
at last /ət ˈlɑ:st/ endlich; schließlich II
at least /ət ˈli:st/ mindestens; wenigstens III
at midnight /æt ˈmɪdˌnaɪt/ um Mitternacht II
at night /æt ˈnaɪt/ nachts II
at that time /æt ˈðæt‿taɪm/ zu jener Zeit V:5/B3
at the moment /ˌæt‿ðə ˈməʊmənt/ im Moment I
at the same time /æt‿ðə ˌseɪm ˈtaɪm/ gleichzeitig V:1/A2

at the time /ˌæt‿ðə ˈtaɪm/ zu dem Zeitpunkt; damals V:3/B3
at the top /ˌæt‿ðə ˈtɒp/ oben V:3/B8
at the weekend /ˌæt‿ðə ˈwi:kend/ am Wochenende I
athletic /æθˈletɪk/ athletisch; sportlich V:6/Project A p. 132
atmosphere /ˈætməsˌfɪə/ Atmosphäre V:6/Project C p. 129
attach /əˈtætʃ/ befestigen; verbinden; *hier:* anfügen V:1/B10
attack /əˈtæk/ angreifen II
attack /əˈtæk/ Angriff V:5/A6
°attempt /əˈtempt/ versuchen V:BS/4
attend /əˈtend/ besuchen IV
attend school /əˌtend ˈsku:l/ in die Schule gehen IV
attendance /əˈtendəns/ Anwesenheit V:5/B3
attention /əˈtenʃn/ Aufmerksamkeit V:3/B6
attic /ˈætɪk/ Dachboden V:4/B2
attitude /ˈætɪˌtju:d/ Haltung; Einstellung IV
attraction /əˈtrækʃn/ Attraktion V:2/A4
attractive /əˈtræktɪv/ attraktiv; reizvoll IV
attractive /əˈtræktɪv/ *hier:* ansprechend V:3/A11
audience /ˈɔ:diəns/ Publikum II
audio feature /ˈɔ:diəʊ ˌfi:tʃə/ Hörbeitrag V:2/B9
audio recording /ˈɔ:diəʊ rɪˌkɔ:dɪŋ/ Audioaufnahme V:1/B11
audition /ɔ:ˈdɪʃn/ Vorsprechen, Vorsingen, Vortanzen V:6/Project A p. 120
August /ˈɔ:gəst/ August I
aunt /ɑ:nt/ Tante I
Aussie *(informal)* /ˈɒzi/ Australier/in; australisch V:1/P4
Australia /ɒˈstreɪliə/ Australien V:1/I
Australia /ɒˈstreɪliə/ V:1/A6
Australian /ɒˈstreɪliən/ Australier/in; australisch V:1/A2
authentic /ɔ:ˈθentɪk/ authentisch V:5/A7

°authenticity /ˌɔːθenˈtɪsəti/ Echtheit; Authentizität V:BS/8
authority /ɔːˈθɒrəti/ Autorität V:6/Project p. 115
automatically /ˌɔːtəˈmætɪkli/ automatisch V:4/A8
autumn /ˈɔːtəm/ Herbst I
available /əˈveɪləbl/ verfügbar III
average /ˈævərɪdʒ/ durchschnittlich III; Durchschnitt V:5/B3
avoid /əˈvɔɪd/ (ver)meiden IV
°awake /əˈweɪk/ wach V:BS/3
award /əˈwɔːd/ Preis; Auszeichnung V:5/B8
be aware of sth /ˌbi‿əˈweər‿əv ˌsʌmθɪŋ/ sich einer Sache bewusst sein IV
awareness /əˈweənəs/ Bewusstsein V:4/A5
away /əˈweɪ/ weg II
awesome /ˈɔːsm/ spitze; super; beeindruckend II
awful /ˈɔːfl/ schrecklich IV

B

babysit /ˈbeɪbiˌsɪt/ babysitten V:3/A4
back /bæk/ Rücken I; zurück I
°back /bæk/ Heck, Rücksitz V:BS/7
back country skiing /ˈbæk‿kʌntri ˌskiːɪŋ/ Skilanglauf V:2/A7
back then /ˌbæk ˈðen/ damals V:1/B10
backache *(no pl)* /ˈbækeɪk/ Rückenschmerzen III
background /ˈbækˌɡraʊnd/ Hintergrund IV
bacon /ˈbeɪkən/ Schinkenspeck I
bad /bæd/ schlecht; schlimm II
bad luck /ˌbæd ˈlʌk/ Pech II
badly /ˈbædli/ sehr, dringend IV
bag /bæɡ/ Tasche II
baked beans *(pl)* /ˌbeɪkt ˈbiːnz/ Bohnen in Tomatensauce I
baker /ˈbeɪkə/ Bäcker/in II
°balance /ˈbæləns/ Gleichgewicht, Balance V:BS/4
ballet /ˈbæleɪ/ Ballett V:6/Project p. 116
balloon /bəˈluːn/ Luftballon I
banana /bəˈnɑːnə/ Banane I
bandage /ˈbændɪdʒ/ Verband III
bar /bɑː/ Riegel V:5/B5
bar chart /ˈbɑː tʃɑːt/ Balken-/Säulendiagramm V:4/A1
barren /ˈbærən/ unfruchtbar V:1/B5
°barrier /ˈbæriə/ Barriere, Hindernis V:1/O
base /beɪs/ Grundlage, Basis V:4/A1
°based on /ˈbeɪst‿ɒn/ basierend auf V:BS/7
°basically /ˈbeɪsɪkli/ im Wesentlichen V:BS/6
basis /ˈbeɪsɪs/ Grundlage; Basis V:2/A10
on a regular basis /ˌɒn‿ə ˈreɡjʊlə ˌbeɪsɪs/ regelmäßig V:2/A1
basket /ˈbɑːskɪt/ Korb V:2/B3
bat /bæt/ Fledermaus I
°bat /bæt/ Schläger V:BS/8
bath /bɑːθ/ Bad V:5/A2
bathing suit /ˈbeɪðɪŋ suːt/ Badeanzug V:1/P4
bathroom /ˈbɑːθˌruːm/ Badezimmer I
battlefield /ˈbætlˌfiːld/ Schlachtfeld V:5/A1
battler /ˈbætlə/ Kämpfer/in V:1/B5
BC (= before Christ) /ˌbiː ˈsiː, bɪˌfɔː ˈkraɪst/ v. Chr., vor Christus; *hier: Wortspiel mit Bezug auf die Ankunft Cooks in Australien* V:1/B3
be *(irr)* /biː/ sein I
be able to do sth /ˌbi‿ˌeɪbl tə ˈduː ˌsʌmθɪŋ/ etw tun können II
be about /ˌbi‿əˈbaʊt/ gehen um; handeln von IV
be afraid of /ˌbi‿əˈfreɪd‿əv/ Angst haben vor III
be allowed to /ˌbi‿əˈlaʊd‿tə/ dürfen II
be around *(informal)* /ˌbi‿əˈraʊnd/ da sein V:3/B8
be asleep /ˌbi‿əˈsliːp/ schlafen IV
be aware of sth /ˌbi‿əˈweər‿əv ˌsʌmθɪŋ/ sich einer Sache bewusst sein IV
be based /biː ˈbeɪst/ seinen Sitz haben V:5/B3
be born /biː ˈbɔːn/ geboren werden III
be committed /ˌbiː kəˈmɪtɪd/ sich widmen V:5/B3
be considered /ˌbiː kənˈsɪdəd/ gelten als V:1/A2
be good at sth /ˌbiː ˈɡʊd‿æt ˌsʌmθɪŋ/ gut in etw sein II
be in high demand /ˌbi‿ɪn ˌhaɪ dɪˈmɑːnd/ sehr gefragt sein V:3/B3
be made /ˌbiː ˈmeɪd/ gemacht werden III
be made up of /biː ˌmeɪd‿ˈʌp‿əv/ zusammengesetzt sein aus V:1/A7
be off /ˌbi‿ˈɒf/ *hier:* frei haben V:3/B3
be one's turn /ˌbiː wʌnz ˈtɜːn/ an der Reihe sein I
be out of breath /ˌbi‿ˌaʊt‿əv ˈbreθ/ außer Atem sein; atemlos sein III
be out of sth /ˌbi‿ˌaʊt‿əv ˈsʌmθɪŋ/ etw nicht mehr haben V:4/A8
be popular with /ˌbiː ˈpɒpjʊlə wɪð/ beliebt sein bei III
be prepared /ˌbiː prɪˈpeəd/ vorbereitet sein auf V:2/A4
be proud of /ˌbiː ˈpraʊd‿əv/ stolz sein auf IV
be right /ˌbiː ˈraɪt/ recht haben II
be scared (of) /ˌbiː ˈskeəd‿əv/ Angst haben (vor) II
be stuck /ˌbiː ˈstʌk/ *hier:* feststecken, festhängen V:3/B3
be supposed to do sth /ˌbiː səˌpəʊzd‿tə ˈduː ˌsʌmθɪŋ/ etw tun sollen IV
be up to sth /ˌbi‿ˈʌp tə ˌsʌmθɪŋ/ etw vorhaben V:4/A3
be wrong /ˌbiː ˈrɒŋ/ sich irren V:1/A4
beach /biːtʃ/ Strand II
°beak /biːk/ Schnabel V:BS/3
baked beans *(pl)* /ˌbeɪkt ˈbiːnz/ Bohnen in Tomatensauce I
beat /biːt/ Takt V:6/Project A p. 120

beat *(irr)* /biːt/ schlagen I
beautiful /ˈbjuːtəfl/ schön II:4/A1
beauty /ˈbjuːti/ Schönheit V:6/Project A p. 119
because /bɪˈkɒz/ weil; da I
become *(irr)* /bɪˈkʌm/ werden II
bed /bed/ Bett I
bed and breakfast /ˌbed‿ən ˈbrekfəst/ Frühstückspension V:2/B5
bedroom /ˈbedruːm/ Schlafzimmer V:4/B2
beetle /ˈbiːtl/ Käfer V:1/A4
before /bɪˈfɔː/ vor I; bevor II; vorher; zuvor II
begin *(irr)* /bɪˈgɪn/ anfangen; beginnen II
beginning /bɪˈgɪnɪŋ/ Anfang V:4/B5
behave /bɪˈheɪv/ sich verhalten, sich benehmen V:6/Project C p. 127
behaviour /bɪˈheɪvjə/ Benehmen; Verhalten V:2/A3
behind /bɪˈhaɪnd/ hinten IV; hinter I
Belgium /ˈbeldʒəm/ Belgien V:3/A2
belief /bɪˈliːf/ Glaube V:2/B9
believe (in) /bɪˈliːv‿ɪn/ glauben (an) III
belong (to) /bɪˈlɒŋ/ gehören (zu) II
belonging /bɪˈlɒŋɪŋ/ Zugehörigkeit V:6/Project A p. 132
below /bɪˈləʊ/ unten, unter IV
beneath /bɪˈniːθ/ unter IV
benefit /ˈbenɪfɪt/ Vorteil; *hier:* Sozialleistung V:3/B3
berry /ˈberi/ Beere V:1/B4
best /best/ beste(r, s) I; am liebsten II
like best /ˌlaɪk ˈbest/ am liebsten mögen I
best wishes /ˌbest ˈwɪʃɪz/ viele Grüße II
bet *(irr)* /bet/ wetten V:6/Project A p. 120
better /ˈbetə/ besser I
like better /ˌlaɪk ˈbetə/ lieber mögen III

between /bɪˈtwiːn/ zwischen I
beyond /bɪˈjɒnd/ jenseits V:5/B3
in the back of beyond /ˌɪn ðə ˌbæk‿əv bɪˈjɒnd/ am Ende der Welt V:1/B10
biased /ˈbaɪəst/ voreingenommen V:5/A6
bicycle /ˈbaɪsɪkl/ Fahrrad III
big /bɪg/ groß I
bike /baɪk/ Fahrrad I
by bike /ˌbaɪ ˈbaɪk/ mit dem Fahrrad I
ride a bike /ˌraɪd‿ə ˈbaɪk/ Fahrrad fahren I
bill /bɪl/ Rechnung III
billion /ˈbɪljən/ Milliarde V:1/A7
bin /bɪn/ Abfalleimer I
bind *(irr)* /baɪnd/ binden, fesseln V:1/B5
biodiversity /ˌbaɪəʊdaɪˈvɜːsəti/ Artenvielfalt V:1/A4
biological /ˌbaɪəˈlɒdʒɪkl/ biologisch V:2/A3
biology /baɪˈɒlədʒi/ Biologie V:2/P12
biosecurity *(no pl)* /ˈbaɪəʊsɪˌkjʊərəti/ *Sicherheitsvorkehrungen gegen biogene Probleme* V:2/B7
bird /bɜːd/ Vogel I
birthday /ˈbɜːθdeɪ/ Geburtstag I
Happy birthday (to you)! /ˌhæpi ˈbɜːθdeɪ tʊ juː/ Herzlichen Glückwunsch zum Geburtstag! I
birthplace /ˈbɜːθˌpleɪs/ Geburtsort V:2/A4
biscuit /ˈbɪskɪt/ Keks I:4/B5
a (little) bit /ə ˌlɪtl ˈbɪt/ ein (kleines) bisschen II
°bit /bɪt/ Stück V:BS/3
bite *(irr)* /baɪt/ beißen III
black /blæk/ schwarz I
Black Forest /ˌblæk ˈfɒrɪst/ Schwarzwald V:5/B3
blackboard /ˈblækˌbɔːd/ Tafel I
blackfella *(informal)* /ˈblækˌfelə/ *austral. Ureinwohner/in* V:1/B3
blackout /ˈblækaʊt/ Verdunkelung V:5/A2
blank out /ˌblæŋk‿ˈaʊt/ verdrängen; ausstreichen V:4/B2

blend in /ˌblend‿ˈɪn/ sich vermischen, passen zu V:6/Project B p. 123
°blimey *(informal)* /ˈblaɪmi/ (ach) du liebe Zeit!
blister /ˈblɪstə/ Blase V:5/A2
the Blitz /ðə ˈblɪts/ *deutsche Luftangriffe auf brit. Städte im Zweiten Weltkrieg* V:5/A2
blood /blʌd/ Blut V:2/A4
blow off /ˌbləʊ‿ˈɒf/ wegreißen; abreißen V:5/A3
blue /bluː/ blau I
BMXing /ˌbiː‿em‿ˈeksɪŋ/ BMX-Rad fahren V:2/A1
board /bɔːd/ Tafel; Brett III
board /bɔːd/ *hier:* Verpflegung V:3/A2; Amt; Behörde V:3/O
board a ship /ˌbɔːd‿ə ˈʃɪp/ ein Schiff besteigen IV
boarding school /ˈbɔːdɪŋ skuːl/ Internat V:1/B10
boat /bəʊt/ Boot II
body /ˈbɒdi/ Körper I
body /ˈbɒdi/ *hier:* Leiche V:5/B4
body language /ˈbɒdi ˌlæŋgwɪdʒ/ Körpersprache V:6/Project C p. 127
boil /bɔɪl/ kochen *(Wasser)* III
bomb /bɒm/ Bombe V:5/A2
bone /bəʊn/ Knochen III
book /bʊk/ Buch I
exercise book /ˈeksəsaɪz ˌbʊk/ Heft I
book /bʊk/ buchen, reservieren V:2/A5
boot /buːt/ Stiefel I
border /ˈbɔːdə/ Grenze V:5/B3
°bored /bɔːd/ gelangweilt V:BS/4
boring /ˈbɔːrɪŋ/ langweilig I
borrow /ˈbɒrəʊ/ (aus)leihen II
both /bəʊθ/ beide III
bottle /ˈbɒtl/ Flasche III
bottom /ˈbɒtəm/ Boden, Grund V:2/A5
bouldering /ˈbəʊldərɪŋ/ Bouldern V:2/A1
boundary /ˈbaʊndri/ Grenze V:6/Project A p. 119
bowl /bəʊl/ Schüssel, Schale III
box /bɒks/ Kasten; Kiste II

Boxing Day /ˈbɒksɪŋ deɪ/ zweiter Weihnachtsfeiertag II
boy /bɔɪ/ Junge I
°boycott /ˈbɔɪˌkɒt/ Boykott V:BS/7
boyfriend /ˈbɔɪˌfrend/ Freund *(Partner)*; Partner III
bracelet /ˈbreɪslət/ Armband V:6/Project A p. 121
brain /breɪn/ Gehirn V:2/A3
°brainwashing /ˈbreɪnˌwɒʃɪŋ/ Gehirnwäsche V:5/O
brand /brænd/ Marke V:5/B5
brave /breɪv/ mutig V:2/P7
bread /bred/ Brot III
break /breɪk/ Pause I
break *(irr)* /breɪk/ brechen; zerbrechen; kaputt machen II
break *(irr)* /breɪk/ *hier:* überschreiten V:6/Project A p. 119
break down /ˌbreɪk ˈdaʊn/ liegen bleiben V:2/A2
break into /ˌbreɪk‿ˈɪntuː/ einbrechen V:4/A3
break out /ˌbreɪk‿ˈaʊt/ ausbrechen V:5/A2
break up /ˌbreɪk‿ˈʌp/ Schluss machen III
break up /ˌbreɪk‿ˈʌp/ zerstören V:1/B8
breakfast /ˈbrekfəst/ Frühstück I
for breakfast /fə ˈbrekfəst/ zum Frühstück I
have breakfast /ˌhæv ˈbrekfəst/ frühstücken I
be out of breath /ˌbi‿ˌaʊt‿əv ˈbreθ/ außer Atem sein; atemlos sein III
°breathe in /ˌbriːð‿ˈɪn/ einatmen V:BS/8
bricklayer /ˈbrɪkˌleɪə/ Maurer/in II
bridge /brɪdʒ/ Brücke II
bright /braɪt/ intelligent; strahlend, hell III
brilliant /ˈbrɪljənt/ genial, klasse III
bring *(irr)* /brɪŋ/ mitbringen I
bring in /brɪŋ/ *hier:* einbringen V:3/B6
bring together /ˌbrɪŋ təˈgeðə/ zusammenbringen IV
Brit *(informal)* /brɪt/ Brite/Britin V:5/B3
Britain /ˈbrɪtn/ Großbritannien III
British /ˈbrɪtɪʃ/ britisch III
bro *(informal)* /brəʊ/ Bruder; Kumpel V:2/B8
broadband /ˈbrɔːdˌbænd/ Breitband V:1/B10
broadcast /ˈbrɔːdˌkɑːst/ Übertragung; Sendung V:1/B10
broadcasting /ˈbrɔːdˌkɑːstɪŋ/ Rundfunk; Fernsehen V:5/A6
brochure /ˈbrəʊʃə/ Broschüre V:1/A10
broken /ˈbrəʊkən/ zerbrochen; gebrochen; kaputt III
brother /ˈbrʌðə/ Bruder I
brotherhood /ˈbrʌðəˌhʊd/ Brüderlichkeit V:5/B2
brothers and sisters /ˈbrʌðəz‿ænd ˌsɪstəz/ Geschwister II
brown /braʊn/ braun I
bruised /bruːzd/ geprellt III
brush /brʌʃ/ putzen; bürsten I
brush one's teeth /ˌbrʌʃ wʌnz ˈtiːθ/ sich die Zähne putzen I
bubble /ˈbʌbl/ Blase V:4/B5
budgie /ˈbʌdʒi/ Wellensittich I
bug /bʌg/ Wanze; Ungeziefer V:2/B7
build *(irr)* /bɪld/ bauen II
build *(irr)* /bɪld/ *hier:* schaffen, aufbauen V:5/B3
build up /ˌbɪld‿ˈʌp/ aufbauen V:6/Project C p. 129
building /ˈbɪldɪŋ/ Gebäude III
bully /ˈbʊli/ mobben II
bullying /ˈbʊliɪŋ/ Mobben II:5/I
burn *(irr)* /bɜːn/ (ver)brennen II
bury /ˈberi/ be-/vergraben V:1/B4
by bus /ˌbaɪ ˈbʌs/ mit dem Bus I
go by bus /ˌgəʊ baɪ ˈbʌs/ mit dem Bus fahren I
bus stop /ˈbʌs‿stɒp/ Bushaltestelle II
bushy /ˈbʊʃi/ Hinterwäldler/in V:1/B5
business /ˈbɪznəs/ Geschäft; Handel III
busy /ˈbɪzi/ belebt; verkehrsreich IV; arbeitsreich; beschäftigt I
but /bʌt/ sondern IV; aber I
butterfly /ˈbʌtəˌflaɪ/ Schmetterling II
°buttock /ˈbʌtək/ (Po)backe; (Hinter)backe V:2/O
button /ˈbʌtən/ Knopf V:4/A3
buy *(irr)* /baɪ/ kaufen I
by /baɪ/ von; mit II; *hier:* (spätestens) bis II
by /baɪ/ *hier:* per V:1/B10; *hier:* an V:5/A2
by accident /ˌbaɪ‿ˈæksɪdnt/ zufällig; aus Versehen III
by bike /ˌbaɪ ˈbaɪk/ mit dem Fahrrad I
by bus /ˌbaɪ ˈbʌs/ mit dem Bus I
by the thousand /ˌbaɪ ðə ˈθaʊznd/ zu Tausenden V:5/B3
by the way /ˌbaɪ ðə ˈweɪ/ übrigens II
bye /baɪ/ tschüs(s) I

C

cabin /ˈkæbɪn/ Hütte V:5/A3
cabin boy /ˈkæbɪn bɔɪ/ Schiffsjunge V:2/B3
cage /keɪdʒ/ Käfig II
cake /keɪk/ Kuchen I
calculate /ˈkælkjʊleɪt/ berechnen V:4/B2
calendar /ˈkælɪndə/ Kalender I
call /kɔːl/ anrufen I; rufen II; Anruf; Gespräch II; nennen III
call sb names /ˌkɔːl ˌsʌmbədi ˈneɪmz/ jdn beschimpfen II
called /kɔːld/ genannt; namens II
calm /ˌkɑːm/ ruhig; gelassen V:5/A3
camel /ˈkæml/ Kamel V:1/A2
camera /ˈkæmrə/ Kamera; Fotoapparat III
camera shot /ˈkæmrə ʃɒt/ Aufnahme; (Film)sequenz V:6/Project B p. 124
campaign /kæmˈpeɪn/ Kampagne V:5/B8
campaign /kæmˈpeɪn/ kämpfen; sich engagieren V:6/Project C p. 126
camper trailer /ˈkæmpə ˌtreɪlə/ Wohnwagenabstellplatz V:1/A4

campfire /ˈkæmpˌfaɪə/ Lagerfeuer V:5/B3
can /kæn/ Dose; Büchse III
can /kæn/ können I
cancer /ˈkænsə/ Krebs V:1/P6
°candidate /ˈkændɪdeɪt/ Kandidat/in V:3/O
candle /ˈkændl/ Kerze I
cane /keɪn/ Zuckerrohr V:1/A4
cane toad /ˈkeɪn təʊd/ Agakröte V:1/A4
canoe /kəˈnuː/ Kanu V:1/B4
canyon /ˈkænjən/ Schlucht V:2/A4
cap /kæp/ Mütze I
capable /ˈkeɪpəbl/ fähig V:2/A3
capital /ˈkæpɪtl/ Hauptstadt IV
captain /ˈkæptɪn/ Kapitän/in; Mannschaftsführer/in V:1/A8
caption /ˈkæpʃn/ Bildunterschrift IV
car /kɑː/ Auto I
card /kɑːd/ Karte I
care /keə/ sich kümmern um; achten auf IV; Betreuung; Pflege; Sorgfalt IV
care about /ˈkeər‿əˌbaʊt/ Wert legen auf IV
career /kəˈrɪə/ Karriere, Laufbahn IV
career expert /kəˈrɪər‿ˌekspɜːt/ Berufsberater/in V:3/A3
careful /ˈkeəfl/ vorsichtig III
carefully /ˈkeəfli/ *hier:* genau IV:4/B7; vorsichtig II
°caretaker /ˈkeəˌteɪkə/ Hausmeister/in V:3/O
carnival /ˈkɑːnɪvl/ Karneval III
°carpenter /ˈkɑːpɪntə/ Zimmermann; Schreiner/in V:BS/6
°carpet snake /ˈkɑːpɪt sneɪk/ Teppichpython V:BS/1
carpooling /ˈkɑːpuːlɪŋ/ *Bildung einer Fahrgemeinschaft* V:2/A7
carry /ˈkæri/ tragen II
carry on /ˌkæri‿ˈɒn/ weitermachen III
carry out /ˌkæri‿ˈaʊt/ durchführen, betreiben V:5/B3
carve /kɑːv/ schnitzen; meißeln V:2/B3
case /keɪs/ Fall V:3/B6
pencil case /ˈpensl ˌkeɪs/ Federmäppchen I
cash /kæʃ/ Geld; Bargeld IV
cash register /ˈkæʃ ˌredʒɪstə/ Registrierkasse V:3/B3
cast /kɑːst/ Besetzung V:1/B6
casual /ˈkæʒuəl/ lässig V:6/Project B p. 122
cat /kæt/ Katze I
catastrophe /kəˈtæstrəfi/ Katastrophe V:2/A7
catch *(irr)* /kætʃ/ fangen II
catch a train /ˌkætʃ‿ə ˈtreɪn/ einen Zug nehmen II
cause /kɔːz/ verursachen III
cause /kɔːz/ Grund, Ursache; *hier:* Sache V:5/B5
cautious /ˈkɔːʃəs/ vorsichtig; achtsam V:2/A3
cave /keɪv/ Höhle V:2/A4
caver /ˈkeɪvə/ Höhlensportler/in V:2/A4
caving /ˈkeɪvɪŋ/ *hier:* Höhlenerforschen V:2/A4
ceasefire /ˈsiːsˌfaɪə/ Waffenruhe V:5/B4
celebrate /ˈseləˌbreɪt/ feiern II
celebration /ˌseləˈbreɪʃn/ Feier II
celebrity /səˈlebrəti/ Berühmtheit; Star V:6/Project A p. 120
cellphone *(AE)* /ˈsel fəʊn/ Handy V:3/B3
center *(AE)* /ˈsentə/ Zentrum V:5/B3
central /ˈsentrəl/ zentral; wesentlich; Zentral- V:5/A2
centre /ˈsentə/ Zentrum; Mitte IV
century /ˈsentʃəri/ Jahrhundert IV
°ceremonial /ˌserəˈməʊniəl/ zeremoniell V:BS/3
°ceremony /ˈserəməni/ Zeremonie V:2/O
certain /ˈsɜːtn/ bestimmt; gewiss V:6/Project p. 114
certainly /ˈsɜːtnli/ sicher; gerne III
chain /tʃeɪn/ Kette V:1/B5
chair /tʃeə/ Stuhl I
chalk /tʃɔːk/ Kreide I
challenge /ˈtʃæləndʒ/ Herausforderung IV
challenge /ˈtʃælɪndʒ/ *hier:* infrage stellen V:6/Project B p. 133
challenging /ˈtʃælɪndʒɪŋ/ (heraus)fordernd V:3/B3
championship /ˈtʃæmpiənʃɪp/ Meisterschaft V:6/Project A p. 120
chance /tʃɑːns/ Möglichkeit; Gelegenheit III
change /tʃeɪndʒ/ wechseln; umsteigen I; Wechselgeld I; (ver)ändern II; Veränderung V:6/Project p. 115
change-maker /ˈtʃeɪndʒ ˌmeɪkə/ *jd, der eine Veränderung in die Wege leitet* V:6/Project C p. 129
channel /ˈtʃænl/ Kanal V:6/Project A p. 119
°chant /tʃɑːnt/ Sprechgesang V:BS/3
character /ˈkærəktə/ *hier:* Figur IV; Charakter; Wesen V:4/B7
character /ˈkærəktə/ *hier:* (Schrift)zeichen V:3/B8; Wesen, Charakter V:4/B2
characteristic /ˌkærɪktəˈrɪstɪk/ charakteristisch V:6/Project A p. 132
charge /tʃɑːdʒ/ aufladen III
charity /ˈtʃærəti/ Wohltätigkeitsorganisation III
chart /tʃɑːt/ Diagramm IV
chat /tʃæt/ chatten V:4/A1
cheap /tʃiːp/ billig II
check /tʃek/ Kontrolle IV; überprüfen; kontrollieren II
check out *(informal)* /ˌtʃek‿ˈaʊt/ sich etw ansehen V:1/A2
checklist /ˈtʃeklɪst/ Checkliste; Kontrollliste V:4/A5
°cheeky /ˈtʃiːki/ frech V:BS/3
cheerful /ˈtʃɪəfl/ fröhlich; vergnügt; heiter V:4/P14
cheers *(informal)* /tʃɪəz/ danke; tschüss V:3/B6
cheese /tʃiːz/ Käse I
chemical /ˈkemɪkl/ Chemikalie V:2/A3; chemisch V:1/O
chewing gum /ˈtʃuːɪŋ ˌɡʌm/ Kaugummi V:3/B1
chicken /ˈtʃɪkɪn/ Huhn I
chicken /ˈtʃɪkɪn/ *hier:* Angsthase V:2/A2

°chief /tʃi:f/ Leiter/in V:5/O
child (*pl* **children**) /tʃaɪld, ˈtʃɪldrən/ Kind I
childcare /ˈtʃaɪldˌkeə/ Kinderbetreuung V:3/A2
childhood /ˈtʃaɪldˌhʊd/ Kindheit V:5/B3
°chin /tʃɪn/ Kinn V:2/O
chips(*pl*) /tʃɪps/ Pommes frites II
chiselled /ˈtʃɪzld/ scharf geschnitten V:5/B5
chocolate /ˈtʃɒklət/ Schokolade I
hot chocolate /ˌhɒt ˈtʃɒklət/ (heißer) Kakao I
choice /tʃɔɪs/ Wahl III; Auswahl V:2/A2
choir /ˈkwaɪə/ Chor V:6/Proj. p. 130
choose *(irr)* /tʃu:z/ wählen; sich entscheiden I
chore /tʃɔ:/ lästige Aufgabe, Hausarbeit V:3/B1
°chorus (*pl* choruses) /ˈkɔ:rəs, ˈkɔ:rəsɪz/ Refrain V:1/B5
Christmas /ˈkrɪsməs/ Weihnachten V:1/A2
Christmas carol /ˌkrɪsməs ˈkærəl/ Weihnachtslied V:5/B4
Christmas Day /ˌkrɪsməs ˈdeɪ/ erster Weihnachtsfeiertag II
Christmas Eve /ˌkrɪsməs‿ˈi:v/ Heiligabend II
church /tʃɜ:tʃ/ Kirche II
cigarette /ˌsɪgəˈret, ˈsɪgəˌret/ Zigarette IV
cinema /ˈsɪnəmə/ Kino I
circle /sɜ:kl/ Kreis III
citizen /ˈsɪtɪzn/ Bürger/in V:1/B3
citizenship /ˈsɪtɪznʃɪp/ Staatsbürgerschaft V:5/B3
city /ˈsɪti/ Stadt; Innenstadt I
city centre /ˌsɪti ˈsentə/ Innenstadt V:1/A7
°civil rights *(pl)* /ˌsɪvl ˈraɪts/ Bürgerrechte V:BS/7
civil society /ˌsɪvl səˈsaɪəti/ Zivilgesellschaft V:5/B3
°civil war /ˌsɪvl ˈwɔ:/ Bürgerkrieg V:5/O
civilian /səˈvɪliən/ Zivil-; *hier:* für Zivilisten V:5/A2
claim /kleɪm/ Anspruch erheben auf V:1/A8
claim /kleɪm/ *hier:* behaupten V:1/O
class /klɑ:s/ Klasse I
class /klɑ:s/ *hier:* (Unterrichts) stunde V:1/B10
classical /ˈklæsɪkl/ klassisch V:6/Project A p. 118
classify /ˈklæsɪfaɪ/ klassifizieren V:6/Project B p. 133
classmate /ˈklɑ:sˌmeɪt/ Klassenkamerad/in II
classroom /ˈklɑ:sˌru:m/ Klassenzimmer I
clean /kli:n/ sauber IV; sauber machen I
clean up /ˌkli:n‿ˈʌp/ sauber machen II
clear /klɪə/ klar; deutlich III
clear /klɪə/ beseitigen V:5/A3; beseitigen, räumen, reinigen V:5/A4
clenched fist /ˌklentʃt ˈfɪst/ geballte Faust V:5/B1
clever /ˈklevə/ klug; schlau II
click /klɪk/ klicken V:4/A3
client /ˈklaɪənt/ Kunde/Kundin V:5/B3
cliff /klɪf/ Klippe, Kliff V:1/A4
climate /ˈklaɪmət/ Klima V:6/Project C p. 129
°climate change /ˈklaɪmət tʃeɪndʒ/ Klimawandel V:1/O
climb /klaɪm/ auf etw (hinauf) steigen; klettern IV
climbing /ˈklaɪmɪŋ/ Kletter- V:2/A5
clock /klɒk/ Uhr I
close /kləʊs/ nah(e) III
close /kləʊz/ zumachen; schließen III
closely /ˈkləʊsli/ eng V:2/A3
closeness /ˈkləʊsnəs/ Nähe V:6/Project A p. 119
°cloth /klɒθ/ Tuch; Stoff V:2/O
clothes *(pl)* /kləʊðz/ Kleider, Kleidung I
clothing /ˈkləʊðɪŋ/ Kleidung IV
cloud /klaʊd/ Wolke I
cloudy /ˈklaʊdi/ bewölkt; bedeckt I
club /klʌb/ Klub; AG I
clumsy /ˈklʌmzi/ ungeschickt; unbeholfen V:2/A5
coastal /ˈkəʊstl/ Küsten- V:2/A8
coffee /ˈkɒfi/ Kaffee III
coin /kɔɪn/ Münze II:6/B11
cold /kəʊld/ kalt I; Erkältung I
colleague /ˈkɒli:g/ Kollege/ Kollegin V:3/A1
collect /kəˈlekt/ sammeln I
°collect /kəˈlekt/ *hier:* einsammeln, abholen V:3/O
collection /kəˈlekʃn/ Sammlung I
college /ˈkɒlɪdʒ/ Universität, College V:3/B2
college education /ˈkɒlɪdʒ‿edjʊˌkeɪʃn/ Hochschulbildung/-studium V:3/B3
°collision /kəˈlɪʒn/ Zusammenstoß V:1/O
colony /ˈkɒləni/ Kolonie V:1/A7
°color *(AE)* /ˈkʌlə/ Farbe V:BS/7
colour /ˈkʌlə/ Farbe I
colourful /ˈkʌləfl/ farbenfroh; bunt II
°combination /ˌkɒmbɪˈneɪʃn/ Kombination, Mischung V:3/O
combine /kəmˈbaɪn/ verbinden IV
come *(irr)* /kʌm/ kommen I
come to mind /ˌkʌm tə ˈmaɪnd/ einfallen V:1/A1
come on /ˌkʌm‿ˈɒn/ *hier etwa:* Jetzt hör(t) aber auf! V:4/A3
come out /ˈkʌm‿aʊt/ herauskommen; *hier:* sich outen V:3/B6
come together /ˌkʌm təˈgeðə/ zusammenkommen V:6/Project A p. 120
come up /ˈkʌm‿ʌp/ aufkommen V:3/B3
come up with /ˌkʌm‿ˈʌp wɪð/ auf etw kommen V:6/Project C p. 126
comfortable /ˈkʌmftəbl/ bequem I
comment /ˈkɒment/ Kommentar, Bemerkung IV
comment /ˈkɒment/ kommentieren V:3/B6
commentary /ˈkɒməntri/ Kommentar; Stellungnahme V:5/A2
commission /kəˈmɪʃn/ Kommission; Ausschuss V:5/B3

committed /kə'mɪtɪd/ engagiert V:5/B3
common /'kɒmən/ üblich V:2/B5; *hier:* gemeinsam V:6/Project A p. 119
commonwealth /'kɒmənwelθ/ Staat, Republik V:1/A8
communicate /kə'mju:nɪkeɪt/ kommunizieren, sprechen IV
communication /kə,mju:nɪ'keɪʃn/ Verständigung; Kommunikation IV
community /kə'mju:nəti/ Gemeinde, Gemeinschaft IV
compare /kəm'peə/ vergleichen III
compared to /kəm'peəd‿tʊ/ im Vergleich zu IV
compassion /kəm'pæʃn/ Mitgefühl, Mitleid V:5/B3
compete /kəm'pi:t/ wetteifern; kämpfen V:6/Project A p. 120
competent /'kɒmpɪtənt/ fähig; kompetent V:3/A4
competition /,kɒmpə'tɪʃn/ Wettbewerb II
complain /kəm'pleɪn/ sich beklagen IV
complete /kəm'pli:t/ vervollständigen; zu Ende bringen IV; vollständig, komplett III
complete /kəm'pli:t/ *hier:* absolvieren V:1/B10
completely /kəm'pli:tli/ völlig, absolut V:6/Project B p. 123
°complex /'kɒmpleks/ Komplex V:2/O
composer /kəm'pəʊzə/ Komponist/in V:6/Project A p. 120
comprehensive school /kɒmprɪ'hensɪv sku:l/ Gesamtschule V:3/A4
compromise /'kɒmprəmaɪz/ Kompromiss V:1/A2
computer game designer /kəm'pju:tə geɪm dɪ,zaɪnə/ Computerspielentwickler/in II
concentrate /'kɒnsn,treɪt/ sich konzentrieren II
concept /'kɒnsept/ Entwurf; Konzept V:4/A9
concerning /kən'sɜ:nɪŋ/ bezüglich V:5/B1
concert /'kɒnsət/ Konzert III
condition /kən'dɪʃn/ Zustand; Bedingung IV
conduct /kən'dʌkt/ (durch)-führen V:3/A8
confidence /'kɒnfɪdns/ Vertrauen; Zuversicht V:1/B8
confident /'kɒnfɪdnt/ selbstsicher; selbstbewusst V:2/P7
conflict /'kɒnflɪkt/ Konflikt IV
Congratulations! /kən,grætʃʊ'leɪʃnz/ Glückwunsch!; Gratuliere! II
°congress /'kɒŋgres/ Kongress V:BS/6
connect /kə'nekt/ verbinden V:4/A8
conscientious /,kɒnʃi'enʃəs/ gewissenhaft; pflichtbewusst V:3/A2
consequence /'kɒnsɪkwəns/ Konsequenz; Folge V:4/B7
°conservation /,kɒnsə'veɪʃn/ Schutz; Erhaltung V:BS/3
consider /kən'sɪdə/ halten für; nachdenken; betrachten III; denken an; in Betracht ziehen V:2/B9
considerable /kən'sɪdrəbl/ erheblich; beträchtlich V:2/B3
consistent /kən'sɪstənt/ beständig; gleich bleibend V:3/B6
console /kən'səʊl/ Konsole V:4/A8
°constant /'kɒnstənt/ dauernd; ständig V:1/O
constantly /'kɒnstəntli/ ständig; dauernd V:3/B6
consume /kən'sju:m/ konsumieren; verbrauchen V:2/A7
consumerism /kən'sju:mə,rɪzm/ Konsum; Konsumdenken V:6/Project B p. 124
-consuming /kən'sju:mɪŋ/ verzehrend V:2/A7
contact /'kɒntækt/ Kontakt IV
contact sb /'kɒntækt ,sʌmbədi/ sich mit jdm in Verbindung setzen IV
contain /kən'teɪn/ enthalten V:6/Project A p. 121
contemporary /kən'tempri/ zeitgenössisch V:6/Project A p. 121
content /'kɒntent/ Inhalt V:1/B11; *hier:* Content V:3/B6
contest /'kɒntest/ Wettbewerb V:4/B5
context /'kɒntekst/ Kontext; Zusammenhang V:5/A1
continent /'kɒntɪnənt/ Kontinent V:1/A2
continue /kən'tɪnju:/ andauern, weitergehen III; fortführen; weitermachen V:3/B6
contribute /kən'trɪbju:t/ beitragen V:5/B3
contribution /,kɒntrɪ'bju:ʃn/ Beitrag; Spende V:6/Project p. 131
control /kən'trəʊl/ Kontrolle III; kontrollieren III
controversial /,kɒntrə'vɜ:ʃl/ umstritten; kontrovers V:6/Project A p. 120
conversation /,kɒnvə'seɪʃn/ Gespräch; Unterhaltung III
convict /'kɒnvɪkt/ Sträfling V:1/P4
°convince /kən'vɪns/ überzeugen V:3/O
convincing /kən'vɪnsɪŋ/ überzeugend V:4/A8
cook /kʊk/ Koch/Köchin III; kochen; braten; backen III
cookie /'kʊki/ Keks; Plätzchen V:3/B1
do the cooking /,du: ðə 'kʊkɪŋ/ kochen I
cooperation /kəʊ,ɒpə'reɪʃn/ Zusammenarbeit V:5/B3
copy /'kɒpi/ abschreiben V:2/A5
°coral /'kɒrəl/ Korallen-; Koralle V:1/O
coral reef /,kɒrəl 'ri:f/ Korallenriff V:1/A7
corner /'kɔ:nə/ Ecke II
correct /kə'rekt/ richtig, korrekt IV
correct /kə'rekt/ korrigieren V:2/B4; verbessern V:5/P4

cosmetics *(pl)* /kɒzˈmetɪks/ Kosmetika; Kosmetikartikel V:6/Project C p.128
cost *(irr)* /kɒst/ kosten II:4/A7
costume /ˈkɒstjuːm/ Kostüm III
cotton /ˈkɒtn/ Baumwolle II
could /kʊd/ könnte(st, n, t) I
council /ˈkaʊnsl/ Rat V:5/B3
count /kaʊnt/ zählen; wichtig sein; ankommen auf II
country /ˈkʌntri/ Land II:1/A11
countryside /ˈkʌntriˌsaɪd/ Landschaft V:2/A4
county /ˈkaʊnti/ (Verwaltungs)bezirk; (Stadt)bezirk V:4/B2
couple /ˈkʌpl/ Paar IV:
courage /ˈkʌrɪdʒ/ Mut IV
courageous /kəˈreɪdʒəs/ mutig V:5/B4
course /kɔːs/ Kurs I
cousin /ˈkʌzn/ Cousin/e I
cover /ˈkʌvə/ bedecken III
cover /ˈkʌvə/ *hier:* abdecken V:1/B10; *hier:* Dickicht, Unterholz V:2/B4; sich befassen mit; behandeln V:5/A6; Abdeckung, Hülle V:1/O
cover letter /ˈkʌvə ˌletə/ Anschreiben V:3/A6
coverage /ˈkʌvrɪdʒ/ Berichterstattung V:5/A6
cow /kaʊ/ Kuh I
crane /kreɪn/ Kran V:2/A10
°crash /kræʃ/ abstürzen V:3/O
craving /ˈkreɪvɪŋ/ heftiges Verlangen V:2/A3
°crawl /krɔːl/ krabbeln; kriechen V:BS/4
crazy /ˈkreɪzi/ verrückt; wahnsinnig II
cream /kriːm/ Sahne II; Creme; Salbe III
create /kriˈeɪt/ erschaffen; erzeugen III
create /kriˈeɪt/ *hier:* erstellen V:2/B9
creation /kriˈeɪʃn/ (Er)schaffung IV
°creation myth /kriˈeɪʃn mɪθ/ Schöpfungsmythos V:2/O
creative /kriˈeɪtɪv/ kreativ V:3/A4
creature /ˈkriːtʃə/ Kreatur; Lebewesen V:1/I
creepy /ˈkriːpi/ gruselig V:1/A4
criminal /ˈkrɪmɪnl/ Verbrecher/in V:4/A3
crinkly /ˈkrɪŋkli/ zerknittert V:4/B2
crisps *(pl)* /krɪsps/ Chips I
criterion (*pl* criteria) /kraɪˈtɪəriən/ Kriterium V:3/B8
critical /ˈkrɪtɪkl/ kritisch V:5/A6
criticise /ˈkrɪtɪsaɪz/ kritisieren V:5/A6
criticism /ˈkrɪtɪˌsɪzm/ Kritik V:5/A6
crocodile /ˈkrɒkədaɪl/ Krokodil I
crop /krɒp/ Ernte V:1/A4; *hier:* Feldfrucht V:2/B7
cross /krɒs/ überqueren II
cross /krɒs/ *hier:* durchqueren V:1/B6
crossword puzzle /ˈkrɒsˌwɜːd ˌpʌzl/ Kreuzworträtsel V:1/P12
crowd /kraʊd/ Menschenmenge III
°crown /kraʊn/ Krone V:BS/8
cruelty-free /ˌkruːəlti ˈfriː/ *nicht an Tieren getestet* V:6/Project p.116
cruise /kruːz/ Kreuzfahrt V:1/A7
cry /kraɪ/ weinen; schreien III
cuddly /ˌkʌdli/ knuddelig V:1/A4
cuddly toy /ˌkʌdli ˈtɔɪ/ Kuscheltier I
cue /ˈkjuː/ Stichwort; *hier:* Zeichen V:6/Project A p.119
cue card /ˈkjuː kaːd/ *Stichwortkarte* V:5/A7
cultivate /ˈkʌltɪveɪt/ anbauen V:2/B3
culture /ˈkʌltʃə/ Kultur IV
cup /kʌp/ Tasse I
cup final /ˈkʌp ˌfaɪnl/ Pokalendspiel, Cupfinale I
cupboard /ˈkʌbəd/ Schrank I
cure /kjʊə/ heilen V:1/B5
curl up /ˌkɜːl‿ˈʌp/ sich einrollen V:6/Project A p.120
current /ˈkʌrənt/ Strömung V:2/B3
curriculum /kəˈrɪkjʊləm/ Lehrplan V:5/B3
customer /ˈkʌstəmə/ Kunde/Kundin I
customs officer /ˈkʌstəmz‿ˌɒfɪsə/ Zollbeamter/in V:2/B7
cut *(irr)* /kʌt/ schneiden II
cute /kjuːt/ süß; niedlich II
CV (= curriculum vitae) /ˌsiː ˈviː/ Lebenslauf V:3/A4
cycle /ˈsaɪkl/ Rad fahren IV
Czech Republic /ˌtʃek riˈpʌblɪk/ Tschechische Republik V:3/A2

D

dad /dæd/ Papa; Vati I
°daily /ˈdeɪli/ täglich V:BS/6
damage /ˈdæmɪdʒ/ beschädigen, schaden III
damage /ˈdæmɪdʒ/ Schaden V:2/B7
damn *(informal)* /dæm/ verdammt, verflucht V:4/A8
dance /daːns/ tanzen I; Tanz II
dancer /ˈdaːnsə/ Tänzer/in V:6/Project A p.118
dancing /ˈdaːnsɪŋ/ Tanzen II
danger /ˈdeɪndʒə/ Gefahr V:2/A3
dangerous /ˈdeɪndʒərəs/ gefährlich III
daredevil /ˈdeəˌdevl/ Draufgänger/in V:2/A2
daring /ˈdeərɪŋ/ kühn; wagemutig V:2/A2
dark /daːk/ dunkel I
°darkness /ˈdaːknəs/ Dunkelheit V:2/O
data *(pl)* /ˈdeɪtə/ Daten V:4/A3
data protection /ˈdeɪtə prəˌtekʃn/ Datenschutz V:4/A9
data security *(no pl)* /ˈdeɪtə sɪˌkjʊərəti/ Datensicherheit; Datenschutz V:2/P12
date /deɪt/ Datum; Termin; Verabredung IV
daughter /ˈdɔːtə/ Tochter I
day /deɪ/ Tag I
one day /ˌwʌn ˈdeɪ/ eines Tages II
day care centre /ˈdeɪ keə ˌsentə/ *hier:* Kindertagesstätte V:3/A2
dead /ded/ tot IV
deal /diːl/ Geschäft V:5/B3
deal with /ˈdiːl wɪð/ sich befassen mit IV

dear /dɪə/ liebe/r *(Anrede)* II
Dear Sir or Madam, … /ˌdɪə ˌsɜːr‿ɔː ˈmædəm/ Sehr geehrte Damen und Herren, … *(als Anrede in Briefen, wenn der Empfänger namentlich nicht bekannt ist)* V:3/A6
death /deθ/ Tod IV
death toll /ˈdeθ təʊl/ Zahl der Todesopfer V:5/B4
debate /dɪˈbeɪt/ Debatte; Diskussion IV
decade /ˈdekeɪd/ Jahrzehnt IV
December /dɪˈsembə/ Dezember I
decide /dɪˈsaɪd/ entscheiden; sich entscheiden II
decision /dɪˈsɪʒn/ Entscheidung III
declare /dɪˈkleə/ verkünden, erklären V:5/A1
declare /dɪˈkleə/ deklarieren; verzollen V:2/B7
°decline /dɪˈklaɪn/ sinken; nachlassen V:1/O
dedication /ˌdedɪˈkeɪʃn/ Engagement V:6/Project B p.125
deep /diːp/ tief III
defend /dɪˈfend/ verteidigen V:2/B5
definitely /ˈdefnətli/ eindeutig, definitiv V:1/A4
degradation /ˌdegrəˈdeɪʃn/ Erniedrigung V:1/B8
°degree /dɪˈgriː/ Abschluss; Titel V:5/O
delicious /dɪˈlɪʃəs/ köstlich, lecker III
°deliver /dɪˈlɪvə/ *hier:* halten; verkünden V:BS/7
demanding /dɪˈmɑːndɪŋ/ anstrengend V:2/A5
democracy /dɪˈmɒkrəsi/ Demokratie IV
democratic /ˌdeməˈkrætɪk/ demokratisch V:5/B3
demonstrate /ˈdemənˌstreɪt/ zeigen, vorführen IV
demonstrate /ˈdemənˌstreɪt/ *hier:* demonstrieren V:6/Project C p.126
department store /dɪˈpɑːtmənt stɔː/ Kaufhaus II
depressed /dɪˈprest/ deprimiert V:4/P14
depression /dɪˈpreʃn/ Wirtschaftskrise V:1/B5
descendant /dɪˈsendənt/ Nachkomme V:1/B3
describe /dɪˈskraɪb/ beschreiben I
description /dɪˈskrɪpʃn/ Beschreibung V:2/A4
desert /ˈdezət/ Wüste V:1/A2
design /dɪˈzaɪn/ Entwurf, Design IV; entwerfen II
computer game designer /kəmˈpjuːtə geɪm dɪˌzaɪnə/ Computerspielentwickler/in II
desk /desk/ Schreibtisch I
desperate /ˈdesprət/ verzweifelt III
despondent /dɪˈspɒndənt/ niedergeschlagen V:4/P14
despondently /dɪˈspɒndəntli/ niedergeschlagen V:4/B5
dessert /dɪˈzɜːt/ Nachtisch III
destination /ˌdestɪˈneɪʃn/ Ziel V:2/A7
destruction /dɪˈstrʌkʃn/ Zerstörung V:1/B4
detail /ˈdiːteɪl/ Detail, Einzelheit IV
detailed /ˈdiːteɪld/ detailliert, genau V:6/Project p.117
details *(pl)* /ˈdiːteɪls/ Personalien; persönliche Daten V:4/A3
detective /dɪˈtektɪv/ Detektiv/in V:3/B7
detention /dɪˈtenʃn/ Nachsitzen V:5/P8
determined /dɪˈtɜːmɪnd/ entschlossen V:1/B6
develop /dɪˈveləp/ erarbeiten; entwickeln IV
developing /dɪˈveləpɪŋ/ sich entwickelnd; heranreifend V:6/Project B p.123
development /dɪˈveləpmənt/ Entwicklung IV
device /dɪˈvaɪs/ Gerät; Apparat V:4/A8
diagram /ˈdaɪəgræm/ Diagramm V:1/B2
dial /ˈdaɪəl/ Skala V:4/B2
dialect /ˈdaɪəlekt/ Dialekt V:1/A2
dialogue /ˈdaɪəˌlɒg/ Gespräch, Dialog II
diameter /daɪˈæmɪtə/ Durchmesser V:2/B4
diamond /ˈdaɪəmənd/ Diamant V:3/B3
diary /ˈdaɪəri/ Tagebuch II
dictionary /ˈdɪkʃənri/ Lexikon; Wörterbuch I
die /daɪ/ sterben II
diet /ˈdaɪət/ Ernährung; Diät V:6/Project C p.126
different /ˈdɪfrənt/ anders; andere(r, s); verschiedene(r, s) II
differently /ˈdɪfrəntli/ verschieden; unterschiedlich V:4/B2
difficult /ˈdɪfɪklt/ schwierig; schwer II
difficulty /ˈdɪfɪklti/ Schwierigkeit; Problem V:1/B6
digger /ˈdɪgə/ (Gold)gräber/in V:1/B5
dignity /ˈdɪgnəti/ Würde; Achtung V:5/B3
dilate /daɪˈleɪt/ sich weiten V:2/A3
dinner /ˈdɪnə/ Abendessen I
°dinosaur /ˈdaɪnəˌsɔː/ Dinosaurier V:BS/3
direct speech /daɪˌrekt ˈspiːtʃ/ direkte Rede, wörtliche Rede II
director /dəˈrektə/ Regisseur/in IV
dirty /ˈdɜːti/ dreckig; schmutzig II
disability /ˌdɪsəˈbɪləti/ Behinderung; Einschränkung V:6/Project B p.125
disagree /ˌdɪsəˈgriː/ nicht zustimmen; nicht übereinstimmen V:3/B5
disappear /ˌdɪsəˈpɪə/ verschwinden IV
disappointed /ˌdɪsəˈpɔɪntɪd/ enttäuscht V:3/B6

disco /ˈdɪskəʊ/ Disko V:5/B3; Diskomusik V:6/Project A p. 118
discover /dɪˈskʌvə/ entdecken III
discrimination /dɪˌskrɪmɪˈneɪʃn/ Diskriminierung; Benachteiligung V:1/A9
discuss /dɪˈskʌs/ besprechen; diskutieren III
discussion /dɪˈskʌʃn/ Diskussion V:1/B10
disease /dɪˈziːz/ Krankheit IV
disempower /ˌdɪsɪmˈpaʊə/ entmachten V:5/A6
disgusting /dɪsˈɡʌstɪŋ/ widerlich III
dish (*pl* **dishes**) /dɪʃ, ˈdɪʃɪz/ Gericht III
dislike /dɪsˈlaɪk/ nicht mögen IV
dislike /dɪsˈlaɪk/ Abneigung V:6/Project p. 131
dispirited /dɪˈspɪrɪtɪd/ niedergeschlagen; entmutigt V:5/A2
display /dɪˈspleɪ/ *hier:* Ausstellung V:1/B9; aushängen V:5/A7
°disposal /dɪˈspəʊzl/ Beseitigung, Entsorgung V:1/O
dispose of /dɪˈspəʊz‿əv/ entsorgen V:2/B7
dispute /dɪˈspjuːt/ bestreiten; über etw streiten V:4/B2; Streit V:5/B3
distance /ˈdɪstəns/ Distanz, Entfernung V:2/A7
distribute /dɪˈstrɪbjuːt/ verteilen V:6/Project A p. 121
°dive /daɪv/ tauchen V:3/O
do *(irr)* /duː/ tun; machen I
do a paper round /ˌduː‿ə ˈpeɪpə ˌraʊnd/ Zeitungen austragen V:3/B1
do gymnastics /ˌduː dʒɪmˈnæstɪks/ Turnen I
do research /ˌduː rɪˈsɜːtʃ/ *hier:* recherchieren V:6/Project A p. 120
do without /ˌduː wɪðˈaʊt/ auskommen ohne III
dock /dɒk/ anlegen V:4/B5
doctor /ˈdɒktə/ Arzt/Ärztin II
document /ˈdɒkjʊmənt/ Dokument V:4/A3
document /ˈdɒkjʊmənt/ dokumentieren, belegen V:5/B4
dog /dɒɡ/ Hund I
walk the dog /ˌwɔːk ðə ˈdɒɡ/ den Hund ausführen I
°dolphin /ˈdɒlfɪn/ Delfin V:BS/3
door /dɔː/ Tür I
dopamine /ˈdəʊpəmiːn/ Dopamin V:2/A3
double /ˈdʌbl/ doppelt IV
doubt /daʊt/ (be)zweifeln V:2/A7
down /daʊn/ hinunter; (nach) unten II
down under *(informal)* /ˌdaʊn‿ˈʌndə/ Australien; Neuseeland V:1/I
Down's syndrome /ˈdaʊnz‿ˌsɪndrəʊm/ Down-Syndrom; Trisomie 21 V:6/Project B p. 125
downhill /ˈdaʊnhɪl/ Abfahrt V:2/A7
Dr (= Doctor) /ˈdɒktə/ Dr. (= Doktor) V:6/Project p. 115
dramatic /drəˈmætɪk/ dramatisch V:4/A3
draw *(irr)* /drɔː/ zeichnen I
°draw strength from /ˌdrɔː ˈstreŋθ frɒm/ Kraft ziehen aus V:5/O
drawing /ˈdrɔːɪŋ/ Zeichnung III
drawing room /ˈdrɔːɪŋ ruːm/ Empfangszimmer; Salon; Gesellschaftszimmer V:5/A2
dream /driːm/ Traum II
dream *(irr)* /driːm/ träumen I
dreamer /ˈdriːmə/ Träumer/in V:5/B2
dreaming story /ˈdriːmɪŋ ˌstɔːri/ *Traumzeitgeschichte* V:1/B3
Dreamtime /ˈdriːmˌtaɪm/ *zentraler Begriff der Aborigine-Mythologie, etwa: Traumzeit* V:1/B3
dress /dres/ Kleid I
dress up /ˌdres‿ˈʌp/ (sich) verkleiden III
drift /drɪft/ treiben; schweben V:2/A4
driller /ˈdrɪlə/ Bohrarbeiter/in V:3/B3
drink /drɪŋk/ Trinken; Getränk I
drink *(irr)* /drɪŋk/ trinken I
drive *(irr)* /draɪv/ fahren II
drive *(irr)* /draɪv/ treiben, vertreiben V:1/A8
driving lesson /ˈdraɪvɪŋ ˌlesn/ Fahrstunde V:3/P2
driving license /ˈdraɪvɪŋ ˌlaɪsns/ Führerschein V:3/P5
drown /draʊn/ ertränken; überfluten V:1/B5
dry /draɪ/ trocken V:1/B5
due /djuː/ fällig IV
due to /ˈdjuː tʊ/ wegen IV
during /ˈdjʊərɪŋ/ während II
dusk /dʌsk/ (Abend)dämmerung V:5/A2
dusty /ˈdʌsti/ staubig V:1/B5
Dutch /dʌtʃ/ holländisch; niederländisch V:1/A8
duvet /ˈduːveɪ/ Steppdecke; Daunendecke I
dynamic /daɪˈnæmɪk/ dynamisch V:6/Project p. 115

E

each /iːtʃ/ jede(r, s) II; je(weils) III
each other /ˌiːtʃ‿ˈʌðə/ einander II
ear /ɪə/ Ohr I
earlier /ˈɜːliə/ vorhin V:1/B10
early /ˈɜːli/ früh II
earn /ɜːn/ verdienen III
°earn a degree /ˌɜːn‿ə dɪˈɡriː/ einen Abschluss erlangen V:5/O
earth /ɜːθ/ Erde II
earthquake /ˈɜːθˌkweɪk/ Erdbeben V:5/A1
°earthy /ˈɜːθi/ erdig V:2/O
ease /iːz/ Leichtigkeit; Mühelosigkeit V:2/A3
easily /ˈiːzɪli/ leicht; mühelos II
east /iːst/ Osten III
East India /ˌiːst‿ˈɪndiə/ ostindisch V:2/B3
Easter /ˈiːstə/ Ostern II
easy /ˈiːzi/ leicht; einfach I
eat *(irr)* /iːt/ essen I
eat out /ˌiːt‿ˈaʊt/ auswärts essen; im Restaurant essen III
eating habit /ˈiːtɪŋ ˌhæbɪt/ Essgewohnheit III

eco- /ˈiːkəʊ/ Öko- V:6/Project C p.126
eco-friendly /ˌiːkəʊ ˈfrendli/ umweltfreundlich IV
economic /ˌiːkəˈnɒmɪk/ wirtschaftlich V:2/B3
edit /ˈedɪt/ bearbeiten II
educate /ˈedjʊkeɪt/ ausbilden; unterrichten V:1/A8
educational /ˌedjʊˈkeɪʃnəl/ Bildungs-; pädagodisch V:1/B3
effect /ɪˈfekt/ Effekt, Wirkung V:5/I
effective /ɪˈfektɪv/ wirksam, effektiv IV
effort /ˈefət/ Mühe, Anstrengung V:6/Project A p.119
egg /eg/ Ei I
fried egg /ˌfraɪd‿ˈeg/ Spiegelei I
either /ˈaɪðə/ *hier:* jede/r V:6/Project B p.124
either … or … /ˌaɪðə ˈɔː/ entweder … oder … III
elastic /ɪˈlæstɪk/ elastisch; flexibel V:2/A4
election /ɪˈlekʃn/ Wahl V:1/A8
electric /ɪˈlektrɪk/ elektrisch; Elektro- IV
electrical /ɪˈlektrɪkl/ elektrisch V:6/Project A p.120
electricity /ɪˌlekˈtrɪsəti/ Elektrizität, Strom III
electronics *(pl)* /ˌelekˈtrɒnɪks/ Elektronik V:6/Project B p.124
elementary education /elɪˌmentri‿edjʊˈkeɪʃn/ Elementarbildung; Grundschulausbildung V:3/A6
elementary school /elɪˈmentri skuːl/ Grundschule V:6/Project A p.121
elephant /ˈelɪfənt/ Elefant I
else /els/ anders; sonst III
anything else /eniˌθɪŋ‿ˈels/ noch etwas I
'em = them *(informal)* /em/ sie; ihnen V:6/Project A p.121
email /ˈiːmeɪl/ mailen V:1/B10
embarrassing /ɪmˈbærəsɪŋ/ unangenehm; peinlich II
embedded /ɪmˈbedɪd/ eingebettet V:5/A6
emergency /ɪˈmɜːdʒnsi/ Notfall IV
emigration /ˌemɪˈgreɪʃn/ Auswanderung; Emigration IV
emotion /ɪˈməʊʃn/ Emotion; Gefühl V:3/P5
empathy /ˈempəθi/ Einfühlungsvermögen; Empathie V:5/B3
emphasise /ˈemfəsaɪz/ betonen; hervorheben V:5/A6
employer /ɪmˈplɔɪə/ Arbeitgeber/in IV
empower /ɪmˈpaʊə/ stärken, befähigen V:6/Project B p.125
empowerment /ɪmˈpaʊəmənt/ Stärkung; Unterstützung V:6/Project A p.118
empty /ˈempti/ ausleeren; ausräumen I; leer (stehend); unbewohnt II
enable /ɪnˈeɪbl/ ermöglichen V:1/B10
enclose /ɪnˈkləʊz/ *hier:* beilegen; beifügen V:3/A6
encounter /ɪnˈkaʊntə/ treffen; begegnen V:1/B6
encourage /ɪnˈkʌrɪdʒ/ ermutigen IV
encouraging /ɪnˈkʌrɪdʒɪŋ/ ermutigend V:3/B6
end /end/ enden; beenden I; Ende; Schluss II
in the end /ˌɪn ðiˈ‿end/ schließlich III
put an end to /ˌpʊt‿ən‿ˈend‿tʊ/ ein Ende setzen V:5/A1
end up *(informal)* /ˌend‿ˈʌp/ schließlich landen V:3/B3
°endangered /ɪnˈdeɪndʒəd/ stark gefährdet; vom Aussterben bedroht V:BS/3
°endemic /enˈdemɪk/ einheimisch V:BS/3
ending /ˈendɪŋ/ Ende; Schluss V:4/B5
endure /ɪnˈdjʊə/ ertragen V:1/B5
enemy /ˈenəmi/ Feind/in IV
°energetic /ˌenəˈdʒetɪk/ voller Energie; energiegeladen V:3/O
energy /ˈenədʒi/ Energie; Kraft IV
engineer /ˌendʒɪˈnɪə/ Ingenieur/in III
English /ˈɪŋglɪʃ/ Englisch; englisch I
in English /ˌɪn‿ˈɪŋglɪʃ/ auf Englisch II
English-speaking /ˈɪŋglɪʃ‿ˌspiːkɪŋ/ englischsprachig V:1/B2
enjoy /ɪnˈdʒɔɪ/ genießen II
enjoy oneself /ɪnˈdʒɔɪ wʌnˌself/ sich amüsieren IV
°enormous /ɪˈnɔːməs/ enorm, riesig V:3/O
enough /ɪˈnʌf/ genug II
enter /ˈentə/ betreten III
entertain /ˌentəˈteɪn/ unterhalten V:3/B6
entertainment /ˌentəˈteɪnmənt/ Unterhaltung V:4/A1
enthusiasm /ɪnˈθjuːziˌæzəm/ Enthusiasmus V:2/A5
enthusiastic /ɪnˌθjuːziˈæstɪk/ enthusiastisch; begeistert V:2/A10
entire /ɪnˈtaɪə/ ganz; gesamt V:6/Project A p.119
entry /ˈentri/ Eintritt V:1/A4
entry /ˈentri/ Eintrag V:1/A4
envelope /ˈenvələʊp/ Briefumschlag II
environmental /ɪnˌvaɪrənˈmentl/ Umwelt- V:2/A3
environmental organisation /ɪnvaɪrənˌmentl‿ɔːgənaɪˈzeɪʃn/ Umweltschutzorganisation V:6/Project C p.126
environmentalist /ɪnˌvaɪrənˈmentlɪst/ Umweltschützer/in V:1/O
equal /ˈiːkwəl/ gleich V:5/B3
equality /ɪˈkwɒləti/ Gleichberechtigung; Gleichheit V:5/B3
equipment /ɪˈkwɪpmənt/ Ausrüstung; Ausstattung II
°era /ˈɪərə/ Epoche V:BS/3
erase /ɪˈreɪz/ auslöschen V:1/A8
error /ˈerə/ Fehler V:4/A3
escape /ɪˈskeɪp/ fliehen; entkommen III
escape /ɪˈskeɪp/ Flucht; Entkommen V:6/Project A p.119

especially /ɪˈspeʃli/ besonders; vor allem III
essential /ɪˈsenʃl/ unverzichtbar, unbedingt erforderlich V:3/A2
establish /ɪˈstæblɪʃ/ schaffen; einführen; durchsetzen V:5/A1
estimate /ˈestɪmeɪt/ schätzen; einschätzen V:5/A5
ethical /ˈeθɪkl/ ethisch V:6/Project B p. 124
ethnic /ˈeθnɪk/ ethnisch; Volks- V:6/Project p. 115
ethos /ˈiːθɒs/ Gesinnung; Ethos V:5/B3
euphoric /juːˈfɒrɪk/ euphorisch V:2/A3
Europe /ˈjʊərəp/ Europa II
European /ˌjʊərəˈpiːən/ Europäer/in; europäisch IV
even /ˈiːvn/ selbst; sogar II
even though /ˌiːvn ˈðəʊ/ obwohl V:3/B3
evening /ˈiːvnɪŋ/ Abend I
event /ɪˈvent/ Ereignis, Veranstaltung III
°eventually /ɪˈventʃuəli/ irgendwann V:BS/4
ever /ˈevə/ jemals II
every /ˈevri/ jede(r, s) I
everybody /ˈevriˌbɒdi/ alle; jeder I
everyday /ˈevriˌdeɪ/ alltäglich, Alltags- V:1/I
everyday life /ˌevrideɪ ˈlaɪf/ Alltag V:2/B3
everyone /ˈevriwʌn/ alle; jeder I
everything /ˈevriθɪŋ/ alles I
everywhere /ˈevriweə/ überall V:4/A3
evil /ˈiːvl/ böse V:1/B6
°evolve /ɪˈvɒlv/ sich entwickeln V:BS/3
exactly /ɪgˈzækli/ genau III
exam /ɪgˈzæm/ Prüfung III
for example /fər‿ɪgˈzaːmpl/ zum Beispiel II
set a positive example /ˌset‿ə ˌpɒzətɪv‿ɪgˈzaːmpl/ mit gutem Beispiel vorangehen V:3/A6
°excellent /ˈeksələnt/ ausgezeichnet V:3/O

except /ɪkˈsept/ außer II
excerpt /ˈeksɜːpt/ Auszug V:1/B8
exchange /ɪksˈtʃeɪndʒ/ austauschen V:5/B4
exchange /ɪksˈtʃeɪndʒ/ Austausch- V:1/A3
exchange student /ɪksˈtʃeɪndʒ ˌstjuːdnt/ Austauschschüler/in V:2/B6
excited, excitedly /ɪkˈsaɪtɪd, ɪkˈsaɪtɪdli/ aufgeregt II
excitement /ɪkˈsaɪtmənt/ Aufregung V:2/A5
exciting /ɪkˈsaɪtɪŋ/ aufregend II
exclamatory remark /ˌeksˌklæmətəri rɪˈmaːk/ Ausruf V:2/A5
exclude /ɪkˈskluːd/ ausschließen V:6/Project A p. 121
Excuse me! /ɪkˈskjuːz ˌmi/ Entschuldigung! III
exercise /ˈeksəsaɪz/ trainieren IV:2/A9; Bewegung; Übung III
exercise book /ˈeksəsaɪz ˌbʊk/ Heft I
exhibition /ˌeksɪˈbɪʃn/ Ausstellung II
exist /ɪgˈzɪst/ existieren IV
expect /ɪkˈspekt/ erwarten V:2/A5
expensive /ɪkˈspensɪv/ teuer II
experience /ɪkˈspɪəriəns/ Erfahrung III; erfahren III; erleben, kennenlernen V:2/A4
gain experience /ˌgeɪn‿ɪkˈspɪəriəns/ Erfahrungen sammeln V:3/A2
experienced /ɪkˈspɪəriənst/ erfahren V:2/A5
experiment /ɪkˈsperɪmənt/ Experiment, Versuch III
experiment /ɪkˈsperɪˌment/ expe- rimentieren V:6/Project B p. 123
expert /ˈekspɜːt/ Experte/ Expertin V:2/A3; erfahren; ausgezeichnet V:2/B3
explain /ɪkˈspleɪn/ erklären IV
explanation /ˌekspləˈneɪʃn/ Erklärung IV
explode /ɪkˈspləʊd/ explodieren V:5/A3

explore /ɪkˈsplɔː/ erforschen; untersuchen IV
explorer /ɪkˈsplɔːrə/ Forscher/in V:1/A8
extend /ɪkˈstend/ sich erstrecken V:1/A7
extinct /ɪkˈstɪŋkt/ ausgestorben V:2/B3
°extinction /ɪkˈstɪŋkʃn/ Aussterben V:BS/3
extra /ˈekstrə/ zusätzlich V:3/B1
extreme /ɪkˈstriːm/ äußerste(r, s); extrem IV
extreme sport /ɪkˈstriːm spɔːt/ Extremsportart V:2/A1
eye /aɪ/ Auge I

F

face /feɪs/ gegenüberstehen IV; Gesicht I
fact /fækt/ Tatsache; Fakt III
fact file /ˈfækt faɪl/ Steckbrief IV
factory /ˈfæktri/ Fabrik III
fail /feɪl/ durchfallen IV
°fail /feɪl/ versagen; scheitern V:BS/8
fail *(informal)* /feɪl/ *etwa:* Dumm gelaufen! V:2/A5
failure /ˈfeɪljə/ Scheitern, Versagen V:6/Project C p. 129
fairly /ˈfeəli/ ziemlich; recht V:2/A1
fall *(AE)* /fɔːl/ Herbst IV
fall *(irr)* /fɔːl/ fallen II
fall asleep /ˌfɔːl‿əˈsliːp/ einschlafen IV
°fall down /ˌfɔːl ˈdaʊn/ hinfallen V:BS/8
fall in love /ˌfɔːl‿ɪn ˈlʌv/ sich verlieben III
fall off /ˌfɔːl‿ˈɒf/ (herunter)-fallen III
fall over /ˌfɔːl‿ˈəʊvə/ (um)fallen; *hier:* hinfallen V:2/A1
false /fɔːls/ falsch V:5/P4
fame /feɪm/ Ruhm V:3/B6
familiar /fəˈmɪliə/ vertraut, bekannt IV
family /ˈfæmli/ Familie I
famous /ˈfeɪməs/ berühmt II
fanmail /ˈfænmeɪl/ Fanpost V:3/B6
fantastic /fænˈtæstɪk/ fantastisch; super I

far /fɑː/ weit II; *hier:* fern II
°far /fɑː/ viel V:BS/8
far away /ˌfɑːr‿əˈweɪ/ weit weg II
farm /fɑːm/ Bauernhof I
farmer /ˈfɑːmə/ Bauer/Bäuerin II
farmhand /ˈfɑːmˌhænd/ Landarbeiter/in V:3/A2
°farmland /ˈfɑːmˌlænd/ Ackerland V:BS/3
fascinating /ˈfæsɪneɪtɪŋ/ faszinierend V:1/A2
fashion /ˈfæʃn/ Mode IV
fashion hack /ˈfæʃn hæk/ *Mode-trick* V:6/Project B p.124
Fashion Parade /ˈfæʃn pəˌreɪd/ Modenschau V:6/Project B p.125
fashionable /ˈfæʃnəbl/ modisch; extravagant V:6/Project B p.122
fast /fɑːst/ schnell I
father /ˈfɑːðə/ Vater I
fault /fɔːlt/ Schuld III
favourite /ˈfeɪvrət/ Liebling; Lieblings- I
fear /fɪə/ Angst haben; fürchten IV; Angst IV
°fearful /ˈfɪəfl/ ängstlich V:BS/8
°feather /ˈfeðə/ Feder V:BS/3
feature /ˈfiːtʃə/ zeigen; erscheinen V:6/Project B p.125
February /ˈfebruəri/ Februar I
federal government /ˌfedrəl ˈɡʌvənmənt/ Bundesregierung V:6/Project C p.129
feed *(irr)* /fiːd/ *hier:* ernähren IV; füttern I
feedback /ˈfiːdbæk/ Feedback, Rückmeldung IV
feel *(irr)* /fiːl/ (sich) fühlen II
feel about /ˈfiːl‿əˌbaʊt/ halten von V:6/Project p.130
feel sorry for /ˌfiːl ˈsɒri fə/ leid tun III
feeling /ˈfiːlɪŋ/ Gefühl III
fellow /ˈfeləʊ/ Mitbürger/in V:1/B8; Mit- V:5/B4
°fellow men *(pl)* /ˌfeləʊ ˈmen/ Mitmenschen V:BS/8
°female /ˈfiːmeɪl/ weiblich V:BS/6
fence /fens/ Zaun V:1/B6
°ferocious /fəˈrəʊʃəs/ wild V:1/O
ferry /ˈferi/ Fähre II
festival /ˈfestɪvl/ Fest; Festival II

fever /ˈfiːvə/ Fieber V:5/A3
a few /ə ˈfjuː/ einige; wenige III
fifth /fɪfθ/ Fünftel V:1/B2
fight /faɪt/ Kampf; Streit IV
fight *(irr)* /faɪt/ kämpfen II; bekämpfen; ankämpfen gegen III; sich streiten III
figure /ˈfɪɡə/ Zahl; Wert V:4/A1
°figure /ˈfɪɡə/ Gestalt; Figur V:BS/7
fill /fɪl/ füllen V:2/A5
fill in /ˌfɪl‿ˈɪn/ eintragen, ausfüllen V:1/B4
final /ˈfaɪnl/ letzte(r, s), endgültig V:6/Project p.115
finally /ˈfaɪnli/ schließlich; endlich II
find *(irr)* /faɪnd/ finden I
find out /ˌfaɪnd‿ˈaʊt/ herausfinden II
finding /ˈfaɪndɪŋ/ Ergebnis V:1/A1
fine /faɪn/ fein IV
in Ordnung, gut II
finish /ˈfɪnɪʃ/ beenden; enden I
fiord /ˈfiːɔːd/ Fjord V:2/B4
fire /ˈfaɪə/ Feuer II
°fire /ˈfaɪə/ feuern V:BS/4
fireplace /ˈfaɪəˌpleɪs/ Kamin V:5/A3
fireworks *(pl)* /ˈfaɪəˌwɜːks/ Feuerwerk II
first /fɜːst/ zuerst I; erste(r, s) I
first aid kit /ˌfɜːst‿ˈeɪd kɪt/ Verbandskasten III
first name /ˈfɜːst neɪm/ Vorname V:3/A4
first of all /ˌfɜːst‿əv‿ˈɔːl/ zuallererst V:3/B6
fish /fɪʃ/ fischen; angeln V:1/B4
fish hook /ˈfɪʃ hʊk/ Angelhaken V:2/B3
fish (*pl* **fish** *or* **fishes**) /fɪʃ, fɪʃ, fɪʃɪz/ Fisch I
fisherman (*pl* fishermen) /ˈfɪʃəmən/ Fischer; Angler V:2/B3
fishing net /ˈfɪʃɪŋ net/ Fisch(er)netz V:2/B3
fit /fɪt/ entsprechen V:4/B2; passen; anpassen V:6/Project B p.122

fit in /ˌfɪt‿ˈɪn/ *hier:* dazugehören V:6/Project B p.123; sich einfügen V:BS/8
flag /flæɡ/ Fahne, Flagge IV
flame /fleɪm/ Flamme V:1/B5
flash /flæʃ/ *hier:* anzeigen V:4/B2
flat /flæt/ Wohnung III
°flat /flæt/ flach V:BS/4
flee *(irr)* /fliː/ fliehen IV
fleet /fliːt/ Flotte V:1/A8
flight /flaɪt/ Flug II
float /fləʊt/ schwimmen; sich treiben lassen V:2/A4
flood /flʌd/ überschwemmen V:1/B5
floor /flɔː/ *hier:* Stockwerk IV; Fußboden I
flour /ˈflaʊə/ Mehl II
flower /ˈflaʊə/ Blume II
flowering plant /ˌflaʊərɪŋ ˈplɑːnt/ Blütenpflanze, Zierpflanze V:1/A2
fly /flaɪ/ Fliege I
fly *(irr)* /flaɪ/ fliegen I
flying fox /ˌflaɪɪŋ ˈfɒks/ *eine der schnellsten Stahlseilrutschen der Welt* V:2/A4
focus on /ˈfəʊkəs‿ɒn/ sich konzentrieren auf V:6/Project p.131
focused, focussed /ˈfəʊkəst/ fokussiert V:2/A3
folder /ˈfəʊldə/ Mappe; Schnellhefter; Ordner V:3/A11
folks *(informal)* /fəʊks/ Leute V:3/B6
follow /ˈfɒləʊ/ (ver)folgen II
follow /ˈfɒləʊ/ *hier:* befolgen V:2/A8
following /ˈfɒləʊɪŋ/ folgende(r, s) III
food /fuːd/ Essen I
foot (*pl* **feet**) /fʊt, fiːt/ Fuß I
on foot /ˌɒn ˈfʊt/ zu Fuß II
football /ˈfʊtˌbɔːl/ Fußball I
football player /ˈfʊtbɔːl ˌpleɪə/ Fußballspieler/in II
footwear /ˈfʊtˌweə/ Schuhe; Schuhwerk V:6/Project B p.123
for /fɔː/ für I
for /fɔː/ *hier:* aus V:6/Project A p.119

for *(+ Zeitraum)* /fɔː/ … lang II
for a start /fər‿ə ˌstɑːt/ zunächst (einmal) V:5/B3
for a while /fər‿ə ˈwaɪl/ eine Weile V:4/B2
for breakfast /fə ˈbrekfəst/ zum Frühstück I
for example /fər‿ɪgˈzɑːmpl/ zum Beispiel II
for free /fə ˈfriː/ gratis II
for help /fə ˈhelp/ nach Hilfe, als Hilfe II
for now /fə ˈnaʊ/ für den Augenblick V:1/B10
for sure *(informal)* /fə ˈʃɔː/ ganz sicher, bestimmt V:2/A3
for the first time /fə ðə ˈfɜːst‿taɪm/ zum ersten Mal III
°for the taking /ˌfɔː ðə ˈteɪkɪŋ/ umsonst sein V:BS/8
°for this reason /fə ðɪs ˈriːzn/ aus diesem Grund V:BS/3
force /fɔːs/ Kraft; Wucht IV
force /fɔːs/ Gewalt V:5/B1; zwingen V:5/O
foreign /ˈfɒrɪn/ ausländisch; fremd V:3/A3
forest /ˈfɒrɪst/ Wald II
forethought /ˈfɔːˌθɔːt/ Weitblick V:5/A2
forget *(irr)* /fəˈget/ vergessen I
fork /fɔːk/ Gabel I
form /fɔːm/ Klasse IV; bilden V:1/A8; Formular V:3/A2
°formal /ˈfɔːml/ formell V:2/O
found /faʊnd/ gründen V:5/B3
foundation /faʊnˈdeɪʃn/ Stiftung V:5/B3
founder /ˈfaʊndə/ Gründer/in V:5/P8
fourth /fɔːθ/ vierte(r, s) I
fox /fɒks/ Fuchs I
fraction /ˈfrækʃn/ Bruch *(mathematisch)* V:4/B2
fragile /ˈfrædʒaɪl/ brüchig; unsicher; zerbrechlich V:5/A5
France /frɑːns/ Frankreich V:1/B2
free /friː/ frei; kostenlos III
for free /fə ˈfriː/ gratis II
free time /friː ˈtaɪm/ Freizeit I

freezing /ˈfriːzɪŋ/ frostig; eiskalt V:2/A5
French /frentʃ/ Franzose/Französin; französisch V:3/A2
frequently /ˈfriːkwəntli/ häufig V:6/Project A p. 121
fresh /freʃ/ neu; frisch III
Friday /ˈfraɪdeɪ/ Freitag I:1/B2
fridge /frɪdʒ/ Kühlschrank II
fried egg /ˌfraɪd‿ˈeg/ Spiegelei I
friend /frend/ Freund/in I
friendly /ˈfrendli/ freundlich I
friendship /ˈfrenʃɪp/ Freundschaft IV
frightened /ˈfraɪtnd/ verängstigt II
frog /frɒg/ Frosch I
frolic /ˈfrɒlɪk/ herumtollen V:5/B5
from /frɒm/ von; aus I
front /frʌnt/ Vorderseite IV
front line /ˌfrʌnt ˈlaɪn/ Frontlinie; vorderste Front V:5/A6
°frown /fraʊn/ Stirnrunzeln V:BS/8
fruit *(no pl)* /fruːt/ Frucht; Obst I
frustrated /frʌˈstreɪtɪd/ frustriert II
frustrating /ˈfrʌˌstreɪtɪŋ/ frustrierend V:3/B3
fuel /ˈfjuːəl/ Benzin, Brennstoff III
°fuel /ˈfjuːəl/ nähren; anheizen V:5/O
full /fʊl/ voll; satt III
full of /ˈfʊl‿əv/ voller V:2/B3
fun /fʌn/ Spaß I; lustig; witzig I
be (good/great) fun /ˌbiː ˌgʊd/ ˌgreɪt ˈfʌn/ (viel) Spaß machen II
have (a lot of) fun /ˌhæv‿ə ˌlɒt‿əv‿ˈfʌn/ (viel) Spaß haben II
fund /fʌnd/ Fonds; finanzielle Mittel V:5/B3
fundraising *(no pl)* /ˈfʌndreɪzɪŋ/ *Geldbeschaffung zu Wohltätigkeitszwecken* V:6/Project p. 131
°funeral /ˈfjuːnrəl/ Beerdigung V:2/O
funny /ˈfʌni/ lustig; komisch I

°furious /ˈfjʊəriəs/ wütend V:BS/4
furniture /ˈfɜːnɪtʃə/ V:6/Project B p. 124
further /ˈfɜːðə/ weiter II
future /ˈfjuːtʃə/ zukünftig IV; Zukunft II

G

G'day *(AusE, informal)* /gəˈdeɪ/ Tag; hi V:1/B10
gain /geɪn/ bekommen; gewinnen IV
gain experience /ˌgeɪn‿ɪkˈspɪəriəns/ Erfahrungen sammeln V:3/A2
gain weight /ˌgeɪn ˈweɪt/ zunehmen IV
gallery /ˈgæləri/ Galerie V:5/A7
gallery walk /ˈgæləri wɔːk/ *Gruppendiskussion in Stationsarbeit* V:5/I
game /geɪm/ Spiel I
gamer /ˈgeɪmə/ Spieler/in V:5/A4
gap /gæp/ Lücke V:1/B4; *hier:* Unterschied V:4/O
garden /ˈgɑːdn/ Garten I
gardener /ˈgɑːdnə/ Gärtner/in II
gardening /ˈgɑːdnɪŋ/ Gartenarbeit; Gärtnern V:3/B1
gas mask /ˈgæs mɑːsk/ Gasmaske V:5/A2
°gather /ˈgæðə/ sammeln; holen V:BS/1
gatherer /ˈgæθərə/ Sammler/in V:2/B3
gay /geɪ/ homosexuell V:3/B6
gear /gɪə/ Ausrüstung III
gear /gɪə/ *hier:* einstellen; schalten V:4/B2
gee *(AE, informal)* /dʒiː/ Wahnsinn, Mannomann V:4/B2
gender /ˈdʒendə/ Geschlecht; Geschlechter- V:5/B3
General Assembly /ˌdʒenrəl‿əˈsembli/ (UNO-) Vollversammlung V:6/Project C p. 129
°generate /ˈdʒenəreɪt/ hervorrufen; erzeugen V:5/O
genre /ˈʒɒnrə/ Genre; Gattung V:4/I

ladies and gentlemen /ˌleɪdiz‿ən‿ˈdʒentlmən/ (meine) Damen und Herren III
geography /dʒiːˈɒɡrəfi/ Erdkunde I
German /ˈdʒɜːmən/ Deutsch; deutsch I
in German /ˌɪn ˈdʒɜːmən/ auf Deutsch I
the German Graves Commission /ðə ˌdʒɜːmən ˈɡreɪvz kəˌmɪʃn/ Volksbund Deutsche Kriegsgräberfürsorge V:5/P9
Germany /ˈdʒɜːməni/ Deutschland I
gesture /ˈdʒestʃə/ Geste V:5/B4
get *(irr)* /ɡet/ werden IV; bekommen I; kommen; gelangen II; *hier:* kaufen II
get a tan /ˌget‿ə ˈtæn/ braun werden V:2/A2
get detention /ˌɡet ˈdɪˈtenʃn/ nachsitzen müssen V:5/B3
°get to do sth /ˌɡet tə duː ˈsʌmθɪŋ/ schaffen, etw zu tun; die Möglichkeit haben, etw zu tun V:BS/3
get familiar with /ˌɡet fəˈmɪliə wɪð/ vertraut werden mit V:6/Project p. 114
get in sb /ˌɡet‿ˈɪn ˌsʌmbədi/ jdn kommen lassen V:2/B7
get into groups /ˌɡet‿ɪntʊ ˈɡruːps/ in Gruppen zusammenkommen V:6/Project p. 116
get into /ˌɡet‿ˈɪntʊ/ *hier:* sich auseinandersetzen mit V:6/Project p. 114
get into trouble /ˌɡet‿ɪntʊ ˈtrʌbl/ in Schwierigkeiten geraten II
get involved /ˌɡet‿ɪnˈvɒlvd/ sich engagieren V:6/Project C p. 129
get to know sb /ˌɡet tə‿ˈnəʊ ˌsʌmbədi/ jdn kennenlernen IV:3/B1
get lost /ˌɡet ˈlɒst/ sich verirren II
get lucky /ˌɡet ˈlʌki/ Glück haben V:2/A5
get on well /ˌɡet‿ɒn ˈwel/ sich gut verstehen III
get out /ˌɡet‿ˈaʊt/ aussteigen I:4/B3
°get tired of sth /ˌɡet‿ˈtaɪəd‿əv ˌsʌmθɪŋ/ einer Sache überdrüssig werden V:BS/4
get together /ˌɡet‿təˈɡeðə/ zusammenkommen IV
get up /ˌɡet‿ˈʌp/ aufstehen I
get used to /ˌɡet ˈjuːst‿tuː/ sich gewöhnen an III
Get well soon! /ˌɡet ˌwel ˈsuːn/ Gute Besserung! II
geyser /ˈɡiːzə/ Geysir V:2/B1
ghost /ɡəʊst/ Geist; Gespenst I
ghostly /ˈɡəʊsli/ geisterhaft; gespenstisch V:1/B5
giant /ˈdʒaɪənt/ Riese V:2/A7
gift /ɡɪft/ Geschenk IV
giraffe /dʒəˈrɑːf/ Giraffe I
girl /ɡɜːl/ Mädchen I
girlfriend /ˈɡɜːlˌfrend/ Freundin *(Partnerin)*; Partnerin II
give *(irr)* /ɡɪv/ geben I
give *(irr)* /ɡɪv/ *hier:* wiedergeben; mitteilen V:5/B3
give a lift /ˌɡɪv‿ə ˈlɪft/ mitnehmen V:2/A2
give a presentation /ˌɡɪv‿ə ˌpreznˈteɪʃn/ eine Präsentation halten V:2/A6
give a reason /ˌɡɪv‿ə ˈriːzn/ einen Grund nennen IV
°give a speech /ˌɡɪv‿ə ˈspiːtʃ/ eine Rede halten V:BS/6
give a summary /ˌɡɪv‿ə ˈsʌməri/ eine Zusammenfassung erstellen V:4/A6
give advice /ˌɡɪv‿ədˈvaɪs/ Rat geben III
°give away /ˌɡɪv‿əˈweɪ/ verschenken V:BS/8
give evidence /ˌɡɪv‿ˈevɪdns/ belegen IV
give up /ˌɡɪv‿ˈʌp/ aufgeben III
given /ˈɡɪvn/ gegeben V:1/B1
glacier /ˈɡlæsiə/ Gletscher V:2/I; V:2/P6
glad /ɡlæd/ glücklich, froh III
glass /ɡlɑːs/ Glas III
glasses *(pl)* /ˈɡlɑːsɪz/ Brille I
glazed /ɡleɪzd/ glasig V:5/A1
glimpse /ɡlɪmps/ flüchtiger Blick V:5/A5
°glisten /ˈɡlɪsn/ glitzern; glänzen V:BS/8
gloss over /ˌɡlɒs‿ˈəʊvə/ flüchtig abhandeln V:5/B5
glove /ɡlʌv/ Handschuh I
glow /ɡləʊ/ leuchten, glühen V:2/A5
glow-worm /ˈɡləʊ wɜːm/ Glühwürmchen V:2/A4
go *(irr)* /ɡəʊ/ gehen; fahren I; werden III
go abroad /ˌɡəʊ‿əˈbrɔːd/ ins Ausland fahren II:1/A3
go away /ˌɡəʊ‿əˈweɪ/ weggehen; verschwinden V:6/Project C p. 128
go for /ˈɡəʊ fɔː/ gelten für V:4/A3
go further /ˌɡəʊ ˈfɜːðə/ weitermachen V:6/Project p. 117
go green /ˌɡəʊ ˈɡriːn/ umweltbewusst werden IV:6/I
go hiking /ˌɡəʊ ˈhaɪkɪŋ/ wandern gehen V:2/A7
go in for *(informal)* /ˌɡəʊ‿ˈɪn fə/ abfahren auf; mögen V:6/Project A p. 120
go kayaking /ˌɡəʊ ˈkaɪækɪŋ/ Kajak fahren V:2/A10
go on /ˌɡəʊ‿ˈɒn/ fortsetzen; fortfahren IV; passieren; weitergehen/-fahren/-reden III
go on holiday /ˌɡəʊ‿ɒn ˈhɒlɪdeɪ/ in Urlaub fahren II
go out /ˌɡəʊ‿ˈaʊt/ (hinaus)gehen; ausgehen III
go out of date /ˌɡəʊ‿ˌaʊt‿əv ˈdeɪt/ *hier:* ablaufen V:4/A8
go out with sb /ˌɡəʊ‿ˈaʊt wɪð ˌsʌmbədi/mit jdm ausgehen IV
go round /ˌɡəʊ ˈraʊnd/ *hier:* sich drehen V:3/B2
go shopping /ˌɡəʊ ˈʃɒpɪŋ/ Einkaufen gehen II
go skydiving /ˌɡəʊ ˈskaɪˌdaɪvɪŋ/ Fallschirmspringen gehen V:2/A10
go swimming /ˌɡəʊ ˈswɪmɪŋ/ Schwimmen gehen I
go through /ˌɡəʊ ˈθruː/ durchmachen V:6/Project A p. 121; durchgehen V:3/O

go together /ˌɡəʊ təˈɡeðə/ zusammenpassen V:1/B2
°go up /ˌɡəʊ‿ˈʌp/ steigen V:BS/4
go with /ˌɡəʊ ˈwɪθ/ gehören zu; passen zu II
go wrong /ˌɡəʊ ˈrɒŋ/ schiefgehen V:3/A10
goal /ɡəʊl/ Tor III
score a goal /ˌskɔːr‿ə ˈɡəʊl/ ein Tor schießen I
God (= god) /ɡɒd/ Gott V:2/B5
be going to do sth /biː ˌɡəʊɪŋ tə ˈduː ˌsʌmθɪŋ/ etw tun werden II
goldfish (*pl* **goldfish**) /ˈɡəʊldˌfɪʃ/ Goldfisch I
gonna (= going to) *(informal)* /ˈɡʌnə, ˈɡəʊɪŋ tʊ/ werden V:6/Project A p. 121
good /ɡʊd/ gut I
be good at sth /ˌbiː ˈɡʊd‿æt ˌsʌmθɪŋ/ gut in etw sein II
be good fun /biː ˌɡʊd ˈfʌn/ viel Spaß machen I
Good luck! /ˌɡʊd ˈlʌk/ Viel Glück! I
Good morning! /ˌɡʊd ˈmɔːnɪŋ/ Guten Morgen! I
good-looking /ˌɡʊdˈlʊkɪŋ/ gut aussehend I
Goodbye. /ˌɡʊdˈbaɪ/ Auf Wiedersehen. I
goods *(pl)* /ɡʊds/ Waren V:2/B7
goodwill /ɡʊdˈwɪl/ guter Wille V:5/B4
goth /ɡɒθ/ Gothic V:6/Project p. 130
government /ˈɡʌvənmənt/ Regierung IV
grab /ɡræb/ sich schnappen V:2/A2
°graduate *(AE)* /ˈɡrædʒueɪt/ die Abschlussprüfung bestehen V:BS/6
graduation /ˌɡrædʒuˈeɪʃn/ (Studien)abschluss V:5/B3
grandad /ˈɡrænˌdæd/ Opa III
granddaughter /ˈɡrænˌdɔːtə/ Enkelin I
grandfather /ˈɡrænˌfɑːðə/ Großvater I
grandmother /ˈɡrænˌmʌðə/ Großmutter I:5/B7
grandparent /ˈɡrænˌpeərənt/ Großelternteil I:5/B7
grandparents *(pl)* /ˈɡrænˌpeərənts/ Großeltern II
grandson /ˈɡrænˌsʌn/ Enkel I
grass /ɡrɑːs/ Gras; Wiese II
grateful /ˈɡreɪtfl/ dankbar III
grave /ɡreɪv/ Grab V:5/B3
great /ɡreɪt/ groß; großartig I
Great Barrier Reef /ˌɡreɪt ˈbæriə riːf/ Großes Barriereriff V:1/A4
Great Britain /ˌɡreɪt ˈbrɪtn/ Großbritannien II
greatly /ˈɡreɪtli/ sehr V:5/B3
Greece /ɡriːs/ Griechenland V:1/B2
greed /ˈɡriːd/ Gier V:5/B2
green /ɡriːn/ *hier:* umweltbewusst IV; grün I
greetings *(pl)* /ˈɡriːtɪŋz/ Grüße II
grey /ɡreɪ/ grau I
grid /ɡrɪd/ Gitter; Raster V:3/A2
grief /ɡriːf/ Trauer V:1/B8
grocery /ˈɡrəʊsəri/ Lebensmittel- V:4/A8
ground /ɡraʊnd/ Boden III
group /ɡruːp/ Gruppe II
grow *(irr)* /ɡrəʊ/ werden IV; anbauen III:4/A1; wachsen III
grow up /ˌɡrəʊ‿ˈʌp/ erwachsen sein/werden II
grower /ˈɡrəʊə/ Pflanzer/in V:1/A4; Züchter/in V:2/B3
guess /ɡes/ (er)raten II; annehmen; vermuten II
guessing game /ˈɡesɪŋ ˌɡeɪm/ Ratespiel V:1/P12
guest /ɡest/ Gast II
guide /ɡaɪd/ Führer/in III
guide /ɡaɪd/ Reiseführer V:2/B7; führen; leiten V:6/Project C p. 127
guided /ˈɡaɪdɪd/ geführt V:1/A7
guinea pig /ˈɡɪni ˌpɪɡ/ Meerschweinchen I
guitar /ɡɪˈtɑː/ Gitarre I
play the guitar /ˌpleɪ ðə ɡɪˈtɑː/ Gitarre spielen II
gum /ɡʌm/ Gummibaum V:1/B5
gun /ɡʌn/ Waffe V:2/B3
gym (= gymnasium) /dʒɪm, dʒɪmneɪziəm/ Turnhalle I
do gymnastics /ˌduː dʒɪmˈnæstɪks/ Turnen I

H

haberdasher /ˈhæbəˌdæʃə/ Kurzwarenhändler/in V:5/A2
°habit /ˈhæbɪt/ Gewohnheit V:BS/3
habitat /ˈhæbɪtæt/ Lebensraum V:2/A7
habitually /həˈbɪtʃuəli/ ständig V:6/Project A p. 121
hair /heə/ Haar I
hairdresser, hair stylist /ˈheəˌdresə, heə ˈstaɪlɪst/ Friseur/in II
hairstyle /ˈheəˌstaɪl/ Frisur V:6/Project B p. 123
half /hɑːf/ halb I
half (*pl* **halves**) /hɑːf, hɑːvz/ Hälfte III
halo /ˈheɪləʊ/ Heiligenschein V:6/Project C p. 129
°halve /hɑːv/ sich halbieren V:1/O
hamster /ˈhæmstə/ Hamster I
handkerchief (*pl* **handkerchiefs/ handkerchieves**) /ˈhæŋkəˌtʃɪf, ˈhæŋkəˌtʃɪfs, ˈhæŋkəˌtʃiːvz/ Taschentuch II
handle /ˈhændl/ bewältigen; regeln; behandeln V:2/A3
handsome /ˈhænsm/ gut aussehend II
handy /ˈhændi/ praktisch IV
hang around *(informal)* /ˌhæŋ‿əˈraʊnd/ rumhängen V:5/B3
°hangi /ˈhæŋi/ *eine im Erdofen zubereitete Mahlzeit* V:BS/3
happen /ˈhæpən/ geschehen; passieren II
happiness /ˈhæpinəs/ Glück; Zufriedenheit V:3/B2
happy /ˈhæpi/ glücklich I
Happy birthday (to you)! /ˌhæpi ˈbɜːθdeɪ tʊ juː/ Herzlichen Glückwunsch zum Geburtstag! I
Happy New Year! /ˌhæpi njuː ˈjɪə/ Frohes Neues Jahr! II

harassment /'hærəsmənt/ Belästigung; Schikane V:3/B6
harbour /'hɑ:bə/ Hafen V:2/A10
hard /hɑ:d/ hart; anstrengend II:2/B2; schwierig V:2/A1
hard skill /ˌhɑ:d 'skɪl/ *berufstypische Qualifikationen* IV
hardly /'hɑ:dli/ kaum III
hardship /'hɑ:dʃɪp/ Not; Elend V:5/B4
harm /hɑ:m/ Schaden zufügen, schaden V:2/A7
harmful /'hɑ:mfl/ schädlich V:2/A7
harmless /'hɑ:mləs/ harmlos V:2/A7
hat /hæt/ Hut I
hate /heɪt/ hassen; nicht ausstehen können I
hate /heɪt/ Hass V:3/B6
hate speech /'heɪt spi:tʃ/ Hassrede; Hetzrede V:5/B3
°hater /'heɪtə/ jd, der etw hasst V:BS/8
have *(irr)* /hæv/ haben; essen, trinken I
have a look at /ˌhæv‿ə 'lʊk‿ət/ sich ansehen IV
have (a lot of) fun /ˌhæv‿ə ˌlɒt‿əv‿'fʌn/ (viel) Spaß haben II
have a picnic /ˌhæv‿ə 'pɪknɪk/ ein Picknick machen I
have a temperature /ˌhæv‿ə 'temprɪtʃə/ Fieber haben III
have breakfast /ˌhæv 'brekfəst/ frühstücken I
have got /ˌhæv 'gɒt/ haben I
have in common /ˌhæv‿ɪn 'kɒmən/ gemeinsam haben V:4/A6
have the bug *(informal)* /ˌhæv ðə 'bʌg/ jdn hat es gepackt V:2/A5
have to /'hæv tə/ müssen I
he /hi:/ er I
head /hed/ Kopf; *hier:* Hörer/in V:6/Project A p. 119
headache /'hedeɪk/ Kopfschmerzen III
headed /'hedɪd/ mit der Überschrift V:4/B2
heading /'hedɪŋ/ Überschrift, Titel IV
headquarters *(pl)* /hed'kwɔ:təz/ Hauptquartier, Zentrale V:5/B3
headstone /'hedˌstəʊn/ Grabstein V:5/B3
healing /'hi:lɪŋ/ Heilung V:1/B8
health /helθ/ Gesundheit III
healthy /'helθi/ gesund III
hear *(irr)* /hɪə/ hören II
heart /hɑ:t/ Herz III
heart rate /'hɑ:t reɪt/ Pulsfrequenz V:2/A3
heartbroken /'hɑ:tˌbrəʊkən/ todunglücklich; untröstlich V:4/P14
°heat /hi:t/ Hitze V:2/O
heaven /'hevn/ Himmel V:5/B2
heavy /'hevi/ schwer II
hedgehog /'hedʒˌhɒg/ Igel I
height /haɪt/ Höhe IV
heighten /'haɪtn/ steigern; erhöhen; verstärken V:2/A3
heli-hike /'heli haɪk/ Heli-Wanderung V:2/A5
heli-hiking /'heli ˌhaɪkɪŋ/ Heli-Wandern V:2/A5
helicopter /'helɪˌkɒptə/ Hubschrauber; Helikopter V:2/A5
hell /hel/ Hölle V:5/B2
hello /hə'ləʊ/ hallo I
help /help/ helfen I; Hilfe II
for help /fə 'help/ nach Hilfe, als Hilfe II
help out /ˌhelp‿'aʊt/ aushelfen V:3/A6
helper /'helpə/ Helfer/in V:3/B3
helpful /'helpfl/ hilfreich; nützlich III
helpless /'helpləs/ hilflos V:5/A5
hemisphere /'hemɪˌsfɪə/ Halbkugel V:1/A2
her /hɜ:/ ihr / ihre; sie I
here /hɪə/ hier; hierher I
Here you are. / Here you go. /ˌhɪə ju‿'ɑ: / 'gəʊ/ Hier, bitte! I
heritage /'herɪtɪdʒ/ Erbe V:2/B5
hero (*pl* **heroes**) /'hɪərəʊ, 'hɪərəʊz/ Held II
hers /hɜ:z/ ihre(r, s) III
herself /hə'self/ sich; sich selbst IV
hide *(irr)* /haɪd/ (sich) verstecken IV
high frequency /haɪ 'fri:kwənsi/ Hochfrequenz- V:1/B10
high rope course /'haɪ rəʊp ˌkɔ:s/ Hochseilgarten V:2/A2
high school *(AE)* /'haɪ sku:l/ Highschool, weiterführende Schule V:3/B3
high score /'haɪ skɔ:/ *erreichter Punktestand bei der Wertung von Computerspielen* V:4/A3
hike /haɪk/ Wanderung V:2/A5
hiker /'haɪkə/ Wanderer / Wanderin V:2/A7
hiking /'haɪkɪŋ/ Wandern V:2/A7
hill /hɪl/ Hügel V:2/A4
him /hɪm/ ihm, ihn I
himself /hɪm'self/ sich; sich selbst IV
hind /haɪnd/ Hinter- V:1/P2
his /hɪz/ sein; seine(r, s) I
historical /hɪ'stɒrɪkl/ historisch V:1/A9
history /'hɪstri/ Geschichte I
hit *(irr)* /hɪt/ treffen, stoßen gegen; schlagen III
hold *(irr)* /həʊld/ (fest)halten II
hole /həʊl/ Loch II
holiday(s) /'hɒlɪdeɪ(z)/ Ferien;Urlaub II
go on holiday /ˌgəʊ‿ɒn 'hɒlɪdeɪ/ in Urlaub fahren II
holiday /'hɒlɪdeɪ/ *hier:* Feiertag V:3/B3
holistic /həʊ'lɪstɪk/ ganzheitlich V:5/B3
holy /'həʊli/ heilig V:1/A7
home /həʊm/ Zuhause; Haus I; nach Hause II
home country /ˌhəʊm 'kʌntri/ Heimatland V:1/B1
home group /'həʊm gru:p/ *Ursprungsgruppe* V:5/B3
homeland /'həʊmˌlænd/ Heimat(land) V:2/B3
homeless /'həʊmləs/ heimatlos; obdachlos V:3/A2
homestay /'həʊmˌsteɪ/ *Aufenthalt in einer Gastfamilie* V:3/A2
homework /'həʊmwɜ:k/ Hausaufgaben I

honest /ˈɒnɪst/ ehrlich V:6/Project A p. 120
honesty /ˈɒnɪsti/ Ehrlichkeit V:6/Project C p. 127
hope /həʊp/ Hoffnung IV; hoffen I
hopeful /ˈhəʊpfl/ zuversichtlich V:4/P14
hormone /ˈhɔːməʊn/ Hormon V:2/A3
horrifying /ˈhɒrɪˌfaɪɪŋ/ schrecklich; grauenhaft V:5/A3
horse /hɔːs/ Pferd I
ride a horse /ˌraɪd‿ə ˈhɔːs/ reiten I
hospital /ˈhɒspɪtl/ Krankenhaus III
host family /ˈhəʊst ˌfæmli/ Gastfamilie V:1/A4
hostile /ˈhɒstaɪl/ feindselig; *hier:* gefährlich V
hot /hɒt/ heiß I; scharf III
hot chocolate /ˌhɒt ˈtʃɒklət/ (heißer) Kakao I
hour /ˈaʊə/ Stunde II
hour /ˈaʊə/ Zeit V:4/B2
house /haʊs/ Haus I
household /ˈhaʊsˌhəʊld/ Haushalt V:3/A2
how /haʊ/ wie I
How come? *(informal)* /ˌhaʊ ˈkʌm/ Wieso? V:6/Project A p. 119
how many /haʊ ˈmeni/ wie viele I
how much /haʊ ˈmʌtʃ/ wie viel I
how to /ˈhaʊ tʊ/ wie man I
How're you going? *(AusE, informal)* /ˌhaʊəjə ˈɡəʊɪŋ/ V:1/B10
°hug /hʌɡ/ umarmen V:5/O
huge /hjuːdʒ/ riesig II
human /ˈhjuːmən/ menschlich; Mensch V:2/A3
human rights *(pl)* /ˌhjuːmən ˌraɪts/ Menschenrechte V:5/B3
humanity /hjuːˈmænəti/ Menschlichkeit; Menschheit V:5/B4
hungry /ˈhʌŋɡri/ hungrig I
hunt /hʌnt/ jagen V:1/B4
hunter /ˈhʌntə/ Jäger/in V:2/B3
hurry (up) /ˌhʌri‿ˈʌp/ sich beeilen I
hurt /hɜːt/ Schmerz V:1/B8; gekränkt; verletzt V:4/B2
hurt *(irr)* /hɜːt/ wehtun, schmerzen III
hurt oneself /ˈhɜːt wʌnˌself/ sich verletzen III
hut /hʌt/ Hütte V:2/A8

I

I /aɪ/ ich I
I betcha *(informal)* /aɪ ˈbetʃə/ ich wette darauf V:4/B2
I'd rather ... /ˌaɪd ˈrɑːðə/ Ich würde lieber ... I
I'll take it. /ˌaɪl ˈteɪk‿ɪt/ Ich nehme es. I
ice /aɪs/ Eis V:2/A5
ice age /ˈaɪs‿eɪdʒ/ Eiszeit V:1/B4
ice axe /ˈaɪs‿æks/ Eispickel V:2/A5
ice cream /ˈaɪs ˌkriːm/ Eis II
ice cube /ˈaɪs kjuːb/ Eiswürfel V:2/A5
ice-climber /ˈaɪs ˌklaɪmə/ Eiskletterer/in V:2/A5
iceberg /ˈaɪsˌbɜːɡ/ Eisberg V:6/Project C p. 127
ICT (= Information and Communication Technology) /ˌaɪˌsiːˈtiː, ɪnfəˈmeɪʃn‿ən kəˌmjuːnɪˈkeɪʃn tekˌnɒlədʒi/ Informationstechnologie, IT I
icy /ˈaɪsi/ eisig (kalt) V:2/A5
idea /aɪˈdɪə/ Idee II; *hier:* Vorstellung II
idea /aɪˈdɪə/ *hier:* Ahnung V:1/A2
identify /aɪˈdentɪfaɪ/ identifizieren IV
identity /aɪˈdentɪti/ Identität V:1/A8
if /ɪf/ wenn; falls II; ob II
ignore /ɪɡˈnɔː/ ignorieren II
ill /ɪl/ krank II
illness /ˈɪlnəs/ Krankheit III
illustrate /ˈɪləstreɪt/ illustrieren V:1/B6
image /ˈɪmɪdʒ/ Bild IV
imaginary /ɪˈmædʒɪnəri/ imaginär; ausgedacht V:2/A10
imagination /ɪˌmædʒɪˈneɪʃn/ Fantasie, Vorstellungskraft V:1/B1
imagine /ɪˈmædʒɪn/ sich etw vorstellen III
imitate /ˈɪmɪteɪt/ imitieren; kopieren V:6/Project B p. 123
immediately /ɪˈmiːdiətli/ sofort IV
immigrant /ˈɪmɪɡrənt/ Einwanderer/in; Immigrant/in III
immigration /ˌɪmɪˈɡreɪʃn/ Einwanderung; Immigration IV
impact /ˈɪmpækt/ Auswirkung V:1/A4
implement /ˈɪmplɪˌment/ einführen, umsetzen V:2/A7
import /ɪmˈpɔːt/ importieren, einführen IV
importance /ɪmˈpɔːtns/ Bedeutung; Wichtigkeit IV
important /ɪmˈpɔːtnt/ wichtig II
impossible /ɪmˈpɒsəbl/ unmöglich IV
impression /ɪmˈpreʃn/ Eindruck IV
impressive /ɪmˈpresɪv/ beeindruckend III
imprisonment /ɪmˈprɪznmənt/ Gefängnisstrafe V:1/P2
in /ɪn/ in; auf I
in addition to /ˌɪn‿əˈdɪʃn tʊ/ zusätzlich zu V:5/A3
in case /ˌɪn ˈkeɪs/ für den Fall, dass V:1/A4
in detail /ɪn ˈdiːteɪl/ ausführlich V:6/Project B p. 124
in fact /ɪn ˈfækt/ tatsächlich; in Wirklichkeit V:1/B2
in front /ɪn ˈfrʌnt/ vorn IV
in front of /ˌɪn ˈfrʌnt‿əv/ vor I
in my opinion /ɪn ˈmaɪ‿əˌpɪnjən/ meiner Meinung nach III
°in need /ɪn‿ˈniːd/ bedürftig V:BS/7
in order to /ˌɪn‿ˈɔːdə tʊ/ um zu IV
in pairs /ˌɪn ˈpeəz/ paarweise V:1/A3
in search of /ɪn ˈsɜːtʃ‿əv/ auf der Suche nach V:6/Project A p. 119
in short /ɪn ˈʃɔːt/ in der Kurzform V:5/B3
in sight /ɪn ˈsaɪt/ in Sicht V:5/B5
in spite of /ɪn ˈspaɪt‿əv/ trotz V:5/B4

in the afternoon /ˌɪn ðiˌɑ:ftəˈnu:n/ am Nachmittag II
in the back of beyond /ˌɪn ðə ˌbækˌəv bɪˈjɒnd/ am Ende der Welt V:1/B10
in the end /ˌɪn ðiˌˈend/ schließlich III
in time /ɪn ˈtaɪm/ rechtzeitig; pünktlich II
in-flight /ˌɪnˈflaɪt/ Bord- V:4/B5
°inch /ɪntʃ/ Zoll *(2,54 cm)* V:BS/4
incident /ˈɪnsɪdnt/ Vorfall; Ereignis III
include /ɪnˈklu:d/ beinhalten; einbeziehen IV
including /ɪnˈklu:dɪŋ/ einschließlich III
inclusive /ɪnˈklu:sɪv/ allumfassend V:6/Project p. 130
income /ˈɪnkʌm/ Einkommen V:6/Project B p. 124
increase /ɪnˈkri:s/ erhöhen; verstärken V:5/B3
increase /ɪnˈkri:s/ (an)steigen; zunehmen V:2/A3
incredible /ɪnˈkredəbl/ unglaublich II
independence /ˌɪndɪˈpendəns/ Unabhängigkeit V:6/Project B p. 123
independent /ˌɪndɪˈpendənt/ unabhängig V:1/A8
India /ˈɪndiə/ Indien V:3/B3
indigenous /ɪnˈdɪdʒənəs/ einheimisch V:1/A2
indignity /ɪnˈdɪgnəti/ Demütigung V:1/B8
indirect /ˌɪndəˈrekt/ indirekt V:5/P10
individual /ˌɪndɪˈvɪdʒuəl/ individuell; einzeln IV
individual /ˌɪndɪˈvɪdʒuəl/ Einzelperson; Einzelne/r V:6/Project A p. 119
individuality /ˌɪndɪˌvɪdʒuˈæləti/ Individualität V:6/Project B p. 123
Indonesia /ˌɪndəʊˈni:ʒə/ Indonesien V:1/B2
indoor climbing /ˌɪndɔ: ˈklaɪmɪŋ/ Hallenklettern V:2/A1
industry /ˈɪndəstri/ Industrie III
infection /ɪnˈfekʃn/ Infektion V:5/A3
inflict /ɪnˈflɪkt/ zufügen V:1/B8
influence /ˈɪnfluəns/ beeinflussen V:6/Project p. 115
influence /ˈɪnfluəns/ Einfluss V:2/A3
info bubble /ˈɪnfəʊ ˌbʌbl/ Info-Blase V:4/A7
inform /ɪnˈfɔ:m/ informieren III
informal /ɪnˈfɔ:ml/ informell V:5/B3
information *(no pl)* /ˌɪnfəˈmeɪʃn/ Informationen II
information technology (= IT) /ˌɪnfəˌmeɪʃn tekˈnɒlədʒi, ˌaɪ ˈti:/ Informationstechnologie, IT III
ingredient /ɪnˈgri:diənt/ Zutat III
°inhabit /ɪnˈhæbɪt/ bewohnen V:1/O
injection /ɪnˈdʒekʃn/ Spritze; Injektion III
injure /ˈɪndʒə/ verletzen V:5/A3
ink /ɪŋk/ Tinte V:4/P9
inner /ˈɪnə/ innere(r, s) V:2/A4
inner-city /ˌɪnə ˈsɪti/ Innenstadt-; innerstädtisch V:5/B3
°insect /ˈɪnsekt/ Insekt V:BS/3
insert /ɪnˈsɜ:t/ einwerfen; (hinein)stecken; einfügen V:4/B2
inside /ˈɪnˌsaɪd/ innen; drinnen; hinein II
inside cover /ˌɪnsaɪd ˈkʌvə/ Innenseite des Einbands V:1/A1
inspector /ɪnˈspektə/ Inspektor/in V:4/B2
inspire /ɪnˈspaɪə/ inspirieren V:3/B6
instead /ɪnˈsted/ stattdessen III
instead of /ɪnˈstedˌəv/ anstatt IV
institution /ˌɪnstɪˈtju:ʃn/ Einrichtung; Institution V:5/B3
instruction /ɪnˈstrʌkʃn/ Anweisung; Instruktion III
insulting /ɪnˈsʌltɪŋ/ beleidigend V:3/P11
insurance /ɪnˈʃʊərəns/ Versicherung V:3/B3
intelligence /ɪnˈtelɪdʒns/ Intelligenz V:3/B3
intense /ɪnˈtens/ intensiv V:2/A3
interact /ˌɪntərˈækt/ interagieren; kommunizieren V:1/B10
interaction /ˌɪntərˈækʃn/ Interaktion V:1/B10
interactive /ˌɪntərˈæktɪv/ interaktiv V:1/B10
intercultural /ˌɪntəˈkʌltʃrəl/ interkulturell V:5/B3
interest /ˈɪntrəst/ Interesse, Hobby II
°interested /ˈɪntrəstɪd/ interessiert V:3/O
be interested in /ˌbiˌˈɪntrəstɪdˌɪn/ interessiert sein an III
interesting /ˈɪntrəstɪŋ/ interessant I
internment camp /ɪnˈtɜ:nmənt kæmp/ Internierungslager V:1/B6
interrupt /ˌɪntəˈrʌpt/ unterbrechen IV
interview /ˈɪntəˌvju:/ Vorstellungsgespräch IV; interviewen, befragen III
into /ˈɪntu:/ in I
intonation /ˌɪntəˈneɪʃn/ Satzmelodie V:2/A10
introduce /ˌɪntrəˈdju:s/ einführen V:2/B9
introduce /ˌɪntrəˈdju:s/ *hier:* einschleppen V:1/A8; vorstellen V:4/P10
introduction /ˌɪntrəˈdʌkʃn/ Einleitung IV:6/Project p. 116
invasion /ɪnˈveɪʒn/ Invasion; Eindringen V:5/A6
invasive /ɪnˈveɪsɪv/ invasiv V:1/A4
invent /ɪnˈvent/ erfinden III
invention /ɪnˈvenʃn/ Erfindung III
inventor /ɪnˈventə/ Erfinder/in III
invitation /ˌɪnvɪˈteɪʃn/ Einladung II
invite /ɪnˈvaɪt/ einladen I
involve /ɪnˈvɒlv/ beinhalten; umfassen V:2/A7
involve sb in sth /ɪnˈvɒlv ˌsʌmbədiˌɪn ˌsʌmθɪŋ/ jdn an etw beteiligen V:5/B3

Iraq /ɪˈrɑːk/ Irak V:5/A5
Ireland /ˈaɪələnd/ Irland II
Irish /ˈaɪrɪʃ/ irisch V:6/Project A p. 120
iron /ˈaɪən/ Eisen V:1/B5
°irrigation /ˌɪrəˈgeɪʃən/ Bewässerung V:1/O
island /ˈaɪlənd/ Insel III
isolated /ˈaɪsəˌleɪtɪd/ isoliert, einsam; abgelegen V:1/B4
issue /ˈɪʃuː/ Frage; Thema; Problem V:4/A9; *hier:* ausrufen V:4/B5
it /ɪt/ es I
Italy /ˈɪtəli/ Italien V:1/B2
item /ˈaɪtəm/ Artikel V:6/Project B p. 124
its /ɪts/ sein(e), ihr(e) *(sächlich)* II

J

jacket /ˈdʒækɪt/ Jacke I
jam /dʒæm/ Marmelade I
jandal /ˈdʒændl/ *neuseel. für Flip-Flop* V:2/B8
January /ˈdʒænjuəri/ Januar I
jet boating /ˈdʒet ˌbəʊtɪŋ/ Jetbootfahren V:2/A4
jewellery *(no pl)* /ˈdʒuːəlri/ Schmuck V:3/B1
job /dʒɒb/ Aufgabe I:4/A6; Stelle; Job; Beruf II
°job interview /ˈdʒɒb‿ˌɪntəvjuː/ Bewerbungsgespräch V:3/O
join /dʒɔɪn/ sich zu jdm gesellen IV:5/B3; mitmachen I
°join /dʒɔɪn/ *hier:* verbinden V:2/O
join in /ˌdʒɔɪn‿ˈɪn/ sich beteiligen an; mitmachen bei V:6/Project C p. 126
°join the army /ˌdʒɔɪn ði‿ˈɑːmi/ Soldat werden V:5/O
joke /dʒəʊk/ Spaß; Witz II
You must be joking! *(informal)* /juː məs bi ˈdʒəʊkɪŋ/ Das soll wohl ein Witz sein! II
journey /ˈdʒɜːni/ Reise III
°jr. (= junior) /ˈdʒuːniə/ V:BS/7
judge /dʒʌdʒ/ (be)urteilen, (ein) schätzen V:6/Project B p. 122
juice /dʒuːs/ Saft II
orange juice /ˈɒrɪndʒ‿ˌdʒuːs/ Orangensaft I
July /dʒʊˈlaɪ/ Juli I
jump /dʒʌmp/ springen I
jump /dʒʌmp/ Sprung V:2/A10
jumper /ˈdʒʌmpə/ Pullover I
June /dʒuːn/ Juni I
just /dʒʌst/ gerade I; nur; bloß II; einfach; wirklich II
justify /ˈdʒʌstɪfaɪ/ rechtfertigen; begründen V:3/B8

K

kai *(informal)* /kaɪ/ *austral./ neuseel. für Essen, Futter* V:2/B8
kangaroo /ˌkæŋgəˈruː/ Känguru V:1/A2
kayaking /ˈkaɪækɪŋ/ Kajakfahren V:2/A1
be keen on doing sth /ˌbiː ˌkiːn‿ɒn ˈduːɪŋ ˌsʌmθɪŋ/ etw mit Begeisterung tun V:2/P9
keep *(irr)* /kiːp/ halten; behalten; aufbewahren III
°keep *(irr)* /kiːp/ *hier:* einhalten V:BS/1
keep doing sth /ˌkiːp ˈduːɪŋ sʌmθɪŋ/ etw weiter tun III
keep fit /ˌkiːp ˈfɪt/ fit bleiben, (sich) fit halten III
keep going /ˌkiːp ˈgəʊɪŋ/ in Gang halten; am Laufen halten III
keep in mind /ˌkiːp‿ɪn ˈmaɪnd/ etw im Gedächtnis behalten V:4/B7
keep in touch /ˌkiːp‿ɪn ˈtʌtʃ/ Kontakt halten; in Verbindung bleiben IV
keep one's eyes peeled for /ˌkiːp wʌnz‿aɪz ˈpiːld fə/ Ausschau halten nach V:2/A4
keep sth in mind /ˌkiːp ˌsʌmθɪŋ‿ɪn ˈmaɪnd/ etw im Gedächtnis behalten V:3/B6
keeper /ˈkiːpə/ Inhaber/in; Wärter/in V:1/B5; (Zoo)wärter/in V:BS/4
key /kiː/ Schlüssel V:3/B2
keyword /ˈkiːˌwɜːd/ Schlüsselwort V:5/B1; Stichwort V:6/Project p. 115
kick /kɪk/ treten III
kid /kɪd/ Kind II
°kidnap /ˈkɪdnæp/ entführen V:5/O
kill /kɪl/ töten III
°kilogram /ˈkɪləˌgræm/ Kilogramm V:BS/3
kind /kaɪnd/ Art; Sorte I; freundlich III:2/A7
kind of *(informal)* /ˈkaɪnd‿əv/ irgendwie, ziemlich V:5/B3
kindergartener /ˈkɪndəˌgɑːtnə/ Kindergartenkind V:5/B3
all kinds of /ˌɔːl ˈkaɪndz‿əv/ alle möglichen II
king /kɪŋ/ König III
kiss /kɪs/ küssen IV
kitchen /ˈkɪtʃən/ Küche I
kite surfing /ˈkaɪt ˌsɜːfɪŋ/ Lenkdrachensegeln V:2/A1
kiwi, Kiwi /ˈkiːwiː/ *Vogel, Frucht und Spitzname für Neuseeländer/in* V:2/A5
km (= kilometre) /ˈkɪləˌmiːtə/ Kilometer V:1/A2
knee /niː/ Knie I
knife (*pl* **knives**) /naɪf, naɪvz/ Messer I
know *(irr)* /nəʊ/ wissen; kennen I
knowledge /ˈnɒlɪdʒ/ Kenntnis; Wissen V:6/Project p. 117

L

label /ˈleɪbl/ beschriften I
label /ˈleɪbl/ Etikett, Schildchen V:5/A2; *hier:* abstempeln V:6/Project B p. 123; *hier:* Label; Marke V:6/Project B p. 125; *hier:* kategorisieren V:6/Project B p. 133
ladies and gentlemen /ˌleɪdiz‿ən‿ˈdʒentlmən/ (meine) Damen und Herren III
lady /ˈleɪdi/ Frau; Dame III
lake /leɪk/ See II
lamp /læmp/ Lampe I
land /lænd/ landen V:2/A5
landscape /ˈlænˌskeɪp/ Landschaft V:1/A4

language /ˈlæŋgwɪdʒ/ Sprache IV
lapel /ləˈpel/ Kragen(aufschlag); Revers V:5/A2
large /lɑːdʒ/ groß II
lash /læʃ/ Peitsche V:1/B5
last /lɑːst/ letzte(r, s) I
last /lɑːst/ (an)dauern V:2/B9
last but not least /ˌlɑːst bət nɒt ˈliːst/ nicht zuletzt; nicht zu vergessen V:5/B3
last night /ˌlɑːst ˈnaɪt/ gestern Abend II
lasting /ˈlɑːstɪŋ/ dauerhaft; andauernd V:5/A1
late /leɪt/ (zu) spät I
latest /ˈleɪtɪst/ neueste(r, s) IV
Latin American /ˌlætɪn‿əˈmerɪkən/ Lateinamerikaner/in; lateinamerikanisch V:6/Project A p. 132
laugh /lɑːf/ lachen II
launch /lɔːntʃ/ *hier:* starten; einführen V:6/Project B p. 125
law /lɔː/ Gesetz; Recht V:1/B6
lawn /lɔːn/ Rasen V:3/B1
lawsuit /ˈlɔːˌsuːt/ Klage; Gerichtsverfahren; Prozess V:6/Project C p. 129
lay *(irr)* /leɪ/ legen II
lay the table /ˌleɪ ðə ˈteɪbl/ den Tisch decken II
layout /ˈleɪaʊt/ Layout; Aufbau V:3/A5
lead *(irr)* /liːd/ führen IV
leaf (*pl* **leaves**) /liːf, liːvz/ Blatt III
learn *(irr)* /lɜːn/ lernen I
learn *(irr)* /lɜːn/ *hier:* erfahren V:5/A3
at least /ət ˈliːst/ mindestens; wenigstens III
least /liːst/ am wenigsten V:2/A6
leave *(irr)* /liːv/ verlassen; abfahren I; zurücklassen; (übrig) lassen III
°leave *(irr)* /liːv/ weggehen V:5/O
leave behind /ˌliːv bɪˈhaɪnd/ zurücklassen V:1/B1
leave out /ˌliːv‿ˈaʊt/ auslassen; weglassen III
left /left/ (nach) links II
be left /ˌbiː ˈleft/ übrig bleiben III
have sth left /ˌhæv sʌmθɪŋ ˈleft/ etw übrig haben II
on the left/on your left /ˌɒn ðə/jɔː ˈleft/ links, auf der/deiner linken Seite II
on the left side /ɒn ðə ˌleft ˈsaɪd/ links II
leftovers *(pl)* /ˈleftˌəʊvəz/ (Über)reste; Überbleibsel V:5/A3
leg /leg/ Bein I
°legacy /ˈlegəsi/ Vermächtnis; Erbe V:BS/7
legal /ˈliːgl/ rechtlich; gesetzlich V:4/A3
legend /ˈledʒnd/ Legende V:2/B1
leisure /ˈleʒə/ Freizeit; Freizeit- V:5/B3
lemonade /ˌleməˈneɪd/ Limonade II
°length /leŋθ/ Länge V:BS/3
lens /lenz/ Objektiv; Linse V:3/B6
lesbian /ˈlezbiən/ lesbisch V:3/B6
less /les/ weniger III
lesson /ˈlesn/ Stunde; Unterricht I
let *(irr)* /let/ lassen II
letter /ˈletə/ Brief; Buchstabe II
level /ˈlevl/ Stufe; Level V:3/B3
liberty /ˈlɪbəti/ Freiheit IV
library /ˈlaɪbrəri/ Bücherei I
lie *(irr)* /laɪ/ liegen II
life (*pl* **lives**) /laɪf, laɪvz/ Leben II
life-changing /ˈlaɪf ˌtʃeɪndʒɪŋ/ lebensverändernd V:2/A5
lifestyle /ˈlaɪfˌstaɪl/ Lebensstil V:6/Project A p. 119
lift /lɪft/ (hoch)heben III
light /laɪt/ Licht I
lighting /ˈlaɪtɪŋ/ Beleuchtung V:3/B6
like /laɪk/ mögen I; wie I
like /laɪk/ ähnlich V:4/A7; Vorliebe V:6/Project p. 131
°-like /laɪk/ -haft; -ähnlich V:1/O
like best /ˌlaɪk ˈbest/ am liebsten mögen I
like better /ˌlaɪk ˈbetə/ lieber mögen III
like doing sth /laɪk ˈduːɪŋ ˌsʌmθɪŋ/ etw gern tun I
like this /ˌlaɪk ˈðɪs/ so II
like-minded /ˌlaɪk ˈmaɪndɪd/ gleich gesinnt V:6/Project A p. 120
likely /ˈlaɪkli/ wahrscheinlich IV
limit /ˈlɪmɪt/ (Höchst)grenze; Limit V:2/A8
line /laɪn/ Linie; Zeile I
lingo *(informal)* /ˈlɪŋgəʊ/ Sprache, Jargon V:2/B8
linked /lɪŋkt/ gekoppelt; verbunden V:2/A3
lion /ˈlaɪən/ Löwe I
°lip /lɪp/ Lippe V:2/O
list /lɪst/ auflisten IV; Liste I
listen (to) /ˈlɪsn/ zuhören I
listener /ˈlɪsnə/ Zuhörer/in V:3/A6
lit up /ˌlɪt‿ˈʌp/ beleuchtet V:4/B2
literally /ˈlɪtrəli/ (wort)wörtlich V:2/A4
litter /ˈlɪtə/ Abfall; Müll II
little /ˈlɪtl/ klein I; *hier:* wenig V:3/B6
a little /ə ˈlɪtl/ ein bisschen III
live /lɪv/ leben; wohnen I
live on /ˌlɪv‿ˈɒn/ leben von V:3/B3
live on the edge /ˌlɪv‿ɒn ði‿ˈedʒ/ ein extremes Leben führen V:2/P7
living /ˈlɪvɪŋ/ lebend V:1/A2
make one's living /ˌmeɪk wʌnz ˈlɪvɪŋ/ leben können von V:3/B6
living room /ˈlɪvɪŋ ˌruːm/ Wohnzimmer I
°lizard /ˈlɪzəd/ Eidechse; Echse V:BS/3
local /ˈləʊkl/ örtlich; hiesig
local /ˈləʊkl/ Ortsansässige/r, Heimische/r V:1/A7
locally /ˈləʊkli/ am/vor Ort V:2/A7
location /ləʊˈkeɪʃn/ Lage; Standort V:1/B6
loftily /ˈlɒftili/ hochmütig; stolz V:4/B2
lolly /ˈlɒli/ Lolli, Lutscher V:2/B5
lonely /ˈləʊnli/ einsam II
long /lɒŋ/ lang I
°long ago /ˌlɒŋ‿əˈgəʊ/ vor langer Zeit V:BS/1

long-term /ˌlɒŋ ˈtɜːm/ langfristig V:5/A5
longing /ˈlɒŋɪŋ/ Sehnsucht; Verlangen V:6/Project A p. 119
look /lʊk/ Blick IV; aussehen I
look /lʊk/ Aussehen; Look V:6/Project B p. 122
look after /ˌlʊk‿ˈɑːftə/ sich kümmern um; aufpassen auf II
look after sb /ˌlʊk‿ˈɑːftə ˌsʌmbədi/ sich um jdn kümmern I
look (at) /ˈlʊk‿ət/ (an)sehen, (an)schauen I
look for /ˈlʊk fə/ suchen nach I
look forward to /ˌlʊk ˈfɔːwəd‿tʊ/ sich freuen auf IV
°look on /ˌlʊk‿ˈɒn/ betrachten; zusehen V:BS/4
look up /ˌlʊk‿ˈʌp/ nach oben sehen V:4/B2; hochschauen V:BS/4
loosen /ˈluːsn/ lockern V:6/Project p. 115
lorry driver /ˈlɒri ˌdraɪvə/ Lastwagenfahrer/in II
lose *(irr)* /luːz/ verlieren III
loss /lɒs/ Verlust IV
get lost /ˌget ˈlɒst/ sich verirren II
a lot (of) /ə ˈlɒt/ viel(e), jede Menge I
lots of /ˈlɒts‿əv/ viel, jede Menge I
loud /laʊd/ laut I
love /lʌv/ lieben, sehr mögen I; Liebe III
love doing sth /lʌv ˈduːɪŋ ˌsʌmθɪŋ/ etw sehr gern tun II
lovely /ˈlʌvli/ schön II
°lover /ˈlʌvə/ Liebhaber/in V:BS/3
low /ləʊ/ niedrig III
low-income /ˌləʊ ˈɪnkʌm/ einkommensschwach V:5/B3
lower school /ˌləʊə ˈskuːl/ *hier:* Unterstufe V:5/B3
bad luck /ˌbæd ˈlʌk/ Pech II
Good luck! /ˌgʊd ˈlʌk/ Viel Glück! I

°luckily /ˈlʌkɪli/ zum Glück; glücklicherweise V:5/O
lucky /ˈlʌki/ glücklich II
lunch /lʌntʃ/ Mittagessen I
lunchtime /ˈlʌntʃtaɪm/ Mittagszeit, Mittagspause I
lyrics *(pl)* /ˈlɪrɪks/ Liedtext V:1/B5

M

machine /məˈʃiːn/ Maschine; Apparat I
magazine /ˌmægəˈziːn/ Zeitschrift I
magical /ˈmædʒɪkl/ magisch V:2/A5
mail /meɪl/ Post V:1/B3
main (course) /ˈmeɪn kɔːs/ Hauptgericht III
mainland /ˈmeɪnˌlænd/ Festland V:1/A2
mainly /ˈmeɪnli/ hauptsächlich V:1/B2
maintain /meɪnˈteɪn/ erhalten; pflegen V:5/B3
major /ˈmeɪdʒə/ *hier:* groß V:2/A3
make *(irr)* /meɪk/ machen I
make a decision /ˌmeɪk‿ə dɪˈsɪʒn/ eine Entscheidung treffen V:6/Project C p. 128
make a difference /ˌmeɪk‿ə ˈdɪfrəns/ einen Unterschied machen; verändern V:6/Project C p. 127
make a living /ˌmeɪk‿ə ˈlɪvɪŋ/ seinen Lebensunterhalt verdienen V:1/A9
make an effort /ˌmeɪk‿ən‿ˈefət/ sich bemühen V:2/A7
make friends (with) /ˌmeɪk ˈfrends/ sich anfreunden (mit) II
make fun of /ˌmeɪk ˈfʌn‿əv/ sich lustig machen über V:6/Project A p. 121
make (good) money /ˌmeɪk ˈmʌni/ (gut) verdienen; (viel) Geld verdienen II
make notes /ˌmeɪk ˈnəʊts/ sich Notizen machen V:1/A8
make one's living /ˌmeɪk wʌnz ˈlɪvɪŋ/ leben können von V:3/B6

make one's way /ˌmeɪk wʌnz ˈweɪ/ sich seinen/ihren Weg bahnen V:1/B6
make sb do sth /ˌmeɪk ˌsʌmbədi ˈduː ˌsʌmθɪŋ/ jdn dazu bringen, etw zu tun III
make sure /ˌmeɪk ˈʃɔː/ darauf achten, dass … III
make up /ˌmeɪk‿ˈʌp/ erfinden, sich ausdenken III
make use of /ˌmeɪk ˈjuːs‿əv/ benutzen; verwenden V:1/A9
mammal /ˈmæml/ Säugetier V:1/A2
man (*pl* **men**) /mæn, men/ Mann I:5/B7; Mensch V:4/B2
manage /ˈmænɪdʒ/ schaffen III
manage /ˈmænɪdʒ/ verwalten; organisieren V:3/B2
mankind /mænˈkaɪnd/ Menschheit V:5/A1
manner /ˈmænə/ Verhalten; Manieren IV
manufacture /ˌmænjʊˈfæktʃə/ herstellen V:2/A7
how many /haʊ ˈmeni/ wie viele I
many /ˈmeni/ viele I
many times /ˌmeni ˈtaɪmz/ oft II
map /mæp/ Karte I
map /mæp/ kartografieren; eine Karte machen von V:2/B3
mapmaker /ˈmæpˌmeɪkə/ Kartograph/in; Kartenhersteller/in V:2/B3
marble /ˈmɑːbl/ Murmel I
March /mɑːtʃ/ März I
march /mɑːtʃ/ Demonstration V:6/Project C p. 128
°marine /məˈriːn/ Meeres-, See- V:1/O
mark /mɑːk/ Note; Zensur III
market /ˈmɑːkɪt/ Markt I
°marriage /ˈmærɪdʒ/ Ehe; Heirat V:2/O
marry /ˈmæri/ heiraten II
marsupial /mɑːˈsuːpiəl/ Beuteltier V:1/A4
match /mætʃ/ Spiel I; zuordnen; passen zu II
match (*pl* **matches**) /mætʃ, ˈmætʃɪz/ Streichholz III

mate /meɪt/ Freund/in; Kumpel V:1/A3; Kumpel, Freund/in V:1/B10
maths /mɑːθs/ Mathe I
matter /ˈmætə/ von Bedeutung sein; wichtig sein IV
matter /ˈmætə/ Materie; Stoff V:2/B3
°mature /məˈtʃʊə/ erwachsen V:BS/6
May /meɪ/ Mai I
may /meɪ/ können; dürfen II
maybe /ˈmeɪbi/ vielleicht II
(to) me /miː/ mir; mich; ich I
meal /miːl/ Mahlzeit; Essen II
mealtime /ˈmiːlˌtaɪm/ Essenszeit V:3/A6
mean /miːn/ Mittel V:5/B1
mean *(irr)* /miːn/ meinen; bedeuten II
meaning /ˈmiːnɪŋ/ Bedeutung III
meaningful /ˈmiːnɪŋfl/ bedeutsam; wichtig V:6/Project C p. 126
measure /ˈmeʒə/ messen V:3/B6
meat /miːt/ Fleisch III
mechanic /mɪˈkænɪk/ Mechaniker/in II
mechanical /mɪˈkænɪkl/ mechanisch V:4/B2
the media /ðə ˈmiːdiə/ die Medien V:5/A6
mediation /ˌmiːdiˈeɪʃn/ Vermittlung; Mediation V:5/B3
mediator /ˈmiːdieɪtə/ Vermittler/in; Schlichter/in V:5/B3
medic /ˈmedɪk/ Mediziner/in V:5/A5
medicine *(no pl)* /ˈmedsn/ Medizin, Medikamente III
medium /ˈmiːdiəm/ Medium; Mittel V:6/Project A p. 119
meet *(irr)* /miːt/ treffen; sich treffen I
Nice to meet you. /ˌnaɪs tə ˈmiːt jə/ Schön, dich/euch/Sie zu treffen. I
meet up /ˌmiːt‿ˈʌp/ (sich) treffen III
°meeting /ˈmiːtɪŋ/ Versammlung; Sitzung V:2/O
meeting ground /ˈmiːtɪŋ graʊnd/ Begegnungsort V:2/I
melody /ˈmelədi/ Melodie V:5/B2
member /ˈmembə/ Mitglied II
memorial /məˈmɔːriəl/ Denkmal; Ehrenmal V:5/B3
memory /ˈmemri/ Erinnerung; Gedächtnis V:5/A2
mention /ˈmenʃn/ erwähnen V:1/A3
mentor /ˈmentɔː/ Mentor/in V:3/A6
menu /ˈmenjuː/ Speisekarte; Menü III
merrily /ˈmerəli/ vergnügt V:5/B5
merry /ˈmeri/ fröhlich V:5/B4
message /ˈmesɪdʒ/ Nachricht; Botschaft III
°method /ˈmeθəd/ Methode V:BS/6
metre /ˈmiːtə/ Meter II
microphone /ˈmaɪkrəˌfəʊn/ Mikrofon V:3/B6
mid-August /ˌmɪd‿ˈɔːgəst/ Mitte August V:3/A6
middle /ˈmɪdl/ Mitte II
migrant /ˈmaɪgrənt/ Zuwanderer/in V:5/B3
mile /maɪl/ Meile V:1/B6
military forces *(pl)* /ˌmɪlɪtri ˈfɔːsɪz/ Streitkräfte V:5/A6
milk /mɪlk/ Milch I
mill around /ˌmɪl‿əˈraʊnd/ umherlaufen V:3/A2
mime /maɪm/ mimen, pantomimisch darstellen V:3/A1
mind /maɪnd/ Geist; Verstand V:4/B2
to my mind /tə ˈmaɪ ˌmaɪnd/ meiner Meinung nach IV
mind /maɪnd/ etw dagegen haben V:2/B7
mindfulness /ˈmaɪnfəlnəs/ Achtsamkeit V:5/B3
mine /maɪn/ meine(r, s) III
mine /maɪn/ Mine; Bergwerk; Fundgrube V:5/P3
mirror /ˈmɪrə/ Spiegel IV
misguided /mɪsˈgaɪdɪd/ fehlgeleitet V:1/B6
miss /mɪs/ verpassen; vermissen II
missionary /ˈmɪʃnri/ Missionar/in V:2/B3
mistake /mɪˈsteɪk/ Fehler, Irrtum III
misunderstanding /ˌmɪsʌndəˈstændɪŋ/ Missverständnis V:2/B3
mix /mɪks/ (ver)mischen III
mixed /mɪkst/ gemischt V:1/B6
mobile home /ˌməʊbaɪl ˈhəʊm/ Wohnwagen V:3/A2
mobile (phone) /ˈməʊbaɪl/ Handy I
modal verb /ˈməʊdl vɜːb/ Modalverb V:2/P7
model /ˈmɒdl/ Modell V:2/B4
model /ˈmɒdl/ modeln V:6/Project B p. 125
model text /ˈmɒdl ˌtekst/ Modelltext V:2/A7
modelling /ˈmɒdlɪŋ/ Modeln V:6/Project B p. 125
°mole /məʊl/ Muttermal; Leberfleck V:BS/8
°mollusc /ˈmɒləsk/ Weichtier V:1/O
at the moment /ˌæt‿ðə ˈməʊmənt/ im Moment I
Monday /ˈmʌndeɪ/ Montag I
money /ˈmʌni/ Geld II
make (good) money /ˌmeɪk ˈmʌni/ (gut) verdienen; (viel) Geld verdienen II
raise money /ˌreɪz ˈmʌni/ Geld aufbringen II
spend money on /ˌspend ˈmʌni‿ɒn/ Geld ausgeben für II
money machine /ˈmʌni məˌʃiːn/ Bankautomat V:3/B2
monkey /ˈmʌŋki/ Affe I
°monkey business /ˈmʌŋki ˌbɪznəs/ Blödsinn; faule Tricks V:BS/4
month /mʌnθ/ Monat II
moon /muːn/ Mond II
moral /ˈmɒrəl/ moralisch; ethisch V:6/Project C p. 134
morally /ˈmɒrəli/ moralisch V:5/B5
more /mɔː/ mehr; weitere I
morning /ˈmɔːnɪŋ/ Morgen I
Good morning! /ˌgʊd ˈmɔːnɪŋ/ Guten Morgen! I

in the morning /ˌɪn ðə ˈmɔːnɪŋ/ am Morgen I
this morning /ðɪs ˈmɔːnɪŋ/ heute Morgen II
tomorrow morning /təˌmɒrəʊ ˈmɔːnɪŋ/ morgen Vormittag II
mosque /mɒsk/ Moschee II
most /məʊst/ die meisten; am meisten III
most of all /ˈməʊst‿əv‿ˌɔːl/ am allermeisten III
mostly /ˈməʊstli/ meistens IV
mother /ˈmʌðə/ Mutter I
mother lode /ˈmʌðə ləʊd/ *hier:* Goldader V:1/B5
mother tongue /ˌmʌðə ˈtʌŋ/ Muttersprache V:3/A4
motivate /ˈməʊtɪveɪt/ motivieren V:3/A6
motive /ˈməʊtɪv/ Motiv V:4/P10
motorbike /ˈməʊtəˌbaɪk/ Motorrad II
mountain /ˈmaʊntɪn/ Berg I
mountain biking /ˈmaʊntɪn ˌbaɪkɪŋ/ Mountainbike fahren V:2/A1
mountaineer /ˌmaʊntɪˈnɪə/ Bergsteiger/in V:2/A5
mouse (*pl* **mice**) /maʊs, maɪs/ Maus I
mouth /maʊθ/ Mund I
move /muːv/ umziehen IV; sich bewegen III
move forward /ˌmuːv‿ˈfɔːwəd/ vorrücken V:1/B8
move on /ˌmuːv‿ˈɒn/ weitergehen IV
movement /ˈmuːvmənt/ Bewegung V:6/Project C p. 129
moving /ˈmuːvɪŋ/ bewegend V:1/B6; ergreifend V:5/B3
moving company /ˈmuːvɪŋ ˌkʌmpni/ Umzugsfirma V:2/B7
mow /məʊ/ mähen V:3/B1
Mr /ˈmɪstə/ Herr *(Anrede)* I
Mrs /ˈmɪsɪz/ Frau *(Anrede)* I
much /mʌtʃ/ viel I; sehr II
how much /haʊ ˈmʌtʃ/ wie viel I
How much is it? /ˌhaʊ mʌtʃ‿ˈɪz‿ɪt/ Wie viel kostet es? I
mud /mʌd/ Schlamm V:5/B5
mug /mʌg/ Becher I
multi- /mʌlti/ multi-, viel- V:2/A8
multicultural /ˌmʌltiˈkʌltʃərəl/ multikulturell V:1/A7
multiplier /ˈmʌltɪplaɪə/ Multiplikator/in V:5/B3
mum /mʌm/ Mama I
music /ˈmjuːzɪk/ Musik II
musical /ˈmjuːzɪkl/ musikalisch; Musik- V:3/A6
musician /mjʊˈzɪʃn/ Musiker/in III
must /mʌst/ müssen II
mustn't (= must not) /ˈmʌsnt, mʌst ˈnɒt/ nicht dürfen II
my /maɪ/ mein(e) I
to my mind /tə ˈmaɪ ˌmaɪnd/ meiner Meinung nach IV
myself /maɪˈself/ mir / mich / ich (selbst) III

N

name /neɪm/ (be)nennen V:1/A8
call sb names /ˌkɔːl ˌsʌmbədi ˈneɪmz/ jdn beschimpfen II
nana *(informal)* /ˈnænə/ Oma V:1/B3
narrator /nəˈreɪtə/ Erzähler/in V:4/P10
narrow /ˈnærəʊ/ eng; knapp III
national park /ˌnæʃnl ˈpɑːk/ Nationalpark V:1/A4
nationalism /ˈnæʃnəˌlɪzm/ Nationalismus V:5/B3
nationality /ˌnæʃəˈnæləti/ Nationalität V:1/B1
native /ˈneɪtɪv/ beheimatet; einheimisch V:1/B6; Einheimische/r
Native American /ˌneɪtɪv‿əˈmerɪkən/ amerik. Ureinwohner/in IV
natural /ˈnætʃrəl/ natürlich V:2/B7
natural disaster /ˌnætʃrəl dɪˈzɑːstə/ Naturkatastrophe IV
naturally /ˈnætʃrəli/ natürlich V:2/A3
nature /ˈneɪtʃə/ Natur III
navigate /ˈnævɪgeɪt/ navigieren V:2/B2
navigation bar /ˌnævɪˈgeɪʃn bɑː/ Navigationsleiste V:6/I
near /nɪə/ nahe, in der Nähe von II
nearby /ˌnɪəˈbaɪ/ in der Nähe (gelegen) III
nearly /ˈnɪəli/ fast; beinahe II
necessarily /ˈnesəsərəli/ notwendigerweise; unbedingt V:6/Project B p. 123
neck /nek/ Hals; Nacken I
need /niːd/ brauchen I; Notwendigkeit, Bedürfnis V:5/B2
need to /ˈniːd‿tʊ/ müssen II
needless to say /ˌniːdləs tə ˈseɪ/ selbstverständlich V:3/B6
negative /ˈnegətɪv/ negativ V:4/A9
neighbour /ˈneɪbə/ Nachbar/in I
neighbourhood /ˈneɪbəˌhʊd/ Viertel; Nachbarschaft I
neither ... nor ... /ˈnaɪðə ... ˈnɔː/ weder ... noch ...
nervous /ˈnɜːvəs/ nervös III
the Netherlands /ðə ˈneðələndz/ die Niederlande V:2/A2
network /ˈnetˌwɜːk/ Netzwerk V:4/A3
never /ˈnevə/ nie, niemals I
new /njuː/ neu I
New South Wales /ˌnjuː saʊθ ˈweɪlz/ Neusüdwales V:1/A4
New Year /ˌnjuː ˈjɪə/ Neujahr II
New Zealand /nju ˈziːlənd/ Neuseeland V:1/B2
New Zealander /nju ˈziːləndə/ Neuseeländer/in V:2/A8
news *(no pl)* /njuːz/ Neuigkeit; Nachrichten II
news report /ˈnjuːz rɪˌpɔːt/ Nachrichtenmeldung V:5/A5
newspaper /ˈnjuːzˌpeɪpə/ Zeitung III
next /nekst/ nächste(r, s) I; dann, als Nächstes III
next to /ˈnekst‿tə/ neben I
nice /naɪs/ schön; nett I
°nickname /ˈnɪkˌneɪm/ Spitzname V:BS/3
last night /ˌlɑːst ˈnaɪt/ gestern Abend II

night /naɪt/ Nacht; Abend III
night shift /ˈnaɪt ʃɪft/ Nachtschicht V:3/P9
no /nəʊ/ nein I; kein(e) I
no longer /ˌnəʊ ˈlɒŋgə/ nicht mehr IV
No Man's Land /ˈnəʊ mænz lænd/ Niemandsland V:5/B4
no matter what /nəʊ ˌmætə ˈwɒt/ was auch (immer) passiert V:6/Project A p. 118
no matter where /nəʊ ˌmætə ˈweə/ wo auch (immer) V:1/B10
no one /ˈnəʊ wʌn/ keiner V:4/A3
No worries. *(informal)* /ˈnəʊ ˌwʌriz/ Gern geschehen.; Kein Problem. V:3/B6
no-one, no one /ˈnəʊ wʌn/ keiner II
the Nobel Peace Prize /ðə nəʊˌbel ˈpiːs praɪz/ Friedensnobelpreis V:5/B3
nobody /ˈnəʊbədi/ niemand; keiner I
noise /nɔɪz/ Geräusch II
noisy /ˈnɔɪzi/ laut II
non- /nɒn/ nicht V:1/B1
non-profit /ˌnɒn ˈprɒfɪt/ gemeinnützig; nicht gewinnorientiert V:5/B3
°non-violence /ˌnɒn ˈvaɪələns/ Gewaltfreiheit V:BS/7
°non-violent /ˌnɒn ˈvaɪələnt/ gewaltfrei V:BS/7
nonchalantly /ˈnɒnʃələntli/ gleichgültig V:4/B2
none /nʌn/ keine(r, s); nichts IV
normality /nɔːˈmæləti/ Normalität V:5/A5
normally /ˈnɔːmli/ normalerweise IV
north /nɔːθ/ Norden III
north /nɔːθ/ nördlich, Nord- V:1/O
°north-east /ˌnɔːθˈiːst/ nordöstlich V:1/O
nose /nəʊz/ Nase I
not /nɒt/ nicht I
not … either /ˌnɒt‿ˈaɪðə/ auch nicht III
not any /ˌnɒt‿ˈeni/ kein(e) III
not anymore /ˌnɒt‿ˌeni ˈmɔː/ nicht mehr III
not anyone /ˌnɒt‿ˈeniwʌn/ niemand II
not anything /ˌnɒt‿ˈeniˌθɪŋ/ nichts II
not at all /ˌnɒt‿ət‿ˈɔːl/ überhaupt nicht III
not even /ˈnɒt‿iːvn/ nicht einmal II
not quite /nɒt ˈkwaɪt/ nicht ganz V:5/A2
not yet /nɒt ˈjet/ noch nicht II
note /nəʊt/ Nachricht; Notiz II
note /nəʊt/ Note; Ton V:6/Project A p. 119
nothing /ˈnʌθɪŋ/ nichts III
notice /ˈnəʊtɪs/ bemerken; wahrnehmen III
noun /naʊn/ Hauptwort; Substantiv; Nomen V:6/Project B p. 133
novelty /ˈnɒvlti/ Neuheit; Neuartigkeit V:2/A3
now /naʊ/ jetzt I
now and again /ˌnaʊ‿ən‿əˈgen/ ab und zu V:2/P7
nowadays /ˈnaʊəˌdeɪz/ heutzutage V:2/B5
°nowhere /ˈnəʊweə/ nirgends; nirgendwo V:BS/3
number /ˈnʌmbə/ Zahl; Nummer I
number /ˈnʌmbə/ Anzahl V:5/P4
numerous /ˈnjuːmərəs/ zahlreich V:5/B3
nurse /nɜːs/ Krankenschwester; Krankenpfleger II
nursing /ˈnɜːsɪŋ/ Krankenpflege; Pflege V:3/B3
nurture /ˈnɜːtʃə/ Erziehung V:2/A3; fördern V:5/B3
nutrition /njuːˈtrɪʃn/ Ernährung V:6/Project C p. 126

O

o'clock /əˈklɒk/ Uhr I
object /ˈɒbdʒekt/ Gegenstand III
obvious, obviously /ˈɒbviəs, ˈɒbviəsli/ offensichtlich V:2/A7
occasionally /əˈkeɪʒnəli/ gelegentlich; hin und wieder V:4/A1
occupant /ˈɒkjʊpənt/ Bewohner/in V:5/A5
ocean /ˈəʊʃn/ Ozean; Meer V:1/A4
October /ɒkˈtəʊbə/ Oktober I
odd /ˌɒd wʌn‿ˈaʊt/ *das Wort, das nicht zu den anderen passt* V:2/P14
of /əv/ von I
Of course! /əv ˈkɔːs/ Natürlich! I
of one's own /əv wʌnz‿ˈəʊn/ eigene(r, s) III
off /ɒf/ von; hinunter, herunter III
off /ɒf/ *hier:* frei V:3/A2; *hier:* vor V:1/O
off to work /ˌɒf tʊ ˈwɜːk/ *hier:* auf zur Arbeit V:3/I
°offer /ˈɒfə/ Angebot V:5/O
office /ˈɒfɪs/ Büro II
official /əˈfɪʃl/ Amtsperson; Beamte/Beamtin V:1/B6
official, officially /əˈfɪʃl, əˈfɪʃli/ offiziell V:1/B4
often /ˈɒfn/ oft; häufig I
oil /ɔɪl/ Öl IV
old /əʊld/ alt I
on /ɒn/ auf; an; in I
be on a high *(informal)* /ˌbi‿ɒn‿ə ˈhaɪ/ *hier:* einen Adrenalinstoß haben V:2/A1
on a regular basis /ˌɒn‿ə ˈregjʊlə ˌbeɪsɪs/ regelmäßig V:2/A1
on foot /ˌɒn ˈfʊt/ zu Fuß II
on its own /ˌɒn‿ɪts‿ˈəʊn/ von alleine II
on one's own /ˌɒn ˌwʌnz‿ˈəʊn/ allein V:1/A10
on request /ˌɒn rɪˈkwest/ auf Anfrage V:3/A4
on the left/on your left /ˌɒn ðə/jɔː ˈleft/ links, auf der/deiner linken Seite II
on the move /ˌɒn ðə ˈmuːv/ unterwegs IV
on the one hand … /ˌɒn ðə ˈwʌn hænd/ einerseits … IV
on the other hand … /ˌɒn ði‿ˈʌðə hænd/ andererseits … IV
on the phone /ˌɒn ðə ˈfəʊn/ am Telefon I

on the right/on your right /ˌɒn ðə/jɔː ˈraɪt/ rechts, auf der/deiner rechten Seite II
on the run /ˌɒn ðə ˈrʌn/ auf der Flucht V:1/B5
on time /ˌɒn ˈtaɪm/ pünktlich IV
on top /ˌɒn ˈtɒp/ (oben) auf II
once /wʌns/ früher IV; einmal II; sobald; wenn, als III
°once again /ˌwʌns‿əˈgen/ abermals V:BS/6
once in a lifetime /ˌwʌns‿ɪn‿ə ˈlaɪfˌtaɪm/ einmalig V:1/A4
the red one /ðə ˈred wʌn/ der/die/das rote III
this one /ˈðɪs wʌn/ diese(r, s) hier III
one /wʌn/ eine(r, s) V:2/P6
one another /ˌwʌn‿əˈnʌðə/ einander V:2/B3
one day /ˌwʌn ˈdeɪ/ eines Tages II
ongoing /ˈɒnˌgəʊɪŋ/ laufende(r, s) V:2/A3
only /ˈəʊnli/ nur; bloß I; einzige(r, s) III; erst V:1/A8
onto /ˈɒntə/ auf, in III
open /ˈəʊpən/ öffnen; aufmachen I; offen; geöffnet II
opening /ˈəʊpnɪŋ/ *hier:* Möglichkeit V:3/A2
opening hours *(pl)* /ˈəʊpənɪŋ‿ˌaʊəz/ Öffnungszeiten III
opera /ˈɒprə/ Oper V:1/A4
operate /ˈɒpəreɪt/ tätig sein V:5/B3
in my opinion /ɪn ˈmaɪ‿əˌpɪnjən/ meiner Meinung nach III
opinion /əˈpɪnjən/ Meinung; Ansicht IV
opportunity /ˌɒpəˈtjuːnəti/ Gelegenheit; Chance, Möglichkeit V:1/B3
opposing /əˈpəʊzɪŋ/ entgegengesetzt, gegnerisch V:5/B4
optimistic /ˌɒptɪˈmɪstɪk/ optimistisch V:4/P14
option /ˈɒpʃn/ Wahlmöglichkeit III
or /ɔː/ oder I
oral /ˈɔːrəl/ mündlich V:2/A10

orange /ˈɒrɪndʒ/ orange I; Orange; Apfelsine III:1/A3
orange juice /ˈɒrɪndʒ‿ˌdʒuːs/ Orangensaft I
orchestra /ˈɔːkɪstrə/ Orchester V:6/Project A p. 119
order /ˈɔːdə/ bestellen III; anordnen, befehlen III
order /ˈɔːdə/ Reihenfolge V:3/P7
in order to /ˌɪn‿ˈɔːdə tʊ/ um zu IV
ordinary /ˈɔːdnri/ gewöhnlich; normal V:6/Project B p. 125
organise /ˈɔːgənaɪz/ organisieren II
organism /ˈɔːgəˌnɪzm/ Organismus V:1/A2
originally /əˈrɪdʒnəli/ ursprünglich IV
originate /əˈrɪdʒəneɪt/ entstehen, seinen Anfang nehmen V:6/Project A p. 120
°ostrich /ˈɒstrɪtʃ/ Strauß V:3/O
other /ˈʌðə/ andere(r, s) I
our /aʊə/ unsere(r, s) I
ourselves /aʊəˈselvz/ uns; wir selbst IV
out /aʊt/ heraus, hinaus; aus II
out of /ˈaʊt‿əv/ aus IV
out of control /ˌaʊt‿əv kənˈtrəʊl/ außer Kontrolle V:6/Project p. 115
out of sight /ˌaʊt‿əv ˈsaɪt/ außer Sichtweite III
out of work /ˌaʊt‿əv ˈwɜːk/ arbeitslos III
°out there /ˌaʊt ˈðeə/ da draußen V:BS/8
outback /ˈaʊtˌbæk/ Hinterland (Australiens) V:1/I
outdoor /ˌaʊtˈdɔː/ draußen; im Freien V:2/A2
the outdoors *(only pl)* /ðiˌ‿aʊtˈdɔːz/ Natur V:2/A8
the great outdoors *(only pl)* /ðə ˌgreɪt‿aʊtˈdɔːz/ die freie Natur V:2/A8
outer space /ˌaʊtə ˈspeɪs/ Weltraum, Weltall V:1/A2
outlet /ˈaʊtˌlet/ Medien; Verlag; Fernsehsender V:5/A6

outside /ˌaʊtˈsaɪd/ außen; (nach) draußen II; vor; außerhalb II
over /ˈəʊvə/ über, hinüber; vorbei II
°over /ˈəʊvə/ über V:3/O
over there /ˌəʊvə ˈðeə/ dort (drüben) I
Over to you. /ˌəʊvə tə ˈjuː/ Jetzt bist du dran. I
overall /ˌəʊvərˈɔːl/ allgemein; Gesamt- V:4/B2
overcome *(irr)* /ˌəʊvəˈkʌm/ bewältigen; überwinden V:5/B1
overcrowded /ˌəʊvəˈkraʊdɪd/ überfüllt V:1/A8
overlook /ˌəʊvəˈlʊk/ überblicken V:5/A2
overnight stay /ˌəʊvəˈnaɪt steɪ/ Übernachtung V:2/A8
overseas /ˈəʊvəsiːz/ Übersee-; aus Übersee V:2/B7
on its own /ˌɒn‿ɪts‿ˈəʊn/ von alleine II
own /əʊn/ eigene(r, s) I
own /əʊn/ besitzen V:1/B1
owner /ˈəʊnə/ Besitzer/in IV

P

p (= penny, pence) /piː, ˈpeni, pens/ Pence I
pace /peɪs/ Tempo V:6/Project A p. 120
°pacifism /ˈpæsɪˌfɪzm/ Pazifismus V:BS/6
°pacifist /ˈpæsɪfɪst/ pazifistisch V:BS/6
pack /pæk/ packen V:2/B7
pack up /ˌpæk‿ˈʌp/ zusammenpacken V:2/B7
packet /ˈpækɪt/ Packung III
page /peɪdʒ/ Seite III
pain /peɪn/ Schmerz IV
painful /ˈpeɪnfl/ schmerzhaft V:5/A5
paint /peɪnt/ (an)malen III; Farbe III
painting /ˈpeɪntɪŋ/ Bild, Gemälde III
pair /peə/ Paar IV
a pair of /ə ˈpeər‿əv/ ein Paar II

a pair of scissors /ə ˌpeər‿əv ˈsɪzəz/ Schere III
paper /ˈpeɪpə/ Papier III
parachute /ˈpærəˌʃuːt/ Fallschirm V:2/A4
paradise /ˈpærədaɪs/ Paradies V:2/A8
paraglide /ˈpærəˌglaɪd/ Paragliding machen V:2/A2
paragliding /ˈpærəˌglaɪdɪŋ/ Gleitschirmfliegen V:2/A1
paragraph /ˈpærəˌgrɑːf/ Absatz; Abschnitt IV
parent contribution /ˈpeərənt kɒntrɪˌbjuːʃn/ Elternbeitrag V:6/Project B p. 124
parents *(pl)* /ˈpeərənts/ Eltern I
parliament /ˈpɑːləmənt/ Parlament V:1/B8
parrot /ˈpærət/ Papagei I
°part /pɑːt/ teilweise; zum Teil V:3/O
part-time /ˌpɑːt‿ˈtaɪm/ Teilzeit- V:3/B5
°partake in /pɑːˈteɪk‿ɪn/ teilnehmen an V:2/O
participant /pɑːˈtɪsɪpənt/ Teilnehmer/in V:5/B3
participation /pɑːˌtɪsɪˈpeɪʃn/ Teilnahme; Beteiligung V:5/B3
particular /pəˈtɪkjʊlə/ bestimmt IV
°partly /ˈpɑːtli/ zum Teil; teilweise V:1/O
pass /pɑːs/ vorbeigehen an IV; vergehen *(Zeit)*; verstreichen *(Zeit)* III; bestehen V:5/B3
pass /pɑːs/ bestehen; *hier:* erfolgreich absolvieren V:5/P8
°pass a law /ˌpɑːs‿ə ˈlɔː/ ein Gesetz verabschieden V:BS/7
°pass by /ˌpɑːs ˈbaɪ/ vorbeigehen V:BS/8
°passage /ˈpæsɪdʒ/ Durchfahrt V:1/O
passenger /ˈpæsɪndʒə/ Fahrgast, Passagier/in III
passionate /ˈpæʃnət/ leidenschaftlich V:3/B6
passive /ˈpæsɪv/ Passiv V:1/A9
passport /ˈpɑːspɔːt/ (Reise)pass V:1/B3
password /ˈpɑːsˌwɜːd/ Passwort V:4/A3
past /pɑːst/ nach I; vorbei; vorüber II; vergangen; letzte V:5/A3
past /pɑːst/ Vergangenheit V:1/A8
past progressive /ˌpɑːst prəʊˈgresɪv/ Verlaufsform der Vergangenheit V:5/P3
pat /pæt/ tätscheln; einen Klaps geben V:4/B2
patience /ˈpeɪʃns/ Geduld V:3/A2
patient /ˈpeɪʃnt/ geduldig IV
patriotic /ˌpætriˈɒtɪk/ patriotisch V:5/A6
pattern /ˈpætən/ Muster V:4/B2
pay /peɪ/ Lohn V:3/B3
pay *(irr)* /peɪ/ (be)zahlen III
pay attention to /ˌpeɪ‿əˈtenʃn tʊ/ achten auf V:1/A9
payment /ˈpeɪmənt/ Bezahlung; Vergütung V:3/A2
PE (= physical education) /ˌpiː ˈiː, ˌfɪzɪkl‿edjʊˈkeɪʃn/ Sport *(Schulfach)* I
peace /piːs/ Frieden IV:Quiz
peaceful /ˈpiːsfl/ friedlich; friedfertig; ruhig V:5/B1
peer /ˈpɪə/ Kollege/Kollegin; Mitschüler/in V:5/B3
pen /pen/ Stift I
pencil /ˈpensl/ Bleistift I
pencil case /ˈpensl ˌkeɪs/ Federmäppchen I
penguin /ˈpeŋgwɪn/ Pinguin I
people /ˈpiːpl/ Leute; Menschen I
people *(pl)* /ˈpiːpl/ Volk V:1/B8
per /pɜː/ pro III
percent *(AE)* **= per cent** *(BE)* /pəˈsent/ Prozent IV
perception /pəˈsepʃn/ Wahrnehmung; Auffassung V:6/Project B p. 125
perfect /ˈpɜːfɪkt/ perfekt V:1/A7
perform /pəˈfɔːm/ aufführen IV
perform /pəˈfɔːm/ *hier:* auftreten V:6/Project A p. 121
performance /pəˈfɔːməns/ Aufführung; Darbietung II
perfume /ˈpɜːfjuːm/ Parfüm, Duft II
perhaps /pəˈhæps/ vielleicht II
period /ˈpɪəriəd/ Zeitspanne; Zeitraum V:3/B3
permission /pəˈmɪʃn/ Erlaubnis; Genehmigung; Berechtigung V:4/A3
personal /ˈpɜːsnəl/ persönlich IV
personal care /ˌpɜːsnəl ˈkeə/ Körperpflege V:6/Project B p. 124
personality /ˌpɜːsəˈnæləti/ Persönlichkeit IV
personnel /ˌpɜːsəˈnel/ Personal V:5/A5
perspective /pəˈspektɪv/ Perspektive, Blickwinkel V:4/B5
pessimistic /ˌpesəˈmɪstɪk/ pessimistisch V:4/P14
pest /pest/ Schädling V:2/B7
pesticide /ˈpestɪsaɪd/ Pestizid; Schädlingsbekämpfungsmittel V:6/Project C p. 129
pet /pet/ Haustier I
PG (= parental guidance) /ˌpiː ˈdʒiː, pəˌrentl ˈgaɪdəns/ nicht jugendfrei V:1/B6
phenomenally /fəˈnɒmɪnli/ phänomenal V:5/B3
phone /fəʊn/ Telefon; anrufen III
answer the phone /ˌɑːnsə ðə ˈfəʊn/ ans Telefon gehen I
on the phone /ˌɒn ðə ˈfəʊn/ am Telefon I
photo /ˈfəʊtəʊ/ Foto II
photographer /fəˈtɒgrəfə/ Fotograf/in V:5/I
take photos /ˌteɪk ˈfəʊtəʊz/ Bilder machen II
phrase /freɪz/ Satz; Ausdruck II
physical /ˈfɪzɪkl/ körperlich IV
°physically /ˈfɪzɪkli/ körperlich V:3/O
physiological /ˌfɪziəˈlɒdʒɪkl/ physiologisch V:2/A3
pick /pɪk/ aussuchen; pflücken, sammeln V:1/B4
pick sb up /ˌpɪk ˌsʌmbədi‿ˈʌp/ jdn abholen I
°pick up /ˌpɪk‿ˈʌp/ aufheben V:BS/8
picnic /ˈpɪknɪk/ Picknick V:1/A4

have a picnic /ˌhæv‿ə ˈpɪknɪk/ ein Picknick machen I
picture /ˈpɪktʃə/ Bild I
pie chart /ˈpaɪ tʃɑːt/ Kreisdiagramm V:1/B2
piece /piːs/ Stück; Teil III
piece of art /ˌpiːs‿əv‿ˈɑːt/ Kunstwerk III
piecework /ˈpiːsˌwɜːk/ Akkordarbeit V:3/A2
pig /pɪg/ Schwein I
pile /paɪl/ Stapel; Haufen V:5/A3
pillow /ˈpɪləʊ/ Kissen I
°pit /pɪt/ Grube; (Erd)loch V:2/O
place /pleɪs/ Ort; Platz I
°place /pleɪs/ platzieren; stellen V:2/O
place of birth /ˌpleɪs‿əv ˈbɜːθ/ Geburtsort V:3/A4
placement /ˈpleɪsmənt/ Stelle; *hier:* Praktikumsstelle V:3/A1
plain /pleɪn/ Ebene V:1/B5; einfach V:6/Project A p. 121
the plains *(pl)* /ðə ˈpleɪnz/ Flachland V:1/B5
plan /plæn/ planen II
plane /pleɪn/ Flugzeug II
plant /plɑːnt/ Pflanze II
plant /plɑːnt/ pflanzen V:6/Project C p. 126
plastic /ˈplæstɪk/ Plastik III
plate /pleɪt/ Teller I
platform /ˈplætˌfɔːm/ Bahnsteig; Plattform II
play /pleɪ/ Spiel; (Theater)stück IV; spielen I
play the guitar /ˌpleɪ ðə gɪˈtɑː/ Gitarre spielen II
player /ˈpleɪə/ Spieler/in III
playground /ˈpleɪˌgraʊnd/ Spielplatz I
please /pliːz/ bitte I
pleased /pliːzd/ erfreut; zufrieden V:3/A6
plenty *(informal)* /ˈplenti/ viel V:4/B2
plenty of /ˈplenti‿əv/ reichlich; genug V:1/B3
plot /plɒt/ Handlung, Plot IV
plus /plʌs/ plus; zuzüglich V:4/A3
pm (= post meridiem) /ˌpiːˈem, ˌpəʊst məˈrɪdiəm/ nachmittags; abends *(nur hinter Uhrzeit zwischen 12 Uhr mittags und Mitternacht)* I
pocket /ˈpɒkɪt/ Tasche III
pocket money /ˈpɒkɪt ˌmʌni/ Taschengeld II
poem /ˈpəʊɪm/ Gedicht II
point (at/to) /pɔɪnt/ deuten (auf); zeigen (auf) III
point of view /ˌpɔɪnt‿əv‿ˈvjuː/ Ansicht; Perspektive V:4/B3; Sicht V:5/A5
polar bear /ˌpəʊlə ˈbeə/ Eisbär I
police /pəˈliːs/ Polizei II
police force /pəˈliːs fɔːs/ Polizei V:1/P4
police officer /pəˈliːs‿ˌɒfɪsə/ Polizeibeamte(r)/-beamtin II
policeman *(pl* **policemen)** /pəˈliːsmən/ Polizist III
policy /ˈpɒləsi/ Programm; Politik V:1/A9
polite /pəˈlaɪt/ höflich IV
political /pəˈlɪtɪkl/ politisch IV
°politician /ˌpɒləˈtɪʃn/ Politiker/in V:BS/6
politics *(pl)* /ˈpɒlətɪks/ Politik V:5/A1
pollute /pəˈluːt/ verschmutzen IV
Polynesia /ˌpɒlɪˈniːziə/ Polynesien V:2/B3
Polynesian /ˌpɒlɪˈniːziən/ polynesisch V:2/B2
swimming pool /ˈswɪmɪŋ puːl/ Schwimmbad I
poor /pɔː/ arm II
pop *(informal)* /pɒp/ Paps; Papa V:1/B3
be popular with /ˌbiː ˈpɒpjʊlə wɪð/ beliebt sein bei III
popular /ˈpɒpjʊlə/ beliebt IV
°population /ˌpɒpjʊˈleɪʃn/ *hier:* Population; Bestand V:1/O
port /pɔːt/ Hafen V:2/A10
portray /pɔːˈtreɪ/ porträtieren, darstellen V:5/B4
pose /pəʊz/ posieren V:6/Project C p. 127
positive /ˈpɒzətɪv/ positiv V:4/A9
°positivity /pɒzəˈtɪvəti/ positive Einstellung V:BS/8
possession /pəˈzeʃn/ Besitz V:5/B2
possibility /ˌpɒsəˈbɪləti/ Möglichkeit V:3/B1
possible /ˈpɒsəbl/ möglich II
post /pəʊst/ posten; bekannt geben V:4/A3; Post; Eintrag V:6/Project p. 115
postcard /ˈpəʊstˌkɑːd/ Postkarte; Ansichtskarte I
potato *(pl* **potatoes)** /pəˈteɪtəʊ, pəˈteɪtəʊz/ Kartoffel II
potential /pəˈtenʃl/ Potenzial V:3/B3
potentially /pəˈtenʃəli/ potenziell V:6/Project p. 115
pound /paʊnd/ Pfund I
poverty /ˈpɒvəti/ Armut IV
power /ˈpaʊə/ Strom; Kraft III
powerful /ˈpaʊəfl/ mächtig; stark III
°practically /ˈpræktɪkli/ praktisch V:3/O
practice /ˈpræktɪs/ Praxis; Übung III
°practice *(AE)* /ˈpræktɪs/ üben; praktizieren V:BS/7
Practice matters. /ˌpræktɪs ˈmætəz/ *etwa:* Übung macht den Meister. V:2/P1
practise /ˈpræktɪs/ üben I
practise /ˈpræktɪs/ praktizieren V:5/B6
prayer /preə/ Gebet II
precise /prɪˈsaɪs/ genau; präzise V:3/B8
prefer /prɪˈfɜː/ vorziehen; bevorzugen III
preparation /ˌprepəˈreɪʃn/ Vorbereitung V:2/A3
prepare /prɪˈpeə/ vorbereiten II
prepared /prɪˈpeəd/ vorbereitet V:4/B2
preposition /ˌprepəˈzɪʃn/ Präposition V:2/P4
present /ˈpreznt/ Geschenk I
present /ˈpreznt/ Gegenwart V:2/B6

present /prɪ'zent/ *hier:* vorstellen V:3/A10
present (to) /prɪ'zent/ präsentieren I
presentation /ˌprezn'teɪʃn/ Präsentation, Vortrag III
presenter /prɪ'zentə/ *hier:* Moderator/in V:6/Project B p. 123
preserve /prɪ'zɜːv/ erhalten V:5/B3
president /'prezɪdənt/ Präsident/in; Vorsitzende/r IV
press /pres/ Presse III
pretend /prɪ'tend/ vorgeben; vortäuschen IV
pretty /'prɪti/ hübsch II; ziemlich II
pretty much *(informal)* /ˌprɪti 'mʌtʃ/ ziemlich V:6/Project A p. 118
prevention /prɪ'venʃn/ Vorbeugung V:6/Project A p. 121
price /praɪs/ Preis II
pride /praɪd/ Stolz IV
primary education /ˌpraɪməri 'edjʊ'keɪʃn/ Grundschul(aus)bildung V:5/B3
primary school /'praɪməri skuːl/ Grundschule V:3/A4
prime minister /ˌpraɪm‿'mɪnɪstə/ Premierminister V:1/A8
principle /'prɪnsəpl/ Prinzip V:6/Project C p. 134
print /prɪnt/ drucken V:4/B2
priority /praɪ'ɒrəti/ Priorität V:5/B3
prison /'prɪzn/ Gefängnis V:1/A9
prisoner /'prɪznə/ Gefangene/r III
privacy policy /'prɪvəsi ˌpɒləsi/ Datenschutzbestimmungen; Datenschutzrichtlinie V:4/A3
privacy protection /'prɪvəsi prəˌtekʃn/ Privatsphäreschutz V:4/A9
private /'praɪvət/ privat V:3/A2
prize /praɪz/ Preis; Gewinn II
probably /'prɒbəbli/ wahrscheinlich II
problematic /ˌprɒblə'mætɪk/ problematisch V:2/B3
procedure /prə'siːdʒə/ Verfahren; Vorgang; Vorgehensweise V:5/A3
process /'prəʊses/ Prozess; Verlauf V:3/B6
produce /prə'djuːs/ herstellen III
produce /prə'djuːs/ *hier:* produzieren V:5/B8
produce *(pl)* /'prɒdjuːs/ Erzeugnisse; Produkte V:2/B4
profession /prə'feʃn/ Beruf V:3/B3
professional /prə'feʃnəl/ professionell; beruflich III; Profi III
profit /'prɒfɪt/ Gewinn III
profound /prə'faʊnd/ tief V:1/B8; tiefgehend; heftig V:6/Project A p. 119
program *(AE)* /'prəʊgræm/ Programm V:5/B3
program *(AusE)* /'prəʊgræm/ Programm V:1/B10
programme /'prəʊgræm/ Programm II
programme /'prəʊgræm/ programmieren V:2/A3
project /'prɒdʒekt/ Projekt III
prominent /'prɒmɪnənt/ deutlich sichtbar V:2/B3
promise /'prɒmɪs/ versprechen IV
promote /prə'məʊt/ fördern, werben für; befördern V:5/B3
pronounce /prə'naʊns/ aussprechen V:4/B2
proper /'prɒpə/ richtig V:4/B2
proper /'prɒpə/ anständig, richtig V:1/B7
proper fraction /ˌprɒpə 'frækʃn/ echter Bruch *(mathematisch)* V:4/B2
properly /'prɒpəli/ richtig III
prosper /'prɒspə/ gedeihen V:2/A3
protect /prə'tekt/ beschützen III
protect /prə'tekt/ schützen V:1/P6
protected /prə'tektɪd/ geschützt V:2/A7
protection /prə'tekʃn/ Schutz V:5/B3
protective clothing /prəˌtektɪv 'kləʊðɪŋ/ Schutzkleidung V:1/P6
proud /praʊd/ stolz III
prove *(irr)* /pruːv/ beweisen III
proven /'pruːvn/ nachgewiesen; bewährt V:5/B3
provide /prə'vaɪd/ zur Verfügung stellen V:3/A2
provider /prə'vaɪdə/ Anbieter/in V:4/A5
psychologist /saɪ'kɒlədʒɪst/ Psychologe / Psychologin V:6/Project p. 115
puberty /'pjuːbəti/ Pubertät V:6/Project p. 115
public /'pʌblɪk/ öffentlich V:5/A2
publish /'pʌblɪʃ/ veröffentlichen; herausgeben II
puddle /'pʌdl/ Pfütze I
pull /pʊl/ ziehen III
pump /pʌmp/ pumpen V:2/A4
punch code /'pʌntʃ kəʊd/ Stanzcode; Lochcode V:4/B2
punish /'pʌnɪʃ/ bestrafen V:1/P2
punishment /'pʌnɪʃmənt/ Bestrafung; Strafe V:2/A10
pupil /'pjuːpl/ Schüler/in I
pupil /'pjuːpl/ Pupille V:2/A3
purchase /'pɜːtʃəs/ Kauf; Einkauf V:3/B1
pure /pjʊə/ rein; klar V:2/A5
purple /'pɜːpl/ violett; lila I
purpose /'pɜːpəs/ Ziel, Sinn IV
purpose /'pɜːpəs/ Grund; Zweck V:4/P2
put *(irr)* /pʊt/ setzen; stellen; legen I
put *(irr)* /pʊt/ *hier:* (auf)hängen V:1/A1; *hier:* ausdrücken V:4/A3
put an end to /ˌpʊt‿ən‿'end‿tʊ/ ein Ende setzen V:5/A1
put first /ˌpʊt 'fɜːst/ an die erste Stelle setzen V:6/Project C p. 128
put into action /ˌpʊt‿ɪntʊ 'ækʃn/ in die Tat umsetzen V:6/Project p. 117
put on /ˌpʊt‿'ɒn/ anziehen; auflegen; auftragen III
put on /ˌpʊt‿'ɒn/ *hier:* veranstalten V:6/Project p. 130
put out /ˌpʊt‿'aʊt/ ausmachen IV

put together /ˌpʊt‿təˈgeðə/ zusammenstellen; zusammensetzen; zusammenbauen V:6/Project p. 130
put up /ˌpʊt‿ˈʌp/ aufhängen III

Q

°qualification /ˌkwɒlɪfɪˈkeɪʃn/ Qualifikation V:3/O
qualified /ˈkwɒlɪfaɪd/ qualifiziert; ausgebildet V:3/B3
quality /ˈkwɒləti/ Qualität V:3/A2
quarter /ˈkwɔːtə/ Viertel I
queen /kwiːn/ Königin III
question /ˈkwestʃn/ Frage II; befragen; verhören III
question /ˈkwestʃn/ *hier:* hinterfragen V:6/Project A p. 119
questionnaire /ˌkwestʃəˈneə/ Fragebogen V:6/Project p. 117
quick, quickly /kwɪk, ˈkwɪkli/ schnell II
quiet /ˈkwaɪət/ leise; ruhig III
quite /kwaɪt/ ziemlich II
quotation /kwəʊˈteɪʃn/ Zitat III
quote /kwəʊt/ Zitat IV

R

rabbit /ˈræbɪt/ Kaninchen I
rabbit-proof fence /ˌræbɪt ˌpruːf ˈfens/ *Schutzzaun in Westaustralien, der gezogen wurde, um die Ausbreitung von Kaninchen auf Ackerland zu vermeiden* V:1/B6
race /reɪs/ Rasse IV; Rennen II
race /reɪs/ *hier:* heftig schlagen; rasen V:2/A4
racism /ˈreɪˌsɪzm/ Rassismus V:5/B3
racist /ˈreɪsɪst/ Rassist/in; rassistisch IV
raft /rɑːft/ Floß V:1/B4
rage /reɪdʒ/ Wut; Zorn V:6/Project A p. 119
railway station /ˈreɪlweɪ ˌsteɪʃn/ Bahnhof II
rain /reɪn/ regnen IV; Regen I
rainbow /ˈreɪnbəʊ/ Regenbogen V:1/B3
rainforest /ˈreɪnˌfɒrɪst/ Regenwald V:1/A7
the rains *(pl)* /ðə ˈreɪnz/ Regenzeit V:1/B5
rainwater /ˈreɪnˌwɔːtə/ Regenwasser V:1/A7
rainy /ˈreɪni/ regnerisch I
raise /reɪz/ heben; erhöhen V:5/B3
raise awareness /ˌreɪz‿əˈweənəz/ Bewusstsein schärfen V:2/B3
raise money /ˌreɪz ˈmʌni/ Geld aufbringen II
°ranch /rɑːntʃ/ Farm V:BS/6
°rancher /ˈrɑːntʃə/ Viehzüchter/in; Farmarbeiter/in V:BS/6
range /reɪndʒ/ Reichweite III
range /reɪndʒ/ *hier:* Bandbreite V:6/Project A p. 119
range from … to … /ˈreɪndʒ frəm ... tʊ .../ eine Bandbreite von … bis … haben V:5/B3
°rank /ræŋk/ Position V:2/O
°rare /reə/ selten V:BS/3
rarely /ˈreəli/ selten IV
rat /ræt/ Ratte I
rather /ˈrɑːðə/ eher, lieber III
I'd rather … /ˌaɪd ˈrɑːðə/ Ich würde lieber … I
rather than /ˈrɑːðə ðæn/ anstatt IV
rating /ˈreɪtɪŋ/ Bewertung V:1/B6
°ray /reɪ/ Rochen V:1/O
re /riː/ betrifft; Betreff V:1/B10
RE (= religious education) /ˌɑːr‿ˈiː, reˌlɪdʒəs‿edjʊˈkeɪʃn/ Religion *(Schulfach)* I
reach /riːtʃ/ erreichen IV
reach an agreement /ˌriːtʃ‿ən‿əˈgriːmənt/ sich einigen V:5/B3
react /riˈækt/ reagieren V:3/B6
reaction /riˈækʃn/ Reaktion V:1/B11
read *(irr)* /riːd/ lesen I
read along /ˌriːd‿əˈlɒŋ/ mitlesen V:1/B2
read on /ˌriːd‿ˈɒn/ weiterlesen IV
read out /ˌriːd‿ˈaʊt/ (laut) vorlesen V:2/A10
read up on /ˌriːd‿ˈʌp‿ɒn/ sich informieren über V:1/I
reader /ˈriːdə/ Leser/in V:4/B7
reading /ˈriːdɪŋ/ Lesen II
ready /ˈredi/ fertig, bereit III
real /rɪəl/ wirklich; echt III
real time /ˌrɪəl ˈtaɪm/ Echtzeit V:1/B10
real-life /ˌrɪəl‿ˈlaɪf/ real V:4/A7
realistic /ˌrɪəˈlɪstɪk/ realistisch III
reality /riˈæləti/ Realität, Wirklichkeit V:5/I
realize (= realise) /ˈrɪəlaɪz/ erkennen, sich bewusst sein IV
really /ˈrɪəli/ wirklich I
reason /ˈriːzn/ Grund II
give a reason /ˌgɪv‿ə ˈriːzn/ einen Grund nennen IV
reassure /ˌriːəˈʃʊə/ beruhigen V:4/B5
rebel /ˈrebl/ rebellieren V:6/Project A p. 120
rebellious /rɪˈbeljəs/ aufsässig; widerspenstig V:6/Project A p. 120
recall /rɪˈkɔːl/ sich erinnern an V:5/A2
receive /rɪˈsiːv/ erhalten; empfangen III
receive /rɪˈsiːv/ *hier:* entgegennehmen V:1/B8
recent /ˈriːsnt/ jüngste(r, s); letzte(r, s) V:1/B6
recently /ˈriːsntli/ vor Kurzem; neulich V:1/B3
recess /rɪˈses/ (Schul)pause V:6/Project A p. 121
recipe /ˈresəpi/ Rezept III
reclaim /rɪˈkleɪm/ *hier:* zurückholen; zurückfordern V:4/B5
recognise /ˈrekəgnaɪz/ erkennen II
recommend /ˌrekəˈmend/ empfehlen III
recommendation /ˌrekəmenˈdeɪʃn/ Empfehlung V:5/B8
reconsider /ˌriːkənˈsɪdə/ überdenken; neu erwägen V:3/B3
record /riˈkɔːd/ aufnehmen III
record /ˈrekɔːd/ Rekord V:4/A7
record /riˈkɔːd/ aufzeichnen, festhalten V:5/B4
recording /riˈkɔːdɪŋ/ Aufnahme V:2/A10

recover /rɪˈkʌvə/ sich erholen IV
°recruit /rɪˈkruːt/ Rekrut/in V:5/O
recycle /riːˈsaɪkl/ recyceln; wiederaufbereiten IV
red /red/ rot I
reduce /rɪˈdjuːs/ reduzieren V:6/Project p.116
reef /riːf/ Riff V:1/O
refer to /rɪˈfɜː tuː/ betreffen; sich beziehen auf V:6/Project p.115
refer to /rɪˈfɜː tuː/ *hier:* bezeichnen als V:5/B4
referee /ˌrefəˈriː/ Referenz V:3/A6
reference /ˈrefrəns/ Referenz; Zeugnis V:3/A4
reflect /rɪˈflekt/ sich spiegeln in, zeigen, zum Ausdruck bringen IV
reflection /rɪˈflekʃn/ Reflexion V:6/Project p.117
°refreshed /rɪˈfreʃt/ erholt V:BS/1
refugee /ˌrefjʊˈdʒiː/ Flüchtling IV
°refuse /rɪˈfjuːz/ ablehnen; verweigern V:BS/6
°regardless /rɪˈɡɑːdləs/ trotz, ungeachtet V:BS/6
registration /ˌredʒɪˈstreɪʃn/ *Überprüfung der Anwesenheit* I
°regret /rɪˈɡret/ bedauern V:BS/6
regular /ˈreɡjʊlə/ regelmäßig; üblich, normal IV
on a regular basis /ˌɒn‿ə ˈreɡjʊlə ˌbeɪsɪs/ regelmäßig V:2/A1
regularly /ˈreɡjʊləli/ regelmäßig III
rehearse /rɪˈhɜːs/ proben; durchgehen V:2/B9
reject /rɪˈdʒekt/ ablehnen V:6/Project p.114
relate to /rɪˈleɪt‿tʊ/ *hier:* sich identifizieren mit V:6/Project p.115
related /rɪˈleɪtɪd/ verbunden; verwandt V:1/B3
relationship /rɪˈleɪʃnʃɪp/ Beziehung III
relative /ˈrelətɪv/ Verwandte/r; Angehörige/r III
relatively /ˈrelətɪvli/ relativ V:2/B5
relaxed /rɪˈlækst/ entspannt V:2/A3
release /rɪˈliːs/ veröffentlichen; herausbringen IV
release /rɪˈliːs/ Entlassung; Freigabe; *hier:* Entweichen V:2/A3
relevant /ˈreləvnt/ entsprechend; wichtig III
reliable /rɪˈlaɪəbl/ verlässlich; zuverlässig III
relief /rɪˈliːf/ Erleichterung V:2/A10
religion /rɪˈlɪdʒn/ Religion IV
rely on /rɪˈlaɪ‿ɒn/ sich verlassen auf III
rely on /rɪˈlaɪ‿ɒn/ *hier:* abhängen von V:2/B7
remark /rɪˈmɑːk/ Bemerkung IV
remember /rɪˈmembə/ sich erinnern an II
remind sb /rɪˈmaɪnd ˌsʌmbədi/ jdn erinnern IV
remote /rɪˈməʊt/ fern; abgelegen V:2/A7
removal /rɪˈmuːvl/ Umzug; Beseitigung V:1/B8
remove /rɪˈmuːv/ entfernen III
renewable /rɪˈnjuːəbl/ erneuerbar V:2/A7
rent /rent/ Miete IV
rent /rent/ mieten; vermieten V:3/A9
repair /rɪˈpeə/ reparieren II
repeat /rɪˈpiːt/ wiederholen V:1/P5
replace /rɪˈpleɪs/ ersetzen V:1/A8
reply /rɪˈplaɪ/ antworten; erwidern II
report /rɪˈpɔːt/ Bericht V:1/A8
report /rɪˈpɔːt/ berichten; wiedergeben V:1/A3
reported speech /ˌrɪ pɔːtɪd ˈspiːtʃ/ indirekte Rede V:3/P11
reporting /rɪˈpɔːtɪŋ/ Berichterstattung V:5/A6
represent /ˌreprɪˈzent/ präsentieren, vertreten IV
represent /ˌreprɪˈzent/ darstellen V:4/O
representation /ˌreprɪzenˈteɪʃn/ Vertretung; Darstellung V:2/B3
representative /ˌreprɪˈzentətɪv/ (Stell)vertreter/in V:2/B3
°reptile /ˈreptaɪl/ Reptil V:BS/1
reputation /ˌrepjʊˈteɪʃn/ Ruf IV
request /rɪˈkwest/ Wunsch, Anfrage V:4/A5
on request /ˌɒn rɪˈkwest/ auf Anfrage V:3/A4
request /rɪˈkwest/ um etw bitten V:1/B8
require /rɪˈkwaɪə/ brauchen; verlangen; erfordern V:2/A4
require sb to do sth /rɪˌkwaɪə ˌsʌmbədi tə ˈduː ˌsʌmθɪŋ/ von jdm verlangen, etw zu tun V:3/A2
required /rɪˈkwaɪəd/ erforderlich V:3/A2
rescue /ˈreskjuː/ Rettung V:2/A9
research /rɪˈsɜːtʃ/ recherchieren IV; Forschung V:5/A2
°reserve /rɪˈzɜːv/ Naturschutzgebiet; Reservat V:BS/3
resident /ˈrezɪdnt/ Bewohner/in IV
resistance /rɪˈzɪst(ə)ns/ Widerstand V:5/B8
°resolution /ˌrezəˈluːʃn/ Lösung V:5/O
resolve /rɪˈzɒlv/ lösen V:5/B3
resort /rɪˈzɔːt/ Urlaubsort V:2/A7
resource /rɪˈzɔːs/ Quelle; Ressource V:2/A7
respect /rɪˈspekt/ respektieren V:1/A7
respectful /rɪˈspektfl/ respektvoll V:1/B8
respond /rɪˈspɒnd/ antworten; reagieren V:1/B10
response /rɪˈspɒns/ Antwort; Reaktion IV
responsibility /rɪˌspɒnsəˈbɪləti/ Verantwortung; Pflicht IV
responsible /rɪˈspɒnsəbl/ verantwortungsbewusst IV; verantwortlich III
restriction /rɪˈstrɪkʃn/ Begrenzung; Einschränkung V:5/B4
result /rɪˈzʌlt/ Ergebnis IV; Folge; Resultat V:5/B3

as a result /əz‿ə rɪˈzʌlt/ als Folge IV
retail /ˈriːteɪl/ Einzelhandel; Kleinhandel V:3/B3
retell *(irr)* /ˌriːˈtel/ nacherzählen V:2/A9
retrieve /rɪˈtriːv/ bergen V:5/B4
return /rɪˈtɜːn/ zurückgeben II; zurückkehren; -kommen III
reuse /riːˈjuːz/ wiederverwenden IV:6/Project p. 116
review /rɪˈvjuː/ Kritik; Rezension III
reviewer /rɪˈvjuːə/ Kritiker/in V:1/B6
°revival /rɪˈvaɪvl/ *hier:* Comeback V:2/O
revolutionize /ˌrevəˈluːʃəˌnaɪz/ revolutionieren V:6/Project A p. 119
reward /rɪˈwɔːd/ belohnen; Belohnung V:4/A7
rewarding /rɪˈwɔːdɪŋ/ befriedigend; dankbar V:3/B3
rewrite *(irr)* /ˌriːˈraɪt/ überarbeiten, umschreiben V:3/P7
Rhine /raɪn/ Rhein V:5/B3
rhythm /ˈrɪðəm/ Rhythmus V:6/Project A p. 120
rice /raɪs/ Reis III
rich /rɪtʃ/ reich II
ride /raɪd/ Fahrt V:2/A2
ride *(irr)* /raɪd/ fahren; reiten I
ride a bike /ˌraɪd‿ə ˈbaɪk/ Fahrrad fahren I
ride a horse /ˌraɪd‿ə ˈhɔːs/ reiten I
ridicule /ˈrɪdɪˌkjuːl/ verspotten V:6/Project A p. 121
right /raɪt/ Recht IV; richtig I; (nach) rechts II; genau; direkt III
right /raɪt/ *hier:* wiedergutmachen V:1/B8
be right /ˌbiː ˈraɪt/ recht haben II
on the right/on your right /ˌɒn ðə/jɔː ˈraɪt/ rechts, auf der/deiner rechten Seite II
You're right. /ˌjɔː ˈraɪt/ Du hast recht. I
ring *(irr)* /rɪŋ/ klingeln; läuten I; anrufen III
°rise /raɪz/ Aufstieg V:BS/7
rise *(irr)* /raɪz/ aufgehen; steigen II
risk /rɪsk/ Risiko; Gefahr V:2/A3; riskieren V:5/A6
risk-taker /ˈrɪsk ˌteɪkə/ *risikofreudiger Mensch* V:2/A3
risky /ˈrɪski/ riskant V:2/A6
river /ˈrɪvə/ Fluss IV
road /rəʊd/ Straße II
roam /rəʊm/ umherstreifen; umherziehen V:1/A2
roast lamb /ˌrəʊst ˈlæm/ Lammbraten V:2/B5
robot /ˈrəʊbɒt/ Roboter V:4/B3
rock /rɒk/ Stein; Fels III
rocky /ˈrɒki/ felsig V:1/B5
role model /ˈrəʊl ˌmɒdl/ Vorbild V:6/Project p. 114
role play /ˈrəʊl pleɪ/ Rollenspiel III
roll down /ˌrəʊl ˈdaʊn/ hinunterrollen; herunterrollen V:2/A4
roller coaster /ˈrəʊlə ˌkəʊstə/ Achterbahn V:2/A2
rolling /ˈrəʊlɪŋ/ sanft ansteigend V:2/B4
room /ruːm/ Raum; Zimmer I
root /ruːt/ Wurzel V:2/B3
rope /rəʊp/ Seil III
round /raʊnd/ um … herum III
round /raʊnd/ rund V:4/B2; *hier:* umher V:BS/4
route /ruːt/ Strecke, Route V:1/A7
row /rəʊ/ rudern V:2/B2
royal /ˈrɔɪəl/ königlich V:1/A2
°rubber /ˈrʌbə/ Gummi V:BS/3
rubbish /ˈrʌbɪʃ/ Müll I
rude /ruːd/ unhöflich; primitiv V:3/B3
ruin /ˈruːɪn/ Ruine V:5/A5; zerstören; verderben V:6/Project A p. 121
rule /ruːl/ Regel II
°rule /ruːl/ *hier:* entscheiden V:BS/1
ruler /ˈruːlə/ Lineal I
run /rʌn/ Lauf III
run /rʌn/ *hier:* Land V:1/B5
run *(irr)* /rʌn/ *hier:* betreiben, leiten; *hier:* in Betrieb sein IV; laufen; rennen I; *hier:* fließen V:1/A7
run away /ˌrʌn‿əˈweɪ/ weglaufen III
running time /ˈrʌnɪŋ taɪm/ Laufzeit V:1/B6
rural /ˈrʊərəl/ ländlich V:2/B3
rush /rʌʃ/ eilen V:5/A2
Russia /ˈrʌʃə/ Russland V:4/P12

S

sad /sæd/ traurig I
sadness /ˈsædnəs/ Traurigkeit V:6/Project A p. 132
safe /seɪf/ sicher; ungefährlich II
safety /ˈseɪfti/ Sicherheit; Sicherheits- IV
saga /ˈsɑːgə/ Saga; Geschichte V:4/I
sail /seɪl/ segeln V:1/A2
sailing /ˈseɪlɪŋ/ Segeln V:2/A2
salad /ˈsæləd/ Salat III
°salary /ˈsæləri/ Gehalt V:BS/4
sale /seɪl/ Verkauf III
sales pitch /ˈseɪlz pɪtʃ/ Verkaufsgespräch V:4/A8
sales rep *(informal)* /ˈseɪlz rep/ Vertreter/in V:3/B3
sales representative /ˈseɪlz reprɪˌzentətɪv/ Vertreter/in V:4/A8
salt /sɔːlt/ Salz III
the same /ðə ˈseɪm/ der/die/das Gleiche; der-/die-/dasselbe III
°the same /ðə ˈseɪm/ *hier:* gleich V:BS/3
sandbag /ˈsænˌbæg/ Sandsack V:5/A2
sanddune /ˈsænddjuːn/ Sanddüne V:1/A7
sandstone /ˈsænˌstəʊn/ Sandstein V:1/A7
sane /seɪn/ geistig gesund; normal V:2/A3
satellite /ˈsætəlaɪt/ Satellit V:1/B10
satisfaction /ˌsætɪsˈfækʃn/ Zufriedenheit V:3/B3

satisfactory /ˌsætɪsˈfæktri/ zufriedenstellend V:4/B2
satisfied /ˈsætɪsfaɪd/ zufrieden V:3/B3
Saturday /ˈsætədeɪ/ Samstag I
sauce /sɔːs/ Soße III
Saudi Arabia /ˌsaʊdi‿əˈreɪbiə/ Saudi-Arabien V:1/A2
sausage /ˈsɒsɪdʒ/ Wurst, Würstchen I
save /seɪv/ retten III; sparen; aufheben V:3/B2
save up /ˌseɪv‿ˈʌp/ sparen V:3/B1
say *(irr)* /seɪ/ sagen I
saying /ˈseɪɪŋ/ Sprichwort V:6/Project A p. 121
scared /skeəd/ verängstigt III
be scared (of) /ˌbiː ˈskeəd‿əv/ Angst haben (vor) II
scarf (*pl* **scarfs** *or* **scarves**) /skɑːf, skɑːfs, skɑːvz/ Schal I
scary /ˈskeəri/ Furcht erregend, unheimlich V:2/A2
scary /ˈskeəri/ unheimlich V:2/P7
scene /siːn/ Szene III
scheme /skiːm/ Projekt; Programm; Plan V:5/B3
schmaltz *(informal)* /ʃmɔːlts/ Schmalz V:1/B6
°scholarship /ˈskɒləʃɪp/ Stipendium V:BS/6
school /skuːl/ Schule I
attend school /əˌtend ˈskuːl/ in die Schule gehen IV
school day /ˈskuːl ˌdeɪ/ Schultag I
school report /ˌskuːl rɪˈpɔːt/ Schulzeugnis III
school trip /ˈskuːl ˌtrɪp/ Schulausflug II
school uniform /ˌskuːl ˈjuːnɪfɔːm/ Schuluniform II
schoolbag /ˈskuːlˌbæg/ Schultasche I
schoolroom /ˈskuːlruːm/ Klassenzimmer V:4/B2
schoolwork /ˈskuːlˌwɜːk/ Schularbeiten III
schoolyard /ˈskuːlˌjɑːd/ Schulhof V:4/B2
science /ˈsaɪəns/ Naturwissenschaft I
scientist /ˈsaɪəntɪst/ Wissenschaftler/in III
scooter /ˈskuːtə/ Roller V:2/A1
score /skɔː/ Punktestand V:2/A2
score a goal /ˌskɔːr‿ə ˈgəʊl/ ein Tor schießen I
scoring /ˈskɔːrɪŋ/ Abschneiden V:5/B3
scornful /ˈskɔːnfl/ verächtlich V:4/B2
Scotland /ˈskɒtlənd/ Schottland II
scrambled /ˈskræmbld/ durcheinander gebracht V:1/P3
°scream /skriːm/ schreien V:BS/4
scream with laughter /ˌskriːm wɪð ˈlɑːftə/ vor Lachen brüllen V:4/B2
screen /skriːn/ Bildschirm V:4/B2
script /skrɪpt/ das Drehbuch zu etw schreiben V:2/B9
scripted /ˈskrɪptɪd/ vorbereitet V:5/B3
sea /siː/ Meer; See II
sea level /ˈsiː ˌlevl/ Meeresspiegel V:1/B4
seafood /ˈsiːˌfuːd/ Meeresfrüchte V:2/B5
sealer /ˈsiːlə/ Robbenfänger/in V:2/B3
sealife /ˈsiːlaɪf/ *hier:* Unterwasserwelt V:2/A2
search /sɜːtʃ/ suchen V:3/B3
search for /ˈsɜːtʃ fɔː/ suchen nach V:2/B3
search term /ˈsɜːtʃ tɜːm/ Suchbegriff V:6/Project A p. 120
seashell /ˈsiːˌʃel/ Muschel I
seaside /ˈsiːˌsaɪd/ (Meeres)küste; Meer V:1/A7
seasonally /ˈsiːznəli/ saisonbedingt; saisonal V:6/Project C p. 128
seat /siːt/ Sitz III
second /ˈsekənd/ zweite(r, s) I; Sekunde II
the Second World War /ðə ˌsekənd ˌwɜːld ˈwɔː/ Zweiter Weltkrieg V:2/B3
secondary school /ˈsekəndri skuːl/ weiterführende Schule V:3/A4
secondary student /ˈsekəndri ˌstjuːdnt/ *Schüler/in einer weiterführenden Schule* V:1/B10
secret /ˈsiːkrət/ Geheimnis III; heimlich III
secretary /ˈsekrətri/ Sekretär/in V:6/Project p. 131
section /ˈsekʃn/ Teil, Stück, Abschnitt IV
section /ˈsekʃn/ *hier:* Gruppe V:6/Project A p. 119
sector /ˈsektə/ Bereich; Sektor V:4/B2
secure /sɪˈkjʊə/ (ab)sichern V:2/B3
security /sɪˈkjʊərəti/ Sicherheit V:3/B3
security camera /sɪˈkjʊərəti ˌkæmrə/ Überwachungskamera V:4/A8
see *(irr)* /siː/ sehen I
Nice to see you. /ˌnaɪs tə ˈsiː jə/ Schön, dich/euch/Sie zu sehen. I:5/B3
See you (soon)! /ˌsiː juː ˈsuːn/ Bis bald! I:3/A5
seek *(irr)* /siːk/ suchen V:1/P6; suchen, streben nach V:1/B5
seeking /siːkɪŋ/ Suchen V:2/A3
seem /siːm/ scheinen IV
seldom /ˈseldəm/ selten; fast nie V:4/A1
selected /sɪˈlektɪd/ ausgewählt V:5/B3
selection /sɪˈlekʃn/ Auswahl III
self (*pl* selves) /ˈself, selvz/ Selbst; Ich V:6/Project B p. 123
self-confidence /ˌself ˈkɒnfɪdəns/ Selbstvertrauen; Selbstbewusstsein V:5/B3
self-confident /ˌself ˈkɒnfɪdnt/ selbstsicher; selbstbewusst V:6/Project C p. 128
self-esteem /ˌself‿ɪˈstiːm/ Selbstwertgefühl V:3/B6
selfish /ˈselfɪʃ/ selbstsüchtig V:6/Project p. 116
sell *(irr)* /sel/ verkaufen II

seller /ˈselə/ Verkäufer/in I
send *(irr)* /send/ schicken II
send for /ˈsend fɔː/ rufen V:4/B2
send in /ˌsend‿ˈɪn/ einsenden; einschicken V:3/A6
senior /siːniə/ Oberstufenschüler/in; Senior/in V:5/B3
senior citizens *(pl)* /ˌsiːniə ˈsɪtɪznz/ ältere Menschen V:5/B3
sensationalist /senˈseɪʃnəˌlɪst/ Sensations- V:5/A6
sense /sens/ Sinn; Gefühl V:6/Project p.115
sense of belonging /ˌsens‿əv bɪˈlɒŋɪŋ/ Zusammengehörigkeitsgefühl V:6/Project A p.119
sensitive /ˈsensətɪv/ verständnisvoll V:1/B6
sensitive /ˈsensətɪv/ empfindlich V:2/B7
sentence /ˈsentəns/ Satz II
separate /ˈsepəreɪt/ trennen V:1/B10
serpent /ˈsɜːpənt/ Schlange V:1/B3
serve /sɜːv/ servieren; bedienen III
°serve /sɜːv/ helfen; dienen V:5/O
serve on /ˈsɜːv‿ɒn/ angehören V:6/Project C p.129
set /set/ Drehort V:2/B6; Set; Garnitur V:6/Project B p.133
set a positive example /ˌset‿ə ˌpɒzətɪv‿ɪgˈzɑːmpl/ mit gutem Beispiel vorangehen V:3/A6
set apart /ˌset‿əˈpɑːt/ abheben von V:6/Project A p.119
set foot on /ˌset ˈfʊt‿ɒn/ betreten V:2/B3
set off /ˌset‿ˈɒf/ aufbrechen; auf den Weg machen V:2/A5
set out /ˌset‿ˈaʊt/ aufbrechen; sich auf den Weg machen V:5/A2
set up /ˌset‿ˈʌp/ aufbauen III; einrichten V:4/A8
set to work /ˌset‿tʊ ˈwɜːk/ sich an die Arbeit machen V:5/A2

setting /ˈsetɪŋ/ Lage; Schauplatz IV
setting /ˈsetɪŋ/ Einstellung V:4/A5
settle /ˈsetl/ sich niederlassen; sich einigen V:1/A8
°settle a dispute /ˌsetl‿ə ˈdɪspjuːt/ einen Streit beilegen V:BS/6
settlement /ˈsetlmənt/ Siedlung V:1/B6
settler /ˈsetlə/ Siedler/in IV
several /ˈsevrəl/ einige; verschiedene II
severe /sɪˈvɪə/ schlimm, stark IV
shade /ʃeɪd/ Schatten V:1/P6
shadow /ˈʃædəʊ/ Schatten IV
shake *(irr)* /ʃeɪk/ schütteln V:5/B1
shake one's head /ˌʃeɪk wʌnz ˈhed/ den Kopf schütteln V:4/B2
shall /ʃæl/ sollen; werden III
shame /ʃeɪm/ Schande V:6/Project p.130
shape /ʃeɪp/ (aus)formen; prägen V:6/Project B p.124
share /ʃeə/ teilen II
share /ʃeə/ (An)teil V:6/Project C p.134
shark /ʃɑːk/ Hai V:1/A4
she /ʃiː/ sie I
sheep farmer /ˈʃiːp ˌfɑːmə/ Schafzüchter/in V:1/A8
sheep (*pl* **sheep**) /ʃiːp/ Schaf I
sheet /ʃiːt/ Blatt; Bogen III
shelf (*pl* **shelves**) /ʃelf, ʃelvz/ Regal I
shift /ʃɪft/ Schicht IV
°shining /ˈʃaɪnɪŋ/ glänzend, strahlend V:BS/8
board a ship /ˌbɔːd‿ə ˈʃɪp/ ein Schiff besteigen IV
ship /ʃɪp/ Schiff II
shirt /ʃɜːt/ Hemd I
°shock /ʃɒk/ Schock V:BS/4
shocked /ˈʃɒkt/ schockiert, entsetzt V:5/B3
shocking /ˈʃɒkɪŋ/ schockierend V:5/B3
shoe /ʃuː/ Schuh I
shoot /ʃuːt/ Aufnahme V:6/Project B p.125
shoot *(irr)* /ʃuːt/ schießen II

°shoot *(irr)* /ʃuːt/ erschießen V:BS/7
shop /ʃɒp/ Geschäft; Laden I
shop assistant /ˈʃɒp‿əˌsɪstnt/ Verkäufer/in V:3/B3
shopping /ˈʃɒpɪŋ/ Einkaufen; Einkaufs- I
do the shopping /ˌduː ðə ˈʃɒpɪŋ/ einkaufen I
go shopping /ˌgəʊ ˈʃɒpɪŋ/ Einkaufen gehen II
shore /ʃɔː/ Küste, Ufer V:1/B5
short /ʃɔːt/ kurz I
short story /ˌʃɔːt ˈstɔːri/ Kurzgeschichte V:1/A6
should /ʃʊd/ sollte(st, n, t) III
shoulder /ˈʃəʊldə/ Schulter I
shout /ʃaʊt/ rufen; schreien II
shout at sb /ˈʃaʊt‿ət ˌsʌmbədi/ jdn anschreien V:6/Project C p.127
show *(irr)* /ʃəʊ/ zeigen II
show up /ʃəʊ ʌp/ erscheinen V:5/B3
°shut up /ˌʃʌt‿ˈʌp/ *hier:* den Mund halten V:BS/4
shy /ʃaɪ/ schüchtern III
shy away /ˌʃaɪ‿əˈweɪ/ zurückschrecken vor; scheuen V:2/P7
°sibling /ˈsɪblɪŋ/ Geschwister V:BS/6
sick /sɪk/ krank IV
side (dish) /ˈsaɪd‿dɪʃ/ Beilage III
sigh /saɪ/ Seufzer V:4/B2
sight /saɪt/ Sehenswürdigkeit II
sight /saɪt/ sichten V:2/B3
sign /saɪn/ Zeichen; Schild III; unterschreiben; unterzeichnen V:2/B3
sign up /ˌsaɪn‿ˈʌp/ *hier:* sich anmelden V:4/A3
silence /ˈsaɪləns/ Stille; Ruhe V:5/A2
silent /ˈsaɪlənt/ still; ruhig V:5/A5
silly /ˈsɪli/ albern; dumm II
similar /ˈsɪmɪlə/ ähnlich III
similarity /ˌsɪməˈlærəti/ Ähnlichkeit, Parallele V:2/B3
simple /ˈsɪmpl/ einfach; simpel V:2/A8

simple past /ˌsɪmpl ˈpɑːst/ einfache Vergangenheit V:1/B4
simply /ˈsɪmpli/ einfach IV
since /sɪns/ seit III
since /sɪns/ da; weil V:2/A3
since then /sɪns ˈðen/ seitdem, seither V:5/B3
sing *(irr)* /sɪŋ/ singen I
sing along /ˌsɪŋ‿əˈlɒŋ/ mitsingen III
singer /ˈsɪŋə/ Sänger/in I
single /ˈsɪŋgl/ einzige(r, s) V:4/B7
sink *(irr)* /sɪŋk/ sinken V:1/B4
sir, Sir /sɜː/ Sir; Herr *(Anrede vor Vornamen)* V:5/A2
siren /ˈsaɪrən/ Sirene V:5/A2
sister /ˈsɪstə/ Schwester I
sit *(irr)* /sɪt/ sitzen I
sit down /ˌsɪt‿ˈdaʊn/ sich hinsetzen IV
sit still /ˌsɪt ˈstɪl/ stillsitzen V:6/Project A p. 120
site /saɪt/ *hier:* Seite V:4/A3
size /saɪz/ Größe III
skate /skeɪt/ inlineskaten I
skateboarding /ˈskeɪtbɔːdɪŋ/ Skateboardfahren V:2/A1
ski /skiː/ Ski fahren / laufen I
skier /ˈskiːə/ Skifahrer/in V:2/A7
skiing /ˈskiːɪŋ/ Skifahren V:2/A1
skilful /ˈskɪlfl/ geschickt III
skill /skɪl/ Fähigkeit; Geschick IV
skilled /skɪld/ ausgebildet; geschickt V:2/A3
skim /skɪm/ überfliegen V:2/B3
skin /skɪn/ Haut IV
skirt /skɜːt/ Rock I
sky /skaɪ/ Himmel II
skydive /ˈskaɪˌdaɪv/ Fallschirmsprung V:2/A10
skydiving /ˈskaɪˌdaɪvɪŋ/ Fallschirmspringen V:2/A1
slap on *(informal)* /ˈslæp‿ɒn/ draufklatschen V:1/P6
°sleep /sliːp/ Schlaf V:BS/1
sleep *(irr)* /sliːp/ schlafen I
sleepover /ˈsliːpˌəʊvə/ Übernachtung I
slide on *(informal)* /ˈslaɪd‿ɒn/ *hier:* aufsetzen V:1/P6
slim /slɪm/ schlank I
slip – slop – slap /ˌslɪp slɒp ˈslæp/ *Name einer austral. Gesundheitskampagne* V:1/P6
slip on /ˌslɪp‿ˈɒn/ anziehen V:1/P6
slop on *(informal)* /ˈslɒp‿ɒn/ schütten; *hier:* großzügig auftragen V:1/P6
slot /slɒt/ Schlitz V:4/B2
slow, slowly /sləʊ, ˈsləʊli/ langsam II
slow up /ˌsləʊ‿ˈʌp/ verlangsamen V:4/B2
small /smɔːl/ klein I
°smaller /ˈsmɔːlə/ kleiner V:BS/3
smart /smɑːt/ schlau; clever V:4/A9
smear /smɪə/ Fleck V:5/B5
smell /smel/ Geruch III
smell *(irr)* /smel/ riechen II
smile /smaɪl/ lächeln I; Lächeln III
smoke /sməʊk/ rauchen IV
°smokey /ˈsməʊki/ rauchig V:2/O
snatch /snætʃ/ schnappen V:1/B6
sneaker *(AE)* /ˈsniːkə/ Turnschuh V:3/B1
°snorkel /ˈsnɔːkl/ schnorcheln V:3/O
snorkelling /ˈsnɔːklɪŋ/ Schnorcheln V:2/A2
snow /snəʊ/ Schnee I
snowboarding /ˈsnəʊˌbɔːdɪŋ/ Snowboardfahren V:2/A1
snowman (*pl* **snowmen**) /ˈsnəʊmæn, ˈsnəʊmen/ Schneemann I
snowy /ˈsnəʊi/ verschneit, schneereich I
so /səʊ/ deshalb; daher II; *hier:* also II
so as to /ˈsəʊ‿əz tʊ/ dass, damit; um V:5/B3
so far /ˈsəʊ fɑː/ bisher V:1/A9
so that /ˈsəʊ ðæt/ damit III
soap /səʊp/ Seife I
social /ˈsəʊʃl/ gesellschaftlich; sozial IV
social media /ˌsəʊʃl ˈmiːdiə/ soziale Medien V:4/A5
social network /ˌsəʊʃl ˈnetwɜːk/ soziales Netzwerk V:4/A3
sock /sɒk/ Socke I
soft /sɒft/ weich IV
soft skill /ˌsɒft ˈskɪl/ *persönliche, soziale und methodische Kompetenzen* IV
software developer /ˈsɒfˌweə dɪˌveləpə/ Softwareentwickler/in V:4/A2
soil /sɔɪl/ Boden, Erde IV
soldier /ˈsəʊldʒə/ Soldat/in V:5/A1
solution /səˈluːʃn/ Lösung IV
solve /sɒlv/ lösen III
some /sʌm/ einige, ein paar; etwas I
somebody /ˈsʌmbədi/ jemand; irgendwer IV
someday /ˌsʌm ˈdeɪ/ irgendwann (einmal) V:4/B5
somehow /ˈsʌmhaʊ/ irgendwie IV
someone /ˈsʌmwʌn/ jemand; irgendwer II
something /ˈsʌmθɪŋ/ etwas I
sometimes /ˈsʌmtaɪmz/ manchmal I
somewhere /ˈsʌmweə/ irgendwo II
son /sʌn/ Sohn I
song /sɒŋ/ Lied III
songline /ˈsɒŋlaɪn/ *Begriff aus der Aborigine-Kultur* V:1/B9
songwriter /ˈsɒŋˌraɪtə/ Texter/in; Songwriter V:6/Project A p. 121
soon /suːn/ bald II
See you (soon)! /ˌsiː juː ˈsuːn/ Bis bald! I
sore throat /ˌsɔː ˈθrəʊt/ Halsschmerzen III
sorrowfully /ˈsɒrəʊfli/ traurig; betrübt V:4/B2
Sorry. /ˈsɒri/ Es tut mir leid., Entschuldigung. I
sorry /ˈsɒri/ traurig V:4/P14
sort /sɔːt/ sortieren IV
sort into /sɔːt ˈɪntuː/ einsortieren V:4/P14
sort out /ˌsɔːt‿ˈaʊt/ ordnen; aussortieren III
sort out /ˌsɔːt‿ˈaʊt/ klären V:5/B3
soul /səʊl/ Seele III

sound /saʊnd/ Geräusch; Klang II; klingen, sich anhören II
sound /saʊnd/ gesund; vernünftig V:2/A8; *hier:* vertretbar V:5/B5
soup /suːp/ Suppe III
sour /ˈsaʊə/ sauer III
source /sɔːs/ Quelle V:4/A1
south /saʊθ/ Süden IV
°South Africa /ˌsaʊθ‿ˈæfrɪkə/ Südafrika V:5/O
South America /ˌsaʊθ‿əˈmerɪkə/ Südamerika V:1/A4
South Australia /ˌsaʊθ‿ɒˈstreɪliə/ Südaustralien V:1/A8
°the South Pacific /ˌsaʊθ pəˈsɪfɪk/ Südsee V:1/O
South Pacific Ocean /ˌsaʊθ pəˌsɪfɪk‿ˈəʊʃn/ südpazifischer Ozean; Südpazifik V:2/B3
°south-east /ˌsaʊθ‿ˈiːst/ Südosten V:BS/3
southern /ˈsʌðən/ südliche(r, s) V:1/A2
Southern /ˈsʌðən/ südliche(r, s) V:2/B3
soy /sɔɪ/ Soja V:6/Project C p. 127
space /speɪs/ Raum; Platz IV; Weltall III
spade /speɪd/ Spaten V:5/A2
speak *(irr)* /spiːk/ sprechen; reden I
speak out /ˌspiːk‿ˈaʊt/ seine Meinung deutlich vertreten V:6/Project C p. 129
°**speaker** /ˈspiːkə/ Sprecher/in IV
special /ˈspeʃl/ besondere(r, s) II
special /ˈspeʃl/ *hier:* besonders, speziell V:4/B2
specialize in *(AE)* = specialise in *(BE)* /ˈspeʃəlaɪz‿ɪn/ sich spezialisieren auf V:6/Project A p. 121
species *(pl)* /ˈspiːʃiːz/ Art; Spezies V:1/A2
spectacular /spekˈtækjʊlə/ atemberaubend; spektakulär V:1/A4
speculation /ˌspekjʊˈleɪʃn/ Spekulation; Vermutung V:4/B2
speech /spiːtʃ/ Rede V:1/A8
direct speech /daɪˌrekt ˈspiːtʃ/ direkte / wörtliche Rede II

speechless /ˈspiːtʃləs/ sprachlos V:2/A5
speed *(irr)* /spiːd/ sausen, flitzen V:2/A4
spell *(irr)* /spel/ buchstabieren I
spelling /ˈspelɪŋ/ Buchstabieren; Rechtschreibung V:3/A5
spelunker /spɪˈlʌŋkə/ Hobbyhöhlenforscher/in V:2/A4
spend *(irr)* /spend/ verbringen; ausgeben II
spend money on /ˌspend ˈmʌni‿ɒn/ Geld ausgeben für II
spending power /ˈspendɪŋ ˌpaʊə/ Kaufkraft V:3/B1
spice /spaɪs/ Gewürz III
spicy /ˈspaɪsi/ würzig; scharf V:1/A4
°spider /ˈspaɪdə/ Spinne V:BS/3
°spill /spɪl/ Verschüttetes V:1/O
°spill out /ˌspɪl‿ˈaʊt/ herausschwappen V:BS/1
spirit /ˈspɪrɪt/ Geist; Stimmung V:1/B5
split up /ˌsplɪt‿ˈʌp/ aufteilen V:6/Project p. 116
spokesman /ˈspəʊksmən/ Sprecher V:6/Project C p. 129
°sponge /spʌndʒ/ Schwamm V:1/O
spooky /ˈspuːki/ schaurig; unheimlich I
spoon /spuːn/ Löffel I
sport /spɔːt/ Sport, Sportart I
sports carnival *(AusE)* /ˈspɔːts ˌkɑːnɪvl/ *Sportfest* V:1/B10
sports centre /ˈspɔːts‿ˌsentə/ Sportcenter I
sports field /ˈspɔːts fiːld/ Sportplatz I
sports hall /ˈspɔːts hɔːl/ Sporthalle I
sporty /ˈspɔːti/ sportlich V:2/P7
spot /spɒt/ Fleck; Pickel III
spotlight /ˈspɒtˌlaɪt/ Scheinwerfer; Aufmerksamkeit V:6/Project p. 117
spread *(irr)* /spred/ verbreiten V:5/B5; ausbreiten V:6/Project A p. 121
spring /sprɪŋ/ Frühling I

squirrel /ˈskwɪrəl/ Eichhörnchen I
stage /steɪdʒ/ Bühne II
stall /stɔːl/ Stand III
stamina /ˈstæmɪnə/ Durchhaltevermögen; Ausdauer V:3/A2
stamp /stæmp/ Briefmarke III
stand *(irr)* /stænd/ stehen II
°stand down /ˌstænd‿ˈdaʊn/ zurücktreten V:BS/8
stand out /ˌstænd‿ˈaʊt/ herausstechen aus V:6/Project B p. 122
stand up /ˌstænd‿ˈʌp/ aufstehen; *hier:* gerade stehen V:5/A2; aufstehen V:BS/8
standard of living /ˌstændəd‿əv ˈlɪvɪŋ/ Lebensstandard IV
star /stɑː/ Stern V:1/A2
stare at /ˈsteər‿æt/ anstarren IV
starship (= star ship) /ˈstɑːˌʃɪp/ Raumschiff V:4/B5
start /stɑːt/ Anfang; Beginn IV; anfangen; beginnen I
starter /ˈstɑːtə/ Vorspeise III
state /steɪt/ (Bundes)staat IV; Zustand, Verfassung IV
state /steɪt/ *hier:* festlegen V:1/B6
statement /ˈsteɪtmənt/ Äußerung, Stellungnahme; Aussage V:5/A7
statement /ˈsteɪtmənt/ Äußerung; Stellungnahme; Aussage V:4/A5
station /ˈsteɪʃn/ U-Bahn-Station; Bahnhof I
station *(AusE)* /ˈsteɪʃn/ große Farm V:1/B10
railway station /ˈreɪlweɪ ˌsteɪʃn/ Bahnhof II
statistics *(pl)* /stəˈtɪstɪks/ Statistik V:1/B2
stay /steɪ/ bleiben; wohnen II
stay away from /ˌsteɪ‿əˈweɪ frɒm/ meiden; sich fernhalten von II
stay in touch /ˌsteɪ‿ɪn ˈtʌtʃ/ in Verbindung / Kontakt bleiben V:3/B3
steal *(irr)* /stiːl/ stehlen III
step /step/ Stufe; Schritt IV steigen; treten III

step out /ˌstep‿ˈaʊt/ *hier:* heraustreten, sich hervortun V:5/B4
stereotype /ˈsteriəˌtaɪp/ Stereotyp; Klischee V:6/Project p. 116
stick /stɪk/ Stock; kleben III
stick to /ˈstɪk tʊ/ an etw (fest) halten V:4/A3
sticker /ˈstɪkə/ Aufkleber I
stiff /stɪf/ steif V:5/A2
still /stɪl/ (immer) noch II
still /stɪl/ reglos; bewegungslos V:4/B2
stilt /stɪlt/ Pfahl V:2/B3
stock /stɒk/ füllen; bestücken V:3/B3
stomach /ˈstʌmək/ Magen; Bauch III
stomach ache /ˈstʌmək‿ˌeɪk/ Bauchschmerzen III
stone /stəʊn/ Stein I
stop /stɒp/ stehen bleiben; anhalten; aufhören II
store /stɔː/ lagern V:2/B3
store *(AE)* /stɔː/ Laden IV
storehouse /ˈstɔːˌhaʊs/ Warenhaus; Schatzkammer V:2/B3
storm /stɔːm/ Sturm III
story /ˈstɔːri/ Geschichte I
straight /streɪt/ gerade(aus); direkt V:3/B3
straight on /ˌstreɪt‿ˈɒn/ geradeaus II
strange /streɪndʒ/ sonderbar; merkwürdig III; fremd; unbekannt V:4/B2
stranger /ˈstreɪndʒə/ Fremde/r V:1/B7
strawberry /ˈstrɔːbri/ Erdbeere V:3/A2
stream /striːm/ (Berg)bach; Flüsschen V:2/A5
street /striːt/ Straße I
in the street /ˌɪn ðə ˈstriːt/ auf der Straße I
°street performer /ˈstriːt pəˌfɔːmə/ Straßenkünstler/in V:BS/4
strength /streŋθ/ Kraft; Stärke V:3/B3
stress /stres/ Betonung V:2/P14
stressed /strest/ gestresst III
stressful /ˈstresfl/ stressig; anstrengend V:3/B3
strong /strɒŋ/ stark I
struggle /ˈstrʌgl/ sich abmühen; sich quälen V:2/A5
student *(AE)* /ˈstjuːdnt/ Schüler/in; Student/in IV
studies *(pl)* /ˈstʌdis/ Studium V:1/B10
study /ˈstʌdi/ studieren; lernen IV
stuff *(informal)* /stʌf/ Zeug III
stunning /ˈstʌnɪŋ/ toll, fantastisch V:1/A4
stupid /ˈstjuːpɪd/ dumm, blöd IV
stupid *(informal)* /ˈstjuːpɪd/ Blödmann; Dummkopf V:4/B2
style /staɪl/ Stil III
stylish /ˈstaɪlɪʃ/ modisch V:6/Project B p. 122
°sub- /sʌb/ Unter- V:2/O
subject /ˈsʌbdʒɪkt/ Schulfach I; Thema V:1/B10
subject /ˈsʌbdʒɪkt/ *hier:* Staatsbürger/in V:2/B3
submit /səbˈmɪt/ einreichen V:4/B5
subscribe /səbˈskraɪb/ abonnieren V:3/P12
subscriber /səbˈskraɪbə/ Abonnent/in V:3/B6
success /səkˈses/ Erfolg III
successful /səkˈsesfl/ erfolgreich III
°successfully /səkˈsesfli/ erfolgreich V:BS/7
successive /səkˈsesɪv/ aufeinanderfolgend V:1/B8
such /sʌtʃ/ so; solch II
sudden /ˈsʌdn/ plötzlich V:2/A3
suddenly /ˈsʌdnli/ plötzlich II
suffer from /ˈsʌfə frəm/ leiden an; erleiden V:5/A3
suffering /ˈsʌfərɪŋ/ Leiden V:1/B8
sufficient /səˈfɪʃnt/ genug; ausreichend; genügend V:2/A8
sugar /ˈʃʊgə/ Zucker II
suggest /səˈdʒest/ vorschlagen II
suggestion /səˈdʒestʃn/ Vorschlag III
°suit /suːt/ Anzug; Kostüm V:BS/4
suitable /ˈsuːtəbl/ geeignet; passend IV
suitcase /ˈsuːtˌkeɪs/ Koffer V:5/A2
summarise /ˈsʌməraɪz/ zusammenfassen V:3/B6
summary /ˈsʌməri/ Zusammenfassung V:4/A3
summer /ˈsʌmə/ Sommer I
sun /sʌn/ Sonne I
sunbathe /ˈsʌnˌbeɪð/ sonnenbaden V:2/A2
Sunday /ˈsʌndeɪ/ Sonntag I
sunglasses *(pl)* /ˈsʌnˌglɑːsɪz/ Sonnenbrille I
sunny /ˈsʌni/ sonnig I
sunscreen /ˈsʌnˌskriːn/ Sonnenschutzmittel V:1/P6
sunshine /ˈsʌnˌʃaɪn/ Sonnenschein II
superior /sʊˈpɪəriə/ überlegen; überheblich V:4/B2
supermarket /ˈsuːpəˌmɑːkɪt/ Supermarkt I
supply /səˈplaɪ/ Vorrat V:2/A8
support /səˈpɔːt/ Unterstützung; Hilfe III
supportive /səˈpɔːtɪv/ unterstützend V:3/B6
suppose /səˈpəʊz/ vermuten; annehmen II
be supposed to do sth /ˌbiː səˌpəʊzd‿tə ˈduː ˌsʌmθɪŋ/ etw tun sollen IV
sure /ʃɔː/ sicher II
sure /ʃɔː/ *hier:* natürlich; na klar V:4/B2
surf the Internet /ˌsɜːf ˌðiˌˈɪntəˌnet/ im Internet surfen II
surfing /ˈsɜːfɪŋ/ Surfen V:1/B1
surname /ˈsɜːˌneɪm/ Nachname V:3/A4
surprise /səˈpraɪz/ Überraschung II
surprised /səˈpraɪzd/ überrascht; erstaunt II
surprising /səˈpraɪzɪŋ/ überraschend V:1/A2
surprisingly /səˈpraɪzɪŋli/ überraschenderweise V:1/B6
surreal /səˈrɪəl/ surreal; (traumhaft-)unwirklich V:2/A5

surround /sə'raʊnd/ umgeben V:6/Project p. 116
survey /'sɜːveɪ/ Umfrage V:5/B7
survival /sə'vaɪvl/ Überleben V:1/O
survive /sə'vaɪv/ überleben III
suspension /sə'spenʃn/ Suspendierung V:5/B3
sustainable /sə'steɪnəbl/ nachhaltig V:2/A7
swap /swɒp/ tauschen V:2/B3
sway /sweɪ/ schwanken, sich wiegen V:2/A10
sweater /'swetə/ Pullover I
Sweden /'swiːdn/ Schweden V:6/Project C p. 129
sweet /swiːt/ süß III; Süßigkeit V:3/B1
sweet as *(informal)* /'swiːt‿əz/ super, klasse V:2/B8
sweet potato /ˌswiːt pə'teɪtəʊ/ Süßkartoffel V:2/B3
swim *(irr)* /swɪm/ schwimmen I
swim *(no pl)* /swɪm/ Schwimmen V:1/A4
swimmer /'swɪmə/ Schwimmer/in III
go swimming /ˌgəʊ 'swɪmɪŋ/ Schwimmen gehen I
swimming /'swɪmɪŋ/ Schwimmen I
swimming pool /'swɪmɪŋ puːl/ Schwimmbad I
°swing /swɪŋ/ Schlag V:BS/8
°swing *(irr)* /swɪŋ/ schwingen V:BS/4
switch off /ˌswɪtʃ‿'ɒf/ ausschalten IV
switch on /ˌswɪtʃ‿'ɒn/ einschalten I
Switzerland /'swɪtsələnd/ Schweiz V:1/A4
swollen /'swəʊlən/ geschwollen III
syllable /'sɪləbl/ Silbe V:2/P14
symbolise /'sɪmbəlaɪz/ symbolisieren V:5/B1

T

table /'teɪbl/ Tisch I
table /'teɪbl/ Tabelle V:2/A5
lay the table /ˌleɪ ðə 'teɪbl/ den Tisch decken II
table tennis /'teɪbl ˌtenɪs/ Tischtennis I
tablespoon /'teɪblˌspuːn/ Esslöffel III
°tail /teɪl/ Schwanz V:BS/3
take *(irr)* /teɪk/ erfordern; benötigen IV; nehmen; bringen I; brauchen; dauern II
take *(irr)* /teɪk/ *hier:* übernehmen V:5/B3; *hier:* machen V:BS/8
take a chance /ˌteɪk‿ə 'tʃɑːns/ die Gelegenheit nutzen V:6/Project C p. 128
take a form /ˌteɪk‿ə 'fɔːm/ Gestalt annehmen V:6/Project p. 130
take a look at /ˌteɪk‿ə 'lʊk‿ət/ sich ansehen III
take a quiz /ˌteɪk‿ə 'kwɪz/ ein Quiz machen V:2/I
take a rain check *(informal)* /ˌteɪk‿ə 'reɪn tʃek/ verschieben V:2/A2
take a risk /ˌteɪk‿ə 'rɪsk/ ein Risiko eingehen V:2/A3
take a seat /ˌteɪk‿ə 'siːt/ sich setzen IV
take a step /ˌteɪk‿ə 'step/ einen Schritt machen V:5/A3
take a test /ˌteɪk‿ə 'test/ einen Test machen III
take a toll on /ˌteɪk‿ə 'təʊl‿ɒn/ seinen/ihren Tribut fordern von V:3/B6
take action /ˌteɪk‿'ækʃn/ handeln V:6/Project p. 131
take apart /ˌteɪk‿ə'pɑːt/ auseinandernehmen V:4/B2
take care of /ˌteɪk‿'keər‿əv/ sich kümmern um IV
take notes /ˌteɪk 'nəʊts/ sich Notizen machen V:1/A3
take on /ˌteɪk‿'ɒn/ annehmen V:4/A9
°take on sth /ˌteɪk‿'ɒn ˌsʌmθɪŋ/ *hier:* es mit etw aufnehmen V:3/O
take one's breath away /ˌteɪk wʌnz 'breθ‿əˌweɪ/ jdm den Atem rauben V:2/A4
take out /ˌteɪk‿'aʊt/ hinausbringen I
take part in /ˌteɪk 'pɑːt‿ɪn/ teilnehmen an I
take photos /ˌteɪk 'fəʊtəʊz/ Bilder machen II
take pictures /ˌteɪk 'pɪktʃəs/ Bilder machen; fotografieren V:5/A5
take responsibility /ˌteɪk rɪˌspɒnsə'bɪləti/ Verantwortung übernehmen V:6/Project C p. 129
take sb's mind off sth /ˌteɪk ˌsʌmbədiz 'maɪnd‿ɒf ˌsʌmθɪŋ/ jdn auf andere Gedanken bringen; jdn ablenken V:6/Project A p. 118
take the tube /ˌteɪk ðə 'tjuːb/ die U-Bahn nehmen I
take time /ˌteɪk 'taɪm/ Zeit lassen/beanspruchen; dauern V:6/Project p. 114
take to /'teɪk tʊ/ Gefallen finden an V:2/A7
take turns /ˌteɪk 'tɜːnz/ sich abwechseln V:1/P9
take up /ˌteɪk‿'ʌp/ *hier:* hinaufbringen; aufheben V:6/Project A p. 121
take up time /ˌteɪk‿ʌp 'taɪm/ Zeit beanspruchen V:3/B6
takeaway /'teɪkəˌweɪ/ Essen zum Mitnehmen V:1/A4
°tale /teɪl/ Geschichte; Erzählung V:5/O
talented /'tæləntɪd/ talentiert V:6/Project B p. 125
talk /tɔːk/ Gespräch; Vortrag V:1/A7
talk about /'tɔːk‿əˌbaʊt/ sprechen über I
talk (to) /tɔːk/ sprechen (mit); reden (mit) I
tall /tɔːl/ groß I
tap /tæp/ Wasserhahn V:6/Project C p. 128
tap dance /'tæp ˌdɑːns/ Stepptanz V:6/Project A p. 118
task /tɑːsk/ Aufgabe III
target task /'tɑːgɪt ˌtɑːsk/ Zielaufgabe II
Tasmania /tæz'meɪniə/ Tasmanien V:1/A8

taste /teɪst/ schmecken II; Geschmack V:6/Project p. 131
°taste /teɪst/ *hier:* probieren V:3/O
tasty /ˈteɪsti/ lecker III
tea /tiː/ Tee I
teach *(irr)* /tiːtʃ/ unterrichten I
teacher /ˈtiːtʃə/ Lehrer/in I
°teaching /ˈtiːtʃɪŋ/ Lehre(n) V:BS/6
°teaching *(no pl)* /ˈtiːtʃɪŋ/ Lehre(n) V:BS/7
tease /tiːz/ hänseln, ärgern V:6/Project A p. 121
teasing /ˌtiːzɪŋ/ Hänseln; Ärgern V:6/Project A p. 121
teaspoon /ˈtiːˌspuːn/ Teelöffel III
technician /tekˈnɪʃn/ Techniker/in III
technology /tekˈnɒlədʒi/ Technologie, Technik III
teen /tiːn/ Teenager V:6/I; jugendlich; Teenager- V:6/Project A p. 119, 120
teen mag *(informal)* /ˈtiːn mæg/ Jugendzeitschrift V:6/Project p. 115
teen magazine /ˈtiːn ˌmægəziːn/ Jugendzeitschrift V:3/B6
teenage /ˈtiːnˌeɪdʒ/ jugendlich; Teenager- V:1/A3
brush one's teeth /ˌbrʌʃ wʌnz ˈtiːθ/ sich die Zähne putzen I
telephone /ˈtelɪˌfəʊn/ Telefon V:3/A4
television /ˈtelɪˌvɪʒn/ Fernseher, Fernsehen V:4/B2
tell *(irr)* /tel/ erzählen I
tell *(irr)* /tel/ *hier:* sagen V:3/A4
teller /ˈtelə/ Erzähler/in V:1/B5
have a temperature /ˌhæv‿ə ˈtemprɪtʃə/ Fieber haben III
temple /ˈtempl/ Tempel II
tent /tent/ Zelt V:2/A8
term /tɜːm/ Begriff III
terrible /ˈterəbl/ schrecklich I
terrific /təˈrɪfɪk/ großartig; fantastisch V:1/B6
°terrified /ˈterəfaɪd/ erschrocken, verängstigt V:BS/4
territory /ˈterətri/ Gebiet; Territorium V:1/A8
terrorism /ˈterəˌrɪzm/ Terrorismus IV
test /test/ prüfen; testen IV
take a test /ˌteɪk‿ə ˈtest/ einen Test machen III
tester /ˈtestə/ Prüfer/in V:3/A9
testing /ˈtestɪŋ/ Testen; Prüfen V:5/B3
text /tekst/ eine SMS schreiben V:2/A2
text message /ˈtekst ˌmesɪdʒ/ SMS II
textbook /tekst bʊk/ Lehrbuch; Schulbuch V:4/B2
than /ðæn/ als II
thank /θæŋk/ sich bedanken III
Thank you. /ˈθæŋk ju/ Danke. I
thanks /θæŋks/ danke I:2/B1
I'm fine, thanks. /aɪm ˈfaɪn ˌθæŋks/ Es geht mir gut, danke. I
that /ðæt/ das I; dass II; der, die, das; jene(r, s) III
that /ðæt/ so V:2/A10
that's (= that is) /ðæts, ˈðæt‿ɪz/ das ist; das kostet I
that's why /ˈðæts ˌwaɪ/ deshalb V:2/A1
the /ðə/ der/die/das I
the … the … /ðə ðə/ je … desto … III
to the days *(informal)* /ˌtʊ ðə ˈdeɪz/ *nachgestellt:* sehr V:2/B8
theatre /ˈθɪətə/ Theater III
their /ðeə/ ihr(e) I
them /ðem/ sie; ihnen I
theme /θiːm/ Thema; *hier:* Kapitel II
theme song /ˈθiːm sɒŋ/ Titelmelodie V:6/Project A p. 121
themselves /ðəmˈselvz/ sich; sie selbst IV
then /ðen/ dann I
then /ðen/ damals V:4/B2
there /ðeə/ dort; dahin I
there is/are / ðeər‿ˈɪz / ðeər‿ˈɑː/ dort ist/sind; es gibt I
therefore /ˈðeəfɔː/ deshalb; deswegen; daher V:3/B3
these (*pl* **of this**) /ðiːz/ diese; das I
they /ðeɪ/ sie I
°thigh /θaɪ/ (Ober)schenkel V:2/O
thing /θɪŋ/ Ding; Gegenstand I
think *(irr)* /θɪŋk/ denken; glauben I
think about /ˈθɪŋk‿əˌbaʊt/ nachdenken über I
think about /ˈθɪŋk‿əˌbaʊt/ *hier:* halten von V:3/O
think hard /ˌθɪŋk ˈhɑːd/ scharf nachdenken V:5/A1
think of /ˈθɪŋk‿əv/ denken an, sich ausdenken II
think of /ˈθɪŋk‿əv/ *hier:* halten von V:5/B2
third /θɜːd/ Drittel V:1/B2
this /ðɪs/ diese(r, s) I
this morning /ðɪs ˈmɔːnɪŋ/ heute Morgen II
°this way /ˈðɪs weɪ/ so; auf diese Weise V:BS/1
those (*pl* **of that**) /ðəʊz/ diese, jene I
though /ðəʊ/ obwohl II
though *(nachgestellt)* /ðəʊ/ jedoch V:1/A4
thought /θɔːt/ Gedanke II
threat /θret/ Drohung II; Bedrohung, Gefahr V:5/A3
threaten /ˈθretn/ (be)drohen II
through /θruː/ durch II
throughout /θruːˈaʊt/ im ganzen/in der ganzen IV
throw *(irr)* /θrəʊ/ werfen III
thumb /θʌm/ Daumen III
Thursday /ˈθɜːzdeɪ/ Donnerstag I
thus /ðʌs/ folglich; so; diese Weise V:5/B3
°tickle /ˈtɪkl/ kitzeln V:BS/1
tidy /ˈtaɪdi/ ordentlich; aufgeräumt; aufräumen I
tie /taɪ/ binden IV; Krawatte I
tiger /ˈtaɪgə/ Tiger I
till /tɪl/ bis I
time /taɪm/ Zeit I; Mal II
all the time /ˌɔːl ðə ˈtaɪm/ die ganze Zeit II
for the first time /fə ðə ˈfɜːst‿taɪm/ zum ersten Mal III
free time /friː ˈtaɪm/ Freizeit I

in time /ɪn ˈtaɪm/ rechtzeitig; pünktlich II
What time is it? /wɒt‿ˈtaɪm‿ɪz‿ɪt/ Wie spät ist es? I
time shift /ˈtaɪm ʃɪft/ Zeitverschiebung V:3/P11
timeline /ˈtaɪmlaɪn/ Zeitachse IV
many times /ˌmeni ˈtaɪmz/ oft II
timetable /ˈtaɪmteɪbl/ Stundenplan I
tiny /ˈtaɪni/ winzig IV
tip /tɪp/ Tipp V:2/B7
tired /ˈtaɪəd/ müde II
title /ˈtaɪtl/ Titel; Überschrift II
to /tʊ/ in; nach; zu I; *hier:* vor I; (um) zu II
to-do list /tə ˈduː ˌlɪst/ To-do-Liste V:3/A9
toad /təʊd/ Kröte V:1/I
today /təˈdeɪ/ heute I
today /təˈdeɪ/ heutzutage V:5/P4
toe /təʊ/ Zeh II
together /təˈgeðə/ zusammen II
togs *(pl)* /tɒgz/ *austral./neuseel. für Schwimmsachen* V:2/B8
toilet /ˈtɔɪlət/ Toilette II
tomato (*pl* **tomatoes**) /təˈmɑːtəʊ, təˈmɑːtəʊz/ Tomate I
tomorrow /təˈmɒrəʊ/ morgen II
tonight /təˈnaɪt/ heute Abend I
too /tuː/ auch I; zu II
tool /tuːl/ Mittel; Instrument V:3/B6; Werkzeug V:3/P11
tooth (*pl* **teeth**) /tuːθ, tiːθ/ Zahn I
toothbrush /ˈtuːθbrʌʃ/ Zahnbürste I
toothpaste /ˈtuːθpeɪst/ Zahnpasta I
top /tɒp/ oberes Ende; Spitze IV; beste(r, s) III
on top /ˌɒn ˈtɒp/ (oben) auf II
topic /ˈtɒpɪk/ Thema III
torch (*pl* **torches**) /tɔːtʃ, ˈtɔːtʃɪz/ Taschenlampe I
torn /tɔːn/ hin- und hergerissen V:1/B1
Torres Strait Islander /ˌtɒrɪs‿ˌstreɪt‿ˈaɪləndə/ der Torres Strait Insulaner V:1/B8
totally /ˈtəʊtli/ völlig, total V:6/Project A p. 120
touch /tʌtʃ/ berühren III
tough /tʌf/ zäh; schwierig III
tour guide /ˈtʊə gaɪd/ Reiseführer/in V:2/B4
toward(s) /təˈwɔːdz/ in Richtung, zu; gegenüber IV
tower /ˈtaʊə/ Turm II
town /taʊn/ Stadt I
toxic /ˈtɒksɪk/ giftig IV
cuddly toy /ˌkʌdli ˈtɔɪ/ Kuscheltier I
toy /tɔɪ/ Spielzeug V:3/B1
track /træk/ Weg, Pfad; Spur V:2/A9
trade /treɪd/ Geschäft machen; handeln V:2/B3; Handwerk V:3/B3
traditional /trəˈdɪʃnəl/ traditionell IV
°traditionally /trəˈdɪʃnəli/ traditionell; üblicherweise V:2/O
traffic /ˈtræfɪk/ Verkehr III
trail /treɪl/ Weg; Pfad V:2/A8
catch a train /ˌkætʃ‿ə ˈtreɪn/ einen Zug nehmen II
train /treɪn/ Zug I
trainee /treɪˌniː/ Auszubildende/r V:4/A2
trainer /ˈtreɪnə/ Trainer/in V:6/Project C p. 128
trainers /ˈtreɪnəz/ Turnschuhe I
training /ˈtreɪnɪŋ/ Ausbildung, Schulung IV
tram /træm/ Straßenbahn; Tram V:1/A7
tramping /ˈtræmpɪŋ/ *neuseeländisch für Wandern* V:2/A8
transceiver /trænˈsiːvə/ Sende- und Empfangsgerät V:1/B10
transcribe /trænˈskraɪb/ umschreiben V:5/A2
transform /trænsˈfɔːm/ verwandeln; umwandeln V:4/I
°trap /træp/ *hier:* einschließen V:2/O
travel /ˈtrævl/ reisen II
travel /ˈtrævl/ *hier:* bereisen V:2/P11
travel blog /ˈtrævl blɒg/ Reiseblog V:2/A5
traverse /trəˈvɜːs/ *hier:* queren V:2/A5
treasure /ˈtreʒə/ Schatz V:2/B3
treat /triːt/ behandeln V:3/B2
treaty /ˈtriːti/ Vertrag; Abkommen V:2/B3
tree /triː/ Baum II
tremble /ˈtrembl/ zittern; beben V:2/A10
tremendous /trəˈmendəs/ enorm; riesig V:5/B3
trench /trentʃ/ Schützengraben V:5/B4
trial and error /ˌtraɪəl‿ən‿ˈerə/ Ausprobieren V:6/Project p. 115
°tribal /ˈtraɪbl/ Stammes- V:2/O
tribe /traɪb/ Stamm V:1/A7
°tribute /ˈtrɪbjuːt/ Tribut; Zeichen V:BS/7
trick /trɪk/ Trick, Kunststück V:2/A1
trickle /ˈtrɪkl/ sickern; tröpfeln V:2/A5
trigger /ˈtrɪgə/ auslösen V:2/A3
trip /trɪp/ Reise; Fahrt III; *hier:* Ausflug V:1/A4
tripod /ˈtraɪpɒd/ Stativ V:3/B6
°tropical /ˈtrɒpɪkl/ tropisch V:1/O
get into trouble /ˌget‿ɪntʊ ˈtrʌbl/ in Schwierigkeiten geraten II
°trouble /ˈtrʌbl/ Ärger; Schwierigkeiten V:BS/1
(a pair of) trousers /ˈtraʊzəz/ Hose I
truce /truːs/ Waffenstillstand V:5/B4
true /truː/ wahr II
truly /ˈtruːli/ wirklich, wahrhaftig V:2/A5
trust /trʌst/ Vertrauen V:6/Project p. 131
trust (in) /trʌst/ vertrauen (auf) IV
truth /truːθ/ Wahrheit II
try /traɪ/ probieren; versuchen II
try on /ˌtraɪ‿ˈɒn/ anprobieren III
take the tube /ˌteɪk ðə ˈtjuːb/ die U-Bahn nehmen I
tuck /tʌk/ stecken; klemmen V:4/B2
Tuesday /ˈtjuːzdeɪ/ Dienstag I
tummy *(informal)* /ˈtʌmi/ Bauch I
°tune /tjuːn/ Melodie V:BS/8

be one's turn /ˌbiː wʌnz ˈtɜːn/ an der Reihe sein I
turn /tɜːn/ abbiegen II; *hier:* umblättern V:4/B2
turn /tɜːn/ werden V:6/Project C p.126
turn a page /ˌtɜːn‿ə ˈpeɪdʒ/ *hier:* ein neues Kapitel aufschlagen V:1/B8
turn around /ˌtɜːn‿əˈraʊnd/ sich umdrehen II
turn back /ˌtɜːn ˈbæk/ zurückblättern V:4/B2
turn into /ˌtɜːn‿ˈɪntʊ/ umwandeln in V:1/A8
turn off /ˌtɜːn‿ˈɒf/ ausschalten II
turn on /ˌtɜːn‿ˈɒn/ einschalten I
turn out /ˌtɜːn‿ˈaʊt/ ausschalten I
turn out /ˌtɜːn‿ˈaʊt/ *hier:* herausstellen V:6/Project A p.119
turn to /ˈtɜːn tʊ/ (sich) wenden an III
°turn to /ˈtɜːn tʊ/ *hier:* umwandeln in V:BS/1
TV (= television) /ˌtiː ˈviː, ˈtelɪˌvɪʒn/ Fernsehen; Fernseher III
TV station /ˌtiːˈviː ˌsteɪʃn/ Fernsehsender V:5/A6
twice /twaɪs/ zweimal III
twist /twɪst/ *hier:* Wendung V:4/B6
type /taɪp/ Art V:1/A7
°type /taɪp/ Typ V:3/O
type in /ˌtaɪp‿ˈɪn/ eingeben V:6/Project p.116
typical /ˈtɪpɪkl/ typisch III
°tyre /ˈtaɪə/ Reifen V:BS/4

U

ugly /ˈʌgli/ hässlich IV
the UK (= United Kingdom) /ðə ˌjuː ˈkeɪ, juːˌnaɪtɪd ˈkɪŋdəm/ Vereinigtes Königreich IV
unable /ʌnˈeɪbl/ unfähig; außerstande III
unbelievable /ˌʌnbɪˈliːvəbl/ unglaublich V:5/B3
uncertainty /ʌnˈsɜːtnti/ Ungewissheit; Zweifel V:6/Project p.115
uncle /ˈʌŋkl/ Onkel I
under /ˈʌndə/ unter I
underground /ˈʌndəˌgraʊnd/ *hier:* unter der Erde V:3/B3
underline /ˌʌndəˈlaɪn/ unterstreichen IV
understand *(irr)* /ˌʌndəˈstænd/ verstehen I
understandable /ˌʌndəˈstændəbl/ verständlich V:2/A3
understanding /ˌʌndəˈstændɪŋ/ Verständnis; Übereinkunft V:5/B1
°undertake *(irr)* /ˌʌndəˈteɪk/ durchführen V:5/O
°unemployed /ˌʌnɪmˈplɔɪd/ arbeitslos V:BS/6
unemployment /ˌʌnɪmˈplɔɪmənt/ Arbeitslosigkeit V:5/B3
unforgettable /ˌʌnfəˈgetəbl/ unvergesslich V:2/A5
unfortunately /ʌnˈfɔːtʃnətli/ unglücklicherweise V:3/B3
unfriendly /ʌnˈfrenli/ unfreundlich III
unhappy /ʌnˈhæpi/ unglücklich III
°union /ˈjuːnjən/ Vereinigung; Verband V:BS/6
unique /juːˈniːk/ einzigartig V:1/A4
the United Nations /ðə juːˌnaɪtɪd ˈneɪʃnz/ die Vereinten Nationen V:5/A3
United Nations Children's Fund (UNICEF) /juːˌnaɪtɪd ˌneɪʃnz ˈtʃɪldrəns fʌnd (ˈjuːnɪsef)/ Kinderhilfswerk der Vereinten Nationen V:5/B3
the United States /ðə juːˌnaɪtɪd ˈsteɪts/ die Vereinigten Staaten II
university /ˌjuːnɪˈvɜːsəti/ Universität IV
unknown /ʌnˈnəʊn/ unbekannt V:1/A9
unlock /ʌnˈlɒk/ aufschließen; *hier:* freisetzen V:4/A7
unnatural /ʌnˈnætʃrəl/ unnatürlich V:2/A3
unrealistic /ˌʌnrɪəˈlɪstɪk/ unrealistisch V:5/B2
unscramble /ʌnˈskræmbl/ wieder ordnen V:1/A5
unsuccessful /ˌʌnsəkˈsesfl/ erfolglos V:2/B3
unsure /ʌnˈʃʊə/ unsicher V:6/Project C p.128
untidy /ʌnˈtaɪdi/ unordentlich; unaufgeräumt I
until /ənˈtɪl/ bis II
unusual /ʌnˈjuːʒuəl/ ungewöhnlich IV
up /ʌp/ nach oben; hinauf; oben III
up to /ˈʌp tuː/ bis (zu) II
upload /ˈʌpˌləʊd/ laden; hochladen V:3/B6
upon /əˈpɒn/ auf; an V:1/B5
upset /ʌpˈset/ aufgeregt; traurig III
upsetting /ʌpˈsetɪŋ/ schlimm; erschütternd V:4/A5
upstairs /ˌʌpˈsteəz/ (nach) oben II
urban /ˈɜːrbən/ städtisch IV:6/Project p.118
us /ʌs/ uns I
(the) US (= United States) /ðə ˌju‿ˈes, juːˌnaɪtɪd ˈsteɪts/ US (= Vereinigte Staaten); US- IV
the USA (= United States of America) /ðə ˌju‿es‿ˈeɪ, juːˌnaɪtɪd ˌsteɪts‿əv‿əˈmerɪkə/ USA, Vereinigte Staaten von Amerika III
use /juːz/ benutzen I
use /juːs/ Verwendung; Einsatz; Nutzung V:4/I
used to + *infinitive* /ˈjuːst‿tuː/ früher + Vergangenheitsform
useful /ˈjuːsfl/ nützlich II
°useless /ˈjuːsləs/ zu nichts brauchbar V:5/O
user /ˈjuːzə/ Benutzer/in III
username /ˈjuːzəˌneɪm/ Benutzername V:4/A5
usually /ˈjuːʒuəli/ gewöhnlich; normalerweise I

V

vacation /vəˈkeɪʃn/ Ferien; Urlaub V:5/A2
vacuum /ˈvækjuəm/ staubsaugen I

valley /ˈvæli/ Tal V:1/B5
valuable /ˈvæljʊbl/ wertvoll V:2/A3
value /ˈvælju:/ Wert V:2/B9
value /ˈvælju:/ schätzen; wertschätzen V:5/B3
variation /ˌveərɪˈeɪʃn/ *hier:* Variante V:2/A7
variety /vəˈraɪəti/ Vielfalt IV
various /ˈveəriəs/ verschieden V:6/Project A p. 119
vegan /ˈvi:gən/ Veganer/in; vegan V:6/Project p. 114
vegetable /ˈvedʒtəbl/ Gemüse I
vegetarian /ˌvedʒəˈteəriən/ Vegetarier/in; vegetarisch III
veggie *(informal)* /ˈvedʒi, ˈvedʒtəbl/ Gemüse II
venture /ˈventʃə/ sich vorwagen V:5/B4
verdict /ˈvɜ:dɪkt/ Urteil V:1/B6
version /ˈvɜ:ʃn/ Version, Fassung III
very /ˈveri/ sehr I
vet /vet/ Tierarzt/-ärztin II
via /ˈvaɪə/ über V:3/B3
victim /ˈvɪktɪm/ Opfer V:5/A3
video game /ˈvɪdiəʊ geɪm/ Videospiel V:6/Project B p. 124
video message /ˈvɪdiəʊ ˌmesɪdʒ/ Videobotschaft V:1/B11
view /vju:/ Ansicht, Meinung; Aussicht V:1/A4
view /vju:/ *hier:* Betrachtung, Klick V:3/B6; betrachten V:6/Project B p. 124
viewer /ˈvju:ə/ Zuschauer/in V:3/B6
village /ˈvɪlɪdʒ/ Dorf II
violation /ˌvaɪəˈleɪʃn/ Verletzung; Verstoß V:5/B3
°violence /ˈvaɪələns/ Gewalt V:5/O
violent /ˈvaɪələnt/ gewalttätig, brutal V:5/A4
°visible /ˈvɪzəbl/ sichtbar V:1/O
vision /ˈvɪʒn/ Vorstellung; Vision V:5/B2
visit /ˈvɪzɪt/ besuchen; Besuch I
visitor /ˈvɪzɪtə/ Besucher/in V:1/A7
vital /ˈvaɪtl/ essenziell; entscheidend V:5/B3

vivid /ˈvɪvɪd/ anschaulich; leuchtend V:1/A4
vlog /vlɒg/ vloggen V:3/B6
vocabulary /vəʊˈkæbjʊləri/ Vokabular; Wortschatz V:4/P5
vocal /ˈvəʊkl/ Vokalmusik V:6/Project A p. 118
vocational school /vəʊˈkeɪʃnəl sku:l/ Berufsschule V:3/B3
voice /vɔɪs/ Stimme V:1/B5
voice recognition /ˈvɔɪs rekəgˌnɪʃn/ Spracherkennung V:4/A9
voluntarily /ˌvɒlənˈteərɪli/ freiwillig V:5/B3
voluntary /ˈvɒləntri/ freiwillig V:3/A2
volunteer /ˌvɒlənˈtɪə/ sich freiwillig melden; ehrenamtlich arbeiten V:6/Project C p. 126
vote /vəʊt/ Stimme; Abstimmung, Wahl III; *hier:* Wahlrecht; wählen; abstimmen V:1/A8
vs. (= versus) /ˈvɜ:səs/ gegen V:3/B6

W

wage /ˈweɪdʒ/ Lohn V:3/A2
wait /weɪt/ (er)warten III
wait for /ˈweɪt fɔ:/ warten auf I
waiter/waitress /ˈweɪtə, ˈweɪtrəs/ Kellner/in II
waiting room /ˈweɪtɪŋ ˌru:m/ Wartezimmer III
wake *(irr)* /weɪk/ aufwecken IV
wake up /ˌweɪk‿ˈʌp/ aufwachen III
walk /wɔ:k/ gehen I; Spaziergang III
walk /wɔ:k/ *hier:* Wanderung, Wanderweg V:1/A4
walk of life /ˌwɔ:k‿əv ˈlaɪf/ Gesellschaftsschicht; soziale Schicht V:6/Project B p. 125
walk the dog /ˌwɔ:k ðə ˈdɒg/ den Hund ausführen I
walker /ˈwɔ:kə/ *hier:* Wanderer V:2/A8
°walking tour /ˈwɔ:kɪŋ tʊə/ Wanderung; Führung V:BS/3

wall /wɔ:l/ Wand I
wallet /ˈwɒlɪt/ Brieftasche V:3/P9
wallow /ˈwɒləʊ/ ausgiebig baden V:5/A2
waltz /wɔ:ls/ Walzer V:6/Project A p. 118
waltz Matilda /ˌwɔ:ls məˈtɪldə/ *umherreisen auf der Suche nach Arbeit* V:1/B5
want /wɒnt/ wollen I
want sb to do sth /wɒnt ˌsʌmbədi tə ˈdu: ˌsʌmθɪŋ/ wollen, dass jd etw tut III
war /wɔ:/ Krieg IV
war zone /ˈwɔ: zəʊn/ Kriegsgebiet V:5/A4
wardrobe /ˈwɔ:drəʊb/ Schrank I
warm /wɔ:m/ warm I
warn /wɔ:n/ warnen III
warp speed /ˈwɔ:p spi:d/ *Geschwindigkeit, die schneller als Lichtgeschwindigkeit ist* V:4/B5
wash /wɒʃ/ waschen; sich waschen I
do the washing up /ˌdu: ðə ˌwɒʃɪŋ‿ˈʌp/ abspülen I
waste /weɪst/ verschwenden IV; Verschwendung; Vergeudung; Abfall V:4/B2
watch /wɒtʃ/ beobachten; ansehen I; Uhr III
watch TV /ˌwɒtʃ ti: ˈvi:/ Fernsehen gucken I
water /ˈwɔ:tə/ Wasser I
water baby /ˈwɔ:tə ˌbeɪbi/ *hier:* Wasserratte V:2/A4
water-resistant /ˌwɔ:tərɪˈzɪstənt/ wasserbeständig V:1/P6
wave (at/to sb) /weɪv/ jdm zuwinken V:1/A7
way /weɪ/ Weg; Art; Weise I
way of living /ˌweɪ‿əv ˈlɪvɪŋ/ Lebensweise V:6/Project A p. 132
way of thinking /ˌweɪ‿əv ˈθɪŋkɪŋ/ Denkweise V:6/Project C p. 134
we /wi:/ wir I
°wealth /welθ/ Reichtum; Vermögen V:5/O
wear *(irr)* /weə/ tragen I
weary /ˈwɪəri/ müde; erschöpft V:5/A2

weather /ˈweðə/ Wetter I
weave *(irr)* /wiːv/ weben; flechten V:2/B3
web /web/ Netz V:1/B10
Wednesday /ˈwenzdeɪ/ Mittwoch I:1/B2
week /wiːk/ Woche I:4/A11
all week /ˌɔːl ˈwiːk/ die ganze Woche lang II
weekend /ˌwiːkˈend/ Wochenende I
°weigh /weɪ/ wiegen V:BS/3
weight /weɪt/ Gewicht III
weird /wɪəd/ merkwürdig; seltsam V:5/B3
welcome /ˈwelkəm/ willkommen II
You're welcome. /ˌjɔː ˈwelkəm/ Gern geschehen. III
°welcoming /ˈwelkəmɪŋ/ freundlich V:2/O
well /wel/ nun I:3/A5; gut II; gesund II
Get well soon! /ˌget ˌwel ˈsuːn/ Gute Besserung! II
well done /ˌwel ˈdʌn/ gut gemacht II
well-equipped /ˌwel‿ɪˈkwɪpt/ gut vorbereitet V:2/A8
wellie /ˈweli/ Gummistiefel I
wellness /ˈwelnəs/ Wohlbefinden V:5/B3
west /west/ Westen III
west coast /ˌwest ˈkəʊst/ Westküste V:2/A5
Western /ˈwestən/ West-, westlich V:2/B6
Western Australia /ˌwestən‿ɒˈstreɪliə/ Westaustralien V:1/A8
wet /wet/ nass I
whale /weɪl/ Wal V:1/A7
whaler /ˈweɪlə/ Walfänger/in V:2/B3
what /wɒt/ was; welche(r, s) I
what else /ˌwɒt‿ˈels/ was sonst I
whatever /wɒtˈevə/ was (auch immer) IV
wheel /wiːl/ Rad III
wheelchair /ˈwiːltʃeə/ Rollstuhl II
when /wen/ wann I; wenn; als I
where /weə/ wo; wohin I
whereas /weərˈæz/ während; wohingegen IV
whether /ˈweðə/ ob IV
which /wɪtʃ/ welche(r, s); was I
while /waɪl/ während II
while /waɪl/ Weile V:5/B3
whilst /waɪlst/ während V:2/A7
whistle /ˈwɪsl/ pfeifen V:4/B2
white /waɪt/ weiß I
white-water rafting /ˌwaɪtwɔːtə ˈrɑːftɪŋ/ Wildwasserrafting V:2/A1
who /huː/ wer; der/die/das I
whole /həʊl/ ganz, gesamt IV
whom /huːm/ wem; wen; der/die/das V:4/A3
whose /huːz/ wessen I; dessen V:1/B6
why /waɪ/ warum I
wide /waɪd/ breit IV
widely /ˈwaɪdli/ weit verbreitet V:5/B4
WiFi /ˈwaɪ faɪ/ WLAN III
wild /waɪld/ Wildnis V:1/A7
wildlife /ˈwaɪldˌlaɪf/ Tier- und Pflanzenwelt V:1/A4
will /wɪl/ werden II
willing /ˈwɪlɪŋ/ bereit; gewillt V:5/A4
win *(irr)* /wɪn/ gewinnen II
wind /wɪnd/ Wind I
°winding /ˈwaɪndɪŋ/ gewunden; kurvenreich V:BS/1
window /ˈwɪndəʊ/ Fenster I
°windscreen wiper /ˈwɪnskriːn ˌwaɪpə/ Scheibenwischer V:BS/3
windy /ˈwɪndi/ windig I
wing /wɪŋ/ Flügel IV
winner /ˈwɪnə/ Gewinner/in II
winter /ˈwɪntə/ Winter I
wipe out /ˌwaɪp‿ˈaʊt/ auslöschen V:1/B3
wire /ˈwaɪə/ Draht V:1/B6
wireless /ˈwaɪələs/ Radio; (Rund)funk V:5/A2
wish /wɪʃ/ wünschen V:5/B4
wish for /ˈwɪʃ fɔː/ sich wünschen V:4/B7
best wishes /ˌbest ˈwɪʃɪz/ viele Grüße II
with /wɪð/ mit; bei I
without /wɪðˈaʊt/ ohne II
witness /ˈwɪtnəs/ Zeuge/Zeugin V:5/A2
woman (*pl* **women**) /ˈwʊmən, ˈwɪmɪn/ Frau I
won't /wəʊnt/ nicht werden II
wonder /ˈwʌndə/ sich fragen II
wonderful /ˈwʌndəfl/ wunderbar, wundervoll II
wood /wʊd/ Holz II
woodland /ˈwʊdlənd/ Waldgebiet V:2/B4
wool /wʊl/ Wolle V:1/A8
word /wɜːd/ Wort I
word processing /ˈwɜːd ˌprəʊsesɪŋ/ Textverarbeitung V:3/A4
word web /ˈwɜːd web/ Wortnetz V:2/P13
work /wɜːk/ arbeiten I; funktionieren II; Arbeit; Werk III
work camp /ˈwɜːk‿kæmp/ *Lager, in dem Freiwillige gemeinnützige Arbeiten verrichten* V:5/B3
work experience /ˈwɜːk‿ɪkˌspɪəriəns/ Praktikum; Berufserfahrung IV
work out /ˌwɜːk‿ˈaʊt/ errechnen; ausarbeiten V:2/A2
work out /ˌwɜːk‿ˈaʊt/ *hier:* sich erschließen V:1/B8
work placement /ˈwɜːk ˌpleɪsmənt/ Praktikum IV
workbook /ˈwɜːkbʊk/ Arbeitsheft III
worker /ˈwɜːkə/ Arbeiter/in V:3/A2
working day /ˈwɜːkɪŋ deɪ/ Arbeitstag II
working hours *(pl)* /ˈwɜːkɪŋ‿ˌaʊəz/ Arbeitszeiten IV
working knowledge /ˌwɜːkɪŋ ˈnɒlɪdʒ/ Grundkenntnisse V:3/A2
working life /ˈwɜːkɪŋ laɪf/ Berufsleben V:3/B3
world /wɜːld/ Welt I
around the world /əˌraʊnd ðə ˈwɜːld/ weltweit, überall auf der Welt IV

all over the world /ˌɔːl‿ˌəʊvə ðə ˈwɜːld/ auf der ganzen Welt V:5/B3
°World Heritage Site /ˌwɜːld ˈherɪtɪdʒ ˌsaɪt/ Weltkulturerbe V:1/O
World War II /ˌwɜːld ˌwɔː ˈtuː/ der Zweite Weltkrieg V:5/I
worry /ˈwʌri/ sich Sorgen machen III
worried /ˈwʌrid/ beunruhigt II
Don't worry. /ˌdəʊnt ˈwʌri/ Mach dir keine Sorgen. II
worth /wɜːθ/ (lohnens)wert III
would /wʊd/ würde(st, n, t) II
°wrap /ræp/ einwickeln V:2/O
write *(irr)* /raɪt/ schreiben I
write down /ˌraɪt‿ˈdaʊn/ aufschreiben V:1/A1
write out /ˌraɪt‿ˈaʊt/ aufschreiben; ausschreiben V:4/B2
writer /ˈraɪtə/ Autor/in III
written /ˈrɪtn/ schriftlich V:5/A5
wrong /rɒŋ/ falsch II
go wrong /ˌgəʊ ˈrɒŋ/ schiefgehen V:3/A10
wrong /rɒŋ/ Unrecht V:1/A8

Y

yeah /jeə/ ja V:4/A3
year /jɪə/ Jahr; Schuljahr, Klasse I
°yell /jel/ laut schreien; brüllen V:BS/4
yellow /ˈjeləʊ/ gelb I
yes /jes/ ja I
yesterday /ˈjestədeɪ/ gestern II
yet /jet/ trotzdem IV; schon; noch IV; bis jetzt III
not yet /nɒt ˈjet/ noch nicht II
you /juː/ du; dich; dir; man; ihr; euch; Sie; Ihnen I
You're right. /ˌjɔː ˈraɪt/ Du hast recht. I
You're welcome. /ˌjɔː ˈwelkəm/ Gern geschehen.; Keine Ursache. III
young /jʌŋ/ jung II
young /jʌŋ/ Junge V:1/P2
youngster /ˈjʌŋstə/ Jugendliche/r V:6/Project C p. 128
your /jɔː/ dein(e); euer/eure I
yours /jɔːz/ deine(r, s); eure(r, s); Ihre(r, s) III
yours faithfully /ˌjɔːz ˈfeɪθfli/ mit freundlichen Grüßen V:3/A6
yourself (*pl* **yourselves**) /jɔːˈself, jɔːˈselvz/ dich I
youth /juːθ/ Jugend; Jugendliche/r IV
youth club /ˈjuːθ ˌklʌb/ Jugendzentrum I
youth council /ˈjuːθ ˌkaʊnsl/ Jugendrat V:6/Project C p. 129

Z

°Zambian /ˈzæmbiən/ sambisch V:5/O
zip /zɪp/ Reißverschluss III
zip-line /ˈzɪplaɪn/ Seilrutsche V:2/A4
zoo /zuː/ Zoo I:WB/1
zoo-keeper /ˈzuːˌkiːpə/ Tierpfleger/in; Wärter/in II

A

abbiegen turn
Abend evening
heute Abend tonight
gestern Abend last night
Abend night
Abendessen dinner
abends *(nur hinter Uhrzeit zwischen 12 Uhr mittags und Mitternacht)* pm (= post meridiem)
Abenteuer adventure
abenteuerlich adventurous
aber but; however
abfahren leave *(irr)*
Abfall litter, waste
Abfalleimer bin
abgesehen von apart from
jdn abholen pick sb up
Abkommen treaty
ablehnen reject
Absatz paragraph
Abschnitt paragraph
abspülen do the washing up
abstimmen vote
Abwesenheit absence
darauf achten, dass ... make sure
achten auf; Zuneigung fühlen care
Ackerbau agriculture
Adjektiv adjective
Adresse address
Affe monkey
Afroamerikaner/in; afroamerikanisch African American
AG; Klub club
ähnlich similar
Ähnlichkeit similarity
Aktivität activity
Akzent accent
akzeptieren accept
albern silly
alle all
alle möglichen all kinds of
alle; jeder everybody; everyone
allein alone
von alleine on its own
am allermeisten most of all
alles everything; all
allgemein overall
im Allgemeinen in general
alltäglich, Alltags- everyday
Alphabet alphabet
als *(bei Vergleich)* than
als; wenn when
als; wie; während as
als Folge as a result
also so
alt old
Alter age
am allermeisten most of all
am Laufen halten keep going
am liebsten best
am liebsten mögen like best
am Morgen/Nachmittag in the morning/afternoon
am Telefon on the phone
am Wochenende at the weekend
Amerika America
Amerikaner/in; amerikanisch American
amerikanische/r Ureinwohner/in Native American
sich amüsieren enjoy oneself
an at; about; on
an der Reihe sein be one's turn
anbauen grow *(irr)*
anbieten offer
andauern continue
ein anderer/eine andere /ein anderes another
andere(r, s) other
andererseits ... on the other hand ...
ändern change
anders else
anders; andere(r, s) different
anerkennen accept
Anfang start; beginning
anfangen start; begin *(irr)*
sich anfreunden (mit) make friends (with)
anfügen attach
Angehörige/r relative
angeln fish
angreifen attack
Angst fear
Angst haben (vor) fear, be afraid (of), be scared (of)
anhalten stop
sich anhören sound
ankämpfen gegen fight *(irr)*
ankommen arrive
ankommen auf count
Ankunft arrival
(an)malen paint
annehmen guess; suppose
anordnen, befehlen order
anprobieren try on
Anruf call
anrufen call; phone; ring *(irr)*
ans Telefon gehen answer the phone
anschließend afterwards
Anschreiben cover letter
(sich) ansehen look at, take a look at, watch
Ansicht opinion, view
Ansichtskarte postcard
Anspruch erheben auf claim
anstarren stare at
anstatt instead of; rather than
anstrengend hard; stressful
Antwort answer
Antwort; Reaktion response
(be)antworten answer; reply
antworten; reagieren respond
Anweisung instruction
Anzeige advertisement (= advert)
anziehen attract; put on
Apfel apple
Apfelsine orange
Apparat machine
April April
Arbeit; Werk work
arbeiten work
Arbeiter/in worker
Arbeitgeber/in employer
Arbeitsheft workbook
arbeitslos out of work
Arbeitslosigkeit unemployment
arbeitsreich busy
Arbeitstag working day
Arbeitszeiten working hours *(pl)*
arm poor
Armut poverty
arrangieren arrange
Art kind; species *(pl)*; type; way
Artikel article
Arzt/Ärztin doctor
Aspekt aspect
außer Atem sein; atemlos sein be out of breath
atemberaubend spectacular
Attraktion attraction
attraktiv; reizvoll attractive
auch too; also; as well
auch nicht not ... either
auf on; onto

(oben) auf on top
auf den Weg machen set off
auf der ganzen Welt all over the world
auf der Straße in the street
auf Deutsch in German
auf Englisch in English
auf etwas (hinauf)-steigen climb
Auf Wiedersehen. Goodbye.
aufbauen set up
aufbewahren keep *(irr)*
aufbrechen set off
Geld aufbringen raise money
aufführen perform
Aufführung performance
Aufgabe job; task
aufgeben give up
aufgehen; steigen rise *(irr)*
aufgeräumt tidy
aufgeregt excited, excitedly
aufgeregt; traurig upset
aufhängen put up
aufhören stop
Aufkleber sticker
aufladen charge
auflegen put on
auflisten list
aufmachen open
Aufmerksamkeit attention
aufnehmen record
aufpassen auf look after
aufräumen tidy
aufregend exciting
aufstehen get up
auftragen put on
aufwachen wake up
aufwecken wake *(irr)*
Auge eye
August August
aus out of; out; from
aus der ganzen Welt from all over the world
aus Versehen by accident
ausarbeiten work out
ausbilden educate
Ausbildung education; training
sich ausdenken think of, make up
Ausdruck expression
zum Ausdruck bringen reflect
Ausdruck; Satz phrase
ausdrücken express
Ausflug trip
den Hund ausführen walk the dog
ausgeben spend *(irr)*
Geld ausgeben für spend money on
ausgebildet qualified
mit jemandem ausgehen go out with somebody
ausgehen go out
auskommen ohne do without
im Ausland, ins Ausland abroad
ins Ausland fahren go abroad
ausländisch foreign
auslassen; weglassen leave out
ausleeren; ausräumen empty
(aus)leihen borrow
ausmachen put out
ausprobieren try out
ausreichend sufficient
Ausrüstung equipment; gear
ausschalten switch off; turn out; turn off
aussehen look
Aussehen appearance
gut aussehend good-looking; handsome
außen; (nach) draußen outside
außer except
außer Atem sein; atemlos sein be out of breath
außer Sichtweite out of sight
außerhalb outside
außerordentlich extremely
äußerst, höchst extremely
außerstande unable
äußerste(r, s) extreme
Äußerung; Aussage statement
Aussicht view
aussortieren sort out
Ausstattung equipment
nicht ausstehen können hate
aussteigen get out
Ausstellung exhibition
austauschen exchange
austral. Ureinwohner/in; der Aboriginals Aboriginal; Aborigine
Australien Australia
Auswahl selection; choice
auswandern emigrate
Auswanderung emigration
auswärts essen eat out
Auswirkung impact
Auszeichnung award
Auto car
Autor/in writer; author

B

backen cook
Bäcker/in baker
Bad bath
Badezimmer bathroom
Bahnhof railway station; station
Bahnsteig platform
bald soon
Banane banana
Bauch tummy *(informal)*; stomach
Bauchschmerzen stomach ache
bauen build *(irr)*
Bauer/Bäuerin farmer
Bauernhof farm
Baum tree
Baumwolle; Baumwoll- cotton
(be)antworten answer
bearbeiten edit
Becher mug
Bedarf need
bedecken cover
bedeckt cloudy
bedeuten mean *(irr)*
bedeutend, wichtig major
Bedeutung importance; meaning
von Bedeutung sein matter
bedienen serve
(be)drohen threaten
bedroht threatened
Bedrohung, Gefahr threat
Beeil dich! Hurry up!
sich beeilen hurry (up)
beeindruckend impressive; awesome
beeinflussen influence; affect
beenden finish; end
sich befassen mit deal with
befestigen attach
befragen question
begeistert enthusiastic
Beginn start
beginnen start; begin *(irr)*
begleiten accompany
Begriff term
behalten keep *(irr)*
behandeln treat
bei with; at
beide both
beifügen enclose

Beilage side (dish)
beilegen enclose
Bein leg
beinahe nearly; almost
beinhalten include; involve
Beispiel example
zum Beispiel for example
beißen bite *(irr)*
beitragen contribute
bekämpfen fight *(irr)*
bekannt well-known
bekannt geben announce
bekannt sein be known
Bekanntmachung announcement
sich beklagen complain
bekommen get *(irr)*
bekommen; gewinnen gain
belebt; verkehrsreich busy
belegen give evidence
beliebt popular
beliebt sein bei be popular with
bemerken; wahrnehmen notice
Bemerkung remark
(be)nennen name
benötigen take *(irr)*
benutzen use
Benutzer/in user
Benzin, Brennstoff fuel
beobachten watch
bequem comfortable
Berechtigung permission
Bereich area
bereits already
Berg mountain
Bericht report; account
Beruf profession; job
beruflich professional
Berufserfahrung work experience
berufstypische Qualifikationen hard skill
berühmt famous; well-known
berühren touch
beschädigen damage
beschäftigt busy
jemanden beschimpfen call somebody names
beschreiben describe
beschriften label
beschützen protect
Besitzer/in owner
besondere(r, s) special
besonders especially; particularly
besorgt worried
besprechen discuss
besprechen, rezensieren review
besser better
Gute Besserung! Get well soon!
bestehen pass
bestehen aus consist of
ein Schiff besteigen board a ship
bestellen order
Möchten Sie bestellen? Are you ready to order?
beste(r, s) best; top
bestimmt particular; certain
Besuch visit
besuchen attend; visit
Besucher/in visitor
beträchtlich considerable
Betrag amount
Betreff re
betreffen affect; refer to
betreiben, leiten run *(irr)*
betreten enter
Betreuung care
betrifft re
Bett bed
beunruhigt worried
Bevölkerung population
bevor before
bevorzugen prefer
sich bewegen move
Bewegung exercise
beweisen prove *(irr)*
sich bewerben um apply for
Bewerbung application
Bewohner/in resident
bewölkt cloudy
sich bewusst sein, erkennen realize (= realise)
sich einer Sache bewusst sein be aware of something
Bewusstsein schärfen raise awareness
(be)zahlen pay *(irr)*
Bezahlung payment
Beziehung relationship
(be)zweifeln doubt
Bild image; picture
Bild, Gemälde painting
bilden form
Bilder machen take photos
Bildschirm screen
Bildung education
Bildunterschrift caption
billig cheap
binden tie
bis till; until
(spätestens) bis by
Bis bald! See you (soon)!
bis jetzt yet
bis (zu) up to
ein (kleines) bisschen a (little) bit
bitte please
bitten ask
Blatt leaf (*pl* leaves); sheet
blau blue
bleiben remain; stay
Bleistift pencil
Blick look
bloß only; just
Blume flower
Blut blood
Boden bottom; ground; soil
Bogen sheet
Bohnen in Tomatensauce baked beans
Bombe bomb
Boot boat
böse evil
Botschaft message
braten cook
brauchen need; take *(irr)*
brauchen; verlangen require
braun brown
brechen break *(irr)*
breit wide
Brennstoff fuel
Brett board
Brief letter
Briefmarke stamp
Briefumschlag envelope
Brille glasses *(pl)*
bringen take *(irr)*
jdn dazu bringen, etw zu tun make sb do sth
britisch British
Brot bread
Brücke bridge
Bruder brother
Buch book
Bücherei library
Büchse can
Buchstabe letter
buchstabieren spell *(irr)*
Bühne stage
(Bundes)staat state
bunt colourful
Bürger/in citizen
Büro office
bürsten brush
mit dem Bus (fahren) (go) by bus
Bushaltestelle bus stop

C

Charakter character
Chips crisps *(pl)*
Computerspielentwickler/in computer game designer
Cousin/e cousin
Creme; Salbe cream
Cupfinale cup final

D

da because; as
daher so; therefore
dahin there
Dame lady
(meine) Damen und Herren ladies and gentlemen
damit so that
danach after that
dankbar grateful
danke thanks
Danke. Thank you.
danken, sich bedanken thank
dann then
dann, als Nächstes next
darauf achten, dass ... make sure
Darbietung performance
das that
das ist, das kostet that's (= that is)
dass that
dass, damit; um so as to
Daten data *(pl)*
Datum date
dauern take *(irr)*
dauernd constantly
Daumen thumb
Daunendecke duvet
Debatte debate
den Tisch decken lay the table
dein(e) your
deine(r, s) yours
Demokratie democracy
demokratisch democratic
denken think *(irr)*
denken an consider
denken an, sich ausdenken think of
der, die, das; jene(r, s) that
der/die/das the; who
der/die/das Gleiche; der-/die-/dasselbe the same
der/die/das rote the red one
deshalb so; that's why; therefore
dessen whose
deswegen therefore
Detail, Einzelheit detail
deuten (auf) point (at/to)
deutlich clear
Deutsch; deutsch German
auf Deutsch in German
Deutschland Germany
Dezember December
Diagramm chart
Dialekt dialect
Dialog dialogue
dich yourself (*pl* yourselves); you
Dichter/in poet
Dienst service
Dienstag Tuesday
diese Weise thus
diese(r, s) this
diese(r, s) hier this one
diese; das these (*pl* of this)
diese, jene those (*pl* of that)
Ding thing
dir you
direkt right
direkte Rede direct speech
Diskussion discussion; debate
diskutieren discuss
Distanz distance
Doktor doctor
Dokument document
Donnerstag Thursday
doppelt double
Dorf village
dort there
dort (drüben) over there
dort ist; es gibt there is
dort sind; es gibt there are
Dose can
Jetzt bist du dran. Over to you.
draußen outdoor
(nach) draußen outside
dreckig dirty
drehen, filmen film
drinnen inside
dritte(r, s) third
(be)drohen threaten
Drohung threat
drucken print
du you
Du hast recht. You're right.
nicht dürfen mustn't (= must not)
dumm silly
dumm, blöd stupid
dunkel dark
durch through
durchfallen fail
Durchsage announcement
Durchschnitt average
durchschnittlich average
durchsetzen establish
dürfen be allowed to; may

E

echt real
Ecke corner
Effekt, Wirkung effect
ehemalige(r, s) former
eher, lieber rather
Ei egg
Eichhörnchen squirrel
eigene(r, s) of one's own; own
eigentlich actually
ein anderer/ein anderes/eine andere another
ein bisschen a little
ein (kleines) bisschen a (little) bit
ein Paar a pair of
ein Picknick machen have a picnic
ein Schiff besteigen board a ship
ein Tor schießen score a goal
noch ein/e another
einander each other
einbeziehen include
eindeutig definitely
Eindruck impression
ein(e) a/an
einerseits ... on the one hand ...
eines Tages one day
einfach easy; just; simple; simply
einfügen insert
einführen introduce; establish
einige several; few
einige, ein paar; etwas some
Einkauf purchase
einkaufen do the shopping
Einkaufen gehen go shopping
einladen invite
Einladung invitation
Einleitung introduction
einmal once
einrichten set up
einsam lonely
einschalten turn on; switch on
einschätzen estimate
einschlafen fall asleep

einschließlich including
Einstellung attitude
Eintritt entry
Einwanderer/in immigrant
Einwanderung immigration
einwerfen insert
Einwohner/in inhabitant
einzige(r, s) only; single
Eis ice cream; ice
Eisbär polar bear
Elefant elephant
elektrisch electric
Elektrizität electricity
Elektro- electric
Eltern parents *(pl)*
Emigration emigration
empfehlen recommend
Ende end; ending
zu Ende bringen complete
enden end; finish
endlich at last; finally
Energie energy
eng narrow
Englisch; englisch English
auf Englisch in English
englischsprachig English-speaking
Enkel grandson
Enkelin granddaughter
entdecken discover
entfernen remove
enthusiastisch enthusiastic
entkommen escape
sich entscheiden choose *(irr)*; decide
entscheidend vital
Entscheidung decision
entschlossen determined
sich entschuldigen apologize (= apologise)
Entschuldigen Sie bitte!, Entschuldigung! Excuse me!
Es tut mir leid., Entschuldigung. I'm sorry.; Sorry.
entsprechend; wichtig relevant
enttäuscht disappointed
entweder ... oder ... either ... or ...
entwerfen design
entwickeln develop
Entwicklung development
Entwurf, Design design
er he
erarbeiten develop
Erde earth
Erdkunde geography
Ereignis event; incident
erfahren experience
Erfahrung experience
Erfahrungen sammeln gain experience
erfinden invent; make up
Erfinder/in inventor
Erfindung invention
Erfolg success
erfolgreich successful
erfordern take *(irr)*; require
erforschen explore
erfreut pleased
Ergebnis result
erhalten maintain; preserve
erhalten; empfangen receive
erheblich considerable
erhöhen increase
sich erholen recover
jemanden erinnern remind somebody
sich erinnern an remember
Erinnerung memory
Erkältung cold
erkennen realize (= realise); recognise
erklären explain
Erklärung explanation
erlauben allow
Erlaubnis permission
erleben, kennenlernen experience
erleiden suffer from
ermöglichen enable
ermutigen encourage
ermutigend encouraging
ernähren feed *(irr)*
ernst serious
Das meinst du doch nicht im Ernst! You must be joking! *(informal)*
(er)raten guess
errechnen work out
erreichen reach; achieve
erschaffen create
(Er)schaffung creation
erscheinen, auftauchen appear
Erscheinen, Aussehen appearance
ersetzen replace
erst only
erstaunt surprised
erster Weihnachtsfeiertag Christmas Day
erste(r, s) first
erwachsen sein, erwachsen werden grow up
Erwachsene/r adult
(er)warten wait
erwidern reply
erzählen tell *(irr)*
erzeugen create
Erzeugnisse produce *(pl)*
es it
Essen food
essen eat *(irr)*; have *(irr)*
auswärts essen eat out
Essen meal
Essen zum Mitnehmen takeaway
essenziell vital
Essgewohnheit eating habit
Esslöffel tablespoon
etwas some; something
noch etwas anything else
euch you
euer/eure your
eure(r, s) yours
Europa Europe
Europäer/in; europäisch European
existieren exist
Experiment experiment
exportieren export
extrem extreme
Extremsportart extreme sport

F

Fabrik factory
fähig competent
Fähigkeit skill; ability
Fahne, Flagge flag
Fähre ferry
fahren go *(irr)*; drive *irr)*
fahren; reiten ride *(irr)*
Fahrrad fahren ride a bike
in Urlaub fahren go on holiday
ins Ausland fahren go abroad
Fahrer/in driver
Fahrgast, Passagier/in passenger
Fahrrad bike; bicycle
mit dem Fahrrad by bike
Fahrrad fahren ride a bike
Fahrt ride; trip
Fakt fact
Fall case
fallen fall *(irr)*
fällig due
falls if
falsch wrong

Familie family
fangen catch *(irr)*
fantastisch fantastic; terrific
Farbe colour; paint
farbenfroh colourful
fast nearly; almost
fast nie seldom
Februar February
Federmäppchen pencil case
Feedback feedback
Fehlen absence
Fehler error; mistake
Feier celebration
feiern celebrate
fein fine
Feind/in enemy
Feld field
Fels rock
Fenster window
Ferien holiday(s)
fern far
sich fernhalten von stay away from
Fernsehen; Fernseher TV (= television)
Fernsehen gucken watch TV
fertig, bereit ready
Fest festival
(fest)halten hold *(irr)*
Festival festival
Feuer fire
Feuerwerk fireworks *(pl)*
Fieber haben have a temperature
Figur character
finden find *(irr)*
Firma company
Fisch fish (*pl* fish *or* fishes)
fischen fish
fit bleiben, (sich) fit halten keep fit
Flasche bottle
Fleck; Pickel spot
Fledermaus bat
Fleisch meat
Fliege fly
fliegen fly *(irr)*
fliehen flee *(irr)*; escape
fließen run *(irr)*
Flüchtling refugee
Flug flight
Flügel wing
Flughafen airport
Flugzeug plane
Fluss river
Folge consequence; result
als Folge as a result
folgen follow
folgende(r, s) following
folglich thus
fördern promote
Formular form
Forscher/in explorer
Forschung research
fortfahren go on
fortführen continue
fortgeschritten advanced
fortsetzen go on
Foto photo
Fotoapparat camera
Frage question
fragen ask
sich fragen wonder
Fragen stellen ask questions
Frau woman (*pl* women); Mrs *(Anrede)*; lady
frei; kostenlos free
Freiheit liberty
Freitag Friday
freiwillig voluntary
Freizeit free time
fremd strange; foreign
sich freuen auf look forward to
Freund/in friend
Freund *(Partner)* boyfriend
Freundin *(Partnerin)* girlfriend
freundlich friendly; kind
Freundschaft friendship
Frieden peace
frisch fresh
Friseur/in hairdresser, hair stylist
Frohes Neues Jahr! Happy New Year!
Frosch frog
Frucht fruit *(no pl)*
zum Frühstück for breakfast
früh early
früher once
früher + *Vergangenheitsform* used to + *infinitive*
frühere(r, s) former
Frühling spring
Frühstück breakfast
frühstücken have breakfast
frustriert frustrated
Fuchs fox
(sich) fühlen feel *(irr)*
führen lead *(irr)*
Führer/in guide
füllen fill
fünfte(r, s) fifth
funktionieren work
für for
für den Fall, dass in case
Furcht erregend scary
fürchten fear
Fuß foot (*pl* feet)
zu Fuß on foot
Fußball football
Fußballspieler/in football player
Fußboden floor
füttern feed *(irr)*

G

Gabel fork
in Gang halten keep going
ganz all; whole
den ganzen Nachmittag lang all afternoon
die ganze Zeit all the time
die ganze Woche lang all week
Garten garden
Gärtner/in gardener
Gast guest
Gebäude building
geben give *(irr)*
Gebet prayer
Gebiet area; district
geboren werden be born
gebrochen broken
Geburtsdatum date of birth
Geburtsort birthplace; place of birth
Geburtstag birthday
Herzlichen Glückwunsch zum Geburtstag! Happy birthday (to you)!
Gedächtnis memory
Gedanke thought
Gedicht poem
Geduld patience
geduldig patient
geeignet suitable
gefährlich dangerous
Gefangene/r prisoner
Gefühl feeling
gegen against
Gegenstand object; thing
gegenüberstehen face
Geheimnis secret
gehen; fahren go *(irr)*
gehen walk
Lass(t) uns gehen! Let's go!
Schwimmen gehen go swimming
Einkaufen gehen go shopping
in die Schule gehen attend school
gehen um be about
gehören zu go with; belong (to)
Geist ghost; mind
gelangen get *(irr)*
gelassen calm
gelb yellow
Geld money

(gut) verdienen; (viel) Geld verdienen make (good) money
Geld aufbringen raise money
Geld ausgeben für spend money on
Geld; Bargeld cash
gelegen situated
Gelegenheit chance
Gelegenheit; Chance, Möglichkeit opportunity
gelegentlich occasionally
gelten als be considered
gut gemacht well done
gemacht werden be made
Gemälde painting
gemäß according to
Gemeinde, Gemeinschaft community
gemischt mixed
Gemüse vegetable; veggie *(informal)*
genannt called
genannt werden be called
genau carefully; right; exactly
genau, bestimmte(r, s); spezifisch specific
Genehmigung permission
genial, klasse brilliant
genießen enjoy
genug enough; sufficient
genügend sufficient
geöffnet open
geprellt bruised
gerade just
geradeaus straight on
gerade(aus); direkt straight
Geräusch sound; noise
Gericht dish (*pl* dishes)
etw gern tun like doing sth
Hättest du gern ...? / Hättet ihr gern ...? Would you like ...?
etw sehr gern tun love doing sth
Gern geschehen. You're welcome.
gerne certainly
Geruch smell
Gesamt- overall
Geschäft shop; business; deal
geschehen happen
Geschenk gift; present
Geschichte story; history
Geschick skill
geschickt skilful
Geschmack taste
Geschwister brothers and sisters
geschwollen swollen
Gesellschaft society
gesellschaftlich; sozial social
Gesetz law
gesetzlich legal
Gesicht face
Gesichtspunkt aspect
Gespenst ghost
Gespräch conversation; call *(Telefon)*
Gespräch, Dialog dialogue
Gespräch; Vortrag talk
gestern yesterday
gestern Abend last night
gestresst stressed
gesund well; healthy
Gesundheit health
Getränk drink
Gewicht weight
Gewinn profit; prize
gewinnen win *(irr)*
Gewinner/in winner
gewiss certain
gewissenhaft conscientious
sich gewöhnen an get used to
gewöhnlich usually
Gewürz spice
es gibt there is/there are
Gibt es ...? Is there ...?/Are there ...?
giftig toxic
Giraffe giraffe
Gitarre guitar
Gitarre spielen play the guitar
Glas glass
Glaube belief
glauben think *(irr)*
glauben (an) believe (in)
der/die/das Gleiche the same
Glück; Zufriedenheit happiness
glücklich happy; lucky
glücklich, froh glad
Glückwunsch! Congratulations!
Viel Glück! Good luck!
Herzlichen Glückwunsch zum Geburtstag! Happy birthday (to you)!
Goldfisch goldfish (*pl* goldfish)
Gras grass
gratis for free
Gratuliere! Congratulations!
grau grey
Grenze border
groß big; tall; large
groß; großartig great; terrific
Großbritannien Great Britain; Britain
Größe size
Großeltern grandparents *(pl)*
Großelternteil grandparent
Großmutter grandmother
Großvater grandfather
die grünen the green ones
grün green
Grund reason
einen Grund nennen give a reason
gründen found
Grundkenntnisse working knowledge
Grundlage, Basis base
Gruppe group
Grüße greetings *(pl)*
viele Grüße best wishes
Gummistiefel wellie
gut good; well
sich gut verstehen get on well
in Ordnung, gut fine
gut aussehend good-looking; handsome
gut gemacht well done
gut in etwas sein be good at something
Gute Besserung! Get well soon!
Guten Morgen! Good morning!

H

Haar hair
haben have *(irr)*; have got
halb half
Hälfte half (*pl* halves)
hallo hello
Hals neck
Halsschmerzen sore throat
halten keep *(irr)*
halten für consider
Was hältst du davon? What do you think?
Haltung attitude
Handel trade; business
handeln act; take action
handeln von be about
Handlung action
Handlung, Plot plot
Handschuh glove
Handy mobile (phone)
hängen hang *(irr)*
harmlos harmless

hart hard; tough
hassen hate
hässlich ugly
häufig often
Haupt- main
Hauptgericht main (course)
hauptsächlich mainly
Hauptstadt capital
Haus home; house
Hausaufgaben homework
zu Hause at home
nach Hause home
Haustier pet
Haut skin
Heft exercise book
Heiligabend Christmas Eve
heimlich secret
heiraten marry
heiß hot
(heißer) Kakao hot chocolate
Ich heiße ... I'm (= I am); My name is ...
heißen, genannt werden (be) called
Held hero (*pl* heroes)
helfen help
Kann ich dir/Ihnen helfen? Can I help you?
hell bright
Hemd shirt
heraus, hinaus out
herausbringen release
herausfinden find out
(heraus)fordernd challenging
Herausforderung challenge
herausgeben publish
Herbst fall *(AE)*; autumn
Herr *(Anrede)* Mr
(meine) Damen und Herren ladies and gentlemen
herstellen produce
herum around
(herunter)fallen fall off
Herz heart
Herzlichen Glückwunsch zum Geburtstag! Happy birthday (to you)!
heute today
heute Abend tonight
heute Morgen this morning
hier; hierher here
Hier, bitte! Here you are.; Here you go.
hiesig local
Hilfe help
nach Hilfe, als Hilfe for help
Hilfe support
hilfreich helpful
Himmel sky
hin und wieder occasionally
hinauf up
hinausbringen take out
(hinaus)gehen go out
hinein inside
(hinein)stecken insert
sich hinsetzen sit down
hinten behind
hinter behind
Hintergrund background
hinüber; vorbei over
hinunter; (nach) unten down
hinweisen auf refer to
hinzufügen add
hoch high
(hoch)heben lift
(Höchst)grenze limit
hoffen hope
Hoffnung hope
höflich polite
Höhe height
Holz wood
hören hear *(irr)*
Hose (a pair of) trousers
hübsch pretty
Hügel hill
Huhn chicken
Hund dog
den Hund ausführen walk the dog
hungrig hungry
Hut hat

I

ich I; me
Ich würde lieber ... I'd rather ...
Idee idea
Identifikation identification
identifizieren identify
Identität identity
Igel hedgehog
ignorieren ignore
ihm, ihn him
ihnen them
Ihnen you
ihr you
ihr/ihre her
ihr(e) their
ihre(r, s) hers
Ihre(r, s) yours
immer always
(immer) noch still
immerhin after all
Immigrant/in immigrant
Immigration immigration
importieren import
in in; into; to; at; on
indem by (+ *-ing*) *(oder nur Verbform mit -ing)*
individuell; einzeln individual
Industrie industry
Informationen information *(no pl)*
Informationstechnologie, IT ICT (= Information and Communication Technology); information technology (= IT)
informieren inform
Ingenieur/in engineer
Injektion injection
inlineskaten skate
innen inside
Innenstadt city (centre)
innere(r, s) inner
innerhalb within
insbesondere in particular
Insel island
insgesamt altogether
Instruktion instruction
intelligent bright
Intelligenz intelligence
interessant interesting
Interesse, Hobby interest
interessiert sein an be interested in
im Internet surfen surf the Internet
interviewen, befragen interview
(irgend)ein(e) any
irgendetwas anything
(irgend)jemand anyone
irgendjemand; jede(r, s) anybody
irgendwer somebody; someone
irgendwie somehow
irgendwo anywhere; somewhere
Irland Ireland

J

ja yes
Jacke jacket
jagen hunt
Jahr year
Frohes Neues Jahr! Happy New Year!
Jahrhundert century
Jahrzehnt decade
Januar January
jdn abholen pick sb up
je ... desto ... the ... the ...
irgendjemand; jede(r, s) anybody

jedenfalls anyway
alle; jeder everybody; everyone
jede(r, s) anyone
jede(r, s) every; each
jederzeit at any time
jedoch though *(nachgestellt)*
jemals ever
jemand somebody; someone
jene(r, s) that
jene those (*pl* of that)
jenseits beyond
jetzt now
Jetzt bist du dran. Over to you.
je(weils) each
Job job
Jugend; Jugendliche/r youth
Jugendzentrum youth club
Juli July
jung young
Junge boy
jüngste(r, s) recent
Juni June

K

Kaffee coffee
Käfig cage
(heißer) Kakao hot chocolate
Kalender calendar
kalt cold
Kamera camera
Kampagne campaign
Kampf; Streit fight
kämpfen fight *(irr)*
Kaninchen rabbit
Kapitel theme
kaputt broken
kaputt machen break *(irr)*
Karneval carnival
Karriere career
Karte map; card
Kartoffel potato (*pl* potatoes)
Käse cheese
Kasten box
Katze cat
Kauf purchase
kaufen buy *(irr)*; get *(irr)*
Kaufhaus department store
kaum hardly
kein(e) no; not any
Keine Ursache. You're welcome.
keiner no-one, no one; no one; nobody
keine(r, s); nichts none
Keks biscuit
Kellner/in waiter/ waitress
kennen know *(irr)*
jemanden kennenlernen get to know somebody
Kerze candle
Kilometer kilometre; km (= kilometre)
Kind child (*pl* children); kid
Kino cinema
Kirche church
Kissen pillow
Kiste box
Klang sound
klar clear
Klasse form; class; year
Klassenkamerad/in classmate
Klassenzimmer classroom
kleben stick
Kleid dress
Kleider, Kleidung clothes *(pl)*
Kleidung clothing
klein little; small
ein (kleines) bisschen a (little) bit
klettern climb
klicken click
klingeln ring *(irr)*
klingen, sich anhören sound
Klub; AG club
klug clever
knapp narrow
Knie knee
Knochen bone
Knopf button
Koch/Köchin cook
kochen do the cooking; cook
kochen *(Flüssigkeit)* boil
Vergangenheitsform von can't couldn't (= could not)
etwas tun können able to do something
Kollege/Kollegin colleague
komisch funny
kommen come *(irr)*; get *(irr)*
Kommentar comment
Komm(t) herein! Come in.
Kommunikation communication
kommunizieren, sprechen communicate
kompetent competent
komplett complete
Konflikt conflict
König king
Königin queen
können may
können/nicht können can/can't
könnte(st, n, t) could; might
Konsequenz consequence
konsumieren consume
Kontakt contact
Kontakt halten keep in touch
Kontinent continent
Kontrolle control
kontrollieren control; check
sich konzentrieren concentrate
Konzert concert
Kopf head
Kopfschmerzen headache
Korb basket
Körper body
körperlich physical
kosten cost *(irr)*
kostenlos free
es kostet it's (= it is)
Wie viel kostet es? How much is it?
köstlich, lecker delicious
Kostüm costume
Kraft strength; energy
Kraft; Wucht force
krank sick; ill
Krankenhaus hospital
Krankenpfleger nurse
Krankenschwester nurse
Krankheit disease; illness
Krawatte tie
kreativ creative
Kreatur creature
Kreide chalk
Kreis circle
Krieg war
Kritik review
Krokodil crocodile
Küche kitchen
Kuchen cake
sich kümmern um look after; take care of
sich um jdn kümmern look after sb
Kuh cow
Kühlschrank fridge
Kultur culture
kulturell cultural
Kunde/Kundin customer; client
Kunst art
Künstler/in artist
Kunstwerk piece of art
Kurs course
kurz short
Kuscheltier cuddly toy
küssen kiss
Küste coast

L

lächeln smile
Lächeln smile
lachen laugh
Laden store *(AE)*; shop
Lage location; setting
Lampe lamp
Land country; nation
landen land
Landschaft landscape; countryside
Landwirtschaft agriculture
landwirtschaftlich agricultural
lang long
… lang for *(+ Zeitraum)*
langsam slow, slowly
langweilig boring
lassen let *(irr)*
lass(t) uns … let's (= let us)
Lass(t) uns gehen! Let's go!
lästige Aufgabe chore
Lastwagenfahrer/in lorry driver
Lauf run
Laufbahn career
laufen run *(irr)*
laut loud; noisy
läuten ring *(irr)*
leben live
Leben life *(pl* lives)
lebendig alive
Lebensbedingung living condition
Lebenslauf CV (= curriculum vitae)
Lebensstandard standard of living
Lebewesen creature
lecker delicious; tasty
leer (stehend) empty
legen lay *(irr)*; put *(irr)*
Lehrer/in teacher
leicht easy; easily
leid tun feel sorry for
Es tut mir leid. Sorry.
leiden an suffer from
leidenschaftlich passionate
leise quiet
sich leisten afford
lernen learn *(irr)*
lesen read *(irr)*
Lesen reading
Leser/in reader
letzte past
letzte(r, s) last; recent
Leute people
Lexikon dictionary
Licht light
Liebe love
liebe/r *(Anrede)* dear
lieben love
Ich würde lieber … I'd rather …
lieber mögen like better
Liebling; Lieblings- favourite
am liebsten mögen like best
Lied song
liegen lie *(irr)*
lila purple
Limit limit
Limonade lemonade
Lineal ruler
Linie; Zeile line
links on the left side
(nach) links left
links, auf der/deiner linken Seite on the left/on your left
Liste list
Loch hole
Löffel spoon
Lohn wage; pay
(lohnens)wert worth
lösen solve
Lösung solution
Löwe lion
Luft air
Luftballon balloon
lustig funny; fun

M

machen do *(irr)*; make *(irr)*
ein Picknick machen have a picnic
einen Test machen take a test
mächtig powerful
Mädchen girl
Magen stomach
Mahlzeit meal
Mai May
mailen email
Mal time
zum ersten Mal for the first time
Mama mum
man you
manchmal sometimes
Manieren manner
Mann man *(pl* men)
Mappe folder
Markt market
Marmelade jam
März March
Maschine engine; machine
Mathe maths
Maurer/in bricklayer
Maus mouse *(pl* mice)
Mechaniker/in mechanic
Medikamente medicine *(no pl)*
Meer ocean; sea
Meerschweinchen guinea pig
Mehl flour
mehr more
Mehrheit majority
meiden avoid; stay away from
Meile mile
mein(e) my
(meine) Damen und Herren ladies and gentlemen
meinen; bedeuten mean *(irr)*
Meinung opinion
meiner Meinung nach to my mind; in my opinion
meine(r, s) mine
die meisten; am meisten most
meistens mostly
Menge amount
viel, jede Menge a lot (of); lots of
Mensch man *(pl* men)
Menschen people
Menschenmenge crowd
Menschenrechte human rights *(pl)*
Menü menu
merkwürdig strange
Messer knife *(pl* knives)
Meter metre
mich me
Miete rent
Milch milk
mindestens at least
mir (to) me
mir/mich/ich (selbst) myself
Mischung mixture
mit with; by
mit dem Bus by bus
mit dem Bus fahren go by bus
mit dem Fahrrad by bike
mit freundlichen Grüßen yours faithfully
mit jdm ausgehen go out with sb
mitbringen bring *(irr)*
Mitglied member
mitmachen join
mitnehmen take away
mitsingen sing along
Mittagessen lunch
Mittagspause, Mittagszeit lunchtime
Mitte centre; middle
in der Mitte von in the middle of
Mitteilung announcement
um Mitternacht at midnight
Mittwoch Wednesday

Mobben bullying
mobben bully
Mode fashion
Modell model
mögen like
sehr mögen love
Ich mag ... nicht. I don't like ...
lieber mögen like better
am liebsten mögen like best
alle möglichen all kinds of
möglich possible
Möglichkeit chance; possibility
im Moment at the moment
Monat month
Mond moon
Montag Monday
Morgen morning
morgen tomorrow
Guten Morgen! Good morning!
am Morgen in the morning
heute Morgen this morning
morgen Vormittag tomorrow morning
morgens, vormittags *(nur hinter Uhrzeit zwischen Mitternacht und 12 Uhr mittags)* am (= ante meridiem)
Moschee mosque
Motorrad motorbike
müde tired
mühelos easily
Müll rubbish; litter
multikulturell multicultural
Mund mouth
Münze coin
Murmel marble
Muschel seashell
Musik music
Musiker/in musician
müssen have to; must; need to
Mut courage
Mutter mother
Muttersprache mother tongue
Mütze cap

N

nach past; after; according to; to
nach Hause home
nach/als Hilfe for help
(nach) links left
(nach) oben upstairs
nach oben up
(nach) rechts right
Nachbar/in neighbour
Nachbarschaft neighbourhood
nachdem after
nachdenken über think about
nachhaltig sustainable
Nachmittag afternoon
am Nachmittag in the afternoon
den ganzen Nachmittag lang all afternoon
nachmittags pm (= post meridiem)
Nachname surname
Nachricht message; note
Nachrichten news *(no pl)*
nachspielen act out
nächste(r, s) next
Nacht night
Nachtisch dessert
nachts at night
Nacken neck
als Nächstes next
nahe close, near
namens called
Nase nose
nass wet
Nation nation
Nationalität nationality
Natur nature
Naturkatastrophe natural disaster
natürlich of course
Naturwissenschaft science
neben next to
negativ negative
nehmen take *(irr)*
Ich nehme es. I'll take it.
die U-Bahn nehmen take the tube
einen Zug nehmen catch a train
nein no
nennen call
einen Grund nennen give a reason
nervös nervous
nett nice
Netz web
Netzwerk network
neu new; fresh
neueste(r, s) latest
Neuigkeit; Nachrichten news *(no pl)*
Neujahr New Year
neulich recently
nicht not
nicht dürfen mustn't (= must not)
nicht einmal not even
nicht mehr no longer; not anymore
nicht mögen dislike
nicht werden won't
nichts not anything; nothing
nie, niemals never
niedlich cute
niedrig low
niemand nobody; not anyone
noch; schon yet
(immer) noch still
noch ein/e another
noch einmal again
noch etwas anything else
Sonst noch etwas?, Darf es noch etwas sein? Anything else?
noch nicht not yet
Norden north
normalerweise normally; usually
Note mark
Notfall emergency
Notwendigkeit, Bedürfnis need
November November
Nummer number
nun well
nur only; just
nützlich useful; helpful

O

ob whether; if
oben up
(nach) oben upstairs
(oben) auf on top
oberes Ende top
Obst fruit *(no pl)*
obwohl although; though; even though
oder or
offen open
offensichtlich obvious, obviously
öffentlich public
offiziell official, officially
öffnen open
Öffnungszeiten opening hours *(pl)*
oft often; many times
ohne without
Ohr ear
Oktober October
Öl oil
Onkel uncle
Opa grandad
Opfer victim
orange orange
Orange orange
Orangensaft orange juice
ordentlich tidy
ordnen sort out
Ordner folder
in Ordnung, gut all right; fine
organisieren organise; arrange
Organismus organism

Ort place; site
örtlich local
Osten east
Ostern Easter
Ozean ocean

P

Paar pair; couple
ein paar some
ein Paar a pair of
Packung packet
Papa dad
Papagei parrot
Papier paper
Paradies paradise
Parfüm perfume
Partner boyfriend
Partnerin girlfriend
passen zu go with; match
passend suitable
passieren go on; happen
Passwort password
Pause break
Pech bad luck
peinlich embarrassing
Pence p (= penny, pence)
perfekt perfect
Personalien details *(pl)*
persönlich personal
persönliche Daten details *(pl)*
persönliche, soziale und methodische Kompetenzen soft skill
Persönlichkeit personality
Pfad trail
Pferd horse
Pflanze plant
Pflege; Sorgfalt care
pflegen maintain
Pflicht responsibility
pflichtbewusst conscientious
Pfund pound
Pfütze puddle
Pickel spot
ein Picknick machen have a picnic
Pinguin penguin
Plan scheme
planen plan
Plastik plastic
Plattform platform
Platz place; site; space
plötzlich suddenly
plus plus
Pokalendspiel cup final
Politik politics *(pl)*
politisch political
Polizei police
Polizeibeamte(r)/-beamtin police officer
Polizist policeman *(pl* policemen)
Pommes frites chips *(pl)*
positiv positive
Postkarte postcard
Potenzial potential
Praktikum work experience; work placement
praktisch handy
Präsentation presentation
präsentieren present (to)
präsentieren, vertreten represent
Präsident/in president
Praxis practice
Preis price; prize; award
Premierminister prime minister
Presse press
privat private
pro per; a
probieren try
Produkt product
Produkte produce *(pl)*
Produktion production
Produzent/in producer
professionell professional
Profi professional
Programm programme; scheme
Projekt project; scheme
Prozent per cent *(BE)* = percent *(AE)*
Prozess process
prüfen test
Prüfung exam
Publikum audience
Pullover sweater; jumper
Punkt point
pünktlich on time; in time
(sich die Zähne) putzen brush (one's teeth)

Q

qualifiziert qualified
Qualität quality
Quelle resource; source
quer durch across

R

Rad wheel
Rad fahren, radeln cycle
Rasse race
Rassist/in; rassistisch racist
Rat geben give advice
raten advise
Rat(schlag) advice *(no pl)*
Ratte rat
rauchen smoke
Raum space; room
reagieren react
realistisch realistic
Realität reality
recherchieren research
Rechnung bill
Recht law; right
Du hast recht. You're right.
recht haben be right
recht, ziemlich fairly
rechtlich legal
(nach) rechts right
rechts, auf der/deiner rechten Seite on the right/on your right
rechtzeitig in time
recyceln recycle
Rede speech
direkte/wörtliche Rede direct speech
reden speak *(irr)*
reden (mit) talk (to)
reduzieren reduce
Regal shelf (*pl* shelves)
Regel rule
regelmäßig regular(ly)
Regen rain
Regenwald rainforest
Regierung government
Region area
Regisseur/in director
regnen rain
regnerisch rainy
reich rich
Reichweite range
Reihe, Folge series (*only plural*)
an der Reihe sein be one's turn
Reis rice
Reise trip; journey; travel
reisen travel
(Reise)pass passport
Reißverschluss zip
reiten ride a horse
Religion religion; RE (= religious education) *(Schulfach)*
Rennen race
rennen run *(irr)*
reparieren repair
Respekt respect
respektieren respect
Ressource resource

im Restaurant essen eat out
Resultat result
retten save
Rezension review
Rezept recipe
richtig correct; right; proper(ly)
in Richtung, zu toward(s)
riechen smell *(irr)*
riesig huge
Rock skirt
Rolle role
Rollenspiel role play
Rollstuhl wheelchair
rot red
Rücken back
Rückenschmerzen backache *(no pl)*
Ruf reputation
rufen shout; call
Ruhe silence
ruhig calm

S

Saft juice
sagen say *(irr)*
Sahne cream
Salat salad
Salbe cream
Salz salt
sammeln collect
Sammlung collection
Samstag Saturday
Sänger/in singer
satt full
Satz sentence; phrase
sauber clean
sauber machen clean; clean up
sauer sour
schaden damage
schädlich harmful
Schaf sheep (*pl* sheep)
schaffen manage; establish
Schal scarf (*pl* scarfs *or* scarves)
scharf hot; spicy
Schatten shadow
schätzen estimate
Schauplatz setting
schaurig spooky
Schauspieler/in actor/actress
scheinen seem
Schere a pair of scissors
Schicht shift
schicken send *(irr)*
schieben push
schießen shoot *(irr)*
ein Tor schießen score a goal
Schiff ship
ein Schiff besteigen board a ship
Schild sign
Schinkenspeck bacon
schlafen be asleep; sleep *(irr)*
schlagen beat *(irr)*; hit *(irr)*
schlank slim
schlau clever
schlecht; schlimm bad
schließen close
schließlich finally; in the end; at last; after all
schlimm, stark severe
schlimmer worse
schlimmste(r, s) worst
Schluss end; ending
Schluss machen break up
Schlüssel key
schmecken taste
Schmerz pain
schmerzen hurt *(irr)*
Schmetterling butterfly
schmutzig dirty
Schnee snow
Schneemann snowman (*pl* snowmen)
schneereich snowy
schneiden cut *(irr)*
schnell fast; quick, quickly
Schnellhefter folder
Schokolade chocolate
schon already
schön beautiful; lovely; nice
schon; noch yet
Schottland Scotland
Schrank wardrobe; cupboard
schrecklich awful; terrible
schreiben write *(irr)*
Schreibtisch desk
schreien shout; cry
schüchtern shy
Schuh shoe
Schularbeiten schoolwork
Schulausflug school trip
Schuld fault
Schule school
in die Schule gehen attend school
Schüler/in pupil; student *(AE)*
(Schüler)versammlung assembly
Schulfach subject
Schuljahr, Klasse year
Schultag school day
Schultasche schoolbag
Schulter shoulder
Schuluniform school uniform
Schulzeugnis school report
Schüssel bowl
schütteln shake *(irr)*
Schutz protection
schwarz black
Schwein pig
schwer heavy; difficult
Schwester sister
schwierig difficult; hard; tough
in Schwierigkeiten geraten get into trouble
Schwimmbad swimming pool
schwimmen swim *(irr)*
Schwimmen swimming
Schwimmen gehen go swimming
Schwimmer/in swimmer
See lake; sea
Seele soul
sehen see *(irr)*
(an)sehen, (an)schauen look (at)
Sehenswürdigkeit sight
sehr very; much
sehr, dringend badly
Seife soap
Seil rope
sein be *(irr)*
sein; seine(r, s) his
sein(e), ihr(e) *(sächlich)* its
seit since
Seite page; side
rechts, auf der/deiner rechten Seite on the right/on your right
links, auf der/deiner linken Seite on the left/on your left
Sekunde second
der-/die-/dasselbe the same
selbst even
Selbstbewusstsein self-confidence
Selbstvertrauen self-confidence
selten rarely; seldom
September September
Service service
servieren serve
setzen put *(irr)*
sich setzen take a seat
sich amüsieren enjoy oneself
sich anfreunden (mit) make friends (with)
sich anmelden sign up
sich ansehen have /take a look at

sich beeilen hurry (up)
sich befassen mit deal with
sich beklagen complain
sich bewegen move
sich bewerben um apply for
sich bewusst sein realize (= realise)
sich beziehen auf refer to
sich die Zähne putzen brush one's teeth
sich einer Sache bewusst sein be aware of something
sich entschuldigen apologize (= apologise)
sich erholen recover
sich erinnern an remember
sich erstrecken extend
sich etwas vorstellen imagine
sich fragen wonder
sich freuen auf look forward to
(sich) fühlen feel *(irr)*
sich gewöhnen an get used to
sich gut verstehen get on well
sich hinsetzen sit down
sich irren be wrong
sich konzentrieren concentrate
sich konzentrieren auf focus on
sich kümmern um care; look after; take care of
sich leisten afford
sich mit jemandem in Verbindung setzen contact somebody
sich niederlassen settle
sich setzen take a seat
sich Sorgen machen worry
sich spiegeln in reflect
sich streiten argue; fight *(irr)*
(sich) treffen meet up
sich um jdn kümmern look after sb
sich umdrehen turn around
sich verirren get lost
(sich) verkleiden dress up
sich verlassen auf rely on
sich verletzen hurt oneself
sich verlieben fall in love
(sich) verstecken hide *(irr)*
(sich) wenden an turn to
sich zu jdm gesellen join
sich; sich selbst herself; himself
sich; sie selbst themselves
sicher sure; safe; certainly
Sicherheit security
Sicherheit safety
sie she; they; them; her
Sie you
Siedler/in settler
Siedlung settlement
simpel simple
singen sing *(irr)*
Sinn; Gefühl sense
Sitz seat
sitzen sit *(irr)*
Ski fahren/laufen ski
Sklave slave
SMS text message
so such; like this; thus
so ... wie as ... as
so genannt so-called
sobald once
Socke sock
sofort immediately
sogar even
Sohn son
solch such
Soldat/in soldier
sollen; werden shall
etwas tun sollen be supposed to do something
sollte(st, n, t) should
Sommer summer
sonderbar strange
sondern but
Sonne sun
Sonnenbrille sunglasses *(pl)*
Sonnenschein sunshine
sonnig sunny
Sonntag Sunday
sonst else
was sonst what else
Sonst noch etwas?, Anything else?
sich Sorgen machen worry
Mach dir keine Sorgen. Don't worry.
Sorte kind
sortieren sort
Soße sauce
sowieso anyway
sowohl ... als auch ... both ... and ...
soziales Netzwerk social network
(zu) spät late
Wie spät ist es? What time is it?
sparen save
Spaß fun; joke
(viel) Spaß haben have (a lot of) fun
(viel) Spaß machen be (good/great) fun
später later; afterwards
(spätestens) bis by
Spaziergang walk
Speisekarte menu
spektakulär spectacular
Spezies species *(pl)*
Spiegel mirror
Spiegelei fried egg
sich spiegeln in reflect
Spiel play; match; game
spielen act; play
Spieler/in player
Spielplatz playground
Spielzeug toy
Spielzeugauto toy car
spitze awesome
Spitze top
Sport, Sportart sport; PE (= physical education) *(Schulfach)*
Sportcenter sports centre
Sporthalle sports hall
Sportplatz sports field
Sprache language
sprechen speak *(irr)*
sprechen, kommunizieren communicate
sprechen (mit) talk (to)
sprechen über talk about
Sprecher/in speaker
springen jump
Spritze injection
Staatsoberhaupt head
Stadt city; town
städtisch urban
Stamm tribe
Stand stall
ständig constantly
stark strong; powerful
Stärke strength
stattdessen instead
stattfinden take place
staubsaugen vacuum
Steckbrief fact file
stehen stand *(irr)*
stehen bleiben stop
stehlen steal *(irr)*
steigen step
steigen; aufgehen rise *(irr)*
Stein stone; rock

Stelle site; job
stellen put *(irr)*
(Stell)vertreter/in representative
Steppdecke duvet
sterben die
Stern star
Stiefel boot
Stift pen
Stil style
Stille silence
Stimme; Abstimmung, Wahl vote
Stock stick
Stockwerk floor
Stolz pride
stolz proud
stolz sein auf be proud of
stoßen push
stoßen gegen hit *(irr)*
strahlend, hell bright
Strand beach
Straße street; road
auf der Straße in the street
Streichholz match (*pl* matches)
Streit argument
Streit; Kampf fight
sich streiten argue; fight *(irr)*
stressig stressful
Strom electricity; power
Stück piece
studieren; lernen study
Stufe; Schritt step
Stuhl chair
Stunde lesson; hour
Stundenplan timetable
Sturm storm
suchen nach look for
Süden south
südliche(r, s) southern
super fantastic; awesome
Supermarkt supermarket
Suppe soup
im Internet surfen surf the Internet
süß cute; sweet
Süßigkeit sweet
Szene scene

T

Tafel blackboard
Tafel; Brett board
Tag day
Tagebuch diary
eines Tages one day
Tante aunt
Tanz dance
tanzen dance
Tanzen dancing
Tasche bag; pocket
Taschengeld pocket money
Taschenlampe torch (*pl* torches)
Taschentuch handkerchief (*pl* handkerchiefs / handkerchieves)
Tasse cup
Tatsache fact
tatsächlich in fact
tausend thousand
Techniker/in technician
technisch technical
Technologie, Technik technology
Tee tea
Teelöffel teaspoon
Teil part; piece
Teil, Stück, Abschnitt section
teilen share
teilnehmen participate
teilnehmen an take part in; compete in
Telefon phone; telephone
ans Telefon gehen answer the phone
am Telefon on the phone
Teller plate
Tempel temple
Termin date
Terrorismus terrorism
einen Test machen take a test
testen test
teuer expensive
Theater theatre
(Theater)stück play
Thema theme; topic; subject
tief deep
Tier animal
Tierarzt/-ärztin vet
Tierpfleger/in zoo-keeper
Tiger tiger
Tisch table
den Tisch decken lay the table
Tischtennnis table tennis
Titel title
Tochter daughter
Tod death
Toilette toilet
toll amazing *(informal)*
Tomate tomato (*pl* tomatoes)
Tor goal
ein Tor schießen score a goal
tot dead
töten kill
Tourismus tourism
traditionell traditional
tragen wear *(irr)*; carry
trainieren exercise; train
Traum dream
träumen dream *(irr)*
traurig sad
treffen; sich treffen meet *(irr)*; meet up
treffen, stoßen gegen hit *(irr)*
treten kick; step
trinken drink *(irr)*; have *(irr)*
Trinken drink
trotzdem yet
tschüs(s) bye
tun do *(irr)*
etwas tun sollen be supposed to do something
etw gern tun like doing sth
etw sehr gern tun love doing sth
etwas tun können be able to do something
etw tun werden be going to do sth
jdn dazu bringen, etw zu tun make sb do sth
etw weiter tun keep doing sth
Tür door
Turm tower
Turnen do gymnastics
Turnhalle gym (= gymnasium)
Turnschuhe trainers
typisch typical

U

die U-Bahn nehmen take the tube
U-Bahn-Station station
üben practise
über about; across; above; over
überall everywhere; all over
Übereinkunft understanding
überhaupt at all; anyway
überhaupt nicht not at all
überleben survive
Übernachtung sleepover
überprüfen check
Überprüfung der Anwesenheit registration
Überprüfung, Kontrolle check

überqueren cross
überraschend surprising
überrascht surprised
Überraschung surprise
Überschrift title
Überschrift, Titel heading
übrig bleiben be left
übrigens by the way; actually
Übung practice; exercise
etw übrig haben have sth left
Uhr o'clock; clock; watch
um at; around
um ... herum round
um Mitternacht at midnight
um zu in order to
(um) zu to
umblättern turn
sich umdrehen turn around
umfassen involve
Umfrage survey
umgeben surround
Umgebung environment
umher around
umsteigen change
umwandeln in turn into
umweltbewusst (werden) (go) green
umweltfreundlich eco-friendly
umziehen move
unabhängig independent
unangenehm embarrassing
unaufgeräumt untidy
unbedingt erforderlich essential
unbekannt strange
unbewohnt empty
und and
unfähig unable
Unfall accident
unfreundlich unfriendly
ungefähr about; around
ungefähr, etwa approximately
ungefährlich safe
ungewöhnlich unusual
unglaublich incredible
unglücklich unhappy
unglücklicherweise unfortunately
unheimlich spooky
unhöflich; primitiv rude
Universität university
unmöglich impossible
unordentlich untidy
uns us
uns; wir selbst ourselves
unsere(r, s) our
(nach) unten down
unten, unter below
unter beneath; under; amongst
unter; zwischen among
unterbrechen interrupt
unterhalten entertain
Unterhaltung conversation
Unterricht lesson
unterrichten teach *(irr)*; educate
Unterschied difference
unterschreiben sign
unterstreichen underline
(unter)stützen support
unterstützend supportive
Unterstützung support
untersuchen explore
unterwegs on the move
unterzeichnen sign
Urlaub holiday(s)
in Urlaub fahren go on holiday
ursprünglich originally
US; US- (the) US
USA the USA

V

Vater father
Vati dad
Vegetarier/in; vegetarisch vegetarian
Verabredung date
verändern change
Veränderung change
verängstigt frightened; scared
Veranstaltung event
verantwortlich responsible
Verantwortung; Pflicht responsibility
verantwortungsbewusst responsible
verärgert angry, angrily; annoyed
Verband bandage
Verbandskasten first aid kit
verbessern improve
verbinden combine; attach
in Verbindung bleiben keep in touch
(ver)brennen burn *(irr)*
verbringen spend *(irr)*
verdienen earn
(viel) Geld verdienen make (good) money
Vereinigte Staaten von Amerika United States of America
die Vereinigten Staaten the United States
Vereinigtes Königreich the UK (= United Kingdom)
verfolgen follow
verfügbar available
vergangen past
Vergangenheitsform von can't couldn't (= could not)
vergehen *(Zeit)* pass
vergessen forget *(irr)*
Vergeudung; Abfall waste
im Vergleich zu compared to
vergleichen compare
Vergütung payment
Verhalten manner
verhören question
sich verirren get lost
Verkauf sale
verkaufen sell *(irr)*
Verkäufer/in seller; shop assistant
Verkehr traffic
(sich) verkleiden dress up
verkünden, erklären declare
verlangen require
sich verlassen auf rely on
verlassen; abfahren leave *(irr)*
verlässlich reliable
Verlauf process
sich verletzen hurt oneself
sich verlieben fall in love
verlieren lose *(irr)*
Verlust loss
vermeiden avoid
(ver)mischen mix
vermissen; verpassen miss
vermuten suppose; guess
veröffentlichen release; publish
verrückt crazy
(Schüler)versammlung assembly
verschiedene several
verschiedene(r, s) different
verschmutzen pollute
verschneit snowy
verschwenden waste
Verschwendung waste
verschwinden disappear

Versicherung insurance
Version version
versprechen promise
Verstand mind
Verständigung communication
Verständnis understanding
verständnisvoll sensitive
verstärken increase
(sich) verstecken hide *(irr)*
verstehen understand *(irr)*
Ich verstehe es nicht. I don't understand.
sich gut verstehen get on well
verstreichen *(Zeit)* pass
Versuch experiment
versuchen try
Vertrag treaty
Vertrauen trust
vertrauen (auf) trust (in)
vertraut, bekannt familiar
verursachen cause
vervollständigen complete
Verwandte/r relative
Verwendung use
verzweifelt desperate
viel much
wie viel how much
Viel Glück! Good luck!
(viel) Spaß haben/ machen have/be (a lot of) fun
viel lots of
viele many
wie viele how many
viele Grüße best wishes
viel(e), jede Menge a lot (of)
Vielfalt variety; diversity
vielfältig, unterschiedlich diverse
vielleicht maybe; perhaps
Viertel neighbourhood; quarter
vierte(r, s) fourth
violett purple
Vogel bird
voll full
voller full of
völlig all
vollständig, komplett complete
von by; from; of
von alleine on its own
von; hinunter, herunter off
vor before; to; in front of; ago
vor allem especially; particularly
vor Kurzem recently
vor; außerhalb outside
voraus ahead
vorbei over; past
vorbeigehen an pass
vorbereiten prepare
vorbereitet sein auf be prepared
Vorderseite front
Vorfall incident
vorgeben pretend
vorher before
morgen Vormittag tomorrow morning
morgens, vormittags *(nur hinter Uhrzeit zwischen Mitternacht und 12 Uhr mittags)* am (= ante meridiem)
vorn in front
Vorrat supply
Vorschlag suggestion
vorschlagen suggest
vorsichtig carefully; careful
Vorspeise starter
vorspielen act out
sich etwas vorstellen imagine
Vorstellung idea
Vorstellungsgespräch interview
vortäuschen pretend
Vorteil advantage
Vortrag presentation
vorüber past
vorziehen prefer

W

wachsen grow *(irr)*
während as
Wahl choice; election
wählen; sich entscheiden choose *(irr)*
wählen vote
Wahlmöglichkeit option
Wahlrecht vote
wahnsinnig crazy
wahr true
während while; during; whilst
während; wohingegen whereas
Wahrheit truth
wahrscheinlich likely; probably
Währung currency
Wald forest
Wand wall
wann when
warm warm
warnen warn
warten auf wait for
Wärter/in zoo-keeper
Wartezimmer waiting room
warum why
welche(r, s); was which
was (auch immer) whatever
was sonst what else
was; welche(r, s) what
waschen; sich waschen wash
Wasser water
Wechselgeld change
wechseln; umsteigen change
Wecker alarm clock
weder ... noch ... neither ... nor ...
Weg way
weg away
Weg trail
wegen because of; due to
weglaufen run away
wegnehmen take away
wehtun hurt *(irr)*
weich soft
Weihnachten Christmas
erster Weihnachtsfeiertag Christmas Day
zweiter Weihnachtsfeiertag Boxing Day
weil because; as
weinen cry
Weise way
weiß white
weit far
weit weg far away
weiter further
etwas weiter tun keep doing something
mehr; weitere more
weitergehen move on
weitergehen/-fahren/ -reden go on
weiterlesen read on
weitermachen carry on; continue
welche(r, s) what; which
Wellensittich budgie
Welt world
aus der ganzen Welt from all over the world
Weltall space
weltweit around the world
(sich) wenden an turn to
wenig little
wenige few
weniger less
wenigstens at least
wenn; als when
wenn; falls if
wer who

Werbung advert, advertisement
werden get *(irr)*; grow *(irr)*; become *(irr)*; will; go *(irr)*
nicht werden won't
etw tun werden be going to do sth
werfen throw *(irr)*
Wert value; figure
Wert legen auf care about
Wesen character
wesentlich central
wessen whose
Westen west
Wettbewerb competition
Wetter weather
wichtig important; relevant
wichtig sein matter; count
Wichtigkeit importance
widerlich disgusting
Widerstand resistance
wie how; like; such as
wie; als as
wie auch immer however
wie man how to
wie viel how much
wie viele how many
wieder again
wiederaufbereiten recycle
Auf Wiedersehen. Goodbye.
wiederverwenden reuse
Wiese grass
willkommen welcome
Wind wind
windig windy
Winter winter
winzig tiny
wir we
wirklich really; real; just
wirksam, effektiv effective
Wirtschaft economy
wissen know *(irr)*
Ich weiß es nicht. I don't know.
Wissenschaftler/in scientist
Das soll wohl ein Witz sein! You must be joking! *(informal)*
Witz joke
witzig fun
WLAN WiFi
wo; wohin where
Woche week
die ganze Woche lang all week
Wochenende weekend
am Wochenende at the weekend
Wohltätigkeits-organisation charity
wohnen live; stay
Wohnung flat
Wohnzimmer living room
Wolke cloud
wollen want
wollen, dass jd etw tut want sb to do sth
Wort word
Wörterbuch dictionary
wunderbar, wundervoll wonderful
Wunsch, Anfrage request
wünschen wish
würde(st, n, t) would
Wurst, Würstchen sausage
Wurzel root
würzig spicy
Wüste desert

Z

zäh tough
Zahl number; figure
zählen count
Zahn tooth (*pl* teeth)
Zahnbürste toothbrush
Zahnpasta toothpaste
sich die Zähne putzen brush one's teeth
Zeh toe
Zeichen sign
zeichnen draw *(irr)*
Zeichnung drawing
zeigen reflect; show *(irr)*
zeigen (auf) point (at/to)
zeigen, vorführen demonstrate
Zeile line
Zeit time
die ganze Zeit all the time
Zeitachse timeline
Zeitraum period
Zeitschrift magazine
Zeitspanne period
Zeitung newspaper
Zensur mark
zentral central
Zentrum centre
zerbrechen break *(irr)*
zerstören destroy
Zeug stuff *(informal)*
Zeuge/Zeugin witness
ziehen pull
Ziel destination; aim
Ziel, Sinn purpose
Zielaufgabe target task
ziemlich quite; pretty; fairly
Zigarette cigarette
Zimmer room
Zitat quote; quotation
Zoo zoo
zu too; to
zu Fuß on foot
zu Hause at home
(zu) spät late
zuallererst first of all
Zucker sugar
zuerst first; at first
zufällig by accident
zufrieden satisfied; pleased
Zug train
einen Zug nehmen catch a train
zugeben admit
Zuhause home
zuhören listen (to)
Zukunft future
zukünftig future
zum Beispiel for example
zum ersten Mal for the first time
zum Frühstück for breakfast
zumachen close
zunehmen gain weight
Zuneigung fühlen care
Zuneigung affection
zuordnen match
zurück back
zurückgeben/-kehren/-kommen return
zurücklassen leave *(irr)*, leave behind
zusammen together
zusammen mit along with
zusammenbringen bring together
zusammengesetzt sein aus be made up of
zusammenkommen get together
zusätzlich extra
Zustand, Verfassung state
Zustand; Bedingung condition
zustimmen agree
Zutat ingredient
zuverlässig reliable
zuvor before
jdm zuwinken wave (at/to sb)
zuzüglich plus
Zweig(stelle) branch
zweimal twice
zweiter Weihnachts-feiertag Boxing Day
zweite(r, s) second
zwischen between; amongst

Names

Girls/Women
Aisha /aɪ'i:ʃə/
Alana /ə'lænə/
Alexa /ə'leksə/
Amalia /ə'ma:liə/
Amiria /ə'miriə/
Anastasia /ˌænə'steɪziə/
Anita /ə'ni:tə/
Becca /'bekə/
Becky /'beki/
Bindi /'bɪndi/
Cara /'ka:rə/
Carla /'ka:lə/
Charlotte /'ʃa:lət/
Chloe /'kləʊi/
Claire /kleə/
Daisy /'deɪzi/
Dgudu /d'gu:du:/
Doris /'dɒrɪs/
Eleanor /'elənə/
Everlyn /'evəlin/
Grace /greɪs/
Gracie /'greɪsi/
Indira /'ɪndɪrə/
Jamila /dʒə'milə/
Janis /'dʒænɪs/
Jeanette /dʒɪ'net/
Joan /dʒəʊn/
Karla /'ka:lə/
Katie /'keɪti/
Laura /'lɔ:rə/
Layla /'leɪlə/
Liz /lɪz/
Lizzie /'lɪzi/
Madeline /'mædəlɪn/
Margie /'ma:dʒi/
Maria /mə'ri:ə/
Marsha /'ma:ʃə/
Martha /'ma:θə/
Mary /'meəri/
Michelle /mi:'ʃel/
Mimi-Ali /ˌmi:mi'æli/
Miriam /'mɪriəm/
Molly /'mɒli/
Nancy /'nænsi/
Nellie /'neli/
Nugi /'nu:gi/
Pari /'pa:ri/
Sam /sæm/
Sandy /'sændi/
Sara /'seərə/
Scarlett /'ska:lət/
Tianna /ti'ænə/
Tina /'ti:nə/
Zani /'za:ni/

Boys/Men
Abel /'eɪbl/
Adam /'ædəm/
Aidan /'eɪdn/
Albert /'ælbət/
Ali /'æli/
Amaral /'æmərəl/
Andres /'ændrəs/
Anthony /'æntəni/
Aristotle /'ærɪstɒtl/
Atman /'a:tmən/
Ben, Benjamin /ben, 'bendʒəmɪn/
Billy /'bɪli/
Brian /'braɪən/
Christian /'krɪstʃən/
Crispin /'krɪspɪn/
Damon /'deɪmən/
David /'deɪvɪd/
Diego /di'eɪgəʊ/
Frank /fræŋk/
Harry /'hæri/
Hassan /hə'sa:n/
Herbert /'hɜ:bət/
Isaac /'aɪzək/
Jack /dʒæk/
Jake /dʒeɪk/
James /dʒeɪmz/
Jan /jæn/
Jarly /'dʒa:li/
Jimi /'dʒɪmi/
Jo, Joe /dʒəʊ/
John /dʒɒn/
Kenneth /'kenɪθ/
Kevin /kevɪn/
Lachlan /'lɒklən/
Luis /'lu:ɪs/
Luther /'lu:θə/
Mahatma /mə'ha:tmə/
Martin /'ma:tɪn/
Mason /'meɪsn/
Mike /maɪk/
Ned /ned/
Nick /nɪk/
Nigel /'naɪdʒəl/
Oliver /'ɒlɪvə/
Peter /'pi:tə/
Phil, Philip /fɪl, 'fɪlɪp/
Ralph /rælf/
Randy /'rændi/
Robin /'rɒbɪn/
Ronald /'rɒnld/
Saddam /sə'dæm/
Scott /skɒt/
Sultan /'sʌltən/
Thomas /'tɒməs/
Tom, Tommy /tɒm, 'tɒmi/
Trevor /'trevə/
Woodrow /'wʊdrəʊ/
Xiuhtezcatl /'ʃu:tezkæt/

Families
Aldiss /'ɔ:ldɪs/
Asimov /'æsɪmɒv/
Bernard /'bɜ:nəd/
Branagh /'brænə/
Carlin /'ka:lɪn/
Chamberlain /'tʃeɪmbəlɪn/
Charles /tʃa:lz/
Clancy /'klænsi/
Cook /kʊk/
Einstein /'aɪnstaɪn/
Elliot /'eliət/
Ferguson /'fɜ:gəsən/
Finn /fɪn/
Franklin /'fræŋklɪn/
Fugill /'fju:dʒɪl/
Gandhi /'gændi/
Garimari /ˌgærɪ'ma:ri/
Glasbergen /'glæsˌbɜ:gən/
Gonzalez /gɒn'za:lɪz/
Hall /hɔ:l/
Hendrix /'hendrɪks/
Hoover /'hu:və/
Hussein /hu'seɪn/
Jackson /'dʒæksən/
Jones /dʒəʊnz/
Kelly /'keli/
Kennedy /'kenədi/
King /kɪŋ/
Kupe /'ku:peɪ/
Lauren /'lɔ:rən/
Lennon /'lenən/
Littlewood /'lɪtlwʊd/
Marks /ma:ks/
Martinez /ma:'ti:nez/
Melrose /'melrəʊz/
Monaghan /'mɒnəhən/
Montessori /ˌmɒntə'sɔ:ri/
Namatjira /næmə'tʃɪərə/
Noyce /nɔɪs/
Obama /əʊ'ba:mə/
Pilkington /'pɪlkɪŋtən/
Rankin /'ræŋkɪn/
Reagan /'reɪgən/
Riggs /rɪgz/
Roosevelt /'rəʊzəvelt/
Rosen /'rəʊzn/
Rudd /rʌd/
Samacumbi /ˌsæmə'kʌmbi/
Sampi /'sæmpi/
Sanders /'sa:ndəz/
Sansbury /'sænzbəri/
Shorthouse /'ʃɔ:thaʊs/
Sider /saɪdə/
Smith /smɪθ/
Southall /'sʌðɔ:l/
Stoddart /'stɒdət/
Stuart /'stju:ət/
Tasman /'tæzmən/
Tickell /'tɪkl/
Valencia /və'lenʃiə/
Vivaldi /vɪ'vældi/
Wilson /'wɪlsn/
Wright /raɪt/

Other Names
AIDS /eɪdz/
All Blacks /ði‿'ɔ:l blæks/
American Eagle /əˌmerɪkən‿'i:gl/
Anangu /ə'næŋgu/
anemone /ə'neməni/
Anzac /'ænzæk/
Aotearoa /ˌa:əʊti:ə'rəʊə/
Australia Act /ɒ'streɪliə‿ækt/
Australia Day /ɒ'streɪliə deɪ/
Ayers Rock /ˌeəz 'rɒk/
B-boying/B-girling /'bi: ˌbɔɪɪŋ/'bi: ˌgɜ:lɪŋ/
basketball /'ba:skɪtˌbɔ:l/
the Blitz /ðə 'blɪts/
Bondi Beach /ˌbɒndaɪ 'bi:tʃ/
the British Empire /ðə ˌbrɪtɪʃ‿'empaɪə/

Bromley /ˈbrɒmli/
cane toad /ˈkeɪn təʊd/
Commonwealth of Australia /ˌkɒmənwelθ‿əv‿ɒˈstreɪliə/
Commonwealth of Nations /ˌkɒmənwelθ‿əv ˈneɪʃnz/
CoolX3000 /ˌku:l‿ˌeks ˌθri:ˈθaʊznd/
didgeridoo /ˌdɪdʒəriˈdu:/
DSLR /ˌdi‿es‿el‿ˈɑ:/
Earth Guardians /ˈɜ:θ ˌgɑ:diənz/
East India Company /ˌi:st‿ˌɪndiə ˈkʌmpni/
fashionista /ˌfæʃəˈni:stə/
Fiordland /fiˈɔ:dlənd/
First World War /ˌfɜ:st ˌwɜ:ld ˈwɔ:/
flying fox /ˌflaɪɪŋ ˈfɒks/
folk /fəʊk/
Forever 21 /fərˌevə ˌtwenti ˈwʌn/
Fox /fɒks/
Fox Glacier /ˌfɒks ˈglæsiə/
fracking /ˈfrækɪŋ/
FriendsShare /ˈfrendzʃeə/
Georgia Peace Society /ˌdʒɔ:dʒə ˈpi:s‿səˌsaɪəti/
Great Barrier Reef /ˌgreɪt ˈbæriə ri:f/
Haka, haka /ˈhɑ:kə/
hangi /ˈhæŋgi/
haul girl /ˈhɔ:l gɜ:l/
Hector's dolphin /ˈhektəz ˌdɒlfɪn/
high score /ˈhaɪ skɔ:/
hip hop /ˈhɪp hɒp/
HIV /ˌeɪtʃ‿aɪ ˈvi:/
hobbit /ˈhɒbɪt/
hockey /ˈhɒki/
Holistic Life Foundation /həʊˌlɪstɪk ˈlaɪf‿faʊnˌdeɪʃn/
Hyde Park /ˌhaɪd ˈpɑ:k/
InsideOut /ˌɪnsaɪd‿ˈaʊt/
Instagram /ˈɪnstəgrəm/
jazz /dʒæz/
Jerry /ˈdʒeri/
judo /ˈdʒu:dəʊ/
Ka Mate /kə ˈmɑ:ti/
Kakadu /ˌkækəˈdu:/
Kakadu National Park /kækəˌdu: ˌnæʃnl ˈpɑ:k/
kea /ˈki:ə/
Kiwi, kiwi /ˈki:wi:/
Kullilla /kʊˈlɪlə/
kumara /kʊˈmɑ:rə/
L & P /ˌel‿ən ˈpi:/
Lady Gaga /ˌleɪdi ˈgɑ:gɑ:/
latin /ˈlætɪn/
League of Legends /ˌli:g‿əv ˈledʒndz/
LGBTQ /ˌel dʒi: bi: ti: ˈkju:/
Lord of the Rings /ˌlɔ:d‿əv ðə ˈrɪŋz/
Mangaotaki /ˌmæŋgaʊˈtæki/
Maori /ˈmaʊri/
marae /ˈmæræ/
moa /ˈməʊə/
moko /ˈmɒkəʊ/
Moore River /ˌmʊə ˈrɪvə/
Moore River Native Settlement /ˌmʊə ˌrɪvə ˌneɪtɪv ˈsetlmənt/
Mount Cook /ˌmaʊnt ˈkʊk/
Muriwari /mʊrɪˈwɑ:ri/
the National Council for the Prevention of War /ðə ˌnæʃnəl ˌkaʊnsl fə ðə prɪˌvenʃn‿əv ˈwɔ:/
New Zealander /nju ˈzi:ləndə/
Nickelodeon /ˌnɪkəˈləʊdiən/
Nike /ˈnaɪki/
the Nobel Peace Prize /ðə nəʊˌbel ˈpi:s praɪz/
Pakeha /ˈpɑ:kihɑ:/
Papatuanuku /ˌpæpətuəˈnu:ku:/
pataka /ˈpɑ:təkɑ:/
Piccadilly /ˌpɪkəˈdɪli/
Pohutu /pəˈhu:tu:/
powhiri /paʊˈhɪərɪ/
punk /pʌŋk/
R&B /ˌɑ:r‿ən ˈbi:/
Ranginui /ræŋˈgɪnwɪ/
rap /ræp/
reggae /ˈregeɪ/
Remembrance Day /rɪˈmembrəns deɪ/
rock /rɒk/
rock 'n' roll /ˌrɒk‿ən ˈrəʊl/
Roma /ˈrəʊmə/
the Royal British Legion /ðə ˌrɔɪəl ˌbrɪtɪʃ ˈli:dʒn/
the Royal Flying Doctor Service of Australia /ðə ˌrɔɪəl ˌflaɪɪŋ ˈdɒktə ˌsɜ:vɪs/
rugby /ˈrʌgbi/
Sainsbury's /ˈseɪnzbəri z/
salsa /ˈsælsə/
School of the Air, SOA /ˌsku:l‿əv ði‿ˈeə, ˌes‿əʊ‿ˈeɪ/
science fiction /ˌsaɪəns ˈfɪkʃn/
Southern Cross /ˌsʌðən ˈkrɒs/
Sparky /ˈspɑ:ki/
Star Trek /ˈstɑ: trek/
Star Wars /ˈstɑ: wɔ:z/
Staten Landt /ˈstætn lænd/
Stolen Generations /ˌstəʊlən dʒenəˈreɪʃnz/
straight-edge punk /ˌstreɪt‿ˌedʒ ˈpʌŋk/
Sunday Telegraph /ˌsʌndeɪ ˈtelɪˌgrɑ:f/
Ta Moko /tə ˈmɒkəʊ/
Tane Mahuta /ˌteɪn məˈhu:tə/
tango /ˈtæŋgəʊ/
Taronga /təˈrɒŋgə/
Taronga Zoo /təˌrɒŋgə ˈzu:/
Teentalk /ˈti:ntɔ:k/
tennis /ˈtenɪs/
The Internet of things /ði‿ˌɪntənet‿əv ˈθɪŋz/
Tommy /ˈtɒmi/
Tuatara /ˌtu:əˈtɑ:rə/
Uluru /ˌu:ləˈru:/
UNESCO /juˈneskəʊ/
The United Nations /ðə ju:ˌnaɪtɪd ˈneɪʃnz/
United Nations Children's Fund (UNICEF) /ju:ˌnaɪtɪd ˌneɪʃnz ˈtʃɪldrəns fʌnd (ˈju:nɪsef)/
Waitangi /waɪˈtæŋi/
waka /ˈwakə/
waka hourua /ˌwakə huˈru:ə/
Wharariki /ˌwɒrəˈri:ki/
whisky /ˈwɪski/
Wikipedia /ˌwɪkiˈpi:diə/
Wimbledon /ˈwɪmbldən/
Women's Peace Union /ðə ˌwɪmɪnz ˈpi:s ˌju:njən/
World eSports Association (WESA) /ˌwɜ:ld‿ˈi: spɔ:ts‿əˌsəʊsiˌeɪʃn/
World Wildlife Fund /ˌwɜ:ld ˈwaɪldlaɪf‿fʌnd/
X-factor /ˈeks ˌfæktə/
Yarra /ˈjærə/
Yellow-eyed penguin /ˌjeləʊ‿ˌaɪd ˈpeŋgwɪn/
yoga /ˈjəʊgə/
ziplining /ˈzɪpˌlaɪnɪŋ/
zorbing /ˈzɔ:bɪŋ/
zumba /ˈzʊmbə/

Geographical Names

Afghanistan /æfˈgænɪstɑ:n/
Africa /ˈæfrɪkə/
Alabama /ˌæləˈbæmə/
Alice Springs /ˌælɪs ˈsprɪŋz/
Angola /æŋˈgəʊlə/
Asia /ˈeɪʒə/
Auckland /ˈɔ:klənd/
Australia /ɒˈstreɪliə/
Baghdad /ˌbægˈdæd/

Names

Baltimore /ˈbɔːltɪmɔː/
Belgium /ˈbeldʒəm/
Black Forest /ˌblæk ˈfɒrɪst/
Bow /bəʊ/
Breclav /ˈbretslæv/
Brisbane /ˈbrɪzbən/
Bristol /ˈbrɪstl/
Britain /ˈbrɪtn/
Canberra /ˈkænbərə/
Canterbury /ˈkæntəbəri/
Chief /tʃiːf/
China /ˈtʃaɪnə/
Czech Republic /ˌtʃek riˈpʌblɪk/
Dubai /ˌduːˈbaɪ/
Dublin /ˈdʌblɪn/
Dunedin /dʌnˈiːdɪn/
England /ˈɪŋglənd/
Ethel Creek /ˌeθl ˈkriːk/
Europe /ˈjʊərəp/
France /frɑːns/
Fraser Island /ˌfreɪzər‿ˈaɪlənd/
Georgia /ˈdʒɔːdʒə/
Germany /ˈdʒɜːməni/
Gisborne /ˈgɪzbən/
Glasgow /ˈglɑːzgəʊ/
Godarville /ˈgɒdəvɪl/
Greece /griːs/
Hamilton Island /ˌhæmltən‿ˈaɪlənd/
Hawaii /həˈwaɪi/
Hawaiki /həˈwaɪki/
Helen /ˈhelən/
Holland /ˌhɒlənd/
India /ˈɪndiə/
Indonesia /ˌɪndəʊˈniːʒə/
Iraq /ɪˈrɑːk/
Italy /ˈɪtəli/
Japan /dʒəˈpæn/
Jigalong /ˈdʒɪgəlɒŋ/
Kashmir /ˌkæʃˈmɪə/
Korea /kəˈrɪə/
Liverpool /ˈlɪvəpuːl/
London /ˈlʌndən/
Los Angeles /lɒs‿ˈændʒəliːz/
Maidstone /ˈmeɪdstən/
Marble Bar /ˌmɑːbl ˈbɑː/
Maryland /ˈmeərɪlənd/
Melbourne /ˈmelbən/
Montana /mɒnˈtænə/
Montgomery /məntˈgʌməri/
the Netherlands /ðə ˈneðələndz/
New South Wales /ˌnjuː saʊθ ˈweɪlz/
New York /ˌnjuː ˈjɔːk/
New Zealand /nju ˈziːlənd/
Newcastle /ˈnjuːˌkɑːsl/
Nullagine /ˈnʌləgɪn/
Oxford /ˈɒksfəd/
Patterson /ˈpætəsən/
Pilbara /pɪlˈbɑːrə/
Polynesia /ˌpɒlɪˈniːziə/
Port Jackson /ˌpɔːt ˈdʒæksən/
Queensland /ˈkwiːnzlənd/
Rhine /raɪn/
Rotorua /ˌrəʊtəˈruːə/
Routeburn /ˈruːtbɜːn/
Roy Hill /ˌrɔɪ ˈhɪl/
Russia /ˈrʌʃə/
San Francisco /ˌsæn frənˈsɪskəʊ/
Sarajevo /ˌsærəˈjeɪvəʊ/
Saudi Arabia /ˌsaʊdi‿əˈreɪbiə/
South Africa /ˌsaʊθ‿ˈæfrɪkə/
South America /ˌsaʊθ‿əˈmerɪkə/
South Australia /ˌsaʊθ‿ɒˈstreɪliə/
South Pacific /ˌsaʊθ pəˈsɪfɪk/
Spokane /spəʊˈkæn/
Sweden /ˈswiːdn/
Switzerland /ˈswɪtsələnd/
Sydney /ˈsɪdni/
Tahiti /təˈhiːti/
Tasmania /tæzˈmeɪniə/
Thailand /ˈtaɪlænd/
USA (= United States of America) /ðə ˌju‿es‿ˈeɪ, juːˌnaɪtɪd ˌsteɪts‿əv‿əˈmerɪkə/
Victoria /vɪkˈtɔːriə/
Vietnam /ˌviːetˈnæm/
Washington /ˈwɒʃɪŋtən/
Washington, D.C. /ˌwɒʃɪŋtən diː ˈsiː/
Wellington /ˈwelɪŋtən/
Western Australia /ˌwestən‿ɒˈstreɪliə/
Whitsunday Islands /ˌwɪtsʌndeɪ‿ˈaɪləndz/
Wirral /ˈwɪrəl/

infinitive	German	simple past	past participle
be /biː/	sein	was / were /wɒz / wɜː/	been /biːn/
beat /biːt/	schlagen; besiegen	beat /biːt/	beaten /ˈbiːtən/
become /bɪˈkʌm/	werden	became /bɪˈkeɪm/	become /bɪˈkʌm/
begin /bɪˈɡɪn/	anfangen; beginnen	began /bɪˈɡæn/	begun /bɪˈɡʌn/
bind /baɪnd/	binden, fesseln	bound /baʊnd/	bound /baʊnd/
bite /baɪt/	beißen	bit /bɪt/	bitten /ˈbɪtn/
break /breɪk/	brechen; kaputt machen; zerbrechen	broke /brəʊk/	broken /ˈbrəʊkən/
bring /brɪŋ/	mitbringen	brought /brɔːt/	brought /brɔːt/
broadcast /ˈbrɔːdˌkɑːst/	senden	broadcast / broadcasted /ˈbrɔːdˌkɑːst / ˈbrɔːdˌkɑːstɪd/	broadcast / broadcasted /ˈbrɔːdˌkɑːst / ˈbrɔːdˌkɑːstɪd/
build /bɪld/	bauen	built /bɪlt/	built /bɪlt/
burn /bɜːn/	(ver)brennen	burnt / burned /bɜːnt / bɜːnd/	burnt / burned /bɜːnt / bɜːnd/
buy /baɪ/	kaufen	bought /bɔːt/	bought /bɔːt/
catch /kætʃ/	fangen	caught /kɔːt/	caught /kɔːt/
come /kʌm/	kommen	came /keɪm/	come /kʌm/
cost /kɒst/	kosten	cost /kɒst/	cost /kɒst/
cut /kʌt/	schneiden	cut /kʌt/	cut /kʌt/
choose /tʃuːz/	wählen; sich entscheiden	chose /tʃəʊz/	chosen /ˈtʃəʊzn/
do /duː/	machen; tun	did /dɪd/	done /dʌn/
draw /drɔː/	zeichnen	drew /druː/	drawn /drɔːn/
dream /driːm/	träumen	dreamt / dreamed /dremt / driːmd/	dreamt / dreamed /dremt / driːmd/
drink /drɪŋk/	trinken	drank /dræŋk/	drunk /drʌŋk/
drive /draɪv/	fahren	drove /drəʊv/	driven /ˈdrɪvn/
eat /iːt/	essen	ate /et/eɪt/	eaten /ˈiːtn/
fall /fɔːl/	fallen	fell /fel/	fallen /ˈfɔːlən/
feed /fiːd/	füttern; ernähren	fed /fed/	fed /fed/
feel /fiːl/	(sich) fühlen	felt /felt/	felt /felt/
fight /faɪt/	kämpfen; sich streiten	fought /fɔːt/	fought /fɔːt/
find /faɪnd/	finden	found /faʊnd/	found /faʊnd/
flee /fliː/	fliehen	fled /fled/	fled /fled/
fly /flaɪ/	fliegen	flew /fluː/	flown /fləʊn/
forget /fəˈɡet/	vergessen	forgot /fəˈɡɒt/	forgotten /fəˈɡɒtən/
get /ɡet/	bekommen; gelangen; kaufen; kommen; werden; holen	got /ɡɒt/	got /ɡɒt/
give /ɡɪv/	geben	gave /ɡeɪv/	given /ˈɡɪvn/
go /ɡəʊ/	gehen; fahren	went /went/	gone /ɡɒn/
grow /ɡrəʊ/	wachsen	grew /ɡru/	grown /ɡrəʊn/
have /hæv/	haben; essen, trinken	had /hæd/	had /hæd/
hear /hɪə/	hören	heard /hɜːd/	heard /hɜːd/
hide /haɪd/	verstecken	hid /hɪd/	hidden /ˈhɪdn/
hit /hɪt/	schlagen; treffen, stoßen gegen	hit /hɪt/	hit /hɪt/

Irregular Verbs

infinitive	German	simple past	past participle
hold /həʊld/	(fest)halten	held /held/	held /held/
hurt /hɜ:t/	wehtun, schmerzen	hurt /hɜ:t/	hurt /hɜ:t/
keep /ki:p/	(be)halten	kept /kept/	kept /kept/
know /nəʊ/	kennen; wissen	knew /nju:/	known /nəʊn/
lay /leɪ/	legen	laid /leɪd/	laid /leɪd/
lead /li:d/	führen	led /led/	led /led/
learn /lɜ:n/	lernen	learnt/learned /lɜ:nt / lɜ:nd/	learnt/learned /lɜ:nt / lɜ:nd/
leave /li:v/	verlassen; abfahren; weggehen	left /left/	left /left/
let /let/	lassen	let /let/	let /let/
lie /laɪ/	liegen	lay /leɪ/	lain /leɪn/
lose /lu:z/	verlieren	lost /lɒst/	lost /lɒst/
make /meɪk/	machen	made /meɪd/	made /meɪd/
mean /mi:n/	meinen; bedeuten	meant /ment/	meant /ment/
meet /mi:t/	treffen; sich treffen	met /met/	met /met/
overcome /ˌəʊvəˈkʌm/	bewältigen; überwinden	overcame /ˌəʊvəˈkeɪm/	overcome /ˌəʊvəˈkʌm/
pay /peɪ/	(be)zahlen	paid /peɪd/	paid /peɪd/
prove /pru:v/	beweisen	proved /pru:vd/	proved/proven /pru:vd / ˈpru:vn/
put /pʊt/	legen; setzen; stellen	put /pʊt/	put /pʊt/
read /ri:d/	lesen	read /red/	read /red/
retell /ˌri:ˈtel/	nacherzählen	retold /ˌri:ˈtəʊld/	retold /ˌri:ˈtəʊld/
rewrite /ˌri:ˈraɪt/	überarbeiten, umschreiben	rewrote /ˌri:ˈrəʊt/	rewritten /ˌri:ˈrɪtn/
ride /raɪd/	fahren; reiten	rode /rəʊd/	ridden /ˈrɪdn/
ring /rɪŋ/	anrufen; klingeln; läuten	rang /ræŋ/	rung /rʌŋ/
rise /raɪz/	aufgehen; steigen	rose /rəʊz/	risen /ˈrɪzn/
run /rʌn/	laufen; rennen	ran /ræn/	run /rʌn/
say /seɪ/	sagen	said /sed/	said /sed/
see /si:/	sehen	saw /sɔ:/	seen /si:n/
seek /si:k/	suchen, streben nach	sought /sɔ:t/	sought /sɔ:t/
sell /sel/	verkaufen	sold /səʊld/	sold /səʊld/
send /send/	schicken	sent /sent/	sent /sent/
set /set/	stellen; handeln; spielen	set /set/	set /set/
shake /ʃeɪk/	schütteln	shook /ʃʊk/	shaken /ˈʃeɪkən/
shoot /ʃu:t/	schießen; filmen	shot /ʃɒt/	shot /ʃɒt/
show /ʃəʊ/	zeigen	showed /ʃəʊd/	shown /ʃəʊn/
sing /sɪŋ/	singen	sang /sæŋ/	sung /sʌŋ/
sink /sɪŋk/	sinken	sank /sæŋk/	sunk /sʌŋk/
sit /sɪt/	sitzen	sat /sæt/	sat /sæt/
sleep /sli:p/	schlafen	slept /slept/	slept /slept/
smell /smel/	riechen	smelt/smelled /smelt / smeld/	smelt/smelled /smelt / smeld/
speak /spi:k/	reden; sprechen	spoke /spəʊk/	spoken /ˈspəʊkən/
speed /spi:d/	sausen, flitzen	sped /sped/	sped /sped/
spell /spel/	buchstabieren	spelt/spelled /spelt / speld/	spelt/spelled /spelt / speld/

infinitive	German	simple past	past participle
spend /spend/	ausgeben; verbringen	spent /spent/	spent /spent/
spread /spred/	verbreiten	spread /spred/	spread /spred/
stand /stænd/	stehen	stood /stʊd/	stood /stʊd/
steal /stiːl/	stehlen	stole /stəʊl/	stolen /ˈstəʊlən/
swim /swɪm/	schwimmen	swam /swæm/	swum /swʌm/
swing /swɪŋ/	schwingen	swung /swʌŋ/	swung /swʌŋ/
take /teɪk/	bringen; dauern; brauchen; nehmen	took /tʊk/	taken /ˈteɪkən/
teach /tiːtʃ/	unterrichten	taught /tɔːt/	taught /tɔːt/
tell /tel/	erzählen; sagen	told /təʊld/	told /təʊld/
think /θɪŋk/	denken; glauben	thought /θɔːt/	thought /θɔːt/
throw /θrəʊ/	werfen	threw /θruː/	thrown /θrəʊn/
understand /ˌʌndəˈstænd/	verstehen	understood /ˌʌndəˈstʊd/	understood /ˌʌndəˈstʊd/
wake /weɪk/	aufwecken	woke / waked /wəʊk / weɪkt/	woken / waked /ˈwəʊkən / weɪkt/
wear /weə/	tragen	wore /wɔː/	worn /wɔːn/
weave /wiːv/	flechten; weben	wove / weaved /wəʊv / wiːvd/	woven / weaved /ˈwəʊvn / wiːvd/
win /wɪn/	gewinnen	won /wʌn/	won /wʌn/
write /raɪt/	schreiben	wrote /rəʊt/	written /ˈrɪtn/

Tipp:
Einige Verben bilden das *simple past* und das *past participle* nach einem ähnlichen Muster. Wenn du sie dir in Gruppen sortierst, kannst du dir die Formen vielleicht besser merken.

bring – brought – brought
buy – bought – bought
fight – fought – fought
think – thought – thought
catch – caught – caught
teach – taught – taught

ring – rang – rung
sing – sang – sung
swim – swam – swum

draw – drew – drawn
fly – flew – flown
grow – grew – grown
know – knew – known
throw – threw – thrown

cut – cut – cut
hit – hit – hit
hurt – hurt – hurt
let – let – let
put – put – put

Bildquellen
Umschlag außen: Dirk Schmidt/dsphotos.de
Innenumschlag vorn: Joachim Zwick, Gießen
Innenumschlag hinten: Technisch-Grafische Abteilung Westermann

123RF GmbH, Berlin: 37 (M. Lupascu), 46 (P. Sangsawang), 50 (P. Bird), 51 (J. Stitt), 56 (C. Howey), 126; 123RF.com, Hong Kong: 114 (palangsi), 122 (adam121), 126 (dolgachov); akg-images GmbH, Berlin: 49, 94, 102, 143 (Glasshouse Images); alamy images, Abingdon/Oxfordshire: 18 (nagelestock.com), 28 (Paul Mayall), 30 (Bill Bachman), 36, 41, 56 (Dan Santillo NZ), 67 (T.M.O.Pictures), 75, 77, 80, 84, 84, 92 (North Wind Picture Archives), 96, 100, 112 (Jack Picone), 114 (Angela Hampton Picture Library), 114 (Cultura RM), 116 (imagebroker), 126 (David Grossman), 128 (imagebroker), 167 (© Jim Holden); Arco Images GmbH, Lünen: 137 (Owen Newman); Australian Embassy, Berlin: 21; Bridgeman Images, Berlin: 135 (© Heini Schneebeli, Australien); CartoonStock.com, Bath: 123 (Dan Reynolds), 127 (Brian Fray); Colditz, Margit, Halle: 164; Colourbox.com, Odense: 39 (Scigelova), 41 (Scigelova); ddp images GmbH, Hamburg: 103 (defd); Demmrich, André, Berlin: 3; dreamstime.com, Brentwood: 13, 16 (Chu-wen Lin), 26 (Nikol Senkyrikova), 30 (Klorklor), 33 (Nikol Senkyrikova); Druwe & Polastri, Cremlingen/Weddel: 58; ecopix Fotoagentur, Berlin: 58 (Reiner Zensen); fotolia.com, New York: 14 ((c) picture-optimize), 16 (hotshotsworldwide), 16 (mgkuijpers), 24 (Infinite XX), 24 (Corbis), 24 (Blend Images), 26, 32 (Corbis), 32 (Blend Images), 36 (oneinchpunch), 47 (ADESIGN), 50 (cassam), 51 (millefloreimages), 58 (Oksana Kuzmina), 64 (SeanPavonePhoto), 65 (Gina Sanders), 78 (Africa Studio), 80 (Klaus Eppele), 117 (Thomas Söllner), 120 (Mario Thiele), 121 (Thomas Söllner), 122 (Andrey_Arkusha), 123, 125 (Thomas Söllner), 127 (travelbook), 128 (wildworx), 128 (Yuri Arcurs), 129 (Thomas Söllner), 144 (ragaly), 168 (auremar), 169 (denisismagilov), 171 (Heiko Kverling), 171 (Andrzej Fryda), 173, 173 (Maksim Toome); Getty Images, München: 15 (Bec Parsons), 19 (Hulton Archives), 22 (Stephen Frink), 29 (Andrew Sheargold), 31 (Patrick Ward), 34 (Stephen Frink), 34 (Jeff Hunter), 58 (Mark Lewis), 102 (Monitor Picture Library/Photoshot), 111 (Mansell/Time & Life Pictures), 120 (2012 Gilbert Carrasquillo), 129; Holistic Life Foundation, Inc., Baltimore: 105, 110; Imago, Berlin: 166 (reemedia); Interfoto, München: 108 (Mary Evans Picture Library); iStockphoto.com, Calgary: 15 (Mark Evans), 17 (HyunJung_Jane_Kim), 17 (John Carnemolia), 19 (zbindere), 24, 24 (poco_bw), 33 (John Carnemolia), 34 (David Coleman Photography), 37 (Andrey Armyagov), 37 (mashabuba), 39 (VisualCommunications), 40 (agustavop), 46 (K. ONeill), 46 (nealec), 49 (ZambeziShark), 50 (tane-mahuta), 66, 67 (Juanmonino), 68 (agnormark), 68 (Stuart Jenner), 69 (agnormark), 69 (Stuart Jenner), 70 (Ridofranz), 72 (Stuart Jenner), 79 (monkeybusinessimages), 88 (Sylphe_7), 113 (oneinchpunch), 114 (damircudic), 116 (Wavebreakmedia), 118 (Digital Vision), 118 (Drazen_), 119 (Wavebreakmedia), 122 ((c) Morgan Lane Studios), 122 (Yuri), 122, 122 (Tempura), 123 (lesleywang2015), 124 (minemero), 126 (Highwaystarz-Photography), 138 (swissmediavision), 139 (Ian Knox), 139 (David Turton), 168 (JackF), 170 (monkeybusinessimages), 172 (JackF), 172, 173 (David Callan); juniors@wildlife Bildagentur GmbH, Hamburg: 111; Lea Gonsior, Augsburg: 106; Library of Congress, Washington, D.C.: 91 (Phillip Leonian from New York World-Telegram & Sun); Lizzie Sider Music, Boca Raton: 121, 121; Madeline Stuart Modelling/www.madelinestuartmodel.com, Brisbane: 125, 125, 125; mauritius images GmbH, Mittenwald: 165 (age), 167 (Pixtal); Miguel Amortegui, Rottingdean: 109; OKAPIA KG - Michael Grzimek & Co., Frankfurt/M.: 46, 94; Panther Media GmbH (panthermedia.net), München: 42 (baranq), 66 (denizo), 67, 67 (Lenets_Tatsiana); Picture-Alliance GmbH, Frankfurt/M.: 17 (AtC), 19, 34 (HB Verlag/Holger Leue), 37 (Bildagentur Huber), 59 (dpa/Frm), 59 (dpa), 74 (dpa), 94, 97 (ZUMAPRESS.com), 98, 98 (AP Photo), 98 (epa Hadi Tabrizi), 101, 138 (dpa/epa Southland Museum), 166, 169 (H. FOHRINGER), 171 (Helga Lade Fotoagentur GmbH, Ger), 172 (Image Source/HBSS, Frankfurt/M.); Rieke, Michael, Hannover: 14, 22; SeaTops, Pirmasens: 18 (Mark Conlin); Shutterstock.com, New York: 18 (Janelle Lugge), 18 (Mo Wu), 18 (Aleksandar Todoro), 21 (Mo Wu), 36, 36 (A. Jack), 36, 38 (R. Caucino), 39 (Woody Ang), 39 (B. Ionescu), 40 (olalaja), 40 (ChameleonsEye), 40 (Niradj), 41 (Woody Ang), 41, 42 (J. Cejpek), 43 (T. Lusth), 46 (neftali), 46 (byvalet), 46 (ChameleonsEye), 46 (Paolo Bona), 46 (neftali), 48 (aaron choi), 48 (ChameleonsEye), 50 (R. Lesniewski), 50 (Don Fink), 50 (LaMiaFotografia), 50 (D. Naumov), 51 (P. Bona), 51 (freevideophotoage), 56 (P. Hofmeester), 68 (Monkey Business Images), 69 (Monkey Business Images), 76, 76, 76, 79 (MJTH), 80 (REDPIXEL.PL), 84, 114 (margo_black), 114 (ArtWell), 114 (Charles Knox), 114 (Ms Jane Campbell), 115 (Zsschreiner), 118 (PrinceOfLove), 118 (Photobank gallery), 118 (Jose Luis Carrasc), 118 (CREATISTA), 118 (DavidTB), 119 (Air Images), 122 (oneinchpunch), 122 (Max Topchii), 126 (studiolaska), 126 (dominika zarzycka), 138 (John Carnemolla), 163 (Diriye Amey), 164 (John Carnemolla), 167 (racorn), 170, 172 (wavebreakmedia), 173 (William Perugini); Specialist Stock, Berlin: 112 (Christian Aid/Karen Hedges); stock.adobe.com, Dublin: 16 (Taras Vyshnya), 36, 36, 52 (PhotoSG), 57 (Christian Schwier), 74 (Darren Tierney), 78, 80, 80, 80, 80, 81, 84, 93; Süddeutsche Zeitung - Photo, München: 92 (SSPL/Science Museum), 95 (SSPL/National Media Museum); Technisch-Grafische Abteilung Westermann: 25, 156; Thomson Reuters (Markets) Deutschland GmbH, Berlin: 19 (POOL New); ullstein bild, Berlin: 16, 92 (Heilke Heller), 92, 94 (Roger Viollet), 96 (Lineair), 102 (JOKER/Walter G. Allgöwer/© VG Bild-Kunst, Bonn 2015), 102 (AP), 103 (Hohlfeld); UNICEF Deutschland, Köln: 97 (© UNICEF/UN013170/ Halldorsson), 107 (© UNICEF/UNI168670/), 107; vario images, Bonn: 168; Visum Foto GmbH, Hannover: 14 (Woodfall); wikimedia.commons: 47 (public domain/NordNordWest); Wolf, H.-U., Steinheim: 104; www.glasbergen.com, SHERBURNE: 63 (From the collection of Randy Glasbergen); Zoonar.com, Hamburg: 37 (Christian Colista), 136 (Christian Beier).

Textquellen

26 „My story“ adaptiert von „My Story“ von Taylar-Jo Connolly in *Praxis Englisch* 1/2009 S.31.
27 „I am Australian“ von *The seekers*, Newton, Dobe/Woodley, Bruce, Orient Pacific Music Pty Ltd. BMG Rights Management GmbH, Berlin
28 Filmkritik zu „Rabbit-proof fence“ adaptiert von http://www.empireonline.com/movies/rabbit-proof-fence/review/
29 „Sorry speech“ von Kevin Rudd: http://www.australia.gov.au/about-australia/our-country/our-people/apology-to-australias-indigenous-peoples, CC BY 3.0
42 „The Outdoor Safety Code“ aus: http://www.doc.govt.nz/parks-and-recreation/know-before-you-go/safety-in-the-outdoors/, CC BY 4.0
85/86 Isaac Asimov, „The fun they had“ in: *Earth is room enough*, 1957, Doubleday, New York
88 Holand, Gil „Colony 4.“ In: Proges, Wilfried (Hg). *Mini-Sagas. An anthology of fifty word short stories*, 2007, Stuttgart: Reclam
95 „War memories“: Textauszüge aus Bob Willey (Hg.). *From all Sides: Memories of World War II*, 1989, Alan Sutton Publishing, Gloucester
98 Zitat von Adam Ferguson: https://www.theguardian.com/media/2011/jun/18/war-photographers-special-report, Zitat von Dar Yasin: http://time.com/kashmir-unrest-dar-yasin/
103 „Imagine“, Text und Musik: John Lennon, EMI Records Ltd.
104 „The Maidstone Mediation Scheme“ adaptiert von: http://www.maidstonemediation.co.uk/resources/Maidstone-Mediation-Secondary-Schools.pdf
105 „Teaching mindfulness“, Holistic Life Foundation, adaptiert von: https://www.indiegogo.com/projects/mindful-moment-program-at-patterson-high-school#/
108 „A Christmas truce advert“ Auszug aus: http://www.independent.co.uk/voices/comment/sainsburys-christmas-advert-nothing-says-merry-xmas-folks-like-trench-warfare-9861367.html
136/137 „The dingo“ adaptiert von: Mackenzie Cottrell: *Don't Shoot the Dingo, Father!*
139 „Monkey business“ adaptiert von: http://jokes4all.net/joke-2975.html
140/141 Auszug aus Nina Bawden: *Carrie's war*. 1973.
144 Alexa Carlin „A Poem For Being Yourself“: http://alexacarlin.com/a-poem-be-yourself/

Alaska (USA)
Anchorage
CANADA
Vancouver
Winnipeg
NORTH AMERICA
Ottawa
Montreal
Chicago
San Francisco
UNITED STATES
New York
Washington, D.C.
Los Angeles
Miami
BAHAMAS
ST. KITTS AND NEVIS
JAMAICA
ANTIGUA AND BARBUDA
BELIZE
Kingston
DOMINICA
ST. VINCENT AND THE GRENADINES
ST. LUCIA
BARBADOS
GRENADA
TRINIDAD AND TOBAGO
Pacific Ocean
GUYANA
Georgetown
SOUTH AMERICA
Atlantic Ocean
IRELAND
Dublin
UNITED KINGDOM
London
EUROPE
MALTA
AFRICA
GAMBIA
Abuja
NIGERIA
Freetown
SIERRA LEONE
LIBERIA
Accra
GHANA
Yaoundé
CAMEROON
NAMIBIA
Windhoek
Cape Town
English-speaking countries
members of the Commonwealth
mother-tongue use
official or semi-official use
non-members of the Commonwealth
mother-tongue use
official or semi-official use
capital
city
0
2000
4000 km